To

THAT AUSTRIAN STATESMAN
WHO SHALL POSSESS THE GENIUS AND THE COURAGE
NECESSARY TO SOLVE
THE SOUTHERN SLAV QUESTION,
THIS BOOK IS RESPECTFULLY
DEDICATED.

DOCH ach! Was hilft dem Menschengeist Verstand,
Dem Herzen Güte, Willigkeit der Hand,
Wenn's fieberhaft durchaus im Staate wütet,
Und Übel sich in Übeln überbrütet?
Wer schaut hinab von diesem hohen Raum
Ins weite Reich, ihm scheint's ein schwerer Traum
Wo Missgestalt in Missgestalten schaltet,
Das Ungesetz gesetzlich überwaltet,
Und eine Welt des Irrtums sich entfaltet. . . .

Und " Schuldig! " hörst du ausgesprochen,
Wo Unschuld nur sich selber schützt.
So will sich alle Welt zerstückeln,
Vernichtigen, was sich gebührt;
Wie soll sich da der Sinn entwickeln
Der einzig uns zum Rechten führt? . . .

Ich malte schwarz—doch dichtern Flor
Zög ich dem Bilde lieber vor.

GOETHE, *Faust*, II.

THE SOUTHERN SLAV QUESTION

THE
SOUTHERN SLAV
QUESTION

AND THE

HABSBURG MONARCHY

By

R. W. SETON-WATSON

HOWARD FERTIG

NEW YORK · 1969

First published in 1911

HOWARD FERTIG, INC. EDITION 1969
Published by permission of Constable and Co. Ltd.,
and copyright under the Berne Convention.

Library of Congress Catalog Card Number: 68-9666

PRINTED IN THE UNITED STATES OF AMERICA
BY NOBLE OFFSET PRINTERS, INC.

Preface

NO country in Europe presents such a variety of complicated problems for solution as the Austro-Hungarian Monarchy; and among these, none is more important and more pressing than the Southern Slav Question. In it are involved the future fortunes of the whole Croat and Serb race, and through them the fate of the Western half of the Balkan Peninsula—from the Gulf of Trieste to the Bulgarian frontier, from the plains of Southern Hungary to the mountains of Albania. On it depends the balance of power on the Adriatic, with all its bearings upon the international situation. Above all, the Southern Slav Question may at any moment exercise a decisive influence upon the foreign policy of Vienna, and upon the internal development of the Dual Monarchy. For on the one hand Austria cannot hope to extend her influence in the Balkans, unless she enlists in her cause the sympathies and support of her eight millions of Southern Slav subjects; while on the other hand, the Croato-Serb race, by reason of its geographical and strategic position, has it in its power by a strict alliance with Austria against Hungary, to destroy completely in favour of the former the balance upon which the Dual System is based, and so to play havoc with the entire mechanism and pave the way for that compromise between federalism and centralism through which alone the acute racial problems of the Dual Monarchy can be solved.

The present volume attempts to trace the growth of national feeling among the Croats and Serbs of the Dual Monarchy, and to describe in fuller detail the more recent movement in favour of Croato-Serb Unity. The fact that the English language contains no book devoted to the history of this movement, must be my excuse for occasional prolixity; not merely the main building, but even the substructure had to be created.

The second portion of the book deals with the Annexation of Bosnia, with the international crisis to which that event gave rise, and with the subsequent exposure of the methods which underlay Count Aehrenthal's whole policy, and under which the Southern Slavs were the chief sufferers. The history of the Friedjung Trial and of the Vasić forgeries sheds such a flood of light upon the political situation alike among the Southern Slavs and in the Dual Monarchy as a whole, that I make no apology for treating it in detail—the more so, since detailed treatment was essential to a fair statement of the rival views.

It was inevitable that any book dealing with this subject should contain an open, and often severe, criticism of Count Aehrenthal's diplomatic methods. The interests of international decency demand that theft, forgery and espionage should cease to be the main pillars of foreign policy in any state which deserves the title of a Great Power. There are occasions when the surgeon's knife is more necessary than the nurse's bandage ; and in the same way I should be neglecting the elementary canons of honest criticism, were I to slur over the facts of this monstrous diplomatic scandal. It is Austria who has been the chief sufferer, alike in prestige and materially, and thus their exposure, so far from being inspired by hostility to Austria, is a pre-eminently Austrian interest. Acting in this belief, I have repeatedly emphasized the contrast between Austria's true political mission in the Balkans, and the foul intrigues which have brought her into unmerited disrepute. There are certain things in the Austria of to-day, of which it is impossible to approve ; but to the impartial observer new life and the desire for progress are everywhere apparent, and not merely this, but a steady growth in the conception of political and constitutional liberty and an increasing distaste for the old methods which still linger on in certain departments of public life. Hence any book which aims at the elucidation of the truth in this direction, may fairly claim to be credited with friendly intentions.

The official press of Vienna has a characteristic habit of treating any criticism of Austro-Hungarian diplomatic methods towards Servia as an apology for the latter state, and indeed of treating any criticism of the Foreign Minister as a proof of hostility towards the Dual Monarchy. The very contrary is the case ; if I were hostile, I should leave the canker untouched, instead of trying to expose it to view. In any case, no one who reads my book will be able to charge me with condoning the corruption and abuses which disfigure political life in Servia and make it impossible to sympathize with Pan-Serb aspirations. Their triumph would indeed be a disaster to European culture, which it is the mission of the Dual Monarchy, with its many races, to represent in South-East Europe.

Incidentally I would recommend a close study of the Aehrenthal policy to all believers in Disarmament; for it is not too much to assert that that must remain a mere dream so long as international policy is conducted on such lines.

To the student of British politics the Croatian problem should be of special interest at the present time; for Croatia supplies the sole genuine analogy upon the Continent of Europe to the position which Ireland would occupy under a system of Home Rule. A careful study of the relations of Hungary and Croatia would be of the utmost value alike to the convinced Unionist and to the thoughtful advocate of devolution, Federalism or any other scheme of constitutional readjustment among the four sister nations of these islands. Those who are reluctant to learn from the past history of Ireland itself, may learn from the history of Hungary and Croatia, how Ireland should NOT be treated, and how ineffectual are repression and lack of sympathy in the solution of any national or racial question.

For a long time past I have regretfully foreseen that I should be driven to criticize Dr. Friedjung, for whose historical writings I have the utmost admiration and whose personal kindness I greatly valued during my visits to Vienna. Fate assigned him a prominent part in the political development of Croatia, and it was therefore inevitable that he should figure prominently in these pages. I can only assure him that I have done my utmost to do justice to his motives, and that while I have not hesitated to criticize his attitude where criticism seemed necessary, nothing has shaken my high estimate of his character as a man and a historian.

I have resolved to ignore the personalities in which my " critics " in Hungary have indulged since the publication of my last two books, *Racial Problems in Hungary* and *Corruption and Reform in Hungary*. But I am obliged to make one brief exception in favour of a former countryman of my own. Professor Arthur Yolland, of Budapest University, has seen fit to publish an article in the April number of *Magyar Figyelö* (a Hungarian review published under the imprimatur of the ex-Premier Count Stephen Tisza), containing longwinded insinuations to the effect that I was paid for my book *Racial Problems in Hungary* by some person or persons unknown. If this lie is not based upon sheer ignorance (and Professor Yolland has had ample opportunity of informing himself through

PREFACE

mutual acquaintances) it can only be a deliberate slander ; and I hereby challenge him either to withdraw his insinuation or to justify his attitude in an English court of law.

Finally, I must express my deep obligation to Mr. Gladstone's Trustees, who have kindly permitted me to publish as an Appendix to this volume the interesting series of letters addressed to Mr. Gladstone by the Croatian patriot Bishop Strossmayer ; and also to Mr. A. Tilney Bassett, for his courteous and ready assistance in this connexion. I have also been fortunate enough to obtain, through friends in Croatia, copies of the replies written by Mr. Gladstone ; and these have been included in the correspondence in their proper chronological order.

In preparing the map, I have been materially assisted by my friend Dr. Joseph Smodlaka, who represents Spalato (Dalmatia) in the Austrian Parliament. It may, however, be well to point out that neither he nor any other Croat politician is in any way responsible for the opinions expressed in my book.

R. W. SETON-WATSON.

AYTON HOUSE, ABERNETHY,
July 20, 1911.

Contents

	PAGE
PREFACE	vii
GEOGRAPHICAL AND STATISTICAL NOTE	1

CHAPTER I
CROATIA FROM THE EARLIEST TIMES TILL 1849 . . . 15

CHAPTER II
THE SERBS OF HUNGARY AND CROATIA 36

CHAPTER III
THE ERA OF EXPERIMENT (1849–1868) 52

CHAPTER IV
THE COMPROMISE BETWEEN HUNGARY AND CROATIA (1868) . 65

CHAPTER V
CROATIA UNDER THE DUAL SYSTEM (1868–1905) . . . 85

CHAPTER VI
BISHOP STROSSMAYER AND THE RENAISSANCE OF CROATIAN CULTURE 118

CHAPTER VII
AN OUTLINE OF CROAT AND SERB LITERATURE . . . 129

CHAPTER VIII
THE RESOLUTION OF FIUME AND ITS CONSEQUENCES (1905–1908) . 142

CHAPTER IX
THE ANNEXATION OF BOSNIA AND THE AGRAM HIGH TREASON TRIAL—ABSOLUTISM IN CROATIA 174

CHAPTER X
THE FRIEDJUNG TRIAL 209

CONTENTS

PAGE

CHAPTER XI

THE SUPILO-CHLUMECKY INCIDENT 288

CHAPTER XII

THE VASIĆ FORGERIES AND COUNT AEHRENTHAL—A CRITICISM
AND AN INQUIRY 303

CHAPTER XIII

MAGYAR RAILWAY POLICY 329

CHAPTER XIV

CROAT AND SERB—THE PROBLEM OF UNITY 335

APPENDICES—
(1.) The Election of Ferdinand I as King of Croatia (1527) 347
(2.) The Croatian Pragmatic Sanction (1712) . . 349
(3.) The Address of the Croatian Diet, June 5, 1848 . 350
(4.) Article XLII (1861) of the Croatian Diet . . 357
(5.) Instructions to the Croatian Delegates during the
    Negotiations with Hungary (1867) . . . 359
(6.) The Hungaro-Croatian Compromise (1868) . . 361
(7.) The Croatian Government (Act II, 1869) . . 379
(8.) The Croatian Diet (Act II, 1870). . . . 383
(9.) The Croatian Budget 387
(10.) Croatia's Economic Position 388
(11.) The Programme of the Party of Pure Right (1893) . 392
(12.) The Resolution of Fiume (1905) . . . 393
(13.) The Resolution of Zara (1905) 395
(14.) The Forged Report of Dr. Spalajković . . . 397
(15.) The Forged Despatch of Dr. Milovanović . . 401
(16.) The Condition of Dalmatia (1910) . . . 406
(17.) The Correspondence of Bishop Strossmayer and Mr.
    Gladstone 416

BIBLIOGRAPHY 445

MAP . . . . *To face* 454

INDEX 455

GEOGRAPHICAL AND STATISTICAL NOTE

THE name of " Southern Slav " is in its widest sense a geographical term. The Slavonic races fall naturally into two groups—the northernmost, comprising the Russians, Ruthenes, Poles, Czechs, Slovaks ; the southernmost, the Slovenes, Croats, Serbs and Bulgars. The two groups are completely cut off from each other by three non-Slav races—the Germans, the Magyars and Roumanians, who occupy a continous territory from the Baltic to the Black Sea.

Thus from a purely geographical point of view, it is correct to describe as Southern Slav the whole tract of country between Görz Klagenfurt and Cilli on the north-west, and Varna, Drama and Salonica on the south-east, between Neusatz and Temesvár on the north and Dulcigno, Ipek and Monastir on the south. The Southern Slav population of this territory may be estimated in round figures as follows :—

I. Slovenes			1,400,000	1,400,000
II. Serbo-Croats—				
A. Croats in Dalmatia . .	500,000			
in Istria . . .	200,000			
in Croatia-Slavonia	1,750,000			
in Bosnia-Herzego-				
vina	400,000			
in Hungary . .	300,000			
		3,150,000		
B. Serbs in Dalmatia . .	100,000			9,200,000
in Croatia-Slav. .	650,000			
in Bosnia-Herz. .	850,000			
in Hungary . .	500,000			
in Montenegro. .	300,000			
in Servia . . .	2,600,000			
in Turkey . . .	300,000			
		5,300,000		
C. Mohammedan Serbo-Croats				
in Bosnia . . .	650,000			
in Turkey . . .	100,000			
		750,000		
III. Bulgars in Bulgaria	3,000,000			
in Turkey	1,600,000			
		4,600,000	4,600,000
	Total . .	15,200,000		

In view of the impossibility of obtaining really accurate statistics for the whole of this territory, we must be content with the approximate total of 15,600,000.

The political problem to which the present volume is devoted, and which has come to be widely known as "the Southern Slav question," deals with a more limited field.

This question in its present-day bearings, may be defined as the problem of Serbo-Croatian unity. Its centre of gravity lay, even before the annexation of Bosnia, within the bounds of the Habsburg Monarchy ; and it is in Croatia and Bosnia that it must reach its solution. With this Bulgaria has nothing directly to do [1] and may therefore be eliminated from the present survey. For an entirely different reason the Slovenes are omitted. They have no distinct history of their own : their voice cannot be decisive in any solution of the problem ; and urgent reasons of strategy and geography make it impossible for them to be included in any unified Southern Slav state of the immediate future.

The history of the two independent Serb states, Servia and Montenegro, requires a special volume to itself. It has hitherto been the fashion abroad to regard them as co-extensive with the Southern Slav question, or at any rate as the decisive factors in it, and to omit from the calculation those Southern Slav countries which own allegiance to the House of Habsburg. In the present volume the process is reversed. Its whole contention, based upon a reading of past history, is that Servia and Montenegro can only watch, and are helpless to hinder, the process of evolution which is gradually making for Serbo-Croat Unity under Habsburg sway. Their gallant struggles for independence in the past may kindle regret in the heart of the sentimental onlooker ; but it cannot obscure the inexorable lesson of history.

The Croats and Serbs are by origin two kindred Slavonic tribes who followed the Avars to the territory which they now occupy, in the course of the sixth and seventh centuries.[2] Living on the frontier between east and west, they have for centuries been exposed to the rival influence of Rome and Byzantium and the eternal strife of these two opposing systems of thought and culture has given to the Croato-Serb race its dual nature, and is at once its strength and its weakness— its weakness in long centuries of seemingly futile strife and disunion, its strength in a still distant future which shall have attained the higher and more complex "Unitas in Diversitate." Linguistic unity has already been achieved ; for the Croat language is Serb written with Latin, the Serb language, Croat written with Cyrillic characters : other difference there is none. The true line of cleavage is religious, every Croat being a Roman Catholic, every Serb a member of the Orthodox Church. To this there are virtually no exceptions.

The Croato-Serb race is at present cut up into eight distinct political entities. Istria and Dalmatia are provinces of Austria, each possessing its own Diet and local institutions. Croatia-Slavonia is an autonomous kingdom [3] under the Crown of St. Stephen, but in all matters of international policy must be reckoned as an integral portion of the kingdom

---

[1] Though indirectly its solution and the consequent increase in Austrian prestige and power in the Balkans would of course vitally affect its foreign policy.
[2] Philologists have derived the name "Hrvat" (Croat) and "Srb" (Serb) from the same root. They base their argument on the grammatical rule which converts "h" into "s" and the kinship between "v" and "b."
[3] Nominally two kingdoms.

of Hungary. The former Serb Voivody forms part of the South Hungarian counties of Bács-Bodrog, Torontál and Temes ; while the city of Fiume enjoys a special autonomous position, under a Governor appointed from Budapest. Bosnia and Herzegovina are administered in the name of Austria and Hungary by the Joint Minister of Finance, their exact constitutional position being still undefined owing to the rival claims of the Dual States. Servia and Montenegro form independent Serb states, under native dynasties ; while Old Servia as the northernmost vilayet of Macedonia, still acknowledges the Sultan's sway. A brief survey of the geographical and economic conditions of these countries will show how untenable the present situation is.

A. CROATIA-SLAVONIA (16,423 square miles).

The secret of Croatia-Slavonia's geographical importance lies in the fact that it blocks Hungary's only access to the sea. The river Drave, from the point where it leaves Austrian territory, to the point where it flows into the Danube forms the northern boundary between Hungary and Croatia, which is continued by the Danube as far as Semlin, opposite Belgrad. At Semlin the southern frontier of Slavonia, towards Bosnia, is formed by the Save, which joins the Danube at Belgrad. Further west, the frontier at first follows the River Una (a tributary of the Save) and then takes an irregular course, first south, then north-west, across the Dinaric Alps to the Adriatic. The Croatian coastline extends from Fiume (outside which town Istria and Croatia meet), for some ninety miles in a south-easterly direction ; but the large islands of Veglia, Arbe and Pago, which adjoin it, belong to the Austrian provinces of Istria and Dalmatia.

Croatia-Slavonia thus falls naturally into two main divisions : (1) the broad and fertile plains which lie between the Drave and Save, interspersed by low hills in the neighbourhood of Pakrac and Požega, and (2) the lofty and barren mountain region which cuts off these plains from the Adriatic, and whose two main ranges are the Kapela and further south the Velebit Mountains.

Zagreb (Agram), the capital, lies above the River Save, on the last low spurs of what are really the Styrian Alps ; for Zagreb is only sixteen miles from the Austrian frontier. Zagreb is a flourishing town of over 80,000 inhabitants (61,002 in 1900), with a fine cathedral and many handsome public buildings (the National Theatre, the Southern Slav Academy, the University, the Art Galleries, the Chamber of Commerce, etc.). Osijek (Essek) the capital of Slavonia, has 25,000 inhabitants ; all the other towns are small, 82 per cent. of the population being engaged in agricultural pursuits.[4] For administrative purposes Croatia is divided into five counties (Zagreb, Modruš-Fiume, Lika-Krbava, Varaždin, and Bjelovar), Slavonia into three counties (Virovitica (Verőcze), Požega and Syrmia (Srijem, Szerém). Zagreb is the seat of an Archbishop ; the two remaining dioceses are Zengg (Senj) and Djakovo, in the latter of which Bosnia was included until the erection of an archiepiscopal see in Sarajevo (1882). The bishops of Zagreb and Djakovo dispose over enormous revenues. The little town of Karlovci (Karlowitz) on the Danube is the seat of the Serb Orthodox Patriarch,

---

[4] According to census of 1900. See *Ung. Stat Jahrbuch* xii, p. 21.

who is metropolitan of all the Serbs of Transleithania, and has under him the bishoprics of Pakrac (Slavonia), Karlovac (Croatia), Versecz, Temesvár, Neusatz and Ofen (Buda).

Agriculture is the main occupation of the people ; but the timber industry is also of importance, there being 3,734,000 acres covered by forest in the year 1895.[5] Factories are few and far between.

The railways of Croatia are under the control of the Hungarian State, and are constructed and managed in the interests of Budapest and in open defiance of the pressing needs of Croatia. The sole artery of any importance is that which runs through Zagreb, Karlovac (Karlstadt) and Ogulin to Fiume. To this everything is sacrificed. Between Fiume and Agram there is no sideline connecting with Austria. On the line connecting Agram with Steinbrück on the Südbahn, there are no express trains ; while through Nagykanizsa and Steinamanger (the direct route to Vienna) there is no quick service during the daytime. The direct connexion between Agram and Graz has hitherto been prevented, despite Croatia's urgent need for improved access to the markets of Styria. South of Ogulin there is no railway at all. The settled policy of the Magyar Government has hitherto prevented the establishment of a railway connexion between Croatia and Dalmatia, between Croatia and Western Bosnia, between Bosnia and Dalmatia. The connexion between Zagreb and Belgrad is better, but everything is done to force all commerce and traffic between Austria and Bosnia to go by Budapest to Bosnisch-Brod instead of by the much shorter and more natural route through Zagreb.

The total population of Croatia-Slavonia amounted in 1900 to 2,400,766, an increase of 688,413 in twenty years. Of these, 1,482,353 were Croats, 607,381 Serbs—or a total of 2,089,734 Serbo-Croats, as opposed to 311,032 of other races (including 90,180 Magyars and 134,000 Germans). By religion, 1,710,425 were Roman Catholics, 612,604 Serb Orthodox, 43,628 Protestant and 20,032 Jewish.

B. Southern Hungary.

According to the census of 1900 there were 434,641 Serbs in Hungary proper. The mere fact that this involves a decrease of 60,492 since 1880 shows that these statistics must be treated with extreme caution. The Serbs are strongest in three counties : Torontál 183,771 (or 31·2 per cent) ; Bács-Bodrog 114,685 (or 19 per cent.), and Temes 85,000 (or 21·4 per cent.). Their chief centre is Neusatz (Novi Sad, Ujvidék) on the Danube, opposite the great fortress of Peterwardein ; but though the home of the Srpska Matica (Serb literary Academy), a Serb gymnasium and two Serb newspapers, this town has lost its Serb character, at the expense of the Magyar and German elements. Other South Hungarian towns where there is a considerable Serb element are Zombor, Temesvár, Pancsova, Versecz and Bečkerek.

The Croats in Hungary proper amount to 188,552, or only 1·1 of the total population. Their settlements lie for the most part along the frontier of Croatia and Styria, in the counties of Zala (84,356) and Vas (17,847), and even as far north as Oedenburg (Sopron) (30,342). The former county includes the so-called " Medjumurje "—the district lying between the Rivers Drave and Mur and the Styrian frontier—which has

[5] *Enc. Brit.* p. 472.

been a continual bone of contention between Hungary and Croatia. The Magyar Government, while steadily erecting fresh Magyar schools in Croatia and Slavonia through the medium of the Julian Society, has on the other hand, succeeded in almost entirely rooting out the Croat schools of Hungary. At present only four are left.

C. ISTRIA (1,908 square miles).

Istria is after Trieste, Görz and Vorarlberg, the smallest of the seventeen Austrian provinces. It consists of a pear-shaped peninsula, extending from the suburbs of Trieste to the suburbs of Fiume. Its northern boundary adjoins the provinces of Trieste (Küstenland), Görz and Carniola. Pola, the capital, a strong naval base and dockyard, with 45,052 inhabitants, lies close to Cape Promontore, the southernmost extremity of Istria. It possesses a local Diet of thirty-three members, sitting at Parenzo.

Its total population amounted in 1900 to 335,965, of whom 38 per cent. (136,191) were Italians, 15 per cent. (47,717) Slovenes and 45 per cent. (143,057) Croats. All are Roman Catholics. The western coastline from Trieste to Pola is almost entirely Italian ; the uplands of the north-west are Slovene, while the eastern half of the peninsula and the islands of Cherso and Veglia are Croat almost to a man. There is a curious little *enclave* of Roumanians, who settled in Istria during the Middle Ages and still preserve their identity.

D. DALMATIA (4,923 square miles).

The kingdom of Dalmatia, though *de jure* part of the Triune kingdom of Croatia-Slavonia-Dalmatia, has *de facto* been in the possession of Austria since the expulsion of the French in 1815. Dalmatia is little more than a strip of coastline, flanked by innumerable islands ; its greatest breadth is forty miles, and in many places it is as narrow as one to ten miles. Its greatest length, from the islands of the Quarnero to the fortress of Spizza on the Montenegrin frontier, is 210 miles. It is a land of striking contrasts, from the barren mountain barriers of Mosor and Orjen, where the peasantry live under the most adverse possible circumstances and where there is scarcely any soil to cultivate, to the fertile vineyards of the coast and the larger islands.

Zara (Zadar), the capital (with 16,000 inhabitants), is the seat of the Diet, the Governor, and the Archbishop and is an important garrison town ; its chief industry is the production of *maraschino*. Spalato (Split), with a population of 24,000, is already the chief commercial port between Fiume and Patras, and is growing every year. It is the natural outlet for the trade of Bosnia, and has an important future before it, when once the sorely-needed railway connexion has been established between Dalmatia and the outer world. Sebenico (Šibenik) with 11,000 inhabitants, is an important naval base, whose value is enhanced by the great waterfalls of the Krka River. Ragusa (Dubrovnik, 10,000), with its harbour of Gravosa, at present forms the Bosnian railway's first outlet to the Adriatic, and attracts by its beauty and antiquities a growing number of foreign visitors. The Bocche, or narrows of Cattaro, with the little town nestling under precipitous crags, is one of the most impregnable natural harbours on the Mediterranean and serves

5

as a strong Austrian naval base. The principal islands are Brazza (170 square miles), Lesina, Lissa, Curzola, Meleda, Pago and Arbe.

At two separate points—near the mouth of the River Narenta, and at Castelnuovo in the Bocche—Herzegovina reaches the sea for a few miles, thus indicating the ancient boundaries between Turkish and Venetian territory. Neither strip possesses a harbour of any consequence, though Castelnuovo, as the terminus of the railway which links Austria's southernmost naval base with the rest of the monarchy, has a certain strategic importance.

The Dalmatian Croats are one of the finest seafaring races in Europe, and the cream of the Austro-Hungarian navy is recruited from among them. Owing to the poverty of the soil, and the neglected state of the province, most of which has no railway connexions with the rest of Europe and at whose expense the last Austro-Italian commercial treaty was concluded, emigration is widely prevalent ; and there are certain districts, notably the peninsula of Sabbioncello and the island of Curzola, where a large proportion of the male inhabitants can speak English, having either served on British ships or spent some years in America, New Zealand, Queensland or South Africa.

In 1900 the total population amounted to 584,823, of whom only 15,279 were Italians ; of the remaining 97 per cent. (565,276), 80 per cent. were Croats and 16 per cent. Serbs. The rapidity with which the Italian element has decayed during the last thirty years is shown by the example of Lesina. In 1880 as many as 314 per 1,000 of the inhabitants appeared in the census as Italians ; in 1890 there were only 27 Italians left.[6] But Italy has left a permanent impress upon the culture, the architecture and the commerce of Dalmatia and will long remain the *lingua franca* of the coast towns. In Dalmatia as elsewhere among the Serbo-Croats, religion is the only real distinguishing feature between the two races ; the Croats are Roman Catholic, the Serbs are Orthodox. Zara is the seat of a Catholic Archbishop, and there are no fewer than six other bishoprics—Sebenico, Spalato, Lesina, Makarska, Ragusa and Cattaro. The ancient Slavonic liturgy known as the Glagolitic rite, is still in use in several hundred churches along the Adriatic ; but the recognition which Bishop Strossmayer's influence had won for it under Leo XIII, was partially withdrawn by the fanatical Jesuit advisers of the present Pope. At present the controversy is dormant ; but so strong is the affection for the Slav rite that among the Dalmatian peasantry an application of the clumsy tactics for which Vatican diplomacy has become a byeword in the last eight years, might easily provoke a movement for union with the Orthodox Church. The Orthodox Church in Dalmatia has bishops at Zara and Cattaro, its membership being strongest in the extreme north and the extreme south. Strangely enough, it is in connexion with the Orthodox Metropolitan of Bukovina, not with those of Bosnia or Servia. The language of the administration and of education is Serbo-Croat ; in the chief towns the Italian language enjoys equal rights.

E. Bosnia and Herzegovina (19,696 square miles).

The two sister provinces of Bosnia and Herzegovina are bounded by Croatia-Slavonia on the north, by Dalmatia on the west, by Servia,

[6] Auerbach, *Les Races et nationalités en Autriche-Hongrie*, p. 221.

BOSNIA-HERZEGOVINA

Turkey and Montenegro on the east, and are roughly shaped like a heart, which tapers to a narrow point near Castelnuovo (Zelenika) on the Bocche di Cattaro. Though both are mountainous throughout—forming the highlands of the Dinaric Alps, they still show considerable differences of soil and climate. Bosnia, which is more than twice as large as Herzegovina, belongs entirely to the central European system, its chief rivers, the Drina (forming the frontier with Servia), the Bosna, the Vrbas and the Una, all flowing northwards into the Save. Herzegovina, on the other hand, lies to the south of the high watershed formed by the peaks of Konjica and Prozor ; and its only important river, the Narenta, forces its way through a splendid defile until it reaches the Adriatic beyond the wide marshes of Metković and Fort Opus.

In Bosnia the vegetation is later, and the cold in winter is extreme ; while in Herzegovina the heat of summer is semi-tropical. Eighty-eight per cent. of the population are engaged in agriculture or forestry. The magnificent forests, entirely neglected under the Turks, have been to some extent exploited by foreign firms since the Austrian occupation. The burning agrarian question has also been left unsolved for thirty years ; but the first step was taken in April 1911, when the new Diet sanctioned a partial scheme of land purchase. Before criticising the Government too severely for its agrarian and educational omissions, it must be remembered that the army of occupation found a savage wilderness, where the dreadful blight of Ottoman rule had lain for centuries, and a beginning had to be made with such elementary requirements as houses, roads and railways. Too little effort has been made to win the hearts of the people ; but no sane critic can deny the enormous advance in material prosperity made since 1877. Nothing can be more striking than the contrast between Belgrade, which has enjoyed virtual independence for close upon 100 years, and Sarajevo, which thirty years ago was on a level with Broussa or Erzeroum. To-day Sarajevo, with its clean streets and handsome public buildings, entirely eclipses the Servian capital. In 1895 Sarajevo had 41,543 inhabitants, but its population is now estimated at 60,000. It is the seat of the Governor (Landeschef), the provincial government with its four departments of the Interior, Education, Finance and Justice, and since 1910 of the provincial Diet.

Sarajevo and Mostar, the capital of Herzegovina (with over 17,000 inhabitants), are important garrison towns, as also are the frontier fortresses of Trebinje, Bilek, Foča and Višegrad. The only other town of any size is Banjaluka, in the northwest, the terminus of a line originally designed by the Turks to connect Europe with Salonica, but soon abandoned like most Turkish designs.

The population of Bosnia-Herzegovina amounted at the census of 1895 to 1,568,092, and is now estimated at 1,800,000. Of these, at least 96 per cent. are Serbo-Croats.

The attempt of the late Baron Kállay to create an artificial "Bosnian" language was merely a skilful manœuvre, intended to hamper the promoters of Serbo-Croat Unity ; it in no way corresponds to the true facts of the case. The entire native population of the two provinces— with the exception of the 8,000 Jews of the capital—is Serbo-Croat by origin and by language. But as in other Balkan countries, the line of cleavage has hitherto been religious rather than racial. Thus divided, the population is as follows :

Orthodox	670,000
Mohammedan	550,000
Roman Catholics	334,000

All the Orthodox, without exception, regard themselves as Serbs, all the Roman Catholics as Croats. The Mohammedans, on the other hand,—the descendants of the old Slav nobility which foreswore its faith in order to retain its lands—have no strong national consciousness, and are content to remain merely Bosnians. But for the unwise and ineffective proselytism of Archbishop Stadler, the Moslems might ere now have joined the Croat camp ; and signs are not wanting that such a process may take place during the next few years.

The Serb Orthodox Church is under a metropolitan in Sarajevo and three bishops in Mostar, Banjaluka and Tuzla. The Roman Catholics also have an Archbishop in Sarajevo and bishops in Mostar and Banjaluka ; bnt the real backbone of Catholicism in Bosnia is the Franciscan Order, which always identified itself with the popular cause during the Turkish occupation, and still follows with effect its democratic methods. The Vakuf, a wealthy fund, from which the Moslem clergy are paid, has its central offices in Sarajevo ; the ecclesiastical affairs of the Moslems are controlled by the central committee (Medžlis) of four members, under the Reis-ül-Ulema, all of whom are nominated by the Government.

The language of administration, of the Courts,[7] of education and of the Diet is Serbo-Croat.

Sarajevo contains over 8,000 Spagnolan or Sephardic Jews, the descendants of refugees from Spanish persecution in the sixteenth century, and like their kinsmen in Salonica still speaking a mixed Italo-Spanish dialect, in which numerous Slav and Turkish words occur.

F. Servia (18,782 square miles).

The kingdom of Servia is bounded on the north by the Save and the Danube, at whose junction lies the capital, Belgrad, on a ridge commanding an extensive view of the plains of Syrmia and the Banat. The Western, or Bosnian frontier, follows the winding course of the River Drina, the chief tributary of the Save. On the south and south-east lies Macedonia, its northern division, the Sanjak of Novibazar, interposing a wedge of Turkish territory between Servia and Montenegro. On the east Servia is separated from Roumania by the Danube, from Bulgaria by the little river Timok and then by an irregular mountainous boundary to a point south-east of Vranja where Turkey, Servia and Bulgaria meet. The greater part of Servia is mountainous, but its peaks are lower and less barren than those of Bosnia and Montenegro. Its main artery, the river Morava, flows from Vranja on the Turkish frontier, into the Danube east of Semendria, and forms the sole link connecting Europe with the port of Salonica and the Aegean.

The capital, Belgrad, had 69,097 inhabitants in 1900, and to-day over 90,000 ; but despite its fine situation, it has no fine streets or public buildings, and cannot be compared in any way to the rival Southern Slav cities of Zagreb, Sarajevo and Fiume. There are no large towns in

---

[7] Though German litigants can obtain justice in their own tongue.

8

SERVIA

Servia, Niš coming second with 24,451, Kragujevac third, with 14,160 inhabitants.[8]   The great mass of the population lives upon the soil.

While in Bosnia the Serb nobles accepted Islam in order to save their estates, the nobility of Servia was extirpated by the Turks ; and the modern kingdom is composed of peasant proprietors, with only a small middle class.   Even more important than agriculture is the pig-feeding industry, to which the chief families of the country owe their rise, and which has more than once had a decisive influence upon its foreign policy.

After 350 years of Turkish rule, Servia asserted her autonomous position in 1817, and thirteen years later became an hereditary principality under the Obrenovitch dynasty.   Its progress has been seriously hampered by the evil rivalry of the two native dynasties of Obrenovitch and Karageorgevitch, a rivalry which has been marked by a series of atrocious crimes.   In 1817 Kara George was murdered by the orders of Milosch Obrenovitch, and in 1868 the murder was avenged upon the latter's son, Prince Michael, the ablest ruler whom modern Servia has produced.   Michael's nephew Milan inherited much of his uncle's brilliancy and statesmanship ; but though he set the seal to Servia's independence and proclaimed her as a kingdom, the erratic and scandalous habits of his private life undermined his position and finally led him to abdicate in favour of his only son Alexander (March 3, 1889).   The last and most unfortunate of the Obrenovitch dynasty was also by no means devoid of talent ; but a faulty education and the evil example of his parents rendered stability of character impossible.   A passion for coup d'états and his foolish marriage with Draga Mašin made Servia the pariah of European royalty and led to the inevitable catastrophe.   On June 11, 1903, a gang of officers in uniform brutally murdered the King and Queen ; and a few days later, the Pretender, Prince Peter Karageorgevič, whom scandal accused of complicity in the murder, as in the death of Prince Michael thirty-six years before—was proclaimed King as Peter I.

The liberal constitution which King Milan had granted in 1889 and which his son arbitrarily superseded five years later, was now restored ; and since then, whatever may be said of Peter Karageorgevič, he has fully earned the title of Servia's first *constitutional* sovereign.   Unhappily, the corruption which had already deeply infected Servian public life, has gathered strength from the rivalry of regicides and anti-regicides.   The Radical party, which has dominated Servia since the assassination, has shown leanings for an adventurous foreign policy, but the country entirely lacks either the resources or the energy to carry it into effect.   The megalomania which led public opinion to compare Servia with Austria-Hungary, was responsible for the cruel but inevitable disillusionment of March 1909.[9]

Since the outbreak of the tariff war (1907) Servia has been able to emancipate herself to some extent from the economic thraldom of the Dual Monarchy, and to find new markets for her produce.   But the absence of direct railway connexions with the West, the huge burdens which her army imposes upon her, and the bad state of her finances, fatally handicap Servia in her efforts to keep abreast of

---

[8] Požarevac, Leskovac, Šabac, Vranja, Pirot and Kruševac also exceed 10,000 inhabitants.

[9] See Chapter ix.

other Balkan states. While Bulgaria and Roumania have a bright future before them, and have progressed during the last generation by leaps and bounds, Servia, on the other hand, has been at the mercy of rival dynastic and party feuds and occupies a position between the upper and the nether millstone.

The population of Servia amounted in 1900 to 2,493,770, and is calculated at 2,750,000 in 1910. Of these, over 90 per cent. are Serbs ; but there are at least 200,000 Roumanians in the north-east district adjoining Negotin, and no fewer than 47,000 gipsies. Almost the entire population belongs to the Orthodox Church, which has a Metropolitan in Belgrad and four bishops at Niš (south), Šabac (north-west), Užice (west) and Negotin (east). Like other would-be " national " states, Servia is not specially tolerant of other races or creeds. The Roumanians of East Servia are not allowed to employ their own language in the schools, and in some cases not even in the churches. Though religious liberty is guaranteed by law, the Roman Catholic Church is virtually proscribed in Servia ; though it is fair to add that this is a form of retaliation against the Catholic propaganda in Bosnia and other Orthodox countries. That intolerance does exist in Servia, is best proved by the treatment of the great Southern Slav patriot Bishop Strossmayer, to whose diocese the Catholics of Belgrad belong.

Education in Servia is also extremely backward. Though by law primary education is free and compulsory, only 17 per cent. of the population could read and write in 1910.[10] In such circumstances the outcry raised in Belgrad against the backward state of Bosnian education, would appear to be somewhat uncalled for.

G. MONTENEGRO (3,255 square miles).

The other independent Serb state is the little principality of Montenegro, proclaimed a kingdom in 1910, on the occasion of Prince Nicholas' Jubilee. Little as it is, it was even smaller before the year 1880, when it first gained access to the sea at Dulcigno and Antivari. Its natural harbour, Cattaro, has become an important Austrian naval base : the roadstead of Antivari is commanded by the Austrian guns at Spizza. This harbour, of which so much is vaguely written in West Europe, is only accessible by a steep mountain railway (built by an Italian company) which climbs up 3,000 feet from Virpazar on the Lake of Skutari, merely in order to descend still more abruptly to the sea. Whatever it may become in the future, its present traffic, both by sea and by rail, is far less important than that of Mallaig, on the West Highland Railway ! Dulcigno and the only promising connexion between the coast and the interior would appear to be the regulation of the River Bojana, which connects the lake and town of Skutari with the sea, and forms for part of its course the southern frontier of Montenegro. For this the co-operation of Turkey is required ; and as Turkey has never done anything for Albania, she is less likely than ever to do so now. The only hope is that the present movement in Albania may lead to an extension of Montenegrin territory to the south.

The existing frontier, after leaving the Bojana, crosses the centre of the Lake of Skutari, and then follows an irregular north-easterly direc-

---

[10] *Encycl. Brit.* (11th ed.) xxiv. p. 690.

tion to a point only ten miles west of Ipek (Peč in northern Macedonia. From here it proceeds northwest, bounding with the Sandjak of Novibazar, until it reaches Herzegovina ; for nearly fifty miles it follows the course of the river Tara.   On the west it is bounded by Herzegovina and Dalmatia, the latter country tapering into a narrow strip of land thirty miles long by barely four miles broad, from Cattaro to Spizza.

Cetinje, the tiny capital, had 5,138 inhabitants in 1907 (including the foreign residents).   Podgorica, on the Morača river, with 12,347 inhabitants, Nikšić with 6,872, and Dulcigno with 5,166 are the chief commercial centres.

The total population in 1900 was estimated at 311,564,[11] of whom all save an infinitesimal number are Serb by nationality and Orthodox by religion.   The barren nature of the country—the southern half is a mere rocky wilderness, though round Nikšić there is good corn land [12]— has driven increasing numbers to emigrate ; and the return of such as make their fortune, is naturally effecting the same transformation of the old national ideas as is noticeable in Hungary, Dalmatia and other primitive countries where emigration and reimmigration is prevalent.

The Petrović dynasty, which has ruled Montenegro since the year 1696, was originally a race of prince-bishops, or Vladikas, in which the nephew followed the uncle.   It has produced more than one remarkable figure—Peter I (1782–1830), who won from the Turks a definite recognition of Montenegrin independence and temporarily occupied the Bocche di Cattaro ; Peter II (1830–1851), who holds a foremost place among Servian poets ; and not least of all, Prince, now King, Nicholas, who has reigned since 1860.   As a mountain fastness, where war against the Turks has for centuries been the main business of life, Montenegro had no need for a prince who was not at the same time an autocrat ; and it was not till 1905 that the country obtained a constitution.   Even since then the old methods have survived in a thinly-disguised form ; and since the notorious Treason Trial of 1908, ministers have been mere creatures of the Prince, and representative government little better than a farce.   To those who insist upon judging Montenegro by the standards of the twentieth century in Paris or London, King Nicholas may well seem a monster of reaction.   In reality he and his state still belong to the heroic Middle Ages, and need not fear comparison with the warriors of Bruce, Du Guesclin or John Hunyády.   Under Nicholas' successors an era of transition must set in ; Montenegro will be adapted to Western conditions and will doubtless lose in the process many of its primitive virtues.

The Orthodox Church of Montenegro consists of two dioceses, Cetinje and Ostrog.   In striking contrast to Servia, where no Catholic hierarchy is tolerated, there is a Catholic Archbishop at Antivari (Bar), with ten parishes and about 6,000 adherents.

H. Turkey.

In dealing with the Serb population, we are confronted by the complete absence of reliable statistics.   The Hamidian régime did not trouble about censuses, and such estimates as exist are almost avowedly based

---

[11] *Encycl. Brit.* xviii. p. 768.
[12] Yet Montenegro, despite its small population, has to import corn.

upon the wishes of their compilers, Greek, Serb or Bulgar as the case might be, rather than on the actual facts of the case. The Macedonian practice of the forcible conversion of villages by the rival bands, has still further complicated the problem, until it is by no means easy to form any definite judgment, even upon seemingly first-hand evidence, as to the true nationality of many districts. Roughly speaking, the territory inhabited by Serbs comprises the whole Sandjak of Novibazar (which separates Servia from Montenegro and was from 1878 to 1908 garrisoned by Austrian troops), the district of Ipek, Jakova and Prisrend (from the Sandjak as far south as the river Drin) ; and the plain of Kossovo, from Mitrovica on the north extending through Pristina and Üsküb to Istib on the south. South and east of this point there may be isolated Serb colonies ; but if so, they are doomed to rapid absorption by the Bulgar element. Even in the neighbourhood of Prisrend the Serbs are steadily losing ground at the expense of the Albanians. Since the accession of King Peter, Servia has made more desperate efforts than ever to arrest the fatal process in Macedonia which is destined some day to decide the struggle of races in favour of Bulgar and Albanian, and against Serb and Greek. But the efforts of the Servian bands have not as a rule been successful. While the Serbs talk and sentimentalize, the Bulgars act and the Albanians shoot.

If the total population of Macedonia be reckoned at 2,500,000, the most liberal allowance cannot assign more than 400,000 of these (including 100,000 Moslems) to the Serb element.

A general survey of the Croato-Serb race may be obtained from the following table :—

	Catholic.	Orthodox.	Mohammedan.
Istria	200,000	—	—
Dalmatia	500,000	100,000	—
Croatia-Slavonia	1,750,000	650,000	—
Bosnia-Herzegovina	400,000	850,000	650,000
Hungary.	250,000	500,000	—
Servia	—	2,600,000	—
Montenegro	10,000	280,000	10,000
Turkey	10,000	300,000	100,000
	3,120,000	5,280,000	760,000
	(34 p.c.)	(58 p.c.)	(8 p.c.)

Croats and Serbs in Europe 9,160,000
„ „ in America 300,000

9,460,000

Pronunciation.

c	=ts in the English	" lots "	
č	= ch	"	" church "
ć	= t	"	" tune "
gj	= j	"	" June "
j	= y	"	" yet "

lj	= gl in the Italian	" meglio "
nj	= gn	"	" degno "
š	= sh in the English	" show "
ž	= j in the French	" jour "
vj	= vi in the English	" view "

all other letters as in English.

CHAPTER I

Croatia from the Earliest Times till 1848

Regnum Regno non praescribit leges.

THE modern Croats, although they occupy the ancient territory of the Illyrians, trace their descent not from these re-
doubtable opponents of Roman rule upon the Adriatic, but from
one of the Slavonic tribes which followed in the rear of the advancing Lombards and Avars. From the scanty records which
have survived, it would seem probable that the Chrobati or
Chorvati were invited by the Emperor Heraclius to free Illyria
from the Avars (634) and that, after the completion of their
task, they remained for many generations as the nominal
vassals of the Eastern Empire. About the same time a kindred Slavonic tribe, the Serbs, were encouraged to settle
further to the east, and thus became masters of the greater
part of the modern Servia, Bosnia and Montenegro, with a
coastline stretching roughly from Almissa to Durazzo. In the
maritime towns of Dalmatia Roman institutions and Roman
culture survived until the rise of Venice as a sea-power finally
prevented Dalmatia from drifting out of the sphere of Western
civilization. Had it not been for Venice there can be little
doubt that the eastern Adriatic would have been lost to Rome.
For when the Exarchate of Ravenna was conquered by the
Lombards (752), Zara had become the Byzantine headquarters
on the Adriatic; and, although the civil authority of the
Emperor grew every year more shadowy, the influence of the
Eastern Church was very far from nominal. The final schism
between east and west coincides with the first mission of the
great Slav apostles, Cyril and Methodius, (865–885), and
explains the readiness with which Rome recognized their introduction of a Slav liturgy. This momentous concession was,
it is true, revoked soon after the death of Methodius; but a
thousand years of opposition on the part of Rome have not
availed to extirpate the Slav liturgy. The mountainous

character of the country, the vicinity of the Serbs, and at a later date the rise of the Bogumile heresy in Bosnia, kept the ancient traditions alive ; and when the national revival of the nineteenth century once more directed attention to the subject, the Glagolitic rite was still in use in several hundred parishes in Dalmatia, Istria and Southern Croatia.

Thus from the very outset the most marked feature in Southern Slav history is its dual character. The struggle between Latin and Slav culture, between the traditions of Rome and Byzantium, made itself continually felt alike in Church and in state, and led to an estrangement between the kindred races of Croat and Serb, which rendered their national consolidation impossible and made the two rivals the prey of foreign conquerors. Not till the nineteenth century did they begin to comprehend the simple truth that union is strength.

The conquests of Charles the Great had shown the Croats that they had little to fear from Constantinople, and under his degenerate successors they felt themselves strong enough (or remote enough) to defy both empires. During the first quarter of the t :nth century Duke Tomislav assumed the royal title,[1] recognizing, like St. Stephen of Hungary three generations later, the suzerainty of the Papal See ; and the most famous of his successors, Zvonimir, actually received the crown in Spalato from the hands of the Legate of Gregory VII (1076). But Zvonimir's greatness died with him. The extinction of the national dynasty plunged Croatia into civil war, and in 1102 the Croat nobles recognized Coloman King of Hungary as their sovereign. Coloman asserted the triple claims of conquest, inheritance and election. His own armies had completed the half-finished work of his uncle Ladislas I : the widow of the childless Zvonimir had been a Hungarian princess, and Coloman now wisely set a seal to these doubtful pretensions by his coronation at Zaravecchia and by the assumption of the title " Rex Hungariae Croatiae atque Dalmatiae."

It would be a mistake to suppose that the mutual relations of Hungary and Croatia had already been closely defined under Coloman ; but there is abundant evidence that the great king, following the tolerant traditions of the House of Árpád, respected the privileges and independent position of Croatia,

[1] In the decrees of a council held at Spalato in the year 914, in the presence of the Legate of Pope John X., Tomislav already bears the title of Chroatorum Rex. Kukuljević, *Jura Regni Croatiae Dalmatiae et Slavoniae,* i. p. 8, copied from Farlati, *Illyricum Sacrum,* iii. p. 93.

and that as yet the sole link between the two kingdoms was the person of the monarch. During the two centuries following upon the Union, more than one Hungarian sovereign entrusted his son with the government of Croatia.[2] It is true that the practice of a separate coronation as King of Croatia was gradually allowed to fall into abeyance ; but that this did not involve the incorporation of Croatia in Hungary is shown by the fact that in 1301, on the extinction of the House of Árpád, the Croatians crowned the Angevin prince Charles Robert as their king in the Cathedral of Zagreb (Agram), while Hungary elected first the King of Bohemia and then Otto of Bavaria. It was not till six years later that the recognition of Charles Robert by the Hungarians restored the personal union between the two kingdoms. But under Charles Robert's son Louis the Great, Hungary reached the zenith of her power and Croatia sank, in fact, if perhaps not in theory, to the rank of a vassal state. Louis showed special favour to Bosnia, whose Ban he allowed to assume the royal title (1376), partly, no doubt, from family reasons, for his wife was a cousin of the Ban Stephen Tvrtko, but probably still more from strategic reasons, since Bosnia was a valuable outpost against Servia, which under Stephen Dushan (1336–1356) had become the most formidable Balkan state. On the other hand Louis brought nothing but misery upon Croatia and Dalmatia, by his ruthless infringement of ancient charters, and his continual wars with Venice and Naples. This may perhaps account for the zeal with which the sister kingdoms abandoned Louis' daughter Mary and supported the candidature of Charles of Durazzo, King of Naples, and later on of his son Ladislas, whose coronation as King of Hungary and Croatia took place at Zara in 1403.

While the weak successors of Louis the Great became involved in internecine war, Stephen Tvrtko was raising the

---

[2] *See* Farlati, *Illyricum Sacrum*, T. v. p. 65, cit. Kukuljević, op. cit. vol. i. p. 35.   A Spalatan Charter of 1194 contains the phrase, "Regnante Domino nostro Bela, Serenissimo Rege Hungariae Dalmatiae Croatiae atque Ramae et Almerico (Emerich) filio super Dalmatiam et Chroatiam." Ibid. ex tabulario Jadertino. "Anno 1195. Regnante D. N. Bela Ungariae Dalmatiae Ramae Rege, et Enrico (i.e. Emerich) eius filio, bis coronato, Dalmatiam et Croatiam feliciter gubernante. . . ." In 1198 and 1199 Bela III.'s other son, Prince Andrew, as Duke of Dalmatia and Croatia, grants charters to the Archbishop of Spalato. ("Ego Andreas tertii Belae Regis filius, Dei gratia Dalmatiae Croatiae Ramae Chulmaeque Dux in perpetuum ") Kukuljević, i. pp. 36–7.

Bosnian kingdom to a position of importance. In the very year when Servia's greatness was overthrown by the Turks on the fatal field of Kossovo (1389) Tvrtko, intent upon his own aggrandisement, gained possession of the whole Dalmatian littoral from Zara to Cattaro. But his greatness did not survive his death in 1391. The Republic of Venice and the King of Naples were soon the only serious rivals for the spoils of Dalmatia. The Magyar nobility's opposition to a foreign king, the decisive advantage which Venice derived from her navy, and the first mutterings of the Turkish storm, gradually withdrew Hungary from the competition.

The failure of Ladislas to make good his claims marks an era in Croatian history out of all proportion to the trivial character of the Neapolitan King. For in 1409 Venice bought from him what remained of his Dalmatian possessions, and by 1420 practically the whole Dalmatian coast, with the exception of the little Republic of Ragusa, was in her hands. Henceforward Croatia and Dalmatia remain apart. The fringe of coast remained for almost three centuries a Venetian colony, systematically neglected and exploited and used merely as a stepping-stone to the Levant. The whole *Hinterland* gradually fell into Turkish hands, until the Crescent waved over the fortress of Clissa, in full sight of Spalato. By comparison with the rest of the Balkans, Dalmatia seemed to enjoy a high level of culture ; but in reality it was already stagnant and living upon its past. The Republic of Ragusa alone shone like a beacon amid the surrounding gloom. Its poets, satirists and dramatic writers—notably Gundulić, the famous author of *Osman*— prepared the way for a renaissance of the Croat language and of Serbo-Croatian national feeling in the nineteenth century.

Sigismund of Luxemburg, the successful rival of Ladislas, showed a not unnatural resentment towards the subjects who had so long disputed his title to the throne. From his reign dates the final abandonment of a separate coronation ceremony for Croatia ; henceforth the Holy Crown of St. Stephen was held to be sufficient for the two kingdoms, and the mystic halo with which long centuries of tradition have gradually surrounded it, seemed in the eyes of the Magyars a symbol of inviolable union between the two countries.

But while Croatia contented herself with a separate *diploma inaugurale* [3] at each fresh accession, she had by no means

[3] The formal document embodying the King's oath and his subjects' fealty and privileges.

renounced her ancient independence, and reasserted her freedom of action on more than one important occasion. In 1490 the estates of Croatia declined to recognize Vladislav II until he had taken oath to respect their liberties, and insisted upon his erasing from the diploma certain phrases which seemed to reduce Croatia to the rank of a mere province.[4]

Far more conclusive, however, was the action of the Croats after the battle of Mohács (1526), where the Hungarian army was annihilated by the Turks and Louis II himself perished. Central Hungary—the real Magyar kernel of the country—became a Turkish province, Transylvania secured its independence by owning the Sultan's suzerainty, while the north and east remained for fourteen years a bone of contention between John Zápolya and Ferdinand of Habsburg. But Croatia had not shared in the fatal defeat ; for the incapable Louis and his arrogant nobles, unwilling to share with others the glory of certain victory, had intentionally given battle two days before the arrival of the Croatian army.[5] While Hungary fell a prey to anarchy and a contested succession, the Croatian Diet sitting at Cetin on January 1, 1527, unanimously elected Ferdinand of Austria as their king, and confirmed the succession to him and his heirs.[6] Thus while in Hungary the Crown remained elective till 1687, it had already become hereditary in Croatia 160 years earlier.

[4] See Kukuljević, iii. p. 9. The original diploma ran, " Regnum Ungariae cum ceteris regnis et partibus subjectis." The final version, as accepted by the Croats in 1492 and inserted in the Corpus Juris Hungarici, ran as follows : " Regnum Ungariae cum caeteris regnis scilicet Dalmatiae Croatiae et Slavoniae et partibus Transylvanis ac provinciis sibi subjectis."

[5] An interesting sidelight is thrown upon the relations between Magyars and Croats in the sixteenth century by the letter which the Ban, Krsto Frankopan, wrote to the Bishop of Zengg on September 15, 1526, upon the first (and incomplete) news of the Battle of Mohács " Since the king has escaped, God Almighty has clearly permitted this defeat of the king and the Hungarians, not for the misfortune and ruin of this country, but on the contrary for its lasting salvation. For if the Hungarians had now defeated the emperor (i.e. Sultan) where would have been the end of their unworthy aggression (reženju, literally the snarl of a quarrelsome dog), and who could have continued to exist under them ? " Cit. Klaić, *Povjest Hrvata*, iii. pp. 357–8.

[6] On the other hand, the Estates of Slavonia (*Universitas Regni Sclavoniae*) sitting in the Castle of Dubrava, elected John Zápolya as their King (January 5, 1527) ; but the latter's chief supporter, Krsto Frankopan falling in battle the following autumn, Zápolya soon lost ground, and a new Diet at Križevci (Kreuz) declared for Ferdinand.

The Sultan's overwhelming victory at Mohács marked a fresh stage in the westward advance of the Turks, who had been a standing menace to Croatia ever since the conquest of Bosnia by Mohammed II (1463). In 1528 the strong garrison town of Jajce fell before the Turks and within a few years they had captured Banjaluka and occupied the whole of Syrmia and what is now known as Slavonia. Finally in 1537 the Crescent gained entrance to the mountain fortress of Clissa, and thus threatened Spalato and the coastline of mid-Dalmatia. Though the position of Croatia was never so desperate as that of the sister kingdom of Hungary, the struggle with the Turks rendered all progress and real culture impossible, and effectually undermined the prosperity of the country. The natural result was a desperate Peasant Rising in the year 1573, which still further weakened Croatia and was suppressed with the utmost cruelty.

The Turkish danger and the increasingly despotic leanings of the later Habsburgs drew Croatia and Hungary once more together. Rudolf II's attempt to curtail the power of the Ban [7] induced the *Sabor* (Diet) to send its representatives

---

[7] The office of Ban is of great antiquity. That it already existed under the native Croat dynasty is proved by its mention in a Diploma of King Krešimir in 1063 (quoted by Lucius, the Dalmatian historian. *See* Virozsil, ii. 335 n., 387). After the union in 1102 the Ban naturally acquired greater importance, as the representative of the Royal power in Croatia. At first all Croatia and Slavonia (which then denoted a somewhat different territory) were under a single Ban ; but from time to time, when special causes, such as Byzantine and Venetian aggression, impaired the authority of the Hungarian King, we meet with a special Ban of Slavonia (Banus totius Slavoniae) and even a *Banus Maritimus* (*see* Timon, *Ungarische Verfassungsgeschichte*, pp. 244–50) ; but these dignities were merely conferred temporarily. Previous to 1848 the Ban was, under the Crown, supreme alike in the political, judicial and military spheres. He presided over the Diets : he sat as Croat representative in the Hungarian Council of Lieutenancy, after its formation ; he took precedence immediately after the Palatine and the Judex Curiae, and held the golden apple at the Coronation ; he acted as President of the Banal Table, the supreme Croatian Court, (from which there has been no appeal to any Hungarian court, at any rate, since Louis the Great in 1359 recognized Croatia's full judicial autonomy) and as such appointed the Vice-Ban ; finally he commanded the military levies of Croatia-Slavonia and the Croatian Military Frontiers. In accordance with the Compromise of 1868, the Ban, though expressly made responsible to the Diet of Agram (§§ 50, 51), became the nominee of the Hungarian Premier, and as such, the representative of Budapest rather than of Agram (*see* pp. 78–9).

(*sollemnes oratores et nuntii regni*) to the Hungarian Diet, there
to defend the rights of Croatia (1591) ; and under Ferdinand
II the Ban, at the express desire of the Croats themselves, took
his seat for the first time in the Hungarian House of Magnates
(1625). That this did not involve the dependence of the Croatian upon the Hungarian Diet, is clearly shown by the fact that
the former, in 1608, had formally ratified and accepted the
Treaty of Vienna, concluded between Matthias and the Magyars
for joint action against the Turks. Indeed, this exercise of
sovereign power on the part of Croatia seems to have been
treated at the time as a matter of course.[8]   Yet another striking
proof that the friendship prevailing between the Croats and
the Magyars did not in any way involve the former's subordination to the latter, is supplied by the action of the Croatian
Diet in the year 1620, in entering upon " a mutual bond of
union and confederation " with the Provinces of Styria, Carinthia and Carniola.[9] The Hungarian Parliament was neither
consulted, nor did it raise any protest against the Croats'
independent attitude.

This period of unruffled amity between the two races is per-
sonified in the splendid figure of Count Nicholas Zrinski (known
by the Magyars as Zrinyi) (1620–1664), who though a patriotic
Croat, composed the first great epic poem in the Magyar language,[10] and left to the Magyars a still more precious legacy
in his niece's child, Francis Rákóczy, the now half-legendary
forerunner of Louis Kossuth. The modern Chauvinist of Buda-

---

[8] Kukuljević, op. cit. ii, pp. 66–7. Here the phrase " Regnum
Hungariae et Provinciae Confœderatae " is employed, the latter, of
course, to describe Croatia-Slavonia.

[9] Kukuljević, op. cit. ii, p. 75. Et haec Regna cum praenominatis
Styriae Carynthiae et Carniolae Provinciis mutuam unionis et certae
confederationis devinctionem ineant (always saving the rights and pre-
rogatives of His Imperial Majesty, of the King of Hungary and of
" these kingdoms ").

[10] This poem, " The Siege of Sziget," celebrates the heroic death of
the poet's grandfather, Count Nicholas Zrinsky, in defending the castle
of Sziget against a vast Turkish army under Suleiman the Magnificent
(1566). It shows the influence of Virgil and Tasso. The poet's brother,
the unfortunate Peter Zrinsky, was a Croatian poet of some note. He
translated " The Siege of Sziget " and " The Siren of the Adriatic "
from the Magyar originals into " our Croatian language " (to quote his
own words). Wherever the Magyar text speaks of " our dear home,"
(mi édes hazánk), he rendered the phrase as " obramba hàrvatska,"
(the defence of Croatia) and elsewhere he sought to emphasize whatever
of Croat sentiment the original contains.

pest is wont to claim him as a Magyar, despite the evident pride with which he referred to his Croat ancestry,[11] and he will certainly remain the type of the old fraternal relations of two hostile nations.

By the beginning of the seventeenth century Croatia and Slavonia had already been reduced to a mere fragment of their former territory—reliquiae reliquiarum regni, in the despondent, phrase of that day.[12] The frontier extended from Zengg to the new fortress of Karlovac (Karlstadt) [13] and Sisak, and thence through the county of Križevci (Kreuz) to the river Drave. The wild mountainous district of the Velebit was contested between the Venetians whose authority was confined to the coast towns, the notorious Uskok pirates—Christian refugees from Turkish territory, whose hand was against every man's, and who from their headquarters at Zengg, kept the whole Dalmatian coast in a ferment—and the Turks, who held the whole of Bosnia, Herzegovina and Slavonia and certain points upon the coast. Defence against Turkish aggression formed for many generations the main occupation of the Croatian population, which deserved in the sixteenth and seventeenth centuries the title of *propugnaculum reipublicae christianae* as truly as Hungary in the great age of John Hunyády. In the first period of chaos which succeeded Mohács, the territory between Drave and Save was guarded by an army supported by the Styrian Estates,[14] while the districts lying between the river Kulpa and the Adriatic were left to the care of the Estates of Carniola. In the course of time a special province, subject to the direct authority of the Emperor, was formed under the title of " the Military Frontiers " (Vojna Krajina). It was divided into two " generalates," the " Slavonian " and the " Croatian," with their headquarters in Varaždin [15] and Karlovac respectively,

[11] In 1658 he wrote, in a Latin letter to the Vice-Sheriff of Agram, " Ego mihi conscius aliter sum ; etenim non degenerem me Croatam et quidem Zrinium esse scio." Cit. Andrić, Kroatische Literaturgeschichte. (*Die österreichischungarische Monarchie in Wort und Bild*, Croatian volume, pp. 128–9). That Zrinsky was in his own age generally regarded as a Croat rather than a Magyar, is shown by the writings of an early Croatian poet, Vitezović, who devotes an interminable epic (Odilenje Sigetsko, The Siege of Sziget) to the exploits of Zrinsky as a Croatian hero.

[12] Cit. Bojničić, *Kroatien (Wort und Bild)*, p. 70.

[13] Erected in 1578 by the Archduke Charles, as commander of the frontier forces.

[14] Bojničić, pp. 68, 71.

[15] Afterwards in Koprejinica. A third district, " The Banal Fron-

and these were organized and governed on a purely military basis. Every Granitschar or Frontiersman was liable to military service from his eighteenth year, and must at all times be ready to bear arms against the invader ; but in return for this duty, successive emperors granted substantial privileges, and the Granitschars were justly famous not only for their military prowess but also for their sturdy independence of character. Every commune elected its head, and all the communes of a capitanate, their joint Judge, the election in each case requiring the sanction of the commanding officer.[16] The Orthodox Church enjoyed the same privileges as Catholicism, in striking contrast to more northerly countries.

Early in the eighteenth century the question of the succession again became acute, owing to the failure of male heirs in the House of Habsburg ; and once more Croatia followed an entirely independent course. The efforts of Charles VI (III) to secure the Habsburg inheritance in the female line, met with their first success in Croatia, where the Diet unanimously accepted the Pragmatic Sanction on March 9, 1712. Though the Hungarian Diet withheld its consent to Charles' proposals till 1723, no voice of protest was raised against the action of the Croatian estates, no attempt was made to assert the suzerainty of Hungary.[17] Nor is it easy to ascribe this silence to a careless neglect ; for in the course of the discussion the estates publicly defined their position in the following momentous words. " Neither force nor conquest united us to the Hungarians, but by our spontaneous and free desire we submitted ourselves not to the kingdom [of Hungary] but to their king, so long as he be of the House of Austria. . . . We are freemen, not slaves." [18] Nothing could be more explicit than

tier," or the district of the Ban, between the Kulpa and the Una, was subject to the authority of the Ban and of the Estates. By the peace of Karlovitz (1699) Slavonia and the Lika district were definitely freed from the Turkish yoke ; the former was formed into a third " Generalate," while the latter was incorporated in the " Croatian Frontier." In 1745 the three Slavonian counties (Syrmia, Virovitica and Požega) were cut off from this, and restored to the civil administration.

[16] See Staré, *Die Kroaten*, p. 44. Šišić, *Povijest Hrvatska*, ii, p. 100.

[17] The Croatian Pragmatic Sanction differs in an interesting detail from those of Hungary and Bohemia. It declares that in default of male heirs, Croatia will accept that Habsburg princess who reigning at Vienna also possesses the three duchies of Austria, Styria and Carniola (dum simul Austriam Styriam ac Carniolam possideat atque in Austria resideat). (*See* Kukuljević, ii, p. 110.)

[18] " Partes quidem sumus, uti leges loquuntur, annexae Hungariae,

23

this ; and it is incredible that the Hungarian Diet would have left such a challenge unanswered, if its tenour had not been generally recognized as justified by historic usage and tradition.

But this vindication of Croatian rights was a barren victory. The Hungarian Pragmatic Sanction of 1723, which has been justly regarded as the real basis of Dualism,[19] marks the opening of a new era, in which the Hungarian aristocracy renewed its strength in the sunshine of court favour, and then employed all the weapons which a subtle policy of voluntary Germanization had placed in its hands, to reverse the tolerant policy of St. Stephen and to transfuse the old aristocratic constitution with the virus of racial monopoly. The exhaustion which followed upon the final expulsion of the Turks may account for the impunity with which Charles III and his daughter Maria Theresa ignored all constitutional forms in their dominions ; but under the old constitution the real centre of gravity lay not so much in the central Diet as in the local assemblies, which controlled their delegates with the utmost jealousy ; and for the present it sufficed that the old local autonomy had once more become a reality. Meanwhile the new Council of Lieutenancy which had been established in 1729, while in certain respects obsequious to Vienna, showed by its attitude towards Croatia that it was by no means indifferent to the interests of Hungary. When in 1767 Maria Theresa erected in Zagreb (Agram) a similar Council for Croatia, depending directly from the Aulic Chancellory in Vienna, the Hungarians skilfully won the Croat nobility to their side and induced their sovereign not merely to abandon this scheme, but to subject Croatia directly to the council of Lieutenancy in Pest (1779). The power of the Ban was radically curtailed, and Croatia-Slavonia came to be regarded no longer as *regna socia*, but merely as *partes adnexae* of the Crown of St. Stephen.

At this critical period of her history Croatia, like Bohemia, was at a fatal disadvantage, owing to the disappearance of

non autem subditi ; et nativos olim habebamus non Hungaros Reges ; nullaque vis, nulla captivitas nos Hungaris addixit, sed spontanea nostra ultroneaque voluntate non quidem Regno verum eorundem Regi nosmet subjecimus . . . Liberi sumus, non mancipia." Kukuljević ii. pp. 105–7.

[19] The ablest exponent of this view is M. Eisenmann, whose brilliant study, *Le Compromis Austro-Hongrois* is an indispensable handbook for the student of constitutional development in the Dual Monarchy.

her ancient nobility.   The ruin of the great families of Zrinsky and Frankopan after the conspiracy of 1670, had brought huge tracts of Croatian territory into the hands of alien families, whose interests speedily became identical with those of the Magyar aristocracy.[20]   Thus the reforms of Joseph II completed the bond of union between the nobility of the two kingdoms ;   in the struggle against Viennese encroachment the rights of the Croatian Sabor were neglected.   The Diet of 1791, it is true, solemnly reaffirmed the special character of Croatia, as the sole condition of the union with Hungary [21] ; but its delegates received the fatal instructions to acquiesce in the decisions of the majority in all matters common to the two countries, and only to resist in matters of local concern. As the tiny group of Croats could never be anything save an insignificant minority in the Diet, these instructions were tantamount to a complete surrender of the Croatian position. The folly of such a surrender became only too apparent in the course of the next fifty years, as the current of national feeling grew steadily stronger among the Magyars.   The linguistic question was the cause of ever recurring conflicts in the joint Diet between Magyars and Croats.   While the former sought to Magyarize the whole administration and to introduce Magyar as the language of parliamentary debate, the Croats as yet clung desperately to the prevailing Latin, and deprecated all change.[22]   At first their resistance was inspired by mere conservatism and the reluctance to learn a foreign tongue ; but in 1805 Croat national feeling was already awake, and Bishop Vrhovac of Agram openly urged the Croats to retaliate by introducing the " lingua Illyrica " into the public life of the country.   The higher clergy in Croatia enjoy a well-earned reputation for patriotism and generosity, and Bishop

[20] The territory recovered from the Turks was also granted mainly to foreign families, e.g., Odescalchi, Colloredo, Trenck, Caraffa, Prandau, Rauch.

[21] " Cum regna haec . . . inde ab origine propriam habuerint consistentiam et sub hac unice propriae consistentiae conditione semet regno Hungariae univerint."   Cit. Pliverić, *Beiträge zum ungarisch-kroatischen Bundesrechte*, p. 153 (from Minutes of Sabor, p. 173 in Archives).

[22] It is worth noting that even the Croatian delegates of 1790—the most Magyarophil whom Croatia has ever sent to the joint Hungaro-Croatian Parliament—protested vehemently against the introduction of the Magyar language, and made it clear that its adoption in Hungary proper (intra recinctum Regni Hungariae) would not have any binding effect upon Croatia.

Vrhovac set a splendid example by his various literary enterprises.

Meanwhile the desperate struggle against Napoleon, in which the Habsburg Monarchy was so intimately involved, tended to throw all else into the background. But while in Hungary the progress of the national movement was unquestionably arrested for a time—or at least driven from political into literary channels—in Croatia on the other hand the real awakening of national sentiment dates from the Napoleonic era. Dalmatia, which on the fall of the Venetian Republic (1797) had for the first time become an Austrian possession, was ceded to the French after the defeat of Austerlitz ; and the genius of Napoleon revived the name, and with it perhaps something of the spirit, of ancient Illyria. The new state thus suddenly created, comprised the provinces of Carinthia, Carniola, Görz and Istria, the seacoast of Croatia, Dalmatia with its islands, and from 1808 onwards the republic of Ragusa.[23] In Napoleon's own words, ' Illyria is the guard set before the gates of Vienna.' [24] Under the enlightened if despotic rule of Marshal Marmont the long stagnation of the Middle Ages was replaced by feverish activity in every branch of life. Administration and justice were reorganized, the Code Napoléon superseding the effete mediaeval codes ; schools, primary and secondary, commercial and agricultural, sprang up in every direction : the first Croat and Slovene newspapers appeared : the old Guild System was reformed and commercial restrictions removed : peasant proprietary was introduced : reafforestation was begun, and the splendid roads were constructed which are still the admiration of every tourist. Official business was conducted in French and Croatian, with the addition of Italian along the coast. A well known story relates how the Emperor Francis, during his visit to Dalmatia in 1818, plied his suite with questions as to the origin of the various public works which struck his eye, and met with the invariable answer, " The French, your Majesty." " Wirklich schad' dass s' nit länger blieben sein " (It's a real pity they didn't stop longer), exclaimed the astonished Emperor in his favourite Viennese dialect, and there the matter rested for eighty years.

[23] French Illyria was divided into seven provinces, including Croatie Civile (Karlovac, Fiume and the Quarnero Islands and Croatie Militaire (Gospić and the Velebit), see Bojničić, op. cit. p. 81.
[24] Cit. Smičiklas, *Poviest Hrvatska*, ii, p. 413.

It was not till the twentieth century that "Vienna," under the goad of Magyar aggression, again remembered the existence of Dalmatia.

The newborn Illyrian state did not survive the French occupation ; Dalmatia and Croatia reverted to their former stagnant condition.[25]   Francis I and Metternich, while upholding abroad the dual policy of legitimacy and reaction, devoted all their efforts to the suppression of liberal feeling within the Monarchy itself.   Not merely in Cisleithania, but in Hungary also · all political life was at a standstill.   The Diet which even before Austerlitz had become a mere cipher, summoned only for the formal sanction of war-subsidies and recruits, was from 1811 to 1825 dispensed with altogether.   The leaders of opposition were reduced to silence by the attractions of title and office : strict police censorship stifled public opinion ; and the Hungarian constitution was virtually in abeyance. In Croatia, where the middle class was even weaker than in Hungary, the triumph of reaction was proportionately greater. But the Illyrian idea was not dead, and in the person of Ljudevit Gaj, the younger generation was ere long to find its inspiration and its hope.

Austria had undertaken the impossible task of blocking up a volcano which continually found new vents for its subterranean fires.   In North Italy, in Poland, and in Hungary alike the popular movement smouldered, but never died. That it ran a more legal course in Hungary than in the other provinces was due to the county assemblies, which at once kept constitutional feeling awake and provided it with a safety valve.   At length their stubborn resistance to arbitrary government induced Francis to convoke the Diet in 1825, and thus unwittingly to open the era of constitutional reform in Hungary.   Unhappily constitutional reform went hand in hand with linguistic innovation and racial intolerance ; and each fresh step taken by the Diet towards the Magyarization of Hungary accentuated the opposition of the Croats.   Voices began to be heard even in Parliament, arguing that Croatia differed in no way from the northern counties of Hungary ; and when the Croat delegates cited the Corpus Juris, they were met by the calm rejoinder that the Magyars were after

[25] The "Military Frontiers" were revived, but the remainder of Napoleon's new-formed state survived as "Austrian Illyria" till the year 1822, with a central administration in Laibach. In that year, however, Croatia recovered her old boundaries and county organization.

all in the majority and would vote them down. Their dignified
retort deserves to be placed on record ; Croatia and Slavonia,
they said, " are not subject but associate kingdoms, which
have Hungary not as mother but merely as sister, and existed
long before Hungary." [26] The Croatian Diet declared with
much spirit, " We are resolved not to degenerate from our
fathers and will preserve our nationality at all costs and with
every possible means. Our rights of local government can
never be the subject of negotiations, our internal administration is not within the jurisdiction of the estates of Hungary,
and we protest most solemnly against all innovations." In
1832 the Diet expressed itself with equal clearness against
the introduction of " an unknown language " (ignota lingua)
and instructed its delegates to the Joint Diet to do all in
their power to prevent it.

Croatian national feeling found its first faint literary expression in an anonymous German pamphlet published at Karlstadt
in the year 1832, under the title, *Are we to become Magyars ?
Six Letters from Pest.*[27] Needless to say, its author answered
the question with an emphatic negative. This little book
caused a sensation out of all proportion to its merits ; for
despite its spirited style and singular freedom from invective,
its sole claim to originality lies in the fact that it interpreted
for the first time in print those vague sentiments with which
the atmosphere of Croatia was already charged. Within a
few months it had reached a third edition ; and its object
had already been achieved, when the Hungarian authorities
ordered its confiscation, and deprived the patriotic Croatian
censor, Father Hörmann, of his office.

Neither protest nor argument could avail to check the rising
flood of Magyar Chauvinism. In 1840 Latin was finally superseded by Magyar as the language of the Hungarian Diet, and
in 1843 Magyar became the exclusive language of the legislature, the government and official business, and in theory even
of education.[28] But in addition to all this, special clauses
were directed against the Croats. The three Slavonian coun-

---

[26] Non subiecta verum regna socia, quae Hungariam non pro matre
sed pro sorore solum habent, longeque prius steterunt quam Hungaria.
Cit. Pliverič, op. cit. p. 163.

[27] " Sollen wir Magyaren werden ? " For over half a century its
authorship was attributed to the poet Kollár ; and it was not till 1894
that its real author was revealed, in the person of Antony Vakanović,
at one time Vice-Ban of Croatia. See Tkalac, *Jugenderinnerungen.*

[28] *See* my *Racial Problems in Hungary*, p. 42.

ties and the Croatian coastline were exempted for six years, in order that the officials if not the population might during that period acquire a knowledge of Magyar; but after that date they were to be subject to the same regulations as Hungary proper. In Croatia, though Latin was to remain the language of the courts and of internal administration, Magyar was to be the sole language of intercourse under all circumstances with the Hungarian authorities. Magyar became an obligatory subject in the schools of Croatia, and as a final insult it was declared that the Latin speeches delivered by the Croat delegates should be regarded as not having been made.

Such intolerance gave a powerful incentive to the Illyrian cause in Croatia, and Gaj became the hero of the hour. A man of Western culture and fiery eloquence, Gaj owed much of his inspiration to the poet Kollár, whose famous epic " The Daughter of Slava," and still more his essay on the literary reciprocity of all Slav nations, had been the pioneers of the Slav revival in the Habsburg dominions. The reforms introduced by Gaj into Croatian orthography proved to be the first real step towards an approximation between the various dialects and hence towards the creation of the modern literary language. A happy instinct led him upon lines parallel to the great Servian linguistic reformer, Vuk Karadžić, whose collection of national songs and proverbs is so justly famous. But Gaj was essentially a politician and an agitator rather than a poet [29]; and the great influence acquired by the journals which he founded in 1834 [30] was due not to literary merits, but to the daring political ideas which they expounded. Surrounded by a group of fiery young patriots, he opened a vigorous propaganda in favour of the Illyrian idea, by which he understood an eventual union of all the Southern Slavs.

Comparing Europe to a maiden who sits with a three-cornered lyre in her hand, Gaj indulged in the following strange rhapsody. " In ancient times this lyre resounded naturally and sweetly, when its ordered chords were as yet touched by gentle breezes. But suddenly a dreadful storm arose from

[29] His famous song, " Još Hrvatska ne propala " (Croatia is not yet lost, so long as we live) cannot lay claim to originality, being based on a similar Polish song. Like so many national airs, it is fine patriotism, but poor poetry, and owes its great popularity in large measure to Lisinsky's haunting melody.

[30] *Novine Hrvatske* (*Croatian Gazette*) and *Danica* (*Daystar*), which in 1836 became *Ilirske Narodne Novine* (*Illyrian National Gazette*) and *Danica Ilirska*.

south and west, and then from east and north : the chords
were rent, and the sweet strains were heard no more. This
lyre is Illyria, a triangle between Skutari, Varna and Villach.
Its strained and unharmonious chords are Carinthia, Görz,
Istria, Styria, Croatia, Slavonia, Dalmatia, Ragusa, Bosnia,
Montenegro, Herzegovina, Servia, Bulgaria and Lower Hungary. What more can we wish to-day, when all long for con-
cord, than that on the great lyre of Europe all these discordant
strings should harmonize once more, and by the charm of
their sweet music should celebrate the eternal youth of the
sitting maiden ? " [31]

He made no attempt to conceal his enmity towards the
Magyars, whom he rightly regarded as the main obstacle
to the realization of this fantastic dream. " The Magyars,"
he cried, " are an island in the Slav ocean. I did not create
the ocean nor excite its waves ; see ye to it that they do not
break over your heads and engulf you." In 1840 he flung
at his opponents the confident words : " To-day you are in
the majority ; but the child as it is born is mine." The
sanguinary words of the Illyrian poetaster [32] were doubtless
inspired by a mere desire for rhetorical effect ; but they fore-
cast none the less clearly the inevitable result of the growing
estrangement between Croats and Magyars.

The movement inaugurated by Gaj was viewed with not
unnatural alarm in Pest, and Magyar influence prevailed
upon the Sovereign to issue a decree proscribing the Illyrian
name alike in the press, in the schools and in public debate !
But the methods of repression which were now adopted availed
as little as the transparent attempt to brand as Panslavism
what was essentially a particularist movement. In 1847
the Chauvinism of the Magyars reached white heat at the
Diet of Pressburg and national enthusiasm ran no less high
at Agram. The pent-up feelings of the long linguistic struggle
found vent when the Croatian Diet assembled on October 20,
1847 ; and three days later it resolved by acclamation that
the Croatian language should be introduced in every office

---

[31] *Danica* of December 6, 1835, cit. Wachsmuth, *Geschichte des Illyrismus*, p. 30.

[32] " See how the wild black Tartar tramples on our nation and language. But before he crushes us, let us hurl him into the abyss of Hell.
Forward, brothers, God is with us. Hell's demons are against us. . .
Let us bathe our fame in the blood of the foe, let each hew off a head
(svaki jednu glavu skini) and the end of our woes is reached. Forward,
brothers, etc. . . ." Cit. Wachsmuth, op. cit. p. 81.

and in every school.[33] An open breach naturally ensued between the Croat delegates and the intolerant Magyar majority at Pressburg. The fresh linguistic claims of the Magyars were passionately opposed by the Croats as an outrage upon Croatian nationality. " I know no Croatian nationality," retorted Louis Kossuth,[34] then at the height of his power and arrogance. The words with which Kossuth met a Serb deputation from the Banat in the early days of April, 1848, showed the non-Magyar races what they had to expect. After refusing to entertain their claims for the revival of Serb autonomy, he declared that only the Magyar language could bind the different nationalities together. " Then," replied the fiery young Stratimirović, a member of the deputation, " we must look for recognition elsewhere than at Pressburg." " In that case," was Kossuth's uncompromising answer, " the sword must decide." The fulfilment of Kossuth's racial ideal would have involved national death for all the other races ; and it was directly due to his intolerance that the Magyars found themselves before the end of the summer ringed round by hostile nationalities in arms.

The famous March laws of 1848, voted by the Hungarian Parliament with an enthusiasm which scorned the discussion of details, sought to transform Hungary at one stroke of the pen from a mediaeval to a modern state. But by one of the brutal ironies of history, the two principles which underlay the great awakening of 1848 were in Hungary enrolled upon opposite sides. Constitutional government found its champions in the Magyars, the idea of nationality in the non-Magyar races. The spirit of autocracy and reaction was thus enabled to recover from its first reverses and to sow discord among the forces of progress. The suicidal intolerance of Kossuth and his followers drove Croat and Serb, Slovak,

---

[33] Rudolf Horvat, *Najnovije Doba Hrvatska Povjesti* (The Latest Period of Croatian History), p. 161.

[34] *Memoirs of Ožegović*, p. 46. Cit. Zagorsky, *François Rački et la Renaissance de la Croatie*, p. 17. On another occasion he expressed himself as unable to find Croatia on the map. (*See* Smičiklas, *Poviest Hrvatska*, ii, p. 480.) Kossuth's Slavophobe tendencies are all the more remarkable considering his own purely Slovak origin. His uncle, George Kossuth, was a Slovak minor poet, and Louis' knowledge of the Slovak language is proved by the fact that in his early days at Pest he attended the sermons of the Slovak poet-pastor in the Lutheran church. *See* Tkalac, *Jugenderinnerungen aus Kroatien*, who heard this from Kossuth's own lips.

Roumanian and Saxon alike into the arms of Austria. Nor was it surprising that these races should turn with aversion from the Hungarian Parliament, with its fiery zeal for the extension of the Magyar language, and rest their hopes upon the centralist constitution proclaimed from Vienna, under which the equal rights of all nationalities in the Habsburg Monarchy were solemnly guaranteed. Nothing illustrates so startlingly the Magyar tendency to ride roughshod over the sister nation, as the fact that at Kossuth's instance, the very name of Croatia was omitted from the new electoral law, while the counties of " Körös, Zágráb and Varasd " (= Kri-ževci, Zagreb and Varaždin) figured in the list of Hungarian counties, as though there were no such thing as Croatian autonomy. That the complete destruction of this autonomy was the Magyars' objective, became apparent from the approval which greeted Tarnóczy, the delegate for Nyitra county, when he openly expressed the hope that the Croatian Diet would cease to exist, and that thus the distinction between Hungary and Croatia would vanish.[35]

More especially the Croats had no alternative save to support Austria ; for the laws of 1848 infringed Croatian autonomy at every turn.[36] Their delegates at Pressburg insisted that many of the most serious innovations required ratification by the Croatian Diet ; but their protests were contemptuously ignored by the majority, and the close of the session sent them home to Zagreb full of the bitterest resentment towards the Magyars.[37]

At this critical moment fortune provided the Croats with a national leader of real ability. In the early days of March Gaj had led a Croat deputation to Vienna to plead for separa-

[35] Pesty, " Die Enstehung Croatiens "(*Ungarische Revue*, 1882, p. 174).
[36] Notably Law V (Franchise), XVII (Local Government), XXII (National Guard) and XXVII (re-erection of the special " seadistricts " of Fiume and Buccari). The electoral law treated Croatia as an integral part of Hungary, not entitled to any special treatment. Eighteen deputies were assigned to Croatia, nine to the Slavonian counties, eleven to the Military Frontiers and two to the towns of Fiume and Osijek (Esseg).
[37] The delegate Ožegović had boldly declared : " I feel that the time for convictions is over, and that the honourable Estates will have to do with the firm resolve of the allied kingdoms." Soon after, during the debate on the conferring of citizenship, Kossuth used the same phrase with which he had met the Serb deputation, " Between us only the sword can decide." (*See* Pliverić, op. cit. p. 179. Smičiklas, op. cit. p. 477).

tion from Hungary and for the formation of Southern Slav state under the direct sovereignty of the Emperor ; and it seems to have been indirectly upon Gaj's advice that the Court acted in filling the vacant post of Ban of Croatia (March 23), on the very day when Count Batthyány formed the first responsible Hungarian Cabinet and before he was able to exercise any influence upon the selection.[38] The appointment of Baron Joseph Jellačić, then still a comparatively obscure officer, proved to be one of the decisive events of the revolution ; for it rallied the whole south of the Monarchy against the Magyars and cut off the latter from the sea and hence from all direct intercourse with liberal Europe.

Jellačić in his proclamation to the nation openly declared that recent events " had shaken and destroyed our relation to our ancient ally Hungary, and the necessity arises of placing our alliance with the Hungarian Crown upon a new basis, worthy of a free and heroic nation ; till then the bond between us remains dissolved by the present Government of Hungary." No sooner was he installed in Agram than he set the Magyars at defiance and opened negotiations with the Serb National Assembly which the Patriarch Rajačić had already convoked at Karlowitz, entirely without authorization from Pest. Then himself following the Serb example, Jellačić opened the Croatian Diet early in June, welcomed the seventy Serb delegates in an impassioned harangue, and closed in words of menace towards the Magyars. " The fraternal union of 800 years," he said, " promises us a friendly solution of the prevailing dispute. But should the Magyars assume the rôle of oppressors against us and our kinsmen in Hungary, then let them know that we are determined to follow the saying of our gallant Ban John Erdödy—*regnum regno non praescribit leges*—and that we shall prove to them with weapons in our hands, that the time is long past when one nation can rule over another. Away, then, with the Magyar régime of compulsion—we did not recognize it even before March 15, but after the March

[38] It appears to be certain that Gaj prevailed upon Baron Francis Kulmer to use his strong influence at Court in favour of Jellačić, and that Kulmer won over the Archduke John. *See* Horvat, *Najnovije Doba*, pp. 111–113. Dr. Friedjung in his *Geschichte Oesterreichs* (i, p. 45) ascribes the appointment to the advice of Baron Jósika, the Transylvanian Aulic Chancellor who, as a *Conservative* Magyar statesman looked upon Croatia as a possible stronghold against the Revolution. The influence of the Archduchess Sophia was also exerted in his favour. (Cf. C. E. Maurice, *Revolutionary Movement of* 1848, p. 288.)

Revolution we broke and annihilated it." [39]   The Diet appointed a committee to consider its relations to Hungary and by Article XI declared all actions of the Hungarian Ministry to be null and void, in so far as they were at variance with the rights of Croatia or the jurisdiction of the Ban. The vague words of friendship for the ancient alliance, in which the resolution was clothed, were not calculated to allay the anxiety and resentment of the Magyars ; and Batthyány obtained from the fugitive monarch in Innsbruck a decree depriving Jellačić of his dignities until an inquiry could be instituted.   On his return to Agram, however (June 28), the Diet, so far from yielding to the Magyar claims, invested Jellačić with virtually dictatorial powers, and laid down that in any negotiations the Magyars must recognize the Triune Kingdom and its ally the Serb Voivody as a free people independent of Hungary. [40] Such a concession was obviously not to be expected save from a beaten foe, and the negotiations were a complete failure. At length the news of Radetzky's reconquest of Milan placed the party of reaction completely in the ascendant at court. It was decided to treat the Magyars as rebels, and to take back by the sword those concessions which, it was argued, had only been extorted by headlong revolution and could not be binding on the sovereign.   In September, 1848, Jellačić, restored to Imperial favour and invested with high command, crossed the Drave at the head of 40,000 men.   The motto " What God brings and a hero's fate " (Što Bog dade i sreca junačka) rallied round him all the Croats and Serbs of the Monarchy.

This is not the place to describe the course of events in the revolutionary war, nor even the great services rendered by Jellačić and by the Serb commander Stratimirović to the Habsburg cause.   The stubborn heroism displayed by the Magyars throughout the struggle was worthy of a better cause ; but independence was a mere fantastic dream so long as both the dynasty and the nationalities were opposed to them.   The meteoric Kossuth completely overshadowed the more moderate and really far abler leaders Deák and Széchenyi, and popularity only served to increase his intolerance.   Thus the Hungarian revolution bore from the very first the character of a furious racial war.   On the one side

---

[39] Pejaković, *Aktenstücke*, pp. 29–30.
[40] *See* Pliverić, op. cit. p. 184.

stood the Magyars, aided by a few Polish exiles and a section of the German bourgeoisie, on the other side all the other races of the Monarchy.

On April 14, 1849, Kossuth committed the crowning error of his career, by solemnly deposing the Habsburgs and himself accepting the Governorship of Hungary. The way was thus opened for Russian intervention, and Nicholas I, in the name of outraged legitimacy, poured 180,000 Russian soldiers across the Hungarian frontier. Then at the eleventh hour, when ruin stared him in the face, Kossuth laid before the revolutionary Diet at Szeged a law guaranteeing the free development of all nationalities upon Hungarian soil. Here at length were genuine linguistic concessions—on paper, and on paper that was worthless. A law which if voted in March '48, might perhaps have rallied the whole of Hungary in support of Magyar pretensions, was worse than useless in July '49, when the country was bleeding from the wounds inflicted by a furious racial war and when overwhelming masses of Russian troops were closing in on every side. On August 11 Kossuth renounced his office of governor and fled into Turkish territory, leaving the Magyar army to make what terms it could.

The Szeged concessions contain no allusion to Croatia; and in any case it can hardly be doubted that at that moment nothing short of complete independence under the Habsburg crown would have satisfied Jellačić and his countrymen. Their hopes were soon dashed to the ground. Croatia was, it is true, spared the brutal repression of which Hungary was the scene after the capitulation of Világos (August, 1849). But like the rest of the Monarchy, it became the victim of that absolutist system which will always bear the name of Alexander Bach. As has been well said, what the Magyars received as punishment was bestowed upon the non-Magyars as reward. If the Magyars before 1848 had been bent upon restricting Croatian autonomy, it was now dispensed with altogether by the central government. German became the language of administration, of justice, of education, and as under Joseph II, the Germanization of the entire Monarchy was the avowed object of the authorities.

CHAPTER II

The Serbs of Hungary and Croatia

THE golden era of the Serb race extends from the twelfth to the fourteenth century. Although they made their way into the present Servia and Bosnia as early as the seventh century—at about the same time when the Croats displaced the Avars further north—they remained a loosely knit confederation of clans, whose chiefs or župans were to all intents and purposes independent, though recognizing the sway of a shadowy overlord.

The first Bulgarian Empire, under the powerful Simeon (893–927) and his successors, reduced the Serbs from time to time to its obedience, and after its overthrow Serbs and Bulgars alike acknowledged the suzerainty of Byzantium. But in 1159 the Serbs found their first great national leader in the person of Stephen Nemanja. In 1169 he gained possession of Southern Dalmatia and what is now Montenegro, and after the death of the Emperor Manuel greatly extended his dominions at the expense of the Eastern Empire, refused to pay tribute and treated as an independent sovereign with Barbarossa, the Crusaders and the Pope. In 1195 he withdrew to one of the monasteries on Mount Athos, leaving to his younger son Saint Sava the task of introducing the same order into the Church, which he himself established in the state. Saint Sava crowned his brother Stephen Uroš as the "first-crowned" King of Servia (1222) and became himself the first Archbishop of the Servian Church, with his residence in Užice, "the Servian Mecca," as Ranke has called it. His influence effectively checked the overtures made by Innocent III to the Servian King, and finally identified the cause of the national Church with Constantinople rather than with Rome.[41]

⁴¹ In 1217 Uroš had actually been crowned by a Papal Legate as King of Servia, Diocletia, Travunia, Dalmatia and Chum. The title "Prvenćani," or "first-crowned" bestowed upon him after his corona-

A later sovereign, Uroš II " the Great " (1237–1272) hus-
banded the resources of the Servian state and staved it over
the perilous period of the Mongol invasions. Thus the country
had already enjoyed a century of comparative peace, when
Uroš's second son Stephen Milutin succeeded to the throne
(1275). Milutin pursued an audacious and utterly unscrupulous policy of marriage alliances, putting away wife after
wife, according as it suited his political aims to coalesce with
Hungary, with Bulgaria or with Byzantium. The proud Emperors, from demanding Servia's homage, were reduced to
begging for its military aid ; and the armies of Milutin twice
helped to repel the Turkish onslaughts in Asia Minor. Milutin's successor, Uroš III (1321–1336), waged continual
war with his neighbours, and after inflicting a crushing defeat
upon the Hungarians, finally destroyed the power of mediaeval
Bulgaria at the battle of Velbužd (1330). The fallen Czar's
family continued to rule Bulgaria, but merely as the docile
vassals of Servia.

But Uroš' greatness was shortlived ; for in 1336 he perished
at the hands of his own son. It was under these foul circumstances that Stephen Dušan,[42] the greatest figure in Servian
history, ascended the throne. Equally distinguished for his
personal bravery and for his gifts as a ruler, a general and a
lawgiver, Dušan introduced many much needed reforms at
home, and at the same time by a daring foreign policy extended
Servia to its furthest limits. In the thirteen campaigns which
he waged against Byzantium, he reduced the greater part of
the modern Macedonia, Albania and Montenegro to his sway,
and even penetrated as far as the Gulf of Corinth on the south
and almost to the gates of Adrianople on the east. The
jealousy of the Hungarian King was aroused by Dušan's suc-
cesses, and Louis the Great took the field against him. But
so far from turning the tide of Servian prosperity, this only
paved the way to further triumphs. Belgrad and its territory was wrested from Hungary, and Bosnia reduced to the
condition of a vassal state (1350). But Dušan was politic
enough not to offend the powerful Republic of Venice, which .
he recognized as a valuable ally against Hungary. He there-

tion by St. Sava, was intended to show that the earlier ceremony was
invalid and worthless.—Kállay, *Geschichte der Serben*, p. 47.

[42] More than one historian has derived the name of Dušan from
dušiti, " to strangle." But it now appears to be generally established
that the true derivation is from duša (soul) and signifies " darling."

fore contented himself with Cattaro as his chief port on the Adriatic, and left the other Dalmatian towns undisturbed. This was the less hardship, since the East offered a wider field for his ambitions than the West. In 1348 he had assumed the title of Czar of Macedonia and ruler of Serbs, Greeks and Bulgars and wore the tiara and other Imperial insignia.[43] The crown of the East was his acknowledged aim, and preparations for the conquest of Constantinople were pushed forward on a vast scale. In 1356 the Servian army occupied Adrianople, and encouraged by the panic and dissension which prevailed among the Greeks, its advance guard was already within sight of the Bosphorus, when the great Dušan died suddenly, in the full vigour of his manhood. The suspicions of poison were more than justified by the practice of the Byzantine court, but no proof was ever forthcoming.

The death of Dušan was followed by a rapid decline of the Servian power. The very extent of his conquests was a source of weakness ; when his strong hand was removed, the empire suffered from the diseases natural to an overgrown child. The power of the nobles, and the rivalry of the older families with Dušan's upstart favourites, led to dissensions within the state, with which the feeble character of his son Uroš IV was quite unable to cope. Above all, the progress of the Turks in Europe left no time for that internal consolidation which alone could have arrested Servia's decay. Bosnia, Thessaly and Albania asserted their independence : Belgrad was once more occupied by Louis of Hungary : the Bulgars no longer admitted their vassalage. The capture of Adrianople by Murad I (1360) even drove the rival empires into an unavailing alliance against the invader.

Uroš was murdered in 1367 by Vukašin, his father's most trusted adviser ; and only four years later the usurper and his army were overwhelmed by the Turks in the desperate night battle of Černomen (1371). The Nemanja dynasty had perished with Uroš ; Łazar Grbljanović, a kinsman by marriage, now became the last of the Servian Czars.

The shortsighted policy of the Christian states still further hastened the fall of Servia and rendered the advance of the Turks more easy. While Hungary assailed the northern frontier, the ambitious Tvrtko of Bosnia affected to regard himself as the successor of Dušan, and assumed the title of " Ste-

[43] At the same time the Serb Patriarch was declared independent of Constantinople.

THE TURKISH ADVANCE

phen Tvrtko in Christ God King of the Serbs and of Bosnia and the Coastland " (1376).[44] That this extremely able ruler played only for his own hand and utterly failed to realize the significance of the Ottoman advance, is clearly shown by his intrigues in Dalmatia and Croatia during the anarchy which followed Louis the Great's death in 1382. These intrigues ended in the submission of the Dalmatian towns and even in his recognition as King of Croatia and Dalmatia (1390). But while he was engaged in acquiring Clissa or Traü, the Turkish hordes were surging across the Balkans, and the unhappy Lazar was left to his fate.

Even in 1386 the Sultan had captured Niš and exacted tribute from the Servian Czar. At length on June 15, 1389, on the plain of Kossovo, the famous " field of blackbirds," Servian independence found a sad, but not inglorious end. The incidents of the battle have inspired countless national ballads : to this day the exploits of Czar Lazar, the gallant Miloš Obilić and Vuk Branković the traitor are chanted by the gusla-players of the Slavonic south and find an echo in the heart of every Serb peasant. Lazar fell in the heat of the battle; Sultan Murad shared his fate when the victory was already won : but his death did not affect the issue. Servia was reduced to the level of a tributary state, and Lazar's son Stephen, though recognized as " Despot " by the new Sultan, was subjected to continual humiliation. His sister entered the harem of Bayezid, and his armies were employed as Turkish auxiliaries against Mirtşea of Wallachia and the Crusaders of Sigismund.[45]

If by the close of the fourteenth century there was little or no trace of the Greater Servia of Dušan's dreams, the Greater Croatia to which Tvrtko of Bosnia aspired was equally short-lived. He died within a year of assuming the Croatian king-ship ; his brother and successor, Stephen Dabiša, soon found it impossible to compete either with Sigismund of Hungary or Ladislas of Naples, and by 1393 was satisfied with the former's recognition of his title to Bosnia. In the earlier years of the fifteenth century Sigismund saw himself strong enough to assert Hungarian suzerainty over Bosnia ; with the result that while King Tvrtko II fell into his hands, the rival claimant

[44] Klaić, *Gesch. Bosniens*, p. 201. He was recognized as such by Venice and Ragusa.
[45] At the Battle of Nicopolis (1396) Stephen turned the scale against the Christians.

39

allied himself with the advancing Turks. During the next
fifty years Servia and Bosnia may be compared to a wall from
which the mortar crumbles piece by piece.

In 1420 Cattaro fell into the hands of Venice. In 1427 the
new Despot of Servia, George Branković, was driven to acknowledge Hungarian suzerainty. In 1440 Bosnia submitted to
an annual tribute to the Turks. For the next twenty years
the progress of the Ottoman arms was arrested by the heroic
John Hunyády; but the splendid terms which his prowess
had exacted were rendered worthless by the treachery of his
own sovereign, Vladislav of Hungary and Poland, who refused
to respect a treaty made with infidels. King Vladislav ex-
piated his breach of faith on the field of Varna (1444); but
the issue of the battle sealed the fate of the Balkan Peninsula.
The perjured states were marked out for summary vengeance;
and the fall of Constantinople (1453) which re-echoed through
the Western world, only marked a fresh stage in the victorious
advance of Mohammed II. George Branković had for close
upon thirty years eked out a precarious existence between
Hunyâdy and the Turks, between the rival suzerains in Pest
and Adrianople. Evicted from the wide domains which had
owned the sway of Dušan, he had made his headquarters at
Semendria, in the extreme north of Servia, and found even
the strong defences of that river fortress too weak to protect
him from the invincible Sultan. His death in 1457 was the
signal for family dissensions; his son Lazar purchased the
Sultan's recognition on the most humiliating terms. Within
a year he too was dead; and Stephen Thomas, the King of
Bosnia, who had thrown in his lot with Hungary and the West,
now obtained from Hunyády's son, King Matthias Corvinus,
the investiture of his son Stephen as Despot of Servia. The
sole result was to impose upon himself the task of defending
Servia and thus to involve his own kingdom in its inevitable
fate. In 1459 Mohammed II captured Semendria and destroyed the last vestiges of Servian independence. Stephen of
Bosnia, whom Matthias and the Pope denounced as a traitor
for suffering this disaster to the Christian arms, sought to
vindicate his reputation by accepting the crown from a Papal
Legate and by refusing his annual tribute to the Sultan. In
1463 Mohammed overran Bosnia and ordered the unfortunate
Stephen to be beheaded [46] : and though Matthias soon recovered

---

[46] Stephen's mother, Queen Catharine, died at Rome in 1478; her
tomb is in the Ara Coeli.

the fortress and district of Jajce, the rest of Bosnia and the Duchy or Herzegovina fell into the hands of the Turks.

Henceforth, for over three centuries and a half, Servia and Bosnia formed pashaliks of the Ottoman Empire, with their seats of government in Belgrad and Sarajevo. But while both were entirely subject to orders from Stambul, their treatment was not entirely uniform. In Bosnia a considerable section of the native nobility accepted Islam, thus saving their estates and acquiring a certain influence upon local affairs. In Servia, on the other hand, the old nobility had been decimated in the long wars, and the few survivors had no choice save between serfdom and exile. The conquered Servians were rigorously disarmed; and the presence of the Turkish armies, on their way to perennial wars against Habsburg and the West, held them in the bonds of helpless despair. The terrible tribute of Christian youths, by which the Sultans replenished the ranks of their Janissaries, broke the spirit of the nation and turned its own native strength into an instrument of enslavement.

Even now the Turkish state had not yet exhausted its expansive forces. Hungary, under her great King Matthias, undermined her strength in onslaughts upon her western neighbours, when she should have been husbanding her resources for the coming contest. His weak successors did nothing to arrest the decline; and the battle of Mohács (1526) in which Louis II and the flower of his nobility perished, destroyed at one blow the independence of Hungary, thus eclipsing the disastrous records of Kossovo.

The conquest of Hungary rendered Servia's position still more forlorn: for so long as a Turkish pasha held sway in Buda deliverance was well-nigh impossible. Throughout this gloomy period of Servian history, the sole guardians of national feeling were to be found among the clergy. The Patriarchate, with its seat in Ipek,[47] survived the general ruin; but the difficulties of its position increased from year to year, until towards the close of the seventeenth century the Patriarch himself, with thousands of his compatriots, accepted the protection of the Emperor and migrated northwards. During the eighteenth century the real centre of Serb national life lay within the Habsburg dominions.

Even under Sigismund the first Serb refugees had begun

[47] Or Peč, in what is now known as Old Servia.

to settle in Hungary, and in 1412 there was already a Serb colony in Ofen (Buda). In 1427 George Branković, in return for his surrender of Belgrad to the Hungarian Crown, received enormous grants of land in Hungary [48] and settled many of his Serb vassals in the lower plain of the Tisza (Theiss). When Servia had fallen a prey to the Turks, Stephen Branković, a brother of the last Despot, was recognized by King Matthias as Voivode of the Hungarian Serbs, and in 1471 his kinsman Vuk, confirmed in this dignity, led a regiment of Serbs in the famous " Black Legion " of Matthias. During the next fifty years other Voivodes were appointed at irregular intervals ; and their importance is best illustrated by an enactment of the Hungarian Diet,[49] by which the Voivode, as a Baron of the Kingdom, was bound to raise a banderium of 1,000 hussars in time of war ; in other words to make the same contribution as the King himself. Fresh settlers were established in Syrmia in 1481, with liberty to retain the Orthodox faith and remission of the tithes due to the Catholic clergy [50] ; while in 1496 sixteen villages of Syrmia were granted by charter to the Orthodox cloister of Krusedol.[51] After the defeat of Mohács, the last Voivode, Ivan Cernović, took the side of Ferdinand of Habsburg, and two years later was captured and executed by the supporters of John Zápolya, the rival King of Hungary. No successor could be appointed : for the Serb settlers, like their Magyar neighbours of the Alföld, were submerged by the Turkish flood. From 1541 to 1687 a Turkish pasha ruled in Buda, and Hungary no longer offered a refuge for the Balkan Serbs. During the sixteenth century, however, Serb monks obtained permission to settle in the Croat districts of Varaždin and Križevci (Kreuz), and numerous Serb fugitives from Bosnia and Old Servia acquired land round the monastery of Marča, where an Orthodox bishop was not merely allowed the free exercise of his religion, but was in receipt of an annual grant of 300 florins.[52]

It lies beyond the scope of this volume to describe the long and gradual process by which the House of Habsburg reclaimed Hungary for Europe and the Christian faith. The religious strife of an intolerant age imposed long delays, and it was

[48] Among other concessions, he received a house in Ofen "pro descensu et hospito." Cit. Helfert, *Vad Rácz*, p. 119.
[49] Art XXII of 1498 cit. Stojacskovics, *Aktenstücke*, p. 8.
[50] Helfert, op. cit. p. 119.   [51] Stojacskovics, p. 9.
[52] Stefanovič, *Die Serben*, p. 66.

not till the close of the Thirty Years' War that the Emperors were free to devote their whole energies to the expulsion of the Turks. Even then, despite Montecuccoli's splendid victory at St. Gotthard (1661), almost a generation elapsed before the task was taken up in earnest. The incentive of a Turkish army before Vienna (1683) roused the Imperial armies to aggression, and in a series of glorious campaigns the Duke of Lorraine, Stahremberg and Louis of Baden recovered Buda and expelled the Turks from Central Hungary. Prince Eugene's first great victory at Zenta (1697) set the seal to these operations, and the treaty of Karlovitz left to the Turks nothing of Hungary save the Banat of Temesvár.

On April 6, 1690, Leopold I issued a memorable proclamation to the Christian population of the Balkan Peninsula, urging them to rise against their oppressors and promising them his Imperial protection, the free exercise of their religion and the privilege of electing their own voivode. As a result of this summons, the Patriarch of Ipek, Arsen Crnojević, with 36,000 Serb families migrated to Hungary and occupied the now desolate territory between the Theiss and Danube.[53] The Imperial charters of August 21, 1690, and August 20, 1691, assured to Leopold's new subjects their full recognition as a nation[54]: the free exercise of their religion, national customs and Church calendar ; the right to elect their patriarch and voivode, and to control their own administration.[55] But Jesuit influences at Court led the Emperor to restrict these generous concessions. The first voivode, George Branković, was after a few years arrested and confined till his death in the fortress of Eger. The office of voivode remained unfilled, while Arsen's successor, Isaias Djaković, was forbidden to assume the Patriarchal name and had to rest contented with the lesser dignity of archbishop. The charter of 1690 was repeatedly confirmed,[56] but its contents remained very largely a dead letter

---

[53] The modern county of Bács-Bodrog.

[54] Toti denique communitati eiusdem graeci Ritus et Nationis Rascianorum," so runs the phase. Charles VI also calls the Serbs the "Natio Rasciana."

[55] (*a*) Liceatque vobis inter vos ex propria facultate ex natione et lingua Rasciana constituere Archiepiscopum. (*b*) Promittimus vobis eligendi Vajvodae libertatem. (*c*) Volumos ut sub directione et dispositione proprii magistratus eadem gens Rasciana perseverare et antiquis privilegiis, eidem a Maj. Nostra benigne concessis eiusque consuetudinibus imperturbate frui valeat. (*See* Stojacskovics, op. cit. pp. 17–20).

[56] In 1695 by Leopold himself, in 1706 by Joseph I, in 1713 and 1715

Freedom of religious observance was the only privilege which was fully respected, and this only in view of the keen discontent aroused by the court's efforts to promote a union with Rome.[57]

The territory thus occupied by the Serbs comprised the southern portion of the Bácska, the banks of the Danube, and parts of the counties of Csongrád, Arad, Csanad and Zarand. As Prince Eugene extended his conquests southward, fresh colonists were welcomed in the Banat, and though many of them were Germans from Swabia and Alsace, the Serbs soon formed the most thriving element in such towns as Pancsova, Versecz, Kikinda and Becskerek.

The discontent of the Serbs at the infringement of their charter led to a rising in 1735 ; the leaders were executed, and their rights still further curtailed. Though regarded in Vienna as the direct vassals of the Crown, they came more and more under the control of the Hungarian county authorities, whose autonomy had never been wholly extinguished even under Turkish rule and now began to regain its old dimensions. To check this, Maria Theresa in 1752 created an Illyrian Aulic Council (Hofdeputation) at Essek, for the conduct of Serb affairs, but as not a single one of its members was Serb, it was greeted with indifference by the people itself. After an experiment of twenty-five years, this council was abolished, and its powers were transferred to the Aulic Chancellory in Vienna (1777). In the same year a new constitution was granted to the Serb Orthodox Church (Regulamentum Privilegiorum), but was badly received by both clergy and laity.

The year 1777 also saw a re-organization of the " Military Frontiers," which had gradually been formed along the Save and Danube as a barrier against the Turks, and half of whose inhabitants were Serbs. The famous race of Granitchars, or Frontiersmen, was the outcome of these measures.[58] Every male inhabitant was at once a peasant and a soldier, holding

by Charles VI (III of Hungary) and in 1743 by Maria Theresa. (*See* Stojacskovics, op. cit. p. 15.

[57] From this period date the two Uniate Churches of Hungary, that of the Roumanians, with its centre in Blaj (Balázsfalva) in Transylvania and that of the Ruthenes in Munkács.

[58] According to Fényes, *Statistik des Königreichs Ungarn*, in 1843, the eight frontier districts of Croatia had a total population of 527,752, of whom 246,687 were Serbs : in the two frontier districts of Slavonia 92,986 out of 162,898 were Serbs, and in the two remaining Hungarian frontier districts 90,132 out of 152,990.

his lands direct from the Crown and subject throughout life to military discipline. Their officers formed in time of peace the local authorities, under the generalates of Agram and Peterwardein ; while the supreme control of the entire system rested with the Ministry of War in Vienna.

One consequence of the collapse of Joseph II's centralist experiments was the re-establishment of the Illyrian Aulic Chancellory at Vienna in 1790. At the national Serb congress which was allowed to meet at Temesvár in September of that year, the demand of an autonomous Serb Voivody was openly expressed, although their leader, Sava Tököly, opposed it on the ground that the Hungarian Estates would never tolerate the erection of such a state within the state. His prophecy was only too well founded. Yielding to the pressure of the Diet, Leopold II abolished the Illyrian Chancellory after it had been only sixteen months in existence, and transferred all Serb affairs to the Hungarian Chancellory. The sole compensation for this infringement of their ancient charters, was a law passed by the Diet, granting Hungarian civil rights to members of the Orthodox Church and removing all the religious disqualifications from which they had hitherto suffered.

The Serbs thus found full recognition for their religion, but not for their nationality. Their former claims were not forgotten, but the Napoleonic wars drove politics into the background and the Serbs sought an outlet for their activity in commercial and literary enterprise. During the first half of the nineteenth century most of the trade of Southern Hungary was in their hands, and they still possessed a relatively larger middle class than any of the other nationalities of the Banat and the Bácska.

During the eighteenth century Karlovci (Karlovitz), as the seat of the historic though dormant Patriarchate, became the true centre of Serb culture and extended its influence to the provinces still subject to the Turks. The connexion between Servia and the Serbs under Habsburg rule grew more intimate. The first liberator of modern Servia, Kara George, had served in an Austrian free corps. The first officials of the new principality were largely recruited among the Serbs of Syrmia and the Banat. The first books and newspapers which penetrated into Servia, came from the Serb printing presses of Buda,Karlovitz, and Vienna. The first insurrection in Turkish Servia (1805) received the help of many well-wishers across the Danube ; and when Kara George and his supporters were forced to fly (1813) it was in Austrian territory [59] that they found a refuge.

The growth of national feeling, which formed so conspicuous a feature of the nineteenth century, was as marked among the Serbs of Hungary and Croatia-Slavonia as among the Magyars themselves.[60] The steady encroachments of the Magyar language were as keenly resented in the Banat as in Croatia or among the Slovaks of the northern counties, and the intolerance with which the Croat delegates were treated by the Magyars at the famous Diet of 1847–8, caused great excitement among the Serbs. Soon after the first news of the revolution had reached the south, the town councils of Neusatz, Pancsova, Karlovitz and Semlin introduced Serb as the language of their official business. A meeting in Neusatz drew up the wishes of the Serb people under seventeen heads : and it was decided to send a deputation to Pressburg to lay them before the Diet. On April 8 the Serbs were admitted to the floor of the House, and the leader of the deputation, Alexander Kostić, declared that his compatriots were ready to risk their blood for the Crown of Hungary. But the cheers with which this declaration was greeted were outbalanced by the uncompromising attitude of the ministry. In their private audience with Kossuth, they insisted that the Serb nation regarded the recognition of its language as essential. "What do you understand by 'nation'?" inquired Kossuth. "A race which possesses its own language, customs and culture," was the Serb reply, "and enough self-consciousness to preserve them." "A nation must also have its own government," objected Kossuth. "We do not go so far," Kostić explained ; "one nation can live under several different governments, and again several nations can form a single state." To this the minister replied that the government would not concern itself with the language of the home and would not even object to minor offices being held by non-Magyars, but that the Magyar interest demanded that no second race should be recognized as a nation. Several of the deputation expressed the fear that open resistance might ensue if the southern Slavs should be disappointed

[59] The Military Frontiers, being under the direct control of Vienna, may be accurately described as Austrian up to their incorporation in Croatia.

[60] For some account of the rise of Magyar nationality and its conflicts with Slav national feeling, see my *Racial Problems in Hungary*.

in their hope that the new situation was to end all compulsion in the matter of language. " If the just claims of the Serb nation are not regarded by the Magyars," blurted out the young Stratimirović, " we should be compelled to seek recognition elsewhere than at Pressburg." Kossuth's famous rejoinder, " In that case the sword will decide," put an end to the discussion and gave the first signal for the racial war.[61]

The appointment of Jellačić as Ban of Croatia was hailed with delight among the Serbs. Disturbances broke out in the Bácska : at Szent Tomás and elsewhere the hated Magyar registers were publicly burnt, the Orthodox clergy assisting at the bonfire. An irregular committee was formed at Neusatz, and its members, accompanied by a large crowd chanting the old Serb ballads of Marko Kraljević, made its way to Karlovitz and summoned the Archbishop to convoke a national assembly. On May 13, 1848, this met at Karlovitz ; the original charters of Leopold I were solemnly read aloud before the assembled crowd, and amid general enthusiasm Archbishop Rajačić was acclaimed as Serb Patriarch, and Colonel Šuplikac as Voivode. The ancient dignities of the race having thus been restored, the assembly passed a series of resolutions, declaring the Serb nation as " politically free and autonomous under the House of Austria and Crown of Hungary, and demanding the restoration of the Voivody, and its union with the Triune Kingdom. A central committee (Glavni Odbor) was elected to devise a scheme of union, and deputations were appointed to present a loyal address to the Emperor and to attend both the Croatian Diet and the Slav Congress in Prague.[62] Next day the committee began its sittings in presence of the Patriarch. Orders from Pest forbidding the assembly had only arrived after it was over : a summons from the Commissioner of Neusatz to the Patriarch to renounce his illegal position, was committed unanswered to the flames. On May 18, George Stratimirović was elected president of the committee, which took the name of " provisional administration." The youthful president—he was only 26—came

---

[61] *Die Serbische Bewegung in Süd-Ungarn*, pp 57–9. Helfert, *Vad Rácz*, p. 132.

[62] A notable feature of these resolutions is the formal expression of sympathy with the national claims of the Roumanians. Soon after the Committee issued a proclamation to the Germans of South Hungary, assuring them that they need have no fear for their nationality. (*See Serbische Bewegung*, pp. 82 and 88.)

originally of a Serb family settled in Albania and had resigned his commission as an Austrian hussar officer, in order to make a runaway marriage. But though fiery and erratic, he had already shown political capacity and application, and he rapidly became the life of the movement for resistance to the Magyars.

The Magyar Government not unnaturally took alarm at the course of events ; the assembly of May 15 was declared an act of rebellion, a new Serb congress was convoked at Temesvár on June 27, and General Hrabowsky and the local authorities received orders to suppress the movement by force. The Vice-Sheriff of Temes, a renegade Serb named Saba Vuković, was specially zealous in establishing courts martial and in arming the Magyar population as a national guard.

The Patriarch Rajačić, at the head of a deputation, was present at the opening of the Croatian Diet on June 5 ; he was acclaimed by the people of Zagreb, and actually attended High Mass in the Cathedral, where the Catholic Bishop Ožegović sang the Te Deum in Old Slavonic. The following week he appeared before the Emperor at Innsbruck, but Magyar influences constrained Ferdinand to receive him with cold civility.

During the absence of Rajačić, all control rested with Stratimirović, who on June 10 answered the Magyars by a call to arms. Small committees sprang up in every district, officers were appointed, and a kind of national Serb militia was formed which attracted hundreds of disciplined fighters from the Military Frontiers and even volunteers from the Principality of Servia, under General Kničanin. Throughout July and August there was desultory fighting between Serbs and Magyars throughout the south of Hungary. Hideous excesses were committed on both sides, and it is of little importance to discover where they originated. Certain it is that the Magyar authorities displayed extreme severity towards the non-Magyar races and virtually challenged all who had any spirit, to take the Austrian side. Equally certain is it that the Serbs took a ferocious vengeance for the execution of their leaders [63] and the illtreatment of their peasantry. Serious Magyar historians accuse the Serbs of burning alive and even impaling some of their

---

[63] On July 17, Stanimirović and another Serb officer were hanged at Temesvár. (*See Serbische Bewegung*, p. 114.)

victims.[64]   On the other hand, the Serb apologists describe in plentiful detail, how wounded Serb prisoners and even old women were bound to the stake for days in blazing sunshine.

Maurice Perczel, known to the Serbs as " the hyaena of Kovilj," [65] ordered on a single day in March, 1849, the execution of 45 Serb prisoners, including several women.[66]   As many as 299 Serbs were thus put to death without trial,[67] and Kossuth seems at one time during the war to have seriously entertained the idea of exterminating the Serbs of the Banat and the Bácska and colonizing the vacant territory with the soldiers of his national militia.   Over the horrors of this racial war it is well to draw a veil of silence.

When Jellačić commenced his autumn campaign against the Magyars, the Serbs were organized under Austrian officers, and proved of great assistance to the Imperial cause.   But the long delay in the recognition of their national claims was not without a depressing effect upon the Serbs ; and it was doubtless this consideration which prompted the Imperial manifesto of December 15, 1848. " Our brave and loyal Serb nation," said the Emperor, " has at all times gloriously distinguished itself by its devotion to our Imperial House and by heroic resistance to all enemies of our Throne and Empire.   In recognition of these services and as a special mark of our Imperial favour and regard for the existence and well-being of the Serb nation," the old titles of Patriarch and Voivode are revived and duly confirmed to Archbishop Rajačić and General Šuplikac. This concession is to be regarded as a guarantee of Serb national autonomy, whose introduction will be one of the monarch's first concerns after the restoration of peace. Šuplikac scarcely survived the news of his recognition by the Emperor : the Patriarch, who himself conducted the dead Voivode's body to its last resting place beside the tomb of George Branković, found himself the sole official representative of Serb national claims. The military duties of Šuplikac were assigned provisionally to the Austrian Colonel Mayerhofer, but the office of Voivode remained unfilled.

When Hungary had at last been reduced to submission,

[64] Irányi and Chassin, *Histoire politique de la Révolution en Hongrie*, ii, p. 45.

[65] Helfert, op. cit. p. 192.

[66] At the Court Martial of Szente.

[67] *See* Friedjung, *Geschichte Oesterreichs*, p. 231, quoted from the official list in the *Wiener Zeitung*, of August 28, 1850.

the promises of the December Manifesto, unlike so many others exacted during the Revolution, were carried into execution. By a decree of November 18, 1849, the Banat and Bácska were separated from Hungary, and formed into an autonomous Serb Voivody, with its seat of government in Temesvár. But this experiment was from the first doomed to failure. Instead of restricting the new province to Serb territory, it was made to include large tracts of country where no Serb was to be found—the county of Krassó, where 75 in every 100 inhabitants were Roumanian and 10 German, the county of Torontál, the northern half of which was peopled by Magyars, Germans and Roumanians. Such racial boundaries as did exist, were deliberately ignored : one race was to be played off against the other, according to the foolish old methods of Austrian Absolutism. The attempts of Jellačić to connect the new province with Croatia and the Military Frontiers, merely brought him into collision with Haynau, as commander-in-chief in Hungary. All that he could effect was that the three Slavonian counties [68] were reunited with Croatia. The seat of the Serb Patriarchate, Karlovitz, was thus excluded from the Voivody, an arrangement which was most distasteful to Rajačić and the Orthodox Church. The artificial nature of the new province and its reactionary constitution created universal discontent, alike among the Serbs, the Magyars, the Germans and the Roumanians. The result was continual friction, in which all the progressive elements tended to range themselves on the side of the constitutional movement in Hungary.

With the collapse of the Bach System in 1860, the sorry experiment came to an end. The Voivody was reincorporated with Hungary. Little as they had appreciated the previous ten years, the Serbs bitterly resented their desertion by Vienna. The National Congress, when it met at Karlovitz in April, 1861, was openly hostile to Austria and to Schmerling, and eagerly espoused the cause of the Magyar Liberals. Svetozar Miletić, already the recognized leader of the Hungarian Serbs, pled the cause of union in his newspaper *Srpski Dnevnik* [69] at Neusatz, and trusted to the honour and generosity of Deák and Eötvös to secure free recognition for the Serb nationality and religion within the bounds of the Hungarian state. His trust in those two statesmen was not misplaced, but unhappily

[68] Excepting the districts of Ruma and Illok in Syrmia.
[69] Afterwards *Zastava*.

they could not bind their successors, and the law guaranteeing the equal rights of the nationalities, which was so prominent a feature of the settlement of 1867–8, remained on paper and was never carried into effect.

The history of the Serbs in Hungary since 1860 is one of slow decay. Shut out from all political influence, they found in their Church autonomy the sole outlet for the expression of national individuality. The economic changes of the last fifty years have not been to their advantage, and while Magyarization has thinned their ranks, there has been a corresponding decline in the birthrate of the Serb peasantry. Meanwhile the older culture of Neusatz and Karlovitz exercised a powerful influence upon the neighbouring principality of Servia. The founder of Servian education, Dositej Obradović (1739–1811) was a native of the Banat, and only crossed the Danube on the invitation of Kara George, the insurgent chief. The founder of Servian philology, the Southern Slav Grimm, Vuk Karadžić, though born in Servia, spent the greater part of his life upon Austrian soil and drew his inspiration from Dalmatia, Bosnia and Slavonia, while the acknowledged chief among Serb poets, Zmaj Jovan Jovanović, was a native of Hungary and lived in Agram. The pioneer of Serb literary societies, the Matica Srpska, was founded at Pest in the year 1826, and remained for many years the only institution of its kind. Even since its removal from Pest to Neusatz (Ujvidék) in 1864, it has fully maintained its reputation for scientific and scholarly work.

Neusatz no longer retains its distinctively Serb character, the Magyar and German elements in the town having increased rapidly in the last half century. Serb culture tends to concentrate more and more in Belgrad on the one hand, and at Zagreb and Sarajevo on the other, and such lesser centres as Neusatz and Karlovitz must inevitably suffer. But while the triangular rivalry of these three capitals has many evil effects in the field of politics, its influence upon literary effort can only be welcomed ; for so long as it does not lead to each ignoring the products of the other two, it cannot fail to introduce variety and contrast into literature and art, and thus tends to counteract that curse of Southern Slavonic life the provincial outlook.

CHAPTER III

The Era of Experiment (1849-1868)

Non Regno, verum Regi.

THE name of Illyria vanished in the storms of revolution. It had from the first made its appeal to the educated classes only ; to the vast mass of the population it conveyed little or no meaning. Not even the most conservative peasantry in the world can be roused to enthusiasm by ideas that have lain dormant for 2,000 years ; and to the Croat peasant Illyria meant no more than Dalriada to the Highland crofter. But the idea which underlay " Illyrism "—the perception of the essential unity of the race, despite its numerous political barriers and despite ecclesiastical cleavage—this idea could not be suppressed and soon found a new and more hopeful expression in the Yougo-Slav movement. The Croatian clergy has always been in the forefront of the battle ; but never has this fact been so nobly exemplified as in the case of Bishop Strossmayer, whose whole life was devoted to furthering the cause of Yougoslavism. During the years of reaction and change which preceded the constitutional settlement of 1868, Strossmayer devoted himself tirelessly to the task of fostering the tender plant of Croatian culture ; and though in later life his political influence waned, his striking personality has impressed itself indelibly upon the life of the nation. Almost all that is ideal in the Croatia of to-day is his work.

For ten years (1850–1860) the Bach system lay like an evil nightmare upon the Habsburg Monarchy. Militarism unredeemed by leadership, clericalism in the undiluted form of an all-embracing Concordat, Germanization as a fatal canker in an administration which not even the most hostile critic would dare to call corrupt—such were the main features of this period of transition, from which Croatia suffered at least as much as the sister kingdom. Absolutism thus converted into terms of bureaucracy, was from the first morally bank-

52

rupt ; and the disastrous Italian campaign of 1859 led to a complete collapse of the system. But with the dawn of constitutional government in the Monarchy, the difficulties of Croatia's position were greatly increased, and it tended to become a mere pawn in the political game between Vienna and Budapest. The October Diploma of 1860 offered a reasonable compromise between the principles of federalism and historic tradition, and Strossmayer and his party were not alone in welcoming it. The new Ban, Šokčević, the former adjutant of Jellačić, one of whose earliest steps had been to introduce the Croatian language into the administration and the schools, now summoned a conference of fifty-five leading politicians, to discuss the electoral law and to give voice to the wishes of the nation. To its three chief demands—the recognition of the national language, the union of Dalmatia with Croatia, and the establishment of a Croatian Chancellory in Vienna—the sovereign sent a highly favourable reply ; and preparations were already being made in Agram for the reception of Dalmatian delegates, when a complete reversal of policy took place at Vienna. The February Patent of 1861 represents a desperate effort to reclothe the worn-out centralist system of Bach with constitutional forms, to establish the German hegemony as the keystone of the constitution. The elections to the Croatian Sabor took place under the impressions of this sudden change. The strongest group in the new House, the National Liberal Party, led by Bishop Strossmayer and the historian Rački, viewed Vienna and Budapest with almost equal distrust and thus held the balance between the Independents (under Cardinal Haulik and the poet Mažuranić) who adhered to the centralist programme, and the Unionists or " Magyarones " under Baron Levin Rauch. The resentment and suspicion which the long years of the Bach régime had aroused against Vienna were rekindled into flame by the disappointment of the February Patent ; and the memories of Jellačić's exploits—perhaps too the resounding phrase of those days, " Italia farà da se "—led the Croat leaders to overestimate their strength, and to alienate Austria without making any special effort to conciliate Budapest. This tendency was strikingly illustrated by the words of Antony Starčević, who now first came into note as the leader of the ultra-Croat opposition : " To exist, Croatia only needs God and the Croats " (Bog i. Hrvati).[70] It is the tragedy of small nations

[70] Horvat, op. cit. p. 205.

that such ideals are mere will-o'-the-wisps, leading them into the quagmire of foreign domination.

Yet the historic phrase of Starčević, with its superb defiance of practical possibilities, fired the imagination of the nation and still figures as a distant ideal. He and his adherents founded the Stranka Prava (the Party of Rights), which upheld an unbending theory of Croatian independence ; and to-day this party, despite the dissensions and the lack of talent within its ranks, still occupies a position of great importance in Croatian politics, and might, if it could but purge itself of fanatical and self-seeking elements, exercise a decisive influence upon the future of the Croato-Servian race.

Meanwhile the tactful attitude of the Magyars, and notably the admission of the great Deák,[71] that Croatia occupied " an altogether special position and had never been incorporated in Hungary," were not without their effect upon the Croats, whose foolish policy of coquetting alternately with Vienna and Budapest led eventually to their being jilted by both suitors. The debate on the Address ended in the unanimous refusal of the Diet to send delegates to the Reichsrat ; and the central government, to whom the appearance of the Croats would have been a valuable counterpoise to the

---

[71] A strange myth has arisen, that Deák offered the Croats " a blank sheet," on which to inscribe their wishes and demands. Ferenczi in his *Life of Deák* (iii, p. 350) proves that he never used the expression. Paul Somssich, however, in the Hungarian debate on the Address (1861), used the phrase: "I am of opinion that we shall again come to an understanding with Croatia ; till then we keep for it *a blank page* in our constitution, but never will we enter the sphere of reproaches or compulsion." (Cit. Pliverić, p. 215.) Deák's views upon Croatia may be best studied in his German pamphlet, *Denkschrift über das Verhältniss zwischen Ungarn und Croatien* (Vienna, 1861). In the first address to the Throne, drafted by Deák and submitted to the Hungarian Parliament on May 13, 1861, the following passage occurs : " Croatia possesses its own territory and has a special position, and was never incorporated in Hungary, but stood in a relation with us and was our ally, who shared in our rights and our duties, our good fortune and our miseries. If then Croatia now wishes as a country to take part in our legislation ; if further it wishes to clear up with us those conditions under which it is prepared to connect its constitutional position with Hungary ; if it wishes intercourse with us, *as nation with nation*, we shall not rebuff it. We only wish that Croatia should not be prevented from sending its delegates to our Parliament, and that both we and they should have the opportunity of commencing negotiations on a constitutional basis." (*See* Deák, *Beszédei*, iii, p. 47.) Nothing could be more conciliatory

abstention of the Magyars, had no alternative but to dissolve the Diet (November 8, 1861). The only real fruit of the Diet of 1861 was Article XLII, which gave the Royal sanction to the assertion " that every bond, whether it be legislative, administrative or judicial, between the Triune Kingdom of Dalmatia-Croatia-Slavonia and the Kingdom of Hungary has in consequence of the events of 1848 legally ceased to exist." [72] The sole *caveat* to this weeping declaration is that one and the same coronation ceremony shall suffice for Hungary and Croatia.[73] In other words, the Personal Union in its extremest form was upheld by Croatia, and its existence was admitted by the sovereign. Those patriots to whom the written letter of the law signified more than its practical execution—and this class of patriot has always been plentiful in the Dual Monarchy—were doubtless overjoyed by such unreserved recognition. Far-sighted politicians must, however, have been aware that such recognition was worthless, unless it could be upheld in the teeth of Magyar opposition, and that this was only possible if Croatia flung itself unreservedly into the arms of Austria.

Schmerling, it is true, under the stress of Magyar opposition, did in so far court the favour of the Southern Slavs as to create an Aulic Chancellory for Croatia and Dalmatia, and to erect a supreme court of appeal in Agram. But even this could not undo the bad effect of his earlier intrigues in Dalmatia, where he had encouraged more or less openly the Italian, or Autonomist Party and thus virtually rendered the Unionist movement in Dalmatia ineffective for another generation. This unwise policy, following upon ten years of Absolutism and Germanization, had imbued the Croats with a mistrust of Vienna so deep as to blind them to the fact that the sole strategic value of their position lay in the possibility of disturbing the balance between the rival states of Austria and Hungary. Southern Slav support would, it is true, immensely strengthen Hungary's position in the struggle for the restoration of constitutional rights; but to Austria this support would prove decisive, since it would depress the balance altogether in her favour and enable her, as in 1848, to isolate and eventually overcome Magyar recalcitrance. Unhappily at that stage, Austria could not be trusted, and had indeed done everything in her power to deserve dis-

[72] See Appendix IV.
[73] Pliverić, p. 205; Wertheimer, *Graf Julius Andrássy*, if p. 370.

trust ; while Hungary possessed in Francis Deák a statesman equally distinguished for his scrupulous sense of honour and for his tactful and conciliatory mood towards Croatia. There was no Jellačić to guide events, to seize occasion by the hand and assert for his country its due influence upon the destiny of the Monarchy ; and hence the Croats rebuffed the advances of Vienna [74] and tended more and more to favour an alliance with Budapest. The true alternative to an alliance with Vienna was a whole-hearted and active co-operation with the Magyars in their constitutional demands. But this was rendered impossible by the general indignation kindled by the news of two encroachments upon Croatian territory. Medjumurja—the territory lying between the Drave, the Mur and the Styrian frontier, and inhabited almost exclusively by Croats—was reunited to Hungary ; while the seaport of Fiume, which had since 1848 formed an integral part of Croatia, was now restored to its former autonomous position, under a governor appointed from Budapest direct.[75] This last act was largely due to the folly of the Ban Šokčević, who had taken vengeance for some anti-Croat riots, by placing the town in a state of siege,[76] and thus played into the hands of the Italian party and the Magyars.

These two incidents arrested the movement in Croatia for renewed friendship with Hungary ; and for the four years which followed the dissolution of the Croatian Diet (1861-

[74] The Croatian Address of September 24, 1861, roundly declares that it cannot see in the Diploma of October 20, 1860, anything save a violation of the public law and the constitution of the Triune Kingdom (Šulek, *Naše Pravice*, p. 430) and therefore denies the legality of the Reichsrat, so far as Croatia is concerned.

[75] Fiume, under its earlier name of St. Veit von Pflaum, had been a fief of the powerful Frankopan family, but attained to an autonomous position towards the middle of the fifteenth century. In 1746 Maria Theresa imposed upon it a Captain and four councillors, and assigned all appeals in administrative questions to Graz, and in financial matters to Triest. In 1776 it was formally handed over to Hungary, Count Joseph Mailáth being appointed Governor and High Sheriff. On October 27, 1777, the Croatian Diet entered a solemn protest against the change, but without effect. Fiume's formal incorporation with Hungary was at length carried out by Article IV of 1807. In 1809 Fiume formed part of the new Illyria and after the expulsion of the French it was not restored to Hungary till 1822. In 1848 it was united to Croatia. On this controversy see Ladislas von Szalay, *Zur ungarisch-Kroatischen Frage* and Fr. Rački, *Rieka prema Hrvatskoj* (Fiume and Croatia).

[76] Horvath, p. 185.

November, 1865), Croatian opinion held suspiciously aloof from Vienna and Budapest alike. The abstention of the Magyars from the Central Reichsrat made the adherence of Croatia and Transylvania essential to the success of Schmerling's scheme. Had the little group of Saxon deputies, who alone represented the lands of the Crown of St. Stephen in the Reichsrat, been reinforced by spokesmen of the 2,500,000 Roumanians of Hungary and by the united delegates of the *socia regna* of Croatia-Slavonia-Dalmatia ; then Schmerling might with some plausibility have asserted that the Reichsrat represented a large section of opinion in Transleithania, and its description as a mere Rump Parliament would have lost much of its force. But the Croats wasted their opportunity and by adopting a policy of inaction, accustomed the decisive factors in the Monarchy to omit Croatia from their calculations.

The elections of 1865 returned a fresh federalist majority to the Sabor. But the Royal answer to the Address of the new House was already tinged by Magyar influence ; it admitted that in theory the Military Frontiers and Dalmatia formed part of the Triune Kingdom, but insisted upon the Sabor regulating its relations with Hungary, before the idea of unity could be realized. In conformity with the Royal wishes, a committee of twelve members was elected by the Sabor to negotiate with Hungary. Its president was Bishop Strossmayer, and one of its most prominent members was Francis Rački the historian. In Budapest it met with a Magyar commission of equal numbers, which was presided over by Count George Mailáth, but whose ruling spirit was Francis Deák (April 16–June 22, 1866).

From the first there prevailed a difference of opinion between the two commissions, the Croats maintaining that the events of 1848 had destroyed the legal bond between the two countries,[77] whereas the Magyars would only admit the severance *de facto*, but not *de jure*. The Croats argued that " the Triune Kingdom had always possessed its own distinct legislature for internal affairs," while the Magyars merely recognized Croatia as possessing " only a certain statutory right." The Hungarian deputation declined to admit the Croat claim that " all laws enacted by the Joint Parliament must be proclaimed in the Croatian Sabor, if they are to be binding upon us " ; nor could it be induced to include among the matters under discussion the relationship of Hungary with Austria, which it declared to

[77] Cf. Art. XLII of 1861.

be a matter for the Budapest Parliament. Moreover it refused even to discuss the question of Medjumurje and demanded an explicit renunciation of Croatia's claim to Fiume. Finally Strossmayer openly exclaimed, " The Magyars do not wish to have us beside them as a nation with equal rights, but under them as a subjected nation. The Magyars rely upon their friends (the Unionists) in Croatia and are waiting for events abroad." [78]

After two months' negotiations, a deadlock had been reached, and the Croat delegates returned to Agram without having effected anything. Strossmayer's view was accurate. The imminence of war with Prussia and the prospect of great changes as its result, had rendered the Magyars indifferent to the outcome of the negotiations. But it would be quite unfair to blame them for this ; it merely showed their just appreciation of the situation. While the Croats still clung desperately to theory, the Magyar statesmen reckoned with hard fact and adjusted their theory accordingly.

The eventful war of 1866 need not be dealt with in the present volume. The rapid defeat of Austria by the Prussian armies was balanced by the Archduke Albert's victory at Custozza and the still more brilliant sea action off Lissa, in which Admiral Tegethoff routed a superior Italian fleet and sank his incapable adversary's flagship. In this connexion it is only just to point to the part played by the Croat seamen of Dalmatia and Croatia, upon whom Austria is more and more dependent for manning her navy.

The two months of negotiation in Budapest appear to have completely disillusioned the Croat delegates and to have destroyed their belief in the possibility of coming to terms with the Magyars. The Croatian Diet, when it met in November, 1866, boldly assumed the attitude which, to be effective, should have been adopted at least four years earlier. The Address to the Throne (December 19), taking as its point of departure Article XLII of 1861 (see Appendix IV), expressed the Diet's readiness " to enter upon negotiations with Your Majesty independently as with our most Gracious King, regarding the relations of this kingdom with the Monarchy as a whole." [79] It furthermore protested against the attitude

---

[78] Cepelić-Pavić, *J. J. Strossmayer*, p. 568, cit. Horvat, op. cit. p. 243. *See also* Pliverić, op cit. pp. 229-244.
[79] Pliverić, p. 425, Šulek, p. 400.

of the Hungarian Parliament in seeking to regulate Hungary's relations with Austria, without consulting Croatia. The address was answered by a cautious Rescript of January 4, 1867, promising that the wishes and demands of Croatia would receive careful consideration, but postponing all decision till the result of negotiations with Hungary had been submitted. The Diet was therefore prorogued indefinitely.

Croatia was completely ignored at this decisive moment in the history of the Dual Monarchy. In February, 1867, Count Belcredi's scheme of Federalism was finally abandoned and that statesman was replaced by Beust, who had recently transferred his services from the Court of Dresden to that of Vienna, and who subordinated all matters of internal politics in the Habsburg Monarchy to the one absorbing passion of " Revenge for Königgrätz." Superficial and vain to a degree, he was on the one hand childishly susceptible to Magyar flattery and on the other was no match for Magyar statesmanship, with the result that he soon persuaded himself that the Magyars were the most suitable instrument for humbling Prussian pride and must be humoured accordingly. Not possessing any intimate knowledge of Hungarian problems and scorning the details of racial strife, he naturally felt no scruples in instituting a system which divided the spoils of power between the two strongest races of the Monarchy, at the expense of all the others.

On February 17, Count Julius Andrássy became the first Premier of the new constitutional régime in Hungary, and on March 30 the famous Ausgleich or Compromise beween Austria and Hungary obtained the sanction of the Hungarian Parliament.[80]

Throughout the momentous negotiations which ended in the restoration of harmony between Vienna and Budapest, Croatia was completely ignored, and no Croat politician had any influence upon the discussions which decided the fate of the Triune Kingdom as well as that of Hungary. Deák, it is true, made some overtures to the Croats, with the object of inducing their delegates to attend the so-called " Coronation " Parliament ; but, so far from showing complaisance towards Croat demands, he appears only to have yielded to the persuasion of Andrássy, in offering Croatia more favourable

[80] It cannot be said to have acquired full validity till December, 1867, when its principles were also sanctioned by the Austrian Parliament.

terms than those which he had defined during the negotiations before Königgrätz. The Croats seem to have had some friends in high quarters,[81] though not in the highest of all. But Beust and Andrássy were in full accord, in their disapproval of Croatian claims ; and the Foreign Minister, within a week of Andrássy's appointment as Premier, was exhorting the Ban, Baron Šokčević to destroy the illusions of " those who aim at loosening the constitutional link which has hitherto existed between Croatia and the Royal Crown of Hungary, and who dream of the foundation of a Triune Kingdom, merely bound loosely to the Monarchy as a whole." [82] But for the somewhat threatening nature of the foreign situation and the fear of Russian propaganda among the Southern Slavs, it is probable that Croatia would have received still scanter consideration. As it was, throughout the critical period the Croatian Diet was denied the opportunity of expressing its opinion ; having been prorogued on January 4, 1867, it was again prorogued on April 11, and was not allowed to meet till May 1, when it was already faced by the *fait accompli* of Dualism.

Meanwhile the Hungarian Parliament had defined its views upon the Croatian question, in the Resolution drawn up and submitted by Deák on April 9. It laid down that there could only be a single act of coronation for the two countries, and that in all matters at issue between the halves of the reconstructed Dual state Croatia must ever form a portion of the Hungarian unit, but avoided all aggressive phrases and concluded in conciliatory tones.[83] The Royal Rescript by which

[81] Deák in an important conversation which he had with Beust on December 20, 1866, " The Ban (Šokčević) rejected contemptuously the friendly proposal (of Deák). Letters of his, which had fallen into the hands of a high personage, showed where the flames of discord were being fanned from." (*See* Deák, *Beszédei,* iv, p. 146.)

[82] Beust to Šokčević, February 22, 1867. Cit. Wertheimer, *Graf Julius Andrássy,* vol. i, p. 373). This book—one of the most important political biographies of recent years—contains a valuable account of the Hungaro-Croatian settlement (pp. 369–412). Though he writes from the Magyar point of view, and does not conceal his dislike of Strossmayer and other Croatian leaders, he does not deserve the charges of extreme partisanship which have been made against him by the Croatian Press. Indeed, he generally writes with admirable moderation.

[83] Deák, *Beszedei,* iv, pp. 483–5. " The Hungarian Parliament for its own part will ever be ready both now and in the further course of the agreement, to give to Croatia, Dalmatia and Slavonia all those guarantees respecting their constitutional and national claims, which they can lawfully and fairly desire."

the Croatian Diet was opened, followed similar lines. The sovereign expressed his desire "to preserve undiminished the historic rights of our dear kingdoms Croatia and Slavonia, to secure to them such measure of independence as corresponds to the needs of their national development, and to offer them all those guarantees for their autonomy which we deem to be compatible with the interests of our Monarchy as a whole." The rescript took its stand upon the Pragmatic Sanction, as "the most important fundamental law of the Monarchy," which specially emphasizes the integrity of the Hungarian crown and the essential unity of all its provinces. The wishes revealed in the Croatian Address of December 19, 1866—in other words, Croatia's desire to negotiate with the monarch direct, and to have a voice in the arrangement between Hungary and Austria—are characterized as conflicting with the Pragmatic Sanction; and the hope is expressed that the Diet will not put forward "such demands as would be apt to render impossible a solution" of the constitutional difficulty. The Rescript then invites the Diet to send its delegates to the Hungarian Parliament on the occasion of the Coronation, and ends with the somewhat peremptory command that they "should so hasten their deliberations that their delegates could reach Budapest by May 15 at the latest."[84] Count Andrássy made it clear that any officials who, as members of the Diet of Agram, ventured to oppose the Magyar wishes, as expressed through the mouth of the Sovereign, would be instantly dismissed or pensioned.[85] Even Strossmayer was threatened with the loss of his Bishopric, and a similar pressure was put upon other leaders of the Opposition. But although Strossmayer and Mažuranić absented themselves from the Diet's deliberations, the great majority of its members passed an Address to the Throne (May 18, 1867), declining in respectful terms to send any representatives to Budapest, until an agreement had been reached upon the constitutional relations between Hungary and the Triune Kingdom. Delegates were appointed for the purpose of meeting a similar Hungarian delegation and drawing up conjointly the Coronation Diploma, and detailed instructions were provided for their guidance.[86]

[84] Pliverić, pp. 261–4 ; Šulek, p. 483 ; Horvat, pp. 238–42.
[85] His telegram to the Ban, to this effect, is cited by Wertheimer, p. 374.
[86] See Appendix V.

A week later, May 25, the Croatian Diet was dissolved, the Royal Rescript characterizing the demands of the majority as "unrealizable, some of them altogether, some of them owing to the short time," and as intended to make all constitutional agreement impossible.

On June 8, Francis Joseph was crowned King of Hungary with more than the usual pomp and solemnity; but neither the Parliament nor the nobility of Croatia were represented at the ceremony. Of the higher Croat clergy only the Bishop of Zengg was present,[87] while deputations were sent by the towns of Fiume, Osijek (Essek) and Požega. The Ban, Baron Šokčević, was obliged to attend the Coronation, in his quality of "Baro Regni"; but he was not long in handing in his resignation (June 27).

As Šokčević's successor Count Andrássy, with whom the nomination of the Ban now really lay, appointed Baron Levin Rauch, the leader of the Unionist, or Magyarone, party in Croatia. His mission was to secure the passage of a Hungaro-Croatian Compromise through the Diet of Agram. His reputation for unscrupulous energy rendered it safe to entrust him with the details of the task. A majority had to be found, by hook or by crook; and Rauch was anything but nice in his choice of methods. The most approved methods of the Police State were revived. All officials, professors or schoolmasters suspected of active sympathy with the Opposition were transferred, dismissed or pensioned.[88] The clergy, then as ever enthusiasts for the national cause, were subjected to intimidation or persecution. The Opposition Press was muzzled; and on August 19 its ablest organ *Pozor* was suppressed altogether.[89] By the autumn the ground had been prepared for more radical measures. On October 20 a new electoral law [90]—specially contrived to harass and handicap the Opposition—was pro-

---

[87] Horvat, op. cit. p. 269.

[88] The Slav world owes Rauch a debt of gratitude, in that among other victims of his illegal régime, a young Croat scholar, Vatroslav Jagić, found it advisable to leave his native country. Under happier circumstances he has lived to be acknowledged as the foremost Slavistic scholar of his time in Europe. But he has also lived to see Croatia groaning under the misrule of a second Baron Rauch.

[89] Horvat, p. 274. A new Croat newspaper—*Novi Pozor*—was at once founded in Vienna. In May, 1869, Rauch forbade its sale in Croatia.

[90] Šulek, op. cit. pp. cxxxvi–cxliii.

mulgated by arbitrary decree ; and it was upon this illegal basis that the elections to the new Diet took place. The whole administrative machine was of course enlisted in favour of Rauch's candidates, the elections lasted from November 19 to December 23, and wholesale bribery and corruption decimated the ranks of the Opposition. Out of sixty-six elected deputies [91] no fewer than thirty-four were officials ; the National Party had shrunk to a tiny group of fourteen members,[92] while Starčević and Mrazović, the two leaders of the Radical and anti-Magyar wing were not allowed to secure seats in the new House.

The Diet met in Agram on January 8, 1868 : and the Opposition feeling its impotence and nettled by the contempt with which the majority treated its protests against the arbitrary change in the franchise, decided to adopt the fatal policy of abstention. Its spokesman declared in the opening sitting, that " in withdrawing from the House, we protest against all the decisions of this Sabor, composed on an unconstitutional and illegal basis. Standing inalienably upon Article XLII of the year 1861 (see Appendix IV) and upon His Majesty's Rescript of November 8, 1861, we protest against the subordination of the Triune Kingdom to the Kingdom of Hungary." [93]

In spite of Strossmayer's disapproval, the whole Opposition, with the exception of two members, withdrew from the House ; and the majority was left in undisputed possession of the field. The deputation elected on January 30 to resume the negotiations with Hungary, consisted exclusively of Unionists ; and though they still took the much-cited Article XLII of 1861 as their point of departure, their acceptance of the Magyar draft of the proposed Hungaro-Croatian compromise was of course from the first a foregone conclusion. A minority among the Croat delegates, it is true, held out for financial autonomy, and Deák was not indisposed to make the concession. But a majority was content to leave the draft virtually unaltered, and its reference to a joint committee was very largely a matter of form. On one point only did the Croat delegates stand firm—the question whether Fiume

[91] As opposed to the hereditary members.
[92] Including Rački the historian and Dr. Michael Polit, then a young Serb advocate, now the veteran champion of the Serbs of Southern Hungary, and once more member of the Hungarian Parliament from 1906 to 1910.
[93] Polić, *Parlam. Povjest,* ii, pp. 20–21.

should belong to Croatia or to Hungary; and it will be seen that paragraph 66 of the Compromise postponed the final settlement of this vital issue till a subsequent occasion.[94] On September 24, 1868, after a debate lasting three days, the measure was adopted *en bloc* by the Croatian Diet, without going into committee, and by 69 votes to 4.[95] Four days later it received the unanimous sanction of the Hungarian Parliament.

[94] The sinister history of this paragraph is narrated on page 81.
[95] Horvat, p. 276; Zagorsky, p. 96.

CHAPTER IV

The Compromise between Hungary and Croatia (1868)

IN the preceding chapter I have attempted to summarize the main incidents of Croatian constitutional development and indirectly to prepare the reader for the view that the claims and aspirations of Croatian parties at the present day are not merely based upon some modern theory of the rights of nationality, but upon the persistent traditions of eight centuries. It may be objected that the recital of ancient claims and privileges, which in no way correspond to actual practice, is of merely academic value. Yet in a country of such composite character and mixed races as Austria-Hungary, constitutional law—best referred to under the convenient German name of *Staatsrecht*—exercises a powerful influence upon political development; and its formulae, even when most inaccurate or extravagant, cannot be ignored with impunity, as they might be in our own country, where public men are too often ignorant even of such fundamental laws as the Scottish or Irish Acts of Union.

If this be my apology for the preceding chapter, none should be required for its successor, in the course of which I propose to analyse the Compromise of 1868. Whatever may be its shortcomings or omissions, this document has for over forty years formed the basis of Hungaro-Croatian relations and, as an essential supplement to the more famous Ausgleich between Austria and Hungary, forces itself upon the attention of all students of the Dual Monarchy and of all politicians who are interested in the future of the Southern Slavs.

In reply to the extremists who deny the validity of the Compromise, it must at once be conceded that it rests upon the most doubtful legal basis; for the assembly which sanctioned it owed its existence to an illegal revision of the franchise by arbitrary decree, and to wholesale electoral corruption and intimidation of the very grossest kind. On the other hand, it is equally true that the franchise upon which the earlier Diets of 1861 and 1865 were elected had originally been promulgated by Jellačić in 1848, even if they subsequently received the unanimous sanction of the elected body. But whether lawful or illegal, the Compromise subsists in practice, and must be seriously reckoned with, so long as the short-sighted policy of Viennese statesmen permits the Dualist System to continue in its present form. In other words, the more advanced claims of Croatia must be treated as tem-porarily in abeyance ; and for the present our attention must be confined exclusively to the strict letter of the law which regulates her relationship with the sister kingdom of Hungary.

The exact juridical nature of the Compromise has formed the subject of much lively controversy. Many Magyar politicians and publicists affect to regard it simply as one of the many laws upon the Hungarian statute book, and subject, like them, to parliamentary revision when occasion arises ; while the Croats are practically unanimous in treating it as a solemn contract between two parties enjoying theoretical if not actual equality. In view of the explicit terms of the preamble to the Act, it is difficult to understand how any one can venture to deny the theory of contract. " An agreement having been reached, by joint decision, between the Parliament [96] of Hungary on the one hand and the Parliament of Croatia-Slavonia and Dalmatia on the other hand with a view to composing the constitutional questions pending between them, this agreement, after being approved, confirmed and sanctioned by His Imperial and Apostolic Royal Majesty, is hereby inarticulated as joint fundamental law of Hungary and Croatia-Slavonia-Dalmatia." So runs the preamble to Law XXX of the Hungarian Parliament, which had already received the sanction of the Croatian Diet, as Article I of the same year.

The preamble is carefully worded in order to suggest full parity between the contracting parties, and the whole pro-

[96] The latter received the Royal sanction on November 8, the former on November 17, 1868. It should be noted that the Magyar text employs the same word—országgyülés—to describe both assemblies. This would seem effectively to dispose of the modern Magyar Chauvinist argument, that the Diet of Agram is no Parliament in the true sense of the word. In Croat the word "Sabor" is applied to both.

cedure adopted to pass the Compromise into law, confirms the view that it is, in the words of the concluding paragraph, a "joint fundamental law" of Hungary and the Triune Kingdom, duly inscribed as such upon the statute books of the two countries. On the other hand, it lays down equally clearly that Croatia and Slavonia have belonged for centuries, alike *de jure* and *de facto*, to the Crown of St. Stephen, and that "the lands of the Hungarian Crown are inseparable from one another."

A large section of Croatian opinion contests this view; while Magyar opinion declines to recognize any distinction between the Crown of St. Stephen"[97] and "Hungary" in the narrow sense, thus arriving at the conclusion that Croatia is a mere province of Hungary. The contention of the Croatian Diet, upheld firmly for centuries, is summed up in the brief phrase, "Regi, non Regno."

This pronouncement, which completely ignores the Croatian Pragmatic Sanction of 1712 and treats the Hungarian Pragmatic Sanction as alone binding upon the two countries, follows closely upon the lines of the Austro-Hungarian Ausgleich, which employs the phrases "Hungary and its annexes" (Nebenländer), and "the lands of the Hungarian Crown" as identical and as forming a single unit in the sense of the Pragmatic Sanction. The preamble may thus be described as a compromise, in the fullest meaning of the word, between the two extreme views; for while assuming the parity of the two parties to the treaty, it at the same time pronounces their union to be indissoluble.

This unity once admitted, it must naturally follow that, in the words of paragraph 1, "Hungary and Croatia-Slavonia and Dalmatia form one and the same state-complex (*Staatsgemeinschaft*)[98] alike in their position towards the other territories under His Majesty's rule and towards other countries." Thus so far as international affairs are concerned, Hungary and Croatia form a single unit; but in all internal matters each of the two states preserves its identity, Croatia being expressly recognized as a "political nation possessing a special territory of its own" (§ 59). And again in section 29 of the Law of Nationalities (1868, XLIV) as "a separate nation from a political point of view." In constitutional questions

[97] Despite the mystical qualities which they assign to the Crown in any discussion of their differences with Austria.
[98] államközösség ; državna zajednica.

analogies are always of doubtful value, and as a matter of fact there is no real analogy among the existing states of Europe to the relationship between Hungary and Croatia.[99] Croatia can only be regarded as a sovereign state, shorn by its own act of certain attributes of sovereignty. Its powers would seem to distribute themselves under three heads :—

1. Common affairs between Hungary and Austria, for which Croatia forms an integral part of the Transleithan unit and is only free to communicate with Austria or the outer world through the medium of Budapest—its executive control being almost nil and even its legislative control being limited to the presence of three Croat members in the Hungarian Delegation.

2. Common affairs between Hungary and Croatia, which lie within the province of the Joint Parliament of Budapest.

3. Autonomous affairs, over which the Diet of Agram enjoys the exclusive control.

I now propose to examine the Hungaro-Croatian Compromise from these three points of view, including within my survey the four revisions of the years 1873 (Art. XXXIV), 1881 (Art. XV), 1889 (Art. XL). 1891 (Art. XXVII), and the three Croatian articles of 1869 (II), 1870 (II) and 1888 (September 29), which deal with the composition and powers of the autonomous Government and Diet of Agram.[100]

A. Austro-Hungarian Common Affairs

Under § 4 Croatia is obliged to recognize as valid and binding the Ausgleich of 1867 (in its Hungarian form, as Art. XII of the Hungarian Parliament), and also the three Acts (XV, XVI, XVII, 1867) regulating the commercial and financial relations of the two halves of the Monarchy, all of which had been concluded between Austria and Hungary without Croatia being consulted. In return for this recognition, however, Hungary inserted the explicit pledge that " in the future fundamental laws and agreements of this nature can only be concluded under the lawful collaboration of Croatia-Slavonia and Dalmatia." [101]

[99] With the possible exception of Finland and Russia.
[100] A careful English translation of the Compromise will be found in Appendix VI.
[101] This paragraph contains an interesting distinction between Common Affairs (between the territories of the Crown of St. Stephen and the other territories of His Majesty) and " affairs which are not common but are

As an interesting example of the manner in which this pledge has been fulfilled, it may be pointed out that Croatia has never been consulted on the occasion of any of the revisions of the Austro-Hungarian Ausgleich, and that during the winter of 1907, when the commercial Ausgleich was renewed, the Croatian constitution was actually in abeyance, as the result of a quarrel conjured up by another equally flagrant violation of the Hungaro-Croatian Compromise on the part of the Hungarian Government.[102]

This enables us to realize the disadvantages from which Croatia suffers, owing to the fact that she was confronted with a *fait accompli* in respect of the joint affairs of the Monarchy. There is absolutely no machinery for securing to Croatia even the means of approach to the central organs of Government in the Monarchy—the Joint Ministries of Foreign Affairs, War and Finance—still less to ensure her being consulted even when matters of the most vital interest to all Southern Slavonic countries are under consideration. A very practical illustration was afforded by the crisis of 1908, when Croatian interests were completely ignored at headquarters, though the Croat and Serb race would have been the main sufferer if a war with Servia had resulted from Baron Aehrenthal's policy.

The joint executive is responsible to those clumsiest and most unreal of constitutional machines, the Delegations,[103] in which Croatia is only represented by five members and can therefore exercise no real influence upon their legislative proceedings, or upon those executive changes on which the Delegations may insist.[104] From the Magyar standpoint this is an essentially wise and desirable arrangement ; but it is of

to be disposed of by common agreement." This was undoubtedly intended by its framers to be conciliatory, but since then conciliation has given place to compulsion.

[102] *See* Chapter VIII.

[103] Two Committees of sixty members each, elected annually by the Parliaments of Austria and Hungary, and meeting alternately in Vienna and Budapest for the discussion of all matters pertaining to the three Joint Ministries. They sit and vote separately, and only communicate by "Nuntium" : in the event of a disagreement there is a joint vote.

[104] To judge by a dispute which arose in October, 1910, there is nothing to prevent the Hungarian Government from filling all five places (four from the Lower and one from the Upper House) with its own nominees, and thus excluding Croat opposition opinion from the Delegations.

course quite irreconcilable with even the most moderate Croat theory of state.

In other words, Croatia, though recognized as " a political nation possessing a special territory of its own," has no part in the Central legislature and executive of the Monarchy and exercises absolutely no control over it. The Joint Ministers stand or fall according to the wishes of Vienna or Budapest. The Monarchy embarks upon a momentous Southern Slav policy, involving European issues ; but the Southern Slavs are not consulted. The financial and commercial interests of this " special territory " are not represented at headquarters. The Ban of Croatia, himself a nominee of the Hungarian Premier (§ 51), is only entitled to communicate with the Sovereign through the medium of the Minister for Croatia, who of course also holds his seat in the Hungarian Cabinet at the will of the Premier (§ 44). Thus a Magyar barrier may be said to exist, shutting off Croatia from the outer world, and depriving her of the very slightest influence upon the councils of the Monarchy as a whole.

It would be absurd to blame the Magyars for thus limiting Croatian independence. According to their reading of constitutional law, Croatia has for centuries formed an integral part of the Crown of St. Stephen, and any concessions of autonomy are a free gift, not a privilege legally exacted. The interests of Hungary are paramount, and they alone are to be consulted. But it would be still more absurd to expect the Croats to regard with anything but extreme aversion an arrangement which places them at the mercy of a country whose economic interests are diametrically opposed to their own.

II. HUNGARO-CROATIAN COMMON AFFAIRS

If we turn from Croatia's share in the affairs of the Monarchy as a whole—a share which can hardly even be said to exist at all—to her share in affairs common to the whole of Transleithania, it will be found that the framers of the Compromise conceived it in what from the Magyar standpoint can only be described as exceedingly liberal terms, and that it contains all the elements of a true federal union of two equal sovereign states.

At the same time it must be remembered that the whole conception of " terms " granted by one party to the other, infringes the theory of contract and is therefore highly distasteful to the Croats. In their view, the Compromise ought to embody the rights which they have enjoyed (at least in theory) for centuries, not the concessions which they have obtained from an allied nation.

Hungary and Croatia possess a Joint Government (gemeinsame Regierung) (§ 3), and in all joint affairs the legislative power belongs to the Parliament of Budapest, which therefore should in strict parlance be known as the Hungaro-Croatian Parliament. In it Croatia is represented by forty delegates from the Diet of Agram.[105] who only sit when matters relating to the whole of Transleithania are under discussion and retire when purely Hungarian measures are introduced (§ 31). These forty are strictly speaking not deputies but delegates, being elected by the Croatian Diet out of its own members, for the whole period of the Joint Parliament.[106] If meanwhile the Sabor should be dissolved, the elected forty continue to be members of the Joint Parliament, until the new Diet has been able to elect new delegates (§ 34). This provision, originally inserted merely for convenience' sake, has become latterly one of the most effective constitutional guarantees which Croatia possesses, since it makes it impossible for Hungary, even when the Croatian Constitution has been entirely suspended (as in 1908–1910), to stifle the free expression of Croatian opinion in the Joint Parliament.

All joint laws are published both in Magyar and in Croatian ; and the. Croat delegates have the right to employ their own language in debate (§ 59). During debates on joint affairs, the flag of Croatia is hoisted above the Parliament buildings, side by side with the flag of Hungary (§ 62). The combined arms of Hungary and of the three Southern Slav kingdoms form the emblem of the Joint Government (§ 61). The royal

---

[105] Article XV, 1881, § 2. Under § 22, XXX, 1868, the number had been fixed at 29 : but § 33 laid down that in the event of either the Military Frontiers or Dalmatia being united to Croatia, the number should be increased, in proportion to the increase of population. When therefore the Frontiers were united in 1881, the number was raised from 29 to 40. On a basis of population, there should then have been 51 deputies for Croatia-Slavonia, which in 1880 had 1,892,499 inhabitants out of a total of 15,642,102 for Transleithania. *Ungarisches Statistisches Jahrbuch* XII, p. 18. Forty out of 453 deputies corresponds to 8·8 instead of 11·4 per cent.

[106] The Diet further sends three of its members as delegates to the House of Magnates (§ 36, modified by 1881, XV, § 2).

title " King of Croatia, Slavonia and Dalmatia," is to appear
after " King of Hungary " on all Hungarian coins (§ 64).

The Joint Affairs of Hungary and Croatia are defined as
follows (§§ 6–9) :—

(1) The Civil List.
(2) All laws relating to recruiting and military service.
(3) The financial system.
(4) Coinage, and weights and measures.
(5) Commercial treaties.
(6) All Questions of Banking and Exchange.
(7) Patents, Copyright, etc.
(8) Maritime, Commercial and Mining Law.
(9) Customs and Trade.
(10) Post Office and Telegraphs.
(11) Railways.
(12) Harbours and Shipping.

The executive side of these affairs lies partly with officials
of the central Government and partly with the autonomous
Croatian authorities (§ 45) ; but in each case, Croatian is the
official language for all officials throughout the territory of
Croatia-Slavonia (§ 57).

In addition to the above affairs, a number of minor matters
—industrial regulations, passports, citizenship and naturalization—are placed under the legislative control of the Joint
Parliament, but their supervision lies with the local executive
(§ 10).

The outward and visible sign of union between Hungary
and Croatia is the Coronation ceremony, which is to be a
single act for the two countries (§ 2). The Magyars have
always assigned a peculiar mystic significance to the Crown
of St. Stephen, and regard it as typifying the territorial unity
of their country. As a matter of fact, even the extremist
Croat politicians, while upholding the view that separate
coronations for the two countries took place for many reigns
after the Union, seem to raise no objection to a joint Coronation ceremony, though they demand Croatia's independence
in all else. In other words they favour the Personal Union,
and wish the person of the Sovereign to be the sole link between
Croatia and Hungary.

III. CROATIAN AUTONOMY

All those affairs which are not expressly enumerated fall
under the sphere of Croatian autonomy (§ 47). In effect,

however, this autonomy is threefold—Administration, Justice (with which Church questions are combined) and Education (§ 48), each of which has a Government Department of its own at Agram, bearing the character though not the name of a Ministry, and subject to the three sectional chiefs, who form, under the Ban, the Croatian equivalent for a Cabinet. As the Ban is responsible to the Diet of Agram (XXX, 1868, § 50 and Cro. Art. II, 1869, § 9) and as the sectional chiefs are appointed by him and resign when he resigns,[107] ministerial responsibility may be admitted to form an essential part of Croatian constitutional theory ; but for reasons which will become apparent later, this responsibility is apt to become a mere farce in practice.

Thus in three directions Croatia enjoys absolute " Home Rule," alike legislative and administrative. The whole executive is organized on a Croatian basis, in the national language : education, partial and hampered though it is by lack of funds, is also entirely national and independent of all control from Budapest ; while Croatia has for centuries possessed a complete judicial system of its own, with a supreme Court of Appeal located in Agram. What is most important of all, the recognition which the Compromise secures to the Croatian language is absolutely unqualified. Croatian is recognized as the sole official language throughout the territory of the Triune Kingdom, and must be employed not only by all organs of the Central Government in that territory, but also in all communications of the Central Government to any of the autonomous authorities (§§ 56, 57, 58). The Croatian delegates, who with very few exceptions are quite ignorant of the Magyar language, have the right to employ their own language both in the Joint Parliament of Budapest and in the Hungarian Delegation (§ 59). The laws must be published in Croatian as well as Magyar (§ 60). The Militia throughout Croatian territory employs the Croatian flag and is commanded in the Croatian language.

The weakest points of the Compromise are the financial relations of the two countries and the position of the Ban. As both have led to repeated misunderstandings and acrid controversy, it is necessary to pass them under review before proceeding any further.

[107] The law does not expressly assign these appointments to him, but the invariable practice, and the sense of Article II, 1869, § 16, leave them in his hands.

COMPROMISE BETWEEN HUNGARY AND CROATIA

(a) *Finance*.

The general principle is laid down, that Croatia-Slavonia shall contribute to the Joint Affairs of the Monarchy, in accordance with its taxable capacity ; and in pursuance of this aim, the proportion of contribution was so fixed that 93·5 per cent. of the total expenses of Transleithania should be borne by Hungary, and only 6·4 per cent. by Croatia. This very liberal arrangement was modified still farther in Croatia's favour in 1880 (Art. LIV), when the proportions were changed to 94·4 and 5·5 respectively. But it was again modified in 1889 (Art. XL), when Hungary was burdened with 92 per cent. and Croatia with 7·93 per cent., and again in 1906 (Art. X), when Hungary's share was reduced to 91·3 and Croatia's share increased to 8·1 per cent. In calculating the proportion to be paid by the two countries, the same procedure was adopted as that of the Austro-Hungarian Ausgleich. In the years 1860–1865 the average net revenue of Austria was 1,187,978,418 florins, that of Hungary 484,687,394 florins, giving a percentage of 71·02 and 28·98 respectively ; but their respective contributions were fixed at 70 and 30 per cent. In the same way the average net revenue of Croatia for the same period was 31,217,648 florins, thus giving a percentage of 6·4 as against 93·6 for Hungary.[108] Thus it appears that Hungary's treatment of Croatia was somewhat more generous than Austria's treatment of Transleithania. Considering that Croatia formed 12 per cent. of the population of Transleithania in 1869, and 12·1 per cent. at the last census (1900), she cannot justly describe as excessive her share of the contribution, even though her taxable capacity is generally admitted to be relatively lower than that of Hungary. Moreover a later paragraph lays down that should Croatian revenue, by reason of increased taxable strength, exceed the proportion of joint expenditure to which it is liable (viz. 8·1 per cent. to-day), the surplus is to be retained by Croatia, and that country is not to be held liable for the deficits of former years (§ 27). This provision may reasonably be regarded as a further proof of generous intentions on the part of the Magyar framers of the Compromise.

Paragraph 13 goes on to state that the total income of Croatia-Slavonia would not suffice for the payment of its share, if the requisite charges for internal affairs were not greatly curtailed, and that therefore Hungary, "in view of

[108] Horn, op. cit. pp. 203–4.

the renewal of the brotherly relation which has subsisted for centuries between it and Croatia-Slavonia," is willing to agree that a fixed proportion [109] of Croatia's income should be earmarked for autonomous expenses, and only the remainder applied to joint expenses.

For this purpose, 45 per cent. (since 1889 44 per cent.) of all Croatian revenue were reserved for internal affairs, and the remaining 55 per cent. (since 1889 56 per cent.) transferred to the Central Treasury.[110] The annual interest on the Croatian Land Redemption Debt is to be paid from Croatian revenue ; but any excess upon the sum of 2,660,000 florins (£221,000) is covered by a Joint Guarantee.[111]

A special Finance Office in Agram, subject to the authority and nominations of the Joint Finance Minister, controls all taxation of what we should call an " Imperial " nature, all stamps, imposts, dues and state domains (§ 22). Those departments of this Office which deal with purely autonomous affairs, are " in every respect at the disposal " of the autonomous authorities, but strangely enough no provision is made for the balances being submitted to the Diet but only to the Joint Finance Minister (§ 23), whom the Croatian Government and executive are expressly enjoined to support in all his requirements (§ 24). The object of the omission is quite evident. The details of revenue and expenditure for Croatia-Slavonia are to be drawn up at the same time as those for Hungary, and both are to be laid before the Joint Parliament in Budapest, and after examination by that body, are to be " communicated " to the Croatian Diet " for its cognisance " (§ 28). In other words a vital distinction is tacitly drawn between the *financial* powers of the Hungarian and Croatian parliaments, however carefully the latter's equality as a contracting party may have been safeguarded in other sections of the document. The Compromise makes no attempt to define the Budgetary rights of the Croatian Diet ; and indeed these are involved in great ambiguity. By the Croatian Article II of 1869 which regulates the details of the autonomous government, the latter is obliged to submit an annual Budget

[109] To be fixed by periodical mutual agreement. For the first ten years this sum was fixed at 2,200,000 florins (£183,000).

[110] § 17, modified by 1873, XXXIV, § 3 and 1906, X, § 5). Wine and Meat taxes, and Customs Dues on the Croatian frontier, are specially excluded from the sources of revenue liable to such division (§ 18 ; also two unimportant additions to XL, 1889, § 5).

[111] § 21, modified by XXVII, 1891, § 21.

to the Diet " for constitutional deliberation " (§ 13 II, 1869). But this of course merely deals with the income and expenditure connected with the three autonomous Departments of Local Government, Justice and Education at Agram ; and means have often been found to evade any effective control, even of these, by the Croatian Diet. There can be no question that those Magyar statesmen who were chiefly responsible for the Compromise—Andrássy, Deák and Eötvös—were not merely actuated by the most honourable motives but desired to treat Croatia with the utmost generosity consistent with their views of constitutional unity. The financial arrangement faithfully reflects this attitude and seems at first sight to be highly favourable to Croatia.[112] But the financial side of the Compromise was ill and hastily considered, alike on the Magyar and on the Croatian side ; and while the Magyar delegates genuinely believed themselves to be making substantial financial concessions (especially in §§ 13, 17, 27) the Croat delegates on their side fully accepted the view that they were making a good financial bargain. This fact, and the complete financial ignorance displayed by the Croatian representatives on the occasion of the revision of 1873, may be considered as robbing Croatia of the right of recriminations.

The true test of the financial arrangement is its practical working ; and when this is considered, it is no longer possible to deny that Croatia has a great and crying grievance. On the one hand, the extreme importance of the clauses which appropriate 45 per cent. of Croatian revenues to autonomous Croatian expenditure (under §§ 13 and 17) must not be lost sight of for a moment. But on the other hand it must be remembered that all financial control, and the entire manipulation and interpretation of the accounts are in the hands of the central Government at Budapest. The Budgets of the Central Parliament are voted as single units, and no clue whatever is given as to the respective contributions of the two countries in many of the entries. Indeed there is not the slightest trace of any attempt to distinguish between them, although paragraph 29 expressly provides for separate budgetary entries. There is little or nothing in the Budget itself nor in the manner in which it is introduced and discussed, to suggest that it differs in any way from the budgets of unitary

[112] This is the view of that extremely impartial writer, Mr. Geoffrey Drage. (*See* his *Austria-Hungary*, pp. 470–74.)

national states such as France or Italy; and the Croatian members have no effective means at their disposal for securing the publication of the missing details. In the words of Mr. Drage, " Croatia is in the position of a firm which cannot examine its own books " [113]; and however indisposed we may be to endorse the view, unfortunately widespread in Croatia, that the balances are systematically " cooked " to the advantage of Hungary, there can at any rate be no question that such an obscure arrangement engenders an atmosphere of suspicion and strain between the two countries, and that the full light of publicity ought to be thrown as soon as possible upon the relative financial position of Hungary and Croatia.[114]

The stranger who consults the Hungarian statute book and runs his eye over the various items of one of the Annual Budgets which it contains, would gain the impression that Croatia, as some dependent provincial *annexe* to the Hungarian state, had received a freewill offering from purely Hungarian funds for the behalf of purely Croatian internal administration. This erroneous view can best be met by Pliverić's succinct statement. " It is not the Joint Treasury," he points out, " which hands over a sum of money to Croatia, that it may cover its autonomous expenses; but on the contrary it is the joint financial administration which, in the name of Croatia, makes over to the Joint Treasury a sum amounting to 55 per cent. of the special revenues of Croatia, for the purpose of covering the Joint Expenses." [115]

A further grievance of the Croats is that, since, by contributing 55 per cent. of her revenue to Joint Affairs, Croatia absolves herself from all further financial obligations towards Hungary, she ought not to be held liable for any share in the public loans carried out in Budapest for purely Hungarian

[113] Op. cit. p. 472.

[114] Ivan Bartolović in a Croatian pamphlet cited by Pliverić (p. 457) argues that Croatia with a net revenue of 15,700,000 florins, would, after fulfilment of all its obligations under the Compromise, only have a deficit of 722,000 florins which could be reduced to the nominal figure of 80,000 florins.

[115] Pliverić, op. cit. p. 445. According to table 10 on p. 505 of vol. xv, *Ungarisches Statistisches Jahrbuch*; in 1903 the net revenue of Croatia-Slavonia (after the deduction of 8,405,000 crowns for administrative expenses, was 36,004,000 crowns. Of this (under § 3 XXXIV, 1873) 20,162,000 fell to joint expenditure and 15,842,000 crowns remained for autonomous expenses, 19,374,000 being actually assigned. According to table 11 (same page) the total revenue of Croatia amounted to 20,197,000, the total expenditure to 20,329,000 crowns.

objects.[116] No such liability is imposed by the terms of the Compromise, or even indirectly hinted at ; and yet Croatia not merely has to contribute, but does not receive her fair share of the public moneys expended as a result of such loans. This grievance would presumably disappear if the relative budgetary position of the two countries could once be ascertained in detail and made public ; for these facts, once elicited, would obviously form the basis for apportioning all subsequent loans. Cavillers would then no longer be in a position to assert that this is one of the very reasons why the facts are kept private. Though this would seem to be a needlessly uncharitable view, there can be no question that at present Croatia has no effective guarantee against being burdened with a share of the charges upon purely Hungarian financial operations.[117]

(b) The Position of the Ban.

The position of the Ban is full of irreconcilable contradictions. On the one hand, he is responsible, as head of the autonomous Government, to the Croatian Diet (§ 50). On the other hand, he is appointed by His Majesty on the nomination of the Hungarian Premier (" the Royal Hungarian *Joint* Premier," as he is described in § 51). He may not hold military rank (§ 52), and sits *ex officio* in the House of Magnates at Budapest (§ 53). In accordance with paragraph 54, the organization of the autonomous Government was left in the hands of the Croatian Diet, and was regulated by it in the Croatian Article II. of 1869. In its terms it is the duty of

---

[116] In 1907 the interest on State loans was 288,089,000 crowns (£12,000,000). In the published statistics no attempt is made to apportion this between the two countries ; in this case nothing is heard of Croatia's " taxable capacity," upon which such stress is laid in §§ 13, 27 of the Compromise. (*See* Appendix IX).

[117] The Regnicolar Deputation sent out in 1886 by the Croatian Diet to negotiate a revision of the Compromise, put forward, among others the following demands :—that the Budget Estimates should be submitted in three separate sections (for Joint Austro-Hungarian, Joint Hungaro-Croatian and purely Croatian affairs) ; that the necessary data for ascertaining the details of revenue should be supplied by the Joint Government not merely to the Croatian Government (as is at present done partially and informally) but also to the Croatian Diet ; that the Croatian delegates should henceforth be excluded from all debates relating to the financial affairs of Hungary alone. These proposals were not accepted by Hungary. See Živković, *Zur Sanierung der Verletzungen des kroatisch-ungarischen Ausgleiches,* pp. 34–5.

the Ban to lay before His Majesty, through the medium of the Croatian Minister, all proposals, motions, nominations and decisions, relative to Croatian affairs (§ 11, 1869). He has the right to be present at all debates of the Diet ; as he has the option of standing as a deputy, he is only free to vote in a division in the event of having been actually elected ; but in any case he is bound to answer, either personally or through a representative, any interpellations which may be addressed to him (§ 12, 1869). The Government is bound to submit the Budget annually to the Diet " for constitutional debate " (§ 13, 1869). The right of nomination to all offices of the autonomous Government rests in the hands of the Ban (§ 16, 1869).

It will be seen that though the Ban is legally responsible to the Diet, this guarantee is worthless in the event of any dispute arising between Hungary and Croatia. The office can only be held by a nominee of the Hungarian Government, who thus can be selected and is selected for the post because he adheres to the Hungarian rather than to the Croatian view. Under the existing system, the Ban must inevitably remain an " exponent " of the Hungarian Premier, to use the blunt phrase of Dr. Wekerle, a recent holder of the latter office. He can only communicate with the sovereign on Croatian matters, through the medium of the Croatian Minister, who, being a member of the Hungarian Cabinet, is of course appointed by the Premier. Thus Croatia is doubly fenced off from the Crown, and its wishes and claims reach the royal presence by the mouth of two Magyar nominees. In such circumstances it is difficult to see how the Crown can form a really impartial opinion upon Croatian affairs.

If this be the result in one direction of the Hungarian Premier's power, in another direction it is equally injurious to Croatian interests. Every office of any importance in Croatia is in the gift of the Ban, and thus indirectly exposed to Magyarone influence. This is all the more serious because the administrative officials and the judicature of Croatia do not in any way enjoy an independent position, but are liable to continual and open pressure from above. Officials who do not follow the political guidance of their superiors, may be passed over, transferred, even placed upon the pension list or dismissed altogether. This practice has been almost universal in Croatia for the last thirty years, and serves to explain alike the stagnation of public life under Count Khuen-Héderváry and the emphasis with which all Croatian reformers have demanded a law guaranteeing the independence of the Bench and of officialdom in general. It is equally obvious that the tendency in Budapest is to hinder a reform which would purify public life in Croatia and thus rally the whole nation in defence of national claims. Stagnation and corruption are to-day the only supports of Magyar domination in Croatia ; once modernize the prevailing system, and that domination is instantly at an end.

Perhaps the most serious flaw in the whole document is that it makes no provision for enforcing its observance by the two contracting parties. There has never been any great difficulty in enforcing Croatia's compliance with its provisions. But as national feeling grew more violent and aggressive among the Magyars, infringements on their part became more and more frequent, and protests were unavailing. The revisions of 1880, 1881, 1889 and 1891, were the result of a skilful system of packing the Croatian Diet with subservient elements : while the less unfavourable revision of 1906 was accepted by the Croats, not as in any way dispelling their grievances, but as the price which they had to pay in return for a free hand in internal reform.[118] The really vital infringements of the Compromise continued unabated, and were extended still further in the summer of 1907. Thus Hungary's position has for some years been that of the chairman of a commercial company, who met the indignant protests of shareholders with the curt remark, " Protest away, gentlemen : it will make no difference ! "

Territorial Questions.

We have already seen that Croatia-Slavonia is formally recognized as " a political nation possessing a special territory of its own " (§ 59). But paragraph 65 goes still further and not merely recognizes, in the name of Hungary, " Croatia's territorial integrity," but also promises Hungarian help in the extension of that territory in two directions—the Military Frontiers and Dalmatia. The reincorporation of the former with Croatia did actually take place in 1881, though the military authorities in Vienna had interposed considerable delays. " The reincorporation of Dalmatia " is claimed as a right of " the Holy Hungarian Crown " (§ 65), which had held sway

[118] Of course, a fresh breach occurred before they had had time to effect these reforms. See Chapter VIII.

over that kingdom during the Middle Ages. "Meanwhile, regarding the conditions of this reincorporation Dalmatia is also to be heard."

In other words, the Compromise recognizes the Triune Kingdom as comprising Dalmatia, and tacitly denies the legality of its occupation by Austria. Indeed, in the preamble and elsewhere the document is treated as an agreement between Hungary on the one side and "Croatia-Slavonia *and Dalmatia*" on the other, as though the union were already an accomplished fact. This very practical concession to Southern Slav national sentiment, has had its share in reviving the old Illyrian ideal under the modern name of Trialism. But Croatian patriots base their aspirations for union not upon Hungarian constitutional law, but upon the rival "Staatsrecht" of the Crown of Zvonimir and upon the idea of racial unity. The support which both parties were wont to expect from the German nationalists in Austria—on the ground that the cession of Dalmatia to Hungary would rid Austria of 600,000 Slavs —is less likely to be accorded to-day, when the great importance of the Southern Slav question is being gradually borne in upon the minds of Austrian politicians.

Meanwhile "the territorial integrity" of Croatia, so solemnly affirmed in the Compromise, was violated in one important particular. The town and harbour of Fiume were expressly excluded, as forming "a special body attached to the Hungarian Crown (separatum sacrae regni coronae adnexum corpus)" (§ 66). Its autonomy and constitutional position are to be defined later as the result of a joint agreement between the Parliament of Hungary, the Croatian Diet and the town itself.

This paragraph has an extraordinary history. Incredible as it may seem, the Magyar and Croat texts are completely at variance, and in the explicit form summarized above it has passed into operation without receiving the sanction of the Croatian Diet. The variant texts run as follows :—

Magyar text (§ 66).	*Croat text* (§ 66).
In the sense of the preceding paragraph there are recognized as belonging to the territory of Croatia Slavonia and Dalmatia :—	In the sense of the preceding paragraph it is recognized that the territorial extent of the Kingdoms of Dalmatia, Croatia and Slavonia comprises :—
1. That district which at present together with the town and district of Buccari belongs to the	1. The whole district which at present, together with the town

COMPROMISE BETWEEN HUNGARY AND CROATIA

Magyar text (§ 66).

County of Fiume, with the exception of the town and district of Fiume. The town, harbour and district of Fiume form a special body connected with the Hungarian Crown (separatum sacrae regni coronae adnexum corpus), concerning whose special autonomy and the legislative and administrative affairs relating thereto, an agreement will have to be reached by means of negotiations between the Hungarian Parliament, the Diet of Croatia Slavonia and Dalmatia and the town of Fiume in joint understanding. . . .

Croat text (§ 66).

of Buccari and its district, belongs to the County of Fiume, with the exception of the town of Fiume and its district, *regarding which an agreement could not be reached between the two Regnicolar Deputations.* . . .

The two versions of the document were in due course submitted to His Majesty for signature ; and a thin strip of paper [119] bearing on it a translation of the Magyar version, as given above, was then stuck over the corresponding portion of the Croat text ! ! The original document is preserved in the Croatian Archives, where this singular falsification of an important State document may be verified. The interpolated passage is not even in the same handwriting as the rest of the document.[120]

It thus appears that the definition of Fiume as "separatum sacrae regni coronae adnexum corpus" has never received the sanction of the Croatian Diet, and is a one-sided claim of Hungary, unproved and merely upheld by superior force. The question is still open. In reality, however, it is not and will not be decided by grounds of law and right, but by its strategic importance as Hungary's only possible outlet to the sea and by the expenditure lavished upon its port by the Government of Budapest. At present the Magyars are able to rely upon the Italian element in the town, owing to its fears of the advancing Croats and their foolish persistence in regarding Fiume as an exclusively Croat town. But if an understanding between Croat and Italian could once be reached, —a contingency likely to follow the approaching truce between the two nationalities in Dalmatia—or if the Croat ele-

---

[119] 22·7 × 9·8 centimeters in dimension.
[120] *Zakoni o Ugarsko-Hrvatskoj Nagodi* (*Laws relative to the Hungaro-Croatian Compromise*), edited by Dr. Ivan Bojničić, Zagreb, 1907, pp. 33–34.

ment should once gain the upper hand (and this must of course be a far longer process), Magyar rule will have no basis in Fiume save the bayonet.

Even the Magyar version, however, contemplates an agreement regulating what is avowedly an irregular and provisional situation. But no negotiations have ever taken place since 1868 ; Croatia reasserts from time to time its theoretical right to the possession of Fiume, and Hungary continues to act upon the ancient principle of *Beati possidentes*.

The final paragraph (§ 70) declares the Hungaro-Croatian Compromise to be a "joint fundamental law" of the two countries, which cannot form the subject of debate in either legislature, and can only be altered by a procedure similar to that adopted in 1868, in other words by an agreement between deputations of the two Parliaments.

The Hungaro-Croatian Compromise is susceptible to very varied interpretations. The extreme Magyar view regards it as a law of the Hungarian Parliament, merely *registered* by the Croatian Diet [121] ; while the extreme Croat view declines even to recognize its binding force, and even many of those who recognize it, maintain that Croatia legally enjoys a position of absolute equality with Hungary and a distinct citizenship of its own. Each of these views is equally removed from the truth, for each is based upon what, in its holders' opinion, *ought to be* the relations of the two countries. We may hold what opinion we like as to the former status of Croatia—the betrayals which have robbed her of her ancient rights (so the Croats would argue) or the unwise and excessive concessions which enabled a mere province to pose as a kingdom (so the Magyars would argue). But if we consider the question with an exclusive regard to the document of 1868, only one conclusion is possible. Croatia is a sovereign state, which by a voluntary agreement with her neighbour, definitely surrendered certain attributes of sovereignty, and thus can only recover its full freedom of action by the permission of that neighbour or by force of arms. Thus Croatia cannot be said to fall under any known category of states, but rather occupies a middle position of its own, between that of pure independence and that of pure federalism. That its relations

[121] Even Prof. Kmety, the constitutional authority, takes this view (*Közjog*, p. 397). "Croatia is not a state, but the Croatian people is a nation." So writes the well-known Magyar publicist Beksics in his book *Dualism* (p. 251). This is mere juggling with words.

with Hungary are the result of a solemn contract between two theoretically equal contracting parties, cannot be denied by any one who reads the Compromise of 1868 : it is conclusively proved by the manner in which it was promulgated by the two legislatures, by the use of the identical word to describe them both, and by the clause which makes all revisions dependent upon mutual consent. Nor can it on the other hand be denied that the first four paragraphs impose definite restrictions upon the sovereignty of the Croatian state. The question of the validity of the Compromise and the further question, how far violations on the one side dispense the other side from its obligations, are two entirely separate considerations with which we are not at present concerned.

CHAPTER V

Croatia under the Dual System
(1868–1905)

*" My countrymen have treated Croatia badly, prevented its develop-
ment, and exploited it financially ; they will pay for this one day."—
Baron Kállay in 1903.*[122]

WHATEVER view may be taken of the provisions of the
Hungaro-Croatian Compromise, there can be no
question that it was intensely unpopular in Croatia. The
hasty introduction of an illegal franchise and the gross electoral
abuses thus rendered possible, the casual and inadequate
manner in which a " packed " Diet passed so fundamental a
law, the manipulation of the clause regulating the status of
Fiume—all this aroused general indignation ; and but for
official pressure it would have been quite impossible to obtain
a majority in the Diet ready to sanction what was regarded as
a betrayal of the national cause.

Yet questionable as were the means employed, an open
breach between Croatia and Hungary such as must inevitably
have resulted if the former country had been truly represented
during the negotiations, would have been far more injurious
to Croatian interests than the acceptance of an honourable,
if inadequate Compromise. The political constellation, alike
in the Habsburg Monarchy and in Europe generally, was
highly favourable to Hungary, and Croatia suffered the inevitable fate of a weak and forgotten nation.[123] Nor can the
Magyars be blamed for their attitude towards Croatia. The
statesmen who framed the Compromise, and notably Deák

[122] In conversation with the Vienna Correspondent of the *Times* (see
Times, December 31, 1909).

[123] Mr. Kadlec, professor of constitutional law at Prague University,
is fully entitled to say : " The Hungaro-Croatian Compromise, like
all political questions, is a question of power," *Ustava*, p. 129, cit.
Zagorsky, *François Rački*, p. 100.

and Eötvös, two of the most liberal-minded men that ever lived, were genuinely anxious to revive the former friendly relations between the sister countries ; and indeed, if Magyar theories of State-Right be considered and if due allowance be made for their Imperialist aspirations in the Balkans and on the Adriatic and for the embarrassments afforded by a Chauvinist opposition, their treatment of Croatia must seem most liberal and conciliatory.

Such a point of view, however, could hardly be expected to appeal to Croatian public opinion, which resented the arrangement all the more on account of the apparent unanimity with which it had been concluded. Strangely enough, the National Liberal Party, whose grave tactical error in adopting the policy of political abstention had rendered this unanimity possible, did not thereby lose its popularity with the country. Round it centred the chief opposition against Baron Rauch ; while a little band of resolute extremists under Antony Starčević continued to proclaim the impossible ideal of a purely Personal Union with Hungary and Austria on equal terms.

Baron Rauch allowed no scruples to stand in the way of his political aims, and made a determined effort to crush opposition by disciplinary action against such of his opponents as held official posts, by the dismissal of professors and others, by strict muzzling of the press and by prohibition of meetings and political organization. The struggle was waged on both sides with the utmost violence ; and an evil habit which has so often envenomed and disfigured Southern Slav politics—the tendency to indulge in unmeasured personalities—made itself only too apparent. The leading Opposition newspaper, *Pozor*, which had been suppressed in Croatia but continued to appear in Vienna, was now prohibited altogether (May 6, 1869). In the following September, its owners founded a new paper in Sisak, under the title of *Zatočnik* (The Champion) and opened in its columns a merciless campaign against the misdeeds of Rauch. The Ban was openly accused of using his position as member of a Consortium for draining the Lonjski Polje marshes, in order to enrich himself at the expense of his country. Some colour was given to this accusation by the declaration of Count Julius Janković that he also as member of the same board of directors had been tempted with the prospect of a sum of 40,000 florins (£3,330), but had thereupon resigned his position on the Board. Rauch prosecuted the authors of the libel, but as the newspaper was published on the territory of the Military Frontiers, the case came before a court [124] which was entirely free from the Ban's influence and resulted in the acquittal of the accused (January 8, 1871).

This verdict was, of course, a fatal blow to Baron Rauch's position. He resigned almost immediately, and was succeeded as Ban by Koloman Bedeković (January 26, 1871), a moderate Croat Unionist who had till then held the position of Minister for Croatia and was generally esteemed as an honest if weak politician. The new Government dissolved the Diet and ordered fresh elections, but, deprived of the masterful hand of Rauch, found it impossible to maintain the artificial majority which he had created. The elections resulted in a decisive victory for the National Party, which secured fifty-one out of the sixty-five seats. Only thirteen Unionists were returned, while Starčević entered Parliament as the solitary exponent of the Pan-Croat idea.

The Government, seemingly unprepared for this result and perhaps disheartened by the prospect of a collapse of Dualism,[125] hesitated as to what policy to adopt, and prorogued the Sabor no less than three times. This evoked a counter demonstration from the Opposition, in the shape of the so-called " September Manifesto " (September 20, 1871) signed by fifty-four out of the sixty-six deputies. This document boldly denies the validity of the Compromise of 1868, declares that the Diet which passed it into law had no right to speak in the name of the nation, and that Croatia could not submit to the dependence of the Ban upon the Hungarian Premier.[126]

The general discontent found open expression during the autumn of 1871, when two adherents of the Starčević idea, Eugene Kvaternik and Louis Bach [127] gathered round them several hundred armed Frontiersmen, and incited the peasantry in the neighbourhood of Ogulin to rebellion. They sought to win recruits for their mad project by announcing the prospect of French and Turkish support. Martial law was proclaimed : the insurgents were soon dispersed by General Mollináry and

[124] In Petrinja.

[125] Under Count Hohenwart as Austrian Premier, the Federal idea seemed on the point of triumphing over Dualism, and the Emperor had already consented to be crowned in Prague as King of Bohemia. The Prussian victories over France, and the influence of Count Andrássy, led to Hohenwart's fall and the abandonment of his policy.

[126] For a summary, see Polić, *Parlam. Povijest*, II, p. 152, sqq.

[127] Zagorsky, p. 141.

the garrison of Karlovac ; and the two leaders were shot and other severe punishments imposed.

This hare-brained enterprise sowed discouragement and alarm among the ranks of the National Party, for on the one hand it aroused the suspicions of distant Vienna against Croatia as a whole and on the other hand won for the intrigues of Baron Rauch the waning support of Budapest and of the Sovereign. The result was the formation of a moderate central party in Croatia, under the influence of Archbishop Mihalović of Zagreb ; round it there rallied all those Unionists who though eager to maintain friendship with Budapest, were not inclined to purchase it by the subserviency and corrupt methods of Baron Rauch,[128] and also those members of the National Party who were anxious for peace. This concentration of the moderate elements in the country was under the circumstances the wisest course which could have been adopted, and had been rendered all the more necessary by the renewed activity of Baron Rauch, and his confederate Vakanović, who on the resignation of Bedeković (February 12, 1872) discharged the duties of the Ban's office, pending a new appointment.

The Sabor was dissolved without having been allowed to transact any business, and Vakanović set himself to create an Unionist majority. But despite scandalous electoral abuses the result of the new elections was a decided victory for the National Party, which retained forty-seven seats, eight falling to the Independent Unionists and only the remaining twenty to Rauch and his friends.[129] Vakanović sought to counteract his ill success at the polls by swamping the Sabor with forty-seven Virilists, drawn from the ranks of the nobles and the higher clergy, and carefully selected because of their Unionist views.

Meanwhile, Vakanović and Rauch had inaugurated a violent campaign of calumny, intended to compromise the National Party in the eyes of Budapest and Vienna, and to drive its leaders from public life. To this end the charge was put forward, that two emissaries of the Bohemian Opposition parties, by name Oliva and Skrejšovský, had held political conferences in Agram, at which the National Party had committed itself to negotiations with the exiled Kossuth and to a revolutionary movement among the Southern Slavs. Minutes of these alleged

---

[128] For instance, Count Ladislas Pejačević, afterwards Ban, and the ex-Ban Bedeković.
[129] Horvat, p. 284.

meetings were forthcoming, and seemed to establish the connexion of the leading Croat politicians, notably the poet and
future Ban Mažuranić, Bishop Strossmayer, the historian Rački,
Mrazović and Vončina, with the headquarters of Panslavism in
St. Petersburg and Belgrad. The names of such Russian
statesmen as Miljutin and Tolstoi are repeatedly mentioned :
an emissary of the latter is alleged to have intrigued in Agram
under an assumed name. Strossmayer and Rački are to be
sounded as to their acceptance of Russian decorations. Money
is promised by a Slav committee of action, for the foundation of
a revolutionary paper in Croatia. Plans for a rising in the
Military Frontiers, with the aid of Belgrad, are laid before the
committee. The final document contains a statement of the
electoral funds placed at the disposal of the National Party by
committees in St. Petersburg, Moscow and Odessa, by the
Živnostenska Banka in Prague, and by Jovan Ristić, the Regent
of Servia. It subsequently transpired that these " minutes "
were forgeries of a certain Reichherzer, who himself brought
the facts to light. Though Rauch and Vakanović were directly
and openly accused of inspiring the forger, no attempt was ever
made on their part to rebut the charges ; and rightly or wrongly
their complicity is treated in Croatia to-day as an established
fact. Whatever may be the true secret history of the documents, their purpose is too self-evident to be mistaken. The
Deák Party and its leader, Count Lónyay were to be deterred
from negotiating with the National Party : the Sovereign was
to be persuaded that Strossmayer and the chief Croatian patriots
were traitors and conspirators ; and after the collapse of the
only party capable of upholding Croatian claims, Baron
Rauch was to return to power as the satrap of a submissive
province. The use of forged documents as a political weapon
was thus introduced into Croatian politics.[130] A generation later,

[130] A pamphlet entitled *Croatia on the Torture-Bench,* which appeared
at the end of 1872 and caused a profound sensation in political circles,
professed to expose the scandalous intrigues to which Rauch and
Vakanović resorted, in order to prevent the approaching entente be-
tween the National Party and Count Lónyay. According to its author,
Rauch's emissary in Vienna conducted the intrigue through a certain
Frau Goldmayer, with whom Lónyay was intimate, and even obtained
the indirect support of Count Andrássy for his intrigue. (*See* Zagorsky,
François Rački, p. 143.) For the facts contained in this paragraph,
see the rare pamphlet, *Enthüllungen über die Künste der Kroatischen
Regierung* (Extraabdruck aus der Prager " *Politik*," No. 121, vom 2
Mai 1872) and *Iz crnoga lista nedavne prošlosti* (From a black page
of the Recent Past), Varaždin, 1904.

under Baron Levin Rauch's own son, the same methods of forgery were made the groundwork of Austria's foreign policy, and dragged the name of Croatia into the forefront of a European scandal.

The situation was saved by the tact and conciliatory attitude of Count Lónyay, who had succeeded Andrássy as Hungarian Premier on the latter's appointment as Austro-Hungarian Foreign Minister. Lónyay, who had a year previously conducted negotiations with the leaders of the National Party, endeavoured to find a common basis of action between it and its Unionist rival ; and eventually the two parties agreed to halve between them the Croatian delegation to the Joint Parliament, and also the Regnicolar deputation [131] which was to negotiate with Hungary a revision of the Compromise. The latter, which included Bishop Strossmayer, Mažuranić, Živkovič, Mrazović, appeared in Budapest, and on November 6, formulated its demands in a " Nuntium " or message to the Hungarian delegation. The main demands were five in number.

(1) The five Croat members of the Joint Delegations [132] should be elected by the Croat delegates in the Parliament of Budapest, not by the whole House.[133]

(2) The Ban should be nominated by the King's own act of authority, and not on the proposal of the Hungarian Premier—in other words, the Ban should be released from the humiliating position of an "exponent" of Magyar policy.

(3) The Ban should receive the title of " Minister for Dalmatia-Croatia-Slavonia," a title corresponding to that of " Landes-Minister " in Austria. This would serve to lay further emphasis upon his responsibility to the Croatian Sabor.

(4) Croatia should acquire full control over its own revenues, paying over to the Joint Treasury the regular annual sum due as its contribution to Joint Affairs (cf. p 74).

[131] The formal name given to the committees which negotiate any revision of the Compromise.
[132] § 41, XXX, 1868.
[133] The object of this demand was to ensure that the majority among the delegates to Budapest should obtain a majority of the five seats in the Joint Delegations. Under the present system the Croats, only numbering 40 out of 453, are completely at the mercy of the Magyar majority in the House in the matter of the selection of the five Croat delegates.

(5) The Croatian Minister in Budapest should not be empowered to interfere in any way with Croatian autonomy, but should rather fill the position of representative of Croatian interests at all Cabinet meetings.

As the Hungarian delegation categorically refused its assent to these demands, Strossmayer and certain other delegates who shared his views withdrew from Budapest ; and those who remained had to content themselves with a greatly modified scheme of revision. The position of the Croatian Minister was, it is true, defined more clearly, but he of course remained as before the channel of communication between the Croatian Government and the Sovereign. Henceforth he was bound to submit " unaltered and without delay " all the reports of the Ban to His Majesty, and was only at liberty to add his own commentary, or that of the Hungarian Government, " if doubts should arise respecting the state connexion established by Article XXX of 1868."

Croatia's contribution to the Joint Treasury was definitely fixed at 55 per cent. of her total revenues.[134] Finally, as a constitutional guarantee of some value, it was laid down that the Croatian Sabor must be convoked within three months of its dissolution. Thus such modifications as were introduced into the Compromise were all in favour of Croatia, but most of the changes which its representatives held to be indispensable, fell before the veto of Hungary.[135]

None the less, it was widely felt that they were the best terms obtainable, and when the completed bill was laid before the Sabor in the summer of 1873, only seven deputies—among them the historian Rački—could be found to vote for the hostile motion which described it as satisfying " neither the rights nor the requirements " of the Triune Kingdom. On September 5, the revision was adopted by seventy-nine votes to ten, and the conflict between Hungary and Croatia seemed at length to have been allayed.

On September 20, 1873, the office of Ban, so long administered by the intriguing Vakanović, was at length filled by the appointment of Ivan Mažuranić, who had presided over the Croatian Aulic Chancellory until its dissolution in 1869, but whose eminent political services are less remembered to-day than his authorship of the famous Croat epic " Čengić Aga." The

---

[134] *See* Appendix VI, modification of XXX, § 17 by 1873, XXXIV, § 3.
[135] Horvat, p. 284 ; Zagorsky, p. 145.

appointment of " The Peasant Ban," as Mažuranić was popu-
larly called—being the first Ban ever appointed who was not
of noble rank—was hailed with general enthusiasm and ushered
in a period of important administrative and educational reforms.
Numerous public institutions were founded, the prison system
reorganized, a Statistical Office established. School attendance was made obligatory, and although lack of funds and of
the necessary teaching staff rendered the enforcement of this
measure impossible,[136] a good beginning, at any rate, was made.
Liberty of the Press was extended, the arbitrary methods of
the " Bach Patent " of 1852 (which still remained in force)
being superseded by Jury Trial for all Press offences. A
fairly liberal law was introduced guaranteeing the Right of
Assembly, while another law assigned to the Sabor the right
of holding responsible, or even impeaching, the Ban " for any
act or omission of his " such as might injuriously affect
Croatia's constitutional position.

An act of May 31, 1875, provided for the complete separation of the executive and judicial arms—a separation which
was, unhappily, not destined to maintain itself in practice.[137]

Meanwhile, the seeds of future trouble were sown by a minor
innovation which owed its origin to the Ban's enthusiasm for
Western " liberal " ideas. A bill was passed excluding the clergy
from the management of the schools, while prescribing certain
prayers and recitation of the Catechism as part of the regular
school curriculum. This aroused fierce opposition from the
Orthodox clergy, and was the main cause of the formation of
a Serb party in Croatia and of the subsequent dissensions
between Croats and Serbs which placed the country for
well-nigh thirty years at the mercy of Budapest.

Of all the many changes which took place in Croatia during
Mažuranić's term of office, two events deserve special mention.
On October 19, 1874, the University of Agram was inaugurated,
and the untiring efforts of Bishop Strossmayer in the course of
national culture, were thus after thirteen years crowned with
success.[138] At first a number of its professors had to be re-

---

[136] Even to-day in Croatia, as in Hungary, the number of children
who visit no school is very great. In the years 1891–5 the average
number of children actually visiting school was 179,670, or 64 per cent. ;
in the years 1896–1900, 196,920, or 60·9 per cent. ; in 1901, 199,292
out of 321,451 (i.e., 62 per cent.) ; in 1907, 241,262 out of 370,725
(65 per cent.). See *Ung. Stat. Jahrbuch*, xii, p. 352, and xv, p. 320.

[137] Especially under Khuen Hédervâry and Rauch.

[138] *See* pp. 123–4

cruited from other Slav races, especially from Bohemia [139]; but this difficulty, common to all new institutions, was successfully overcome. Though lacking a medical faculty and though hampered by the refusal of reciprocity of degrees with the universities of Austria, the new University soon became a centre of learning for all the Croats, Serbs and Slovenes of the Habsburg dominions, and can to-day fairly compete with the better endowed university of Belgrad.

While from a cultural point of view nothing could surpass in importance the erection of the first Southern Slav University, the re-incorporation of the old Military Frontiers at length restored Croatia-Slavonia to the position which they had occupied before the Turkish invasion. The first step had already been taken by a Royal Rescript of June 8, 1871, granting to the " Frontiers " constitutional rights corresponding exactly to those enjoyed by Croatia. The perpetual military service to which the Granitchars had hitherto been liable was replaced by the rules of Universal Service applicable to the rest of the Monarchy [140]; and a further stage in the change from a military to a civil régime was now effected by an Act of September 8, 1873. None the less, despite the eagerness displayed by Mažuranić, the union still remained very largely on paper and its consummation was not reached till July 15, 1881, when the old régime in the " Military Frontiers " was finally swept away.

The chief merit of Mažuranić as Ban was the perseverance with which he devoted himself to the task of introducing really modern administrative methods in Croatia. In addressing the newly-appointed High Sheriffs in April, 1875, he had roundly declared, that " an end at last be put to the officials regarding the people as a legacy, whom it was their profession to exploit," and that nothing would please him more than to be remembered as the founder of a good administration. [141] If his successors in office succeeded in infecting the Croatian executive with those habits of intrigue, favouritism and intimidation in which Magyar administration has always excelled, it is at any rate impossible to blame the " Peasant Ban " for this unhappy state of affairs.

The Bosnian insurrection, which broke out in July, 1875, and proved far too formidable for the Turks to quell, placed Mažur-

---

[139] Contemporary scoffers nicknamed Agram University " the University of St. Wenceslas," an allusion to the national Saint of Bohemia.
[140] Horvat, p. 286.
[141] Rogge, *Oesterreich seit der Katastrophe Hohenwart-Beust*, ii, p. 54.

anić in a most equivocal position, which eventually proved altogether fatal to his popularity. Croatian national sentiment was thoroughly roused by the sufferings of the Bosnian population and the endless tales of Turkish atrocities, and clamoured for action ; while in Budapest, on the other hand, enthusiasm for the Turks ran high and the unrest noticeable among the Croats and Serbs of the Triune Kingdom, and the southern counties of Hungary proper[142] was frowned upon by the Magyar Chauvinists as a proof of Panslav sympathies and Russian intrigue. In certain districts of Bosnia Francis Joseph was hailed by the insurgents as the " Croat King " (hrvatski kralj). Volunteers joined them from all the Slav races of the Monarchy. Above all, crowds of refugees, especially women and children, found their way into Croatia and Dalmatia. The maintenance of these unfortunates soon became a serious problem, even affecting the neutrality of the Monarchy ; and it was hardly to be wondered at that, when the new Sabor assembled in August, 1875, and when the Speech from the Throne carefully avoided all reference to the rising, the leader of the extreme Opposition, Makanec, brought an interpellation, urging that the Diet should provide the refugees with money and medical assistance. The Ban in his reply declared such matters to be outside the competence of the Sabor, and warned the Opposition that a continuance of its tactics might easily lead to a dissolution[143] ; and in this attitude he was supported by the great majority of the Diet, despite the sentiments of the country at large.

In the following year (1876) excitement rose to fever pitch ; and when on July 2 Servia and Montenegro declared war upon the Turks, the belief in the re-establishment of a Southern Slav kingdom was already widespread. Meanwhile, public opinion in Budapest was more Turcophil than ever, a torchlight procession appeared beneath the window of the Ottoman Consul ; wreaths were deposited upon the half-forgotten grave of Gül Baba, the Turkish dervish ; and in the late autumn a sword of honour, bought by public subscription, was carried to Constantinople by a special deputation of Magyar students, and presented to Abdul Kerim, the commander of the Turkish armies against Servia. The Hungarian Government—then under the guidance of that masterful and unscrupulous Chauvinist, Coloman Tisza—had already treated the Slovaks, Rou-

[142] The Voivodina of 1851–60.   [143] Rogge, op. cit. ii, p. 66.

manians and Saxons far too brutally to require any further prompting, and repressive measures were now adopted against the Serbs of the Banat. Dr. Svetozar Miletić, the Serb leader, who had offered to raise a corps of Serb volunteers in the cause of Christian Slavdom, was thrown into prison, in defiance of his immunity as member of the Hungarian Parliament. Arrests and inquiries were made throughout the Banat, sixty persons being examined in Versec zalone.[144] By orders of General Mollinary, the commander of the Agram garrison (who was credited with being in secret accord with Rauch, Tisza and Andrássy in the Magyar interest), the former leader of the Serb rising in 1848, General Stratimirović, was arrested in Semlin ; but the absurdity of the suspicions directed against him was clear from the fact that he had just been expelled from Belgrad owing to his bitter hostility to Tschernajev,[145] and he was soon afterwards released. Miletić's colleague Kaspinović shared his fate, and both were put on trial for high treason, on the ground of their connexion with the leaders of the Omladina [146] in Belgrad and their efforts to raise Serb volunteers for Prince Milan's campaign against the Turks. The fact that Miletić had been received in audience by Milan and had publicly toasted the prince as " King of the Serbs " and harangued in favour of " the liberation of the Serbs from Magyar and Mongol yoke," was pounced upon by the Public Prosecutor. The usual methods of the police state were employed to secure his conviction, and a former secretary of Stratimirović was induced to figure as informer. Eventually, Miletić was sentenced for his alleged separatist tendencies to five years' imprisonment ; in prison his reason left him, and he did not long survive his consequent release.

Meanwhile, Mažuranić, in response to peremptory orders from Budapest, joined in the hunt for traitors, and numerous arrests were made in Croatia-Slavonia. A store of pamphlets and flyleaves for the people were found in the possession of the Archpriest Begović in Karlovac. The editor of the frontier newspaper *Graničar* was found to be in correspondence with the Servian statesman Ristič. Four brewery assistants were caught in the attempt to smuggle cases of dynamite into Servia. Finally Axentinović, the President of the Essek Chamber of Commerce, was arrested as an agent of the Belgrad Government. The most childish legends were circulated, and

[144] Ibid. p. 188.   [145] The Russian envoy in Servia.
[146] A well-known student society.

were welcomed by a still more childish credulity on the part of the authorities ; and when in the autumn the inevitable fiasco arrived and most of the prisoners had to be released, no end had been gained save that the Serbs of the Triune Kingdom were thoroughly exasperated and in just such a frame of mind as rendered it easy for the Magyars to play off Croat and Serb against each other and so to reduce the country to long years of impotence.

The outbreak of the Russo-Turkish War transferred the centre of interest from the Western to the Eastern Balkans ; but the Dual Monarchy's period of " masterly inactivity " at length came to an end, when on July 4, 1878, the Congress of Berlin entrusted her with a mandate to occupy Bosnia and Herzegovina in the interests of Western civilization. No time was wasted in acting upon the suggestion, but the two preceding years of neutrality and intrigue had destroyed all sympathy for Austria-Hungary among the inhabitants of the insurgent provinces, who were wellnigh unanimous in their desire for union with Servia and Montenegro. The mandate of Europe had to be imposed by force of arms, and the Austrian troops met with a prolonged and desperate resistance. As on so many other occasions, Croat soldiers played a distinguished part in the campaign, and the supreme command was entrusted to two Croat generals, Filipović and Jovanović. In spite of the large number of troops employed to quell the insurrection— not less than 150,000 in all—a guerilla warfare was prolonged into the winter, the Austrian losses were very considerable, and horrid excesses—natural to a people which had endured for four centuries the atrocities of Turkish rule—were perpetrated against the invaders.[147]   It was not till January 1, 1879, that the new Government could be definitely established at Sarajevo.

The bitter disappointment which the course of recent events had aroused in Croatia was reflected in the Sabor's Address to the Throne on September 28, 1878. In this, not content with repeating its old demands for the reincorporation of Dalmatia, the final absorption of the Military Frontiers, and a clear definition of Fiume's constitutional position, the Diet expressed the conviction that a permanent solution of the task now assumed by the Monarchy could only be attained if in the course of time Bosnia and Herzegovina were annexed to the Triune King-

[147] The Bosnians of that period shared with the Herreros the hideous practice of mutilating their wounded enemies.

dom. The Address was greeted by a storm of abuse from the Magyar press, and at the instance of his Hungarian advisers, Francis Joseph was led to remark that " the Sabor had exceeded its sphere of action, in speaking of Bosnia and Herzegovina." [148] " It is the Dualist policy," wrote the despondent Rački to a friend, " which has prevented the incorporation of Bosnia and Herzegovina in Croatia. The peace of San Stefano is, in my opinion, for the Balkan Peninsula what the peace of Villafranca was for Italy and that of Prague for Germany." [149]

As time passed and the final incorporation of the Military Frontiers was still delayed, Mažuranić grew more and more impatient, and at length was unwise enough to threaten to resign unless some action were taken, both in the matter of the Frontiers and of the revision of the financial provisions of the Compromise. The Magyars, who were only too glad to be rid of Mažuranić, readily accepted his resignation (February 21, 1880).

He was succeeded as Ban by Count Ladislas Pejačević, a Croatian nobleman of high character but of less pronounced national sympathies than his predecessor. His term of office ushered in a period of Magyar aggression, in which the Compromise of 1868 was no longer strictly observed on the part of the Budapest Government, and continual infringements were made upon Croatian autonomy. The appointment of a Magyar official, Antony David, as Director of the Financial Department in Agram, was one of the first slight indications of this changed attitude, which contrasted so unfavourably with the punctilious care with which Deák, Andrássy and Lónyay had always fulfilled their obligations, when once entered upon. In June, 1880, David introduced the seemingly harmless innovation of courses of instruction in the Magyar language, for the benefit of the financial officials in Agram. When, however, it was announced that promotion would be made dependent upon proficiency in Magyar, Croat patriotic sentiment at once took alarm ; and Dr. Mrazović, one of the leaders of the National Party, seceded with twenty-two other deputies and formed the Independent National Party.

The final incorporation of the Military Frontiers (July 15, 1881), so long and so eagerly awaited, had a soothing effect upon Croatian public opinion ; and as the foreign situation was comparatively calm once more, Count Pejačević might have

[148] Horvat, p. 288.
[149] Letter of Rački to Novaković, Ap. 3, 1878, cit. Zagorsky, p. 150.

long continued undisturbed in office, but for an apparently trifling incident. In the summer of 1883 David removed the scutcheons bearing Croat inscriptions, which had hitherto hung above the entrance of the Finance Office and certain other public buildings in Agram, and replaced them by others bearing inscriptions in both Croat and Magyar. This innovation—insignificant as it may seem to those who are not aware of the enormous importance attached throughout Austria-Hungary to such external symbols as flags, colours and inscriptions [150]—was bitterly resented by Croatian opinion as a clear infringement of the Compromise.[151] As paragraph 57 expressly makes Croatian the official language throughout Croatia, even for organs of the Joint Government, it is certainly difficult to realize upon what grounds the Magyar authorities could justify their action.[152] On August 15 riots broke out in Agram, and the obnoxious scutcheons were removed by the crowd. The excitement spread into the provinces, and troops had to be called out to quell the disorders. The Ban, whom David had not consulted, and Bedeković, who was now Croatian Minister, laid the case before the Hungarian Cabinet; but when it decided that in order to vindicate the reputation of the Joint Government, the bilingual scutcheons must be restored wherever they had been forcibly removed, Pejačević at once resigned (August 24) and made his reasons public. This spirited attitude more than atoned, in the eyes of his countrymen, for his previous inactivity, and earned him the name of the " Cavalier-Ban."

Coloman Tisza adhered rigidly to the view that the legal question could not even be considered until reparation had been made for the action of the mob. While doubtless unprepared for so violent an outbreak in Croatia, he was not averse to giving that country a taste of the habitual brutality with which he treated the Slovaks and Roumanians. On September

[150] It is sufficient to refer to such incidents as the Cilli gymnasium, which wrecked an Austrian Government (1886), the part played by the night watchman of Leitmeritz and the postbags of the Nordbahn in the rivalry of Czech and German. In Hungary the authorities have time after time resorted to bloodshed, rather than allow the Roumanian peasantry to wear its national colours.

[151] *See* Appendix V.

[152] The Magyar argument was that the Compromise nowhere lays down what language the inscriptions are to be in, and that therefore it was both legal and reasonable that both languages should be employed on buildings which served both countries.

4, 1883, the Croatian constitution was suspended by the nomination of the commanding officer in Agram, Baron Hermann Ramberg, as Royal Commissioner for Croatia. Ramberg's firm yet tactful behaviour soon restored order. Only three days after his appointment the bilingual scutcheons were back in their places, but on October 16 they were replaced by the so-called " dumb shields," which bore the arms of Hungary and Croatia, but no inscription of any kind.

But though actual disturbances were soon at an end, the appointment of a Royal Commissioner marks an eventful and fatal turning-point in Croatian history. It dealt the death-blow to the Unionist idea in Croatia. In the succeeding period Unionism still could boast prominent adherents and a majority in Parliament, since for opportunists, placehunters and *arrivistes* there were more openings than ever before and since no device was left untried to thin the ranks of Opposition. But the soul of the nation had finally rejected the Hungarian partnership and longed passionately for freedom from its irksome bonds. Save for a few brilliant individual exceptions the party of convinced adherents of the union ceased to exist. The country was divided between Magyarophobes and Mamelukes, and for twenty-five years the Mamelukes were to prevail, for reasons which will soon become clear to the reader.

The chief gainer from the Ramberg interregnum was the Party of Right (Stranka Prava), as the adherents of Antony Starčević were called. Its uncompromising negation of the Compromise with Hungary seemed to be justified, if the fundamental law which regulated the relations of the two countries could be lightly set aside by a stroke of the pen from the Hungarian Premier.[153] With the restoration of order Ramberg's mission was at an end, and Tisza looked about for a suitable candidate for the office of Ban. Overtures were made to Baron Filipović, who as a Croat general was popular and respected, yet free from all party ties ; but he had no inclination to leave his retirement, merely to play the part of a Magyar exponent in his native land. On December 1, 1883, the appointment was announced of Count Charles Khuen-Héderváry, a cousin of Tisza himself. The new Ban had been born in Slavonia, where his chief estate was situated, and had spent two years at the former Academy of Law in Agram, before he went on to Vienna and Budapest Universities. For the three

---

[153] Polić, *Graf Khuen-Héderváry und seine Zeit*, p. 7.

years previous to his appointment as Ban, he had occupied the post of High Sheriff of the county of Györ. This was practically all that the Croatian public knew of the man who was destined to rule their country with a rod of iron for the next twenty years, and for whom history will reserve a special niche as the most successful satrap of any modern European province. The young Ban—he was only thirty years of age—was looked upon by many as a political cipher, and it was prophesied that his term of office would be brief.

Count Khuen-Héderváry's remarkable career is only too open to criticism ; but no one can deny his great political capacity. From the very first he showed a calm energy, coupled with an iron nerve and complete self-restraint such as are strikingly alien to the Croat temperament, and for that very reason made a deep impression upon the Croat mind. Above all, he possessed a remarkable gift of judging character and estimating motives, and as he always knew the weakest spot in his enemy's armour, and spared no pains to collect his information, he gradually succeeded in gathering round him a really able band of fellow-workers in the task of holding down Croatia. Unlike so many men in such a position, he was not satisfied with mere opportunism or ambition in his subordinates ; subservience he never exacted from them, but ability and energy he regarded as indispensable. While this explains his success, it also helps to explain the deep hatred which his name still inspires in Croatia. For when the Croats describe Count Khuen as the corrupter of a whole generation of their countrymen, they are not guilty of mere exaggeration. The essence of his system consisted in closing every public career to men of independent views or strong national feeling and in forcing all who had a career to make or a salary to earn—and in so poor a country as Croatia the exceptions to this class are unhappily rare—to forswear their political convictions and to submit blindly to marching orders from above.

Count Khuen enjoyed one signal advantage which had been denied to all his predecessors since the Compromise. He stood entirely outside and above the parties, no personal ties bound him to this politician or to that. He could pose as impartial, and, it is only fair to add, he often justified the pose, in matters where his predecessors could hardly have failed to betray their party leanings. His very detachment made it the more difficult for his opponents to understand him or to calculate his probable course of action ; while he took a born diplomat's delight in watching and forestalling their designs, from behind the mask of an eternal smile.

Secured in his post by Court favour and the confidence of Colomon Tisza, Count Khuen set himself the thorny task of reducing Croatia to order and of creating a pliant and docile majority, pledged to the Compromise with Hungary and innocuous from the standpoint of " the Magyar State idea " (a Magyar állam eszme) which now formed the main objective of Hungarian statesmen. When he took office, the old National Party was already in the last stage of decay, and its collapse was regarded on all sides as inevitable. Khuen, however, galvanized the corpse, and gave it a new lease of life ; the name and the external trappings of the party survived, but its character underwent a complete transformation, and it richly deserved the epithet of " Mameluke " bestowed upon it by stern critics of its opportunist views.

At this period the moderate Opposition, represented by the Independent National Party (which had seceded from the majority in 1881) was overshadowed by those uncompromising and turbulent elements which followed Antony Starčević. This remarkable man, whose retiring idealistic nature contrasted strongly with the violence of his political opinions, based the programme of the Party of Right (or the Starčević Party, as it came to be called later) upon historic right and racial fanaticism. His sterling honesty of character stands above all question (though the evil Croat propensity of political slander has not left even his name untouched) ; and it was above all this quality which earned him such an unbounded influence over the younger generation of Croats. Unhappily, he carried his horror of compromise to extravagant lengths, and indeed in his rigid adherence to principles often sacrificed the reality which underlay them. His fanaticism was unreasoning to an almost unhealthy degree, and degenerated under his successors into a mere policy of blind hatred. His incapacity to learn from events and his unmeasured use of personalities rob him of the right to the title of statesman ; but his influence in rousing the youth of his country from the swamp of lethargy and corruption into which Magyar rule had plunged it, cannot easily be exaggerated.

The appointment of Count Khuen-Héderváry was of course received most unfavourably by the Party of Right, which vented its ill-humour in stormy outbursts in the Sabor. But from the very first Count Khuen showed a firm hand, and as early as December 19, 1883, several Opposition deputies were excluded from the sittings. Feeling ran higher than ever before in Croatian public life ; the fiercest polemics between the parties were the order of the day. The Opposition indulged in unmeasured abuse, and even violence : the majority retaliated by infringements of the rules of the House. Finally, a few days before the close of the Session, both Opposition parties, by way of protest against such illegal proceedings, decided to absent themselves altogether from the House.

The general election of August, 1884, was contested with the utmost violence, which sometimes degenerated into bloodshed. Gross official pressure on the one hand was met by terrorism and wild invective on the other. In spite of every obstacle which the Government could throw in their way, forty-one members of the Opposition succeeded in running the electoral gauntlet ; of these thirteen belonged to the Independent National Party (including Dr. Joseph Frank [154]), three were non-party, while the remaining twenty-five were followers of Starčević.

Khuen and his confidants, having met with a very partial success at the polls, resorted to even more drastic measures in the new Sabor (October, 1884). The debate on the Address to the Throne gave rise to the usual stormy scenes, the Party of Right moving a rival Address, in which the validity of the Compromise was denied, as created by " an illegal assembly." Hereupon the new President, Mirko Hrvat, one of the most energetic and masterful members of the Government Party, threw aspersions upon the Starčević Address, as calculated to arouse doubts regarding " the innate loyalty of this Diet and the nation which it represents, towards the sacred person of His Majesty," and then solemnly protested against " the bare idea " that the Diet could ever accept such an address. This grave accusation was greeted with fierce cries of " Revoke," but on three successive days the President closed the sitting without allowing the members of the Party of Right any opportunity of defending themselves. On October 24, Hrvat opened the proceedings by a fresh statement, in which he proposed the exclusion of fifteen members of that party from eight sittings of the Sabor, and promptly followed this up by declaring them excluded from that day's sitting. He frankly admitted that he was acting contrary to the Standing Orders

[154] *See* below, p. 110.

of the House, but justified his action on the plea that their framers could not know that deputies would ever find their way into the Diet who would make its work impossible by noise and even howling, and by "insults such as cannot be tolerated even in the lowest grades of society." [155] On the motion of the deputy Lončarić a revision of the Standing Orders was proposed and accepted by the majority without alteration. When the fifteen excluded members sought to gain admission, their way was blocked by gendarmes, at the orders of the Government.

This drastic reform invested the President of the Chamber with well-nigh absolute discretionary powers over the deputies. It introduced a sliding scale of punishments for refractory members, beginning with a call to order and a reproof, and then proceeding to exclusion from eight to thirty sittings; and finally from thirty to sixty sittings, with loss of salary during the period of exclusion. Above all, a vigorous form of closure was adopted ; after the debate on any subject had lasted three days, any member of the Sabor who could obtain the support of ten others, was entitled to move the closing of the discussion, and "on such a motion the Sabor decides immediately without any debate, merely by standing up." [156]

Any Croatian verdict upon this extraordinary incident must inevitably be determined by the party bias of the individual. There can be no question that Hrvat's action was arbitrary to the last degree and involved a gross infringement of the Croatian Constitution. But unless we deny the principle that "the King's Government must be carried on," we shall be constrained to find extenuating circumstances for his action. Under the circumstances of the day, the Opposition had shown itself to be a destructive, not a constructive, force ; and its triumph must inevitably have led to a fresh suspension of the Constitution. Nothing shows more clearly Antony Starčević's complete lack of statesmanship than his adoption of tactics which directly challenged an adversary whom he knew to be greatly superior in strength, to resort to some such drastic measures. No statesman worthy of the name sets himself deliberately to ride for a fall.

With the revision of the Standing Orders, the power of the Opposition was broken ; and the Ban was free to extend that notorious system of repressive Government which will always

[155] Polić, op. cit. p. 39.   [156] Horvat, op. cit. p. 291.

be known to history as " the Khuen Régime." One formidable step in the taming of Croatia was the law which suspended for a period of three years trial by jury for all press actions. Public opinion had favoured the defendants in political cases, and with but few exceptions the juries had acquitted.[157] Now however it was at once possible to muzzle the Opposition press by confiscation and by legal proceedings and to ensure that these took place before courts which were amenable to Government influences.

Meanwhile the Government, by its administrative " reforms," strengthened its hold upon the officials throughout the country and made them more than ever dependent upon their superiors. The High Sheriffs of the counties were invested with fresh powers, in certain respects even over the local town councils. The Ban, it is true, expressly denied the exercise of pressure upon the officials ; but perfunctory denials could deceive nobody, in view of his own significant phrase, " In a country where two parties are struggling, one for the legal status quo, the other against it, the attitude of the officials is clearly marked out." [158]

The Session of 1885 was still marked by scenes of the utmost violence ; but the Party of Right was fatally handicapped by the new Rules of Procedure, and, it must be added, was entirely lacking in the tactical skill and adaptability by which a Parnell might perhaps have continued to defy the Government. The elections of 1887, conducted on the most approved Tammany principles, still further strengthened the " National " party at the expense of the Independents and the Starčevićians ; and Khuen now felt himself strong enough to adapt the franchise to his own requirements. Croatia presents an example, probably unique in modern Europe, of perpetual juggling with the franchise, and Count Khuen may well have felt that one more addition to the long list of electoral " reforms " might be ventured upon with impunity.[159]

---

[157] Polić, op. cit. p. 62.   [158] Ibid. p. 42.

[159] The Diet of 1848 was elected on the basis of an electoral law, hurriedly drawn up under Jellačić by representative Croats summoned for the purpose, but never submitted to full discussion by the Sabor. The Diets of 1861 and 1866 (see Šulek, *Nase Pravice*, pp. 242–46) were also elected on this rough draft, the opportunity not arising for a thorough measure of reform. In 1866 a new franchise bill was laid before the Sabor (*see* Šulek, op. cit. pp. cxxvii–cxxxv) but not passed, and the elections of 1867 were conducted upon a provisional franchise, arbitrarily promulgated (*see* Šulek, pp. cxxxvi–cxliii). In 1870 at

The new electoral law did, it is true, reduce the number of virilists and bring the constituencies of the former Military Frontiers into line with those of the rest of the country.[160] But otherwise all the evil features of the old franchise were retained or accentuated. Public voting and a tax qualification which was extremely high for so poor a country, made "freedom of election" in Croatia a mere farce. Less than 2 per cent. of the population possessed the vote, and from 50 to 60 per cent. of the electors were officials.[161] The Croatian vote was now for the first time extended to the joint officials, even if they possessed a vote in their own homes in Hungary. This provision, which would have been a mere matter of justice under a wide and liberal franchise, was, under the special circumstances of the case—and was of course intended to be—a convenient weapon in the hands of the Government. The official who voted for an Opposition candidate, or even absented himself from the poll, risked, and often lost, his position ; and thus for years the officials were the pliant tools of the Government, turning the scale in a large number of constituencies. A specially valuable asset were the State railway employees—many of them Magyars—who could always be relied upon to vote as their superiors ordered ; and it is this fact which explains the fierce opposition of the Party of Right to the enfranchisement of the joint officials.[162]

This reactionary franchise formed the basis for a complete system of electoral corruption and intimidation. No trick or quibble was neglected to cheat the Opposition of its votes or to deter its supporters from voting. The registers were consistently "doctored," names were omitted or falsely

length a new franchise law was passed by the Sabor. It was specially framed to give the Government organs great power, yet Rauch's Unionist party was twice beaten on its own franchise. In 1874 the National Party, now in power, introduced and passed a much more liberal measure ; but in 1881, after the split in the governing party, a fresh "reform" was carried, again extending the influence of the authorities. This remained in force until Khuen's "reform" in 1887.

[160] Till then, the Frontiers had voted on a special franchise promulgated in 1883.

[161] In 1906 there were 45,381 electors out of a population of 2,416,304, i.e., 1·8 per cent. (Horvat, p. 292).

[162] They further based their opposition upon the view that Hungarian and Croatian citizenship are entirely distinct and not reciprocal. Yet however logical such a distinction might seem to be, it is quite impossible to interpret the Compromise in this sense, in view of its clear recognition of Croatia's identity as a distinct state.

inscribed, while strangers were allowed to vote in the name of dead voters or to impersonate the absent. Bribery was practised openly, and the authorities canvassed actively for the Government candidates. The right of assembly and freedom of speech were suspended without scruple, and even the immunity of Opposition deputies was not respected. In some constituencies the electorate numbered less than a hundred,[163] and here the task of the Government was comparatively simple. Elsewhere, where the Opposition was more formidable, the electors were sometimes in the last resort kept back forcibly from the poll by detachments of gendarmerie or by military cordons. More than one case could be quoted where electors have only reached the poll by lying flat beneath a load of hay on a peasant's cart ; and other equally strange devices have sometimes been required before a Croat citizen could exercise his political rights. Nor was bloodshed unknown at the Croatian elections of the Khuen era. Most notorious of all, but by no means unique, was the fusillade by which eight peasants were killed and sixty others wounded ; numerous sentences of fines or imprisonment being imposed upon those who had dared to survive the massacre.[164]

In 1888 the Opposition was still further weakened by its own intolerant attitude. On the occasion of Bishop Strossmayer's jubilee, when the entire nation should have united in its homage to one of its greatest sons, a discordant note was struck by *Hrvatska*, the organ of the Starčević Party. So violent was its abuse of the Apostle of Southern Slav unity that three members of the Party of Right, including Erasmus Barčić—to-day the " Father " of the Croatian House— seceded and formed a small group of their own, until seven years later they were reinforced by a further secession. The fanaticism of the Starčević party at this period knew no bounds ; charges of atheism and infidelity were showered upon their opponents, and the attempt was even made to discredit such priests as chose to adhere to the National Party. Nothing could better illustrate the intellectual poverty of the party than these supremely foolish tactics. The inevitable result was to strengthen the alliance of the Serbs with the Government and to swell the ranks of its Croat supporters who owed their seats to artifice and trickery of the grossest

[163] In Perušić, Srb, Gračac, Karlobag and Korenica the electors were 61, 74, 74, 75 and 81 respectively, see Horvat, p. 292.
[164] Loiseau, *Le Balkan Slave*, p. 177.

kind, by a solid phalanx of twenty to twenty-five devoted Serb adherents, elected in accordance with the real wishes of the Orthodox population. So long as the only serious party of opposition denied the very existence of the Serbs in the Triune Kingdom, the latter had no choice but to accept Count Khuen's friendly overtures. It was not until the younger generation of Croats assumed a more enlightened and reasonable frame of mind towards their Serb kinsmen, and gave expression to the growing idea of fellowship in a new political organization, that the Serbs ventured to leave the apronstrings of the Government. *Divide et impera* was the secret motto of the Khuen régime. He realized that the two main principles of Antony Starčević were mutually destructive, that the independence of Croatia and the formation of a Greater Croatia were only practicable with the aid of the Serbs. So long, then, as he could retain the Serbs upon his side, the nation must remain weak and divided ; no effort was spared to secure the success of this policy, and so long as he remained Ban that success was strikingly complete.

The powerlessness of the Opposition became more than ever apparent in 1889, when the financial provisions of the Compromise were revised in a sense distinctly unfavourable to Croatia, the quota (or contribution to the joint affairs of the Monarchy) being raised from 6·4 to 7·9 per cent., and the proportion of revenue to be retained for autonomous expenditure being reduced from 45 to 44 per cent. (1889, XL, §§ 1 and 6a).

The elections of 1892 reduced the Party of Right to eight members. Its unfruitful policy of negation had kept the country in a state of feverish exhaustion, at a time when strong purgatives were needed. The urgent need of new tactics had at length become apparent even to its most uncompromising adherents ; and in the autumn of 1892 the Independent National Party and the Party of Right combined to form the so-called " United Opposition " (Sjedinjena Opozicija). But the union was more apparent than real. The broad statesmanship of Strossmayer might have supplied what was lacking in the narrower idealism of Starčević, but it could not hope to assimilate the blind fanaticism of the latter's followers. The only practical fruit of this temporary union was the revision of the Starčevićian programme in 1894. The party abandoned its fiercely anti-Austrian attitude, recognized the existence of Joint Affairs between Hungary and Croatia on the one hand and Austria on the other, but still denied the legality

107

of the Hungaro-Croatian Compromise and demanded its revision on such a basis as would secure absolute parity between the two countries. The union of Croatia, Slavonia, Dalmatia, Bosnia, Herzegovina, Fiume, Istria in a single state —known under the modern name of Trialism—became more than ever the aspiration of all true Croat and Serb patriots within the Habsburg Monarchy.

The year 1895 witnessed a recrudescence of the violent scenes of twelve years before. During the official visit of the Emperor-King to the Croatian capital, the anger of the mob and of the students was excited by the prominence of the Hungarian tricolour and the Serb national colours in the street decorations. An attempt was first made to tear down the latter from the Orthodox Church, and though this was fortunately frustrated by the police, the demonstrations were renewed the following day (October 15, 1895) before the great equestrian statue of Jellačić, which occupies the centre of the principal square of Agram and seems to menace the Magyars with his drawn sword pointing in the direction of Budapest. Here in the presence of a huge crowd, four students soaked a Hungarian flag in alcohol and burnt it to the strains of the old Illyrian hymn, " Yet is not Croatia fallen, while we are yet alive."[165] A similar outburst of feeling marked the following year, when the students of Belgrad burnt the Hungarian flag, in protest against the inclusion of the Servian arms among the symbols of the *partes subjectae* of the Crown of St. Stephen,[166] which decorated the Millenary Exhibition in Budapest. The gradual dawn of friendlier feelings between Croat and Serb was foreshadowed by the reception accorded to the Croat Sokols [167] in Belgrad, by the mutual compliments paid by the two races at the translation of the remains of Vuk Karadžić, the great Serb scholar, and by the cordial declarations of Vaso Gjurgjević, who had succeeded Hrvat as President of the Sabor and was now leader of the Serb faction. " The Serbs and the Croats in the Croatian Kingdom have the same future, the same destiny, the same political aim."

In his declining years Antony Starčević showed a tendency to modify his *non possumus* attitude in the Serb question ; but death removed him in 1896, at the very period when the

[165] " Jos Hrvatska ne propala, Dok mi Živimo."
[166] See Loiseau, op. cit. pp. 172-7.
[167] The famous gymnastic societies, originally developed in Bohemia, but since copied by all Slav nations.

first signs of returning sanity showed themselves in the relations of the " hostile brethren." No one save Bishop Strossmayer has exercised so deep an influence upon Croatia during
the last half century : no one combined such noble idealism
and such simplicity and firmness of character with such lack of
political balance and scorn for the practical possibilities of
public life. His exaggerated praise of past centuries was
redeemed by the earnest ambition to create a new moral basis
for a society which he regarded as corrupt and decaying ; but
it cannot be said that his choice of tactics was calculated to
arrest the decay which he lamented. His strange contempt
for the whole existing national culture and literature might
have been admissible in one who was steeped in the great
literatures of the West ; but of this there was no sign, and his
programme, despite his own keen critical faculty, was sadly
lacking in intellectual background. Hence his followers, who
did not possess his earnestness and reasoning powers, inevitably
tended to lose sight of cultural aims, in the vain pursuit of
political mirages. Starčević's impossible attitude on the Serb
question was largely responsible for the success of the Khuen
régime and the complete subordination of Croatia to the
Magyars ; and it cannot be denied that by his policy of un-
restrained fanaticism he showed himself lacking in the most
essential qualities of statesmanship and played into the hands
of his enemies. Yet it is impossible to withhold our admiration from his passionate consistency and rigid patriotic creed
and still more impossible to doubt his sincerity and honour.
So long as the name of Cato commands the respect of the
modern world, so long must Croatia honour the memory of
Antony Starčević.

The death of Starčević deprived the Party of Right of its
founder and its most outstanding figure ; and the selection of
a successor was influenced by those intrigues and personalities
which are unhappily so characteristic of Croatian public life.
Within the next year the party split into two sections. One
of these united with the old Independent National Party and
other scattered adherents of Strossmayer, and formed the
" Croatian Party of Right " ; while the other, under the title
of the " Party of Pure Right," upheld the theories of Starčević in their most uncompromising form. While the former
gradually formed the nucleus of a new political group, destined
to overthrow the Mamelukes of the governing party, the latter
owed whatever influence it possessed to the great ability and

tactical skill of its leader, Dr. Joseph Frank, who is in many respects the most interesting figure in Croatian public life during the last fifteen years.

Dr. Frank's Jewish birth did not deter him from becoming the mouthpiece of Croat nationalism in its extremest form, and fanning the religious and racial passions of the mob. In this direction his influence has been almost wholly evil and has been mainly responsible for the violence and acrimony of political and press controversy in recent years. But on the other hand, he rendered great services to Croatia by his thorough study of the economic and financial situation and by the renewed attention which he called to that hitherto neglected subject. His chief claim to consideration, however, rests upon his statesmanlike views of foreign policy and of the place which the Croat race and its aspirations should fill in the international situation. He was the first politician since the collapse of Haulik's party in the sixties, and the withdrawal of Strossmayer from active politics, to advocate an alliance between Austria and Croatia, to realize that while on the one hand Croatian national claims must remain a mere dream without the support of Vienna and the dynasty, so on the other hand the economic needs of the two countries and the requirements of a true Imperial policy should lead the dynasty to favour Croat claims. It is a further merit of Dr. Frank, that he has been the most consistent advocate of the union of Bosnia with Croatia. Unhappily his policy has been obscured by a blatant clericalism, which alienated the more thoughtful elements of public opinion, and had as demoralizing an influence upon the peasantry as the equally blatant anti-clericalism which it evoked as protest.

The elections of 1897, despite gross corruption on the part of the authorities, were marked by a fresh rally of the Opposition, which secured twenty-five out of eighty-eight seats. But Khuen promptly took steps to unseat seven of the leading Opposition deputies, including Professor Vrbanić, the well-known constitutional writer, and Dr. Pasarić, who had been returned unopposed. Needless to say the usual pliant instruments and legal quibbles were found to execute and to palliate this high-handed action. In the terse phrase of a modern historian, " it may be said that to Khuen as a rule the constitution was mere padding ; he governed absolutely." [168] It is only fair to add that agrarian disturbances, which broke out in Slavonia during the autumn of 1897, and which culminated

[168] R. Horvat, op. cit. p. 293.

in an assault upon Count Khuen's own country house at Nustar, provided the Government with a pretext for repressive measures.

The Opposition was still too weak to resist Count Khuen successfully : and he, on his side, by skilfully fanning the flame of discord among the rival factions, soon reduced them once more to impotence. The next five years were a period of stagnation, in which the nation groaned in vain under the restraint of the Khuen régime.

Never before had the agitation against the Serbs been conducted with such violence as by Dr. Frank and his followers in the closing years of the century ; while the favour shown to them by the Government not unnaturally served to enhance anti-Serb feeling among wide circles of the Croat population. In 1902 serious anti-Serb riots took place in Agram, under the auspices of the Starčević Party. Spiteful rumours accused Dr. Frank and Count Khuen of secretly working together to maintain unabated that waning discord of Croat and Serb to which the Government owed its majority and the Frank party the most effective point in its programme.

These events, however, gave the first impetus to a change in the policy of the Serbs in Croatia and to the formation of a new political organization, the Independent Serb Party, which has since then played so important a part in the history of the country. " The younger generation of Serbs came to the conclusion that the Khuen régime merely favourized the Serbs in order to play them off against the patriotic Croat parties which were engaged in a struggle for the political rights and liberties of the country. They came to realize that the Magyar onslaughts upon Croatia's language and autonomous position must prove equally injurious to Serb and to Croat : that the Serbs have an equal interest in upholding the rights guaranteed by the Compromise, and should therefore unite in defence of their common fatherland. (In a Magyarized Croatia Serbs and Croats alike would be Magyarized, as is already happening to the Serbs in Hungary. In a Croatia which was flourishing politically and economically, the Serbs would share all the benefits.") [169]

The stagnation to which Khuen's iron rule had reduced Croatia, had rendered the great majority of the older generation impervious to all ideas of progress : and hence it was from abroad that the new movement was forced to draw its inspira-

[169] *Kroatien und dessen Beziehungen zu Bosnien,* p. 82.

tion. Its first beginnings may be traced to the group of Croat students who had been implicated in the " flag-riots " of 1895 and had found it necessary to complete their education at the University of Prague. Here most of them became the disciples of Professor Thomas Masaryk, who had already become an ethical force throughout the whole Slav world and whose influence upon the thought and outlook of so many leaders of public life in Slav countries—alike in Bohemia, Russia and Hungary, in Servia, Croatia and Bulgaria—has since then grown steadily from year to year, until to-day it may safely be described as without any parallel.

Two publications, *Novo Doba* (The New Age) in Prague and *Narodna Misao* (National Thought) in Agram, preached to the younger generation the idea of Croato-Serb brotherhood and unity ; and their staff brought new ideals and enthusiasms into the cynicism and decay of Croatian public life.[170] The outbreak, when at length it came, was sudden and spontaneous. In February, 1903, the Hungarian delegation had abruptly rejected all the Croatian proposals for a revision of the financial Compromise, and on March 11 a public meeting of protest against the Magyar attitude was held in Agram by the Opposition parties. Great enthusiasm prevailed, and similar meetings were organized in the chief provincial towns, while the press, led by *Obzor*, the chief Croatian newspaper, opened a vigorous campaign against Count Khuen and in favour of Croatia's financial autonomy.

Almost daily confiscations were the result, and *Obzor* frequently appeared with ominous blank spaces in its leading articles and sometimes with whole columns of erasures. A Magyar inscription over the new railway station of Agram led to fresh demonstrations, and on March 27 they were renewed with greater violence than before. A general feeling of unrest gained possession of the country. Rioting in Agram was followed by bloodshed in Zaprešića, where a peasant died of his injuries. The troops were called out, sharp measures were adopted. Meetings were prohibited wholesale, and a large number of arrests were made, including the chief members of the *Obzor's* staff. The press was gagged more mercilessly than ever before ; confiscation was an almost daily occurrence,[171] and whole columns of print—articles and news

---

[170] See Marjanović, *Hrvatski Pokret*, pp. 15 seq.

[171] *Obzor*, in its Jubilee number (December, 1910) states that it alone paid about 60,000 crowns in fines, etc., during the Khuen régime.

alike—fell victims to the censor's fury, until it was almost possible to speak of " white editions." [172]

The disturbances of the spring of 1903, though insignificant in themselves, showed that Croatia was at length shaking off the inertia in which it had been sunk for the past twenty years, and roused men to the idea that Count Khuen's position, which they had come to regard as impregnable, might after all be shaken. The movement was greeted with equal surprise and enthusiasm throughout the Southern Slav provinces, and nowhere was the enthusiasm so marked as in Dalmatia. Here the Croat idea had during the past generation shown a steady growth at the expense of the Italian.[173] One by one the municipalities of the Dalmatian coast towns—Spalato, Sebenico, Traù, Lesina, Ragusa, Cattaro—fell into Croat or Serb hands, until Zara alone remained Italian. The Croat language gradually rose from a subordinate to a predominant position in the schools and in the law courts, while the same tendency was noticeable in the provincial press. Enjoying less freedom than the other provinces of Austria, Dalmatia might complain that its economic needs were ignored or neglected by the central Government, and that the methods of bureaucracy and espionage which have been allowed to survive along Austria's southern frontier were not merely superfluous but clumsy and insulting. But despite all its pedantry and suspiciousness, the Austrian administration in Dalmatia has never been accused of corruption ; and if it cannot compare with that of Tirol or Bohemia, it has never led even its bitterest critic to regard with envy the administrative conditions of Croatia, of Servia or of Montenegro. In short, neglected as it was, it enjoyed a privileged position among Southern Slav countries, a fact which is in itself the most glaring proof of the intolerable position of the Croato-Serb race.

The movement in Croatia found a lively echo in Dalmatia, but the strict censorship imposed by Khuen made it difficult

---

[172] In Hungary and Croatia, a newspaper can only be confiscated after publication, but as the first copy must be submitted to the police, confiscation can follow very speedily. A raid is then made upon the postbags and the cafés. The newspaper then reprints, leaving the incriminated passages blank, save for the word zaplijen (" confiscated"). During the three weeks which I spent in Agram at the time of the High Treason Trial, a policeman used sometimes to appear at the door of the Café Corso, and my friends would greet him with the question, " What paper is it to-day ? "

[173] *See* p. 10.

for accurate news to find its way across the frontier. The wholesale arrests in Agram gave rise to the wild rumour that certain Croat leaders were to be hanged. One of those strange frenzies which at rare intervals seize upon a whole nation, ran through the Croat population of Istria and Dalmatia. Everywhere public meetings of protest and sympathy were held, wild abuse was levelled at Count Khuen and his Government, and public collections were made in favour of their victims, the Italians generously contributing side by side with their Croat rivals. Tales of massacre circulated among the peasantry, and until their falsity became apparent many houses were draped in black. The " black days " still form a vivid memory of the Dalmatian people. Acting under the stress of national excitement, over thirty Croat deputies of the Diets of Dalmatia and Istria conceived the idea of seeking an audience with the Emperor and appealing to him for mercy for the victims of the Khuen régime. But, unfortunately, their intention had become known in Budapest, and the Hungarian Government exerted all its influence to prevent the audience. Every Minister—Austrian and Austro-Hungarian alike—turned a deaf ear to their appeals ; and the thirty deputies were obliged to leave the Hungarian capital—Francis Joseph was at the time residing in the palace of Buda—without being admitted to the presence of their sovereign. Whatever may have been the reasons of state which dictated this rebuff —whether Francis Joseph yielded reluctantly to the insistence of his constitutional advisers, or freely followed his own inclinations—it is a notorious fact that this was a turning point in the relations of the Habsburg dynasty and the Southern Slavs. The Dalmatian Croat is proud and sensitive, and still regards the Emperor with very much the same feelings as he regarded in former centuries some powerful voivode in the Turkish wars— as his natural champion and vindicator against all injustice. But while the patriarchal conception of kingship is part and parcel of the people's nature, the monarchical tradition can hardly be said to exist at all, and thus when the nation's representatives were refused access to the steps of the throne, the universal sentiment was one of dismay, resentment and disappointment. The southern mind, at once naïve and passionate, interpreted it as a clear proof of hostility on the part of the dynasty towards the Southern Slavs.[174] A great revul-

[174] The Archduke Maximilian (afterwards Emperor of Mexico) and Crown Prince Rudolf had enjoyed enormous popularity among the

sion of feeling took place. In the Diet of Dalmatia violent speeches were delivered against "Vienna" and Austria. Khuen's henchmen and the instruments of Magyarization in Croatia were openly denounced as the agents of Vienna. The Dalmatian politicians became the moving spirits in the political revival. Encouraged by the sympathy which the events in Croatia aroused in the Italian press, they aimed at kindling the interest of Europe in their cause. The natural channels of redress being resolutely closed to them, they not unnaturally sought to turn the international situation to their own advantage. Brought up in Italian thought and under the spell of the Risorgimento, they modelled their dreams of Southern Slav unity upon the piecemeal advance of Piedmont. Italy, Hungary and the new Jougo-Slavia were to form the three bulwarks of a rejuvenated Southern Europe against the onslaughts of Teuton and Muscovite alike. The steady growth of a powerful ultra-national Opposition in the Hungarian Parliament and the internal crises which had convulsed Austria for some years past, encouraged them in the belief that a new situation was at hand, when Magyar and Croat might reconcile their differences and unite in defence of a common independence.

Calm reflection should have told the incensed Croats that in refusing an audience, the monarch was merely acting on the advice of his constitutional advisers. It is on the statesmen who gave His Majesty such advice, that the responsibility for subsequent events must rest. They were presumably aware of the intention of the Dalmatian leaders, not to mince their phrases, but to lay the whole unpalatable truth before their sovereign ; and they were determined at all costs to prevent him from hearing the Croat point of view in so outspoken and convincing a form. The blame rests not with the sovereign, but with the political system which compels him to base his estimate of one race upon the information supplied by its bitterest enemy.

The fall of the Széll Cabinet in June, 1903, supplied Count Khuen Héderváry with a convenient means of retreat from a position of which he had grown tired. On June 27 he was nominated Hungarian Premier, and in the words of a modern

Croats. Long after the latter's death, the peasantry in remote hill districts of Dalmatia refused to believe his death and maintained that he would come again, like another Barbaróssa or Boabdil.

Croat historian, "All Croatia took a deep breath." [175] But his successor, Count Theodore Pejačević, son of the " Cavalier Ban," though averse to high-handed measures, was at first hampered by illness and delegated the conduct of affairs to the sectional chief for Home Affairs, Dr. Šumanović, one of Khuen's most zealous supporters. The removal of the hated Ban calmed the excitement of the population ; but in its essentials the old system of government survived, and blind subservience to Budapest took the place of Khuen's consistent attitude of " Thus far and no farther." A notable example of this was supplied by the permission granted to the Magyarizing " Julian Society " to erect its schools in Croatia, ostensibly for the benefit of Magyar railway employees and agricultural settlers, but in reality only too often for the Magyarization of Croat and Serb children in places where there were but few Magyar residents.

To Western minds it seems monstrous that any restriction whatever should be placed upon the erection of schools, no matter what their language of instruction may be. In Hungary, on the other hand, private enterprise in education is crippled at every turn, even if it be exercised through the medium of a religious body ; and the restrictions imposed upon the mother-tongue of school children are so severe that two and a half million Slovaks possess only 247 primary schools and not a single secondary school where Slovak is the language of instruction. The linguistic rights of racial minorities simply do not exist except on paper. Under such circumstances it would seem to be a positive inversion of Magyar principles to insist upon the maintenance of Magyar schools for a racial unit which only forms 3·8 per cent of the population. Nor can we be astonished that Croat public opinion should bitterly resent the activity of the Julian Society in Croatia, when we realize that meanwhile the few Croat schools in Hungary are being steadily Magyarized.[176] It is to be feared that many years will elapse before each race is free to build unhindered as many schools as it pleases in the other's country.

[175] Horvat, op. cit. p. 295.

[176] In 1906–7 there were only four Croat schools among a Croat population of 19·4 per cent. in County Zala, and nine among a Croat population of 12·3 per cent. in Co. Sopron, i.e., counting one school in Vas, a total of fourteen Croat schools for a Croat population of 188,552. (See Ung. Stat. Jahrb., xv, p. 322.) By the winter of 1910 there was only one Croat school left in Hungary.

THE END OF THE KHUEN ERA

The withdrawal of Count Khuen signified a change of persons rather than a change of régime ; the old methods were continued, though in a distinctly milder form. The new Ban declared the Compromise with Hungary to be the basis of his policy, and talked vaguely of further guarantees for the Croatian language. But the best commentary on this barren programme were the demands put forward in public meetings, whenever they were allowed : universal suffrage, secret ballot, freedom of elections, of association and assembly, liberty of the press, financial autonomy, independence of judges, guarantees of personal liberty. These demands illustrate better than any book the condition of Croatia under Count Khuen Héderváry.

Croatia was made the subject of debates in the Hungarian Parliament. The Kossuthists found that the Khuen régime in Croatia supplied them with convenient party capital against the new Khuen Cabinet in Hungary, and exploited it accordingly ; while some of its members were genuinely indignant at the estrangement of Croat and Magyar for which the " Liberal " policy was responsible. When the deputy Visontai inveighed against the repression of press freedom in Croatia, the Croatian Minister Dr. Tomašić, Count Khuen's ablest lieutenant, roundly declared that " this was done in the interest of Hungary." This was a practical illustration of Khuen's maxim, that Croatia's policy must be made in Hungary, and of the elder Andrássy's oft-quoted dictum that Croatia can only be governed by alternate doses of " oats and whip." [177]

Under Pejačević the severity of the old régime was somewhat relaxed ; but repressive measures were not altogether abandoned. On July 4 Father Jemeršić and another priest were sentenced to six months' imprisonment for the usual " incitement " ; and on the 19th of the same month the trial of twenty-four citizens of Karlovac resulted in the condemnation of two persons to eight months, eleven others to six months each, in addition to lesser sentences, for demonstrations against Khuen and the Magyars. On August 14 Mr. Stephen Radić, the peasant leader, and Professor Pasarić were sentenced to two and four months' imprisonment, on a charge of incitement against the Ban and the Magyar nation.

[177] Cf. *Neue Freie Presse*, January 11, 1908.

CHAPTER VI

Bishop Strossmayer and the Renaissance of Croatian Culture

Sve za vjeru i za domovinu.
(All for faith and fatherland).—*Motto of Strossmayer.*

THE well-known Italian statesman Marco Minghetti once assured the Belgian publicist Emile de Laveleye that he had had the opportunity of observing at close quarters almost all the eminent men of his time. " There are only two," he added, " who gave me the impression of belonging to another species than ourselves. These two were Bismarck and Strossmayer." The man of whom this high tribute was spoken arrested the attention of Western Europe on the memorable occasion of the Vatican Council, when his eloquence led the opposition to the doctrine of Infallibility and his courage recorded one of the three dissentient votes. But Strossmayer's true claim to immortality rests, not upon his espousal of liberalism in the Church, but upon his services to the cause of Croatian nationality and culture. Rarely has any patriot so completely justified the title of " First Son of the Nation " (Prvi Sin Naroda) ; and Strossmayer must always occupy a prominent place in any account of Croatia.[178]

Joseph George Strossmayer was born on February 4, 1815, at Osijek (Essek), the capital of Slavonia ; his family was of German-Austrian origin, but had long since been completely Croaticized. After studying at the gymnasium of his native town and the seminary of Diakovo, he proceeded to the University of Pest, where he astonished his professors by his brilliant powers of dialectic. " He will be either the chief

---

[178] The standard life of Bishop Strossmayer is in Croatian, by Monsignor Cepelić and Pavić. But it is out of print ; I have failed to secure a secondhand copy in Agram, and it is not in any library which I have been able to consult during the last twelve months.

heretic of the century," exclaimed the president of the examining board, " or the chief pillar of the Catholic Church " (*aut primus haereticus saeculi aut prima columna catholicae ecclesiae*).[179] After three years as chaplain at Peterwardein, he was in 1847 appointed a court chaplain and director of the Augustineum [180] in Vienna.

As one of the most elegant Latinists of his time,[181] he was specially acceptable to the ecclesiastical authorities, while his active enthusiasm for the cause of Croatian nationality and literature brought him into touch with Jellačić, Kulmer and Ožegović. It was their influence at Court which secured for him, at the early age of thirty-four, the vacant Bishopric of Djakovo, to which he was nominated on November 18, 1849. This ancient see, formed out of the united dioceses of Bosnia and Syrmia,[182] is one of the largest in Europe, not only embracing the districts named but also exercising a nominal sway over the Catholics of Servia. For close upon half a century its enormous revenues [183] were devoted by the patriot Bishop to the furtherance of national traditions and culture. The Croat motto which he adopted at his consecration, was realized as truly in a financial as in any other sense, " Sve za vjeru i domovinu "—" All for faith and fatherland." Commencing with the foundation of new schools in his immediate neighbourhood, he steadily increased the endowments of almost all the secondary schools in the country. A fund of £4,000 was devoted to improving the condition of the clergy of Syrmia. A seminary, with Croat language of instruction, was founded for young Bosnian clerics. Bulgarian Uniate students

---

[179] As M. de Laveleye sarcastically adds : " It was not the fault of Pius IX and the Vatican Council if the first part of the prophecy was not fulfilled." (*See* his *Balkan Peninsula*, p. 32.)

[180] One of the most important theological seminaries in Austria.

[181] Long afterwards, at the Vatican Council, "he earned the praise of being *primus orator Christianitatis.*" He told Laveleye that Latin was the language in which he could express himself most clearly (p. 47).

[182] The official title is " Episcopatus bosnensis, diacovensis et sirmiensis." The bishopric of Bosnia was originally subject to the Archbishop of Salona, but in the thirteenth century, owing to troubles with the Bogomile heretics, was transferred to Diakovo. In 1773 Clement XIV united the sees of Bosnia and Syrmia under the Archbishop of Agram. In 1881, however, a special Archbishopric of Sarajevo was erected, which has since then been occupied by Monsignor Stadler.

[183] According to Laveleye (p. 46) they averaged 150,000 florins (= £12,000) a year.

were educated at his expense. The Slav Chapter of St. Jerome in Rome [184] was restored and endowed.

From the very first his interest centred upon literary and philological studies. Acting from the conviction that historic research and accurate knowledge of the past are essential foundations of all national achievement, he sought out such students as would be ready to devote themselves to literary and historical pursuits. Francis Rački, the pioneer of historical research in Croatia, owed his training and leisure to the great Bishop. Theiner, the well-known Vatican librarian, received his support in the collection of Southern Slav documents.[185] The brothers Miladinović edited and published at his expense the first collection of Bulgarian popular songs. Even the great Servian philologists Vuk Karadžić and Daničić, were under deep obligation to his generosity. Indeed there is no learned society among the Southern Slavs which has not at one time or another enjoyed Bishop Strossmayer's benefactions.

But unquestionably his greatest and most lasting achievement was the foundation of the Southern Slav Academy of Science and Art at Agram, which was the result of his generous initiative. In 1860 Strossmayer and Rački discussed the idea, and the Bishop offered the sum of £4,000 as a preliminary subscription, which he afterwards augmented to more than double that amount. The letter in which he announced his intention to Ban Šokčević is a kind of national manifesto, ascribing the backwardness of the Serbo-Croat language and literature to lack of united effort, and insisting upon Zagreb's fitness to become the centre of " a scientific society which is destined to give a common impulse to the intellectual movement among the Bulgars, Serbs and Croats." [186]

Croatia responded to Strossmayer's appeal, and in July, 1861, the Diet made the scheme its own. Long bureaucratic delays ensued before the royal sanction was obtained for the statutes of the new institution, which naturally awakened no enthusiasm among the Viennese advocates of Centralism. At length on July 28, 1867, the Southern Slav Academy was formally opened by its founder and inspirer. M. Louis Leger, who attended as the representative of the Sorbonne, has put

[184] S. Girolamo degli Schiavoni.
[185] *Vetera Monumenta Slavorum Meridionalium historiam illustrantia* (Rome, 1863).
[186] December 10, 1860, cit. Zagorsky, op. cit. pp. 107–8.

upon record that he had " rarely met with so touching a popularity " [187] as that which the ovation accorded to Strossmayer revealed ; but the Government ungraciously forbade all decorations or illuminations in the streets of Zagreb. The Bishop's inaugural address, which is celebrated as a classic example of Croat oratory, was primarily devoted to the relations of science and religion, and to an eulogy of great French thinkers, notably Pascal and Bossuet, Chateaubriand and Montesquieu. At the close, he referred briefly to the hostile charge that he squandered the revenues of the Church upon mundane objects. " Thanks be to God," he said, " I am not the sole culprit : I have as my accomplices our whole clergy, to the very last man. This clergy knows that all which is done for the faith is profitable to science, and that all which is done for science is to the advantage of the faith. Let the whole nation realize that in future we shall not allow ourselves to be deterred by any accusation or insult from the path which we have marked out. We shall discharge conscientiously the duties of our ministry, but we shall also develop with all our powers all those interests which affect the material and moral progress of our people, its existence and its future." [188]

The academy thus constituted consists of thirty-two elected, sixty corresponding and sixteen honorary members. Its activity is divided among various special committees, dealing with antiquities, ancient manuscripts, art, folklore, seismology and zoology. Its publications exceed 300 volumes and include scholarly editions of the earlier Croat poets, collections of documents dealing with Southern Slav history, and a monumental dictionary modelled on that of Littré. The Academy buildings contain an interesting museum of antiquities and a large library.[189] In 1884 Bishop Strossmayer added to his other benefactions by presenting a gallery of over 300 paintings, collected by him during his annual visits to Italy. Though hostile critics have sometimes accused it of being swayed by political passion, it is beyond dispute that the Academy succeeded from the first moment of its existence in concentrating within its walls the best scholarship and scientific talent of which the country was possessed.

[187] Leger, p. 131.　　　[188] Cit. Leger, p. 182.
[189] In 1902 it contained over 1,800 manuscripts, many of great value for the history of Slav literature, and 25,000 charters and other documents.—*Die öst-ung. Mon. in Wort und Bild (Kroatien)*, p. 178.

The first President of the Academy was Don Frane Rački, the real founder of historical criticism among the Southern Slavs. Born in 1828 of a peasant family on the coast of Croatia, Rački was educated for the priesthood. Even as a young seminarist in Vienna, he attracted the attention of Strossmayer ; the enthusiasm with which he studied the charters and the Glagolitic texts of his native diocese won him a vacant canonry at the Illyrian college of San Girolamo in Rome. He soon became a recognized authority on the language and liturgy of the ancient Slavs, and as a result of his researches in the Secret Archives of the Vatican and other libraries, published in 1857 and the following years a work dealing with the Slav apostles Cyril and Methodius and the old Slav alphabet which they had employed. Under his editorship the so-called *Codex Assemanianus* in the Vatican was published in its original alphabet ; and as Cardinal Haulik refused to accept the dedication of the book, owing to its bearing upon the delicate problem of the Slav liturgy, it appeared under the patronage and at the expense of Bishop Strossmayer.[190] Rački's latest biographer seeks, not without success, to prove that his national prejudices influenced his judgment to a far less degree than his Catholic convictions[191] ; but it would be absurd to deny that in all his laborious researches the historian was inspired by the belief that they would serve to kindle the flame of national feeling.

In 1860 Strossmayer invited Rački to take up his residence at Djakovo, and henceforth he became the adviser and collaborator in all his projects, whether literary or political. Four years later he began, in conjunction with Professor Jagić,[192] to publish a review devoted to history and philology, and as the zealous advocate of Vuk Karadžić's reforms in Croat orthography, was exposed to violent opposition from the conservative school of writers ; nor was this opposition diminished when he organized a small conference of competent students to discuss the publication of a philological dictionary of the Croat language. Spite and intrigue secured Rački's dismissal from the post of inspector of secondary schools

[190] Zagorsky, p. 57.
[191] Zagorsky, p. 62. An improved edition was published in 1878 at Rome, by Ivan Crnčić.
[192] Now the chief living Slavistic scholar ; till his retirement in 1908, professor at Vienna University and editor of the *Archiv für slavische Philologie* (Berlin).

which he had held since his return from Rome. It was hoped that the material loss which this involved would compel him to resign the presidency of the new Academy and to leave Zagreb, where his presence was most unwelcome to a Magyarone Government. But here again the situation was saved by the Bishop's generosity. "Brother will not abandon brother," he wrote to Rački. "I guarantee you all you need till you find another post. If the same misfortune occurred to me, we would live together and share between us all we had. On no account abandon the presidency of the Academy." Rački remained at his post, and did much to give the Academy its distinctive note. Above all, it was his enthusiasm for the idea of Southern Slav unity which prevented its outlook from becoming exclusively Croat and won for Agram the services of George Daničić, the most brilliant Serb scholar since Vuk.

Bishop Strossmayer did not rest content with the project of an academy. On April 29, 1861, he laid before the Diet a scheme for the erection of a national Croatian University. The idea was received with acclamation ; statutes were drawn up and embodied in a law, but thanks to the opposition of the Centralists in Vienna the royal sanction was withheld. In October, 1866, during the festivities which celebrated the tercentenary of Zrinsky's heroic defence against the Turks, Strossmayer once more raised the question of an university and not merely started a public fund by subscribing £4,000, but promised his annual salary as High Sheriff as a further contribution. Roused by his example, the city of Agram subscribed an equal amount, and Archbishop Mihalović £2,500 ; and within a short period of time over £30,000 had been collected—a remarkable achievement, when we consider the scanty resources at Croatia's disposal. When Francis Joseph paid his state visit to Agram after the conclusion of the Compromise, the statutes were at length sanctioned (1869) ; but the political differences with Hungary interposed a further delay of five years before the final obstacles were removed. In October, 1874, the University of Agram was opened by the Ban Mažuranić, representing the Sovereign. This time the city was free to don festive dress, and enthusiastic crowds greeted Bishop Strossmayer as the father of his country.[193] The university, though small and lacking a medical faculty, has proved a credit to its originators. Though at first obliged

[193] Laveleye, p. 36.

to recruit its professors from other Slav countries, notably from Bohemia, it has gradually succeeded in filling the necessary posts with native talents, and in its thirty years of life can show the names of many scholars of repute.[194]

No sketch of Bishop Strossmayer would be complete without some reference to the Cathedral of Djakovo, to whose erection he devoted for many years a considerable proportion of the income of his see. It was in the truest sense a labour of love, for it was designed to be an apotheosis in stone of all the ideas which its creator held most sacred—a vindication of Christianity on soil once profaned by Turkish rule, an outpost of the Cross on the frontier of Moslem Bosnia, and at the same time a monument of Croatian art and architecture, in which the reviving national feeling should find its full expression. The Church is built in the ancient Lombard style, with lofty towers similar to those of S. Zeno at Verona.[195] The chief material used is brick of a rich red colour; the mouldings and cornices are of Illyrian limestone. The interior is decorated with national Croat designs and frescoes from the Old and New Testament by the painters Seitz. The centre of the apse shows the Southern Slav peoples, guided by the pious founder to the throne of our Lord and His mother. Other scenes represent the first preaching of the Gospel in Slavonic countries. Apart from its rich artistic treasures, the interior is marked by a severe and medieval simplicity, worthy of that purified Catholicism which filled the dreams of the great bishop.

His keen opposition to the dogma of Infallibility at the Vatican Council of 1869–1870 exposed him to many attacks, and destroyed all hope of his succeeding Haulik in the vacant archiepiscopal see of Zagreb. Incidentally it won him the close friendship of such champions of liberty within the Church as Acton and Döllinger, who were equally attracted by his

[194] It may be worth citing the following names : in history, Smičiklas, Klaić, Nodilo and Sišić ; in constitutional law, Pliverić (the standard Croat authority on the Compromise), Vrbanić (a specialist on the financial relations with Hungary), Tomašić (the present Ban) ; in civil law, Bogišić (author of the Montenegrin Civil Code) ; in criminal law, Šilović and Rojc ; in zoology, Brusina ; in art, Kršnjavi (the translator of Dante and re-organizer of secondary education) ; in literature, Šurmin (author of a standard literary history).

[195] Its height is 84 metres, its length 78, its greatest breadth 60. (See Wort und Bild (Kroatien), p. 500 ; Laveleye, op. cit. pp. 41–2 ; W. Ritter, Évêques Artistes (Gand, 1890).)

saintly personality, his wide culture and the enthralling charm of his Latin oratory. But while the latter carried his resistance to the point of secession, Strossmayer, after gallantly recording his vote in a minority of three, submitted to the superior verdict of the Church, and henceforward abstained from all criticism of the obnoxious dogma. That he welcomed the fall of the Temporal Power as a scarcely disguised blessing, was only to be expected from a man of his wide outlook on the frontier between Western and Eastern culture ; and his interesting correspondence with Gladstone [196] shows that he regarded as its necessary consequence a far-reaching reform of the Roman Curia, such as would curtail the undue influence of Italian prelates and restore to it its former universal character.

He shared with Mr. Gladstone and so many other leaders of thought and opinion the pious wish for the reunion of Christendom. But with him this aspiration had a highly practical side, in his efforts to promote good feeling and if possible union between the Churches of Rome and the East. Realizing keenly the hindrances which religious rivalry placed in the way of national progress among the Southern Slavs, he felt that their removal would be the surest means of realizing alike his national and his religious ideals. Unhappily, his efforts were misunderstood by the Orthodox clergy, especially in Servia and Russia : he was unjustly attacked as a mere agent of Vatican propagandism ; and when in 1885 he proposed to pay a pastoral visit to the Catholics of Belgrad, the Servian Government declined to guarantee his personal safety, and the visit had to be abandoned. [197]

While his schemes of reunion were foredoomed to failure, his zealous advocacy of the neglected Slav Liturgy known as the Glagolitic rite drew upon him the disapproval of the Ultramontane party. But the scholarly Leo XIII, who was keenly interested in all matters concerning the Eastern Church, was fully alive to the important part which the " Glagolitza "

[196] *See* Appendix XVII.

[197] Such is the intolerance of the Servians towards Catholicism, that a Barnabite Father sent by Strossmayer to minister to the thousands of Italian workmen engaged in railway work in Servia, was assaulted, injured and obliged to leave the country. In Servia the clergy are sunk in formalism, and their influence is national, not religious. In Bosnia, on the other hand, the Catholics, under Archbishop Stadler, have shown distinct leanings to aggression and proselytism, but mainly towards the Moslem population, among whom they have met with scanty success.

might play in winning the peoples of the Balkan peninsula to Catholicism. Throughout his pontificate the ancient liturgy was tolerated, and within certain limits actually encouraged, and the publication of Slavonic missals and their distribution permitted. It was only under his less statesmanlike successor and his fanatical advisers that the Glagolitic clergy fell once more into disfavour at Rome and their rite was materially restricted.

In 1885 the thousandth anniversary of the Slav apostle St. Methodius was widely celebrated in Russia, and on this occasion Strossmayer sent a telegram of congratulation. His enemies, especially in Budapest, made much capital out of the incident, and represented his action—prompted as it was by a lifelong veneration for the Slav apostles—as an insult to the Holy See and to the Dual Monarchy! Once more Pope Leo was too sagacious to be misled by such obvious bias, and received him graciously when he appeared in Rome in 1888 at the head of a large Southern Slav pilgrimage. But the Emperor Francis Joseph, misled by his Magyar entourage,[198] was unhappily prevailed upon to administer a public rebuke to the Bishop, when the latter came to pay his respects on the occasion of manœuvres in Slavonia. A rejoinder was naturally impossible ; and the Bishop, now old and frail, was deeply wounded by the unmerited disfavour of his Sovereign, but henceforth abstained from all political action. The most regrettable feature of the incident was that it lent colour to the belief, already widely current among the Southern Slavs, that the Monarch showed a marked preference for the Magyars and disliked the Croats. This unhappy legend will meet us on a later occasion.

A lifelong desire of Bishop Strossmayer was to survive the expulsion of the Turks from Europe, and thus to witness what seemed to him the just retribution for the sufferings inflicted upon his race and his religion. Hence the rising in Bosnia, which formed a titular dependency of his diocese, commanded his whole sympathies and interest. He never lost an opportunity of pleading the cause of the Southern Slavs, whether Bosnia, Servia or Bulgaria were involved ; and by means of his numerous connexions with eminent Frenchmen, he was able to influence very materially French public opinion during

[198] The Chauvinist Coloman Tisza, notorious for his constant violations of the Croatian Compromise and the Law of Nationalities, was then Premier of Hungary (1875–90).

the Eastern crisis. Through the medium of Lord Acton, he entered into correspondence with Mr. Gladstone, and in a series of effective if rhetorical letters expressed his gratitude for the famous pamphlet on "Bulgarian Atrocities" and advocated the liberation and autonomy of the Christian peoples of the Balkans.[199]   It is interesting to note that while in 1876 he urged upon Gladstone that Bosnia should be placed under the protection of Servia, in February, 1878 (soon after the Congress had been decided upon), he already recognized this solution to be impracticable, and favoured the complete autonomy of Bosnia and the cession of Old Servia to Servia by way of compensation. It is impossible not to regret that nothing ever came of his tentative suggestion that he should appear before the Congress to plead the cause of his Bosnian kinsmen. The sight of the great Christian orator before that distinguished gathering of diplomatic freebooters would have afforded equal food for reflection to the cynic and the moralist.

In the following year he expresses his fears lest Austria may introduce into the occupied provinces her old superannuated system, instead of fulfilling her natural mission as the bulwark between Slav and Teuton. Though he "would gladly give his life to save this splendid state," he considered Austria under present conditions less likely to allay complications than to introduce into every question the seed of future discord. In his view the real evil lay in Magyar predominance in the counsels of the state, and in that race's policy "of blind hatred towards the Slavs"; and he had therefore openly deplored the influence exerted by Andrássy upon Disraeli during the Eastern Crisis. In December, 1878, he agreed with M. de Laveleye in regarding Austrian rule in Bosnia as a necessity : "but whether it will be an advantage to Austria will depend upon the policy adopted. If Vienna, or rather Pest, means to govern the new provinces by Hungarians or Germans, and for their profit, the Austrians will finish by being more hated than the Turks."[200]   He was ready to re-echo the cry of the Slovak patriot Hodža in 1848, "Rather the Russians than the Magyars." It was only in this sense that Strossmayer was a Pan-Slav. In the true political significance of the word, he was anything but Pan-Slav. Like Palacky and many other dis-

[199] Strossmayer and Gladstone never met, though a meeting was more than once arranged by their mutual friends, and thus the encounter between Bossuet and Leibnitz, to which the Bishop playfully alludes in one of his letters, remained a dream.

[200] Laveleye, op. cit. pp. 30–31.

tinguished Slavs in the Habsburg Monarchy, he believed it the mission of Austria, and desired to see her great and prosperous. It was his misfortune that his faith in Austria was greater than the faith of those who controlled her destiny, and the bitter disillusionments of his political career would have amply excused an attitude of open hostility on his part. If he still hoped for a brighter future, this was due not to any signs of statesmanship in Vienna—for this the Magyars monopolized till the close of Strossmayer's long life—but solely to the unconquerable optimism of the Christian prelate.

We may conclude this sketch of Bishop Strossmayer's career by quoting the personal impressions of M. de Laveleye on the occasion of their first meeting. " He appeared to me like a saint of the Middle Ages, such as Fra Angelico painted on the walls of the cells of San Marco in Florence. His face was refined, thin, ascetic ; his light hair, brushed back, surrounded his head like a halo ; his grey eyes were clear, luminous, inspired. A sharp yet gentle flame beamed from them, the reflection of a great intellect and a noble heart. His speech is easy, glowing, full of imagery ; but although he speaks French, German, Italian and Latin besides the Slav languages, with equal ease, no one of these dialects can furnish him with terms sufficiently expressive for the complete rendering of his thought, and so he uses them by turns. He takes from each the word, the epithet, he needs, or he even uses the synonyms that come from them all. It is when he finally arrives at Latin that his sentences flow with unequalled breadth and power. He says precisely what he thinks, without reticence, without diplomatic reserve, with the abandon of a child and the insight of genius. Entirely devoted to his country, desiring nothing for himself, he fears no one here below ; as he seeks only what he believes to be good, just and true, he has nothing to conceal." [201]

The great Bishop died, at the age of ninety, on April 10, 1905, on the eve of a new political era in Croatia. As a politician, he lacked balance and restraint, and was swayed by sentiment to an excessive degree. But as an intellectual and moral force, as the patron and inspirer of thought and culture, his influence upon Croatia and the Southern Slav world cannot be exaggerated. As Jellačić typifies the military prowess and loyalty of the Croat, so Strossmayer stands for those qualities of faith and romantic idealism for which the best sons of the race have been distinguished.

[201] Op. cit. p. 30.

CHAPTER VII

An Outline of Croat and Serb Literature

Non erunt ultra duae gentes, nec dividentur in duo regna ; sed fiet unum ovile et unus pastor.—*Križanić*.[202]

BEFORE we return to the less congenial atmosphere of modern politics, it may be well to lay before the reader a brief outline of literary development among the Croats and Serbs.

In striking contrast to many politicians, who seem to take a malicious delight in magnifying imaginary differences, the whole tendency of Southern Slav philologists and literary historians has been directed towards a unified language for the Croat and Serb race. In theory this has already been attained, and to-day every savant whose researches and opinions carry the slightest weight are unanimous in regarding " the Serbo-Croat language," as they prefer to call it, as a literary unit. Indeed, in the field of literature Croat and Serb are but two names for one and the same language, whose divergences of dialect are mainly the result of geography, not of racial or religious distribution. The Croats use the Latin alphabet, modified in accordance with the rules of modern Bohemian orthography, the Serbs, the Cyrillic alphabet as reformed by Vuk Karadžić ; other distinction there is none. But the artificial barrier of the rival alphabets has prevented the consciousness of their essential unity from extending beyond the small educated minority.

As there lurks behind this distinction " the religious Dualism (Catholicism, Orthodoxy) and the Dualism of name (Croat, Serb) with divergent ideals for the future, the external trappings assume a deeper significance than the parallel use of two alphabets in the German language. Indeed, the masses of the people still look upon the literary products of *one* alphabet

[202] So runs the prophecy of one of the earliest Croat writers.

only as their spiritual possession, thereby reducing by half not merely the circulation but also the capacity for production.[203] Instead of a single literature possessed by a race of seven or eight millions, which under favourable circumstances could do splendid work, there really still exist two smaller literatures, each with three to four million adherents." [204]

The Serbo-Croat language falls into three main dialects which are distinguished by the varying form of the word " what," as the " ča," the " što," and the " kaj." The last of these is spoken in north-west Croatia, from the neighbourhood of Karlstadt to the river Mur, and forms the link between Serbo-Croat and Slovene. The first (ča) is confined to Istria, North Dalmatia, the Croatian seacoast, the Dalmatian islands. The central or što-dialect is the most extensively spoken— throughout Slavonia, South-east Croatia, South Hungary, Servia, Bosnia, Herzegovina, South Dalmatia and Montenegro, and now occupies a dominant position in the literature of the race. It is spoken in its purest form in Herzegovina,[205] which

[203] Incredible as it must appear to any foreigner, there is no Anthology in existence which includes both Croat and Serb poets within the same covers. The admirable *Hrvatska Antologija* contains the best work of Preradović, Mažuranić and other Croat poets ; for the Vladika Peter and Jovanović we must go to Serb collections. The two are kept in airtight compartments by what can only be described as childishly provincial bigotry.

A *reductio ad absurdum* of this artificial barrier is supplied by an ostensibly scientific essay published by the " Club of the Starčevićian Academic Youth," in other words, by a group of schoolboys, who in Croatia, instead of rowing and playing football, are encouraged to dabble in politics and to waste their time squabbling in cafés. ' At the present day '—so runs the argument—' almost all savants are of opinion that the Croatian language should be called ' Croat or Serb,' and this phrase has found its way even into the Croatian schools. The Club, on the contrary, being of opinion that such a description is radically false, has requested Mr. G. to treat this question in detail, and this pamphlet is the result.' Mr. G. argues that unity of accent is the best test of unity of language, and as the " što " and " ča " dialects differ greatly in accent, they are two different languages! The name " Serb " is just as false as the name " Bosnian." This sort of rubbish is seriously encouraged by the Frank Party. (*See* Prilog poznavanja akcenatske teorije Mažuranićeve u obziru na komentatorska domišljanja, Zagreb, 1907.)

[204] Jagić, *Die slavischen Sprachen*, p. 22 (Kultur der Gegenwart, vol. ix).
[205] Three sub-dialects can be distinguished, according to pronunciation, e.g. the word for " beautiful " is lijep (lee-ape) in Herzegovina, Montenegro, South Dalmatia ; lep (lape) in Servia ; lip (leep) in Slavonia, Bosnia. This last is no longer written at all, and only the first is regarded as literary. Jagić, p. 26.

is celebrated as the Tuscany of the Southern Slavs, and this fact is admitted by all sections of the race. But the comparative ease with which this dialect won its recognized position was due at least in part to the proximity of Herzegovina to the Republic of Ragusa, which witnessed the first important development of Croat literature. The chief characteristic of the language is its close adherence to the speech of the people : the purest style is that which reflects this most faithfully.

The earliest literature of the Southern Slavs is liturgical in character. The Glagolitic manuscripts of the Adriatic coast-line, the miraculous lives of Servian saints, and the laws of Stephen Dušan are the only literary landmarks of the Middle Ages. The destruction of the Slav states of the Balkans by the Turks arrested all development at the very moment when culture and education were beginning to flourish; and the ignorance and stagnation of the Orthodox Church completed what Turkish barbarism had begun. But the downfall of Servian independence produced a splendid crop of ballad poetry, rude, irregular, but spontaneous and inspired, brimming over from the heart of a proud and unhappy people, and unequalled in Europe save by the Spanish Cid and the bards of the Scottish Border. The whole cycle of ballads is dominated by the fatal defeat of Kossovo, the Flodden of the Balkans, and by the mythical figures of its heroes—Marko Kraljević, the *preux chevalier* of Southern Slav legend ; Miloš Obilić, unjustly charged with treachery and sealing his loyalty with the Sultan's blood ; Vuk Branković, the real traitor, trusted and deceiving, branded by a whole nation's curse. But above all others towers Marko, with his giant frame and charmed life, typifying by his deeds of prowess the ideals of a primitive people, by his death the political death of the nation, by his enchanted slumber its resurrection and future freedom. Such poetry, as an English poet has justly observed, has its origin " not in the heads of a few, but in the hearts of all." " It is the sword of a Crusader in the scabbard of a Turk." [206]

The situation of Dalmatia on the border line between Slav and Latin culture, exposed that province to the influence of the Italian Renaissance and gave it a natural pre-eminence over its kinsmen under Turkish sway. Marko Marulić, a native of Spalato, whose epic poem *Judith* was completed in 1501

[206] " Owen Meredith " (Robert, Earl of Lytton), *Serbski Pesme*, p. x (1861, London).

131

and first printed in 1521, is regarded as "the father of Croat literature," though he himself speaks of earlier poets. But the real cradle of Serbo-Croat literature is the tiny Republic of Ragusa, which by the middle of the sixteenth century was the only fragment of Southern Slav territory which could boast its complete freedom from foreign rule. Its earlier group of poets, whose work was closely modelled on the Italian lyrics and dramas of the late Renaissance from Sannazaro and Politian to Tasso, does not call for comment here. But Ivan Gundulić (1588–1638) demands recognition not merely as the eulogist of that miniature Venice, the gem of medieval Slav towns, but as the first great poet of the Slavonic world. His pastoral play *Dubravka* is modelled on the *Aminta* of Tasso ; but so far from being a mere slavish imitation, treats in a highly original manner the congenial theme of Ragusan liberties. But his masterpiece is the romantic epic *Osman*, which celebrates the struggle of the Cross against the Crescent and the services rendered by the Slav nations in the cause of Christendom. Here again the analogy with Tasso's *Gerusalemme Liberata* is more apparent than real. Gundulić's choice of the octosyllabic metre gives the poem an entirely different flavour, and his fervent, not to say fanatical, Catholicism deterred him from adapting Tasso's fantastic device of a Christian hero as the lover of an infidel. *Osman* is more modern in spirit and construction, and shows real insight into the Turkish character. On its own merits as a work of imaginative genius, it can hardly be compared to its more famous Italian rival ; but when we consider the linguistic difficulties with which its author had to contend and the relative positions of the Italian and Croat languages in his day, we must admit *Osman* to be a work of extraordinary merit.

Gundulić was followed in Ragusa by numerous minor poets ; but the dreadful earthquake of 1667 proved as fatal to the Republic's literary activity as to its commercial prosperity. The censorship which Venice exercised in her Dalmatian dominions and the absence of a printing press on the eastern side of the Adriatic,[207] checked all literary progress in Dalmatia

---

[207] Even Ragusa, from fear of the Turks, printed its books in Italy. Murko, *Die südslavische Literatur* (Kultur der Gegenwart), p. 216.

Baron John Ungnad, the former Governor of Styria, established printing presses in Tübingen and Urach for Southern Slav books, especially in the Glagolitic and Cyrilline alphabets. The object was to

until quite modern times. To this statement there is one brilliant exception—the Franciscan friar, Andrew Kačić, from the neighbourhood of Makarska, who may be regarded as a link between the poets of Ragusa and the modern popular school. During his numerous journeys through Bosnia as a Papal legate, he gathered ancient manuscripts and charters, and listened to the recitations of peasant bards. In 1759 he published a collection of his own poems entitled *Pleasant Sonversations of the Slav People* (Razgovor Ugodni naroda Slovinskoga), afterwards known under the simpler title of *The Book of Songs* (Pjesmarica). In it he celebrates the exploits of Croat, Serb and Bulgar heroes, adhering so closely to popular lines of thought and expression. His book enjoyed immense popularity, and marked out the lines which Vuk Karadžić was to follow sixty years later in his linguistic reforms. The folk-songs scattered through its pages came under the notice of Herder when he was preparing his " Songs of the Nations," and so introduced the popular poetry of the Serbs for the first time to the Western world.

Meanwhile in Croatia there was no favourable field for literary effort ; the whole life of the nation was absorbed by the struggle against the Turks. But two outstanding figures of Croatian history in the seventeenth century left a literary legacy behind them. Francis Frankopan beguiled the last weeks of his imprisonment by composing songs, and his kins-man and fellow-conspirator Count Peter Zrinjsky, published Croat paraphrases of the Magyar poems of his brother Nicholas —*The Siren of the Adriatic* and the *Siege of Sziget*, which cele-brates the exploits and death of their heroic ancestor. The interest which these versions possess is chiefly historical and political.

The eighteenth century is equally barren in literary achieve-ment. The only figure which deserves mention by the side of Kačić is Matthew Reljković, an officer in the Military Frontiers, who was captured by the Prussians during the Seven Years' War and employed his captivity in comparing the situation of his own country to that of the civilized West. The result of his observations was published in the form of a lengthy epic, composed in decasyllables and bearing the strange title of *The Satyr or the Wild Man* (Satir ili divlji čovjek, 1761,

Protestantize the Southern Slavs and through them the whole Balkan Peninsula.—Murko, p. 217.

Dresden). In spite of its didactic tone, its commonplace ideas, and the depreciatory terms in which it refers to many popular customs, Reljković's work enjoyed a popularity almost as great as that of the Franciscan friar.

Napoleon's Illyrian experiment, while responsible for a revival of literary effort among the Slovenes, produced no immediate effect upon the Croats. Nor was Servia's recovery of independence accompanied by any outburst of poetic talent. The vivifying force which led to a literary revival in the nineteenth century, came from among the Serbs ; but it was the Serbs of Hungary, Slavonia and Bosnia, not those of the young principality. We have already seen that Dositej Obradović, the founder of education in Servia, was a native of the Banat. But his autobiography and other didactic works, despite the enormous influence which they undoubtedly exercised in so barren a field as Turk-ridden Servia, do not possess a high literary value and are essentially for his own age rather than for posterity.

A far greater figure was the linguistic reformer Vuk Stefanović Karadzić, best known as Vuk. Born in 1787 at a small village on the frontier between Servia and Bosnia, he acted during the first rising against the Turks as an interpreter of letters to the illiterate Serb commander of his district. But when in 1813 Kara George was forced for a time to abandon the struggle, Vuk found his way to Vienna, and at the instance of Kopitar, the foremost Slavistic scholar of his day, devoted himself to the collection and study of Serb popular poetry and stories. In 1814 he published a hundred of these popular lyrics and six of the " Hero-Songs " (Junačke Pesme) which fill so large a place in the imagination of the Serb and Croat people. A book of such marked originality could not fail to attract attention, and the romantic movement in the West, then at its height, welcomed the popular poetry of the Serbs and made it possible to publish ten years later in Leipzig a greatly enlarged edition in four volumes. Inspired by the purity of language and classic turn of phrase which he found in the ballads and songs of the people, Vuk set himself the task of elevating the vernacular to the position of the literary language and thus superseding the conventional and artificial language which owed its survival to the favour of the Church authorities. To this end he introduced phonetic reforms into the old Cyrillic alphabet, consistently following the principle that a language should be written as it is spoken, and conversely pronounced as it is written. His first grammar, based upon the Herzegovinian dialect, appeared in 1814. But the most decisive influence was exercised by his great Serb dictionary (Srpski Riječnik) published four years later at Vienna. The first edition contained 26,000 words, the second edition over 20,000 more, and is a rich mine for the study not merely of literary evolution, but of folklore and ethnography. For many years Vuk travelled through the various Serb countries gathering fresh material; and the result of his journeys was a whole series of popular tales, proverbs, anecdotes, songs and ballads, which have long since become models of Serbo-Croat literary style. His reforming ideas were bitterly resented by the older generation, especially by the Orthodox clergy, who until very recent times have always opposed every form of innovation. The opposition centred round the Srpska Matica, the earliest Serb literary society, which was founded at Pest in 1826 by Hadžić-Svetić.[208] Yet despite the prestige enjoyed by his opponents and the violence with which he was attacked, Vuk persevered in his course, and strong in the support of all the chief philologists from Kopitar and Grimm to Dobrovsky and Šafařik, he gradually won over to his side the whole of the younger generation. Some idea of the difficulties with which he had to contend may be gathered from the fact that in 1832 his orthography was actually forbidden in Servia and that from 1852 to 1860 even his works were not allowed.[209] But long before his death in 1864, the ideas of Vuk had triumphed; the final blow to the old theories was administered by his brilliant pupil, George Daničić in his *Struggle for the Serb Language* (Rat za srprski jezik, 1847). The same writer, a Serb from Slavonia, and for many years Secretary of the Southern Slav Academy in Agram, gave a practical form to his advocacy of linguistic reform by his eloquent Serb version of the Bible.

A contemporary of Vuk, Simon Milutinović (1791–1847), is the first Serb poet of note whom Bosnia has produced. Born in Sarajevo, he studied in Belgrad and Karlovitz, but afterwards spent a number of years in Germany, where he aroused the interest of Goethe for Serb ballad poetry,[210] became the friend of Grimm and Uhland, and supplied considerable material for Therese von Jakob, who under the pseudonym of

[208] In 1864 it was transferred to Neusatz after the long feud had been decided in Vuk's favour.
[209] Murko, p. 225.
[210] See Geothes Werke, Band xxxvii.

" Talvj " won a high reputation as the pioneer of Slav literary history in western lands. His epic *Srbijanka* is an attempt to achieve for the Servian war of independence what the heroic lays of Kossovo had achieved for that gloomier period of the nation's history. Despite certain obvious faults of style and expression, it was the first poem which could challenge comparison with the *Osman* of Gundulić. The influence of Milutinović, who spent five years in Montenegro before finally settling at Belgrad, inspired his pupil, the future Vladika, Peter II, with a love of poetry, which was soon to bear splendid fruit. This prince, one of the most talented of a long succession of able rulers, is still regarded by many Servians as their foremost poet. His first important poem, which bears the unpromising title of *The Light of the Microcosm*, was composed under the influence of Milton's *Paradise Lost*. But in his later epic *The Mountain Garland* (Gorski Vijenac) he discards philosophy for action, with the most admirable results. Its subject is the Montenegrin struggle for liberty, which culminated in a famous massacre of the Moslem population in 1702.[211] The poem cannot be assigned to any special category : in the strict sense it is neither a drama nor an epic. But as a revelation of Montenegrin character, as a glowing panegyric of one of the few primitive peoples of the West, it ranks high in Serbo-Croat literature. How unfavourable the conditions of Montenegro were to poetic talent, can best be realized from the fact that Peter II found it necessary to melt down the type of his newly-erected printing press as bullets for the Turkish war. Yet the tradition survived in his own family, and his nephew, Prince (now King) Nicholas, achieved wide fame by his patriotic drama, *The Empress of the Balkans* (Balkanska Carica), which has sometimes been regarded as indicating the direction of its author's ambition.

While Prince Peter celebrated the glories of the Black Mountain, Agram became the centre of a remarkable literary renaissance, best known as " The Illyrian movement." Its founder, Ljudevit Gaj (1809–1872) had studied law in Vienna, Graz and Pest, and in the latter capital fell under the influence of the Slovak poet John Kollár, the apostle of " literary reciprocity among all Slav nations."[212] Though full of ideas and

[211] Sometimes known as the " Montenegrin Vespers," by analogy with the Massacre of Sicilian Vespers in 1282.

[212] For an account of Kollár and his works *see* my *Racial Problems in Hungary*, pp. 51–57.

enthusiasm, Gaj had no great literary talent. His function was that of the agitator and journalistic pioneer. His faculty for catching the popular fancy is illustrated by his patriotic song, " Still Croatia is not fallen, while we are yet alive " ; frankly imitated from the famous Polish hymn, and set to a peculiarly haunting melody, it became the " Marseillaise " of Illyrism, and is still one of Croatia's chief national airs. But its literary value is very slight indeed, and his other writings are in no way superior. In the field of orthography and grammar, however, his reforms are almost as important for the Croats as those of Vuk for the Serbs. Based upon the što-dialect and upon the rules of orthography observed among the Czechs, Gaj's reforms were adopted without any serious opposition. His efforts to attain literary unity were of course inspired by the dream of the political union of all Southern Slavs. He was in many respects ahead of his age, and though his ultimate aim is still far from attainment, the immediate object is already an accomplished fact, and his ideal seems less fantastic to-day than it seemed seventy years ago. But his spirit is more needed than ever in the past, to combat the petty forces of provincial conceit and jealousy, which form the great hindrance to progress among the Southern Slavs.

The first real poet of Croat romanticism was Stanko Vraz (1810–1851), who, though a Slovene by birth, wrote all his lyrics in the Croat language. Though an enthusiast for popular poetry, he was under the influence of the romantic poets of the west, and endeavoured to introduce foreign forms of lyrical expression. His contemporary, Ivan Mažuranić (1813–1890), afterwards Ban of Croatia, won the heart of the nation by his noble epic *The Death of Čengić Aga* (Smrt Smail-Aga Čengić), which in a highly dramatic form depicts an incident of the long struggle between Turk and Montenegrin. The poem strangely blends those elements of grim savagery and Christian heroism which the desperate nature of the struggle called forth. A splendid sense of rhythm and a delight in onomatopeic phrases, are further characteristics of the poem. Mažuranić added to his reputation by supplying the two missing cantos of Gundulić's *Osman*—a masterpiece of imitative skill.

The primacy among Croat poets, however, falls to Peter Preradović (1818–1872), an Austrian officer who had originally dabbled in German poetry and only discovered in middle life the possibilities of his native tongue. One of his finest lyrics, *The Wanderer* (Putnik) describes in allegorical phrases his return to national consciousness. His poetry breathes an atmosphere of calm reflection and ripe thought, which only render the more impressive his passionate belief in the future of the race. His intimate friend, Ivan Trnski (1819–1909) also enjoys a high reputation as a lyrical poet and as the translator of many foreign classics ; but his work is less spontaneous in tone and shows traces of artificiality. Meanwhile, Fra Grgo Martić (1822–1902) became the mouthpiece of national feeling among the Croats of Bosnia. His pathetic lyric *The Tears of Bosnia* (Plač Bosne) and his long—indeed, well-nigh interminable—epic *The Avengers* (Ostvetnici), make him a worthy successor of that earlier Franciscan Kačić. But his work is extremely uneven and lends itself to abridgment.

Among the Serbs the most brilliant poet of the last half-century has been Jovan Jovanović (1833–1904), christened Zmaj (or " Dragon ") by his admiring countrymen. Zmaj betrays his origin as a Hungarian Serb ; the great Magyar lyrist Petöfi is one of his favourite models, though it would be useless to pretend that he attains to Petöfi's fiery excellence. In later years Zmaj devoted himself to writing poems for children, and did much to encourage literature for the young in Servia. Other Serb poets of real talent are George Jakšić (1832–1878) and Laza Kostić (born 1841), author of the first Serb drama *Maksim Crnojević* and translator of several plays of Shakespeare.

Dalmatia, the earliest home of Serbo-Croat literature, was the last province to be affected by the revival of the nineteenth century. Count Medo Pučić (1821–1882), the scion of an ancient Ragusan family, and a poet in whom the Italian influences of his native town were strongly marked, was for many years a solitary figure in Dalmatian literature. But he is not without worthy successors. Count Ivo Vojnović, in a brilliant dramatic trilogy (Dubrovačka Trilogija) celebrated the dying glories of the Republic of Ragusa, while his brother treated the same subject from the standpoint of a historian. Antony Tresić-Pavičić (born 1867) [213] in his lyrical poetry, seeks classic and Italian models, and shows remarkable rhythmic gifts and a love for rich effects of sound and colour. He has attempted the drama with considerable success, taking for his theme the fall of the Roman Republic. In Bosnia Tugomir Alaupović

[213] Since 1907 member of the Austrian Reichsrath for his native island of Lesina (with Brazza).

(born 1873) has attracted attention by his pessimistic verse. The revival of Croatian poetry was followed by the appearance of a number of prosewriters, who compare favourably with those of most smaller European nations. Their leader, August Šenoa (1838–1881) may not unfairly be described as the Scott of Croatia, his historical novels illustrating with great force the romantic vicissitudes of his country's history. *The Goldsmith's Daughter, The Peasant's War, Beware of Zengg*, and many others reveal Šenoa as a born storyteller, whose complete mastery of plot and description rivets the attention of the reader and assures him a high and enduring place among modern novelists. A shorter story entitled *The Flower from the Poet's Grave* (Karamfil sa pjesnikova groba) is a charming love idyll skilfully contrived to honour the memory of the Slovene poet Prešeren ; the charming style and breezy atmosphere of this little book would of themselves suffice to win him a niche in Croat literature. Unhappily an early death carried him off at the very height of his activity.

An equally prolific novelist was Joseph Tomić (1843–1906), whose chief works are *The Dragon of Bosnia* and *For King and Home*, and who completed Šenoa's unfinished novel *The Curse*. In the eighties French naturalism found its way into Croatia ; its first notable exponent was Eugene Kumičić (1850–1904), who after publishing a number of novels of almost Zolaesque brutality, reverted in his later years to the historical romance (*The Conspiracy* and *Zrinski and Frankopan*). Ljubomir Babić-Gjalski (born 1854), whose novels have been translated into several languages, is in certain respects the Paul Bourget of Croatia. His love of psychological problems shows to best advantage in his short stories, which are full of French influence, despite their national character (*Janko Borislavić, Dawn, Mors, Radmilović*). Other favourite writers are the satirist A. Kovačić, Joseph Kozarac (born 1858) (*Dead Capital, Three Loves*) and the realist Janko Leskovar (*Ruined Courts*). As was to be expected, the influence of the modern Russian novel is strong and increasing among the Croats.[214]

Unlike the Croats and the Bulgars, among whom Ivan Vazov (born 1850) ranks very high as a story-teller, the Serbs are weak in fiction. Their only novelist of importance is Laza

---

[214] An excellent idea of the modern Croatian novel can be obtained from a collection of stories by various authors (*Hrvatski Pripovjedači*, Zagreb, 1908) well edited by the rising dramatist, Milan Ogrizović.

CROAT AND SERB LITERATURE

Lazarević, who as a country doctor acquired an intimate knowledge of the patriarchal peasant life which still prevails in Servia, and depicted it in a number of admirable short stories. A new period is about to open in Serbo-Croat literature. The absurd cleavage which owes its origin to the misfortune of a dual alphabet, and which has been fostered by unfavourable political conditions, is becoming more unreal with every year. A growing perception of the essential unity of race and language is spreading among Croat and Serb alike, and the old barriers of provincialism and prejudice are slowly yielding to a wider outlook upon life.

NOTE UPON CROATIAN MUSIC AND ART

The Croats have a music of their own, which though it cannot compare with that of Bohemia, is not without charm and originality. The first composer of real merit was Vatroslav Lisinski (1819–1846), who harmonized many of the most popular folksongs, and wrote, in addition to choral music, two important operas, *Porin* and *Ljubov i zloba* (Love and Spite). The most prolific and at the same time the most popular Croat composer was Ivan Zajc (1834–1906), who in 1874 became Director of the Croatian Opera in Agram. His best known operas are *Nicholas Zrinski*, *Lizinka*, *Zlatka*, *Man the Decks* ; but his choral compositions are quite as attractive (e.g. *Evening on the Save*).

Franjo Kuhač (b. 1834) deserves mention as an untiring collector of Southern Slav and Balkan folksongs and dances. In recent years Felix Albini, a Croat with Italian name, has won popularity by the charming operetta *Baron Trenck*, which was well received abroad. In the summer of 1911 it appeared in London in a very mangled form, charmingly staged, but with the characteristic national songs and dances either omitted or consigned to the background.

The fine opera house and theatre—probably the finest in Europe for a town of Agram's size—was completed in 1896, and is the focus of Serbo-Croat music and drama.

In curious contrast to Croatia, the Dalmatian Croats and the Serbs are the least musical of the Slav races. Their national instrument, the gusla, creates an atmosphere of its own, peculiarly suited to the recitative of peasant bards ; but though impressive, it is in no sense musical. An exception must be made in favour of the Serb *Kolo*, one of the most fascinating dances in Europe.

Croatian Art is older than is generally realized abroad. Carpaccio and Schiavone, and Michelangelo's pupil, the miniature painter Clovio, were Croats by birth, though of course their genius was entirely merged in the Italian schools of art. The first names on the roll of modern Croat artists are two Dalmatians—Vlaho Bukovac (b. 1855) and Celestine Medović (b. 1851), both of whom have won recognition in Paris and elsewhere abroad. Another Dalmatian, Ivan Rendić, and Robert Frangeš, are popular sculptors, the former being best known for his sepulchral monuments. For many years Bukovac occupied a dominant position in Art at Agram ; and a number of

ART AND MUSIC

promising pupils owe much to his influence, without adhering at all closely to his ideas—e.g., Ivan Tišov (decorative frescoes), Ferd. Kovačević, Robert Auer (nude studies), Iveković, Crnčić (charming landscapes of the Adriatic coast), Rački (remarkable Dantesque studies). The annual exhibitions in the Art Salon of Agram are quite worthy of attention. A small group of able artists has established itself at Spalato in Dalmatia (Vidović, Katunarić, Meneghello) and publishes a comic illustrated paper *Duje Balavac*. The most remarkable figure in modern Croat art is the young Dalmatian sculptor, Ivan Meštrović, who bids fair to become the Rodin of the Southern Slav world. His wonderful series of figures for a Southern Slav Valhalla, has been recognized by the Italian Press as one of the chief features of the Art Section at this year's Exhibition in Rome.

CHAPTER VIII

The Resolution of Fiume and its Consequences (1905-1908)

THE Hungarian crisis, which was directly responsible for Count Khuen Héderváry's resignation as Ban, now began to influence very materially the course of events in Croatia. Even under Baron Bánffy's premiership (1898) the Party of Independence, which led the Opposition in the Hungarian Parliament, had indulged in obstructive tactics and provoked a so-called Ex-Lex condition in Hungary by preventing the passing of the Budget. As personal motives played an important part in the struggle, the substitution of Mr. Coloman Széll for Baron Bánffy restored peace for some years. But in 1902 Széll's proposals for an increase in the number of recruits led to a fresh outburst of obstruction, more violent than any which had gone before. The year 1903 saw a renewal of the ex-lex condition. For six months obstruction was rampant, and at length Széll, disappointed in his belief that the Opposition would " talk itself quiet," saw no alternative but to resign office. Count Khuen Héderváry, on succeeding to the premiership, made a provisional arrangement with the Opposition ; but within a few weeks the truce was broken, and the implication of his friend, Count Ladislas Szapáry, then Governor of Fiume, in a sordid case of political bribery, rendered the new Premier's position untenable and led to his resignation (August 10, 1903). Meanwhile the demands put forward by the Party of Independence for ultra-Magyar " national " concessions in the Army, had thoroughly alarmed the dynasty, and were met on September 16—while the Khuen Cabinet was still conducting affairs, pending the appointment of a successor—by the famous Army order of Chlopy,[215] in which His Majesty roundly declared that he would never surrender the military powers which the constitution of the Dual Monarchy assured to him. The excitement aroused in Hun-

[215] So-called from the small Bohemian village at which the Emperor dated the Order during the autumn manœuvres of 1903.

gary by this emphatic document spurred on the Opposition to fresh obstruction, and the new Cabinet, which was formed in November, 1903, by Count Stephen Tisza, soon found itself obliged to attempt a revision of the Standing Orders of the House, as the sole means of checking parliamentary anarchy. It was not, however, till October, 1904, that Tisza proceeded in earnest to this revision ; but when his proposals were at length laid before the House, the Opposition attempted to make discussion impossible. On November 17, 1904, a motion for holding two sittings daily was carried by a bare majority, and Count Albert Apponyi, speaking in the name of the whole Opposition, declined to respect this decision of the House. This parliamentary revolution was followed next day by a counter-revolution of the majority, the motion for reform being passed on an improvised vote.

Parliament was at once prorogued, and when it met again on December 13, the Opposition wrecked the House and rendered all debate impossible. At this critical moment Count Tisza, who had frankly admitted the illegality of the means adopted to secure reform, but had sought to justify them on the plea of necessity and *raison d'état*, now suddenly reverted to the strict constitutional view and appealed to the country. The general elections of January, 1905, resulted in the overthrow of the Liberal Party, which had ruled Hungary since 1876. The Party of Independence secured 166 seats, the minor Opposition groups 72, [216] and the Liberals only 159 ; Count Tisza was therefore faced by a hostile Coalition[217] of 231 deputies, and placed his resignation in the King's hands. For some months negotiations were conducted between the Crown and the Coalition, but as the latter persisted in dictating terms for the acceptance of office while the former sought to curtail the programme of his future ministers, no agreement could be reached, and on June 19, 1905, Baron Géza Fejérváry, an old soldier who had held the portfolio of National Defence in several Liberal cabinets, was appointed

---

[216] The so-called Dissidents 27 ; the People's Party (Clerical) 25 ; the New Party 13. There were also 10 Nationalists, 2 Democrats, 2 Socialists and 10 non-party.

[217] In November, 1904, after the parliamentary *coup d'état* the four Opposition groups—the Party of Independence under Mr. Francis Kossuth and Count Albert Apponyi, the Dissidents or Constitutional Party under Count Julius Andrássy, the People's Party under Count Aladar Zichy, and the New Party under Baron Desiderius Bánffy formed themselves into the since famous Coalition.

Premier with a number of little known permanent officials as his ministers. The new Cabinet, being without a majority in Parliament, could only govern by repeated prorogations, and the political situation remained obscure and precarious.

This brief outline of the course of events in Hungary supplies the clue to the political transformation in Croatia which took place under Count Theodore Pejačević. The decay of the Liberal party in Hungary was accompanied by a corresponding decay of its ally the " National " party in Croatia. Their principles, or rather their lack of principles, were similar, and so also were the methods which they employed. In each country successive governments found that an Opposition, tied to a programme so extreme as to be utterly impracticable, was often convenient rather than embarrassing, since it could be used by the authorities in Agram and Budapest against Budapest and Vienna respectively. In Croatia a skilful policy of playing off rival races and party factions against each other and of enforcing a strict political discipline upon every rank of officialdom, had resulted in a prolonged period of stagnation ; but the withdrawal of Count Khuen released forces which had till then been pent up, and the seething cauldron at once emitted steam.

The younger generation in Croatia showed a marked revulsion of feeling in favour of Serbo-Croat friendship, and this tendency was powerfully supported by public opinion in Dalmatia. Mr. Supilo's organ, *Novi List*, which had already won the ear of Croatian patriots by its onslaughts upon Khuen at a time when the press of Agram was effectively muzzled [218]— a Dalmatian leader once not inaptly described it to me as " a dumping place for all new and modern ideas "—now became the chief champion in the press of the idea of Croato-Serb unity. After preparing the ground for some months with great

[218] *Novi List,* being published in Fiume, is subject to the Hungarian Press law which, however susceptible of reactionary interpretation, is at any rate infinitely more liberal than the Croatian press law. Mr. Supilo had originally been editor of *Crvena Hrvatska,* a small weekly newspaper published at Ragusa in the interests of the Party of Right. In 1900 he left Ragusa for Sušak, where he founded a daily paper called *Naša Sloga.* Its main idea was opposition to the Khuen régime, its owners being Ružić, Erasmus Barčić and other wealthy Croats in and around Fiume. In order to evade the muzzling to which Count Khuen subjected the Croatian press, the paper was transferred to Fiume and re-christened *Novi List.* It soon became the leader of the Opposition Press.

skill and caution, it then began to blend the idea of unity with attacks upon Austria and the Viennese " Camarilla," and to prepare the way for a *modus vivendi* with the Magyars. The Dalmatian leaders, who represented the real driving force in this new movement, were far-sighted enough to realize the advantages which Croatia might reap from Magyar party dissensions. Disillusioned and alienated by the rebuff which they had received in Vienna, and interpreting it in the light of a century of past history, they drew the conclusion that no help was to be expected from Austria, who would at the last moment give way to the Magyars, as she had invariably done at every crisis of the past fifty years.[219] With a strange mixture of naïveté and ' slimness,' of lofty idealism and political cynicism, they dreamt of a Southern Slav millennium, as the direct consequence of their alliance with the Magyars, and flattered themselves that they could beat that race of born politicians at its own game. Better at any rate, they argued, to help the Magyars at their need, and thus win the right to share the spoils of victory, than to commit themselves on the side of Austria and then to be left a prey to the incensed Magyars,[220] under circumstances even more unfavourable to Croatia than those of the years 1867, 1883 and 1903.

Mr. Supilo and his friends realized clearly that they need expect nothing from the Liberal party, already on its deathbed, and that the " National " party in Croatia was so closely linked with the Liberals and so impervious to new ideas that the enterprise must be undertaken without its help ; they therefore devoted their attention to the Magyar Opposition parties, whom they knew to be eagerly searching on all sides (both at home and abroad) for allies in their struggle against Vienna. Meanwhile in order to prepare public opinion for so striking a change of tactics, they publicly mooted in Dalmatia

[219] About this time a mischievous legend found its way from mouth to mouth and found wide belief among the credulous Southern Slavs— to the effect that the Emperor, in conversation with a distinguished General, had remarked, *Die Kroaten—das sind Fetzen*. This phrase has been more than once quoted to me by men of standing in Dalmatia and Croatia, where the belief that the Dynasty is anti-Croat has unhappily been widespread since the rejected audience. Though there is no ground for this story, I think it well to refer to it, for, there can be no doubt that it has found credence and helps to explain the revulsion of Croat feeling in favour of the Magyars.

[220] Cf. the argumentation in *Kroatien und dessen Beziehungen zu Bosnien* (p. 87) by a deputy of the Croato-Serb Coalition.

during the summer of 1905 the idea of a conference to be attended by all the Croat deputies in the Viennese Reichsrath and in the Croatian Diet.

Its ostensible aim was to consider the steps necessary to secure the union of Dalmatia with Croatia under the Crown of St. Stephen ; but the tacit design of its organizers was to frame a programme such as would be acceptable to the Magyar Opposition as the basis of a working agreement. A preliminary meeting of twenty-four deputies was held at Ragusa on August 14, and Fiume was fixed upon as the place of the conference. As had been anticipated, the National party declined the invitation to attend and Dr. Frank's party also adopted a hostile attitude, partly owing to personal reasons, partly from religious fanaticism and hostility to the Serbs, but also because despite many shortcomings its leader, alone of all Croatian politicians, had realized the vital need of friendly relations with Austria, and had too clear a grasp of the international situation to be seduced into dubious adventures by the heroes of the Budapest Coalition. Meanwhile the Serb parties preserved a friendly neutrality, and resolved to await the issue of the conference before committing themselves to any public expression of opinion.

On October 2, 1905, forty Croat deputies from Croatia, Dalmatia and Istria met at Fiume. A preliminary motion greeting with sympathy the struggle of the Hungarian nation for its rights, and betraying an anti-Austrian tendency, was put forward by Professor Vrbanić, the well-known Constitutional writer. After a debate lasting several days in which almost all the Dalmatian leaders took part, Dr. Antony Trumbić who had been till recently Mayor of Spalato and enjoyed a wide popularity in Dalmatia, submitted a resolution from his own pen, containing a definite statement of policy. A small minority favoured a declaration of a much more general character and the appointment of a special committee to " sound " official opinion both in Austria and in Hungary before committing themselves to a new policy. The great majority, however, was anxious to commit itself openly to the new policy, and on October 4 the famous Resolution of Fiume was adopted, almost unaltered. A sub-committee consisting of Dr. Pero Cingrija,[221] Dr. Trumbić, Vicko Milić,[222] Harambašić

[221] Mayor of Ragusa and one of the most distinguished Croat politicians in Dalmatia.
[222] Till his death, in 1910, President of the Croat party in Dalmatia.

and Father Zagorac,[223] was appointed to carry out the ideas which it embodied.[224]

The Resolution of Fiume lays down as a general political axiom the view that " every nation has the right to decide freely and independently concerning its existence and its fate," interprets the Hungarian crisis as an attempt to carry this axiom into practice, and affirms it to be the duty and interest of the Croats " to fight side by side with the Hungarian nation for the fulfilment of its constitutional rights and liberties." The price of Croatian support is then defined as twofold—on the one hand the re-incorporation of Dalmatia, which, it might be presumed, would be equally attractive to Magyar and to Croat, and on the other a radical change in " the present intolerable conditions " in Croatia. The reforms necessary to such a change were summed up as follows : Electoral reform and freedom of elections ; complete freedom of the press ; right of assembly and association ; judicial independence, and irremovability of judges, and the formation of special courts to protect the citizen against political tyranny, and to punish arbitrary officials. The compromise of 1868 is to remain the basis of the relations between the Hungarian and Croatian nations, but such changes are to be made as shall assure to the latter an independent development, alike in matters " political, cultural, financial, and economic." In the opinion of *Obzor* the importance of the Resolution consists in defining the minimum of Croatian national claims—in a word, the execution of the compromise, its extension in an autonomous sense and the re-incorporation of Dalmatia. Its real significance, however, lies far deeper than any mere definition of claims. It marks an entirely new departure in Southern Slav politics, the attainment of its majority by a young nation, the adoption for the first time of an independent policy of construction. That this

---

[223] Afterwards one of the most prominent members of the Croato-Serb Coalition in Croatia (*see* pp. 255-8 for the part which he played at the Friedjung Trial), he became discontented with its policy, seceded early in 1909 and joined the so-called Dissident group of Dr. Mile Starčević, of which he is to-day the mainstay.

[224] The real initiative had come from Dalmatia when Mr. V. Milić, the President of the Croatian party, had strongly backed the propaganda of a Magyar journalist, Dr. Rudolf Havas, for the Union of Dalmatia with Hungary. In 1903 the Magyar Deputy, Paul Hoitsy, had published a pamphlet in favour of " Greater Hungary "—a league of Magyars, Roumanians, Serbo-Croats and Greeks, such as would close the gates of the Balkans to Russian aggression.

policy was based upon a radical misconception of their allies' character and honesty of purpose, does not really detract from the boldness of its design or from the energy and skill with which it was initiated and carried through. It can only be understood as a reaction against long years of neglect and desertion on the part of Vienna, ending in the crowning indignity of the rejected audience. Under such circumstances, the hope that the Magyars would, if only in their own interests, adopt a more generous and statesmanlike attitude, was as natural as it was to prove unfounded. Better, it was argued, endeavour to make terms with Budapest direct than to rely upon Viennese support in the struggle against Budapest and then invariably be left to pay the piper.

The newly appointed committee at once proceeded to Agram, where negotiations were opened with delegates from the Serb Independent, the Serb Radical, and the Peasant parties ; the two former assented to the new policy, but Mr. Stephen Radić, the leader of the Peasant party, offended by the anti-Austrian tinge of the proceedings, entered a strong protest and withdrew. Meanwhile a majority of the Dalmatian members of the Reichsrat also defended the Austrophil standpoint and declined to sign the Resolution ; but this did not deter the promoters of the movement from despatching a telegram to Mr. Francis Kossuth, as president of the Hungarian Party of Independence and announcing the success of the Resolution, "despite the efforts of agents of the Viennese Camarilla." The publication of this telegram aroused considerable indignation, but its contents were quite eclipsed by Mr. Kossuth's reply, which ran as follows : " We greet our Croatian and Dalmatian brothers and remind the Croats that we have always shared with them the rights which we had won for ourselves, and that on the contrary they have always been oppressed by Austria. May God bring back Dalmatia through Croatia to the Crown of St. Stephen ! We await you in love and full hope. Francis Kossuth." [225] For plain speaking this left nothing to be desired, and it is hardly surprising that such language in the mouth of a man who aspired to the rank of Hungarian Premier, inspired alarm and resentment, not merely at the Ballplatz, but also in the Hofburg.

Kossuth's telegram led to direct negotiations between Supilo

[225] Milić, *Postanak*, p. 16. As one of the Resolutionist leaders said to me, " We were naïve enough in those days to regard Francis Kossuth as a real Kossuthist."

and Trumbić on the one hand and prominent members of the Hungarian Coalition on the other. The importance which the Magyar Opposition assigned to the negotiations is shown by the fact that no fewer than five future members of the Wekerle Cabinet sat in the committee which the Hungarian Coalition deputed to meet the Croat leaders.[226]

Kossuth himself, writing in his own press organ *Budapest* on October 15, pled the cause of Magyar-Croat friendship, and argued that the deeds of violence which had made the Magyar name detested in Croatia during the past twenty years had been committed by the instruments of the Ban, without the approval of the Hungarian nation, and in accordance with the Camarilla's wishes. Almost at the same time Mr. Supilo's newspaper published a declaration in the name of the executive Committee of the Hungarian Coalition, solemnly pledging its leaders to concede the Croat language of command at the moment the Magyar language of command shall have been secured for Hungary, and in return for this stipulating for Croatian support in the struggle against Austria.

On October 16, twenty-six Serb deputies met at Zara, expressed their agreement with the principles embodied in the Resolution of Fiume and publicly declared themselves in favour of joint political action between Croats and Serbs, in the interest of their common Fatherland. The Resolutions of Fiume and Zara mark the beginning of a new era in Southern Slav politics. Henceforth the old rivalry of Croat and Serb is on the wane, and with each succeeding year fresh recruits have been won for the doctrine that " Croats and Serbs are one nation by blood and language."

During the winter of 1905 the various Opposition parties of Croatia—with the exception of Dr. Frank's adherents and the tiny group of the Peasants' Party, under Stephen and

[226] These five were Count Albert Apponyi (afterwards Minister of Education), Count Julius Andrássy (Minister of the Interior and framer of the notorious abortive Franchise Reform Bill of November, 1908), Baron Bànffy (the Chauvinist ex-premier and leader of the short-lived New Party), Mr. Géza Polónyi (Minister of Justice until driven from office in February, 1907, by the scandalous revelations of Mr. Lengyel and a certain Baroness Schönberger), Count Theodore Batthyány (a prominent Independent and to-day Vice-President of the Justh party), and Count Zichy (leader of the People's party and Minister *a latere*). Mr. Francis Kossuth (afterwards Minister of Commerce and author of the notorious Railway Bill which led to the rupture between Hungary and Croatia in the summer of 1907) was President of the Committee.

Antony Radić—organized themselves as the Croato-Serb Coalition, and conducted an active anti-governmental campaign on parallel lines with their allies, the Hungarian Coalition. The leaders of the " National party " in Croatia were not slow to realize the importance of the new movement. Ultraclerical circles looked with disfavour upon the reconciliation of Catholic Croat and Orthodox Serb, and still more upon the progressive elements to whose influence it was so largely due ; and it was an easy task to persuade the Clericals of Vienna, and even higher personages, that the national evolution of a disunited race was in reality a dangerous conspiracy against the Monarchy and the Habsburg Dynasty. This view was rendered plausible by the distinct anti-Austrian tinge which Croat opinion had assumed since the deputation's fiasco in 1903, and by the open language employed by Mr. Supilo in discussing the dangers of the *Drang nach Osten*. The Austro-Hungarian Foreign Office, with that strange blend of boundless credulity and childish suspicion which characterizes those who rely for their information upon the methods of the Police State, lent a willing ear to the denunciations of party fanatics and to the inventions of spies, informers and *agents provocateurs*— a class of reptile which Turkish misrule and the rival intrigues of Austria and Russia have bred in large numbers throughout the Balkans and the adjoining provinces. Subsequent indiscretions revealed a confidential circular issued by the Ban of Croatia, by order of the Foreign Office, to the High Sheriff of every county, and requesting them to place certain prominent individuals in Agram and other towns under secret observation, to tamper with their correspondence with certain Croat and Serb leaders in Dalmatia and Bosnia, and to submit detailed reports of the results of their inquiries. The ostensible cause for such action was the alleged formation of a Bosnian Committee for smuggling weapons and seditious literature into Bosnia and thus provoking a general rising [227] ; but the real aim was to obtain insight into the plans of the Opposition leaders and, if possible, sow discord between the allied Coalitions.[228]

[227] The absurdity of this story may be gathered from the fact that Professor Cvijić, the well-known; geographer and Rector of Belgrade University, is described as president of the insurrectionary committee.

[228] Karl Hron in *Die Wahrheit über die Wiener Orientpolitik* (p. 49) maintains that the orders for the arrest of the alleged conspirators had already been signed; and that execution was only delayed.

It may be that the Ballplatz was already preparing the campaign of forgery and intrigue which was to prepare the way to annexation, and that Baron Aehrenthal merely took over instead of initiating the " policy " which has since then come to be associated with the lofty names of Nastić and Vasić. Be this as it may, the sudden political transformation which took place in Hungary in the spring of 1906 brought the suspects into power and rendered such intrigues temporarily impossible.

On February 14, 1906, the gorgeous Chamber on the Budapest embankment had been surrounded by troops, and a colonel of militia had read the decree of dissolution to an empty House. No date had been assigned for the new elections, and the Opposition had foretold a whirlwind of indignation throughout the country, as a response to these wanton insults to the Constitution. But the country remained quiet and indifferent; the Government, having over-trumped the Coalition by making Universal Suffrage the main point of its programme, could afford to despise the latter's patriotic phrases and appeals to " State Right." The working classes and the nationalities—in a word a majority of the nation, though a minority of the electorate—favoured the " unconstitutional " government of Baron Fejérváry. The Coalition saw power slipping from its hands, and at the eleventh hour capitulated to the Crown, accepting a " compact " which has since become public and which shelved all the questions which had evoked the crisis, until a radical measure of electoral reform could be adopted. It is difficult to believe that the Coalition leaders ever intended to fulfil their pledge of reform ; for when once normal conditions had been restored they devoted themselves to passing law after law of the most reactionary nature,[229] and allowed two years and a half to elapse without even laying a franchise bill before Parliament.

The appointment of the Coalition Cabinet, under Dr. Wekerle as Premier, was followed by general elections both in Hungary and in Croatia. In the former country the old Liberal party disappeared altogether, its leader, Count Tisza, withdrew from political life, and the Coalition parties divided the

to say, though no arrests were made the rising never took place on the day mentioned in the document.

[229] E.g., Count Apponyi's notorious Education Acts (*see* detailed analysis in my *Racial Problems in Hungary*, pp. 227–233) and Mr. Daranyis' Agricultural Labourers' Act (*see Times*, September 25, 1907).

parliamentary spoils between themselves,[230] the little group of twenty-five non-Magyar deputies forming the only opposition in the House. In Croatia, for the first time for a generation, the Government was not in a position to exercise political pressure upon the elections; and as a natural result, the National Party suffered a decisive reverse, losing all but twenty-one seats. The Croato-Serb Coalition, or Resolutionists, as they were at first called, obtained a relative majority of forty-three seats,[231] while twenty fell to the Starčević Party. It would be absurd to pretend that the Resolution of Fiume awakened any enthusiasm among the Croatian electors; the success of the Coalition was won not by reason of it, but despite it, and was due to the deep relief and satisfaction which had greeted the entente between Croat and Serb.

The result of the elections sealed the bargain which the Croatian leaders had concluded with Mr. Kossuth and his friends. The new Croatian Government was formed out of members of the Coalition while a special arrangement retained Count Theodore Pejačević in his position as Ban, aloof from all party connexions. The Croato-Serb Coalition, not possessing an absolute majority in the Sabor, found itself too weak to adopt an active policy, and was seriously hampered during the winter of 1906 by the obstruction of the Starčević Party under Dr. Frank, furious at the increased influence which the Resolution of Fiume had secured to the Serbs, and still more at the revival of friendship between Agram and Budapest. Thus in a year of government the Coalition practically achieved nothing; of all the wide programme of reform contained in the Resolution of Fiume a law guaranteeing the independence of judges was the solitary fruit, and even this was still awaiting the royal sanction, when a grave crisis arose in the relations of Croatia and Hungary.

In May, 1907, Mr. Francis Kossuth laid before the joint Parliament in Budapest a new railway bill regulating the status of the railway officials, in which Magyar is expressly declared to be the official language of the entire railway system of Transleithania, and thus of Croatia also. This was resented by the Croats as a clear violation of the Hungaro-Croatian Compromise of 1868, § 9 of which declares the railway system

[230] No fewer than 189 seats (or 45·7 per cent.) were left uncontested.
[231] Croatian Party of Right, 19; Independent Serb Party, 16; Progressive Party, 3; Autonomous Club, 3; Serb Radicals, 3; Non-Party, 4.

to be one of the affairs common to the two countries, while § 57 prescribes Croatian as the official language for all organs of the joint government within the borders of Croatia-Slavonia and hence also for the railways.

The Magyar contention was that in practice the Magyar language had always been employed on all the railways, and that the new law was not guilty of any innovation. To this the Croats rejoined that an abuse which had long been reluctantly tolerated was greatly aggravated by the grant of legal sanction, that the law recognized the rights of the Croatian language, and that no modification of any kind could be made in the Compromise, save by consent of two specially convoked deputations of the Hungarian and Croatian legislative assemblies. Although the quarrel would seem to have arisen over a very ordinary measure for the regulation of traffic, the most far-reaching constitutional questions between Hungary and Croatia were involved.

Chauvinist feeling in Hungary which ran riot under the Coalition régime, insisted upon regarding Croatia as an integral part of the Kingdom of Hungary, and her autonomy as the outcome of generous concessions from Budapest, and not of a solemn contract between two equals. From this it of course followed that the language of the Hungarian state was entitled to a special position even on Croatian territory. In other words, the legal recognition of the Magyar language on the railways of Croatia was but the first step in the Magyarization of Croatia, at which the *exaltados* of the Hungarian Coalition aimed. The extreme importance to Hungary of the railway line from Agram to Fiume and the designs entertained by the Magyars for bringing the Croatian coastline under their immediate control, no doubt help to explain why the conflict broke out on this point, and why the Croats resisted so stoutly. But there is good reason to believe that the Magyar Government wished to pick a quarrel with the Croats, and that if the latter had tamely submitted to one violation of the Compromise, they would soon have been confronted with another. Nor is it improbable that the Foreign Office had some share in this result. Even at this date the annexation of Bosnia-Herzegovina was in contemplation, and the existence of a Pan-Serb conspiracy in those provinces had become an *idée fixe* in the official mind. Whether the idea of establishing a connexion between Bosnian intrigue and the political leaders of Croatia, first came from Budapest or from Vienna, it is not easy to determine. But the strategic convenience of having an absolutist régime in Croatia at a time of complications with Servia such as might be evoked by the annexation seems to have already commended itself in influential quarters. Clerical and military interests were strangely intermingled ; some highly placed officers being guided almost equally by strategic considerations and by the desire to overthrow the Croato-Serb Coalition, as a refuge of anti-clerical influences.

From the very first the Croato-Serb Coalition vehemently opposed Mr. Kossuth's illegal innovation ; and as all redress was uncompromisingly refused, its delegates in the Joint Parliament of Budapest resorted to obstruction of the sharpest and most effectual kind. For the first time since 1868 full use was made of the paragraph of the Compromise (§ 59) which entitled the Croatian delegates to speak in Croatian. Interminable Croatian speeches were delivered, minute points of order were raised and every advantage was taken of the somewhat complicated and obsolete Standing Orders. As hardly any of the Magyar members understood a word of Croatian, and as even the President and the Vice-President, from ignorance of the language, were unable to enforce a proper control of the proceedings, it can easily be imagined that the tactics of the Croats infuriated Magyar public opinion and made it less than ever disposed to compromise. After parliamentary business had been at a standstill for a whole month, Mr. Kossuth introduced a Bill consisting of a single sentence—which deserves immortality, if only for its grammatical construction—and empowering the Ministry of Commerce to enforce the provisions of the obstructed bill until such time as it should have received full parliamentary sanction !

The Croato-Serb Coalition, beaten though it was, consoled itself with the thought that it had won for itself in Europe a notoriety equal to that of Mr. Parnell and his friends in 1881, and that its bold resistance to Magyar aggression had won for it great popularity among the electorate of Croatia. On June 25, Count Pejačević, having identified himself with the attitude of the majority, sent in his resignation, and was succeeded as Ban by Dr. Alexander Rákodczay, who had for some yesar past occupied the position of President of the Supreme Court of Appeal in Agram.

As a Magyar by birth and a pronounced Unionist in sentiment, Dr. Rákodczay completely failed to rally a party round him or to allay in any way the general indignation. In the autumn session at Budapest the Premier, Dr. Wekerle, threw out dark hints of treason and unrest and warned the Croats of the dire results to which their obstinacy might lead, if they dared to look across the frontier for their political guidance.[232] This hint of renewed intrigues between Agram and Vienna was occasioned by the interest which the Christian Socialist party displayed in Croatia. But this interest being unhappily identified with narrow clerical influences, did not lead to any positive result.

The Croato-Serb Coalition remained firm in its opposition to the new Ban, and was even taking steps for his impeachment when the Sabor was dissolved and new elections ordered. Dr. Rákodczay's methods proved too moderate—and many would add, too scrupulous—for his masters in Budapest, and, with the best will in the world, he had entirely failed to win any support, save from the small group of discredited Magyarones, who alone survived from the old National party. He was therefore thrown overboard after the electoral campaign had already begun, and his place was filled by Baron Paul Rauch, son of the Ban who had guided the Compromise of 1868 through the Croatian Sabor (January 6, 1908). From the very first Baron Rauch attempted to rule the country with a rod of iron, but during his two years of office anarchy and absolutism went hand in hand, and each fresh act of the Ban merely served to increase the detestation in which he and his taskmasters at Budapest were held. In the first place he failed to realize that the days of Count Khuen were over, and that no human power can force a grown man into the strait jacket which was made to fit a child.[233] Besides, what was equally important, he was as incapable and unbalanced as Count Khuen Héderváry had been adroit and masterly. Hitherto his name had been associated with two clumsy onslaughts upon Count Khuen, conceived with the transparent object of superseding him as Ban, but ending in his complete discomfiture.[234] It is only fair to the Hungarian Premier,

[232] *See* e.g. his speech on November 9, 1907.

[233] A high Bosnian official (one who is anything but anti-Magyar) in conversation with a friend of mine, once characterized the Khuen régime in Croatia as a "strait jacket," from which the prisoner was released under his successor, and added that no power on earth, not even Khuen himself, could ever succeed in forcing the victim's body into it once more.

[234] In 1892 he had compared Khuen to Tanlongo, the Director of the Banca Romana, but withdrew and apologized. His second attack was

Dr. Wekerle, to add that he was from the first sceptical as to Rauch's fitness for the post, but that the latter enjoyed the support of high clerical and military circles to whom Dr. Wekerle thought it expedient to defer. Within a few days of his appointment, even before he had arrived in Agram, Baron Rauch contrived to alienate the only political group upon whose open support he could count, by a reference, all the more offensive because of its truth, to " exhuming the mummies of the National party." [235]

Baron Rauch's arrival at Agram (January 15) was made the occasion of hostile demonstrations from a large crowd, and he was greeted with a shower of rotten eggs in the streets on his way to the Banal Palace. He was not slow to revenge himself by publicly insinuating that the Coalition was guilty of " anti-dynastic and treasonable " tendencies ; and when Father Zagorac as publicly demanded the proofs of his assertion,[236] he remained silent.

Meanwhile every effort was made by Rauch's Government to influence the course of the elections. The voting registers were tampered with ; pressure was brought to bear upon the officials ; troops were called in ostensibly to preserve order but in reality to hamper the Opposition in its exercise of the franchise. The officials were reminded from headquarters that an old decree from the Absolutist régime of Alexander Bach (1855) enjoining upon the officials political subservience was still in force, and that the law of 1907 dealing with electoral purity did not entitle officials to vote for Opposition candidates ! Yet, little as electoral freedom was respected, Rauch's action ended in a complete fiasco. The Elections of February 28 resulted in a decisive victory of the Croato-Serb Coalition, which secured fifty-seven [237] out of eighty-eight seats, while twenty-four fell to the Party of Pure Right under Dr. Frank. For the first time the Croatian officials defied the pressure of the Government, and at the last moment the Unionist Ban was reduced to issue an order to the officials to vote for candi-

on the occasion of a difference between Khuen and Bânffy (then Hungarian Premier).

[235] *Vaterland*, January 10, 1908, cit. Montbel, *La Condition Politique de la Croatie*, p. 271.

[236] In an open letter to the *Hrvatska* of January 21.

[237] Divided as follows : Croatian Party of Right, 26 ; Autonomist Club (under Count Pejačević), 8 ; Serb Independent Party, 19 ; Progressive Party, 4. There were also 2 Peasants Party, 2 Serb Radicals, and 2 Non-party.

dates of the Starčević party against Coalition candidates, in other words, to support the party whose programme denies the legality of the connexion with Hungary which it was the Ban's duty to uphold and defend. Not merely did all three sectional chiefs lose their seats, but Baron Rauch failed to secure the election of a single adherent !

Such an electoral result would be highly remarkable in any country in Europe ; but, when it is remembered that Croatia possessed the narrowest franchise in Europe—not excepting even that of Hungary itself [238]—the issue of these elections may fairly be described as unique. Incidentally they afforded a striking proof of the new Ban's incapacity. It must have been obvious to the Hungarian Cabinet that a Khuen Héderváry would have produced a very different result ; and the fact that they retained Baron Rauch in office and that Dr. Wekerle exerted himself in his defence, goes some way towards proving that no great anxiety prevailed at Budapest to restore harmony between the two countries, and that a state of absolutism in Croatia would be by no means unwelcome. As will become abundantly clear at a later stage of the narrative, absolutism upon the southern frontier of the monarchy formed an essential part of the schemes which were already ripening to completion, and in which the leading parts were assigned to Baron[239] Aehrenthal, Dr. Wekerle and Baron Rauch. The motives of the Hungarian Government itself were threefold ; firstly, the boundless racial fanaticism of its followers, which it felt equally unable and disinclined to check ; secondly, the hope that compliance with the views of Vienna might be rewarded by permission to evade its pledges of electoral reform ; and thirdly, the desire to deprive the Croats of all possibility of intervening in the negotiations for a renewal of the Austro-Hungarian Commercial Ausgleich and thus to escape from the necessity of consulting Croatian as well as purely Hungarian economic interests.[239a] It is notorious that the fulfilment of the Kossuthist ideal—namely, the erection of a Customs-union against Austria and of an independent Hungarian Bank—would have seriously endangered Croatian interests ; and the stalwarts of the Independent Party felt that as a rupture on this point was sooner or later inevitable,

---

[238] *See* my *Corruption and Reform in Hungary* for a full account of the Hungarian Franchise.
[239] Became Count in 1909.   [239a] See pp. 69–70.

it would be better to pick a quarrel at the time most convenient to themselves.

Dr. Joseph Frank in an interview with the Hungarian Premier, which earned him much unmerited abuse in Croatia, assured that astute statesman that twenty years of absolutism under a Royal Commissioner would be required in order to render possible the formation of a new Magyarone party in Croatia.[240] The subsequent course of events has borne out this opinion, and in the spring of 1911 a Magyarone majority in the Sabor seems as far off as ever.

The new Diet was opened on March 12. Mr. Barčić [241] as " Father of the House," occupied the President's chair, and in a fiery speech urged the Diet " to stand firm like one man against the oppressors beyond the Drave " (i.e. the Magyars). " In this difficult moment," he added, " we must be united, and must act as the Italians when they were struggling for unity and chose as their motto ' Fuori gli Stranieri.' . . . The Government, which has suffered such an electoral defeat, will not resign, despite the will of the people. Hence we must call out to the Ban, this lackey of the Magyars, ' Down with the unworthy one! Resign ! ' " The Starčević party provoked the most scandalous uproar in the House, one of its most notorious members, a certain Mr. Elegović, howling down the Serb members as "Wallach pigs," [242] and all vieing with each other in their abuse of the Magyars and the Compromise. So hostile a reception boded ill for Baron Rauch's Parliamentary prospects, and on March 14, the Sabor was prorogued indefinitely, before it had even had time for the formal preliminaries

[240] *See* Dr. Frank's own version of the interview, in *Pester Lloyd*, March 1, 1908.

[241] A veteran Garibaldian, the life-long champion of Fiume's reunion with Croatia, and now a member of the Croato-Serb Coalition and an enthusiast for Croato-Serb unity.

[242] The terms of abuse employed by this individual in the Croatian Sabor during the years 1906–8 are probably a parliamentary record in Europe (see e.g. his abuse of the Ban himself in the Sabor on 19 March, 1910) ; but even they were eclipsed by a disgusting encounter between him and Mr. Stephen Radić, the leader of the Peasants' Party, in April, 1910. It would be unpardonable on my part to reproduce the scene. I must refer the reader to the Croatian press (e.g. *Agramer Tagblatt* of that date). I was in Dalmatia at the time, and I cannot do better than quote the terse comment of one of my Dalmatian friends, a prominent Deputy. He simply quoted the well-known Austrian proverb, " The Orient begins at Bruck on the Leitha " (the frontier station between Austria and Hungary).

of the session or for the election of delegates to the joint Parliament. The Royal Rescript of prorogation was dated March 3, and it was thus apparent that the Hungarian authorities had had no intention of giving the new Diet a fair trial, even if it should have shown itself less refractory than it actually did. It is possible that Baron Rauch entertained the idea of an immediate fresh appeal to the country, but after so decisive a result this would have reduced the representative principle to a mere farce, and was speedily abandoned, if it was ever entertained.

Baron Rauch now threw off all pretence of constitutional government, and for the next two years absolutism prevailed in Croatia. Less than three years had elapsed since the Hungarian Coalition—then still in opposition—was filling Europe with its passionate appeals against the alleged attempt of Austria to introduce absolutism into Hungary. And yet this same Coalition, after sacrificing to its thirst for office the most vital points of its political programme, now proceeded to enforce against the sister-nation of Croatia an absolutism of the most stringent and oppressive nature. Seldom has the irony of history been so strikingly illustrated.[243]

An active campaign of denunciation and slander was now opened by the press organs of the Government [244] against the Croato-Serb Coalition, and the Starčević party, in its blind hatred of the Serbs, was shortsighted enough to swell the chorus. The Coalition press, when it replied to these attacks, was repeatedly confiscated. Even the manifesto to the nation, which the Coalition members issued on March 20, was subjected to the same treatment. A month later the eighteen members of the Serb Independent Party issued an open letter to the Ban, summoning him to substantiate the charges of treasonable and anti-dynastic tendencies, which he and his press had brought against them.[245] They ascribed his slanders to the desire to

[243] See my *Absolutismus in Kroatien* (p. 1) which had the honour of being confiscated by Baron Rauch's Government in October, 1909.

[244] *Narodne Novine* (The Official Gazette), *Agramer Zeitung* (for foreign consumption), and a scurrilous sheet called *Ustavnost* which ceased publication within a week of Rauch's fall.

[245] His first charge appeared in an interview in *Az Ujság* (of Budapest) on January 18, and it was repeated in *Neue Freie Presse* of 19th and the *Narodne Novine* of January 22. After the elections he informed a reporter of the Viennese *Zeit* that the threads of the Coalition extended not only to Bosnia but also to Servia. Soon after he informed the Hungarian Cabinet of the dangers of the Croatian situation, owing to

break up the Coalition by ruining the Serb party and so to
retain his hold upon the office of Ban.[246] They then pledged
themselves that if he would convoke the Sabor, they would
themselves demand of it the suspension of their immunity,
in order that their case might be tried before the public courts,
and concluded by declaring that, if the Ban refused compliance
with their just demand, they would be entitled to assume that
he had "from his lofty position consciously and maliciously
lied, slandered and denounced." To this fiery document Baron
Rauch replied by a brief statement, repeating his former
insinuations and declining to adduce any proofs [247]; whereupon
the Independent Serbs issued a further declaration treating
their assumption as conclusively proved. Baron Rauch's
statement acquired added significance from the fact that it
was issued immediately after his audience with Dr. Wekerle
and Baron Aehrenthal in Budapest, and that the press was
allowed to assume without contradiction that he was acting
with the full approval of those two statesmen.[248] Professor
Manojlović as a member of the Serb Independent party, had
of course signed its manifestoes along with all his colleagues ;
and Baron Rauch now revenged himself by placing him upon
the retired list, a step which roused intense feeling in academic
circles. Professor Šurmin, of the Progressive party, had
already been deprived of his chair, because he had watched a
student demonstration against the Ban at the railway station
of Agram, without making any attempt to intervene. Thus
in the one case Baron Rauch took political vengeance for an

Pan-Serb propaganda ; these remarks were published in the press and
were met by no dementi. (*See* Manifesto of Serb Independent Party
in *Die Ritterliche Affaire des Baron Paul Rauch*, pp. 7–10.)

[246] "You are deliberately and systematically working to represent us
as dangerous and revolutionary elements and you are doing this in
order to convince the decisive factors of the necessity for your remaining in the post of Ban, and of the danger which your removal might
cause to the Dynasty and the Monarchy " (op. cit. p. 9).

[247] " As the Independent Serb Party has seen fit to transfer a purely
political matter to personal ground, I hereby declare that I will not
follow it there, the more so as it did not find it advisable to disprove its
tendencies, which were already sufficiently evident. On the contrary,
the Independent Serb party and its chief organ *Srbobran* prove by their
sympathies for the Pan-Serb dreams, which have publicist representatives outside the bounds of the monarchy, that they indulge in these
dreams with pleasure. My remarks referred to this behaviour, and I
will not enter upon further polemics. April 11, 1908. Baron Paul
Rauch." (*See* op. cit. p. 11.)

[248] *See* e.g. *Neue Freie Presse*, April 11, 1908 (Abendblatt).

attitude which from a drawing-room point of view may not
have been above criticism, but which certainly offended against
no known law ; in the other case, out of even more petty feelings of revenge, he punished a single individual for the sins of
eighteen and sheltered his personal honour behind the armour
of his official position. The University of Agram rightly regarded Rauch's actions as an infringement of its autonomy,
and as a result of the ensuing agitation, the great majority of
students withdrew from Agram and spent the summer semester
at Vienna, Prague or Graz.

From the moment of Baron Rauch's arrival in Agram, Dr.
Joseph Frank, the leader of the Party of Pure Right and his
organ *Hrvatsko Pravo*, had entered with great vigour into the
campaign against the Croato-Serb Coalition, and had rivalled
even the official press in the charges of disloyalty and intrigue.
Dr. Frank's tactics did much to accentuate still further the
extreme bitterness of party feeling in Croatia, and the utterly
reckless personalities exchanged between the parties had a
demoralizing effect upon public life. The attitude adopted by
Dr. Frank, so inconsistent with his programme of uncompromising opposition to the Compromise and to Hungary, at this stage
aroused suspicions among his own followers and (personal differences as usual supervening) led to an open secession from the
party (April 23, 1908).[249] The leader of the Dissidents, as they
came to be called, was Dr. Mile Starčević, a man who atones
for lack of ability by his transparent honesty of purpose, and
whose most valuable asset is the name inherited from his
famous uncle.

Throughout the spring and summer of 1908 an elaborate
campaign was waged by the official press of Agram, Budapest and Vienna against the Croato-Serb Coalition, and its
" treasonable designs." A number of articles began to
appear as early as April in the *Pester Lloyd*, the regular
receptacle of statements intended by the Viennese Foreign
Office for the consumption of the foreign public.[250] The

[249] Only four deputies seceded, but they were joined later on by others,
until the two sections were roughly in the proportion of five to two.

[250] It may be worth while to quote at length from one of the earliest
and most significant of these *inspired* press onslaughts. Readers of my
later chapters will find a great deal between the lines. " In Agram
especially the Serb danger has become serious, for . . . the Serbo-Croat
Coalition to-day no longer makes a Croat policy, but is completely
under the spell of the irreconcilable Pan-Serb Radicalism, which seeks

Serb danger in Croatia is gravely discussed by those who have for the past decades favoured the Serbs at the expense of the Croats. The Coalition is accused of intimate connexions with the Servian Government. The situation of Bosnia is depicted in the gloomiest colours ; the old paeans in praise of Austrian administrative success give place to accounts of sedition, unrest, and Pan-Serb propaganda. Perhaps the most significant feature of all these articles is the author's intimate knowledge of facts—perhaps " surmises " and assertions would be more accurate—which could only be elicited through secret service methods. The movements of Servian Government spies in Dalmatia and Bosnia, their relations with the Serb press in Sarajevo, the intrigues of Belgrad agents among the Serb troops of the Monarchy ; the " huge sums " paid by Servia to English and French publicists, the reception accorded by King Peter to Bosnian deputations—all these details, and many more, are faithfully recorded now by journals of the first rank, now by less reputable organs of opinion, as occasion served. Most sensational of all was the so-called " Coronation pro- gramme," revealed by the *Pester Lloyd* on April 28, and con- taining the plan of action which, it was alleged, Dr. Pašić, the Servian Premier, had laid before King Peter in March, 1904, and which had formed the basis of Servian policy ever since. Needless to say no indication was given of the manner in which access had been gained to so highly confidential a document ; and we shall not go far wrong in ascribing it to the same troubled source as the " documents " upon which Baron Aehrenthal relied to justify his annexation policy. This remarkable programme contained the following eight points,

to have as little to do with Budapest as with Vienna, and sees its aim and desire in a great Southern Slav State, governed from Belgrade. If none the less various politicians of the Serbo-Croat Coalition have recently wooed the help of Vienna, this was solely to mobilise the Viennese Court against Budapest, but, by no means out of love for Austria or the Dynasty. The overtures of the Coalition, which were at once seen through, . . . were without effect, for in Vienna one has and can have no interest in the establishment at Agram, merely out of hatred for Hungary, of a régime in which Pan-Serbism plays first fiddle, and which would finally turn against Austria and the Dynasty as much as against Hungary. The net which the Pan-Serb Propaganda seeks to spread over the whole south and south-east of Austria-Hungary must at last be rent asunder, and the Pan-Serb hydra's head must be hewn off. That can certainly only be achieved, if in Agram and Budapest, in Sarajevo and Vienna a common plan is adopted against the common foe." *Pester Lloyd*, April 18, 1908.

THE PAN-SERB IDEA

(1) Alliance of Servia with Montenegro and a joint foreign policy ; (2) an agreement with Bulgaria regarding the Macedonian reforms ; (3) furtherance of the Coalition idea in Croatia, and encouragement of the Hungarian Party of Independence in its struggle with the Crown·; (4) economic emancipation from Austro-Hungarian markets ; (5) revolutionary agitation in Bosnia, and publicist propaganda in the West, with the object of discrediting the Austrian administration ; (6) agreement with Italy regarding the Adriatic and agitation for a free harbour in Dalmatia ; (7) the formation of a " Wandering " Southern Slav Committee for the purpose of intrigue with Serb politicians in the monarchy ; (8) the Coronation of Peter Karageorgevitch as King of all the Serbs. A special department, it was alleged, had been formed in the Servian Foreign Office, for the purpose of organizing a revolutionary movement in Bosnia ; and the fact that Mr. Spalajković, the official in charge of the so-called " Macedonian " department, was related by marriage to one of the Bosnian Serb leaders, lent colour to the allegation.

As a statement combining the actual motives of Servia's policy with other aims which she ought to but did not follow, and with others again whose truth would tend to palliate measures of repression in Croatia and Bosnia, this document must be pronounced to be highly plausible. That every Servian dreams of a Pan-Serb Empire, no one will be concerned to deny ; but no one who knows anything of the wretched organization of the kingdom and of the glaring contrast between ambitious ideals and big talk on the one hand and on the other complete failure to translate words into action, will be disposed to take the matter seriously. Servia, weakened by the feuds of regicides and anti-regicides, demoralized by the events of 1903 and its aftermath of crime and intrigue, was utterly incapable of undertaking any action which would seriously menace the Dual Monarchy ; and such surplus energy as was left over from internal party strife, was devoted not to Bosnia, but to Macedonia and Old Servia, where the Servian element has for the last ten years been steadily receding before Bulgar and Albanian aggression. The support of Servian bands in Turkey was a sufficiently severe strain upon Belgrade, without its indulging in wild and unpromising adventures west of the Drina. That the new movement for Croato-Serb unity in Croatia was welcomed in Belgrad may be taken for granted, and it is equally certain that Servian *exaltados* believed that the work of the Coalition would redound to Servia's advantage—a belief due partially to their ignorance of their kinsmen across the frontier, and partially to a better founded perception of the shortsightedness and credulity of Vienna. But only this latter quality ought to have deluded Austrian public opinion into regarding Serbo-Croat national feeling as in any way different from similar manifestations among the Germans or Italians of the Monarchy. The movement in Croatia for national unity was a natural development which any student of historic evolution might have foreseen. It was entirely independent of similar movements across the frontier ; and a statesman of real genius would have understood how to use the movement as a powerful instrument in furthering Austrian influence throughout the Balkans, instead of stupidly alienating the race upon whose good-will the ultimate success of a forward policy must depend.

Meanwhile Rauch wreaked his vengeance on the officials who had voted for the Coalition ; many were suspended or transferred, some even sent to posts in Magyar districts of Hungary, where not a word of Croatian was spoken. The usual practices of withdrawing licences, or orders, and inflicting vexatious fines were employed by the authorities. In Bosnia the Serb press was treated with extreme severity ; and virtually the entire staff of Srpski Riječ was sentenced to lengthy terms of imprisonment on charges of sedition.

The persistence of the campaign made it obvious that some important political design was on foot, but during the summer of 1908 suspicion was not yet centred upon the mainspring of the action. The determination of the Magyars to restore discord between Croat and Serb and so to reduce Croatia once more to submission seemed at first to be a sufficient explanation ; and hardly any one realized that a carefully prepared campaign was on foot for the annexation of Bosnia and Herzegovina, and that the Viennese authorities were in search of such facts and material as would render the plea of absolute necessity convincing in the eyes of Europe. In his designs Baron Aehrenthal found a ready accomplice in the Budapest Government, which was determined to crush the Croats at all costs. The Magyar leaders hoped, by a complaisant attitude towards the annexation, to purchase from the Crown a free hand in the matter of electoral reform, and calculated that if complications should arise reform might be indefinitely postponed.

The ancient claims of suzerainty exercised by Hungary over Bosnia, also seem to have influenced the Coalition Cabinet.[251]

The press campaign inaugurated by Rauch, and ably sustained by the Frank party, increased in violence as the summer began. The first arrests soon followed.

In May, 1908, *Hrvatsko Pravo*, the organ of Dr. Joseph Frank, published letters from Kostajnica (a small town on the Bosnian frontier), which were intended to prove the existence of a Pan-Serb revolutionary propaganda. Proclamations, it was reported, had been distributed in the town urging the Croats to revolt and join the kingdom of Servia. Sceptics wondered why a place from which Servia is almost inaccessible, and where a small minority of 300 Serbs is overawed by over 1,500 enthusiastic adherents of Dr. Frank, should have been selected as a centre of Pan-Serb propaganda.[252] None the less on July 1 two shoemaker's assistants and an old woman of seventy-three were arrested on a charge of high treason. The Public Prosecutor hastened down from Agram, and two further victims were found, in a village schoolmaster and a clerk. These five persons remained for many weeks in prison, and were at last released when the absurdity of the charge against them had become too patent, and when more promising victims had been obtained elsewhere.

On July 9 Dušan Mandić, a " traveller " for an Agram friendly society called Srpsko Bratstvo [253] (Serb brotherhood) was suddenly arrested at Rakovica,[254] and handed over not to the local court, but to the Mayor of Agram, a special confident of Rauch, who in his turn consigned him to prison. After a delay of nearly three weeks, the officials who had accused him declared their grounds for the arrest to be an official secret, and Mandić was allowed to remain in prison. In his despair he refused all food, and after six days of this " hungerstrike " was sent to a hospital, where he was shut up for two days in a cell with a madman. At last he was released, without any attempt at explanation or apology.

The Public Prosecutor, Mr. Accurti, who had only recently

---

[251] See Dr. Wekerle's speech in Parliament, July 3, 1907.

[252] In other words Kostajnica is one of the least favourable spots in Croatia for Pan-Serb propaganda, but one of the *most* favourable for trumped-up charges.

[253] A kind of Life Assurance Company. Two of the Serb bishops are its members and the present Patriarch Bogdanović formally recommended it to the lower clergy.

[254] In the County of Modruš-Fiume, close to the Bosnian frontier.

been appointed over the heads of thirty-six of his colleagues, had meanwhile decided upon his line of action ; Mandić and the five prisoners from Kostajnica had served their purpose as " blinds." The real victims were now to be selected ; the necessary tools were also forthcoming. Baron Rauch had wished to proclaim a state of siege in Croatia [255] ; but Dr. Wekerle was not prepared to go to such lengths, and refused to allow an active campaign against the Serbs until the election of the new Serb Patriarch had taken place.[256] This election, upon the result of which the Magyar Government relied to detach the Serb Radicals from the Croato-Serb Coalition, actually passed off without incident on August 1. On July 21, however, a meeting had taken place between Dr. Wekerle, Baron Rauch, Mr. Josipović (the Minister for Croatia) and—Mr. Accurti, who reported upon his preparation for the coming hunt for traitors. The train was now laid ; the first explosion was caused by the notorious pamphlet *Finale*, published by George Nastić in the last week of July. The best service which could be rendered to this individual, is to consign his name to a speedy and lasting oblivion, and it is not the wretched puppet himself, but the wirepullers behind him that compel me to assign to his pamphlets and evidence a prominence which they do not by themselves merit. George Nastić is a native of Sarajevo, and at the time when he first acquired notoriety, was a student at Vienna University, with but little prospect of completing his studies. It has since transpired—and indeed has not even been denied by Nastić himself—that he was in the pay of the Bosnian police,[257]

[255] Masaryk, *Der Agramer Hochverratsprozess*, p. 87. Rauch's interview with Wekerle was on April 25.

[256] The Patriarch is elected by the Church Congress at Karlovitz, though it is in the power of the Hungarian Government to withhold the Royal Sanction and order a new election. On this occasion, active measures against the Serbs would have alienated the Serb Radicals, who were playing a double game with the Government in order to secure the acceptance of their candidate for the Patriarchate.

[257] E.g., Hron, op. cit. (p. 49) states that he was often seen in the antechamber of the Sectional Chief for the Interior, in Sarajevo, in company with a well-known Government agent. *Srbobran*, the organ of the Serb Independent party in Agram, published facsimiles of letters proving this connexion. On August 25, 1908, there appeared in *Srbobran* a signed statement of Risto Radulović, editor of the Serb newspaper *Narod* in Mostar (the little capital of Herzegovina), charging " the spy George Nastić " in the most explicit terms with " espionage, theft and swindle," on various occasions (e.g., the theft of opera glasses in the

and acted as *agent provocateur* at various demonstrations in the Bosnian capital.[258] In December, 1906, he was nominally expelled from Bosnia, and found his way to Belgrad, where he soon ingratiated himself in political circles by the publication of a pamphlet on " The Jesuits of Bosnia." This effusion, which is devoted to an attack upon Archbishop Stadler of Sarajevo and his unwise methods of Catholic propaganda, is, according to its author, based upon information supplied by a land agent in the Archbishop's own service ; on the other hand, *Pokret*, the organ of the Croatian Progressive party, maintains that Nastić did not write a word of it, but merely received the proofs from an agent of the Bosnian Government, which hoped to serve its own ends by the publication of such a pamphlet in Servia. In any case the pamphlet appears to have caused some sensation in Belgrad and secured Nastić the entrée into the *Slovenski Jug* (" The Slav South "), which, according to his own account, was a revolutionary club, having numerous connexions with all the most prominent Southern Slav leaders. It is upon his alleged experiences in this Club that *Finale* is based.

One of its most prominent members, we learn, was Captain Nenadović, a cousin of King Peter ; both the King himself and Prince George took a lively interest in its proceedings. A Conference was held in Belgrad, a policy of active terrorism was approved, arrangements were made through the mediation of the Crown Prince [259] for the manufacture of bombs at the Servian military arsenal in Kragujevac, and money was forthcoming from the Court. The Club meetings were attended by Valerian Pribičević, a professor of theology in the Orthodox Seminary at Karlovitz, and by his brother Milan, who, though formerly an officer of the Austrian army, had deserted it for the service of King Peter. These two had secured as adherents of their designs their third brother Adam, a local administrative official at Vrginmost in Croatia, and Bude Budisavljević, a deputy of the Serb Independent party. Nastić himself was deputed to superintend the bomb making, which he describes in considerable detail. Finally the bombs were

Viennese Burgtheater !) and challenging him to bring an action for libel. Cited verbatim in *Der Hochverratsprozess* (publication of the Defence), p. 113. Nastić ignored this.

[258] For calling out " Long live King Peter " in the streets he was fined 200 crowns, which were never paid. While he was left unassailed others who had joined in the cry at his instigation were put into prison.

[259] *Finale*, p. 18.

packed, brought back to Belgrade and lodged on the premises of the Slovenski Jug.[260] Up to this stage, the bombs were intended for use upon Austrian soil ; but, Nenadović now proposed that they should be sent to Montenegro and justified the suggestion by asserting that Prince Nicholas had sold to Austria-Hungary the Balkan plans of Italy. The scheme met with some opposition from the members, but eventually these very bombs were discovered in Cetinje ! Nastić himself, disgusted at the idea of a plot against Montenegro, returned to Bosnia in September, 1907, and as early as November we find him in Cetinje, in touch with the Montenegrin secret police.[261] In the spring of 1908 he appeared as a witness in the notorious High Treason Trial at Cetinje, and in July he decided " out of higher humanitarian and patriotic grounds " [262] to unmask the criminal designs of his former associates. It is worth noting in this connexion that Nastić admits having received over 4,000 crowns from Montenegro, in order to defend himself against Press attacks, and that he used this to publish *Finale*.[263]

As proof of this revolutionary design Nastić published in an Appendix to *Finale* certain documents in facsimile —firstly some postcards written to Nastić from Brussels by Ljubomir Jovanović, one of the chief members of Slovenski Jug, and secondly, as *pièce de résistance*, a "provisional statute of organization for the liberation of the Southern Slavs " transcribed in the handwriting of Milan Pribičević and accepted by a conference of Slovenski Jug in December, 1907. According to Nastić the apparently harmless references on these postcards to a " library," to Schiller's Song of the Bell, and to a certain "degenerate fellow " called Nicholas who " seems " to have " sealed his fate," must be interpreted as allegorical references,[51] to a collection of bombs, to revolutionary propaganda and to the Prince of Montenegro.[264]

[260] *Finale*, p. 29.
[261] Masaryk, p. 86. The Montenegrin Premier, Dr. Tomanović, admitted this on June 12, 1909, in an interview in the *Narodni Listy* (Prague).
[262] In three instalments of 1,000,300 and 3,000 crowns. *See* his evidence 98th day of Agram Trial. He further admitted having demanded a larger sum later on, to keep himself going.
[263] *Finale*, p. 66.
[264] In reality this wicked "Nicholas " was probably Nicholas Jovičevič, the chief of police in Cetinje, whom Nastić had met and intrigued with in Semlin. *See* Masaryk, op. cit. p. 57.

In the absence of all proof, Nastić's bare assertion is presumably to be accepted as sufficient guarantee of these secret and fantastic meanings. More important, however, is the statute, which subsequent events have shown to be really in the handwriting of Milan Pribičević. This long-winded and ridiculous document aims at "Southern Slav National Unity," to achieve which a "Revolutionary Organization" is to be founded. Its true ideal is "a great Southern Slav federation of Republics," its methods should be revolutionary ; but, as "active terrorism, . . . the so-called Revolution by outrages, is, under our conditions almost impossible and fruitless," these methods resolve themselves into "a question of tactics," which must vary according to the country and province. The sphere of action is limited to Servia, Bosnia, Herzegovina, Dalmatia, Montenegro, Croatia, Slavonia, Istria, the Slovene Country, Hungary, Old Servia, and Macedonia ; co-operation with the Bulgarians is regarded as quite impossible.

An elaborate plan of revolution is to be concocted, with "political, geographical, topographical, economic and statistical data " (!) " for all possible eventualities." [265] Agitation is to be conducted by pamphlets and through the press ; foreign public opinion is to be won ; connexions are to be formed with "similar organizations abroad." A special branch is to be formed in America. Propaganda is to be made in the Austro-Hungarian Army. Then follows a kind of syllabus of membership and organization compiled like the list of contents of some German scientific work ; everything grouped neatly under such headings as provincial, communal, individual organizations, rights and duties of Committees, division of labour, their sphere of influence and relations to each other. The final section lays down the tactics to be observed in the various countries. In Servia " where freedom and popular government prevails," these are to consist in " finding means and persons "; in Hungary, where " a revolution is not possible," in awakening the people's consciousness "; in Bosnia, " where the people has no rights, and in Turkey, where it is in physical slavery," in an extreme democratic struggle against the Government, and in terrorist action ; in Croatia and in Dalmatia, in supporting those elements which are for Union and Serbo-Croat equality ; among the Slovenes, in supporting the Progressives against Austrian Clericalism ; in Montenegro, in "terrorist action against the old régime."

[265] As if the Slovenski Jug was a kind of Statistical Office.

I have treated this fantastic scheme in far greater detail
than it deserves, because it was the only concrete document
which was produced at the Agram High Treason Trial, and
because it would appear to have contributed materially
towards persuading the Viennese authorities of the existence
of a Pan-Serb conspiracy. Yet it is not easy to understand
how any serious politician could take the " Statute " of Milan
Pribičević seriously. Its glaringly unpractical nature is
patent to every reader : for it is obvious that really dangerous
conspirators, so far from compiling for their own guidance
elaborate rules of the most doctrinaire type, have the most
wholesome horror of pen and ink. That the highest circles
in Belgrad, if they really did contemplate the murder of
Prince Nicholas and a revolution in Bosnia, would ever have
employed such a garrulous visionary as Milan Pribičević, is
ludicrously improbable. Certain it is that the frequent
successful conspiracies which have stained the annals of
modern Servia, were conducted on very different lines, or
they would not have been successful. And if Milan Pribičević
was an unlikely instrument, how much more unlikely is it
that George Nastić would have been employed in any capacity
save that of a subordinate spy. Belgrade contains, relatively
to its population, more secret service agents than any European
capital save St. Petersburg ; and Nastić's antecedents would
have been sufficient to deter the Servian Government from
entrusting him with important work, even if it had not had
such a wide and varied choice.

Still more glaring are the contradictions in which Nastić
involves himself in the course of his pamphlet. On the one
hand he gives his readers to suppose that the Slovenski
Jug had important connexions everywhere ; on the other
he poses as the moving spirit of the conspiracy, and hints
that nothing had been done before his arrival in Belgrad.[266]
At one place he tells how the statute was adopted at a large
conference of the Slovenski Jug, headed by the President ;
at another he admits the President to have been in Brussels
at the time.[267] He emphasizes the keen interest shown by
King Peter and Prince George in the proceedings of the
Slovenski Jug [268]; and yet the statute which the Club (including the King's alleged kinsman Nenadović) [269] unanimously

[266] Hron, p. 51.   [267] Masaryk, p. 47.   [268] *Finale*, p. 15.
[269] The relationship was denied in an official dementi of the Servian
Government.

adopts, is avowedly anti-dynastic and republican.[270] At one point he describes Milan Pribičević as the author of the statute, at another, he speaks of its "authors "; in his evidence at Agram he said that it was compiled at the meetings of the Slovenski Jug, while in his final pamphlet " Where is the truth ? " he describes it as the work of the Servian Foreign Office.[271] He tells us how he returned to Bosnia in September, 1907, after taking a leading part in the proceedings of the Slovenski Jug ; and apparently expects us to believe that the Bosnian police knew so little of this (according to his own account) dangerous agitator as to leave him undisturbed.[272]

Most suspicious of all, he assures us that he is acting from the loftiest patriotic motives [273] in the interest of the Southern Slav nation,[274] but a little later he reveals quite another motive, when he writes that, in order to silence the attacks made upon him in connexion with the Cetinje Trial, he must act upon the words, " An eye, for an eye, a tooth for a tooth." [275] Of his motives, indeed, the less said the better, for every line of his pamphlets tells the same sordid story, and reveals an unhealthy craving for notoriety, a weak megalomania which may fairly be said to " think in bombs." [276]

---

[270] *Finale*, pp. 48–9.

[271] *Wo ist die Wahrheit ?* p. 14. Masaryk, pp. 45–6. Nastić in his evidence (95th day of the High Treason Trial) again affirmed that the ideas underlying the statute are not those of Pribičević.

[272] This 'fact is, of course, one of the best proofs of Nastić's connexions with the Bosnian police. A still more decisive proof is a letter addressed to Nastić from Sarajevo on April 10, 1908, by Captain Michael Vorner, a member of the Austrian General Staff, and showing that Nastić supplied the military authorities in Bosnia with secret information, in return for money. This letter was published by *Srobobran* and its genuine character was never disputed.

[273] *Finale*, p. 7.   [274] Ibid. p. 8.

[275] Ibid. p. 16. In his evidence at the High Treason Trial (97th day) he gives as his chief motive in publishing *Finale*, the desire to prevent the bombs being discharged into Austro-Hungarian territory.

[276] It is difficult to realize how Nastić could have expected any sane reader to believe the contents of his pamphlets. For instance, after telling us of his reception at the hands of prominent politicians in Belgrad, and of the keen interest aroused in him as a Bosnian political refugee, he asks us seriously to believe that he went to the little provincial town of Kragujevać, under the assumed name of " Dr. Kraus, engineer from Vienna," and there got into touch with the chief of the arsenal, without the Servian police having any notion of what he was doing. A still more flagrant absurdity. Nastić tells us that his main cause of complaint against his fellow-conspirators was that they were sending bombs against Montenegro instead of against Austria Hungary. He

THE RESOLUTION OF FIUME

The denunciations of Nastić were followed during the first fortnight of August, 1908, by the arrest, on a charge of high treason, of two of Milan Pribičević's brothers, Adam, an official in the small town of Vrginmost and Valerian, a Professor in the Serb Orthodox Theological Seminary in Karlovitz.[277] Nastić, in company with no less a person than Mr. Sporčić, the head of the Croatian police, went from Budapest, where his pamphlet was published, to Vienna and from there to Agram.[278] He was then subjected to a preliminary examination, and the long array of illegalities on the part of the authorities began. According to his own avowal, Nastić was not merely guilty of high treason, but was actually one of the foremost conspirators ; in such cases the Criminal Code of Croatia expressly lays down that no suspect can either be put on oath or allowed to remain at liberty before the trial.[279] Yet Nastić was not arrested, and was allowed to give evidence under oath both at the preliminary inquiry and at the subsequent trial. The inference drawn from this by many acute observers to whom the above-mentioned details were as yet inaccessible, was, that Nastić was a spy and *agent provocateur*.

The arrest of the Pribičević brothers was the signal for a

therefore returns to Bosnia and promptly proceeds to denounce to the Austrian police as " traitors " those persons who had declined to conspire against the Monarchy. Hron (op. cit. p. 53) rightly remarks that this fact alone would suffice to prove the absurdity of the whole High Treason trial.

[277] The fourth brother Svetozar, is editor of *Srbobran* and one of the chief deputies of the Serb Independent party.

[278] *See* p. 324 for the relations of Sporčić with Nastić and other shady individuals. In Cetinje, Nastić had according to his own account (*see* 94th day of High Treason Trial) made the acquaintance of Steinhardt, an Austrian Jewish journalist who had been expelled from Servia and lived in Semlin, the frontier town opposite Belgrad, as correspondent of Viennese journals. Not long after, Steinhardt introduced Nastić to Mr. Leopold Mandl, the editor of Baron Aehrenthal's semi-official organ the *Wiener Allegemeine Zeitung* (author of *Oesterreich-Ungarn and Serbien*, a well-written apology for the Aehrenthal Policy), who made it possible for him to publish the Croatian and Servian editions of *Finale*. As the reader will now realize, we are now in very troubled waters. Nastić maintains that he placed the original of the Statute for safety in Steinhardt's hands. It certainly has not been produced.

[279] The only exception made is in favour of those who supply secret information calculated to frustrate the plot at a time when the authorities were still without information. As Nastić, so far from this, actually published his information (and so, it might be argued, publicly warned the conspirators and gave them time to efface the traces of their plot) the exemption did not apply to his case.

regular campaign against the Serbs on the part of Baron Rauch's Government. By October 1, thirty-three arrests had been made, including six village schoolmasters, six small tradesmen, two students, a mayor, a notary, a forester and two priests, Father Milić and the Archpriest Nicholas Hercegovac. Some were placed in chains on their way to Agram, only one was examined after his arrest, none were allowed to communicate with their lawyers, some were even forced to share cells with condemned criminals of the worst type.

The Government having dispensed with all pretence at constitutional rule, had openly reverted to the old anti-Serb policy which had prevailed under Count Khuen's predecessors. After twenty years of subservience to Magyar aims, the Serbs had dared to unite with their natural allies, the Croats. To punish them for this unwonted self-assertion and to restore the old enmity between the two races, was the task assigned by Budapest to Baron Rauch and his creatures. The motives which led the Ballplatz to associate itself with the anti-Serb campaign, and the events to which this cynical alliance gave rise will be explained in the following chapter.

CHAPTER IX

The Annexation of Bosnia and the Agram High Treason Trial

THE fall of Count Goluchowski in October, 1906, marks the opening of a new era in Austro-Hungarian foreign policy. His successor, Baron Aehrenthal, showed no inclination to follow in the old paths of inaction and self-depreciation on which the Ballplatz had walked since the days of Andrássy. Ten years as ambassador in St. Petersburg had taught him to believe in Austria's strength and mission, and in that essential corollary, Russia's weakness. While fully alive to the value of the German alliance, he understood better than the world at large the essential weakness of the Triple Entente for purposes of aggression ; and having assigned to himself the ambitious rôle of an Austrian Bismarck, he flattered himself that he could impose his wishes upon an unwilling and divided Europe and deliberately set himself to evolve an Eastern policy in which Germany should be led instead of leading.

After a year spent in consolidating his position, Baron Aehrenthal inaugurated the new forward policy in January, 1908, by his scheme for a railway through the Sandjak of Novibazar. The absurd outcry with which this project was greeted in the European Press was not the real reason for its abandonment some months later. This was rather caused by grave engineering and financial difficulties which the minister had strangely overlooked in giving his project to the world. A further important factor in the abandonment was the new strategic theory put forward by the military authorities, that Austria's true line of advance into the Balkans lies not through the barren and worthless Sandjak, but along the valley of the Morava, which forms the backbone of the kingdom of Servia and offers direct access to Salonica and the Aegean. For some years past this secret and unavowed theory has

174

coloured Austria-Hungary's whole attitude towards her Balkan neighbours.

The Turkish Revolution, with its sequel the restoration of the short-lived constitution of 1876, led Baron Aehrenthal to hasten his pace. The difficulties which faced the Young Turkish regime seemed to offer a favourable opportunity for finally legalizing Austria-Hungary's position in the occupied provinces. The nominal survival of the Sultan's suzerainty over Bosnia would, it was argued, inevitably lead to complications now that Turkey had shaken off its long lethargy and showed a genuine tendency to reform. The Bosnian Mohammedans would look more than ever towards Stambul, and might even claim the right of sending deputies to the Ottoman Parliament. Whichever turn affairs might take, prompt action seemed advisable. If the new regime should prove a success, there was a real danger of the Chauvinists of Stambul reasserting obsolete claims ; and it would be well to forestall this possibility. If on the other hand it should prove a failure, Austria-Hungary was but accomplishing, at a time convenient to itself, what was sooner or later inevitable. Russia was known to be unprepared for war since her defeat in the Far East : Germany was at the worst a friendly neutral ; and it was calculated that the Western Powers, even if they opposed, would not push their opposition to extremes.

At the time of the Sandjak scheme, Baron Aehrenthal appears to have still hoped to attain his ends in the Near East by means of a skilful plan of " compensations all round " ; and there is good reason to believe that the opening of the Dardanelles to Russian warships was to have been Russia's share of the spoils. Unfortunately Russian public opinion treated the Sandjak scheme as an infringement of the understanding which had been concluded between Russia and Austria-Hungary at Mürzsteg in 1897 and had regulated their attitude to Macedonia ever since ; while the Reval meeting between King Edward and the Czar (June, 1908) was regarded in Vienna as a fresh stage in a policy of Balkan innovation, inaugurated by Sir Edward Grey's proposals of Macedonian financial reform.[280] Thus on both sides public opinion was already nervous and suspicious, when the international crisis broke out in the autumn of 1908.

[280] There can be little doubt that these proposals really gave an impetus to the Young Turk movement, and thus were partially responsible for the downfall of Hamidian rule.

THE ANNEXATION OF BOSNIA

It seems certain that the annexation of Bosnia and Herzegovina was already being contemplated before the outbreak of the Turkish revolution. But the exact method by which this step was to be accomplished had not yet been determined, when on October 5, 1908, Prince Ferdinand of Bulgaria proclaimed his country's independence and assumed the kingly title. Baron Aehrenthal's hand had again been forced, and immediate action was decided upon. Two days later, the annexation of Bosnia was formally announced in a manifesto of the Emperor Francis Joseph to the inhabitants of the two provinces.

From the very first the legal aspect of the question was entirely ignored, and the idea that an international treaty could be binding in inconvenient circumstances does not appear to have occurred to public opinion in the Monarchy, until it was emphasized by the foreign press. That the action of Austria-Hungary and of Bulgaria alike constituted a clear violation of the Treaty of Berlin and of the earlier Treaty of London,[281] is beyond all dispute. But the indignation expressed abroad was quite excessive.

The attitude of the British press in particular was not unnaturally regarded as hypocritical, in view of the position which Disraeli's Government had adopted towards the question of annexation in 1878, and still more in view of our own record in respect of the Cyprus Convention and the occupation of Egypt. The British Government showed itself to be not so much hypocritical as doctrinaire in its treatment of the situation. In theory, its attitude was unimpeachable, for it was based upon principles of international law such as no amount of sophistry could undermine. But in practice this attitude was open to the gravest objections, since the annexation was frankly based upon the rival principle of brute force. Unless we had been prepared to wage war in defence of an abstract theory of international law, we should have done better to accept the new situation under protest but without reserve or delay. As it was, our attitude exposed the Triple Entente to an inevitable rebuff, and in the meantime led Servia to indulge in false hopes of material aid and thus greatly prolonged the crisis. That the annexation was grossly mis-

[281] By it (1871) it is laid down that " no Power can break its treaty engagements or modify their stipulations except by friendly agreement and with the assent of the other contracting parties.

managed by Baron Aehrenthal and was based upon forgery and intrigue, does not in any way affect the fact that the British Government had only two logical alternatives—either enforcement of the Treaty of Berlin at all costs, or recognition of an act which Britain had eagerly advocated a generation earlier. Meanwhile, there can be no question that Baron Aehrenthal's action dealt a fatal blow to the cause of public law among the nations, and so to the fabric of international agreements to whose erection the reign of Edward VII had been devoted. It was resented equally by British Radicals, who saw their dreams of international disarmament dispelled for an indefinite period, and by British Conservatives, who wrongly suspected German influences. But in many quarters, and especially in Russia, the real motive for the outcry against the Annexation was disappointment and alarm at the sudden resurrection of Austria-Hungary as a Great Power, after many years of impotence and effacement. Baron Aehrenthal and his methods are only too open to criticism ; but one merit cannot be denied to him. He restored the Monarchy to her place in the counsels of Europe, and finally dispelled the absurd myth that it is a weak and decadent state, ready for dismemberment on the death of its present sovereign. Since the Bosnian crisis, every one knows that Austria-Hungary is one of the strongest powers on the Continent, and likely to become stronger, not weaker, in the immediate future.

The disapproval, not to say hostility, with which Europe greeted Baron Aehrenthal's coup d'état, could not be overcome by the plea that Bulgaria had forced his hand. The less disposed foreign opinion showed itself to accept the explanations which he offered, the more important did it become to find proofs of the urgent necessity of annexation.

Aehrenthal's press organs set themselves with praiseworthy zeal to denounce and expose the Pan-Serb revolutionary movement, which, they alleged, was spreading from its headquarters in Belgrad all over Croatia, Dalmatia and above all Bosnia-Herzegovina, and threatened to undermine Habsburg rule throughout the Southern Slav provinces. It was at this point that Baron Aehrenthal found valuable allies in the Hungarian Coalition Government, and in its exponent, Baron Rauch, the Croatian Ban. The complaisant attitude of the Magyars—in striking contrast to their keen disapproval in 1878 of the occupation policy—found its explanation in the internal situation of Hungary. Dr. Wekerle and his colleagues hoped to mollify their sovereign by complete subservience in matters of foreign policy, and thus to win his consent to Count Andrássy's reactionary scheme of plural voting, which, if once passed, might have postponed all genuine reform of the franchise for another generation. At the same time the Magyar Chauvinists had their eyes upon Bosnia, as a future colony of Budapest. To them the chief danger lay in the new-found harmony of Croat and Serb, which seemed to be the precursor of that political unity which, under the elusive name of Trialism, already filled the dreams of so many Southern Slavs. In the Magyar interest, the Croato-Serb Coalition must be shattered at all costs. Baron Rauch's experiment in arbitrary government had hitherto failed of the desired effect ; and it may be that so *rusé* a statesman as Dr. Wekerle would have dispensed with his services, but for the intrigues of certain high officers and ecclesiastics, whose influence at Court was exercised in his favour.[282] But in view of this secret support and of the difficulty of finding a substitute, it was thought wise to leave him at his post, and to rely upon his lack of scruple outbalancing his lack of tact. The most vulnerable section of the Croato-Serb Coalition was the Serb Independent Party : against it, therefore, Rauch concentrated his efforts, acting on parallel instructions from Budapest and Vienna.

The ulterior aims were different, Budapest seeking to sunder Croat and Serb once more, and so to reduce Croatia to political impotence, and if possible the Serbs to their old rôle as obedient " Stimmvieh " for the Magyar cause : Vienna being desirous of proving the existence of widespread unrest and treasonable agitation, such as could only be effectively checked by an energetic foreign policy. But while the aims were different, the means to be adopted were identical. The Serbs must be compromised : the most dangerous leaders of the Coalition must be rendered politically impossible : treasonable propaganda on a large scale must be discovered, or if necessary invented.

We have seen that Baron Rauch, from the very moment of his appointment as Ban, publicly accused the Coalition leaders of anti-dynastic and treasonable dealings, while steadily declining to adduce proofs for his assertion. Direct proceedings against them, however, were impossible, since they were

[282] Cf. Masaryk, op. cit. p. 73.

sheltered by their parliamentary immunity, and very naturally declined to apply for its suspension so long as the Constitution was suspended and the Diet prevented from meeting. Even had Rauch been disposed to override their Croatian immunity, the most important deputies were further covered by their immunity as delegates to the joint Parliament in Budapest, and its violation would have created a most dangerous precedent, of which an unconstitutional Government in Hungary might some day take advantage against Magyar extremist deputies. The leaders being, therefore, for the moment beyond his reach, Rauch had to content himself with smaller game.

Even before October 1 twenty-four persons had been arrested on a charge of treason : on that date eight further arrests were made. During the next three months frequent arrests and domiciliary visits were made in various parts of Croatia, until in January, 1909, no fewer than fifty-eight Serbs were awaiting their trial in the prison of Agram [283]—including the Archpriest of Glina, Nicholas Hercegovac, two other priests and a curate, seven school teachers and two country doctors. The remaining prisoners were for the most part well-to-do tradesmen or petty officials. All without exception were Serbs, and the great majority open adherents of the Serb Independent party. The arrests and the inquisitions which preceded and followed them, naturally caused the greatest panic throughout the country ; and this was not diminished by the treatment meted out to the prisoners, most of whom were brought in chains to the capital, and left for many months untried. Some were even obliged to share the cells of condemned criminals ; for instance, the schoolmaster Borojević and the merchant Gajić were confined with two men who were under sentence of death for murder and robbery. Most of the prisoners were not examined and remained in ignorance of the details of the charge against them. Finally, in their despair, Father Milić, Valerian Pribičević and several others resorted to a " hungerstrike," not in the hope of regaining their liberty, but merely in order to be confronted with their judges.[284]

Needless to say, the whole affair awakened, as was intended

[283] Five were eventually discharged.

[284] Father Milić, after nine days without food, was ordered to be transferred to the hospital, attempted resistance and had to be removed by force.

179

by its promoters, intense resentment and indignation in Belgrad, and fanned to white heat the war fever into which the annexation of Bosnia had plunged the Servian people. How far this effect was calculated beforehand by Baron Aehrenthal and his advisers, is a matter which we shall have to consider later.

At length on January 15, 1909—five months after the first arrests—the indictment against the fifty-three Serbs was issued by the Public Prosecutor, Mr. Accurti.[285] This astonishing document filled over 100 large octavo pages, and was actually published as a supplement to the official Croatian Gazette, *Narodne Novine*, and scattered broadcast in thousands of copies. The natural result of this manœuvre was to stereotype the evidence of the witnesses and to lessen immensely the danger of conflicting statements for the prosecution. At the same time it gave rise to a crop of blackmailing incidents.[286]

The indictment is an unique example of generalization, for it is so worded that if a specific act of treason were proved against a single one of the prisoners, all the others would thereby be implicated in his guilt.[287] Its main charge rests upon the existence of a Pan-Serb and revolutionary movement in Croatia, directed from the Slovenski Jug in Belgrad and aiming at the erection of a Greater Servia at the expense of the Habsburg Monarchy. The revolutionary club itself is alleged to have been under the direct patronage of King Peter and Prince George. Only five of the prisoners are accused of direct relations with Belgrad : ten others are charged with being accomplices, while the remaining thirty-five are only indirectly implicated.

The sole documentary proofs brought forward were the revolutionary statute and letters published by Nastić in his *Finale* ; and even these were not submitted in the original.

---

[285] It is pleasant to be able to record a detail which reveals Dr. Wekerle, the Hungarian Premier, in a pleasant light. The defending counsel appealed to him, and it was as a result of his personal intervention that the opening of the trial was not still further delayed. I give this fact on the authority of Dr. Popović, the Serb deputy, and one of the ablest of the prisoners' counsel.

[286] *Srbobran* of January 22, 1909, published two such letters in facsimile. The paper was promptly confiscated by the Public Prosecutor !

[287] *See* pp. 4–5 of the printed indictment, translated on pp. 31–32 of my *Absolutismus in Kroatien* (Vienna, 1909).

Nastić, the informer, who himself admitted only knowing three of the prisoners, was the only witness cited to prove a connexion with Belgrad. The rest of the evidence relied upon consisted of "phenomena "[288] of a general kind. The indictment openly expounds the ideas of Dr. Frank and the Party of Pure Right. Just as the Magyars argue that in Hungary there is but one nation, the Magyar, and regard every reference to a Slovak or Roumanian nation in Hungary as disloyalty to the State, so Dr. Frank builds all his theories upon the premiss that every citizen of Croatia can only be a Croat and that there can be no such thing as a Serb nation in Croatia. The Public Prosecutor made this line of argument his own, and hence throughout the document the "Serbs" are referred to in inverted commas! It treats as suspicious and "symptomatic" the fact that the "Serbs" of Croatia describe their Church as "Serb Orthodox" and not "Greek Oriental "[289]; yet their Metropolitan's official title is "Serb Patriarch." It treats as symptomatic the use of the Cyrilline alphabet; yet a law of 1887, passed under Count Khuen Héderváry, allows its official use in every commune where there is a Serb majority, and in that case makes it an obligatory subject in the school. It treats as symptomatic the use of Serb national songs; yet these songs, most of which celebrate the great Serb emperor Stephen Dušan and the fall of Serb independence on the fatal field of Kossovo in 1389, have been sung and cherished by every peasant in the Slavonic South during five centuries. It treats as symptomatic the use of the "Serb" arms—the cross and the four letters, "S "—as proving sympathy for the Kingdom of Servia; yet it is a notorious fact that these arms have been borne by the Serb Patriarch ever since he took refuge in Habsburg territory in the seventeenth century, that they have been universal in all Serb lands for centuries, and that Prince Milosch of Servia adopted them as the arms of the new principality in its struggle against the Turks. It puts forward the brazen assertion—surely one of the most monstrous perversions of history ever uttered by a public prosecutor—that among the population of Croatia and Slavonia the use of the "Serb" name only came into

[288] This word continually recurs in the original document.
[289] The nomenclature still employed by the authorities in Austria-Hungary—an anachronism dating from the period when all Orthodox Churches were subject to the Greek Patriarch in Constantinople. No Orthodox ever uses the phrase himself.

vogue since the year 1903, and at once proceeds to connect this with the accession of the Karageorgević dynasty and the growth of the Pan-Serb idea under King Peter's auspices.[290] As the reader is already well aware, the year 1903 marks a change of régime in Croatia as well as in Servia. The murder of King Alexander, and the resignation of Count Khuen Héderváry occurred within a brief space of each other: and the latter event was marked by a distinct growth in Serb national feeling. No one knew better than Mr. Accurti or Dr. Frank [291] that the reaction from the Khuen regime, when the whole country breathed again after twenty years of the "straight jacket" (see p. 155) was in no way influenced from Belgrad, which at that time was entirely occupied by the dynastic crisis and by the rising in Macedonia.

A further proof of treasonable intrigue was the possession of King Peter's portrait, which is as popular among the Serb population of Croatia as those of William II or the Bavarian Royal Family in German Bohemia or Tirol. Several prisoners were accused of shouting "Long live King Peter" in the streets; and one, a shopkeeper, was charged with keeping dynamite, though it transpired eventually that it was merely used in small quantities for ordinary purposes of trade.[292] Still more incredible, the indictment treats as "symptomatic" the assertion of an ignorant villager that the Virgin Mary was a Serb, and the fact that a certain Servian officer, a habitué in the small bath of Lipik, was invariably known as "Mr. President." [293]

Above all, in the fact that the prisoners presume to call themselves "Serbs," and not "Vlachs," [294] the Public Prose-

[290] Yet though this forms his principal argument, Accurti makes on p. 14 of the indictment the astonishing admission that, "as early as the year 1880 all these phenomena were visible; it was known that their source was in Belgrad, but the Government paid no attention to them." What Khuen-Héderváry had tolerated for twenty years suddenly became a danger to the State in 1906.

[291] It subsequently transpired (see p. 307) that Mr. Accurti, in composing the indictment, collaborated with the leaders of the Frank party and used historical notes supplied by them.

[292] Blasting, etc., in a country district.

[293] Because he had been there so often. Cf. Masaryk, p. 24.

[294] The word "Vlah" in the Croatian or Servian language, means "a member of the Orthodox Church," but has the same offensive sound about it as the word "Papist" as applied to Catholics. Needless to say, no Orthodox would dream of applying it to himself or a co-religionist. The Frank party, who deny the existence of Serbs

cutor pretended to find a proof of treasonable leanings, though in so doing, he calmly ignores the fact that successive Habsburg Emperors conferred special national privileges upon the Serb immigrants, and that even the present Emperor has addressed more than one proclamation to " the Serb nation." [295] The reader, unfamiliar with political conditions in Hungary and Croatia, may marvel that such argumentation could be put forward at all; and indeed it takes some time to realize that juggling with such phrases as " nation " and " nationality " is habitual among all races of the Austro-Hungarian Monarchy. Reduced to its elements, the indictment is a political tract, launched by one party against its rival— an attempt on the part of the Frank party to ruin the Croato-Serb Coalition.

An interval of six weeks elapsed between the publication of the indictment and the opening of the Trial, which at last began on March 3 in Agram, before a tribunal of seven judges. Even the most declared opponents of the prisoners freely admitted to me during the trial [296] that these judges were specially selected for the occasion by the Rauch Government, and that neither as judges nor as private individuals did they enjoy sufficient prestige to be entrusted with the most important political trial in Croatia during modern times. Indeed a prominent politician [297] actually assured me that the names of the seven judges were proposed to Rauch by the judicial department, in the deliberate belief that their appointment would lead to a grave scandal and fiasco. Whatever truth there may be in this almost incredible assertion, there is no doubt that the behaviour of the President, Mr. Tarabocchia, and of the second judge, Mr. Pavešić was for weeks the talk

in Croatia, make a point of calling all Orthodox " Vlahi," meaning thereby to be offensive and to suggest that the Serbs of Croatia are really Wallach (i.e. Roumanian) immigrants. The fact that most Roumanians are also Orthodox did lead in former centuries to the two races being confused under the same name and the phrase " Wallach Church " sometimes occurred. Philologists, however, are of opinion that the word " Vlah " is derived from the old High German word " wahla " (a foreigner speaking another tongue) akin to " wälsch," " Wales," " Walloon."

[295] E.g. in 1848, see pp. 47–49.
[296] I spent over three weeks at Agram during the High Treason trial and my impressions, during repeated visits to the court, confirmed all that I heard or read elsewhere.
[297] Who was not and is not an adherent of the Coalition.

of Agram. Their nocturnal revels in the wineshops and cafés of the capital were publicly branded by Professor Masaryk, in his well-known speech in the Austrian Parliament.[298]

It is not my purpose to inflict upon the reader the interminable and dreary annals of the Agram High Treason Trial, which dragged on from March 5 till October, and which long before its close had become fully as great a burden to its authors as to its victims. From the very first it showed itself to be one of the grossest travesties of justice in modern times ; and he would be a bold man who would to-day attempt an apology for the manner in which it was conducted. Lest, however, I should be accused of taking anything for granted without abundant proofs, I propose to summarize a few (but only a few) of the more glaring illegalities of the Trial, under four main headings.

I. THE PRELIMINARY INQUIRY.

The *juge d'instruction* examined no fewer than 276 witnesses for the prosecution, but not a single one out of the 300 proposed by the defence. The hearing of these latter was refused, and the Court informed the defence that they might renew their application during the course of the trial. Thus the proceedings had already lasted *six months*, before a single witness for the defence had been admitted, and even then only twenty were allowed, all the most important being rejected.

The preliminary inquiry had been conducted with such carelessness, that at the main proceedings quite a number of witnesses for the prosecution denied having used the expressions ascribed to them.

One of these, Tanasija Drpa, having obstinately adhered to his denial on essential points, and having further asserted that he had been examined in a drunken condition, was first browbeaten by Mr. Tarabocchia and then arrested in court on a charge of perjury. The President made no secret of the fact that this was intended " pour encourager les autres," and warned the next witness that the same fate awaited him, if he did not tell the truth.[298a]

---

[298] *See* Masaryk, *Der Agramer Hochverratsprozess*, p. 14. This pamphlet is a reprint, with slight alterations, of the speech which Professor Masaryk delivered in the Austrian Parliament on May 17, 1909.

[298a]. 43rd day.

The witness Križnjak denied having ever made the statement ascribed to him, " that this country was Serb and must fall to Servia," and said that the *juge d'instruction* had simply ordered him to put his sign to a written deposition. When warned by the Judge, he persisted in this statement. The assistant *juge d'instruction* was then heard, and while not remembering the details of Križnjak's evidence, was certain that he dictated it in the witness's own presence to the clerk Marijašević. Counsel for the defence here pointed out that though the witness Križnjak can neither read nor write, the first report contains the statement that he saw in Gajić's house the inscription " Long live Peter Karageorgević." When the defence demanded that Marijašević should also be heard, the presiding Judge refused this as " superfluous," and ordered Križnjak's arrest on a charge of perjury.[299] On July 10 he was actually sentenced on that charge to ten months' imprisonment, though absolutely no motive could be adduced for his perjury and everything went to show that he was telling the truth.

The innkeeper Kordić not only denied having said what was ascribed to him, but also maintained that during the examination the *juge d'instruction*, Mr. Košutić, had said to him, that in Croatia there are no Serbs.[300]

Another innkeeper, named Louis Schmidt, who was put on oath in spite of having been convicted of fraud, was accused by two rival witnesses of having bragged that he was a Government detective and would get 1,200 crowns for his services. Schmidt, though he denied this, actually admitted having received instructions from the Public Prosecutor to report on events in the district of Topusko.[301] When Dr. Hinković inquired what Schmidt was living upon in Agram, Mr. Accurti, in great excitement, protested against this question, and it was disallowed by the President.

II. TREATMENT OF THE DEFENDING COUNSEL.

At every turn Dr. Hinković and his colleagues were hampered in their defence of the unfortunate Serbs. Not merely were their formal applications for the hearing of witnesses overruled in the most wholesale manner, and their efforts to obtain evidence from Belgrad—rendered doubly difficult owing to the strained relations with Servia—represented in the " inspired " press as savouring of treason. Day after day during

[299] 48th day.   [300] 54th day.   [301] 40th day.

the cross-examination the presiding Judge ruled out of order the most essential questions to the witnesses ; and counsel's protests against this injustice were repeatedly met by violent outbursts of the Judge and the imposition of heavy fines.

That the defending counsel sometimes went too far in their expression of indignation, is undoubtedly true ; but this was almost inevitable in view of the restrictions imposed by the President. As a fair specimen of the questions tabooed, the following may be quoted. Nastić was asked by Dr. Popović, how he knew that the brothers Pribičević had received money from Servia.[302] This, and literally scores of questions relative to the crucial subject of the Slovenski Jug, were disallowed by the President. One of the accused [303] put to a hostile witness the question whether it was not true that he (accused) had worked to promote Serbo-Croat friendship. The President would not allow an answer.

Dr. Budisavljević was fined 50 crowns for saying that it was superfluous to draw his attention to a certain point.[304] Dr. Popović was fined 120 crowns on the ground that he was bringing an unnecessary plea of nullity.[305] Dr. Medaković was fined 200 crowns for contending that the Judge was infringing the Criminal Code, when he sentenced a prisoner to twenty-four hours in a dark cell for refusing to answer a question.[306] Dr. Mazzura was fined 100 crowns for clapping his hands at a sharp sally of one of his colleagues.

Again Dr. Hinković, having elicited from Nastić the interesting fact that he had not been put on oath at the Cetinje Treason trial, was anxious to learn the reason for this ; but the President would not allow Nastić to answer.

One of the prisoners asserted that the *juge d'instruction* spoke to him of King Peter as " a robber " ; but the President stopped further reference to this. In short, while showing no desire whatever to hasten the pace of the trial, and often even allowing prolix examination, the President showed a tendency to disallow most questions dealing with any really vital points at issue, above all with the relations of the prisoners to Belgrad and Servia.

III. TREATMENT OF THE PRISONERS.

I have already referred to the grave scandals in the prison,

---

[302] 105th day. [303] Borojević, 35th day. [304] 47th day.
[305] 15th day. [306] 32nd day.

where a number of the accused Serbs were forced to share the cells of condemned criminals. After the trial had already begun, the second Judge, Mr. Pavešić, was entrusted with the supervision of the prison : in other words, one of the Judges received discretionary and disciplinary power over the prisoners whom he was trying. It was not till all the counsel for the defence had submitted a joint protest to the presiding Judge, that this decision was revoked.

Many of the prisoners had spent many months in confinement before the trial opened, without any clear idea of the charges which had led to their arrest. The long restraint, the horrible uncertainty and their apparent abandonment to their fate—coupled with anxiety as to the fate of families whose means of subsistence had been removed—were not without their effect. Five of them resorted in their despair to a hunger strike, and Adam Pribičević, his nerves utterly unstrung, even made an unsuccessful attempt to take his own life in prison. None the less, the spirit of the prisoners was not broken, and in court they repelled the charges with the greatest possible vigour, sometimes interpolating remarks when a witness made what they regarded as an unfounded assertion. Their bold protestations of innocence were highly distasteful to the Court, and Mr. Tarabocchia raged against them like a veritable Judge Jeffreys. The accused, who it may be at once admitted, behaved in a childish and aggravating manner,· were treated from the first as naughty children ; were repeatedly excluded from the proceedings in court on the ground of " refractory behaviour," or were sentenced to solitary confinement, to the dark cell, to fasting or to a board bed. For instance, on the 19th day Adam Pribičević interrupted the Public Prosecutor with the remark, " The Slovenes also have created their own institutions." He was promptly excluded from the proceedings for a whole week. On the 41st day the same prisoner was banished from the court for a fortnight, because he had called out something. On the 45th day Vukelić was shut out for the remainder of the trial, on account of his noisy interruptions.

Once when I myself was present in court, one of the prisoners, a consumptive whose appearance was lamentable, ventured to protest when the Judge disallowed a very important question directed by his counsel to the witness. Mr. Tarabocchia sprang from his seat in great annoyance, the Bench withdrew to a private room, and after a few minutes' interval the unfortunate man was sentenced for the third time to twenty-four hours without food in a dark cell !

On the 28th day the Public Prosecutor charged Dr. Gjurić with being a traitor, whereupon he replied, " You incriminate even the Servian Saints ! " " It would be bad," retorted Mr. Accurti, " if all Serbs were like you : for you are a traitor." When Dr. Gjurić violently protested against this offensive remark, the Court sentenced him to two days' fasting in a dark cell.

On the 22nd day the prisoner Konćar suddenly called out that a woman in the gallery was taunting him with mock signs of a rope being placed round the neck. Instead of defending the prisoners against such insults, the Judge sentenced Konćar to three days' exclusion from the court and twenty-four hours' dark cell ; and it was only when the woman greeted Counsel's protests by a loud cry of " You are a liar," that Mr. Tarabocchia requested her to withdraw.

On one occasion the prisoners loudly protested against the help given by the President to an embarrassed witness. " Behave decently," cried the Public Prosecutor to them. " Behave decently yourself," shouted back one of the prisoners. " Do you think you're in your native village ? " said the President, and sentenced him to forty-eight hours' detention in a dark cell, with fasting and without a mattress to the bed, and to exclusion from the proceedings for eight days.[307]

Here was a case of definite impertinence, and it is clear that a Court which tolerated such outbursts must soon cease to command respect. Unhappily the outbursts of the prisoners were the direct result of outrageous conduct on the part of the Judge, and thus won the sympathy even of those who would have been loudest in condemning such behaviour in a properly conducted trial.

IV. The Evidence Allowed.

As we have seen, almost all the witnesses proposed by the defence were disallowed. The 270 witnesses brought by the prosecution were mainly recruited from among the prisoners' bitterest political opponents. Almost all were men who refused to recognize the existence of Serbs in Croatia, and these were supposed to give impartial evidence against the fifty-three Serbs ! A number of them were rival tradesmen,

[307] 36th day.

who had suffered from the prisoners' successful competition. With certain exceptions, their standard of education was low, some being entirely illiterate. Two instances suffice to show how worthless was their opinion on political matters. One witness, when asked if he considered the accused to be loyal, replied, " How can they be loyal to the King, when they're against the Government ? "[308] A female witness, who convulsed the Court by her evidence, was so ignorant as to talk of " Raf " instead of Rauch, and " Daramit " instead of dynamite.[309]

Some idea of the childishness and absurdity of the evidence brought forward in proof of treasonable agitation, may be obtained from the following instances.

Great stress was laid upon the popularity of King Peter's portrait. A witness affirmed on oath that he had seen in the prisoner Živković's house a picture with the inscription " Petar Jurišić, Kralj Srbije"—"Peter *Jurišic*, King of Servia."[310] Another prisoner, an innkeeper, explained that he had had in the taproom a portrait of Gambrinus, whom the peasants mistook for King Peter.[311]

Another witness who spoke of King Peter's portrait, admitted having seen it in *Hrvatski Novosti*, the farthing newssheet of the anti-Serb Party.[312] Mojo Hrvačanin, who during the campaign of 1876 had saved the life of Peter Karageorgević, was treated as a suspect because his old friend had received him in audience after his accession to the throne of Servia.

Ljubomir Milić, a tailor in Glina, was examined by the President. " You trod on a dog's tail," said he, " and when the dog howled, you said, ' How that Croat whines ! ' " *Accused :* " In the first place the dog had no tail ! Secondly it is untrue that I called the dog a Croat." *President :* " But the witnesses say you did." *Accused :* " I only asked, ' Is the dog a Croat, I wonder, as you make out there are only Croats in Croatia ? ' The question was a joke." *Solvuntur tabulae risu.*

Dr. Gjurić was seriously asked by one of the Bench whether his real reason for not wearing a collar was that the word " cravat " was derived from " Croat." The accused replied that this was merely ridiculous, and the public not unnaturally agreed with him. But the Public Prosecutor solemnly declared,

---

[308] 57th day.   [309] 40th day.   [310] 38th day.
[311] 33rd and 39th days.   [312] 54th day.

" There's nothing to laugh at there ! It is proved that as a student you objected to wearing a collar, simply out of hatred towards the Croatian nation." [313] When, however, one of the prisoners suggested that the witness Rebrača could not be a good Croat, because he wore no collar, the President threatened him with punishment.[314]

V. BEHAVIOUR OF THE PRESIDING JUDGE.

It is not too much to say that Mr. Tarabocchia's behaviour during the trial baffles description. A man of slight build, highly nervous manner and unhealthy complexion, he gives the impression of an excitable *avocat*, not of a judge. Where there should be calm and dignity, there is continuous and spasmodic movement. No one who watched him in court could fail to be struck with the open manner in which he espoused the side of the prosecution.

Not content with excluding or punishing the prisoners, he took every opportunity of threatening them. When the prisoner Oblaković replied to a question with the words, " I can't help laughing," the President replied, " I'll impose a disciplinary punishment, so that you may forget how to laugh." [315]

Another day he called out to the accused, " Take care that you don't have to fast at Easter ! " [316] And again, " If even one of you budges, out he flies ! " [317] When one of the witnesses revoked his alleged evidence at the preliminary examination, and was thrown into prison for perjury, Mr. Tarabocchia warned the next witness in a menacing tone that he too would be arrested, if he failed to tell the truth. Often enough he contrived to " suggest " to the witnesses their answers, and in this he was manfully assisted by the second Judge, Mr. Pavešić. Prosecution and defence were treated in an entirely different manner. While, for instance, he forbade the defence to criticise the Public Prosecutor,[318] he declared that it was inadmissible " to emphasize the innocence of the accused ! " [319] According to his mood, he punished them or had his joke at their expense. He ordered Valerian Pribičević to remove a rose from his buttonhole : he shouted the word " Silence " across the Court ; he forbade one of the defending counsel, Dr. Solarić, to address his own father, who was one of the prisoners, in the second person [320] : he dismissed

[313] 28th day.   [314] 49th day.   [315] 31st day.   [316] 26th day.
[317] 55th day.   [318] 7th day.   [319] 26th day.   [320] 29th day.

Dr. Hinković's questions as " gammon " [321] : he forbade counsel to shake hands with their clients when the Court rose.[322] When Oblaković declared that his conscience was clear, the President rejoined, " Very well, just sit down with your clear conscience ! " [323] " You've had your lunch," he cried one day : " after it you're always obstreperous." [324] One day another prisoner protested against the evidence of a man whose father was a criminal and whose two uncles had been hanged ; and when ordered to be silent, announced a plea of nullity. " Put in as many as you like," said the Judge. " You look like a plea of nullity yourself." [325] The prisoner Bekić complained of the vague reference in the indictment to " phenomena " of high treason. " You're a phenomenon yourself," said the Judge. " Yes," cried the prisoner plaintively, " and this phenomenon has been sitting nine months in preventive arrest ! " [326]

The President's ready wit was worthy of a better occasion : it certainly was singularly inappropriate at a momentous political trial. The other judges, selected for their subservience, were in no way qualified for their task, and made a most unfavourable impression upon observers in court. The Public Prosecutor, on the other hand, was elegant and cultured, but his cynical and negligent air was replaced from time to time by menace and intimidation. On the 7th day he said of Adam Pribičević : " If he had a clear conscience, he would not be sitting here." On the 23rd day he interrupted the prisoner Kačar with the words, " That is a lie." On the 46th day he told another prisoner, " At the end of the trial, you will see how serious your situation is." The best that can be said of him, is that he showed far more restraint and good taste than any of the judges.

One gross scandal has still to be added to this plethora of scandals. During the course of the trial, Dr. Hinković, the leading advocate for the defence, and his colleague, Dr. Budisavljević, went to Belgrad to collect material in their clients' interest, and immediately on their arrival informed the Austro-Hungarian Minister, Count Forgách, of their business. On the way home to Agram Dr. Budisavljević was stopped, at the frontier station of Semlin, and searched by the police. All his papers were seized. Later on the Public Prosecutor

---

[321] 39th day. [322] 14th day. [323] 31st day. [324] 29th day.
[325] 57th day. [326] 55th day.

produced Dr. Budisavljević's notes as evidence against the
prisoners. When the defence protested, the Court declared
that it was quite immaterial how the Public Prosecutor had
come into possession of his proofs ! Needless to say, whatever
was favourable to the prisoners in these notes was carefully
suppressed, only such things were used as could be twisted
into an admission of their guilt.

The main object was to prevent any assistance reaching
the prisoners from Belgrad, and indirectly to warn possible
Servian witnesses of the dangers to which they would expose
themselves, if they came to give evidence in Agram. This
incident in itself is a vivid illustration of the complete absence
of constitutional life in Croatia.

*   *   *   *   *

The grave scandals of the Agram trial found an echo throughout the European Press, and Croatia, so long forgotten by the
outside world, acquired an unwelcome notoriety. On May
14, 1909, the distinguished Bohemian philosopher and politician,
Professor Masaryk, brought forward an interpellation on the
subject in the Austrian Parliament, and in a powerful speech
exposed the misdeeds of Baron Rauch and his creatures, and
emphasized their evil effects upon the whole policy of Austria-
Hungary upon its southern frontier. Professor Masaryk did
not mince matters, and spoke quite openly of the notorious
misconduct of some of the judges. One result of the speech,
which naturally caused a great sensation, was that the President of the High Court in Agram strictly prohibited Mr. Tarabocchia and his colleagues on the Bench from frequenting
public places at night, so long as the trial continued ! ! [327]

The speech was received by a chorus of the most virulent
abuse from the organs of Baron Rauch and Dr. Frank. *Narodne
Novine*, the official Government gazette, described Professor
Masaryk as " a vulgar parrot." *Ustavnost*, calmly ignoring
his European reputation, wrote as follows in an article entitled
" Pan Masaryk." " A certain Masaryk, of whom nothing
is known in Croatia save that he is the father of our Progressives . . . this Czech, who is nothing but a Pan-Slav *agent
provocateur* in Servian sheepskin . . . had the boundless
insolence to attack our judges in a manner which baffles criticism, for no dictionary contains the right expression for such
behaviour." The *juge d'instruction*, Dr. Košutić, actually

[327] Masaryk, op. cit. p. 37, note.

published the following statement : " I shall not have your speech in my hands for another forty-eight hours. I declare you beforehand to be a blackguard, a ragamuffin, a man without honour, a nobody, the refuse of human society." On May 24, these scurrilities were endorsed by the *Agramer Zeitung*, Baron Rauch's other organ ! I do not apologize for reproducing them, for they show more clearly than anything else the type of men upon whom Baron Rauch found it necessary to rely.

Needless to say, Baron Rauch spared no efforts to muzzle the Croatian press during the course of the trial. While all the leading newspapers of Europe gave great prominence to the scandals of the Rauch regime and of Mr. Tarabocchia's conduct of the trial, the official organs of Baron Rauch were engaged in a campaign of calumny against the prisoners, the defence and all who dared to espouse its cause, and " the control of Europe " was laughed to scorn as a device of the Freemasons, engineered by Dr. Hinković, the prisoners' brilliant advocate. Confiscations were endless ; *Pokret* and *Srbobran* alone were seized close upon a hundred times under Baron Rauch. On June 26, 1909, *Obzor* was actually confiscated for publishing the official *communiqué* of the conference of the Croato-Serb Coalition ; and all the other Agram papers were obliged to omit the essential portions of this document, though the Budapest papers which had reproduced it were left untouched by the Croatian Public Prosecutor. This was a little too strong even for the Magyars —who in their own relations to the unhappy non-Magyar races, employ, instead of confiscation, the less sensational though equally effective methods of fine and imprisonment. The *Pester Lloyd* even published an article under the title of " Russian Press Censorship in Croatia " ; but this naturally did not deter Baron Rauch from hindering the legal majority of the Sabor in the expression of its views.

We have already seen in the case of Professors Šurmin and Manojlović how readily Baron Rauch vented personal grudges. A less important but still more characteristic instance of this was the treatment of a local town councillor, who was sentenced to three days' imprisonment, because at a meeting of the Council he had referred to Rauch as an " exponent " of Magyar policy, in other words because he had employed the very phrase used by the Hungarian Premier, Dr. Wekerle.

How little personal freedom was respected under Rauch,

was illustrated in a drastic manner by the arrest of Mr. Schlegel, sub-editor of the Progressive organ *Pokret*. After a particularly outrageous incident in the High Treason trial, Mr. Schlegel handed in at the central Post Office in Agram a private telegram to Professor Masaryk, describing briefly what had happened. The same day he was arrested and thrown into prison, on a charge of "*public* incitement against the authorities." There he remained for a fortnight, until the Higher Court ordered his release, without comment or apology.

Even more notorious was the treatment of Father Mathew Novosel, a member of the Croatian Diet, who on the occasion of the Ban's visit to Brod on June 15, 1909, was unwise enough to call out "Down with Rauch." For this "treasonable" action he was promptly arrested by gendarmes, detained for eight hours, and eventually sentenced to fourteen days' imprisonment without the option of a fine, his parliamentary immunity being simply ignored. Twenty-six other persons were sentenced for similar equally harmless demonstrations.

It lies beyond the scope of the present volume to describe the course of events during the protracted Bosnian Crisis of 1908–1909. But a brief summary is inevitable, in order that the reader may be in a position to understand the intimate connexion between events in Croatia and the annexation policy of Baron Aehrenthal.

The annexation of Bosnia and Herzegovina, following closely upon the declaration of Bulgarian independence, had caused intense excitement in Servia, where political phantasts had fancied themselves to possess a reversionary interest in the two provinces. In addition to their other misfortunes, the Servians of the Kingdom have an unhappy tendency to exaggerate their own capabilities, and to underestimate those of their opponents ; and on this occasion public opinion rashly favoured a challenge to the second military power of the Continent.

The recruits were called out, and loud threats of war were uttered; but on October 10 the Skupština had sufficient self-restraint and sanity to decide against war by 93 to 66 votes. The friction which had so long prevailed between Servia and Montenegro vanished in view of the crisis, and General Vukotić was sent to Belgrad as a special envoy of Prince Nicholas. His detention by Baron Rauch's police on his way through Agram was treated by Servian public opinion as a deliberate insult ; and there can be little doubt that its aim was provocative. The Servian claims began to take definite shape ; much was heard of an " irreducible minimum," consisting of (a) the cession of a strip of territory connecting Servia and Montenegro and (b) the grant of autonomy to Bosnia. Crown Prince George went to St. Petersburg, in the hope of inducing the Czar to take up the cudgels for Servia ; and a leading Belgrad news-paper went so far as to declare that " now or never is the moment for trying conclusions with a mediaeval state on the point of dissolution." [328] Meanwhile Russia and the Western Powers adopted the attitude that Austria-Hungary and Bulgaria had, by their one-sided action, infringed an inter-national agreement, and that only an European conference could ratify the changes involved. Baron Aehrenthal, while raising no objection to the summons of a Conference, declined to admit that " the accomplished fact could be questioned there or even made the subject of discussion." [329]

The press—alike in Belgrad, Vienna, Berlin, Paris and London—fanned the growing irritation ; changes of perfidy, intrigue and illegality were bandied about between the various capitals. Above all, Baron Aehrenthal succeeded in mobiliz-ing the entire press of Vienna (with one exception) in favour of his policy. A notable feature of this press campaign were the systematic attacks upon Britain, as the *spiritus movens* of the whole opposition. As a single instance of the absurdities served up for the consumption of the Austrian public, may be quoted the statement of an otherwise sensible newspaper that Mr. Noel Buxton had paid for Servian armaments, by handing over £4,000 in gold ! [330]

Serbophil demonstrations and rioting took place in Prague, and the sixtieth anniversary of the Emperor's accession (December 2) was celebrated in the Bohemian capital by the proclamation of martial law. Turkish opinion had in no way been mollified by the cession of the Sandjak ; and a

[328] *Politika*, October 26, 1908.
[329] Speech in the Austrian Delegation, Budapest, October 27.
[330] As *The Times* correspondent caustically remarked (November 30), "the comic organs will soon be entitled to complain of unfair official competition." As a matter of fact, this yarn was outbid by a report of the *Zeit* (December 3), said to be current in Austrian par-liamentary circles, to the effect that " during the last few weeks a Viennese bank has transmitted £1,500,000 of English money in cheques to Servia ! "

serious boycott of Austrian goods was organized in all the ports of European and Asiatic Turkey. Baron Aehrenthal held resolutely to the view that a conference could only register the *fait accompli*, but agreed to a preliminary exchange of views with the Powers (December 10), and found it necessay to abandon the argument that Turkey was not entitled to any further compensation. Negotiations were opened between Vienna and Constantinople on the basis of a Turkish demand for money compensation (December 21).

The publication of the Russian Circular Note to the signatories of the Congress of Berlin (December 24) was regarded in Vienna as an unfriendly act. It certainly marked the adoption of a more aggressive policy by Mr. Isvolsky, round whose personal duel with Baron Aehrenthal the European crisis tended more and more to revolve. His speech in the Duma on Christmas Day (New Style) was a veiled appeal to the rising tide of Panslavism in Russia. While admitting Russia's engagements in the matter of Bosnia,[331] and arguing that a protest was a grave political blunder unless its author was prepared if necessary to resort to force, he laid renewed emphasis on the need for a conference, in order to vindicate the axiom that international contracts cannot be broken save by consent of all parties. He concluded by openly advocating a league between Turkey and the Christian states of the Balkans for the joint defence of their national and economic development.[332]

Mr. Isvolsky's speech was followed a week later by the speech of Dr. Milovanović, the Servian Foreign Minister (January 2, 1909). He declared the fate of Bosnia to be not merely an eminently Servian, but also an European question, and argued that the mission of Austria-Hungary in the Balkan Peninsula was now at an end. " The freedom," he added, " which the Balkan peoples won from 1812 to 1876, they obtained through Russia, while Austria-Hungary's first step in the Balkans consisted in subjecting the people of two Serb lands. . . . The path of Austria-Hungary to the Aegean Sea must be blocked. She must cease to be a Balkan State." Becoming more conciliatory, he argued that it was not necessary to drive Servia into a struggle of despair ; for " if Austria-Hungary would fulfil her mission as a link between the

---

[331] Viz. the Budapest Convention of 1877 and the Berlin Declaration of 1878.
[332] *Times* December 27.

Germanic Latin and Slav peoples," Servia's interests could be reconciled with her own and all the Balkan states could gather round her. But the Danube and the Save must at all costs remain the legal boundary between the Habsburg Monarchy and the Balkans. The following day the Skupština passed an unanimous resolution, which formulated as the sole guarantees of Servia's political and economic independence, the erection of Bosnia into a vassal state under the Sultan's suzerainty and the grant of a territorial link between Servia and Montenegro.

It was only to be expected that such language should be ill-received in Vienna, where from the first there had been an undue tendency to ignore Servia's vital stake in all questions affecting her Western frontier and to deny any moral claim arising either from racial affinity or from wars which she had waged in defence of Bosnian interests. Nor was any allowance made for the difficult situation of a Minister who had to interpret the national sentiment without challenging that of a neighbouring power. The bad impression was increased by a misleading translation of one of the crucial phrases, in which Milovanović was represented as having said that Austria had "enslaved," not "subjected," the two provinces. Count Forgách, the Austro-Hungarian Minister at Belgrad, was instructed to make inquiries as to the correct version ; and the Foreign Minister's reply, that his speech had no aggressive tendency, merely increased the difficulty of his position and inflamed still further the warlike feeling at Belgrad.

On January 9 the Austrian offer of T. £2,500,000 to Turkey as indemnity for the annexation, was accepted by the Grand Vizier, and, after a little delay, endorsed by the Cabinet and by Parliament. The former suzerain had thus been induced to relinquish his rights, and Baron Aehrenthal scored an important point.

On February 2 Mr. Isvolsky parried with the Russian proposal for a Turko-Bulgarian settlement, by which Russia agreed to liquidate the Turkish war indemnity of 1882 and Bulgaria took up a loan of 82,000,000 francs, paying moderate interest upon it to the Russian Treasury. This ingenious arrangement took Vienna by surprise, and was not unnaturally regarded there as a Pan-Slavistic device for attracting Bulgaria once more into the orbit of St. Petersburg. It also encouraged Servia to fresh exertions, and on February 5 a credit of

33,500,000 francs for armaments was adopted by the Skupština. The war fever in Belgrad continued. The Servian
press lost all self-restraint, and also all sense of proportion.
" Either Europe must concede our demands," wrote *Politika*,[333]
" or it will come to a fearful and bloody war." The situation
seemed to be going from bad to worse. On the part of
Austria-Hungary a powerful and obstinate Minister, unwilling
to admit his faulty tactics ; an " inspired " press, suffering
from a severe attack of Jingo sentiment ; a network of secret
intrigues at Court, clerical, military, political, racial, personal ;
on the part of Russia, an irresponsible desire to score off a
detested rival ; on the part of the Western Powers, a doctrinaire outlook, combined with irresolution and *laisser faire* ;
on the part of Servia a complete lack of balance, a refusal to
reckon with the realities of the situation, an inclination to
stake the country's future upon a gambler's throw. Meanwhile, clumsily as he had managed the actual step of annexation, it must be admitted that Baron Aehrenthal himself
showed very considerable restraint, even when his organs
in the press were most aggressive. Rival diplomats conceded
his faculty for " sitting tight " and awaiting developments.

But now significant *ballons d'essai* found their way into the
Neue Freie Presse and other important newspapers. The
question of an European mandate to Austria-Hungary for
the occupation of Servia was, it was alleged, already under
consideration : for the growth of Servian armaments and
the impossibility of massing troops on the Bosnian frontier
for an indefinite period, rendered some such step inevitable.
Samouprava, the official organ of the Servian Government,
retorted with a long *communiqué*,[334] protesting against the
attacks of the Vienna and Budapest press, and treating as a
gross insult to Servia the idea of a punitory expedition, such
as is only made against wild robber tribes." It appealed to
the signatory Powers of Berlin, and roundly declared that
any such action would be " a brutal and uncalled-for onslaught
upon Servia, meant to provide a cynical pretext for realizing
the second stage in Austria-Hungary's scheme of Balkan
conquest, according to which Servia figures as the next object
of plunder after Bosnia and Herzegovina." The new Servian
Coalition Cabinet, under Stojan Novaković (February 23)
continued its preparations, and an open rupture seemed in

[333] February 6, 1909.   [334] February 22.

sight, when the Powers, on the initiative of France, made joint representations at Belgrad, urging Servia not to insist on her territorial demands. As no change occurred in the situation, Count Forgách, acting on instructions from Vienna, expressed the hope that Servia was prepared to follow the advice of the Powers and change her attitude on the Bosnian question. He added that until Servia intimated to Vienna her desire for friendly relations, no steps could be taken to lay the Servian commercial treaty before the Parliaments of the Dual Monarchy (March 6). Servia left Count Forgách's note unanswered for ten days, but meanwhile (March 10) issued a Circular Note to the Powers, disclaiming all desire to provoke war but reaffirming its view that the Bosnian question is European. In short, Servia placed its case unreservedly in the hands of the Powers as the competent tribunal, "and therefore demands from Austria-Hungary no compensation, territorial, political or economic." The Servian reply to Forgách, when it did come (March 14), was politely evasive, and was regarded in Vienna as inadequate. On March 17 Russia replied to the official intimation of the Austro-Turkish agreement by insisting that this in no way averted the necessity for a Conference : and despite the increasing energy with which the three Western Powers urged pacific counsels in Belgrad, Mr. Isvolsky's step was widely regarded as materially increasing the chances of war. As stronger pressure was brought to bear upon Servia, and as the latter's statesmen showed signs of yielding, Baron Aehrenthal's manner seemed to become stiffer and more uncompromising. The Austrian Premier, Baron Bienerth, spoke of the untenable situation on the frontier : the Joint Army was mobilized and over 200,000 troops were poured into the occupied provinces. The Austrian press was not unnaturally full of articles on military and strategic subjects. The outbreak of war appeared to be only a question of days.

At this critical moment (March 24 and 25) two long interviews with "an Austro-Hungarian Politician in Belgrad," couched in language of thinly veiled menace, appeared in the *Neue Freie Presse*. Both bore many signs of their origin in the Belgrad Legation, and supplied the first public clue to the campaign of calumny and forgery associated with the names of Vasić and Swientochowski. In the first a reference was made to Servia's intrigues in Budapest and to her "suspicious connexions with the Serbo-Croat Coalition, whose intimacy is still by no means known in its entirety." Servian money, it was alleged, was working in Laibach and Prague. In the second it was made clear that the Monarchy would not be satisfied with "a half-success," and that Servia's "Pater Peccavi" (*sic*) must be said direct to Vienna, not through any intermediary.

In the same number as the first of these interviews there appeared an article entitled "Austria-Hungary and Servia," from the pen of Dr. Henry Friedjung, the well-known Austrian historian, written in a most uncompromising style and full of the gravest imputations against the Servian Government and dynasty and their alleged accomplices among the leading politicians of Croatia. Based as it was upon documentary evidence which could only have been supplied by the Ballplatz at its chief's express orders, the article naturally made a deep impression upon the public for which it was intended, and was regarded in diplomatic circles as indicating the lines upon which Baron Aehrenthal proposed to justify the impending occupation of Servia. As a matter of fact it had been intended as merely the first of a series of articles, in which a long array of original documents should have proved the aggressive purpose and scandalous intrigues of the Servian Government, thus fatally compromising it in the eyes of Europe. Two days previously similar charges had appeared in the *Reichspost*, the well-known organ of the Christian Socialist Party in Vienna.

On the very day when this article was published, two events occurred which transformed the international situation. Crown Prince George, who had been the life and soul of the war party in Servia, abdicated his right to the Throne, in consequence of the widespread rumours which charged him with having mortally injured his valet in a fit of passion. The German Ambassador in St. Petersburg asked to be informed of Russia's intentions ; and Mr. Isvolsky, faced by the prospect of Germany's mobilization in aid of her ally, suddenly expressed his readiness to recognize the annexation of Bosnia. The Servian Government, realizing that in the event of war Montenegro would be its only ally, saw no alternative but to submit. On March 27, Servia gave a definite proof of pacific intentions by dismissing the reserves : and three days later, acting on the collective advice of France, Britain, Italy and Russia, addressed to Austria-Hungary a Note, in which she recognized the "*fait accompli* created in Bosnia" as "in no way affecting her rights," and promised to abandon the attitude of protest which she had maintained since the previous autumn, to resume neighbourly relations with the Dual Monarchy, and to restore her army to its ordinary peace footing.

The international crisis was thus at an end, and on April 9 the Great Powers intimated at Vienna their formal recognition of the annexation. The last mutterings of the storm died away when Austria-Hungary consented to abrogate Article XXIX of the Treaty of Berlin and thus to remove the last trammels upon Montenegrin sovereignty. There remained, however, the internal crisis in Croatia, which owed its origin in great measure to what unscrupulous and blundering diplomats conceived to be the necessities of foreign policy, and whose evil influences reacted upon all the provinces of the Slavonic South. So far as Baron Aehrenthal was concerned, the hunt for traitors had ceased to have an object on the day when the annexation was recognized. The real value of the Agram trial had been calculated for the period when the army had crossed the Servian frontier, when the existence of a Pan-Serb conspiracy would justify the proclamation of martial law in Croatia, and when the publication of highly compromising documents would destroy all sympathy in Europe for " the nest of bandits " in Belgrad. But the evil spirits which he had invoked could not be so easily dispelled. Though Baron Aehrenthal's motive for continuing the trial was now gone, the motives of the Hungarian Government and of Baron Rauch were more pressing than ever. Persecution, instead of destroying, seemed to be cementing Croato-Serb unity and rallying all Croatia against Magyar pretensions. The Hungarian Coalition, now tottering to its fall, was more than ever conscious that Croatia formed the Achilles' heel of Hungary, more than ever determined to break the power of the rival Coalition in Croatia. Baron Rauch, furious at his own failure and hopelessly compromised by his clumsy choice of tools, saw his sole hope of continuance in office in the triumph of the Magyar cause. The High Treason trial, with all its attendant scandals, was therefore allowed to continue at Agram : indeed, its " abolition," after it had attained such notoriety, would have constituted a far greater scandal and would have aroused the very suspicions which it was desired to avert.

Had Dr. Friedjung's article never appeared, the true nature of the conspiracy against Croatia might never have transpired : and the whole affair might have flickered out with a grave miscarriage of justice in a Croatian court, speedily to be forgotten by the outside world. But the grave nature of the charges, the deservedly high reputation of their author as a historian and as a man of honour, the political interests involved, above all the patent fact that documents and information alike had been placed at the historian's disposal by the Foreign Office itself—all this would have made it impossible for the matter to be hushed up, even if Rauch's official press and his unofficial supporters in the Frank party had not made it the signal for a fresh campaign of calumny. The Coalition leaders realized, perhaps for the first time, the full strength of the forces arrayed against them, and for that very reason felt that they must fight to the bitter end.

Dr. Friedjung's article, leading as it did to the famous trial of December, 1909, and to the exposure of Count Aehrenthal's diplomatic methods, may fairly be described as one of the most important landmarks in the development of the Southern Slav question ; and therefore I make no apology for analysing it in considerable detail.

The article begins by describing Servia's insolent attitude towards the Dual Monarchy as unparalleled in modern history, and as due to disappointment at the failure of long years of intrigue in Bosnia. In view of the outcry raised in Belgrad, it is high time to expose the conspiracy " against us," which began with the murder of King Alexander in June, 1903. The new King had grown up in an atmosphere of plots and had pledged himself in writing to the leader of the murderous gang. This document, quoted as authentic by Dr. Friedjung, ran as follows : " I, Prince Peter Karageorgevitch, swear by my honour, that so long as I and my heirs are on the Servian throne, the conspirators and their heirs shall not only not be proceeded against before the law, but rather that the highest positions in the country shall be assured to them." The successful conspirators aimed at " erecting a Great Servian Empire on the ruins of Austrian and Turkish rule," and in 1905 conceived the idea of helping the Magyar Party of Independence in the struggle for an independent Hungary. Bosnia was to be the Servian share of the spoils. " Hence from Belgrad was constituted the Serbo-Croatian Coalition, which was intended as a link between the aspirations for the separation of Hungary and of Bosnia from the Habsburg Monarchy. These fantasies were dissipated, it is true, in consequence of the pact concluded by the Party of Independence in April,

1906, with the Emperor Francis Joseph ; but there remained one welcome result for the Pan-Serb leaders. For the kernel of the Serbo-Croatian Coalition, the Serb Independent Party, remained in permanent connexion with Belgrad, took its watchword from there ; and large presents of money to influential Serbs in South Hungary and Croatia nourished the alliance thus concluded." As a proof of this grave charge, Dr. Friedjung adduces a confidential Report, written in 1907 by Dr. Spalajković, under-secretary in the Servian Foreign Office, to his chief, describing his meeting with a certain Coalition deputy [335] at Semlin. " The noble Serb from South Hungary " demanded 50,000 francs, but finally, in return for 12,000 in cash, agreed to place five newspapers of the Serb Independent party at the disposal of the Servian Government! The report contained the further statement that Supilo had advised the Servian Premier, Dr. Pašić, to spend his summer holiday on the Croatian coast, so as to be in touch with " political friends." " Should the sectional chief or the Servian Government dispute any of these assertions, they would be supplied with further details, and the names of bribed deputies could be given, as also the sums supplied to them out of the money of the Servian state."

One of the chief instruments of the conspiracy is the Club Slovenski Jug [336] in Belgrad, whose dealings with bombs and dynamite were partially exposed at the Cetinje Treason trial. The bombs seized in Montenegro are known to have been manufactured in the Servian arsenal of Kragujevac, under the special supervision of Nenadović, a relative of King Peter ; and Prince Nicholas at any rate believed his grandson George of Servia to be privy to the plot for removing a rival Serb dynasty. A letter of Spalajković to a Montenegrin friend is then cited, lamenting the suspicion with which Dr. Pašić is regarded in Cetinje ; and that statesman's share in the plot against Montenegro is assumed to be one of the main causes of friction between the two Serb states.

" Should it be ordained," continues Dr. Friedjung, " that the Austrian arms shall thoroughly purge Belgrad of the nest of conspirators and help the healthy elements of the Servian people to triumph, this would be a civilizing deed of great

---

[335] Dr. Friedjung suppressed the name, because he did not wish to supply proofs for the Agram trial. *See infra*, p. 225.
[336] *See* pp. 167–170.

value—not merely an advantage for the Austro-Hungarian Monarchy, but also the liberation of a whole people from a company of conspirators divided among themselves and sowing evil on every hand, while they plunder the Servian state during the purchase of armaments and the preparations for war." [337] "Deep, however, as is the rottenness of the Servian state, it is not the office of a Great Power to act as controller of morals (Sittenpolizei) on her frontiers. But it is her duty to assure the safety of her own frontiers."

The article then deals with the Slovenski Jug's agitation in Bosnia and the "important material" supplied by one of its emissaries to the Austro-Hungarian Government in August, 1908. [338] " It is a sorry trade which this Nastić pursued, and one can only handle the fellow with gloves, or better with the tongs. He makes no secret of the fact that the Montenegrin Government paid money for his treachery towards his comrades ; and if he denies having likewise received payment from the Ban of Croatia, let him who will, believe this. But that is a matter of indifference in judging the facts." Dr. Friedjung then treats the existence of the " Revolutionary Statute " (see p. 169) in Milan Pribičević's own handwriting, as a conclusive proof of the conspiracy ; but while emphasizing the project of " a league of Southern Slav Republics," he seems completely to forget that he is thereby demolishing the theory that the Servian dynasty was at the head of the movement. He condemns the onesided attacks made at the Agram trial " upon the Serb nationality as such," and admits that a perusal of the indictment suggests that Rauch's government is using its opportunity " to strike a deadly blow at the Coalition." But while not blind to the evil side of the trial, he holds that stern measures were necessary, in order to sever the threads with Belgrad. He gives further details of the Pan-Serb propaganda in Bosnia, and of the control exercised by Spalajković over the Bosnian press ; and he asserts that the accounts of Slovenski Jug show 15,000 francs to have been sent from Belgrad during the communal elections at Sarajevo in 1908.

The remainder of the article deals with an alleged league between the Young Turk Committee and the Slovenski Jug,

---

[337] This and other passages show signs of another hand.
[338] In other words, *after* the publication of *Finale* and during his visit to Agram with Sporčić.

for the contingency of war with Austria-Hungary. When the Austro-Hungarian Consul-General in Salonica was instructed to inform the Committee of the intention to grant a constitution to Bosnia, he received "the deeply insulting answer, that Austro-Hungary did not possess the right, . . . which lay solely in the hands of the lawful sovereign the Sultan." This incident and the danger of Bosnian deputies appearing in Stambul, combined with the Pan-Serb propaganda to render the annexation inevitable, and forced Baron Aehrenthal to place Turkey before a *fait accompli*. Before acting, however, he broached the matter with Russia and Italy, offering to concede to the former the free passage of the Dardanelles ; and at his meeting with Mr. Isvolsky in Buchlau (September 15, 1908) it had been arranged to the two statesmen's mutual satisfaction. The attitude of the Viennese Cabinet was that of a *rocher de bronze*, against which "the loosely-knit Servian state" could easily be shattered.

This singular article, from the pen of the foremost Austrian historian, appeared at a moment when, in the words of the leading article,[339] "the decision as to war and peace is on the razor's edge," and when, "unless to-morrow or at latest on the day after," Servia abandons her mad pretensions, "disaster can hardly be averted." The real significance of the article, however, lies not so much in its author's high reputation as in the source from which he drew his documents and other information. It revealed the fact that the collection of material compromising to Servia formed a definite part of the plan of campaign adopted by the Ballplatz. It revealed the further fact that the theft of important documents formed part of the business of Austro-Hungarian diplomats. How many scandalous secrets lay behind these two facts, the future course of events was to reveal.

On March 27, Mr. Tuškan and Dr. Medaković, in the name of the Croato-Serb Coalition, wired to the *Neue Freie Presse*, declaring all Dr. Friedjung's charges against the Coalition to be "pure inventions," and summoning him to name the guilty deputies, so that the matter might be laid before a court of law. The historian, in a brief reply, declined to be more explicit and encouraged them to bring the threatened action, since he was always ready to produce his proofs. His reputation, he added, proved that he could "distinguish genuine documents and historical sources from false ones,"

[339] *Neue Freie Presse*, March 25, 1909.

and that in testing facts he was "not swayed by political passion or personal spite."

The *Reichspost*, whose sources of information were the same as Dr. Friedjung's, had already published the names of the three deputies alluded to in the Spalajković report ; and these three, Messrs. Supilo, Pribičević and Lukinić, lost little time in suing the editor for libel. The other chief incriminated person, Dr. Spalajković, as a high official in the Servian Foreign Office, had naturally been tongue-tied so long as the crisis lasted : and it was not until after the Montenegrin Note (April 9) and the formal recognition by the Powers (April 10) that he was in a position to vindicate himself against Dr. Friedjung's charges. On April 10, however, he published an answer in the *Neue Freie Presse*, repudiating in the most explicit and detailed manner all the charges levelled against him by Dr. Friedjung. Not merely did he deny the very existence of the alleged Report, but he denied having ever written any of the phrases ascribed to him or having ever met any member of the Croato-Serb Coalition. But a denial, however emphatic, would only convince his own friends and leave his enemies to believe the opposite. " My ' No ' balances his ' Yes ' ; one syllable, the other." Hence the sole remedy for this unsatisfactory position is a court conducted by " scientific experts " (sachkundige Experte).

Dr. Friedjung's rejoinder, printed in the same issue of the *Neue Freie Presse*, declines this proposal, on the ground that legal proceedings are already pending, and that it would be too much to expect him to submit to two tribunals. Though it might be safer to consent to arbitration, he prefers to go before a jury. As for Dr. Spalajković's " No," he somewhat arrogantly concludes, " it is an error to suppose that any critical reader would assign the same weight " to the words of one who was " the soul of the war party against Austria-Hungary " and to " the historian whose quest is truth." Dr. Friedjung's colleagues may regret the tone of this reply and his refusal to submit to an inquiry by a court of impartial foreign savants. But it is quite impossible to blame him for deciding in favour of an ordinary trial. Dr. Spalajković's delay—inevitable though it may have been—had left the choice of tactics entirely in the hands of the Coalition leaders ; and they had adopted the only course open to them, namely a libel action before the Viennese courts. Before the Servian Under-Secretary intervened, they had already entrusted Dr. Harpner, one of the leaders of the Austrian Bar, with the conduct of their case. In these circumstances Dr. Friedjung's attitude was most natural. His researches in the Foreign Office had led him to regard Dr. Spalajković as the ringleader in a dangerous conspiracy for the overthrow of Austrian rule among the Southern Slavs ; and so far from showing him any consideration, he hoped to ruin his political career. Dr. Spalajković thus had no alternative but to await the issue of the libel action, and to watch his opportunity for intervening.

The date of Dr. Friedjung's trial was fixed for the autumn, but for various reasons it was not till December that the proceedings actually opened. By that time the whole subject had become highly distasteful to Baron, now Count, Aehrenthal and his admirers ; and various efforts were made to secure a settlement. But on the one hand, Dr. Friedjung, firmly convinced that he was fighting in a righteous cause, felt his reputation as a historian to be at stake : on the other hand, the Coalition was determined to put an end to the campaign of calumny directed against it, and could have accepted no compromise which left the falsity of the documents in doubt.

Count Aehrenthal, whose estimate of journalists and publicists as a class is said to be low, found that he must pay dearly for having entrusted an eminent historian with the press onslaught upon Servia. An ordinary scribbler might perhaps have been " squared " ; a man of Dr. Friedjung's calibre was immovable in matters which concerned his personal honour.

Meanwhile the High Treason trial dragged on at Agram till at length, after the proceedings had already lasted over 150 days, the verdict was announced on October 5, 1909. Adam and Valerian Pribičević were sentenced to twelve years' imprisonment, Pero Bekić to eight years, three others to seven years each, six others to six years each, and finally nineteen others to five years. The twenty-two other prisoners were acquitted. The total sentences imposed amounted to 184 years !

The verdict was worthy of such a trial : and it is sufficient to point out two of its most flagrant absurdities. (1) The accused were found guilty of conspiring to form a Pan-Serb state under the sceptre of King Peter, and the brothers Pribičević of direct relations with the revolutionary society in Belgrad. Yet the Court affirmed with special emphasis, that it had " relied upon the evidence of the so-called Crown witness Nastić only in so far as . . . it was supported by other unexceptionable evidence or documentary proofs. The rest of his evidence the Court has rejected as irrelevant." In other words, the only witness who even pretended to prove a direct connexion of the prisoners with Belgrad, is put on one side, and yet that connexion is treated as proved ! (2) If the prisoners' guilt was so clearly established, sentence of death was the only adequate punishment for so grave a charge as treason and revolutionary intrigue. In the case of conspiracy against the State there can be no extenuating circumstances—at least in a country where High Treason has not yet been consigned to the lumber-room of mediaeval phrases. Either they are guilty, in which case the full severity of the law should be imposed : or they are innocent, in which case they should be acquitted. Sentences of five or six years' imprisonment for such an offence are obviously inadequate, except as the result of royal clemency. It is always open to the Sovereign to commute the death sentence, and there was no reason why this should not have been done in the case of the Serb prisoners.

Thus ended one of the most scandalous trials of modern times, one which in its own country rivalled even the Dreyfus trial for the fierceness of the party passion which it aroused. Long before its close, it had become obvious to all impartial observers that a gross travesty of justice was being committed.

Dr. Hinković and his colleagues, who had already entered countless pleas of nullity against the rulings of the Court, lodged an appeal against the verdict ; and the monster case was referred to the Septemviral Court. The next scene of the Croatian drama was to be enacted before a Viennese jury ; upon its issue depended the fate of the Rauch regime.

CHAPTER X

The Friedjung Trial [340]

" My defence takes the form of a chapter in the history of the Balkan problem."—*Dr. Friedjung*, December 9, 1909.

I. Dr. Friedjung's Defence (p. 211)—II. Dr. Friedjung's "Documents" (p. 216)—III. The Evidence of Dr. Funder (p. 228)—IV. The *Reichspost* Documents (p. 230)—V. The Evidence of Baron Chlumecky (p. 235)—VI. The Attitude of the Court (p. 240)—VII. The Evidence of Professor Marković (p. 245)—VIII. The Evidence of Professor Masaryk (p. 250)—IX. The Evidence of Father Zagorac (p. 255)—X. Dr. Polit and the Servian Witnesses (p. 259)—XI. The Evidence of Dr. Spalajković (p. 263)—XII. Coalition Witnesses (p. 271)—XIII. Compromise (p. 277).

ON December 9 the long-expected trial opened before a Viennese jury. Three separate actions had been brought : by the fifty-two deputies of the Croato-Serb Coalition against Dr. Friedjung ; by Mr. Supilo alone against Dr. Friedjung ; and by Messrs. Supilo Pribičević and Lukinić against the editor of the *Reichspost*; but being based in each case upon the same material, all three charges were by common consent made the subject of a single trial.

The proceedings were conducted before a court of three judges, their president being Dr. Wach, a counsellor of the Supreme Court (Oberlandesgerichtsrat). Two of the leading members of the Austrian Bar held briefs for the contending parties : Dr. Edmund Benedikt for the defence, Dr. Harpner for the prosecution. Of the two defendants, Mr. Ambros was a mere figurehead, behind whom stood the chief editor, Dr. Friedrich Funder, and the Christian Socialist party, whose chief organ the *Reichspost* is.

[340] All quotations in this chapter are from the very full reports of the trial given in the *Neue Freie Presse*. I was myself present at the proceedings on the seventh and following days (six days in all) and was thus enabled on certain points to form my own impressions, being personally acquainted with the defendants, a number of the plaintiffs and even several of the witnesses.

THE FRIEDJUNG TRIAL

The figure of Dr. Friedjung deserves very different treatment. Born in 1851 of Jewish parents in a small Moravian town, he was educated in Vienna and Prague and in 1873 became professor of history at the Vienna Academy of Commerce. His first book was an admirable monograph on the Emperor Charles IV and his influence upon the culture of Mediaeval Bohemia. In 1877, however, he entered the political arena with a pamphlet on " The Compromise with Austria." The sharp criticisms of the Taaffe Cabinet which this book contained, led to its author's dismissal from his post ; the Minister of Education was unjust enough to refuse a disciplinary inquiry. Young Friedjung joined the staff of the *Deutsche Zeitung*, the leading German National organ of those days, and was for many years an active exponent of what are now known as Pan-German doctrines.[341] Indeed the famous Linz Programme of 1885, containing the political *credo* of the German extremists in Austria, was from his pen. Amid all his activity as a journalist, he still found time for historical research ; but time had already mellowed his political opinions, when in 1896 he published a larger work on *The Struggle for the Supremacy in Germany*. With him as with so many of his contemporaries the Pan-German gradually gave place to the Austrian patriot. The old conception of Austria as a German state fought with the growing perception of Austria's great mission as a Völkerbund [342] a league of races bound together by indissoluble ties of necessity and interest. This new Austrian patriotism—marred, it is true, at times by something of the old German-Austrian narrowness—is the *leitmotif* of all his books, alike of his brilliant study of Austro-Prussian rivalry, and of the later volumes dealing with Austrian Policy during the Crimean War and *Austria since* 1848.[343] The broad perspective and sober judgment which characterise all his writings, won him general recognition alike in Austria and in Germany, and a lucid and attractive style rendered them accessible to a wide public.

[341] He was also for many years correspondent of the Munich *Allgemeine Zeitung*, the *Grazer Tagespost* and the *Vossische Zeitung* of Berlin, to which he still frequently contributes.

[342] *See* article on Dr. Friedjung, by Dr. A. Bettelheim, in *Oesterreichische Rundschau*, January, 15, 1911.

[343] Dr. Friedjung has also shown himself to be a very able military critic, notably in his accounts of Königgrätz, Custozza and the seafight off Lissa. He edited the Papers of Benedek, the unfortunate commander of the Austrian Army in the war of 1866.

DR. FRIEDJUNG'S DEFENCE

Despite his acknowledged rank as the most brilliant historian of modern Austria, Dr. Friedjung had been for years consistently ignored by the *Neue Freie Presse*,[344] the leading German paper of the Monarchy ; and hence the publication of his article by that journal gave rise to much comment. There is good reason to believe that Baron Aehrenthal, who had during the summer of 1908 entered into friendly relations with the chief editor and proprietor of the *Neue Freie Presse* (at about the same time when he first made Dr. Friedjung's acquaintance) arranged the publication of the manuscript without ever consulting its author.[345]   At the trial now opening it was not merely the reputation of Dr. Friedjung that was on trial, but no less a personage than Count Aehrenthal and his diplomatic methods.   Despite the transparent disclaimers of the *Fremdenblatt* and other official organs, the whole atmosphere of the case was purely political, and an issue of European importance was at stake.

I.   DR. FRIEDJUNG'S DEFENCE.

Almost the entire course of the first day's proceedings was occupied by Dr. Friedjung's speech in his own defence.   It was couched in the same grandiloquent strain as the incriminated article, and no one who reads it could pretend that it was worthy of the gifted author of *Der Kampf um die Vorherrschaft*.   His article, he said, was written at a moment when the Emperor " called to arms thousands and ten thousands of our brothers and sons," and reflected the feelings of that exciting time.   Not being in a position to defend his fatherland sword in hand, he conceived it to be his plain duty as a historian and publicist, to place his pen at the service of Austria, and in so doing he was only continuing his lifework of strengthening the consciousness of his fellow-citizens, by an interpretation of their past history.

The main portion of the article was aimed at a foreign foe, with whom at the moment war seemed to be imminent ; its purpose was to expose the threads of Pan-Serb conspiracy, and thus to demonstrate the necessity of the annexation.

---

[344] As the main journalistic bulwark of the Dual System, and organ of the Jewish Liberals, it regarded the Pan-Germans with hostility, partly owing to their anti-Semite tinge.

[345] It is said that when the sudden change from war to peace occurred (March 24), an effort was made at the last moment to withdraw the article, but that it was already too late.

Only in passing did it deal a blow at certain parties and politicians of Transleithania.

Dr. Friedjung went on to admit that the Croats and Serbs of the Monarchy are at bottom loyally devoted to the State and to the dynasty, and impervious to the intrigues of Belgrad, and that these loyal sentiments explain the unusual phenomenon of a whole party of fifty-two members appearing as plaintiffs on the present occasion. But his opponents must be divided into two very unequal halves—on the one hand certain individuals whom he would name and would prove guilty of treasonable practices and the acceptance of foreign bribes, and on the other hand the great majority of the party, whose honour was in no way affected by these charges and who only took action " for the honour of the flag." He rejoiced to think that the whole Southern Slav question had thus been raised, and that the result of the trial would be to effect " a separation between the loyal elements and certain political desperadoes."

Dr. Friedjung then indulged in a sharp attack upon Dr. Tuškan and Mr. Francis Supilo, the president and the real leader of the Coalition, whom he charged with " an incomprehensible, a pitiless hatred towards our Austrian fatherland." The best proof of this was supplied by the words uttered by the former during a heated debate in the Croatian Diet— November 30, 1905—that he was ready to go to war with gun in hand and fire upon Vienna. And here, after another patriotic outburst in defence of " this glorious city," " this ancient seat of culture and education," " against foreign brutality," Dr. Friedjung mildly affirmed that he had no idea of urging the jury to form straight away a damning opinion of his opponents. Alas ! the " Don't put him under the pump " argument in the mouth of the Austrian Froude !

Far worse, however, was the famous speech delivered by Supilo on February 25, 1907, in which he spoke as follows :— " If we are conscious that our task consists in forming a wall of defence for the Balkans against the foreigner, and not a bridge for his advance, then, gentlemen, we must before all reckon with our brethren the Serbs." Austria, then, cries the horrified historian, is a foreigner ! Strange words in the mouth of a Croat, who remembers the long centuries in which Austrian and Croat bled together in the Turkish wars. " Were the verdict of Mr. Supilo not influenced by bribery, then he would never have exposed himself so far, he would never have expressed himself so impudently against Austria-Hungary and for Servia." Are these, one involuntarily exclaims, the words of an accused man defending himself against a grave charge of political libel, or the words of a public prosecutor fulminating against a prisoner in the dock? [346]

Dr. Friedjung then proceeded to fence in the ground : he had charged the plaintiffs [347] with "shady and dishonourable, but not with treasonable relations" (*wohl unlauterer und illoyaler nicht aber hochverräterischer Verbindungen*), and he denied the insinuation that his action made him an accomplice in the oppression of the non-Magyar races of Hungary. He then passed in review Supilo's journalistic activity and affected to discover in him an abrupt change from an Austrophil to a violently Austrophobe policy, from the moment when in 1901 he settled in Fiume as editor of *Novi List.* After rightly placing at Supilo's door the chief responsibility for the Fiume Resolution, he emphasized its anti-Austrian character for the benefit of the jury, and pictured the delight with which Louis Kossuth, " the irreconcilable enemy of the House of Habsburg," would have welcomed this unholy pact and still more the wicked words of Dr. Tuškan. The Fiume and Zara Resolutions he depicted as a conspiracy for the partition of the Monarchy, in accordance with which Hungary would have separated from Austria, Dalmatia would have fallen to Croatia, and Bosnia would have been surrendered to King Peter. He admitted the services rendered by the Croato-Serb Coalition to the cause of racial harmony between Croat and Serb, but his sympathy with this cause was clouded by the anti-Austrian tinge which it had assumed ; and he recounted with indignation the incidents of the short-lived Magyar-Servian entente of 1906, when the fire-eating Kossuthist deputy Zoltán Lengyel, in his speech at Semendria, urged the Servians to perfect their armaments and so increase their value as allies, and when Magyar and Servian sabres were bound together beneath the Hungarian tricolour.

[346] Even the *Neue Freie Presse*, which throughout the trial openly took sides for the defendants, printed in italics what was favourable to them and in its comments slurred over and sometimes even ignored what was unfavourable, wrote of this speech as follows : " His finely conceived remarks, though in form a defence, formed in reality the sharpest and most unsparing attacks upon the Croato-Serb Coalition." (*N.F.P.* December 10, 1909.)

[347] "Meine Prozessgegner." Here then would seem to be no question of individual members, but rather of the whole Coalition.

After a moderate survey of party conditions in Croatia under Pejačević and Rauch, Dr. Friedjung turned to a discussion of the revolutionary and Panserb propaganda in Belgrad. The Servian Budget provides a fund of £55,000 a year " for the worthy defence of national interests," in other words for agitation abroad ; and from this fund not merely are the churches and schools in Old Servia and Macedonia supported, but also large sums are distributed in the southern districts of the Habsburg Monarchy, through the medium of Servian Government officials and also the Belgrad society Slovenski Jug (The Slav South). In directly charging the Coalition deputies, Messrs. Supilo, Medaković, Pribičević, Budisavljević and Lukinić with receiving bribes from Servia, he declared that his evidence was based not upon Austrian or Hungarian reports but exclusively upon documents drawn from the Servian camp. Of these the majority came from the archives of the Slovenski Jug. An important link in the relations between the Croat deputies and Belgrad was the Servian Consul-General in Budapest, Mr. Petković,[348] who was especially active during the sessions of the Hungarian Parliament, and whose agents repeatedly travelled through Hungary. Even the Belgrad press, added Dr. Friedjung, wrote quite openly of " certain Serb politicians of Hungary," especially members of the Serb Radical party, as pensioners of Servia.

After analysing the contents of a number of his " documents," Dr. Friedjung referred to the continual praise of Servia sung by the newspapers of Supilo and Pribičević[349] and quoted—as it subsequently transpired, in a grossly inaccurate form [350]—a speech delivered by Supilo in the Croatian Diet early in 1907, describing Bosnia's severance from the Monarchy as a piece of good fortune and urging Croat and Serb to unite against the stranger, in other words against Austria-Hungary and its German ally.

Dr. Friedjung, when initiated into these details of the pan-Serb conspiracy, felt it to be his patriotic duty to combat it by every means in his power. Its existence rendered the annexation of Bosnia absolutely necessary. But Austria-Hungary would merely have placed itself in a false position by demanding the dissolution of the Slovenski Jug ; for Belgrad was capable of denying that the sky is blue, and in place of

[348] Now Servian Minister in Cetinje.
[349] *Novi List* and *Srbobran.*   [350] *See* page 280.

one secret society three or four new ones would have sprung up. No, the only course for the Monarchy was action so energetic as to make the restless little Balkan states tremble and give the required satisfaction. The news of the annexation roused the Slovenski Jug to fresh activity, and according to the minutes of its central committee, an attempt was made to win the friendly leaders of the Croato-Serb Coalition for a general rising. "I hasten to add," continued Dr. Friedjung, "that this summons to treachery and armed revolt was *not* complied with; but how far must these relations have gone, if the Slovenski Jug could dare to address to these deputies so mad or infamous a summons?" Further, the leaders of the Coalition were largely responsible for the improved relations between the Courts of Belgrad and Cetinje, though the conspirators in Belgrad soon found that all the money devoted by them to intrigues in Bosnia and Croatia was merely thrown away, and that its recipients had no intention of risking their skins for "the Southern Slav King."

Summarizing his results, Dr. Friedjung argued that since the accession of the Karageorgević dynasty in 1903 the Servian state has been the prey of a crowd of Macedonian, Bosnian and Croatian adventurers and political speculators, who fought for the Secret Fund and for pickings from the Army Estimates; while the agents of the pan-Serb propaganda within the Monarchy were above all else political swindlers, even if they were not traitors. "It is no business of the historian," he concluded, "to reduce men's words and deeds to the provisions of a penal code; his task is to examine documents, to establish facts and illustrate characters. I have not charged my opponents with treason, but with an action which is really more disgraceful, even if its consequences are less serious. For there are circumstances in which it is valorous and high-spirited to risk one's head in a conspiracy for the achievement of political and national dreams. But it is utterly contemptible to enter into relations with the enemy of one's country, to ask and to accept money for oneself, for newspapers and for political trials, and then to proclaim oneself as a model of loyalty, and those who say the contrary as slanderers. My lifework has been historic research, and thus my defence takes the form of a chapter in a historical book, the history of the Balkan problem. I have spoken to you, gentlemen, as my judges, but at the same time I address my fellow-historians, who will also give their verdict as to whether in examining these documents I have acted critically and conscientiously, sifting the true from the false. Every impartial person will, I am sure, admit that I have built upon the sure foundation of reliable documents, and hence I await with complete calm the final verdict of the jury."

II. Dr. Friedjung's "Documents."

The "documents" upon which Dr. Friedjung based his defence, were laid before the Court in a printed German translation, generally referred to as the Green Book. They are twenty-four in number, and are preceded by a brief preface giving Dr. Friedjung's idea of the Slovenski Jug society. The reader of the Green Book cannot fail to be struck by the fact that the majority of the "documents" have been very extensively " cut," and are in many cases mere fragments. Whether the omitted portions would have thrown much additional light upon the question at issue, it is of course impossible to say without a study of the original forgeries ; but from a significant admission made by Dr. Friedjung in the course of the trial (*see* p. 260) it would appear that the selection was not carried out on strictly scientific lines.

Nineteen of the "documents" relate to the Slovenski Jug, notably the minutes of a number of its ordinary meetings and of its central committee, the very existence of which was denied by the prosecution. In these minutes Professor Božidar Marković, a young professor of criminal law at Belgrad University, appears as president of the club ; the vice-presidents were Ljubomir Jovanović, fomerly President of the Skupshtina, and since 1909 Servian Minister of the Interior, and Ljubomir Davidović, a former Minister of Education. In No. I the names of Glavinčić and Gjorgević appear as members, but in all subsequent documents only six names occur, namely the president, the two vice-presidents, Michael Jovanović—of whom nothing is known—Rista Odavić and Mile Pavlović, the two latter being professors in Belgrad gymnasia.

I. Minutes of Slovenski Jug, February 1–(14), 1908.[351] (2 " cuts ".)

The president of the club, Professor Marković, reports a conversation with the Servian Premier, Dr. Pašić, who wished

[351] In this and most of the other " documents " both Old and New Style are given ; but it is obvious that no Servian (least of all in a revolutionary club) would ever dream of adding the New Style.

the club's statutes to be altered in such a way that any item of expenditure exceeding 1,000 francs must be referred to the Foreign Minister. The Premier expressed doubts as to Slovenski Jug's agents in Bosnia, and declined to assist the club any farther until he had reliable information. Several members criticized Pašić's attitude very outspokenly, and Davidović used the following words : [352] " It is known to the Premier, and I declare to you, that we must help our friend Supilo. I therefore beg you to send him at once 4,000 crowns." Another member argued that Bosnia was in greater need of help than Croatia, which had neither a Burian [353] nor a Hörman [354] to torment them.[355] After an hour's debate, 3,000 crowns were voted in aid of Supilo.

II. Slovenski Jug, Central Committee, eighth meeting, minutes of February 26 (March 10), 1908. (2 " cuts ".)

The ex-Minister of Education, Davidović, reported upon Supilo's plan of campaign, and the advantages which would accrue to the Serbs from their joint action with the Croats. Above all the Starčević party must be defeated, Serb interests must be defended against Rauch, " the servant of Vienna," and the pledge breakers of Pest must be shown that the Serbs are formidable foes. Davidović therefore proposed that " material aid " should be sent to Supilo, in view of " *the impending elections* to the Diet of the Triune Kingdom." For this purpose it was decided to convey 6,000 dinars (£240) to Supilo through the club's confidential agent.

III. Confidential order of the Servian Foreign Office to assign the sum of " 6,000 francs in gold from the Treasury to the committee of Slovenski Jug, to be paid by them to Mr. Supilo." Signed " Dr. Stefanović," dated February 29 (March 13), 1908.

IV. Payment of 6,000 dinars to Supilo. Order to pay, signed by Marković, as president of the central committee of Slovenski Jug, issued to the treasurer of the club. Dated March 2, 1908.

---

[352] Throughout the following analysis all quotations are translated quite literally from the German text so that the reader may have some idea of its extreme crudity of phrase.

[353] Austro-Hungarian Finance Minister and hence Minister for Bosnia.

[354] A prominent official in Sarajevo, a patriotic Austrian Croat.

[355] Only a supporter of Baron Rauch could have written thus, for it is obvious that not even a Belgrad Chauvinist would have described Burian and Hörman as worse than Rauch.

THE FRIEDJUNG TRIAL

V. Minutes of Slovenski Jug, March 9 (22), 1908.

Marković announced that the Premier had approved a grant of 10,000 francs for the foundation of agricultural societies in Bosnia. It was then decided to request the Foreign Minister to grant " 15,000 francs in gold " in aid of the Serb opposition at the Sarajevo municipal elections, the meeting " being unanimously inspired by the conviction that a contribution is necessary for the preservation of the Serb name and the Serb pride." Marković pointed out that the Premier was not disposed to continue his grants, if their efforts in Sarajevo should prove a failure ; and hence defeat must at least be followed by some protest more effective than a mere deputation to Vienna, or lamentations in the press. The Orthodox and Mohammedan Serbs of Bosnia must unite in circulating a memorandum throughout the European press. Four thousand francs were assigned to *Srpska Riječ*, the leading Serb newspaper in Bosnia, and to another local journal. (A " cut " here suggests that further names are given.)

VI. Report of the central committee of Slovenski Jug to Prince George of Servia. March 17 (30), 1908.

The report submits the minutes and accounts of the last month, which showed an expenditure of 37,890 francs. Its main tenour is a complaint of inadequate financial support by the Minister of Foreign Affairs. One passage is worth quoting, as an illustration of the naïveté of author and recipient alike. " Your Royal Highness must be well aware that public opinion in Servia is devoting its special attention to the movement among our brethren in Bosnia and Herzegovina, and it is equally well known to you that the Servian people, with respect to Macedonia, Old Servia, Bosnia and Herzegovina, possesses its (*sic*) unquestionable historic and traditional rights. Even though the committee has no idea of exceeding the limits of that policy which is suitable for the preservation of peace in the Balkan peninsula, and though the Servian people adheres loyally and honestly to this policy, the committee in its activity cannot be indifferent to eventualities which threaten Serb national interests " . . . etc.

VII. Minutes of Slovenski Jug, March 30, 1908. (Only " the most important passage " is reproduced, and even in it there are 3 " cuts ".)

Jovanović reports a conversation with the Premier, whose first words were, " Ljuba, brother, stop a little . . . with your propaganda." Pašić feared evil results from Slovenski

Jug's activity, both "because the Austrian, Hungarian and Bosnian Governments keep up an extensive system of spies, and might discover everything, and also because railway communications with Italy are at stake." "Besides," added Jovanović, "the minister informed me confider.tially as to the disappearance of certain important documents, among them also one of ours, regarding Supilo. Vice-consul Vintrović sent this document by a courier to the minister, who, however, did not come into possession of it. . . . If our document has fallen into wrong hands, then we must certainly suspend our activity for a certain time." [356]

VIII. Extract from minutes of central committee of Slovenski Jug, July 29, 1908.

Reference is made to the services of Messrs. Supilo and Budisavljević, and as "matters are now approaching the decision whether our Coalition or Rauch in league with Vienna is finally to win the victory," it is decided to assign 3,000 dinars to Mr. Supilo, 5,000 to the newspaper *Srbobran*, and 2,000 to Mr. Budisavljević.

VIII*a*. Balance of accounts of Slovenski Jug for August, 1908, showing expenditure as above.

IX. Minutes of Slovenski Jug, August 21, 1908.

Here Dr. Friedjung, instead of supplying translated extracts, merely summarizes the contents of the minutes in question. In them Professor Marković reported upon his journey to Salonica, and his negotiations with the Young Turk Committee. Their result was an arrangement for joint action on the part of the Orthodox and Mohammedan Serbs of Bosnia for agitation in favour of the extension to Bosnia of the new Turkish constitution, and for the publication of a newspaper in Constantinople to propagate this idea. Jovanović then reported a conversation which he had had with the Foreign Minister, Dr. Milovanović, who expressed the fear that lack of caution on the part of the Slovenski Jug might involve Servia in difficulties abroad. "I convinced him, gentlemen," continued Jovanović, that even if he should meet with difficulties and unpleasantnesses, he only had to contest and deny everything, like Mr. Pašić." [357]

[356] This passage is a very obvious trick, to render more plausible the wholesale methods of theft by which all these "minutes" were ostensibly stolen from the Slovenski Jug. In reality, as will be seen later (Chapter XII), they were manufactured in the Belgrad Legation.

[357] What better proof of the forgery could be supplied than this astounding extract ?

Finally a manifesto intended by Supilo for the use of the Croato-Serb Coalition was submitted to the meeting, and approved on condition that it should be signed jointly by Serbs and Croats.

X. Minutes of Slovenski Jug, September 22 (October 5), 1908, the very day of the annexation. (1 " cut".)

The president refers to the possibility of annexation and moves that their Bosnian friends, Damjanović and Krulj, should be speedily advised " to work with greater energy, and be ready at any moment." Supilo, Medaković [358] and Babić-Djalski [359] must also be warned, and every effort made to win over the Bosnian Mohammedans. After an adjournment Marković, who had been summoned by a minister, announced the *fait accompli* of the annexation, and passed the minutes with the words, " Our action must now begin, and I therefore beg you, gentlemen, to be here to-morrow, that we may consider what we can do to liberate our oppressed brothers."

XI. Resolutions, etc., passed at the twenty-seventh meeting of the central committee of Slovenski Jug, September 22, 1908. In this document, then, we have the central committee, whereas in the previous document, which refers to the same resolutions, only the ordinary meeting is referred to.

(*a*) The president communicates the telegram of the Budapest consulate, announcing the annexation. " I have already informed Hadži Risto (Damjanović) and Krulj of this barbarous action." The vice-president announces that the minister gives the committee a free hand in its efforts " to fan the discontent of the people in Bosnia and Herzegovina, and incite them to armed resistance." A member proposes sending a supply of bombs to the Bosnian frontier.

(*b*) Petition to the minister for a supply of bombs and poison " to poison the springs," 1,000 rifles with ammunition, and a sum of 20,000 francs.

(*c*) Appeal to the Town Council of Belgrad for the support of the club in its efforts " to save Bosnia."

(*d*) A communication to be sent to Babić-Djalski, Supilo and Medaković, urging upon them, in view of the dangers in which the Serb race is placed, to arrange a general rising in Croatia-Slavonia.

(*e*) A similar appeal to be sent to three Bosnian leaders.

[358] President of the Croatian Sabor.
[359] A well-known Croatian novelist and poet, member of the Coalition.

DR. FRIEDJUNG'S " DOCUMENTS "

(f) Captain Manojlović entrusted with the care of the bombs.
XII. Minutes of Slovenski Jug, October 5 (18), 1908. (3
" cuts ".)

An exalted harangue by Marković on the dangers brought
by the annexation upon the Servian Fatherland. " In this
sacred room (sic) a year ago momentous words were heard,
that the young son of the old Prince, Prince Mirko, is working
with certain individuals against our reigning house, that he
is chiefly responsible for preventing every attempt to liberate
the Serbs from Austrian slavery." Mirko and his father have
fortunately renounced this policy, " for he realizes that he
was on false paths, on paths where the fate of Alexander
Obrenović would have reached him." Servia and Montenegro
must at length unite in defence of the national idea and shake
off the chains of " Swabian-Magyar " culture. " The Swabian [360]
bloodsucker already has our brothers by the throat, but he
has not yet strangled them."

Davidović then pled the cause of friendship between Servia
and Montenegro, argued that Jovanović's policy of intrigue
with the Progressive Party in Montenegro had caused great
mischief, and pointed out that " Medaković, Lorković and
Supilo with Djalski describe this as the basis for our further
work." To this Jovanović rejoined that the policy adopted
by him towards Montenegro was not his own, but that of " our
insulted Crown Prince." It was finally agreed that Marković
and Davidović should confer with the Young Turks, and
Jovanović with the Montenegrin Voivode Vukotić. The committee would then draw up a plan for the equipment of the
" Bands."

XIII. Minutes of Slovenski Jug, thirty-first meeting, October 21 (November 3), 1908 (4 " cuts ".)

Marković announces the result of his conference with the
Servian Premier Velimirović, regarding the club's activity
in Bosnia. The Premier had expressed the wish that the
smuggling of arms, ammunition and bombs across the frontier
should no longer be carried on by natives of the kingdom, but by
the Bosnians themselves. But this roused opposition from
Jovanović and Davidović, and Marković, admitting the difficulties involved in a change of tactics, agreed that the old
method of smuggling must be retained.

---

[360] " Švab " is the usual name for the German throughout the Western
Balkans. It is sometimes used to denote any foreigner.

THE FRIEDJUNG TRIAL

XIV. Telegram of Mr. Popović, Servian Minister in St. Petersburg.
[The composition and origin of this "document" is so obscure and suspicious, that I prefer to give an exact translation rather than to offer any comment.]

From the Ministry of Foreign Affairs
13/XI PETERSBURG,
Ljubomir Jovanović, Professor, President of the Skupshtina, Here (="Local," i.e. Belgrad).

Mr. M. Popović announces to you : Messrs. Miljukov, Korabljev, Stohovitch and others have handed me 2,000 roubles, in the desire that you should buy and procure with the money rifles and lead (Blei) against the Austrians. These gentlemen send great greetings, and exhort you not to yield. For the present I can tell you nothing personally from my side. Through the post I send you 2,000 roubles.

M. POPOVIĆ.

It is not clear whether this "document" is a telegram to the President of the Skupshtina, as Dr. Friedjung describes it, or a mere summary of the contents of a telegram received by the Servian Foreign Office. In the latter case it is obvious, from the wording, that something has been suppressed. Schoolboys sometimes begin letters in the third person, and end in the first ; but not even in Servia or in Russia is that customary among diplomats. Dr. Friedjung should have known this.

XV. Extract from minutes of Slovenski Jug, central committee, November 16 (29), 1908. (Beginning and end missing ; 3 " cuts ".)

Marković reports a further conversation with the Foreign Minister, Dr. Milovanović, who informed him that Berlin and London, to say nothing of Vienna, were fully aware that Servia's propaganda was far more active in Bosnia than in Old Servia, Macedonia and the Triune Kingdom. The Minister urged great caution, and insisted that the minutes of Slovenski Jug should be submitted to no one in the Foreign Office save Dr. Spalajković. Jovanović endorsed the view that no junior officials should be allowed to see them ; for " that must be the source from which news of the pan-Serb propaganda get abroad. After all, what else can be expected of officials with a monthly salary of 80 francs, than that if our minutes fall into their hands, they should trumpet them abroad in all

directions." [361]   A contribution from " our Russian brothers "
was then thankfully acknowledged. Jovanović then announced that Messrs. Lorković, Supilo and Medaković, with
other members of the Coalition, decided at their last meeting
to act so as to convince the central committee of the Slovenski
Jug that they know how to adapt their attitude in the Bosnian
question, and that Belgrad need not believe the lies of the
Viennese slaves. Only in view of the uncertainty of the
present time they cannot develop their activity in detail, but
they will do this to the Servian agent [presumably the Budapest
consul], since Francis Supilo is authorized to do so. The
meeting then decided to postpone its decision until it heard
from this agent.

XVI. Telegram of the Servian Consul in Budapest to the
Servian Foreign Minister, December 29, 1908 (January 11,
1909).

" In their conference of yesterday they accepted Supilo's
demand. Inform Professor Pavlović that demonstrations will
take place. I have disbursed the money."

XVII. Minutes of Slovenski Jug, central committee, January 9 (22), 1909. (1 " cut " : end missing).

Present : Marković, Lj. Jovanović, Davidović, Michael Jovanović and the Russian deputy Maklakov as guest. Marković
declares that in entering upon its fourth year of existence,
Slovenski Jug realizes that its patriotic hopes are not in vain.
This is best proved by the attitude of " our brothers in the
Triune Kingdom," who, despite Rauch's pressure, remain
true to " the sacred idea of united and fraternizing Serbdom."
The Bosnians only asked for arms, in order to be at their
enemy's throat.

XVIII. Minutes of Slovenski Jug, central committee, January 22 (February 4), 1909. (3 " cuts " : end missing.)

Davidović reported that his relations with the Croato-Serb
Coalition had suffered interruption, " because Baron Rauch
accidentally is in possession of certain written proofs as also
insinuations of some dishonest people about the connexion
with us. The written proofs with which the servant of the
Viennese and Pest hussars hopes to annihilate the Coalition,
are not of a kind which could compromise us or the leaders
of the Coalition. None the less, our brothers Supilo and Meda-

[361] Here again it is absolutely incredible that any Servian could
have written thus.

223

ković, have requested our Consul-general in Budapest, Mr. Petković, to inform the minister of their wish that our club Slovenski Jug and its reading-room should remain closed so long as that Rauch comedy remains unfinished. The deputies in question will do all in their power, so that the whole affair may end in a *blamage* of the Ban Rauch." Pavlović stated that during his recent visit to Agram, Medaković had expressed the wish that the Slovenski Jug should be closed until after the High Treason trial, since Baron Rauch used the existence of the club as one of his chief arguments.

The committee decided to appeal to the Foreign Minister for a grant of 6,000 francs in aid of the defence of the Serb prisoners in the Agram High Treason Trial, as requested by Messrs. Supilo and Medaković. It was then announced that the Guerilla Bands Committee had assigned 5,000 francs to the Slovenski Jug in support of the rising in Bosnia.

XIX. Extract from minutes of Slovenski Jug, central committee, February 15 (28), 1908.

Marković reports that the Foreign Minister is not disposed to grant the 6,000 francs requested, or to take any action in Croatia so long as the Rauch regime lasts. The committee resolved to renew its application for this money.

XX. Circular of Count Pejačević, as Ban of Croatia, to all the High Sheriffs (February 21, 1906). The only genuine document in the Green Book (*see* p. 272).

This confidential report states that a Bosnian committee in Belgrad, under the chairmanship of Professor Cvijić, is intriguing for a rising in Bosnia, acquiring confidential agents, spreading pamphlets and proclamations, and smuggling arms. It then names seventeen persons in Agram and six other Croatian towns—notably Dr. Medaković and Mr. Pribičević— as agents of this committee, and instructs the High Sheriffs, acting in strict secrecy, to place them under observation and submit a detailed report on the result of their inquiries. " In the interest of a more effective control, I draw your attention to the correspondence carried on between the above-named persons and the following persons living outside the bounds of Croatia-Slavonia " (here follow the names of fourteen Dalmatians and Bosnians, including Mr. Supilo, and also four residents in Belgrad). In the report Dr. Franko Potočnjak[362] is assumed to be the intermediary between the various

---

[362] *See* p. 276.

groups of conspirators. It concludes by emphasizing the need for special watchfulness in regard to "political and publicistic movements and also foreign travellers."

In a footnote Dr. Friedjung points out that this circular was sent out at a time when Count Pejačević, as head of a Unionist Government, had to contend with the opposition of the Croato-Serb Coalition. He is however quite in error in stating that Count Pejačević went over to the Coalition after the latter's victory at the elections of 1906. The true facts are that the Wekerle Coalition Cabinet, two of whose chief members, Kossuth and Polonyi, had been the Magyar representatives at the Resolution of Fiume, gave its Croatian allies a free hand at the elections and the latter having failed to secure an absolute majority in the Diet, Count Pejačević remained Ban as a neutral statesman who belonged to neither Coalition. He did not join the Croato-Serb Coalition until the elections of February 1908, eight months after he had ceased to be Ban.

XXI. Report of Dr. Spalajković, Under-Secretary of State for Foreign Affairs, to the Servian Premier, Dr. Pašić, June 4, 1907.[363]

This longwinded "document" purports to be an account of a meeting at Semlin between Dr. Spalajković and Mr. Svetozar Pribičević. The latter expressed his gratitude for the assurance that " so long as the present Cabinet remains in power, Servia would scrupulously fulfil those pledges which it had given in the sense of the Fiume Resolution." Spalajković pointed out that owing to internal difficulties Servia would be unable to increase the suffi hitherto supplied to " the Croato-Serb Party " (sic !), but would make a special grant in the event of new elections in Croatia, " for the Servian Government is firmly convinced that no other combination could assure to the aims of Southern Slav solidarity a more certain support than that which has acquired its basis in the Fiume Resolution, and which by means of the understanding arrived at in Fiume on the part of Your Excellency and Mr. Protić with Messrs. Supilo and Medaković, was also extended to Servia." Servia, however, owing to its relations with Bulgaria, its unreadiness for war and other reasons, was obliged to aim at improved relations with Austria-Hungary

[363] *See* Appendix XIV.

and consequently to adopt "a certain reserve" towards its friends in the Monarchy. After March, 1908, however, the situation would be different; the Servian army would be then well armed, and above all the new loan, "regarding which the preliminary negotiations are already ended and which the *Skupshtina will vote in the autumn,*" will place increased funds at the disposal of the state. Pribičević admitted the strength of Spalajković's arguments, but urged the grant of 50,000 francs in aid of his party and its action in the Hungarian Parliament. Finally he reduced his demands first to 20,000 and then to 12,000 francs, which were to be consigned within two days to Peter Jelovac, a merchant in Semlin. In return for this sum the Serb Independent party would place at the disposal of the Servian Press Bureau no fewer than five newspapers—*Srbobran* and *Srpsko Kolo* in Agram and three in the provinces. It was agreed that all Bosnian news should so far as possible be first of all submitted to the press bureau to avoid suspicion on the part of the Bosnian authorities. "The foreign publicistic action" was to remain as hitherto in the hands of Dr. Polit,[364] who had already made several "disbursements for certain persons in the entourage of Mr. Josipović.[365]

Finally Mr. Pribičević suggested that the Servian Minister in Vienna should induce the Russian ambassador to employ his intimate relations with the German ambassador to induce the latter to influence the entourage of the Emperor in favour of the Croato-Serb Coalition and against the Hungarian Government. In reply to this suggestion, Spalajković explained that the Servian Government would regard it as a great mistake if the Coalition in return for such services should succumb to the influence of Vienna and the Habsburg policy. For even if such action might commend itself to the Croat deputies, their Serb colleagues could not fail to realize that the aims of the Serb race in regard to Bosnia would be finally compromised, if once Vienna acquired unlimited power to regulate according to its pleasure the fate of the occupied provinces. In this connexion the continuance of a parliamentary government in Budapest such as the present, forms a

[364] The well-known leader of the Serb Liberal party in South Hungary, whose integrity is a household word, and who for many years has been a conspicuous opponent of the very regime in whose interests he is here represented as acting.

[365] Minister for Croatia in the Wekerle Cabinet.

guarantee of decisive and unquestionable value for the Serb race."

After a general disquisition on Servian policy, Spalajković concluded by informing Pribičević that " the chief of the Servian Government " had decided to follow Supilo's advice and spend his summer holidays on the Croatian coast, " where he will await his political friends with a view to closer contact." The report is signed " Dr. Miroslav Spalajković, Božović," the latter being ostensibly cashier in the Foreign Office.

XXII, XXIII, XXIV. Minutes of three joint meetings of the central committee of Slovenski Jug and of the Guerilla Bands Committee, October 6 (19) : October 20 (November 2), 1908 : and January 7 (20), 1909.

Professor Marković as chairman. General Nicholas Stefanović gives his views as to the organization of bands for the inroad into Bosnia, and states that he has received 750 rifles with 87,000 rounds for their equipment.

At the end of the Green Book there is a map, apparently drawn up by the military authorities in Vienna to illustrate the movements of the various guerilla bands referred to in the last three " documents."

Of all the twenty-four " documents " not a single original was forthcoming ; and Dr. Friedjung himself only saw the original of one (No. II), and being ignorant of the Servian language, could not in any case have tested their authenticity. Counsel for the defence, Dr. Benedikt, did however produce original photographs of three " documents," namely the Slovenski Jug minutes of February 26, 1908 (II) and of January 22, 1909 (XVIII) and the money order of 6000 francs for Mr. Supilo (III). Dr. Benedikt also claimed that the handwriting of these minutes was identical and was that of Milan Stefanović, the secretary of Slovenski Jug ; and as a further proof of this he produced an original draft of the minutes of August 30, 1909, which had no direct bearing on the questions at issue but would assist the experts in their comparison of the handwriting.

Counsel for the prosecution, Dr. Harpner, at once contested the very existence of this Milan Stefanović, and summoned the defence to supply information as to his identity, in order that he might be called as a witness, like the other persons whose names figured prominently in the documents. Dr. Benedikt showed a marked reluctance to comply with this request, and argued that it is extremely difficult to prove the existence of any one ! He promised, however, to endeavour to find out about Stefanović in Belgrad. Three days later (December 16) during the cross-examination of Professor Masaryk, Dr. Harpner reverted to this promise, and elicited from Dr. Friedjung the statement that Stefanović is " very closely known by those to whom these minutes were delivered," and that he himself had read detailed descriptions of the man's appearance. He had also written to the Austro-Hungarian Legation in Belgrad—in other words, to the receivers of the " stolen documents "—asking if they could supply the man's address. On December 18, Dr. Friedjung announced the Legation's reply that Milan Stefanović is a student, and secretary of Slovenski Jug, and that though his address is not known, he can be found daily at the Café Slavia. The Legation also reported that there are seventy-nine persons of that name in Belgrad, five of them being students. Dr. Harpner's further attempts to clear up this mysterious personality led the defence to shelter itself behind the dangers which the purveyor of documents would incur if his identity were made public.

III. The Evidence of Dr. Funder.

After Dr. Friedjung, Mr. Ambros, the responsible editor of the *Reichspost*, had the opportunity of defending himself ; but as he was universally recognized as a mere " straw-man," Dr. Friedrich Funder, the principal editor, was allowed to give evidence on Ambros' behalf, and indeed not merely to give evidence but to follow Dr. Friedjung's example by a scarcely veiled *plaidoyer*.

Dr. Funder began by referring to the keen interest with which the *Reichspost* had followed the Southern Slav question for some years past. In attacking individual politicians of Croatia, he and his paper had acted as Great Austrians and as friends of the Croats, in the conviction that unworthy elements were leading astray a brave and deserving nation. As to the documents on which his charges were based, he said, " I have seen them in places where only the most serious documents are employed : I know their origin ; in most cases I know how they were obtained and how carefully their authen-

ticity was tested." As early as 1905 the *Reichspost* published
letters from Croatia charging Supilo with accepting money
from Servia ; and on that occasion he contented himself
with an apology from *Hrvatsko Pravo*,[366] which had published
similar charges, and the *Reichspost* was left unassailed. The
later articles which appeared in the *Reichspost* in October
and November, 1908, were in the main based upon the Report
of Dr. Spalajković to the Servian Premier Dr. Pašić,[367] the
genuineness of which he and Dr. Friedjung had been able
to test from original photographs. " Moreover the genuineness of our documents results not merely from the character
of a single document but far more from their mutual connexion ; and as soon as one part of these documents, and indeed
the very part which contains the most serious charges, is
proved to be unquestionably genuine, then the whole chain
of evidence is complete." Dr. Funder might well have added
that if once this all-important document could be proved
to be unquestionably false, the whole chain of evidence would
fall to pieces. Doubtless that is his private opinion to-day.

Dr. Funder treated the Fiume Resolution not unfairly as
an act of anti-Austrian policy, but proceeded to draw from
this the altogether unwarrantable conclusion that its silence
as to the fate of Bosnia and Herzegovina proved that its
authors had promised those provinces to their allies in Belgrad !
He then cited Mr. Francis Kossuth's telegram of greeting
to the authors of the Resolution, Lengyel's speech in the
Hungarian Parliament on the possibilities of the Magyar-
Servian entente (December 12, 1907) and the advances made
by a Magyar deputation to the Turkish Minister in Belgrad
for Turkey's co-operation in the war against Austria. In
reply to counsel for the defence, Dr. Funder was obliged to
admit that no member of the Croato-Serb Coalition had been
present at the incidents to which he took exception, and that
he only wished to pourtray the *milieu* in which the Coalition worked. As Dr. Harpner very rightly pointed out, it is
hardly fair to describe as a person's *milieu* incidents and places
in which he had never been.

After illustrating by various extracts from *Novi List* Supilo's
anti-Austrian motives in bringing about the Resolution of
Fiume, and his paramount share in its success, Dr. Funder

---

[366] Organ of Dr. Joseph Frank and his party.
[367] *See* Appendix XIV and p. 225.

criticised the cringing attitude at first adopted towards the illegal Railway Bill of Kossuth and Szterényi. Not content with drawing up an absurdly mild peace formula Supilo made a speech in the Hungarian Parliament—June 2, 1907—in which he refused to renounce his belief in the reliability of the Magyars and implored them to reconsider the proposed measure.[368] But, Dr. Funder argued, the enigmatic attitude of Supilo, Pribičević and their friends at that moment, is explained by instructions which they had received from Belgrad, to preserve at all costs the entente with the Kossuthists against Vienna.

IV. THE *Reichspost* " DOCUMENTS."

Dr. Funder then laid before the Court the " documents " upon which the *Reichspost* had based its articles. They were five in number, and were also submitted in a printed German translation.[369] Of the five, two are identical with two of Dr. Friedjung's " documents," namely A. the Spalajković Report and C. the order of payment of 6,000 francs to Mr. Supilo. There remain the three following :—

B. Instructions of the Servian Premier Dr. Pašić to Mr. J. Tomić, librarian of the National Library in Belgrad, in view of his secret mission to Agram. Dated from the Servian Foreign Office, January 19 (Feb. 1), 1908 (both Old and New Style are given).

The Servian Government has intentionally selected a non-political personage for this mission on the eve of the Croatian elections. Though entirely approving of the Fiume and Zara Resolutions, " it looks with suspicion upon the attitude and expressions of opinion of the leading Croatian politicians and their newspapers, especially those of the Croatian Party of Right, as the strongest element in the Coalition." Tomić

[368] It is not easy for a foreigner to realize what else Mr. Supilo could have done under the circumstances. Would Dr. Funder have had him announce to his Chauvinist audience that he had never trusted the Magyar leaders and was therefore not in the least surprised at their breach of faith ? Such action might perhaps have brought water to the Great Austrian mill, but it would hardly have been worthy of so wary a politican as Mr. Supilo.

[369] *Aktenstücke zur grosserbischen Propaganda in Oesterreich-Ungarn.* Den Wiener Geschworenen unterbreitet von Dr. Friedrich Funder, chefredakteur der Reichspost.

is to speak with Tuškan,[370] Šurmin, Lorković,[371] Magdić and others, but not in the presence of persons connected with *Srbobran*,[372] and to test their adherence to the ideas of the Fiume Resolution. He is to reveal himself as an agent of the Servian Government, and to explain that the latter, " as the most important factor among the Southern Slavs to-day, not merely wishes to be informed beforehand of the intentions and steps undertaken by the Croats, but also that they should profit by the opinion and advice of the Royal Government," which is in a better position to judge matters from an international point of view. Servia, as an independent state with a dynasty of its own, has the first word among the Southern Slavs ; solidarity must be attained, irrespective of political boundaries. Servia has been of great assistance to the Croat politicians of Croatia and Dalmatia, " has won over the Slovene and Czech leaders in Austria," " has placed almost all Southern Slav newspapers of importance at the service of the Coalition's aims, and finally has contributed materially to the Coalition's electoral campaign." It has even induced the Serb Radicals at the second ballots to back the candidates of the Coalition, " though this party's good relations with Budapest form an important factor in the special policy of the Kingdom of Servia." Tomić is then to emphasize the advantages accruing to the Coalition from Serb support and to claim increased influence for the Serbs. An understanding with Budapest lies in the interest of Servia and the Serb race, and would be a guarantee for the position of the Serbs in Bosnia. Servia requires friends and kinsmen in the Government of Croatia, who might " help to prevent the fate of Bosnia being decided by foreigners." " Bosnia must be reserved politically to the Orthodox and Moslem elements, and in this there can be no compromise. . . . This is a *conditio sine qua non*, without which Servia and the Serbs will go their own way." Friendship with the Magyars is of great importance to the Serb race.

Tomić is to induce the Croat politicians to agree upon joint principles of action, to be embodied in a formal document. Servia intends to send a retired diplomat to live in Agram, ostensibly for private study, but really as a go-between with Servia.

[370] President of the party mentioned.
[371] The two leaders of the Croat Progressives.
[372] Organ of the Serb Independent Party.

D. Memorial of the Slovenski Jug to the Foreign Minister, Dr. Milovanović. Dated 17 (30) January, 1909. Signed by Professor Ljub. Jovanović, President of the Skupština, as Vice-President of Slovenski Jug.

This long-winded memorial proclaims " the national salvation of Bosnia and Herzegovina " to be the club's first duty. Servia's efforts to prevent an understanding between Austria and Turkey would be materially assisted, if the Moslems of Bosnia could be induced to abandon their passive attitude. The two provinces must be claimed by Servia. Even the most extensive autonomy " under the Viennese Emperor " would merely " mean the creation of a new miserable Croatia where there is no place for the Serbs." The Narodna Obrana, or Committee of Defence, will be ready for action within forty days and " our bloody protest " will force Servia to move.

No one in Servia would consent to Montenegro receiving part of Herzegovina. " The Bocche, Spizza and Albania are there, and the Prince can get his son-in-law to help him to an increase of territory in that direction." All the Slovenski Jug's endeavours to win Russian and Italian support " for the Serb cause are hampered by " the gentleman in Cetinje." Dr. Milovanović's admissions of decreasing support from Europe had exercised a depressing effect upon the Bosnian Serb leaders. The memorial goes on to criticize the Foreign Minister's policy in a highly argumentative and depreciatory tone, and declines in the name of Slovenski Jug and the Narodna Obrana to continue the tactics by which the Ministry has attained " these wretched results." The two societies cannot contribute one farthing to the *Srpska Riječ* nor " to the Bosnian advocates in Budapest, especially as the Serbs of Sarajevo are rich enough to maintain their newspaper without aid from Belgrad. " The two committees are confronted just at present by great tasks, caused by Bosnian affairs." Meanwhile they have contributed as much as 54,000 francs in aid of the victims of the Agram trial, and in order to assure their proper defence have " since the date when this matter was entrusted to them by the Ministry, paid over a further sum of 7,000 dinars to advocates in the Triune Kingdom through Mr. Lukinić. We have subventioned the press of the Triune Kingdom with close on 30,000 dinars, without counting the 28,000 crowns which we sent in two instalments to Budapest and which were employed by Messrs. Supilo and Banjanin according to their approval, for the Hungarian papers." The Slovenski Jug further urges the Foreign Office to advance money for action in the Hungarian Press, through Mr. Tomić or Dr. Polit.[373] It has already agreed to print pamphlets for the defence in the Agram trial, and has " ensured the appearance at the proceedings in Agram of a large number of editors and correspondents of the fraternal Russian and Czech Press and also from England."

E. Instructions of the Servian Foreign Minister Dr. Milovanović to the Servian Minister in Vienna. 4 (17) April 1909.

This " document " consists of a lengthy disquisition upon Servian foreign policy, the attitude of "the Cabinet of St. James," and other matters of international policy. I have translated it *in extenso* in Appendix XV, so that the reader may judge for himself how far the Ballplatz is likely to have been the dupe, rather than the inspirer, of such crude forgeries.

After the documents had been read, Dr. Funder's examination was resumed. When pressed as to whether he had seen the originals, he pleaded official secrecy as a reason for not answering, and in this he was supported by the Court. When pressed by the plaintiff's counsel, however, he admitted that he had received the documents " from such a source that I, and with me every journalist in Austria, could not fail to be convinced, ' here I am certain to get something good '." Not knowing the Cyrilline alphabet, he could not in any case have read the originals, but they were regarded in the highest circles—*an leitender Stelle*—as unquestionably genuine, and this was enough for him. " The work of Messrs. Supilo, Lukinić and Pribičević," he concluded, " are the destruction of the consciousness of the state among their own people, conspiracy and plotting with the enemies of the Monarchy. It was our patriotic duty to oppose such intrigues. I can only hope most earnestly that the Croat and Serb people of the Monarchy, freed from individuals who have poisoned its present, are on the eve of a happier future."

Cross-examined by Dr. Popović, Dr. Funder was obliged to admit that he had no proof whatever that the sum of 12,000 francs alleged to have been paid by the Servian Government to Svetozar Pribičević, had actually been paid over. He

[373] The leaders of two rival sections of Serb opinion in Hungary, and bitter enemies of each other.

had assumed that it had been paid because the " minutes "
stated that it would be paid.

In reply to a further question of Dr. Popović, he claimed
to have carefully verified the facts referred to in the various
documents on which he based his charges. Great then was
his embarrassment, and that of Dr. Friedjung, when the able
Serb advocate pointed out that in the " minutes " of Slovenski
Jug of March 10 (February 26 O.S.), 1908, 6,000 dinars are
alleged to have been voted in aid of " the *impending* elections "
in Croatia, whereas in reality the elections had already taken
place on February 26. Dr. Funder was reduced to silence,
and Dr. Friedjung was constrained to make an admission
peculiarly galling for a historian of European reputation :—
" Knowing that the elections took place early in the year—
im Frühjahre—I can say with a calm mind, that I did not
inquire more closely into the date of the elections." The
feeble effort of defending counsel to throw doubt upon the
accuracy of the printed German translation published by
their client, was promptly silenced by the sworn translator
referring to the photograph of the " original." To the plea
of the Judge that a forger would have taken care not to put
an obviously wrong date upon the documents, Dr. Harpner
retorted that he would prove in the course of the proceedings
that the forger had reckoned with very stupid people !

In order to obtain an authoritative statement as to the
date of the elections, the Judge sent an official telegram
to the Croatian Government, and on Monday, 13th, he
read out the reply in court. Although Baron Rauch's
Government was straining every nerve to ruin the Coalition
and was actually at the very moment scattering flyleaves
broadcast in the streets of Agram, announcing the plaintiffs
in the trial to be fatally compromised, it might still have
been expected that it would adhere strictly to the facts in
its answer to Dr. Wach's inquiry. But the telegram after
correctly stating that the elections took place on February
27 and 28, and that the Diet was opened on March 12
and prorogued on March 14, continued as follows : " Since
this Diet has not yet formally constituted itself, the second
ballots could not take place as yet." As Dr. Harpner at
once pointed out, this statement was flagrantly untrue,
as at least five of the plaintiffs had been actually elected
at second ballots. A second telegram finally elicited an

accurate reply ; the second ballots in those constituencies where no candidate had obtained an absolute majority, took place on February 27 and 28 and March 5 and 10 : certain deputies however had been elected in more than one constituency, and as the prorogation had left them no time to state formally which they had selected, certain bye-elections were still necessary.

The defence tried to argue that the contested passage in the " document " referred to a second general election which Rauch was contemplating within a few days of the result of the first ! Dr. Harpner brushed this quibble aside by citing the phrase, " The Frank and Starčević Party must be defeated." On March 10—the date of the document—this party *was* already defeated, and hence the phrase could not possibly refer to a second election.[374]

At the conclusion of Dr. Funder's examination, the Court dealt with a number of proposals for the hearing of fresh witnesses, and a lengthy discussion arose as to the appointment of experts to deal with the handwriting of Dr. Friedjung's photographs. The names suggested were Professor von Jagić, the foremost Slavistic scholar of the present day, and Dr. Uebersberger, lecturer in East European history at Vienna. The Judge, however, took the strange view that the court interpreter would be able to do all that was required and that no special expert was needed. His reasons for such an attitude were soon to become apparent.

V. The Evidence of Baron Chlumecky.

The first witness for the defence was now called, in the person of Baron Leopold Chlumecky, son of the distinguished financier and railway director.

Baron Chlumecky, who is 35 years of age, is at present a member of the Moravian Diet, a director of the Austrian Lloyd, political editor of the well-known review *Oesterreichische Rundschau*, and author of an extremely able and interesting but violent book on Austria-Hungary and Italy. He began his career as a junior official in the Bezirkshauptmannschaft —Prefecture—of Ragusa, and in this post one of his most important duties was the supervision of the elaborate system of

---

[374] It is probable that the forgers, in concocting this " document," confused the Old and New Styles.

espionage maintained by Austria in the former Republic of Ragusa and along the Montenegrin frontier.[375] At that period the Serb and Italian parties jointly held the commune of Ragusa in their power and enjoyed the support of the local Dalmatian Government. The Croats conducted a bitter opposition against the Serbs, and the local organ of the Croat party, the *Crvena Hrvatska*, was edited by Mr. Supilo, then an unknown journalist. Baron Chlumecky at first inclined towards the Serbs, but confessed to having been greatly influenced by a conversation with Baron Kállay, the administrator of Bosnia, who exposed to him the secret aims of the Serb parties and called out to him as he left, " Le serbisme, voila l'ennemi." Henceforward Chlumecky leant more and more towards the Croat party, and even went so far as to admit that the policy of Vienna towards the Croats was unjust. This attitude earned him the disapproval of his superiors, and he was transferred to the small Dalmatian port of Makarska. In Ragusa he had made the acquaintance of Mr. Supilo, and even after his return to Vienna they corresponded from time to time.

Such are the circumstances which would appear to have induced the defence to summon Baron Chlumecky as a witness, though it is not easy to understand the grounds upon which the Judge allowed him to be called at this stage of the proceedings. As will appear presently, his evidence had absolutely no bearing upon the libel, and took the form of an attempt to smirch the private honour of Mr. Supilo.

" One thing I know," he assured the Court, " that Mr. Supilo received supplies from private Austrian sources, which were certainly not large sums of money but none the less were calculated to assist him in the precarious monetary circum-

[375] " Dr. Harpner : What were you there ?
Witness : I was secretary—Konzipist—at the Prefecture. In a frontier country where a movement known to be dangerous to the State exists, it is a matter of course that the authorities do not confine themselves to documentary information, but draw their information as thoroughly as possible from real life. That happens all over the world. Everywhere the authorities have ways and means of getting information otherwise than by documents. In this extraordinary caution is observed. First of all the individuals and their reliability are tested, and then their information is accepted by no means readily. Traps are laid for them, in order to prove their trustworthiness. It is clear that the authorities deny their relations to such spies, for they can never reveal their sources, otherwise they would learn nothing. Kállay considered it necessary also to have a spy in Ragusa."

stances in which he then found himself. In the same way
Kállay's agent informed me that he also made material grants
to Mr. Supilo." As an illustration of Mr. Supilo's attitude on
the Servian question, Baron Chlumecky then proceeded to
read aloud the following extract from a letter written to him
by Supilo on August 13, 1901. "I have in my hands the draft
of a conspiracy between Mohammedans and Greek Orientals
devised against the existing order of things in Bosnia. The
draft is printed in Belgrad." Needless to say, this letter
served to increase the growing sensation in court and to confirm the impression that Supilo, as a venal agent of the Austrian
Government, was in the habit of transmitting to Chlumecky
secret denunciations of his Serb enemies. It was not till the
following Monday—December 13—when Baron Chlumecky's
version of the facts had held the field for forty-eight hours
and the entire Viennese press had employed the Sunday
interval in heaping abuse upon Supilo's defenceless head—
that the full text of the letter was read aloud in court. The
correct version of the passage quoted by Chlumecky runs as
follows :—" I have in my hands the draft of a conspiracy
between Mohammedans and Greek Orientals devised against
the existing order of things in Bosnia. *I shall publish it with
comments in an article in Novi List, and think that it will be an
interesting matter.* The draft is printed in Belgrad." Thus
it appears that Baron Chlumecky deliberately suppressed a
sentence which would have given the affair a wholly different
complexion—behaviour which seems all the more inexcusable
in view of the fact that the draft of which Supilo wrote had
already become the public property of the entire Agram
press, before its contents were published in *Novi List*.

Questioned as to the sources from which Mr. Supilo received
money, Baron Chlumecky stated that sums of 20 to 30 crowns
had been paid over by the Bosnian agent, and also that on one
occasion a private individual had paid Supilo 200 crowns (£8),
as an earnest of his maintaining his anti-Serb attitude. At
this point Mr. Supilo rose and said : " I declare solemnly on
my word of honour that up till 1903 I was an enemy of the
Serbs." (Cries from the plaintiffs : " We know that ! ")

The Judge : " Is it true that you took money for pursuing
this policy ? "

Supilo (in great excitement) : " I declare that I have never
in my life taken a kreuzer from any one, neither for my policy
nor for altering it . . . neither as subvention nor as charity."

In answer to further questions of Judge and counsel, Supilo denied the charge more emphatically than ever. " Then," said the Judge, " the witness must be lying. . . . I call upon the witness to name the person who gave Mr. Supilo the 200 crowns." Whereupon Baron Chlumecky replied, " If it must be so, well and good," adding ' with a dramatic gesture,' [376] " I myself gave him them."

The sensation in court was profound, but a few incredulous laughs were heard from among the plaintiffs. And here the Judge, yielding completely to the excitement of the moment, exclaimed, " Gentlemen, there is nothing to laugh at. We have just heard that Mr. Supilo here in open court has broken his word of honour, and you will have to consider carefully whether you wish to have further intercourse with such a man." (Turning to the witness.) " So you can testify under oath that you gave Mr. Supilo at least 200 crowns in view of his political attitude ? "

Witness : " Solely with a view to his political attitude."

Judge : " Then there is no more to be said. Mr. Supilo has given his word of honour and has broken it. (Turning to Supilo) I have no further question to put to you."

When Dr. Harpner asked Supilo what he had to say, he could only vaguely stammer, " I can find no words." " That I can believe," cried the Judge. " Now I can easily understand the letter too. When you write to the Baron that a conspiracy is on foot in Bosnia, it can only mean that you simply want more money. That is the whole explanation."

This exciting scene continued. Asked by Supilo where he had handed over the money, Chlumecky stated that he had done so on the open street in Ragusa, on leaving a political conference at the house of Kállay's agent, and when Supilo persisted in his denial, the witness raised his voice and repeated his accusation more emphatically than ever, the Judge promptly backing him up with the words, " Nothing could be clearer : there can be no challenging that."

But Supilo, dazed as he was and intimidated by the violence of the Judge, stood his ground and continued in his stubborn peasant's way to deny his guilt. He had once visited Chlumecky in Vienna, he said, and the latter had requested him to keep him informed on political conditions in Dalmatia. On the same occasion Baron Chlumecky had spoken of being a subscriber to *Novi List* ; but though the paper was sent to

[376] *Times*, December 13, 1909.

him for years, he never paid his subscription in spite of something like twenty formal reminders. Here the Judge again broke in : " You would really do better to keep a little more closely to the truth." " What I say," rejoined Supilo, " is the pure truth." " What interest," cried the Judge, " could the witness have in committing the offence of perjury ? "

" In order to annihilate him politically," came in chorus from the Croatian deputies, who had followed the whole scene with pardonable excitement. Baron Chlumecky indignantly protested, " Perhaps you fight with such arguments, but not I." And the Judge, red with anger, rose from the Bench and shouted at the plaintiffs [377] the now famous words, " I must request you, gentlemen. *We are here in Vienna.* I need say no more ; but I can't allow such things here. In this country— *bei uns*—that is out of the question."

When the various parties had recovered their calm, Baron Chlumecky's place as witness was taken by Mr. William Dorotka, editor of *Ustavnost*, Baron Rauch's most venomous organ, and one of the leaders of the campaign of calumny directed for the previous two years against the Croato-Serb Coalition. If there is one man whom every native Dalmatian would decline to accept as an impartial witness on Dalmatian affairs, that man is Baron Chlumecky. If there is one man whom every native of Croatia would decline to accept as an impartial witness on Croatian politics, that man is Mr. Dorotka.[378] This, of course, accounts for their being summoned as witnesses in a trial whose whole *mise-en-scène* was inspired by the motto *Divide et impera.*

Dorotka related a conversation which he had had in 1903 with Count Ladislas Szapary, then Governor of Fiume. According to the latter, Supilo came regularly to him for orders, with the

[377] I quote the very words of the reporter of the *Neue Freie Presse*, who certainly cannot be accused of partiality for the plaintiffs (*Ruft schreiend und hochangerötet den Anklägern zu*).

[378] Every Croat will admit this to be an understatement of the facts. But for the benefit of British readers I may mention that within a couple of days of Rauch's fall *Ustavnost* ceased to appear.

In the course of conversation with a Dalmatian official some nine months before the trial, I happened to ask him his opinion upon a recent article of Baron Chlumecky on Dalmatia—*Oesterreichische Rundschau*—whose violence had caused some stir. My friend, an Austrian of the Austrians, avoided a direct expression of opinion, but significantly remarked, " Why, Chlumecky is the best hated man in Dalmatia."

obsequious phrase, " Che commanda Eccelenza, Che io scriva."
" I gave him the information," added Szapáry, " and every time
put my hand to my pocket-book and gave him 5 gulden "
(8s.).

Once more Mr. Supilo was at a loss for words and fell a victim
to the Judge's sarcasm ; but he explicitly denied having ever
spoken with Count Szapáry or having ever been at his house.
At this point the proceedings were broken off, and as it was
Saturday afternoon, the general public was left for forty-eight
hours under the impression of the charges against Mr. Supilo,
which were none the less damaging because entirely irrelevant
to the question at issue ; and the defence had scored a tactical
success, thanks to the skill with which the course of the proceedings had been adjusted to the week-end pause. Next
morning the entire Viennese press fell upon Mr. Supilo with all
the violence of inspiration ; and the *Neue Freie Presse*, the
foremost advocate of Count Aehrenthal's policy, outbid all its
rivals in treating the Croatian leader's guilt as a *chose jugée.*
" To-day in court the spine of the deputy Supilo was broken.
A political corpse hangs with shattered bones upon the gallows " . . .—such are merely the opening words of a leading
article which is a monument of bad taste and political bias.
But the *mot d'ordre* which had inspired this general press
onslaught failed to produce the desired intimidation. On the
one hand Mr. Supilo, anxious that the charges against his
person should not confuse the real issues of the trial, loyally
announced his withdrawal from the Coalition ; and on the
other hand his colleagues, realizing the deep-laid intrigues with
which they had to deal, and strengthened in their resolve by
such courageous champions as Professor Masaryk, showed themselves more determined than ever to establish their innocence
in the teeth of a hostile court.

Mr. Supilo vigorously organized the defence of his own cause,
and was fortunate in securing the services of an able advocate,
Dr. Walter Rode. Henceforth the Supilo-Chlumecky feud
runs like an uneven thread through the main texture of the
trial ; but as it does not in any way affect the main issues
involved, I have thought it better to treat it as an entirely
separate incident and to assign to it a separate chapter of its
own.

VI. THE ATTITUDE OF THE COURT.

Monday's proceedings were taken up by a large number of

miscellaneous incidents—proposals and counter proposals by the rival counsel and the discussion of various points which I have preferred to treat in their proper context rather than in the accidental order in which they were brought before the court. More than one sharp passage of arms occurred, and Dr. Harpner took his revenge for the opening polemics of the defendants by asserting that he would prove " that all these documents produced by Dr. Friedjung are a clumsy forgery, which any person of any perception could detect at the first glance."

Before the Court rose, General Tomičić, one of the plaintiffs, was called as witness and cross-examined by the Judge as to a Report of the Austro-Hungarian military attaché in Belgrad describing the movements of Servian guerilla bands along the Bosnian frontier. The General expressed his belief that such a report deserved to be taken seriously, as the result of careful inquiries ; but urged that the Chief of the General Staff, General von Hötzendorf, was the most competent person to express an opinion and should therefore be called as witness.

Dr. Friedjung in laying before the Court the alleged report of Dr. Spalajković, indulged in a violent attack upon its " author." Referring to Spalajković's reported intention of giving evidence in person, he said, " We shall see whether Dr. Spalajković possesses the courage to fulfil this announcement. I shall then have the opportunity of proving that this gentleman held in his hands the threads of Pan-Serb agitation in Bosnia and Croatia ; and while I would fain conduct my lawsuit with the Serb and Croat subjects of our Monarchy calmly and with a certain restraint, shall proceed mercilessly against this Mr. Spalajković as the foreign instigator of treasonable intrigues, and shall give him a passport (*Geleitbrief*) for his diplomatic career which he will not be anxious to produce." Such a diatribe, obviously inspired by a fervent if somewhat narrow patriotism, came naturally enough from the mouth of Dr. Friedjung. But while we may find excuses for a defendant in a political trial indulging in threats against a witness, none can be found for the omission of the Court to repress such excesses, for such an omission is dangerously akin to intimidation, especially when the object of the attack is a foreigner.

The attitude of the Court became still clearer on the fourth day when the prosecution submitted telegrams received by Professor Masaryk, the well-known leader of the Czech Realists, from Dr. Milovanović, the Servian Foreign Minister, and from

Dr. Simić, the Servian Minister in Vienna.[379] Though bearing directly upon the most weighty of all the "documents" and proceeding from the foremost person affected by the charge— Dr. Milovanović—they were not admitted as evidence, the Judge curtly remarking, "It has been said to be a matter of course that official circles must always deny such things." This decision betrays the tendency of both the defence and the Judge himself to throw discredit upon declarations coming from Servia. It was, moreover, a challenge none the less evident because not expressed in words; for it placed Messrs. Milovanović and Simić before the difficult alternative of defying all diplomatic precedents by giving evidence in person, or of seeming to shrink guiltily from a course to which international not personal considerations offered the real obstacle. Dr. Benedikt was not slow to follow up this advantage, and proceeded to expatiate on the dangers involved for the Servian witnesses in their appearance before the Court. If the documents are genuine, he argued, then all the persons mentioned in them, even though foreigners, are by Austrian law guilty of high treason and liable to the penalties which that offence involves. Notably the Servian Minister of the Interior, Dr. Jovanović, is believed to be a fugitive Austrian subject and might consequently have an unpleasant reception: still more so then Mr. Godjevac, who as President of the Servian Bands Committee arranged the despatch of bombs to Austria.[380] "I am far from protesting against these gentlemen coming," added Dr. Benedikt. "In my private capacity there is nothing I would do more reluctantly than help to create a trial for treason. If it be said that the documents are false, then all danger is averted—that is: if this finds belief." Dr. Funder's counsel expressed the same view even more strongly. "Let

[379] "In reply to your telegram I can categorically declare that the Friedjung documents, in so far as they concern the Servian Government and Servian diplomacy, are not only false, but that no veritable document of this kind can exist, because neither Supilo nor Pribičević nor Medaković nor any one of those whom Friedjung has drawn into the affair, has ever, on any score whatever, directly or indirectly, received money from the Servian Government, and because the Servian Government has never organized nor subsidized, nor had any knowledge whatever of such intrigues as are laid by Friedjung to the charge of the Serbo-Croatian Coalition. I add that my alleged instructions to the Servian Minister at Vienna and to the Servian Consul at Budapest are gross inventions of a forger equally ignorant of the form of our written intercourse and of the fundamental lines of our policy"—translation as given in *Times* of December 14, 1909.

[380] According to No. 23, see p. 227.

the gentlemen from Servia come if they want to. But every one will be prepared to draw the consequences. This building contains another authority also,[381] and I don't know what consequences that authority will draw from false evidence."

All this was hardly encouraging, and all that Dr. Harpner could do was to emphasize the fact that despite all these thinly-veiled threats nothing could happen to any one in a legal state like Austria, on the basis of forged documents. He therefore appealed to those who were in a position to prove the forgery to trust themselves to the Court.

Next day Dr. Benedikt returned to the charge. He protested against Professor Masaryk's action in publishing Dr. Milovanović's telegram in the Viennese press and argued that in other countries this would amount to grave contempt of court. Then, by way of illustrating the view that no Servian can be trusted to tell the truth, he proceeded to cite statistics of the political murders which had taken place in Servia previous to the year 1895 !! As 1,200 murders were committed on an average every year in Servia, and as there were only 2,000 persons actually in prison, it followed that ten or twenty thousand murderers are at large in the country—the tacit inference from this being that the witnesses proposed by prosecuting counsel belonged to this numerous army of criminals. This was too much for the Judge, who aptly pointed out that the Kingdom of Servia was not the subject of the present trial.[382] The defence had, however, secured its object, which was to prejudice the jury still further against the Servians.

Hereupon the Judge announced the decision of the Court not to cite the Servian witnesses, first because it had no means of enforcing compliance, second because it seemed inadmissible to demand the presence of persons who would incur serious dangers under the terms of the Austrian Penal Code (§§ 38 and 58c), and thirdly because in giving evidence they might be hampered by their duty as citizens and by pledges of official secrecy. If, however, any of them chose to present themselves voluntarily within the next four days, the Court would be willing to hear their evidence.

It must be admitted that after all these amiable preliminaries, it required considerable courage on the part of the impli-

[381] Viz., the police.
[382] Needless to say, I do not guarantee the accuracy of Dr. Benedikt's statistics.

243

cated Servians to appear before the Court. None the less, Professor Božidar Marković, the President of the Slovenski Jug and the alleged leader of the terrorist organization in Belgrad, had already arrived in Vienna, and was now summoned as a witness.

Before, however, this important witness was heard, Dr. Friedjung made an interesting statement as to the origin of his documents. His informants had since November, 1907, been in a position to secure the minutes of each meeting of Slovenski Jug soon after they were drawn up. The originals were brought each time by a paid agent, " who was naturally regarded with suspicion, since he plied an ugly trade." (Dr. Friedjung did not stop to inquire how far the receiver of stolen goods is superior to the thief.) They were then either copied or at once translated or photographed, and the originals were then handed back to the agent, who restored them to their proper place. That photographs could not be supplied in every case, was due to the fact that no libel action was in view at the time. The main object of this traffic in stolen documents—or as, Dr. Friedjung more elegantly put it, " this watchfulness of the factors in question "—was to secure information as to military movements on the southern frontier and as to possible intrigues in Bosnia ; Croatia was only a secondary consideration. A regular archive was placed at Dr. Friedjung's disposal, and for weeks he studied " hundreds and hundreds " of these documents, including at least as many documents from Slovenski Jug as those which he had laid before the Court.[383] When war with Servia seemed inevitable, he held it to be his duty to make use of this material and wrote the article in the *Neue Freie Presse*, which was to be the first of a series. During the advance of the Austrian army across the Save, he had intended to publish the various documents, and thus to prove to Europe, " that Austria-Hungary had been compelled by Servia's perfidious relations to dishonest elements in our Monarchy, to resort to arms." On the very day of publication, however, Crown Prince George was obliged to resign his rights to the throne, and the danger of war gradually diminished. When Dr. Harpner pressed for the name of the man who supplied the documents, Dr. Friedjung rejoined, " I must confess I was not prepared for such naïveté on the part of Dr. Harpner. I know the man. But do you believe that in a country where

[383] No wonder that spies like Nastić are able to save enough money in a couple of years, to open a café in Vienna.

so many political murders take place, this man would be spared if what he has done became known ? . . . I hand over nobody to the gallows," he added, " I regard the question as ridiculous." Needless to say, the real reason for not revealing his name lay in the natural fear of Count Aehrenthal that his principal spy might indulge in awkward revelations concerning the methods of the Ballplatz.

Asked by his own counsel whether he would characterize more closely the source from which he had received the documents, Dr. Friedjung pointed out that this was immaterial to the question of their authenticity. Dr. Funder, as a busy journalist, was perfectly entitled if he received a document from " leading circles," to regard it as genuine and make use of it without further examination. " But *I* am not in this agreeable situation. For scientific investigations there is no authority . . . for science knows no authority, but only reasons." In other words, he once more staked his reputation as a historian of scientific methods upon the issue of the trial.

VII. THE EVIDENCE OF PROFESSOR MARKOVIĆ.

Mr. Marković, Professor of Criminal Law at Belgrad University, is a pleasant type of young Servian " Gelehrte " and certainly does not convey the impression of a secret terrorist or an organizer of bomb conspiracies. At the request of the Judge he began by describing the activity of the Slovenski Jug, which had originally been founded in 1902—not in 1904 as Dr. Friedjung had asserted—by twenty or thirty young enthusiasts, as a students' club. The columns of their organ, *Slovenski Jug*, which began to appear in November, 1903, give the best idea of the aims of the club. It organized a Southern Slav art exhibition in Belgrad in 1903, a congress of Bulgarian and Servian students at Sofia in 1904, and took an active interest in all cultural affairs of the Southern Slavs. In 1906 it was transformed into an ordinary citizens' club ; and on March 11 of that year a mixed committee drew up the statutes. It never had any relations to the Servian Government, but received a subsidy of 400 francs a month from the Belgrad Town Council, to enable it to maintain a public reading-room. Marković was elected President of the club in July, 1907, but he had spoken with the Servian Premier, Dr. Pašić, for the first and last time in the autumn of 1909.[384]

[384] Not in February, 1908, as Document I states (*See* p. 216).

Professor Marković next proceeded to deny wholesale the authenticity of the alleged minutes of the Slovenski Jug. No central committee—*Zentralleitung*—had ever existed : no report had ever been submitted by the club to Prince George. No one of the name of Jovanović was ever vice-president. He himself had never been in Salonica, though he was represented as conferring with the Young Turk Committee there. More than one of the alleged meetings had never taken place at all. Above all, the minutes of October 21 (November 3), 1908, were an obvious forgery, for so far from presiding over a meeting in Belgrad on that date, he had actually been in Berlin since early in October, attending lectures on penal law and making the acquaintance of eminent German jurists such as Professor von Liszt. Both his arrival and departure were duly intimated to the police, and his statements could be verified, as also the fact that he had stopped en route at certain hotels in Vienna and Budapest which he indicated by name. On November 1, 1908, the club almost ceased to exist, because the Town Council discontinued its subsidy ; and the reading-room had to be closed until November, 1909. Marković further denied having ever met General Stefanović and Dr. Godjevac, whose presence is recorded in the minutes of October 6, 1908 (No. xxii). The Slovenski Jug had never held joint sittings with the Bands Committee ; a committee of National Defence (Narodna Obrana) did indeed exist in Belgrad, and still exists, but he had no knowledge of its proceedings and had never belonged to it. He had never heard of bombs being prepared, or even kept on the premises of the Slovenski Jug. The minutes of the meetings of the society were kept by the secretary ; this post was held during Marković's time as President, by three different men, but no one of the name of Milan Stefanović had ever been secretary, and Marković knew no such person either in Belgrad or in the rest of Servia. When shown Dr. Friedjung's photographs, he was unable to recognize either them or their handwriting.

The explicit nature of Marković's denials and his determined bearing were not without their effect even upon the supporters of the defendants, and by way of redressing the balance, counsel for the *Reichspost* in a loud voice demanded of the witness whether he regarded regicide as justifiable. When the excited protests of the plaintiffs had died down—voices were heard repeating the Judge's already famous phrase, " We are here in Vienna "—Professor Marković declined to answer ; and Dr.

Kienböck added the still more offensive comment, " That also is an answer." Even this was surpassed next day by Dr. Benedikt, who inquired, " Is it usual in Belgrad to fabricate bombs in the reading-rooms, in order to blow up the Prince of Montenegro ? "

Witness (excitedly). I won't answer that question.

Dr. Benedikt : Even that answer is quite enough for us.

Dr. Harpner : I beg to point out that the defendants, but no one else, call your veracity in question.

The witness was now subjected by Dr. Friedjung and the defending counsel to a minute and vigorous cross-examination, in the course of which, while remaining absolutely consistent on every point, he showed an occasional tendency to quibble and a rather too marked disinclination to furnish his opponent with even the most trifling facts. For instance, he had previously stated the perfectly correct fact that there is no " Doctor Stefanović " in the Servian Foreign Office. He now admitted that there is an official called Dragomir Stefanović in that office, and that " Dr. Stefanović " might in Servian stand either for " Doctor " or for " Dragomir," but that the Dragomir in question did not possess the degree of doctor, and had informed the witness before he left Belgrad that on principle he never signed himself " Dr.," lest he should appear to be sailing under false colours.[385] The defence, not without some show of reason, complained that Professor Marković might at least have volunteered this information, without waiting for it to be wrung from him ; but in roundly charging him with suppression and distortion of the facts—*eine rückhältige hinterhältige Aussage*— Dr. Benedikt was guilty of gross exaggeration and failed to allow for the resentment of a man whose name had been misused upon a colossal scale and whose country had been grossly insulted—whether with or without provocation, is immaterial— by the defendants.

The defence next tried to press home the argument that it was well-nigh incredible that a man engaged in politics like Marković, should be unacquainted with so many of the chief political figures in Belgrad, all the more so as the Servian capital still has barely 100,000 inhabitants. In reply, Marković pointed out that he was an university professor, and his first occupa-

---

[385] It is by no means unusual in continental countries for persons with the degree of doctor, to prefix that title to their signature in more or less formal letters or in documents.

tion was scientific study (Wissenschaft); he could naturally give more information about the academic and legal world than about the generals or medical men of Belgrad. Dr. Friedjung was unwise enough to express astonishment that Marković should have selected for a three weeks' visit to Berlin " the most exciting period which the Kingdom of Servia had gone through for years "—forgetting that this very fact, if proved, supplied a very strong presumptive proof against Professor Marković's activity as the leader of a revolutionary committee. How was it that one of the most fervent patriots, one of the most decided politicians in the country, went abroad just at this very moment ? The obvious reply came that he was neither a determined nor an active politician and that for him " Wissenschaft" really was more important than politics.

Here Dr. Benedikt, promptly changing his ground, inquired whether it was not considered more politic that the president of the insurrection committee and of the Slovenski Jug should *not* be in Parliament ?

Witness : " But according to this account, the President of the Skupshtina is my Vice-president.

Dr. Benedikt : It is a curious thing, that at the joint meeting of the central direction of Slovenski Jug and the Bands Commitee, Jovanović was not present." This is a distinctly unfair quibble on the part of Dr. Benedikt, for the " minutes " of the *previous* meeting of the " central direction " *do* contain the name of Mr. Jovanović.[386]

Next day (December 14) the cross-examination was renewed. Marković stoutly denied all knowledge of bombs having found their way into the premises of Slovenski Jug, as the informer Nastić had asserted in the Agram High Treason trial, and insisted that Nastić's evidence was false from beginning to end. A little later he admitted that the newspaper *Slovenski Jug* was since June 3, 1907—the date of his own election as President—the organ of the club. This admission formed a pretext for fresh tirades on the part of the defendants, who argued that he was deliberately suppressing the true facts. But Marković adhered stubbornly to his original standpoint. " To definite questions I answer truly with Yes or No. But to questions which are not put, I do not give any answer. . . . I stake my life that no one can prove me to have spoken falsely."

Intimidation was of no avail ; and the defence made a final

[386] *See* Green Book, p. 55.

attempt to prejudice the jury against this imperturbable young foreigner, by laying before the Court a pamphlet which he had written at the height of the Bosnian crisis. " The Servian View of the Bosnian Question " reflects pretty accurately the attitude of the vast mass of educated Servians towards the Aehrenthal policy. It contains the usual exaggerations as to Austrian rule in Bosnia, but also a summary of the genuine grievances of those provinces. Above all, it deals with the effects of the annexation upon Servia's economic position and concludes with an expression of the opinion—at that time endorsed by the entire Servian Press—that a recognition of the annexation would be a national catastrophe, to which Servia could never submit, even at the risk of war with Austria-Hungary.

It was now the turn of the jurymen ; and their questions, while obviously inspired by an honest desire to be fair to both parties, strikingly illustrate the provincial outlook of the average Viennese tradesman. The most characteristic question ran as follows :—" As you do not know the plaintiffs in this trial, as moreover you are a Servian citizen and a foreigner here, I really can't make out properly what led you to the journey hither which costs so much money and time,[387] in order to give evidence in a private libel action. In my opinion the minutes laid before us by Dr. Friedjung are in no way insulting to you as a Servian citizen (*sic !*), indeed I think you have in this way done some service to your country. I can't then make out why you have come." The answer of Professor Marković, that he had come firstly to clear his own person from the allegations made against him, and secondly to defend his own country, was so obvious that a distinct effort is required in order to grasp the mentality of the questioner. As Dr. Harpner said, " If I were to hear some one was charged with treasonable relations with Austria by an Italian who alleged that I had plotted treason with him, and if I knew it to be untrue, then I too would go off at my own expense and say that it is a lie." In other countries such a statement would have been regarded as a ludicrously superfluous commonplace ; but in view of the jury's attitude it became one of sheer necessity.

Marković might well have added that non-appearance would

---

[387] This shows how little the Viennese tradesman travels ; for it is not farther from Belgrad to Vienna than from Inverness to London.

have been the best proof of guilt.[388] That the defence were fully conscious of this, and for that very reason made a desperate effort to frighten the Servians into remaining away, became apparent from Dr. Benedikt's concluding questions. Why, he argued, had Marković not put in an appearance at the High Treason trial in Agram, in which the relations of the accused to the Slovenski Jug played so prominent a part, and in which Nastić brought such grave charges against the club. But here Dr. Benedikt's attack failed ; for it was pointed out that Nastić's statements referred to incidents previous to Marković's election as president : that Marković's name was not implicated until Friedjung's Green Book appeared : that the Agram court not merely refrained from citing witnesses from Servia, but also expressly declined to examine even those who might appear voluntarily : and that, though his name was among those proposed as witnesses by the defence in Agram, he was at that time at a German watering place, and did not know that his testimony had been invoked.[389]

The attitude of Dr. Friedjung and his counsel towards Professor Marković was unworthy of so distinguished an historian, and *The Times* was well within the mark in describing his criticism as " pettifogging," and in declaring that the adoption of these tactics by a man hitherto regarded as " of considerable mental elevation," produced a painful impression upon the public in court.[390]

VIII. The Evidence of Professor Masaryk.

The first witness at the next day's proceedings was Professor Thomas Masaryk, the well-known Bohemian savant and politician. The important part which he had already played, and was still to play, in the cause of Croatian liberties, entitles

[388] And who is so naïve as to suppose that this would not have been the line adopted by the defence if the Servians had really remained away ?

[389] This is by no means as improbable as it might seem at first sight. Under the Rauch regime, and especially during the whole course of the Agram trial, communication between Agram and Belgrad had its dangers. It was not till June, 1909, that the representatives of the accused dared to go to Belgrad with a view of collecting urgently necessary information for the defence ; and on their way home the private papers of one of their number, Dr. Budisavljević, were arbitrarily seized by Rauch's officials in Semlin, and handed over to the Public Prosecutor for use in the trial.

[390] *Times*, December 16, 1909.

the reader to expect some estimate of the man and his career. By birth a Moravian Slovak from the little frontier town of Göding (Hodonín),[391] he had been intended for the career of a village schoolmaster, but found his way to Vienna, and devoted himself there and in Leipzig to philosophical studies. In 1879 he won his spurs with a remarkable essay on " Suicide as a Social Phenomenon," and in 1882 he was appointed professor at the new Czech University in Prague. A year later he founded a literary review of his own, and it was here that he waged pitiless warfare against one of the chief literary trea-sures of his nation, the famous Königinhof MS. In spite of fierce attacks upon his scholarship and patriotism, Masaryk never faltered until he had established beyond all question that the manuscript was from beginning to end an impudent forgery. " It was not merely a matter of the genuine or false character of the MS.," he declared, " but of vindicating the liberty of every man to give expression at all times and places to his scientific convictions." He had proved the old Hussite spirit to be still alive ; and when in 1891 he turned to politics, he showed the same uncompromising tendencies, though careful to limit his programme to the realm of possibilities. He might well have taken for his motto, " The truth shall make you free!" In 1900, dissatisfied with the barrenness of Czech politics, he formed a party of his own, the so-called Progressives, or Czech Realists. In the new Parliament of Universal Suffrage, he offered a crowning proof of his originality and courage, by expounding the grounds of his religious belief before a House of ultramontanes and agnostics. Freedom of conscience is to him much more than a mere phrase, and in its defence he has incurred much obloquy.[392]

Some idea of the wide field which his studies cover, may be obtained by looking up his name in a library catalogue. In addition to endless smaller essays, we find monographs on John Hus and Havlíček, the O'Connell of Bohemia, on Hume, Pascal and Buckle, a treatise on Logic, essays on Suicide and Hypnotism, The Philosophical Basis of Marxism, Palacky's Idea of the Bohemian People, The Russian Revolution. Too

[391] Born March 7, 1850. *See* an interesting article by J. Vančura, " Unsere Götzenzertrümmerer " (Our Idolbreakers), in *Čechische Revue*, April, 1910, pp. 201–223.

[392] Notably when he fought for a revision of the Polná Ritual Murder Trial (1899), and when he defended Professor Wahrmund's aggressive anti-clerical pamphlet, *Katholische Weltanschauung* (1908).

liberal to be a Pan-Slav in the Russian sense, he believes in Austria's mission and in a great future for the Slavs under Habsburg rule, and he regards Prague, not St. Petersburg, as the focussing point of Slavonic culture.

Impatient of forms and phrases, cold and unexpansive in manner, he goes to essentials, and when he holds the kernel, despises the outer shell. Almost Spartan in his private life, an enemy of alcohol and tobacco, he is no lover of effect or ceremony, and relies upon reason rather than sentiment. Indeed, he is free, almost to brusqueness, from the exaggerated sentimentalism of the Slav. In any country such a man could not fail to exercise a deep influence upon his students : in Bohemia, it is not too much to say that he has become one of the chief moral forces of the country. Moreover Prague, as a brilliant centre of national culture, and as the most untrammelled of all the Slavonic universities, attracts students from every Slav country : and all those who showed sympathy for liberal and progressive principles, fell under the thrall of Masaryk. Thus we are faced by the remarkable fact that not merely in Bohemia itself, but among the Slovenes and the Slovaks, in Croatia, Dalmatia, Bosnia, Servia, Bulgaria, even to some extent in Russia and Poland, the younger politicians, under the age of forty, have been largely recruited from among his stvdents. The idealism of the younger generation of Southern Slavs, the incentive to shake off the corrupt past, were the direct fruit of his teaching. In Croatia especially, the Progressive Party was founded by his pupils, Dr. Lorković and Professor Šurmin, on the lines of his own party. Mr. Supilo, the peasant Cato, was a man after his own heart. The Serb Independent leaders, Messrs. Pribičević, Budisavljević and Popović, were equally under his influence. In Belgrad more than one of the men whose names occurred in Dr. Friedjung's " documents," had held a high place among his pupils and in his own estimation. " For Supilo, Pribičević and Lukinić," he had declared in the Austrian Parliament, " I would lay both my hands in the fire." [393] How was it possible that the very cream of those who had been through his hands, should be accused of actions which ran counter to his whole teaching ? Inevitably he was led to investigate the charges : for the slur upon the pupils reflected upon the master too. And with each step in the inquiry, the conviction ripened in

[393] *See* Masaryk, op. cit. p. 101.

him that their very excellence had exposed them to a shameful plot, which aimed at robbing Croatia of her ablest sons. Once more he was involved in a momentous dispute as to the authenticity of documents, and in challenging Dr. Friedjung's thesis, he had one obvious point in his favour. Professor Masaryk was a recognized authority on Slavonic languages : Dr. Friedjung could not read a word of Servian or any other Slav language. In other words, the one was qualified to criticise the " documents " : the other was not.[394]

Professor Masaryk gave a long and conscientious account of his visits to Belgrad, and the methods which he employed to investigate the allegations brought forward by the Public Prosecutor in Agram, and by Dr. Friedjung's article. In some respects, he argued, he could say more than Marković. On his second visit to Belgrad in July, 1909, he had spoken with Marković, the main object of his inquiry being to discover whether the Slovenski Jug was the central committee of a secret society, or had intimate relations with the Servian Government. He satisfied himself that this was not the case, and was confirmed in this view by the discovery that Slovenski Jug had been in serious financial difficulties and could scarcely have existed but for the Town Council's subsidy. The judge here not unfairly suggested that if a secret society had existed, it was hardly likely that Professor Masaryk, as a foreigner and an Austrian, would have been let into its secrets ; and the fact that on his second visit to Belgrad, several Servian newspapers denounced him as an Austrian spy, seemed to confirm the Judge's scepticism. But Professor Masaryk maintained confidently that he, who had so many intimate friends and former pupils in Servia, could not have failed to detect the existence of revolutionary designs among them. Some of them he knew so well, that they would have told him every-

---

[394] In writing thus of Professor Masaryk, I feel that, like Balaam, I came to curse and stayed to bless. The attitude of his more prominent followers, who have degraded his liberal views into mere anti-clericalism, had prejudiced me against him also ; and even at the time of the Agram Trial, I could not approve of his tactics or his speech in Parliament. But his attitude at the Friedjung Trial, and still more his courageous exposure of Count Aehrenthal and his methods (*see* Chapter XII) completely converted me. He had nothing to gain and has actually gained nothing but insult and abuse. No one can withhold his admiration from his unselfish and loyal defence of his old pupils—or at least none save those who think that the sole lesson to be learnt from a scandal is the best method of avoiding detection on the next occasion.

thing, everything ; nor would he hesitate for a moment to brand Milovanović or Jovanović as liars, if he found their assertions to be untrue. Asked whether he believed that a Foreign Minister would admit the existence of such a conspiracy, he replied, " A small-minded politician would not admit it ; a Bismarck would." Nor was it only to him that Milovanović had expressly denied the charges. He had discussed the matter publicly in the Skupshtina, where he had many enemies. And when during strained relations with Austria a Servian Minister publicly speaks of these things in the Skupshtina, in discussing a universal question—for the Servian question is a universal question in which Austria, Russia, Britain, Italy and Germany are interested—and Count Aehrenthal does not disavow him in the official press, then I must assume that Milovanović is speaking the truth."

Professor Masaryk, in passing to a criticism of Dr. Friedjung's " documents," pointed out that he had devoted four years to the study of documents during the famous literary feud of the Königinhof MS.; and on the present occasion he had employed similar methods. To begin with, the phraseology of the documents was incredible. Not even a schoolboy would write as Pasić, Servia's foremost *Realpolitiker*, is represented as writing in the secret instructions to Tomić. And how could a man like Milovanović, in a confidential document dealing with high politics, write of " Golden Prague " or of " the Czech Kingdom " ?

In reply to Dr. Friedjung, he admitted that on his first visit to Belgrad he only remained two nights, having previously made appointments by letter with those whom he wanted to see. His chief reason for going was that no one in Agram dared to go,[395] and even he as a politician was laying himself open to suspicion, and therefore stopped as short a time as possible. He had not spoken with Marković on that occasion, because the object of his enquiries related to a period previous to the latter's connexion with the club. His interest was concentrated on Milan Pribičević, as the author of the revolutionary statute, and Ljuba Jovanović, as former president of Slovenski Jug. At the Agram trial the statute played the principal part, while the Marković " minutes " had not yet been produced ; and it was therefore only natural that he should concern himself with the former and not the latter. An amusing incident

---

[395] Owing to the attitude of Rauch's absolutist government.

occurred when Dr. Friedjung asked who had told him that the statute had reached Austria from Montenegro. Professor Masaryk replied that he had learnt this fact from several sources which he was not at liberty to mention, and also from no other than George Nastić, who for once in a way appeared to have spoken the truth. Here Dr. Friedjung threw doubt upon Nastić's veracity, though he had not scrupled to cite him in his article in the *Neue Freie Presse*—see p. 204. When Masaryk rejoined that this fact was also published in the *Wiener Allgemeine Zeitung*, one of Count Aehrenthal's organs, Friedjung poured contempt upon the scientific methods of that newspaper. " Then," said Masaryk, " Count Aehrenthal should have published a *dementi*, if the statement was inaccurate." [396]

Strangely enough, this and the fact that the Servian Premier's telegram was published without contradiction in the *Fremdenblatt*, the chief official organ of the Ballplatz, seem to have impressed the Court and the jury far more than anything that Professor Masaryk could say. They were openly sceptical " when he assured them that the word of a Foreign Minister had some claim to consideration, and that a large-minded politician would give an honest answer to an honest question from an intimate friend, or at least would not wilfully mislead him." [397]

Professor Masaryk's evidence was not impressive : like himself, it was not calculated for effect, and indeed, in the hostile court, created an atmosphere of frigid scepticism. The extreme conviction with which he spoke, the evidences of careful and minute investigation which he was able to adduce, were wasted upon a judge and jury with whom it seemed to be an axiom that all Serbs are naturally liars and conspirators.

IX. The Evidence of Father Zagorac.

The next witness presented a complete contrast to Professor Masaryk. Father Stephen Zagorac has been for the last eight years a member of the Croatian Diet. As one of the chief representatives of Croatia at the Resolution of Fiume, he held an influential position in the Croato-Serb Coalition, and was

[396] It is highly significant that the *Neue Freie Presse*, in its ostensibly verbatim reports of the trial, omits all reference to this little incident—doubtless as a result of a hint from the proper quarter. I am relying here upon my own notes taken in court.

[397] *Times*, December 17, 1909.

one of its most active members in Budapest. Despite his natural leanings to the Clericals of Vienna, he showed extreme reluctance to abandon the cause of Magyar-Croat friendship, and in the summer of 1908 he exposed himself to much criticism by attempting to negotiate singlehanded with Budapest. As a result of this incident and of friction with other Coalition leaders, Father Zagorac seceded in the autumn of the same year, and threw in his lot with the small group of Dr. Mile Starčević. Renouncing all hope of an entente with Hungary, he pinned his whole faith upon Austria, the Heir-Apparent, and the Christian Socialist Party, with members of which he was on friendly terms. Thus it was Dr. Funder, the Christian Socialist editor, who cited him as a witness, to report on his former relations with the Croato-Serb Coalition.

Father Zagorac at once admitted that he had heard talk of relations between the Coalition and the Servian Government, but all his information came from Vienna. "Over two years ago certain exalted persons in Vienna are said to have repeatedly affirmed that the Coalition contains antimonarchical and antidynastic elements." He at once discussed the matter with Supilo and other leaders, and regarded their replies as entirely satisfactory. Questioned as to his informant, Father Zagorac declined to give his name, but added, "None the less I learnt that the Archduke Francis Ferdinand stated before various political personages, that the Coalition was connected with treasonable intrigues." Mr. Laginja [398] had repeated to him a similar remark of the Austrian Premier, Baron Beck ; and documents were believed to exist, proving Supilo to be an enemy of the dynasty. From another absolutely authentic source he had heard that Count Aehrenthal had also spoken of anti-monarchical elements in the Coalition. About the same time he himself had an interview with Dr. Gessmann—the well-known Christian Socialist leader in Austria—and found it necessary to defend the Coalition from the charge of being unpatriotic and hostile to the Monarchy. In reply to Dr. Kienböck, he stated that not long before he seceded from the Coalition, he had applied for an audience with the Heir-Apparent, but it was refused without reason stated, and he was merely informed "At present it is impossible." Soon afterwards, however, he met a politician who had actually been received in audience, and it was then that he learnt of the Archduke's remark.

[398] Member of the Reichsrath for a Croat district in Istria.

Father Zagorac then stated the reasons which had prompted him to secede from the Coalition. First, he could no longer submit to the leadership of Supilo. Second, he was dissatisfied with the Coalition's attitude in the Bosnian question. Third, he was no longer willing to accept the Ausgleich with Hungary as the basis of Croatia's policy. And, finally, what he had heard in Vienna had not been without its effect upon him, and he felt that Croatia must in the future at all costs avoid the enmity of Austria. Supilo he described as an intolerably autocratic leader—from this view the plaintiffs at once dissented; any one who differed from him was at once either a fool or an agent of Austria or Hungary. Under his guidance the Coalition had made endless tactical blunders, chiefly owing to the rapidity with which he veered round from Serbophobe to Serbophil, from Magyarophobe to Kossuthist, from an opponent of Austria to an admirer of the "Great Austrian" idea. But though all this made it impossible for him to continue to work with Supilo, he emphatically asserted that he had never doubted Supilo's personal honour, and to-day he was still convinced that Supilo had never accepted a kreuzer from any one. Though up till December, 1908, a member of the executive committee of the Coalition, he had never heard a syllable as to relations with Servia on the part of any of its members. While admitting that he had at the time expressed open disapproval of Supilo's occasional visits to Italy and Servia, and had even described the latter as a "pilgrimage," he vigorously denied that there had ever been any talk of treason inside the Coalition. There have been traitors in the Monarchy, but they are to be sought not in the ranks of the Coalition, but in Budapest and in the Serb-Radical party. He had once asked the deputy Budisavljević his opinion of the Slovenski Jug, and had received the answer, "That is tomfoolery"(*Das sind Dummheiten*). "And I replied," added Father Zagorac, with surprising vigour, "that we too could do with a Slovenski Jug against the Magyars." A chance conversation of his with the deputy Dr. Magdić had been falsely reported as conveying a slur upon the patriotism of the Coalition, and he now corrected it amid loud laughter from all parts of the court. He himself had said that a time might come when bombs would be required; for when a man is attacked by a robber with the words "Your money or your life"—and this was the attitude of the Magyars towards Croatia—weapons are the only resort, and in that case it matters very little where the bombs come from. " Perhaps," replied Magdić, " and I'll be the first to blow up a bridge." "And I the second," added this representative of the Church militant. As he had taken care to warn the Court, the whole affair smacked strongly of an inn parlour (*ein Wirtshausgespräch*). The whole campaign against the Coalition, he added, was in his opinion, even after reading the " documents," a mere political intrigue, whose object was the revival of the old " Magyarone " regime in Croatia. " And what impression did these documents make upon you ? " asked counsel for the prosecution. " I have read carefully every day the reports in the *Reichspost*," replied Father Zagorac, " and one day I said to my curates, ' Gentlemen, I have read the documents of which Dr. Funder told me, but I'm afraid he will be dreadfully let in ' (*Er wird sich schrecklich blamiren*)."

The evidence of Father Zagorac created a profound sensation. The source of the defendants' information had from the first been sufficiently obvious ; but the fact that forged documents had played a decisive part in winning the consent of the dynasty and of the Austrian Government to the Aehrenthal policy, had hitherto been kept discreetly in the background. Father Zagorac's extremely outspoken language tore away the veil for the first time, and the scene which it revealed was far from edifying. Dr. Friedjung rightly felt that such revelations could not be passed over in silence, and standing up in court he made the following statement :—

" Hitherto I have said not a word as to whether His Imperial and Royal Highness, Archduke Francis Ferdinand, or Count Aehrenthal, or the Premier Baron Beck have seen these documents. But as the witness stated here that he knew that these documents have been for years in the possession of, and known to, these highly-placed personages, I am obliged and entitled to declare that these documents were certainly brought to the knowledge of all the authoritative quarters (*leitende Stellen*) which had to conduct the government of the Monarchy. I content myself with pointing out that I was not naïve in producing the documents, for otherwise I should have shared this naïveté with all the authoritative quarters that have been mentioned."

This statement effectively demolished the assurances of Count Aehrenthal's official press, that the Friedjung Trial was in no sense a political affair and that its issue was of no concern to the Foreign Minister. Its eminently political character was now apparent to all the world. The Friedjung Trial was already threatening to compromise the diplomatic methods of the Monarchy, and to become a grave European scandal.

A new witness was now produced in the person of Father Zajnko, who gave a confused account of a conversation which he had had with Zagorac as recently as the autumn of 1909. The latter had confided to him the reasons for which his audience had been refused, and also the account which Supilo had given of his visits to Belgrad ; " I believed him," said Zagorac, " but afterwards, when I heard Spalajković speak, I was convinced that the matter was quite different." Zagorac had further repeated the phrase of Supilo, that he had visited Belgrad " only in the interests of the Coalition."

But Father Zagorac yielded not an inch, and boldly confronting the witness, he denied having ever even mentioned to him the name of Spalajković, or having ever used the phrase " in the interests of the Coalition." " Either you have made a mistake," he cried with his accustomed verve, " Either you have made a mistake, or you are lying." And here the matter rested, though not before it had transpired that Supilo could not possibly have made the remark attributed to him by Zajnko, since his visit to Belgrad had taken place in the first days of April, 1905, at a time when the Coalition had not yet come into being.

X. Dr. Polit and the Servian Witnesses.

The next witness was Dr. Michael Polit-Desančić, a man of seventy-seven, who had for many years been the recognized leader of the Serbs in Southern Hungary. Originally a member of the Croatian Diet in the sixties, he had been settled for forty years in Neusatz (Ujvidék), the home of the Serb Academy (Srpska Matica). During the Bosnian insurrection of 1876–77, he had as a young advocate gallantly defended Svetozar Miletić, when arraigned by the Magyar Government for his Serbophil tendencies. When in 1906 he re-entered the Hungarian Parliament, after an absence of over twenty years, he was able to remind the House of his farewell phrase a generation before, " We meet again at Philippi." As an old-world Liberal, he was bitterly opposed to Dr. Pašić, and the Radical party, which had dominated Servia since King Alexander's murder ; and hence his association with the Pašić Govern ment, as the minutes of the Slovenski Jug alleged, had considerably mystified even Dr. Friedjung himself.

In the course of his evidence, Dr. Polit stated that as a young man he had written regularly on Balkan affairs in the *Augsburger Allgemeine Zeitung*, and his articles had actually been described as inspired by Bismarck's press bureau ! But for the past twenty years he had not written a single article in the foreign press ; and as for conducting a foreign press propaganda in favour of Pašić, it was only necessary to point out that both his party and his newspaper had been for twenty years at enmity with the Radicals both in Servia and in the Banat, that he had repeatedly written articles attacking Pašić and demanding the trial of the regicides. Nor could any one acquainted with his relations to the Magyars fail to realize the sheer absurdity of the charge that he had received money on behalf of the Hungarian press. Here Dr. Friedjung freely admitted that he knew Dr. Polit's high reputation and had consequently been puzzled by the passage referring to him in Spalajković's secret report.[399] Indeed, he had at first been disposed to omit the passage, and had only reluctantly decided to print it in full. As Dr. Harpner afterwards (December 18), pointed out with crushing irony, it would be far better if they had the *complete* documents before them ; so many more absurdities might then become apparent. He admitted Dr. Friedjung's bona fides but claimed that from the point of view of an effective control, these omissions were distinctly unfortunate. A barren dispute followed between the witness and Dr. Friedjung on the academic question whether it was permissible for a newspaper to accept subventions from abroad. Both parties played with the words " criminal " and " natural," until their hearers were genuinely bewildered ; the witness apparently held that to accept a subsidy where there was clearly no treason involved, was not penal, while the defendant regarded all subsidies from abroad as unjustifiable, and unpatriotic. For obvious reasons the discussion must have been followed with some anxiety by numerous representatives of the Viennese and Budapest press.

Mr. Peter Jelovac, the merchant in whose house at Semlin—according to the Spalajković report—the Servian money was paid over to the deputy Pribičević, next categorically denied the allegation and gave details as to the four occasions on which he had met Pribičević.

[399] *See* Appendix XIV.

DR. POLIT AND THE SERVIAN WITNESSES

After Mr. Tončić, the Vice-Governor of Dalmatia, had been examined regarding Mr. Supilo's activity in Ragusa (*see* p. 292) fresh witnesses from Servia were allowed to run the gauntlet of a hostile court.

Mr. Davidović, a former Servian Minister of Education, and Vice-President of the Skupshtina, whose name occurs repeatedly as member and even vice-president of the Slovenski Jug, declared that he had never belonged to the club and denied having ever attended any of the meetings reported in the alleged " minutes." He described the Slovenski Jug as a students' society, which pursued objects of general culture and also sought connexions with similar organizations abroad. Though not intimate with Marković, he belonged to the same party, and was therefore in a position to state that Marković took no active part in politics, except in so far as he voted at elections. When the Judge pointed out that the relations alleged to have subsisted between the witness and Austrian politicians constituted a penal offence, Davidović replied that he was fully aware of this and that it was hardly likely that he would have appeared before the Court if he had felt himself to be guilty. After the Judge had put a number of minor questions, Dr. Benedikt, assuming his most offensive manner, stated that in view of such wholesale denials he had nothing to ask the witness, and Dr. Friedjung tersely added that a cross-examination was superfluous.

Mr. Davidović was replaced by Mr. Mile Pavlović, a professor in one of the Belgrad gymnasia. A little man with pointed beard and bushy moustache, speaking fluent but highly original German, and accompanying his quaint phrases with excitable gestures, he introduced, it must be confessed, an irresistibly comic element into the trial. But unhappily a sense of humour is not Dr. Friedjung's strong point : his counsel was thoroughly nettled by the unfavourable turn which the trial had taken ; and even the Judge, who as the author of light dramas from the life of the people ought to have known better, took the good man more seriously with every fresh sally. Hence the Servians were received with an icy condescension and suspicion which was far more provocative than the vigorous but not unnatural onslaught of the defence upon Professor Marković.[400]

[400] Personally I had from the very first had strong reason to doubt the accuracy of Dr. Friedjung's information ; otherwise I should naturally not have written in defence of the Croato-Servian Coalition in my pamphlet *Absolutismus in Kroatien*—published in Vienna in September,

261

THE FRIEDJUNG TRIAL

The very first words of Mr. Pavlović convulsed his audience; to the Judge's formal question whether he was married, he replied, " Unfortunately a bachelor." " Do you belong to a party ? " asked the Judge a little later. " I might say," answered the good man, " I am myself a party. I was once editor of a newspaper, but left it eight years ago and am now, so to speak, a widow at large ! " *Solvuntur tabulae risu :* but the defence maintained a portentous dignity ; and when Pavlović had declared that though a member of the Slovenski Jug he had never belonged to a committee of any kind and had never signed the minutes, that the club pursued literary and artistic aims, that neither it nor its president Marković had taken an active share in politics, and that he knew nothing of the existence of bombs on its premises,[401] Dr. Benedikt roundly declared that he was not so simple as to ask further questions about the Slovenski Jug, since he was convinced that this witness would not tell the truth ! This exhibition of temper seems to have been due to Pavlović's awkward request to be allowed to see the original of the " minutes " bearing his signature, and to the sarcasm with which he received the reply that the originals were not before the Court.

Dr. Friedjung contented himself with a single question : Do you often travel in Austria-Hungary ? Hereupon this chatty " conspirator " plunged into a highly characteristic account of his last visit to Bosnia in the summer of 1908. He had been commissioned by the Minister of Education to proceed to Ragusa and arrange for the erection of a monument over the grave of Milan Kristić, a well-known Belgrad dramatist who had died during a visit to Ragusa. On the way he decided to stop in Sarajevo, and here he at once called upon Mr. Hörman, one of the highest officials of the Bosnian Government, and

1909. But none the less I entered court full of prejudice and hostility towards the witnesses from Servia, and inclined to suspect the Slovenski Jug of evil practices, even while convinced that it had no accomplices in Croatia. Despite this prejudice (which—as the result of information received in Vienna—was especially strong against Dr. Spalajković) my indignation was roused by the attitude of the Court towards the Servian witnesses ; and it passes my understanding how any sane observer of the proceedings could regard persons like Pavlović, Odavić and Marković—three radically different characters—as dangerous plotters of murder and revolution.

[401] He admitted having written two articles in *Slovenski Jug*, one an attack upon Montenegro, the other on a literary subject. He also stated that certain newspapers had affected to detect revolutionary aims in the fact that the society organized a Southern Slav art exhibition !

explained the object of his journey. He was however neither allowed to remain nor to proceed upon his journey ; gendarmes and detectives promptly fetched him from his hotel and escorted him back across the Bosnian frontier. His explanation of the expulsion was that being an unmarried man he kept a spare room in his house in Belgrad specially for poor students and workmen who came from Bosnia, and that this had made his name known in Bosnia and specially obnoxious to the police authorities. As he remarked—in a phrase of more than questionable taste, but unhappily not wholly devoid of truth— " the nose of the Bosnian police is no mere ordinary nose." But however deserving of criticism and reform the Bosnian police-state may be, Mr. Pavlović's choice of time and place was singularly inopportune. At the same time Dr. Friedjung was merely laying himself open to criticism when he persisted in regarding such a man as Pavlović as one of the ringleaders of a Pan-Serb conspiracy ; for no one who listened to his evidence could fail to realize that he would within a fortnight have proved fatal to the existence of any secret society.

The next witness was Mr. Rista Odavić, formerly professor in a gymnasium, but now playwright and *regisseur* of the Royal Theatre in Belgrad. His evidence contained few points of interest. While admitting that he had been and still was a member of the Slovenski Jug, he denied all other allegations as explicitly as the other witnesses. He helped to smooth the somewhat ruffled dignity of the Court by his mild and conciliatory replies, and concluded by expressing the pious hope that if by his evidence he had contributed to expose the forgeries, Dr. Friedjung, for whom as a historian he had the highest respect, would not fail to be grateful to him.

VIII. THE EVIDENCE OF DR. SPALAJKOVIČ.

Saturday's sitting brought the crowning sensation of this eventful trial, and ruthlessly demolished the last outworks behind which the defence had taken refuge. The notorious Dr. Spalajković, against whom Dr. Friedjung had fulminated in his opening *plaidoyer*, at length confronted his traducer. But instead of the bespectacled bureaucrat of sinister and intriguing aspect whom we had been led to expect, there appeared a tall, elegant figure, of military carriage, whose courteous and dignified demeanour presented a striking contrast to the studied impertinence with which he was received. Under extraordinary provocation, he invariably kept his temper, and showed himself to be a worthy representative of Servian diplomacy.

Dr. Spalajković began his evidence with a slightly long-winded declaration of the motives which had induced him to appear before the Court. In the first place he held it to be a duty of which neither his diplomatic position nor the fact that he was a foreigner could absolve him ; and secondly, he was prompted by the desire to promote good relations between Servia and Austria-Hungary, which were impeded by these "mendacious documents." He could not help regretting that the proposal which he had made when Dr. Friedjung's article appeared —that the whole question should be submitted to the arbitration of a court of savants—had not found acceptance with his opponents. As it was, he appeared to-day, full of confidence in the impartiality of the Viennese jury and in the firm conviction that these lying documents were "a colossal mystification," intended to throw suspicion upon Servia, the Servian Government, the Slovenski Jug, himself and the Croato-Serb Coalition. This view was also shared by his chief, Dr. Milovanović, with whose permission he now proposed to lay his proofs before the Court. " Gentlemen," he continued, "there are clever forgeries and stupid forgeries. The forgeries contained in this pamphlet (Dr. Friedjung's Green Book) do not belong to the former category. That one can see at first glance." He then offered to submit to a technical cross-examination on the handwriting of his alleged secret report, and suggested a comparison of his handwriting with either the original or its photograph. When the Judge explained that the Court had nothing at its disposal save a mere printed copy of the Servian text, Dr. Spalajković expressed his readiness to prove the forgery even on this inadequate basis. The Judge sought to smooth over the absence of originals by the remark that the document might perhaps have been abstracted from the Servian Foreign Office for a brief space of time and then returned before any one had noticed its absence. But this suggestion the witness politely brushed aside by affirming that if such a document, or even anything resembling it, had ever existed, he would scarcely have found courage to appear before the Court.

Dr. Spalajković, with the Judge's permission, then entered upon a detailed criticism of the forged report. (1) Confining himself at first to matters of external form, he contrasted the extreme prolixity of the report with the statement contained in Document XV (Slovenski Jug Minutes of November 16,

THE EVIDENCE OF DR. SPALAJKOVIĆ

1908), that he (Spalajković) would " report briefly to the Minister." The document was headed, " Ministry of Foreign Affairs, political department, Belgrad, June 4, 1907. Confidential No. 3,027 " ; but on referring to the official records it appeared that the total number of numbered documents in that department during 1907 amounted to 1991, the numbers on June 1 and 30 respectively being 832 and 1,040. (2) In the same way, Dr. Funder's chief document—the instructions of Dr. Milovanović to the Servian Minister in Vienna—bears the number 5,703, whereas in reality the first document drawn up on that date by the department in question is numbered 367, and even as late as December 1, 1909, the total only amounted to 2,748.

(3) The Servian text contains a word which he could never possibly have employed either in an official or a private letter, and which was not in use in Servia.[402] As a proof that the style of the text bore no resemblance to his, he ventured to lay before the Court a treatise of his which had appeared in 1906 in the *Archiv für Rechts- und Socialwissenschaft.*

(4) The report is signed by " Miroslav Spalajković," whereas he invariably signed all official documents with " Dr. M. Spalajković " and never with his full Christian name.

(5) It is also signed by Bozović as cashier, whereas in reality no cashier in the Servian Foreign Office had ever signed a political report or had the slightest connexion with the political department.

Passing to the contents of the report, Dr. Spalajković next pointed out that he had never in his life visited Semlin in company with the cashier Bozović and had never met Mr. Svetozar Pribičević. The absurdity and Utopian folly of the report were well illustrated by two striking instances : (1) The report contains the following passage : " Besides the Government will have control over a new extended Budget, and what is the main thing, over larger contributions from the new State Loan, regarding which the preliminary negotiations are already ended, and which the Skupshtina will vote in the autumn." " I would ask you, gentlemen," added Dr. Spalajković, " to note specially that the document is dated June 4, 1907, and speaks of a loan which Parliament will vote in the autumn. But, gentlemen, this whole matter of the loan was already

[402] Uručin—" handed in "—a literal translation of the German phrase " eingehändigt." This Germanism, though unknown in Servia, is quite usual in Croatia, of which the forger is probably a native.

265

settled, both with regard to the preliminary negotiations and also with regard to the Skupshtina—*a year previously* ! " The negotiations had been finally completed in Geneva in 1906 by Dr. Paču and Dr. Spalajković himself, and soon afterwards the Servian Parliament had voted the loan, which amounted to 90,000,000 francs, not 93,000,000, as Dr. Friedjung had erroneously stated.

When the loud applause which greeted this conclusive proof of the forger's ignorance had been sternly repressed by the Judge, Dr. Spalajković turned to the concluding passage of the Report, which contains the request that the Minister should sanction the disbursement of 12,000 dinars, "to debit of No. 190 of Item xxxviiiB. of the fifth Chapter of the Budget." Never, he assured the Court, had any document of the Servian Foreign Office employed such a formula in its references to the Budget. After pointing to the formal phrases and technicalities which would be used under such circumstances, he produced a copy of the Servian Budget for 1906, an examination of which would confirm his statements.

In case, however, doubts should still be entertained as to the authenticity of his facts, he had the following statement to make : "Should it be necessary, the Servian Government will resort to a final measure, in order to repel and rebut such charges as are contained in this document. It will, namely, if necessary, approach all the Great Powers with the request that the representatives of the Great Powers at Belgrad may convince themselves of the accuracy of all these statements and proofs which have been laid before the Court." And then turning to the alleged Instructions of Dr. Milovanović to the Servian Minister in Vienna, he characterized the document as "not only an idiotic and clumsy forgery, but also a feeble attempt to sully the honour of the Minister. His personality, his ability, his *Realismus*, and his services in the cause of European peace are so well known to all authoritative quarters that every one of them before whom this document was placed, would indignantly throw it aside as I myself do."

"So you have nothing more to say on this point," remarked the Judge, who perhaps wished to heighten the impression by a humorous sally. Most people will agree with the plaintiffs that Dr. Spalajković had already said a good deal ! Finally, he stated that the Servian Foreign Minister was not merely willing, but anxious, that the Austro-Hungarian Minister in Belgrad should test the accuracy of his statements and that in response to a telegram the necessary books of the Foreign Office would be immediately placed at Count Forgách's disposal.

In reply to Dr. Harpner, the witness declared, both in his own name and in that of Dr. Milovanović, that the Servian Government had never had any relations with the Coalition, either through the Slovenski Jug or other channels. Asked by the Judge whether he had been relieved of his pledge of official secrecy, he replied that he was authorized to speak freely upon everything relating to the Coalition and the issue involved in this trial. Owing to his position in the Foreign Office no intercourse could have taken place without his knowledge ; but, " Gentlemen," he declared, " my conscience is clear, and I here swear that I do not shelter myself behind any form of immunity, whether legal or conventional ; for me a clear conscience is the best guarantee."

The Judge stubbornly pressed the witness to explain why the Servian Government had made no diplomatic representations on the subject of these charges ; but Spalajković, who showed a marked reluctance to say anything which might offend Austrian susceptibilities, at last reduced him to silence by suggesting that it might be well to institute an inquiry, and both parties could then publish their versions of the reasons which prevented the matter from being settled by diplomacy. The haste with which Dr. Wach relinquished the subject, showed that there was more behind it than the politely cryptic phrase of the Servian official seemed to suggest.

Further questions of the Judge made a still more painful impression. The cross-examination of a high diplomatic official as to the possibility of documents under his care having been purloined by spies or hirelings employed by the questioner's own Foreign Minister, was one of the most repulsive incidents in the whole trial. Nor was it necessary to treat as suspicious the assertion of Dr. Spalajković, that he had other more important things to do during the Bosnian crisis than to read the " red number " of the *Slovenski Jug* newspaper. Sir Edward Grey might well be excused for not reading the *Isis* or the *Granta* at a moment of acute international danger ; and *Slovenski Jug* appears only to have differed from those well-known publications, in that it was more ambitious, less influential, and far worse edited.

At this stage in the proceedings Dr. Friedjung sought to bolster up his tottering cause by reading out a declaration of the Hungarian Premier, Dr. Wekerle, to the effect that he knew

" not only from the Report of Dr. Spalajković but also from numerous other documents, that illicit relations subsisted between Belgrad and the leaders of the Pan-Serb movement in the lands of the Crown of St. Stephen." [403] " I have read this," continued Dr. Friedjung, " because the gentlemen from Servia seem to me to assert rather too much. They have the right to deny everything. But in my opinion they exceed the limits of their right of denial, when they describe the documents which were used by the leading authorities—*leitende Stellen*—of the Monarchy as the basis of their foreign policy, and by the leading authorities entrusted with the Monarchy's defence as the basis of their measures for the defence of our country, when they say of these that they are stupid and ridiculous forgeries." Nothing could have shown more clearly the historian's desperate plight than this strange attempt to restrict his adversaries' right of defence ; at the best Dr. Wekerle's statement merely proved that the forger had made one more dupe in the high places of the Monarchy, and at the worst it might be objected that the man who was responsible for Baron Rauch's absolutist regime and who for the past two years had done all in his power to destroy the Croato-Serb Coalition in the interests of the Magyar hegemony, was the last man in the Monarchy from whom an impartial statement could be expected. Dr. Harpner, moreover, was able to cite Dr. Wekerle's answer to an interpellation in the Hungarian Parliament, which showed that he had not always professed the opinion quoted by Dr. Friedjung.

The time had at length come for the " merciless " exposure with which Dr. Friedjung had threatened this " foreign agitator " ; but the historian's big guns proved as innocuous as any schoolboy's peashooter. While treating the Servian,

---

[403] Those who knew Dr. Friedjung's private opinion of the Wekerle administration and its policy, alike internal and external, could only regard his appeal to the authority of Dr. Wekerle as an admission of weakness and also as an indirect sign that the rats of the Foreign Office were already leaving the sinking ship. Dr. Wekerle's statement is all the more remarkable, when compared with his answer to an interpellation in the Hungarian Parliament on March 30, 1908, regarding Dr. Friedjung's charges. On that occasion he said that he had had the opportunity of examining the document (viz., the Spalajković Report), and that while it might be a sufficient basis for a publicist's charges it did not, *for a minister*, constitute documentary proof ! (*See Pester Lloyd*, March 30.) These two statements are highly characteristic of Dr. Wekerle's methods.

Secretary of State throughout the examination with a studied rudeness [404] which was far more painful to his own friends than to his opponents, Dr. Friedjung could adduce no more damning evidence than a report of the Bosnian police regarding Dr. Spalajković's visit to his father-in-law in Sarajevo, based on information supplied by one of the numerous spies who frequent the Bosnian capital.[405]   Dr. Spalajković had in September, 1907, spent a month's leave with his wife at the house of her father, Mr. Jeftanović, and on that occasion had met Mr. Damjanović, a leader of the Orthodox Serb Opposition in Bosnia and Dr. Gavrila, a well-known Serb advocate resident in Budapest, who was expelled from Bosnia after his meeting with Spalajković.   Both men were admittedly intimate friends of the Jeftanović family and two of the most honoured guests at the Spalajković wedding in 1906.   But Dr. Friedjung argued that their presence in the house was a proof of political intrigue, and maintained that it was Dr. Gavrila who drew up the disloyal Bosnian appeals to the Great Powers, after they had been drafted in Dr. Spalajković's office in Belgrad.   As a last resort, Dr. Friedjung cited from an article by M. René Pinon in the *Revue des Deux Mondes*, where Dr. Spalajković is spoken of as

[404] He did not even take the trouble to stand up while putting his questions, as he had invariably done in all other cases ; and the Judge made no attempt to protect the witness from the defendant's sallies.
At a certain point witness begged the Judge not to allow questions which were quite irrelevant and only wearied him.   Dr. Friedjung : " I shall go on wearying you, Herr Sektionschef.   I shall weary you very, very much.   Do you know Dr. Gavrila's position in the political struggles of the Mohammedan and Serb opposition ? "   Witness : " What do you understand by Serb opposition ? "   Dr. Friedjung : " ' What is a lieutenant ? ' asks the simple maiden."

[405] This report—dated September 15, 1909—contains the following highly instructive passage :—" *A spy announces* that Spalajković brought with him a considerable sum of money from the Servian secret fund for the Serb society ' Prosvjeta ' here, and carried on negotiations with Dr. Milan Skrskić, lawyer's clerk here.   The subject of these *is said to have been* the well-known May Resolution of the Serb ultras and the assembly of the Serb organization, which took place in November, 1907, that is after Spalajković's departure.   Moreover *he is said to have (ferner soll er)*—acquired influence over the editors of *Srpska Riječ* and to have written the articles ' Dogogjaje ' and ' Srbiji ' in praise of Pašić's policy."   These hearsay denunciations of a badly-paid Bosnian spy—for with the exception of George Nastić all the Bosnian spies seem to be badly paid—were eagerly swallowed by the credulous historian. Even if he failed to realize the worthlessness of such evidence, he might surely have shrunk from thus exposing the contemptible and underhand methods of the Bosnian police.

holding in his hands the threads of Pan-Serb propaganda in Old Servia, the Banat, Bosnia and Dalmatia. The witness mildly hinted that he was not responsible for the sources of information of M. Pinon, who had been in Constantinople and Vienna as well as Belgrad. He regretted that he himself had become the bogey of the Viennese Press, but this was not the occasion for clearing himself from all its vague assertions.

But Dr. Friedjung excelled himself when he suggested that the 12,000 francs which the " Report " represents Dr. Spalaj-ković as having paid over to Messrs. Pribičević and Supilo might in reality have found their way into his own private pocket. This supposition he based upon a misinterpretation of Professor Masaryk's speech in the Reichsrat in May, 1909, criticising the conduct of the Agram High Treason Trial.[406] Even here Dr. Spalajković's self-possession did not desert him. Immediately after the speech, he said, he had telegraphed to Professor Masaryk for an explanation, and had received the answer that Masaryk, after expressing his firm conviction that the document was false, had drawn the entirely " hypothetical conclusion " that if genuine it must be regarded as a kind of promissory note for 12,000 francs. " Only if this impossibility were possible," such was Masaryk's process of argument.

After a few more futile questions the long examination was at an end, and Dr. Spalajković as he withdrew heaped coals of fire upon the Judge by thanking him for his " impartial attitude." It is unhappily impossible to congratulate the Judge upon his attitude towards the Servian witnesses, and as I do not belong to the diplomatic corps I am under no obligation to slur over unwelcome facts. It is true that Dr. Wach did not show the same lack of restraint as during the Supilo-Chlumecky incident ; but he none the less openly placed himself upon the side of the defendants, asking the Servian witnesses questions which can only be described as unpardonable, aud more than once assuming the manner of a schoolmaster towards his pupils. In view of the eccentric—his enemies would call it offensive— behaviour of Mr. Pavlović, some excuse might be found for the Judge's sharp command, " Will you be kind enough to stand still ? "—though, as I have already suggested, it would have been wiser to refuse to take the witness seriously. But what can be said of a little incident which the Viennese press unanimously suppressed ? When towards the end of the cross-examination Dr. Spalajković, nettled by the insults of Dr.

[406] Masaryk, *Der Agramer Hochverratsprozess*, p. 105.

Friedjung, showed an apparent disinclination to answer one of the many questions about the Slovenski Jug, and turned for a moment in mute appeal to the jury, the Judge, throwing all politeness to the winds, curtly exclaimed, " Kindly look a little this way " (*Bitte ein bisschen hieher zu sehen*). A forger in the dock might well have complained of the unfriendly tone. The Servian Secretary of State proved his diplomatic training by swallowing in silence so petty an insult.

In justice to Dr. Wach, it must be added that the conduct of such a trial would have taxed the powers of the most experienced judge in Europe, and that however little trouble he took to conceal his own personal sympathies, he at any rate allowed the fullest freedom of speech to both sides and practically never ruled a question out of order. How far the legal profession would count this to him for righteousness is a question which need not concern us.

XII. Coalition Witnesses.

When the court opened on the following Monday, the Judge announced the rejection of the proposal that the Austro-Hungarian Minister in Belgrad should verify Dr. Spalajković's statements, and based his decision on the argument—if argument it can be called—that the proposal had no bearing upon the authenticity of the " documents ! " Needless to say, the true reason was to be sought elsewhere.

He then read aloud a declaration of Dr. Gavrila, who offered to depose on oath, that his intercourse with Dr. Spalajković in Sarajevo was in no way connected with politics : that as lawyer to the latter's father-in-law he was continually in the house on business : that Dr. Spalajković not only avoided political discussions on principle, but was also busily engaged at the time on a work dealing with the Hague Conference, which held the foremost place in all their conversations.

The question of the Servian Loan led to a long argument between the rival counsel, which ended in the confirmation of Dr. Spalajkovič's facts. The last Servian Loan was actually voted in 1906 and was already being quoted on the Paris Stock Exchange before the end of that year ; and Dr. Friedjung, with a frankness which did him honour, now brushed aside the quibbles of his counsel, and admitted that the loan of 1906 was the last of which there could be any question here. As Dr. Harpner pointed out, it was incredible that Dr. Spalajković, one of the men who arranged this very loan at Geneva, could less than a year later in a private statement to his chief have placed the negotiations in the future instead of in the past. After an amusing passage of arms between Dr. Harpner and Dr. Kienböck, in which as usual the former scored brilliantly, a witness from Bosnia was heard, in the person of Mr. Damjanović, an intimate friend of Dr. Spalajković's father-in-law. He denied Dr. Friedjung's description of him as the leader of the Serb Opposition in Bosnia, but admitted that he was chairman of the committee which published *Srpska Riječ*. He denied the assertion of the Bosnian Government that Spalajković influenced the articles published by this newspaper, and added, " Its information comes from one of its spies, who can be had for five crowns." The *Srpska Riječ* was, it is true, in low water and owed the Serb Savings Bank in Bosnia £1,300 ; but it had never received subventions from abroad, as the forged minutes of the Slovenski Jug suggested. The most it had received from Servia was 1,000 francs " from a wellwisher " and 500 francs from guests assembled at a wedding ; and both contributions were publicly acknowledged at the time. When asked by Dr. Friedjung to explain the cause of his party's failure at the Sarajevo communal elections in 1908, Mr. Damjanović stated that the former Town Council had been dissolved because it had ventured to draw up statutes restricting the franchise to Bosnian subjects, and thus affecting those officials who preferred Austrian or Hungarian to Bosnian citizenship. As a result, the Bosnian Government exercised strong pressure ; and the fact that there were over 800 officials in Sarajevo who had to record their vote in presence of their superiors, sufficiently explained the failure of the Serb Opposition. Mr. Damjanović's evidence throws many interesting sidelights upon the situation in Bosnia on the eve of the annexation, but to discuss it at all adequately would lead far too far afield.

It was now the turn of the plaintiffs to be called as witnesses. Above all, Count Pejačević was questioned regarding Document XX of Dr. Friedjung's Green Book, the only genuine article in the collection. Count Theodore Pejačević, who succeeded Count Khuen Héderváry in 1903 as Ban of Croatia, continued to hold office under the Wekerle Cabinet, and eight months after the conflict provoked between Hungary and Croatia by Mr. Kossuth's Railway Bill had led to his resignation, joined the ranks of the Croato-Serb Coalition. In

February, 1906, when still Ban but not as yet member of the Coalition, he had, in accordance with instructions from high quarters, issued to the various High Sheriffs of Croatia-Slavonia a confidential circular instructing them to keep under observation a number of political leaders in the various towns of Croatia and Dalmatia—among others, Messrs. Medaković, Pribičević and Supilo—and even to control their correspondence. Owing to an indiscretion the contents of this circular became public ; and on November 27, 1906, Count Pejačević made a statement on the subject in the Croatian Diet. In assuming full responsibility for the circular, he hinted somewhat vaguely that he had not himself shared the doubts which had prompted the order for such an inquiry, admitted that the wording of the circular was calculated to convey the erroneous idea that not merely an inquiry but definite action against the persons named was intended, and declared that it had been recalled not merely owing to his personal conviction but also because not a shadow of a suspicion had arisen, such as could justify the enquiry. Dr. Friedjung included the circular in his Green Book and treated Count Pejačević's change of front, as revealed in his statement in the Diet, as highly suspicious. Count Pejačević under cross-examination now emphasized the fact that the inquiry had yielded entirely negative results, not one of the High Sheriffs having discovered anything of a compromising nature. He reminded the Court that Dr. Benedikt was wrong in asserting that he had recalled the circular because he was a member of the Coalition ; the Coalition at that time did not possess the majority in the Diet, and he himself, standing outside the parties, governed by means of an understanding between the moribund " National " party and the Coalition, and did not join the latter till after the elections of 1908. He reaffirmed his statement in the Diet, and insisted that the Coalition could not possibly have intrigued with Servia without his knowledge.

Dr. Friedjung pointed out that when in November, 1905, Dr. Tuškan—now President of the Coalition—made his notorious attack upon " Vienna " in the Croatian Diet, Count Pejačević had been the first to raise an indignant protest ; how then was it possible for him, as privy councillor and former Ban, to join a party whose leader had employed such language ? " Political convictions and personal opinions," replied Count Pejačević, " change often enough. There have been men who were condemned to death for high treason and afterwards became Hungarian Premiers." This reference to the great Andrássy did not satisfy Dr. Friedjung, who remarked that eighteen years had elapsed between the day when Andrássy's effigy was burnt by the hangman and the date of his nomination as the first Premier of the new era in Hungary (1849–1867), while less than three years separated Tuškan's speech from Pejačević's entrance into the Coalition. "There are people in Hungary," retorted the witness, "who were involved in the Resolution of Fiume and immediately afterwards became ministers in Hungary." He might have fortified this reference to Francis Kossuth and Polónyi by pointing out that proceedings for *lèse majesté* were actually pending against the latter at the very moment when he was appointed Minister of Justice.

When further asked whether it was possible to maintain a control over the correspondence of private individuals and whether such action was not a felony, Count Pejačević, with a curious smile, replied, " Oh, yes, it is possible ! " This little incident lifts the curtain for a moment from one of the most unsavoury features of Hungarian public life—the violation of postal secrecy for political purposes.

The report of the experts, Professor von Rešetar [407] and Dr. Kraus, upon the Servian text of Dr. Spalajković's " Report," was next submitted to the Court. Referring first to the style, they remarked upon the length of the sentences, the bureaucratic mannerisms, and the frequent Germanisms, of which some might have been used by any educated Servian or Croatian but others only became intelligible when translated literally into German. They then indicated certain crass grammatical errors and expressed the opinion that the report had been written " by some one who is not completely versed either in Servian grammar or in Servian orthography." Not having the original before them, they could not establish with absolute certainty whether some of the worst errors were not those of the printers ; they were at any rate of a kind such as no Servian with the slightest pretence to real culture could have committed. The Judge interpreting this to mean that the " Report " might have been written by a

[407] The son-in-law and successor of the famous Slavistic scholar Professor Vatroslav von Jagić.

diplomat, but not a man who could write good and correct
Servian, drew from Professor Rešetar the following striking
opinion. "Whether a diplomat wrote it or not, I cannot
say. But if a diplomat wrote it, then he was no Servian."
Nothing could be more explicit than this. Dr. Kraus, it is
true, sought to weaken the impression produced in court
by a reference to critics who argued that Goethe and Lessing
had not fully mastered the German language and that Napoleon could not write French! Professor Rešetar however
under cross-examination adhered to the view that no Servian
or Croat of any education could have made such gross mis-
takes, and that after listening to Dr. Spalajković's evidence—
which was delivered in Servian and took up the whole of
Saturday's proceedings—he felt it to be incredible that such
a report could ever have been written by a man who spoke
such admirable Servian.

The plaintiff Mr. Budisavljević now plied the experts with
numerous questions on technical points of style and phraseology. It thus transpired that the printed Servian version
of the Spalajković report which had been supplied to the experts, and from which Document XXI of the Green Book
was translated, was based upon a Cyrilline copy, specially
transcribed for Dr. Friedjung by a Croatian lady doctor
"from the copy at my disposal," in other words from the
copy placed at Dr. Friedjung's disposal by the Ballplatz
authorities. The historian was also constrained to admit
that the proofsheets of this all-important "document" went
back to the printer without having even been submitted
for correction to the lady copyist! "The matter naturally
went through several hands, and in this way of course errors
of style or grammar may have crept in." The course of the
proceedings had already shown that the historian had not
verified the facts which his documents contained—even on
such important details as the Croatian elections and the
Servian Loan ; but it now became evident that he had also
neglected the elementary precautions enjoined by the study
of documents, precautions which in this case were rendered
all the more necessary by his ignorance of the Servian language.

Professor Rešetar and Dr. Uebersberger then submitted
their opinion upon the photographs of the Slovenski Jug
"minutes," and explained in great detail the reasons which
led them to different conclusions. The former held not only
that the handwriting of two of the chief minutes differed

but that one was a deliberate imitation of the other ; while the latter confirmed Dr. Friedjung's assertion that the handwriting of all the minutes was identical. Subsequent developments have confirmed the former's view. But it is obvious that to accept Dr. Friedjung's own view on the matter involved even more fatal consequences : for it would then suffice to prove the falsity of one " document " in order to invalidate all the others.

After Dr. Čingrija had given evidence regarding Supilo's activity in Ragusa [408] Count Kulmer was asked to describe the situation in Croatia, in the name and from the standpoint of the Croat deputies of the Coalition. He frankly admitted that he had never approved of the Fiume Resolution, but none the less held its underlying idea—the reconciliation of Croat and Serb—to be essentially sound, since no Government in Croatia could hope for a majority so long as the Serbs were in opposition. At the elections he himself had stood as an independent candidate, but had afterwards entered the Coalition in answer to a personal appeal from Mr. Supilo, who had succeeded in convincing him that the Fiume Resolution offered guarantees for a genuine constitutional regime in Croatia. He could affirm upon oath that the influence of Servia had never been noticeable within the Coalition, and he declined to take Dr. Tuškan's abuse of " Vienna " seriously, or to regard it otherwise than as an outburst provoked by the unwise policy which was then being pursued towards Croatia.

Dr. Lukinić was next allowed to defend himself against the specific charges made against his person. Early in the notorious Spalajković Report reference is made to a letter addressed to the Servian Consul-General in Budapest by the four deputies Supilo, Potočnjak, Pribičević and Lukinić, offering their services to Servia. In denying emphatically the existence of any such letter, Dr. Lukinić pointed out that at the period when it was supposed to have been written, Pribičević and Supilo were at open feud with Potočnjak, a man who after belonging to and quarrelling with almost all the many parties in Croatia has found it necessary to retire altogether from politics. In the " memorial " of the Slovenski Jug to Dr. Milovanović—No IV in the *Reichspost* brochure—Dr. Kukinić is again referred to, as the recipient of 7,000 francs from Belgrad in aid of the defence of the fifty-three Serb prisoners in the Agram High Treason trial. As he now pointed out, both he and close upon thirty other Croatian advocates had voluntarily undertaken the defence, and though the trial lasted nearly seven months, not one of them received a penny for their trouble, either from Servia or from any other source. On the contrary they had all contributed from their private means towards the support of the families of the persecuted Serbs.

XIII. COMPROMISE.

The crushing nature of Dr. Spalajković's evidence, following upon so many other unpleasant surprises, had not been lost upon the defendants, and above all Count Aehrenthal and the Ballplatz officials watched with growing anxiety the interest displayed by the European press in these scandalous revelations of their incapacity and lack of scruple. When then the official confirmation of Professor Marković's alibi was at length received from the Berlin police authorities, negotiations were opened with the plaintiffs with a view to a compromise. The whole morning of the 21st was occupied by the fruitless endeavour to find a formula acceptable to both parties. Dr. Friedjung, while prepared to admit the questionable origin of Documents XII and XIII—the minutes of the Slovenski Jug of October 5 and 21 (O.S.), 1908, which are directly disqualified by the Berlin alibi—as yet failed to realize that the demolition of two " documents " seriously affected the authenticity of the others also.

As no agreement could be reached, Dr. Wach reopened the proceedings at four o'clock and called as witness Dr. Vladimir von Nikolić, formerly head of the Croatian Department of Justice under Count Pejačević, and since the elections of 1908 chairman of the executive committee of the Croato-Serb Coalition. As he pointed out with evey natural emphasis, this committee controlled every detail of the Coalition's policy, and he had never missed a single meeting ; he was thus in a position to take oath that there had never been the faintest trace of treasonable tendencies among its members. The great aim of the Coalition had been to revive constitutional government in Croatia, to introduce modern institutions such as freedom of elections, right of assembly, postal secrecy and judicial independence, and to settle amicably with the Magyars the numerous violations of the Hungaro-Croatian Compromise which had occurred since the year 1868. When Kossuth's Railway Bill and the Croatian obstruction in Budapest led to an open breach between the two nations, the Hungarian Government resolved at all costs to break up the Croato-Serb Coalition, and hoped to attain this end by casting suspicion upon its individual members. The survival of the Coalition and the maintenance of an entente between Croats and Serbs formed the sole guarantee for the success of Croatia's struggle against Hungary.

In Croatia, continued Dr. Nikolić, it is nothing new for a Government to brand its opponents as traitors and enemies of the dynasty. In 1872 under Baron Levin Rauch—the father of the notorious Baron Paul Rauch—similar forgeries played a great part in Croatian politics, and an attempt was made to implicate the poet Mažuranić and Bishop Strossmayer in treasonable intrigues.[409] On that occasion also the forged " minutes " of revolutionary meetings found credence in authoritative quarters, until in 1879 the forger himself, a certain Reicherzer, published a pamphlet confessing the whole fraud. In short what is impossible in Vienna is only too possible in the south of the Monarchy, where there exist persons who make a living by the fabrication of similar slanders. So far as the alleged money subsidies were concerned, Dr. Nikolić regretfully admitted that he had himself contributed from his own pocket a larger sum to the electoral fund than had, according to Dr. Friedjung's " documents," been sent by the Servian Government ! As chairman of the executive committee, he was naturally familiar with the details of electoral expenditure and the sources from which their funds were derived. Dr. Friedjung drew attention to the fact that Agram, a town of 90,000 inhabitants, had no fewer than twelve daily papers—as many as Vienna with its two millions—and asked whether it was not the case that only three or four of these were self-supporting. The witness, while admitting a certain amount of truth in this suggestion, added that the Agram newspapers served the whole country, with its 2,600,000 inhabitants, and most of them were supported at great sacrifice by their respective parties.

The evidence of Dr. Nikolić produced a distinct effect upon the jury. But the final breach in their armour of suspicion

[409] See p. 89.

against every Serb was made by Dr. Dušan Popovič, the able Serb criminal lawyer, one of the youngest but most popular and influential members of the Croato-Serb Coalition. As one of the defending counsel in the infamous Agram trial, he naturally had a complete mastery of his subject ; and his gift for ready and humorous repartee showed to especial advantage on the present occasion.

Dr. Popović explained that he had been chosen as the spokesman of the Serb members of the Coalition, partly because he had been in Belgrad more than any of them and yet had never been accused of disloyal practices. He then described the activity of the Serb Independent party since its formation in 1883, its support of the Khuen regime and the growing discontent of the new generation. " Till 1905 there were no constitutional guarantees in Croatia, and even to-day there is no law asserting the independence of the judges, the freedom of the press or the right of public assembly ! " The Fiume Resolution was the natural result of such a situation, and was essentially the work of the Croats, not of the Serbs, and least of all of the Kingdom of Servia ; for while thirty Croat deputies took part in the negotiations, no Serb was present, and the Serbs waited till the pact had been completed between Magyars and Croats, before they too declared their adherence in the Resolution of Zara. The real motive which prompted the Croats to come to terms with Budapest, must be sought in their recollection of Vienna's ingratitude after 1848, when despite all their sacrifices in the Habsburg cause, the Croats—to quote again from Dr. Friedjung's own *History of Austria*—received as reward what the Hungarians received as punishment.[410] Above all they were prompted by the fear of " Vienna," by which must not be understood the city of Vienna, the Sovereign or the Monarchy, but " certain powerful political personages who are not eternal but change from time to time, and who . . . wish to give the Magyars *carte blanche* in internal politics (viz. of Transleithania) simply in order that the latter may abandon their military demands." Moreover Dr. Friedjung and Dr. Funder were quite mistaken in regarding the Resolution of Fiume as a mere conspiracy of Budapest and Agram against Vienna ; for the Croats its most important provisions were those relating to internal reforms—electoral, judicial, administrative—and to the union

[410] In reality this famous phrase is merely cited by Dr. Friedjung from an older work.

of Dalmatia with Croatia.[411] In short, the Resolution had nothing whatever to do with Pan-Serb propaganda, and the defendants might learn this fact from the organizer of the present anti-Serb campaign, Baron Paul Rauch, who on November 13, 1905, spoke as follows :—" It seems to me that the honourable name of a ' National ' party is far better deserved by those men who have adhered to the Fiume Resolution and broken away from Vienna, whence we have never experienced anything save bitter disappointments." Since then unhappily political slander and vituperation had grown commoner in Croatia, accusations of Pan-Serbism began to be heard, and in the notorious " Argus " affair (see p. 300) the identical charges were formulated which form the basis of the present trial. "To-day in Croatia," added Dr. Popović, " they adduce as proofs of this (Pan-Serb) propaganda, the very emblems which in the history of the Monarchy have been rendered so famous and so sacred by the blood of our fathers in 1848." [412]

Dr. Popović next confessed that during the campaign of calumny directed against members of his party, he had more than once made inquiries through various relations and friends in Belgrad, and that possibly his southern temperament had engendered temporary suspicions which his confidence in his colleagues should have rendered impossible. His inquiries of course convinced him that the charges were utterly groundless. Perhaps the most interesting feature in Dr. Popović's long and impressive speech was his correction of the misleading extracts quoted by Dr. Friedjung from the speeches of the Coalition leaders.

1. For instance, Dr. Tuškan's famous threat of marching rifle in hand against Vienna, was not part of a speech at all, but a wild interjection uttered during the most disorderly scene which the Croatian Parliament had witnessed in recent years, and from the context it was obvious that his anger was directed against the Dual system, not against Austria or the dynasty.

2. According to Dr. Friedjung, Mr. Budisavljević had declared in the Diet that he would accept money from Servia.

[411] In accordance with § 65 of the Ausgleich.

[412] A reference to the Serb national arms and colours, under which Stratimirović led the Serbs of the Banat in 1848 against the Magyars, but which were treated by the Public Prosecutor in the Agram High Treason trial as " symptomatic " of treason.

The true facts were as follows. In reply to a deputy who accused *Srbobran* of receiving 30,000 francs from Belgrad Budisavljević answered : " I declare openly before the Croatian Sabor that if Servia had given even one halfpenny in the interests of the Southern Slavs, the Croat-Servian and Bulgarian race, I would like Wolf [413] openly acknowledge it in the Diet. Permit me to say frankly that society in Servia has not realized the mission which it has to fulfil towards the Croat Slovene and Bulgarian race as well as towards itself. . . . I know that my words will perhaps be published to-morrow in the foreign press, but that does not disturb me." To Dr. Friedjung's remark, " That means, ' If Servia were to give money, I would take it,' " Dr. Popović neatly retorted, " No, that means, ' If I had received money, I would admit it '."

To those of us who read continually in the newspapers of the relations of the Irish party with Mr. Patrick Ford and the Irish Americans, Dr. Friedjung's point of view is, if not absolutely incomprehensible, at any rate doctrinaire in the highest degree.

3. Dr. Friedjung had charged Supilo with declaring that it would be a blessing for Bosnia if it were detached from the Monarchy. Dr. Popović now read aloud the exact words of Supilo, which ran as follows :—" And if fortune should have it, that Bosnia and Herzegovina leave the complex of the Monarchy, then it is natural that every true and honourable Croat should prefer that if Bosnia cannot be Croatian it should fall to the Servian brother rather than to a stranger. But if fortune decides that Bosnia should enter that organism in which Croatia now is, then it is the duty of every true patriot to strive with fiery zeal, in order that Bosnia and Herzegovina may fall into the hands not of strangers but of their Croatian brothers."

4. Finally Dr. Popović referred to the much quoted article of *Srbobran*, in which the Kingdom of Servia was treated as decisive for the attitude of the Serbs in Croatia-Slavonia. He reminded the defendants that when the breach between Agram and Budapest led to the appointment of Baron Rauch as Ban of Croatia, the Serb Radical party seceded from the Croato-Serb Coalition and coquetted with Rauch and Wekerle. But while almost every newspaper in Belgrad espoused the side of the Coalition, *Samouprava*, the official

[413] A reference to Karl Hermann Wolf, the notorious Pan-German deputy in the Austrian Reichsrat.

organ of the Servian Government, wrote in favour of Rauch and approved the attitude of the Serb Radicals. The latter's chief organ *Zastava*, so far from accusing the Coalition of being under the influence of Belgrad, actually argued that the Belgrad press was inspired from Agram.[414] It was under such circumstances that *Srbobran* wrote as follows :—" Servia as an independent state is in a position to judge what policy best corresponds to general Servian interests. For the Serbs— i.e. of Croatia—it cannot be a matter of indifference what policy the Servian people outside the Monarchy pursues."

" What have you to say to that, Doctor ? " exclaimed the witness, turning to Dr. Friedjung.

" Just as Berlin must not be the standard for the policy of the German Austrians," replied Dr. Friedjung, " in exactly the same way Belgrad must not be the standard for the Serbs of Austria."

" Were you always of this opinion, Dr. Friedjung ? I have been told that you once belonged to the Pan-Germans."

" A Pan-German in the sense that all Germans are one in spirit and in culture—*geistig und kulturell zusammengehören*— a Pan-German in this sense I still am to-day."

" Well, Dr. Friedjung, we Serbs are just the same."

No sooner had the Court risen, than negotiations between the parties were resumed ; but many hours were required that night and the following morning—Wednesday, December 22—before an understanding could be reached. Dr. J. M. Baernreither, one of the most prominent German Austrian politicians and a man who enjoyed the confidence alike of Count Aehrenthal and the Heir-Apparent, appeared upon the scene and made every effort to bring matters to a successful issue. After urging upon Mr. Supilo and his colleagues the grave issues at stake—the reputation of Austrian diplomacy and the honour of the Monarchy—he offered positive assurances that an end would be put to the prevailing absolutist system in Croatia. Their consent could however only be obtained to a compromise whose terms should be explicit enough to preclude the subsequent use against them of any of the famous " documents." Dr. Friedjung, on the other hand, showed extreme reluctance to admit the falsification of any save the

[414] This additional proof of the relations between Dr. Pašić, the Servian Premier and *Zastava*—in Neusatz (Ujvidék) in South Hungary—only serves to confirm the evidence of Dr. Polit (*see* p. 260).

two "documents" directly affected by the Berlin alibi, and seemed to consider that his reputation as a historian would suffer less from this unbending attitude than from a frank admission of his error.

It is an open secret that the compromise was due to direct pressure from the Foreign Office, which on the one hand realized that a condemnation of the defendants would be equivalent to a public vote of non-confidence in itself, but on the other hand feared the bad effect which would have been created abroad, if the jury had acquitted on patriotic grounds. In that event the Servian Government was prepared to appear before the Hague Convention and there to claim the assistance of the Great Powers in exposing the forgeries and in vindicating the good name of Dr. Milovanović.

At last complete agreement was reached ; and a careful programme was drawn up for the concluding scene of the trial. When the court opened, Mr. Supilo was invited to give evidence as to the charges of bribery from Servia contained in the forged documents, and as to the visits to Belgrad which had drawn on him so much suspicion.[415] After polite expressions of regret from Dr. Benedikt and Professor Masaryk for a fierce passage of arms which had taken place between them during the latter's cross-examination, the Judge read aloud the official statement of the Berlin police, proving beyond all possibility of doubt that Professor Marković was actually in Berlin on the very day when he was alleged to have presided over a meeting of the Slovenski Jug in Belgrad. Counsel for the prosecution hereupon asked Dr. Friedjung what he had to say in view of so clear an alibi ; and the historian then read aloud the following declaration :—" I made all the assertions of my article after thorough examination, and only reached the fundamental view expressed in my article after conscientious consideration of all the circumstances before me. I am no swashbuckler—*Klopffechter*— and know how to appreciate the importance as evidence of Professor Marković's stay in Berlin now officially confirmed. I therefore declare loyally that the two documents of October 20 and 21 must be eliminated, and that I should no longer like to base any claim upon (*in Anspruch nehmen*) the remaining documents. Having made this declaration, I can say with a calm conscience that in my whole attitude in the affair

[415] *See* page 295

and also in to-day's declaration I had in view the welfare of our common fatherland."

A brief statement followed on behalf of the responsible editor of the *Reichspost*; and Dr. Harpner then withdrew the prosecution, after briefly stating the motives which had prompted his clients to appeal to the arbitrament of a Viennese court. Unable to trust themselves to an Agram court, they came before a civilized court in a constitutional country, in order that all the world might learn the policy of which they were the victims. No one had ever questioned the good faith of Dr. Friedjung, and after his declaration the Coalition could fairly regard the trial as at an end, since they were convinced that the opinion of the world and the verdict of history would be upon their side. After a similar declaration from Mr. Supilo's counsel, the Judge pronounced the formal verdict of acquittal, and the Court broke up amid general congratulations. Dr. Wach was only voicing the universal sentiment when he expressed the hope that the trial would bear good fruit for Austria. Rarely if ever has so much dirty linen been washed before the Austrian public; and few statesmen will envy Count Aehrenthal his laundry bill.

The manner in which the origin of the forgeries came to light, will be described in a subsequent chapter. Meanwhile it will suffice to summarize in the briefest possible manner the points at which the prosecution successfully effected a breach in the " documents."

Out of the seventeen " minutes " of the Slovenski Jug, two (Nos. XIII and XXIII) were annihilated by the alibi of Professor Marković, which proved beyond all question that at the moment when he was supposed to be presiding over a revolutionary society in Belgrad, he was actually studying law at Berlin University. The defence had specially emphasized the fact that all the " minutes " were in the same handwriting; and in that case, when two had been invalidated, all the rest must also be regarded as worthless. The falsity of another of the " minutes " (No. II) was clearly shown by its reference to the " *ensuing* elections in Croatia," at a date when they were already over. A hundred other details combined to render the " minutes " extremely suspicious—the numerous Croaticisms and Germanisms in ostensibly Serb documents: the use of New Style dates, incredible in an Orthodox country like Servia: the fact that the author sometimes thinks in " crowns," instead of dinars or francs : the variations in the signatures of the president and officials of the Club [416] : the confusion regarding the office-bearers [417] : the fact that a secret central committee was formed, and none the less the really secret business was discussed at the ordinary meetings.[418] Of course the bare idea that a revolutionary committee, above all one composed of Servian students, should have kept minutes at all was highly suspicious, and of itself suggested the bureaucratic origin of the " documents."

The notorious Report of Dr. Spalajković (No. XXI) was not merely headed by imaginary numbers and signed in an impossible manner, but was, in the opinion of the experts, written in a style so ungrammatical and so essentially un-Serb, as to preclude its author from being an educated Servian, still less a Servian diplomat. Its references to the Servian Budget were incorrect. Its use of Dr. Polit's name betrayed the forger's ignorance. Above all, it contained a reference to a State Loan which Parliament was to sanction next autumn, whereas this loan had actually been sanctioned a year previously. As the alleged author of the Report had himself concluded the negotiations for the loan, it was impossible to argue that he could have made so crude an error. The instructions of Dr. Pašić to the librarian Mr. Tomić (No. B of the *Reichspost* " documents ") were such as no serious statesman could have written. The instructions of Dr. Milovanović to the Servian Minister in Vienna (No. E., do.), the most impossible " document " of all, could not survive their perusal in cold blood, and indeed no diplomat in Europe could ever have credited a colleague, however incapable—and Dr. Milovanović is the very reverse of incapable—with writing such an effusion. Its absurd references to the Cabinet of St. James, to " Golden Prague " and " the Czech Kingdom " amply sufficed to prove its falsity, quite apart from its wretched literary style. In short, the diplomatic " documents " were palpable forgeries, but were as palpably not written by a mere spy.

The compromise in which the trial ended for the moment saved the real culprits from well-merited exposure, but left the

[416] The former sometimes appears as B. Marković, sometimes as Božidar, sometimes as the more familiar Božo.

[417] E.g. in No. VI Ljuba Jovanović is given as Vice-president : in No. X Lj. Davidović ; in No. XII again Ljubomir Jovanović.

[418] Cf. No. VII.

world in no doubt as to their identity. The *Zeit* was merely voicing the general opinion, when it described the Friedjung trial as " a cleansing storm " and as " a fiasco of our methods of obtaining diplomatic intelligence," since the documents were not *good*, but *clumsy*, forgeries. The *Neues Wiener Journal* was still more outspoken, and called the issue of the trial " a verdict of ' Guilty ' against the Foreign Office," neatly adding that " the leading authorities " (*Leitende Stellen*) of the Monarchy in reality deserved the title of " misleading " ; while the well-known military journal, *Danzers Armee Zeitung*, concluded a scathing article with the words, " To the devil with the Police Spy System." The *Vaterland*, the organ of the Conservative clericals, argued that the trial had proved that " Vienna wished the Croats well." The " triumph " of the Coalition would, it added, have good results, " if the Croats are now given something more than mere words and friendly phrases."

Perhaps the most effective criticism of the trial is to be found in *Die Fackel*,[419] from the pen of that brilliant and characteristically Viennese satirist, Karl Kraus. " In Court were heard the words : ' These documents were to have supplied Europe with the proof that Austria-Hungary had been compelled to resort to arms by Servia's perfidious connexion with shady elements in our Monarchy.' Thus spoke a misused historian : the documents, which might have deceived the penetration of a public schoolboy, are proved to be forgeries, and the man who misused the good faith of a historian, of a whole population, of Europe, without being able to excuse himself with the plea that he himself was not misused, the statesman who is the victim of a forger of operetta standard—Count Aehrenthal, who has not stinted our money over preparations for war and proofs of its necessity, who has misused our faith in order to sacrifice our blood, *he* does not leave us in the hours of doubt, he does not go into exile among the Eskimos, he, the condemned of this trial, gives us no public apology (*Ehrenerklärung*) and *we* shall pay the costs."

Of the two defendants, Dr. Friedjung had to bear the brunt of criticism. Dr. Funder had merely acted as any journalist would have acted in his place : he had naturally assumed that the Foreign Office dealt only in genuine documents, and the mere fact that he received them from such a quarter, absolved him from all need of inquiry into their general character.

[419] No. 293, January 4, 1910.

Dr. Friedjung, on the other hand, had expressly debarred himself from the privilege of this argument, and had insisted that he had applied to the " documents " all the canons of historical research and the strictest documentary tests. In view of his ignorance of the Serb language and alphabet, it is unfortunately impossible to allow his claim. But it is equally impossible to avoid sympathizing keenly with him ; for never has the confidence of a historian in those who control his country's foreign policy, been more shamefully abused, and there is good reason to believe that Dr. Friedjung, when he at last realized his position, made it a point of honour to adhere to a standpoint from which many a man would have considered himself absolved, in view of the deception practised upon him.

Dr. Friedjung's real fault consisted in yielding to the flattering attentions of the Foreign Minister. His journalistic instincts tempted him to aspire to the position of a new Gentz to the modern Metternich. He, too, like more exalted personages, seems to have assumed that Count Aehrenthal would not work with impudent forgeries as the groundwork of his policy, and hence accepted without further question a series of " documents " in a language which he did not know and therefore could not control. The trial utterly demolished his claim to be regarded as a politician of judgment or acumen ; but it need not affect our verdict upon him as a historian. In writing the fatal article of March 25, 1909, and in all that he said in court, he gave free rein to the somewhat blatant patriotism which the Bosnian crisis had evoked ; in the books which have won him so wide and solid a reputation, this note is happily wanting. In short, the Friedjung Trial has supplied us with yet another proof that " a great historian may also be a naïve politician."

CHAPTER XI

The Supilo-Chlumecky Incident

BEFORE attempting an analysis of the documents or discussing the results of this momentous trial, it is necessary to bring the Supilo-Chlumecky incident to a conclusion. Much as I should have liked to avoid discussing an incident which would appear to involve the grossest perjury on the one side or the other, I cannot unhappily shut my eyes to its extreme importance, both in its bearing upon the political situation in Croatia and Dalmatia and upon the future career of a man who is beyond all question the ablest living Croat politician. The necessity for treating the affair in special detail will, I am persuaded, have already become apparent to the reader; and I can only hope that he will acquit me of laying needless stress upon the personal element in the case.

During Monday's proceedings Mr. Supilo moved that the following witnesses be heard—Mr. Tončić, now Vice-Governor of Dalmatia, but at the time of the alleged bribery Baron Chlumecky's superior in the prefecture of Ragusa, who could affirm that Supilo had never written in favour of the Austrian Government as Chlumecky had alleged; Mr. Karčanski, Kállay's agent in Ragusa, who could affirm that he had never given Supilo a farthing and that Supilo and Chlumecky had never met in his house; and Count Szapáry, the former Governor of Fiume, who could affirm that he had never spoken with Supilo and had never given him money, and that at the time of his alleged remark to Dorotka Supilo's newspaper was being confiscated almost every other day owing to its violent attacks upon the Hungarian Government.

The letter which played so important a part in Baron Chlumecky's evidence, was at last read aloud in court [420] and Mr.

[420] *See* page 237.

Supilo was able to point out that it contained no trace of secret denunciation, but simply related a fact which he was about to publish in *Novi List*.

On Tuesday Dr. Rode, appearing for the first time, proposed as witnesses the Governor of Dalmatia, Baron Nardelli, the Mayor of Ragusa, Dr. Pero Čingrija, and the ex-Ban Count Theodore Pejačević, and sought to justify their summons by the following arguments. " The witness Baron Chlumecky was described by the Judge as a specialist in Bosnian matters, and he himself gave himself out as one who has clear insight into Bosnian chaos and into Servian conditions. I wish to prove through the Governor of Dalmatia what political rôle Chlumecky played in the Governor's office at Zara and in the prefecture of Ragusa : that he was not entrusted with any special political mission : that owing to his attitude in society and owing to certain intrigues he was disciplinarily transferred to Makarska, a circumstance which the witness deliberately suppressed (here Dr. Rode was in error : Baron Chlumecky did *not* suppress the fact) ; that he had to employ the whole influence of himself and his family in order to get back to Ragusa. The Mayor of Ragusa will give evidence that Chlumecky during his stay at Ragusa took very little share in politics, had the reputation of a man who was impossible in Ragusa and was the laughing-stock of the town, run after by the street-arabs (another needless exaggeration). In Hermann Bahr's recently published book *Dalmatinische Reise* [421] it is said of Baron Chlumecky, ' I know too well how he spent his time in Ragusa, what is thought of him in Dalmatia.' I have no intention of bringing up the private affairs of an incriminating witness. But it seems to me important whether this man who pretends to have played a great political rôle in Bosnia and claims to have been drawn into conversation by so important a person as Supilo—whether Supilo ever spoke with him about politics at that period or not." Here again Dr. Rode indulged in needless exaggeration ; for at the time of the alleged bribery Supilo was still an unknown journalist, and Chlumecky a young man of high social standing. The Judge then was only within his rights in insisting that counsel should moderate his attacks upon an absent witness. Dr. Rode then urged that the Mayor of Ragusa could bear witness to the Catonic

[421] One of the best books on Modern Dalmatia.

habits of life of Supilo, who although his party would at any time have placed money at his disposal, had always lived as a poor man—*ein armer Teufel*—and was still one to-day. In the same way Count Pejačević, the former Ban, could give evidence that though he and other members of the party could have assisted Supilo materially, Supilo had never dreamt of asking their help.

Dr. Benedikt opposed the summons of these witnesses and argued that Baron Chlumecky counted as one of the most serious political writers in Austria, and that in any case the discussion on this point was irrelevant, since any person was capable of judging whether he had or had not given 200 crowns to another man. Supilo was again treated with scant courtesy by the Judge, but had perhaps laid himself open to a rebuff by repeating what his counsel had already said for him.

It was not till Wednesday that the first real step was taken towards Supilo's rehabilitation. A letter from Count Ladislas Szapáry was read out by the Judge, in which the ex-Governor of Fiume declared that he had never been personally acquainted with Mr. Supilo. He admitted having once discussed Supilo with Dorotka, but so far as he could remember, " Dorotka's evidence certainly did not entirely correspond with my words. It is certain that I was then and still am of the opinion—so far as I can recollect such trifles after ten years—that the Gubernium often helped Supilo's paper with small contributions. I naturally can neither remember the sum nor the particular instances nor the officials who acted as go-betweens." Mr. Supilo, after pointing out that his disclaimer of personal acquaintance with Count Szapáry was thus confirmed, insisted that the latter's reference to payments made to *Novi List* must rest on a misunderstanding. There are, he said, in Fiume certain proscribed individuals, who are under police supervision and give themselves out as journalists, even of big papers. One of these men pretends to be on the staff of the *Novoje Vremja*. It is by no means impossible that one of these scoundrels, who wheedled sums of five and six florins out of Count Szapáry and his successor Count Nako, has also got money in the name of *Novi List*." Supilo closed his statement with the remark that as a journalist he had been repeatedly slandered by his enemies; but one of the leaders of the Dalmatian Serbs had shortly before his death begged forgiveness for these unjust slanders.

Next day Mr. Rode returned to the charge with still greater

vigour. He begged the Court to summon as a witness Dr. Julius Mogan, advocate in Fiume, who could give evidence on the following point. " Baron Chlumecky affirmed that he had not subscribed to *Novi List* and would have sent it back if it had been sent to him." (Counsel for the defence : " That he didn't say.") " Of course. He made this deposition, and it is from A to Z contrary to the facts. For I can prove that this newspaper was sent regularly to Baron Chlumecky from 1901 to 1907, that he did not send it back, that he did not pay the subscription for it, and that no less than about twenty reminders urging payment of arrears of subscription were sent to him, and that he did not see fit to pay his subscription until the Fiume advocate Dr. Mogan in the name of the publishers sent him a sharp lawyer's letter." This point Dr. Rode regarded as important, as tending to prove his client's contention, that Baron Chlumecky's evidence was false from beginning to end.

Dr. Rode next proposed the summons of Mr. Pavić von Frauenthal, formerly Vice-Governor of Dalmatia, to prove that Baron Chlumecky had spread the rumour that Baron David, at that time Governor of Dalmatia, and his wife stood in treasonable relations with the Prince of Montenegro. Baron David, said Dr. Rode, had expressed the desire not to be summoned as a witness, since he considered it beneath his dignity to refute Chlumecky, but had added that Mr. Pavić could supply the desired information.

Finally Dr. Rode urged the summons of Mr. Ružić, one of the group of wealthy Croats to whom *Novi List* belonged. Mr. Ružić was in a position to prove not only the integrity of Supilo's character, but also the absurdity of the accusation that *Novi List* could ever have been subsidized, directly or indirectly, by the Hungarian Government, to which it had always been so bitterly hostile until the eve of the Resolution of Fiume.

Dr. Benedikt opposed the hearing of these witnesses, on the ground that Dr. Rode was following the old Roman custom of calling in Laudatores ; but Dr. Rode was ready with the crushing retort that the latest methods of Viennese procedure seemed to be the introduction of Calumniatores. " When counsel for the defence speaks of the despairing flap of Supilo's wings, I would beg to remark that Supilo is to-day more alive than ever." Objectionable as all these personalities are, it must not be forgotten that the defence set the example by

291

summoning Chlumecky, whose evidence was in its essence an attempt to rake up Supilo's past and so discredit his present. Two days later Dr. Rode proposed the examination of a high official in the Hungarian Ministry of the Interior, who had been Count Szapáry's right hand in Fiume and would therefore know all about the alleged subsidies to *Novi List*, and also of the chairman of the limited company to which that newspaper belongs, who could prove that Supilo as editor could not have accepted subsidies for the newspaper, while the company was financially independent and obviously not likely to be paid by its bitterest political opponents. Search should also be made among the postal receipts of May to August 1907 in order to prove that Baron Chlumecky did actually send to *Novi List* a postal order of 137 kr. 85 h.

Almost all these motions were rejected by the Judge, who showed a marked reluctance to revive the dispute between Supilo and Chlumecky. He had very probably arrived at the conviction that the whole incident would form the subject of a separate action and need not therefore be mixed up with the present trial.

Of all the witnesses proposed, only two were allowed— Mr. Tončić and Dr. Čingrija. The former, who appeared before the Court on Friday afternoon, was now Vice-Governor of Dalmatia, but at the period in question had been formerly Baron Chlumecky's superior in the prefecture of Ragusa. In the course of his evidence he indicated the modest rôle played by Supilo as journalist and politician at the period in question ; his newspaper had not merely been violently anti-Serb but had criticised so openly certain of the Government officials, " that it had to be confiscated." He inferred rather than stated in so many words, that the paper had not been actually anti-Austrian, since " of course a pronouncedly anti-Austrian attitude would also have been confiscated,"— a phrase which charmingly illustrates the blend of naïveté and reactionary sentiment for which the Dalmatian bureaucrat is justly famous. Supilo, he said, had often lamented to him his own lack of means and the small circulation of his paper, but had never asked or received any material support from the local authorities, nor had he—the witness—ever heard of the alleged bribe until he read the newspaper accounts of the present trial. Mr. Tončić, who under examination showed a marked but not unnatural disinclination to commit himself by a straight answer to a straight question, skilfully avoided expressing any opinion upon Supilo's private character, but assured the Court that Baron Chlumecky had unquestionably been taken seriously in Ragusa and had filled a position far superior to his office.

Only one concrete fact emerged from Mr. Tončić's evidence, but this was not without importance and tended to bear down again the balance as it was rising in Supilo's favour. Mr. Tončić stated that a former official of the Ragusan prefecture had once told him of a conference held between him, Baron Kállay's agent Karčanski, Baron Chlumecky and Mr. Supilo, the aim of which was the formation of an Austrophil and Serbophobe club under the name of " Austria." Supilo's presence at this conference, Mr. Tončić added, had earned for him attacks in the local Serb newspaper, which also accused him of repeatedly accepting money from Karčanski. Mr. Tončić denied all personal knowledge as to the truth of these charges ; the most he could say was that Chlumecky had once asked him whether Supilo was worthy of support and that he had understood the question as an inquiry whether Supilo's political attitude justified material support from the Austrian side.

Mr. Supilo once more had appearances against him. He denied having ever taken part in any such conference, and affirmed that he had only once been in Karčanski's house, and on that occasion the only other persons present had been the latter and his sister. These disclaimers were received by the Court with scarcely veiled scepticism, but were confirmed at a later stage of the trial by a telegram from Mr. Karčanski, who offered to give evidence under oath that throughout his stay at Ragusa Supilo had only once been in his house and had met no one there save himself and his sister : that he, Supilo and Chlumecky had never in their lives all been together, and that he had never given or even offered money to Supilo.

Finally another witness was heard, whose evidence threw new and interesting light upon the incident. This was Dr. Melko Čingrija, a prominent Dalmatian lawyer and politician, and son of the veteran Mayor of Ragusa Dr. Pero Čingrija, who did so much to bring about the Resolution of Fiume. He stated that he himself had been present at the conference with Karčanski, Chlumecky and several other Ragusan politicians ; but he had no recollection of Supilo having been there, though he declined to give a positive assurance after the lapse of so many years. He was however positive that the conference referred to was the only one which ever took place, not merely because his position in the party made it impossible for such a meeting to be held without his knowledge, but also because the Serbs, who at that time controlled the movements of their rivals by a regular service of private spies, would unquestionably have reported the fact in their newspapers. "I remember," he added, "that on that occasion, when we left Karčanski's late at night, a (Serb) vedette was still there."

Cross-examined as to Supilo's financial circumstances, Dr. Čingrija stated that Supilo, whom he had known almost since they were children, lived in a very modest way, worked very hard, and had practically no requirements; he had always acted from conviction or from sentiment and had never allowed any one to influence him. He had more than once found friends who were only too ready to lend him money, but had invariably paid them back. Supilo's policy of hostility to the Serbs had reached its climax at the very period in question, and hence any such incentive as Baron Chlumecky's alleged bribe would have been entirely superfluous. Hence the witness was profoundly convinced of Supilo's innocence.

The morning following Dr. Čingrija's evidence was devoted to fruitless negotiations between the two parties, and when the proceedings were resumed that afternoon, the evidence of Dr. Nikolić and Dr. Popović, full of interest as it was, was already regarded on both sides as something in the nature of a stopgap, pending the resumption of negotiations. When at last on Wednesday morning complete agreement was reached and the proceedings were wound up in accordance with a carefully concerted programme, it was felt that above all full opportunity should be offered to Mr. Supilo to rebut the charges directed against him by the forgers, the more so as the Chlumecky incident had diverted attention from the real issues of the trial. No sooner had the court opened than the Judge, with a courtesy which offered a striking contrast to his former demeanour, invited Mr. Supilo to defend himself against the accusation of bribery by foreign powers.

"Perhaps there is no one in Croatia," began Mr. Supilo, "who has been slandered so much as I, as having received money from every conceivable country and Government." As an illustration of this, he pointed out how he had been charged with receiving 100,000 crowns—£4,160—for his services in bringing about the Resolution of Fiume. In an interview with Dr. Lueger, the latter had frankly apologised for believing this story, adding that if Supilo had received even ten crowns from the Magyars, the famous Croatian obstruction in Budapest would never have taken place.

" I am very poor and have done a lot of political work. . . . I did not create the situation in which our nation was, but as a young man found it so. For some years I went with the stream and thought it my sacred duty to fight for the Croat idea against the Serbs. Later on I came to see that we are a single nation speaking a single language, and that it is mere folly for us to fight against each other. And I had the courage to say this to my countrymen and to preach another policy of unity between Croats and Serbs, and this unity has borne good fruits." Mr. Supilo then explained that despite his limited income he had managed to save a little, and that whenever he had laid by £5 or £10, he had been in the habit of making short journeys abroad, for instance to Italy and Switzerland, as also inside the Monarchy, in order to study on the spot social linguistic or political conditions. In this way he had twice been in Belgrad. During his first visit, in March, 1902, he did not meet any Servian politician, and the dominant topic of the day was the relation of Alexander to the unhappy Draga. His second visit took place in April, 1905, when there were rumours of war between Servia and Bulgaria and of a counter revolution against the regicide regime; and on this occasion, with the aid of a Hungarian acquaintance in Belgrad, he managed to obtain an audience with the Premier, Dr. Pašić. Mr. Supilo gave a humorous description of how that wily old statesman evaded all questions of the still unknown journalist and bowed him out with meaningless compliments. His concluding words deserve to be quoted verbatim :—" I would like to add that all these documents which write of me as receiving money or the value of money from Servia, are a malicious invention. Were I to fall into the bitterest poverty and had not even a crust of bread, I would rather accept support from my worst enemy than from Servia. Do you know why ? In order that no one can reproach me, the former anti-Serb, of having followed for money a Serbophil policy. I wanted to make peace with the Serbs because the struggle between Serbs and Croats would have worn us both out. I succeeded in concluding peace, and no power on earth will avail to destroy the unity between us."

Mr. Supilo's evidence was succeeded by the reading of Professor Marković's Berlin alibi and by Dr. Friedjung's declaration. Dr. Harpner then withdrew the prosecution on behalf of the Coalition, and Dr. Rode followed suit on behalf of Mr. Supilo, after pointing out that much had transpired in the course of the proceedings to rehabilitate his client, and that Croatian public opinion, which alone is qualified to pass judgment upon him, had never for an instant doubted his innocence.

On this note the trial ended, leaving the Coalition as a whole completely victorious. But Mr. Supilo, despite the favourable turn taken by the proceedings, left the court under a cloud, and it is difficult to resist the conclusion that he was mistaken in deciding not to prosecute Baron Chlumecky on a charge of perjury. In most countries such mutual mud throwing would have led inevitably to a special libel action, and this would certainly seem to be the proper means of rehabilitation. But in Croatia charges of bribery are more frequent than in Britain, and the law does not visit them with the same severity. Baron Chlumecky for his part has also seen fit to ignore all the grave charges brought against him both in court and in the public press.[422]

The historian of the trial is unhappily confronted by certain questions which force him to deal with the credibility of these repulsive details. In the first place, how did it happen that Baron Chlumecky was allowed to give evidence at all at so early a stage of the trial ? The point at issue, so far as Mr. Supilo was concerned, was whether or no he had been bribed by Servia in the years 1907–8 ; the fact—assuming it to be correct—that he had been bribed by *Austria* ten years previously, was therefore quite irrelevant even as presumptive proof.

---

[422] The well-known Croatian novelist, Lisičar, published a signed article in *Pokret*—December 13, 1909—the organ of the Progressive party in Croatia, in which he brought terrible personal charges against Baron Chlumecky. I naturally have no intention of reproducing them, but I wish the reader to realize that they are of such a nature that no punishment could be too severe for their author, if he should fail to prove his case. (*See Agramer Tagblatt*, December 14, 1909.)

II. Mr. Supilo in his open letter to his electors—Lettre de Frano Supilo à ses électeurs, French translation, Fiume 1910, p. 33—charges Baron Chlumecky with having received a present (*mandoletta*) of 30,000 crowns for recommending to his father a group of Dalmatian contractors for the construction of the railway between Gravosa and Castelnuovo, and adds that Mr. Antonio Meneghello, a member of the firm in question, and other witnesses, are prepared to testify to this effect. The responsibility for this charge must rest with Mr. Supilo.

When once the authenticity of the documents had been established, such a fact might no doubt fairly be adduced as yet another proof of Mr. Supilo's bad character ; but to give it this strange precedence was equivalent to an open pronouncement in favour of the defence. No one who has studied with any attention the policy inaugurated by Count Aehrenthal, Dr. Wekerle and Baron Rauch in the south of the Monarchy, and the methods by which that policy was furthered alike in Vienna and in Agram, can fail to realize that the summons of Baron Chlumecky as a witness was a carefully preconcerted move, in which the defendants were but the innocent dupes of sinning diplomats. As editor of the *Oesterreichische Rundschau*, Chlumecky was one of the most effective supporters of Aehrenthal's whole policy and had openly espoused the cause of the Coalition's deadliest enemies, the party of Dr. Joseph Frank, in whose organ the first public charges of bribery had been made against Mr. Supilo. During his three years as a " political " official in Dalmatia, he had learnt the methods of espionage and denunciation encouraged by the Ballplatz upon the southern frontier ; and hence his evidence accorded with the best traditions of the Police State of Metternich. The *mise-en-scène* was admirable ; the guilty wirepullers were as yet discreetly veiled from the public gaze. It was calculated that the plaintiffs would lose their nerve in face of Baron Chlumecky's disconcerting *coup de théâtre*, backed by the marked hostility of the Court and the jury and by Rauch's renewed activity in Agram : that the inspired chorus of abuse in the Viennese press would complete their discomfiture : and that dissensions within the Coalition would lead to a collapse of the prosecution.[423] Count Aehrenthal's natural wish to prevent the triumph of his victims, and the fear lest the exposure of his methods might lose him the confidence of the Emperor and the Heir Apparent and discredit him in the eyes of Europe, supply an ample explanation for these intrigues.

If we regard the incident from its psychological side we must endeavour to banish from our minds the actual course of events, and assuming for the moment Mr. Supilo's guilt,

---

[423] The *Neue Freie Presse*, on Sunday morning, gave prominence to the idle rumour that Count Pejačević, General Tomičić and Dr. von Nikolić, three of the most distinguished members of the Coalition, had left its ranks. It at once added a dementi of the rumour ! The origin of this *ballon d'essai* is pretty obvious.

we must ask ourselves how he might reasonably be expected to act under such damning circumstances. Trained in a rough school where political calumny was an almost daily occurrence, combining the caution of the peasant with the suspicion inherent in every Ragusan, Mr. Supilo had been taught by bitter necessity the lessons of perseverance and self-reliance. Sheer force of character had won him the position of the most influential, and at the same time the most " dangerous " Croat politician ; and his success inevitably earned him the enmity of influential quarters. If there was one man in all the Slavonic South whom it was difficult to find napping, that man was Mr. Supilo. For a whole week beforehand he had known that Baron Chlumecky was to be one of the foremost witnesses against him, and he therefore had a whole week to prepare his line of action. If guilty, he must have known only too well what Chlumecky was coming to say, and under such circumstances only a lunatic could have been taken by surprise. For a guilty man who was not prepared to confess his guilt, only two courses were possible. On the one hand he might forestall the coming disclosure by a personal statement—to the effect that, while he had never accepted money from abroad, he had early in his career under the stress of great poverty accepted small loans from various political friends in Ragusa, and among others a sum of £8 from Baron Chlumecky : that this sum was in the nature of an acknowledgment of former work from an acquaintance with whose political opinions he fully agreed. If entirely unscrupulous, he might even have safely asserted that the money had been repaid long ago. Such an admission might have been galling to a man who had since come to play so important a part in Southern Slav politics, but at least it could not be regarded as in any way dishonourable or as having even the remotest bearing upon the present trial.

On the other hand, he might boldly await Baron Chlumecky's appearance as a witness and thunder him down in righteous indignation, or even, in true Southern Slav fashion, threaten him with personal violence. Such a part, if skilfully played, might have thrown dust in the eyes of the court and nullified the effect of Chlumecky's evidence. And what do we actually see ? The most *rusé* of Southern Slav politicians, the only man of whom " Vienna " is really afraid, stands before his accuser in mute astonishment, helpless as a child. His whole behaviour was that of a man staggered by an incredible charge, not of a man overwhelmed with guilt.

The whole problem is one of extreme delicacy ; for the charge of bribery is based upon an incident at which no third party was present, and hence it is a question of one man's word against another's. Thus despite ourselves we are driven back upon two indirect forms of evidence—the sworn statements of the two men, and their character and reputation in public and private life. Unlike the judge, who did not seem to regard bribery as a dishonourable occupation, we must inevitably start from the axiom that the trade of a briber is at least as disreputable as that of an accepter of bribes. So far as the actual incident of the 200 crowns is concerned, Chlumecky's positive assertion is met by Supilo's equally positive denial, and there is no external proof in one direction or the other. But if we consider the statements of the two men in court we find that Chlumecky, whose hostile attitude to Supilo, to the Coalition and to Dalmatia was notorious, deliberately suppressed a vital phrase in a letter which he cited as compromising Supilo, and that he was proved to be in error on more than one point of fact ; while every assertion of Supilo was subsequently borne out by those to whom he appealed. Despite countless libels and the violence of local party strife, I am not aware that any one has thrown a stone at Supilo's private character ; while numerous charges of the gravest nature have been publicly made against Chlumecky, charges which may be absolutely without foundation but which he has taken no steps to disprove. Thus there is not the slightest reason why the impartial observer should regard the latter's word as more reliable than the former's. Baron Chlumecky may in the course of time have succeeded in convincing himself that he actually gave money to Supilo ; similar delusions are by no means rare, and it is a more charitable supposition than the sole alternative. Meanwhile it is a remarkable fact that the very men who know Supilo most intimately and are best qualified to judge, are most firmly convinced of his innocence. And here I do not merely refer to the evidence of Professor Masaryk and Father Zagorac but to the opinion of his Dalmatian friends.[424] It is at least significant that Dr. Baernreither, the *preux chevalier* of German-Austrian politi-

---

[424] All the best men in Dalmatia—e.g., Dr. Čingrija, the well-known Mayor of Ragusa, Dr. Trumbic, the ex-Mayor of Spalato, Dr. Smodlaka, the leader of the Democratic Party, the poets Mr. Tresić and Count Vojnović, Father Biankini, the deputy, and Monsignor Bulić, the archaeologist—are firmly convinced of his innocence.

cians, publicly shook hands with Mr. Supilo at the close of the trial.

It may be regretted that Mr. Supilo did not follow up the Friedjung Trial by a libel action against Baron Chlumecky ; but unhappily his treatment in court had not encouraged him to appear once more before a Viennese tribunal. For him it was sufficient that public opinion throughout the Southern Slav world was practically unanimous in acquitting him. If I do not re-echo the gallant words of Professor Masaryk in the Austrian Parliament—" For Supilo I would lay both hands in the fire "—it [is only because as a foreigner I do not feel called upon to express so outspoken an opinion.]

The whole incident is repulsive in the extreme, and I would gladly have avoided it, were not such important issues involved. The deliberate aim of Supilo's enemies has been to rid themselves of the ablest, most farsighted and most dangerous champion of Southern Slav unity and progress ; and it was therefore inevitable that any account of the Friedjung Trial should treat fully of the Supilo-Chlumecky incident. That they should have raked up a story which even if true would have been discreditable but entirely irrelevant to the question at issue in the trial, shows that they were at their wits' end to find any evidence such as would supplement the forgeries.

The plot has failed ; and the time will come once more for Mr. Supilo to play a decisive part in Southern Slav politics. But the supine incapacity which the Croato-Serb Coalition has displayed ever since intrigue robbed it of its natural leader, is an eloquent proof that the wirepullers of the Friedjung Trial were right in concentrating their efforts against Mr. Supilo.

Note on the Origin of the Charges against Mr. Supilo.

In August and September, 1905, the chief organ of the Frank Party, *Hrvatsko Pravo*, published a series of articles under the pseudonym of " Argus." These contain the germ of the subsequent charges of treason directed against Mr. Supilo, who had become obnoxious to the Frank party owing to his advocacy of Croato-Serb friendship. Supilo brought an action in Agram against the paper, and Dr. Joseph Frank was obliged to admit in court that he had no proof of the allegations. The Christian Socialist organ, *Reichspost*, reproduced them from *Hrvatsko Pravo*, but Mr. Supilo, having won his action in Agram, ignored the Viennese organ, perhaps unwisely.

In April, 1905, when rumours of war between Servia and Bulgaria were in the air, Supilo paid a brief visit to Belgrad. Here he met a Hungarian official, Dr. E—— H——, whom he had known in Fiume. The latter drew his attention to the comments of *Budapesti Hirlap* on a recent article of Supilo advocating a Magyar-Croat entente. At H——'s urgent suggestion, Supilo agreed to write an answer, said that it would appear about a fortnight later in his own paper *Novi List*, and sketched out the lines of argument which it would follow. Through the medium of H——, Supilo obtained an audience with Pašić the Servian Premier, but failed to "draw" him as he had hoped. On his return home he duly wrote the promised article, and thought no more of the incident until it was recalled to him in the following manner.

In July, 1907, a prominent Croatian politician of the older generation was invited by telephone to visit one of the former leaders of the Magyarone party in Croatia. (My informant did not bind me to secrecy ; indeed his omission to do so was rather marked. But I prefer to mention no names, in view of the position of the two men in question.) The latter then produced a document proving treasonable acts on the part of Supilo. He had pledged himself not to show it, but read aloud certain portions, suppressing the names of the writer and the addressee, and holding his fingers over what was evidently the stamp of a Government office in the upper corner. The document described Supilo's visit to Belgrad, his interview and treasonable discussions with Pašić, and then gave the gist of an article which was shortly to appear in the *Novi List*. He then produced a copy of *Novi List* of the period in question, and pointed to a certain article, which the visitor, to his consternation, found to be almost identical with that which was prophesied in the mysterious document. His informant then begged him to admit that the matter was not quite clean, and to take no further action in favour of Supilo. The visitor, however, drew a different conclusion from the incident, and the reader may be left to do the same. The names would of course give added point to the story.

Three Anecdotes.

The political phantasy of the Serb has no bounds ; lack of balance and proportion is combined with inordinate belief in his own destiny, and a corresponding disinclination to work it out for himself. Let me give three illustrations of this from my own experience.

(1) In the spring of 1908 I was talking in Belgrad to a Servian who held a minor diplomatic post. We discussed the short-lived entente between Magyars and Serbs two years previously. My acquaintance lamented over the folly of the Magyars in ruining so promising an alliance ; and when I asked him what he had hoped to achieve, he assured me with enthusiasm, " By this time, my dear sir, we should have had *a million bayonets* (sic !) mobilized against Vienna." After all, this state of mind does not differ essentially from that of the well-known Servian newspaper *Politika*, which on October 27, 1908, after the annexation of Bosnia, wrote, " Now or never is the moment for trying conclusions with a mediaeval state on the point of the dissolution." The Serbs foolishly imagined that Austria-Hungary was about to break up, and it was only the Bosnian crisis which taught them the bitter lesson that the Monarchy is far stronger than ever before.

(2) Among the Serb politicians of Bosnia I found the belief widespread that the Army, the administration and the judicial system of Servia are all greatly superior to those of Austria ! In my opinion this truly comic belief deprives its holders of all claim to be regarded

as serious politicians. In their fanaticism, some even went so far as to defend, not merely the murder of Alexander and Draga—for which some kind of a case can be made out—but actually the *manner* in which it was committed !

(3) A prominent Montenegrin politician, with whom I had a conversation in April, 1909, defined the future relations of the two Serb states to Austria-Hungary in the emphatic phrase " aut-aut " (either-or). Either, he held, the Monarchy must fall in pieces, or Servia and Montenegro must lose their independence. In that case, I felt inclined to reply, " The Serb states must make their will."

The idea that they are quite able to cope with Austria-Hungary is widespread in the Northern Balkans, and is of course largely due to the weak policy of Vienna during the long interval between Count Andrássy's resignation and Baron Aehrenthal's accession to power.

CHAPTER XII

The Vasić Forgeries and Count Aehrenthal —A Criticism and an Inquiry

" It is the duty of History, not only to crown with glory him to whom glory is due, but also when it is necessary, to use the branding iron."

BARON ALFRED BERGER, *Buch der Heimat*, I, p. 66.

THE issue of the Friedjung Trial vindicated the Croato-Serb Coalition from the slanders of its enemies and gravely compromised the Austro-Hungarian Foreign Office in the eyes of Europe. It also completed the discredit into which Baron Rauch's regime had fallen and rendered his position well-nigh untenable. His fall was still further hastened by events in Hungary.

The collapse of the Hungarian Coalition in the autumn of 1909 had led to the final resignation of the Wekerle Cabinet shortly before Christmas, after it had lingered for many months *in statu demissionis*. Dr. Lukács having failed to form a cabinet, the King on January 19, 1910, appointed Count Khuen-Héderváry as Hungarian Premier. Not the least of his qualifications in the eyes of his admirers were his intimate knowledge of Croatian affairs and the extreme awe in which his name was held throughout the Triune Kingdom ; nor indeed did he lose any time in justifying his reputation. The charges brought forward by Baron Chlumecky had forced Mr. Supilo to withdraw from the Croato-Serb Coalition, and although his colleagues rallied round him most gallantly and showed their firm belief in his personal honour, the partnership was thus dissolved at a highly critical moment. The Coalition, once deprived of its natural leader, showed a strange lethargy and indecision, of which Count Khuen-Héderváry made full use. The men who filled Supilo's place had lost their nerve during the trial, and but for Professor Masaryk's insistence, might have been beguiled into dangerous concessions. When after the trial Viennese statesmen were prepared to treat with them for a remedy of their just grievances, they had preferred a night at the theatre to a conference with the most influential German politician in Austria ; and " Vienna " had drawn the natural conclusion that they were impossible allies. Now, like a flock of frightened sheep, they allowed Count Khuen to dictate his own terms for the " pacification " of Croatia. In their anxiety to be rid of the obnoxious person of Baron Rauch, they forgot that the new Premier would under no circumstances retain as Ban a man with whom his personal relations were so strained. Hence in the " compact " which they concluded on January 25, they bartered away most of the principles for which they had fought, in return for their enemy's head upon a charger. Rauch's successor as Ban was Dr. Nicholas Tomašić, for many years Count Khuen's trusted lieutenant in Croatia and by far the ablest exponent of the Union with Hungary. During his retirement from public life since the collapse of the " National " Party, Dr. Tomašić had written a very brilliant monograph on the early constitution of Croatia, and its publication in the autumn of 1909 had done much to dispel his former unpopularity.

Croatia gained nothing save a change of Ban ; instead of one who had proved his glaring incapacity to coerce the country, it now had a past master in the art of political diplomacy. The Rauch regime had become an European scandal ; in coming to terms with Tomašić, the Coalition renounced whatever advantage this fact conferred, and reduced the Croatian question once more to the same level of provincial interest as the question of an Italian University in Trieste or the grievances of Ruthene peasants in Galicia. The new Government, it is true, admitted in theory that Mr. Kossuth's Railway Bill had infringed the Compromise, but the date at which this illegality was to be removed was left absolutely vague.

In adopting a compliant attitude so different from its former bold vindication of Croatian rights, the Coalition was influenced by two important considerations, quite distinct from fear and sloth. Baron Rauch had during his two years of office devoted a strict attention to the electoral rolls, and had succeeded in reducing the number of voters from 49,000 to little over 40,000. The independent voters were thus in a decisive minority ; and it was feared that the exercise of governmental pressure upon the officials who now formed the bulk of the electorate, might enable the Ban, in the event of new elections, to annihilate the Coalition and restore the old Mameluke system of the Khuen era. Meanwhile the Frank party had definitely offered itself as a candidate for office, and set itself to underbid the Coalition at Budapest; its object of course being to secure control of electoral reform and to enforce it in a manner unfavourable to the Serbs.[425] It is scarcely credible that Count Khuen ever seriously thought of accepting the alliance of a party whose programme does not recognize the Hungarian connexion; and Mr. Supilo had good grounds for holding that the nation was ready to support a brave and determined opposition and could defy and defeat the old method of a " packed " Diet. Yet the bogey of Dr. Frank at the head of affairs in Agram, was sufficient to unnerve the national resistance; and the bitter press feud between the Coalition and Supilo, which resulted from his criticisms of the " pact," still further confused the situation.

It is not my purpose to express any definite opinion upon the present Ban and his political methods. I merely wish to lay before the reader in brief outline the events of the past year in Croatia, and then to pass on to the next act in the drama of forgery which characterized Count Aehrenthal's Southern Slav policy.

On February 7, 1910, Dr. Tomašić's appointment as Ban of Croatia was officially announced. In accordance with the pact, the so-called " mummies " of the old National Party were admitted to membership in the Coalition, and were adopted as Coalition candidates for the vacant mandates to the Diet. On March 18 the Diet met once more, after the Constitution had been entirely suspended for 25 months; but this time the majority showed an unwonted docility. The Budget indemnity was meekly passed at the Ban's request, and the proceedings were merely formal, until the new Franchise Bill was laid before the Sabor on May 4. Even then its discussion was entirely perfunctory, though the deputies

---

[425] " You drove us into the pact," cried Svetozar Pribičević, the Serb Independent leader, to the members of the Party of Pure Right, during a sitting of the Sabor in the Spring of 1910. How different was his attitude in June 1907, when Dr. Wekerle said to Professor Šurmin, " If you won't cease your resistance, I will take the man who will accept our standpoint—Dr. Joseph Frank " (see Šurmin's speech in Sabor, April 20, 1910). The Croats did *not* cease their resistance, and Dr. Wekerle did *not* " take " Dr. Frank.

were fully alive to its inadequacy and shortcomings. The only criticism came from the Frank Party, which opposed it as being too favourable to the Serbs. By the third week of May the reform had been hurried through, and on the 24th the Sabor was prorogued. The new reform bears the character of an obvious stopgap. The Hungarian Government had vetoed the introduction of Universal Suffrage, ostensibly on the ground that Croatia must not anticipate the march of events in the sister state. The old faulty distribution of seats was retained; schoolmasters were made ineligible for the Diet; and the solitary improvement was the reduction of the property qualification, with the result that the franchise was enjoyed by over 250,000 individuals, instead of less than 50,000 as hitherto.

When this bill had received the royal sanction, the Coalition fancied itself to be secure, and showed some inclination to hold Dr. Tomašić to his promises. But here again the personal equation took precedence of national claims. A serious dispute arose between Ban and Coalition, because the former declined to dismiss Mr. Aranicky from the department of Justice. On July 18 Dr. Tomašić resigned, but his resignation was not accepted by the sovereign; and henceforth the Ban played with his opponents, avoiding the tactical errors of his predecessor, but adopting a less conciliatory attitude than he had shown on his accession to power.[426] Moving cautiously in a valley of dead bones, he regarded it as his mission to undermine the unity of the Coalition, and to restore the old discord upon which Magyar rule in Croatia was based. To him Croatia's sole hope for the future depends upon the connexion with Hungary, and towards the maintenance of that connexion in its present form his efforts are honestly if mistakenly directed. On August 22 the Sabor was dissolved, and the new elections, which took place in the last week of October, led to a situation which has condemned Croatia to political stagnation ever since. Dr. Tomašić succeeded in detaching the so-called "Slavonian Group" from the Coalition and secured the election of 17 supporters; while the Coalition lost its absolute majority, being reduced from 53 to 35. The rival factions of the Party of Right divided 24 seats between

[426] In this he was encouraged by the astonishing victory of his friend and master Count Khuen at the elections of June, 1910, a victory due to corruption on a scale hitherto unequalled. (See my *Corruption and Reform in Hungary*.)

them, 15 falling to Dr. Frank, 9 to Dr. Starčević. The Peasants' Party, hitherto represented by three members, trebled the number of its seats. Mr. Supilo remained outside the parties, while the Socialists lost their only seat, and a German National- ist was elected in Syrmia. Thus no party obtained a workable majority, and a majority friendly to the Compromise with Hungary seems definitely unattainable. Dr. Tomašić, while careful not to dispense absolutely with constitutional forms, has governed, so to speak, from hand to mouth, by conferences and prorogations. Croatian politics beat time, and wait uneasily for the march of events in Hungary and Austria.

One of the earliest acts of the Tomašić Government had been to secure a revision of the High Treason trial. On April 2, 1910, the Septemviral Table (the Croatian Court of Appeal) quashed the verdict of Mr. Tarabocchia and his col- leagues, on the remarkable ground that the facts adduced in the Public Prosecutor's indictment do not prove the alleged high treason and that the case against the prisoners had not been sufficiently elucidated. Yet it seems quite incredible that after a trial lasting seven months there could be any real doubt upon the matter : either the guilt or the innocence of the prisoners had been clearly established.

On April 30 a strange incident of the trial was brought to light in the Croatian Diet. Dr. Mile Starčević laid before the House the manuscript notes of an article dealing with the history of the Serbs in Croatia, in the handwriting of a promi- nent member of the Frank party. These notes, it was alleged, had been specially written for the use of the Public Prosecutor, Mr. Accurti, and it was thus sought to establish a direct influ- ence of the Frank party on the course of the trial of its political enemies. A comparison of the notes with the actual text of the indictment was found to lend colour to the charge, for certain portions would appear to have been copied by Accurti almost word for word. Their author did not deny their authenticity, but argued that they merely contained the answers to specific questions of a historic nature addressed to him as an authority on Croatian history. On the other hand no indication was given as to the means by which these stolen goods fell into the hands of their present possessor.

The incident, while by no means as discreditable as Dr. Starčević maintained, simply proved what was already notorious, that the Public Prosecutor framed his indictment in accordance with the tenets of an extremist party, and accepted his history ready-made, without in any way troubling to investigate for himself.

Throughout the summer of 1910 the questions raised in the Agram and Vienna trials remained in abeyance. But in the autumn new developments occurred, which raised the controversy once more in a highly dramatic form.

It will already have struck the English reader as remarkable that Count Aehrenthal should not have been immediately called to account in Parliament for the grave scandals revealed in the Friedjung trial. That he was able to evade parliamentary criticism for ten whole months after the trial, was due solely to the peculiarities of the Dual System in Austria-Hungary. The Delegations, which are alone competent to discuss matters affecting foreign policy, are two entirely distinct bodies, recruited from the Austrian and from the Hungarian Parliament. While the Austrian delegation had been elected in the ordinary way, the Hungarian Government, being without a majority or even a party in the Hungarian Parliament, was unable to procure the election of a Hungarian Delegation. Thus it was not till after Count Khuen-Héderváry's great victory at the polls in June 1910, that the necessary election of delegates could take place : and it was then already too late for a summer session, owing to the pressure of parliamentary business. When the Delegations did at length meet on November 8, 1910, the Premier and the Ban by a skilful manœuvre contrived to eliminate the Croats from the Hungarian Delegation [427] and thus saved Count Aehrenthal from the criticism of the men whom he had wronged. But although the Croats were thus reduced to silence, the Austrian delegation contained their most formidable champion in the person of Professor Masaryk, who had since the Friedjung trial devoted a great deal of time to careful investigation of the forgeries and their origin.

In the autumn Mr. Supilo had received a letter from a certain

[427] They selected three excellent but colourless Croat deputies, without even consulting the forty Croat members in Budapest, from among whom the selection had to be made : then when the three indignantly laid down their mandates, three Magyar substitutes were declared elected to the vacant places !

Vasić in Belgrad, declaring himself to be identical with the mysterious Milan Stefanović (see p. 246) and asserting that the forgeries were fabricated in the Belgrad Legation with Count Forgách's knowledge, and that one copy of the photographs that were made there, was sent to Count Aehrenthal and a second to the Archduke Francis Ferdinand. The originals, he added, were now in Servian hands, and the material against the Legation was overwhelming. Mr. Supilo at once communicated with Professor Masaryk, who then paid visits to Agram and Belgrad to investigate the matter. It was the outcome of these inquiries that finally decided him to raise the whole question of the forgeries at the Delegation.[428]

In his speech on November 8, Professor Masaryk addressed two direct questions to Count Aehrenthal. How was it possible that the forgeries were not recognized as such by the Austro-Hungarian Legation in Belgrad, by the Foreign Office in Vienna, and by the Ministry of War which based its plans upon them ? And did Count ehrenthal and his press bureau know the contents of Dr. Friedjung's article before it appeared, and even prompt its publication ? It was no mere case of a duped Minister, he continued ; " the forgeries proceed from the Austro-Hungarian Legation in Belgrad." Mr. von Svientochovski, secretary of that legation, engaged in February, 1909, a young journalist named Vladimir Vasić to teach his children Servian. Soon afterwards a number of documents purporting to be "minutes" of the Slovenski Jug were placed before him, and he was entrusted with the task of removing the " Croaticisms " with which they were replete. Finally in November, 1909, on the eve of the Friedjung Trial, he had to copy them out in the name of the mysterious " Milan Stefanović." [429] The work was done in Svientochovski's study and in the house of another member of the legation. Vasić himself retained some of these " documents " in his own hands, and though pressed to return them, evaded doing so. Count Forgách, who knew of the work, had promised Vasić a career

---

[428] The reader will find an admirable summary of events relating to the Vasič forgeries in the telegrams of *The Times* correspondent in Vienna. (See *Times* of November 9, 10, 11, 14, 17, 19, December 7, 8, 23, 24, 30, 31, 1910.) I take this opportunity of drawing attention to the important part which he has played in elucidating the truth on matters of Austrian and Hungarian politics.

[429] See p. 246.

in Vienna, and in April, 1910, he was at last enticed as far as Agram, where he lived some weeks in the house of an Austrian officer called Captain Cvitaš. Finally he took alarm and fled back to Belgrad, still without having disgorged the documents. It would be the simplest thing in the world, added Professor Masaryk, to prove the truth of these assertions. "Count Aehrenthal only has to lay the forgeries before the House. I have here some of these false minutes, which he was to have got, but did not get. Let us compare the handwriting, and instantly the matter is cleared up." After stating that he had been refused access to the "documents" and photographs which had figured in the Friedjung trial, he concluded with the following words : "After this accusation of mine Count Aehrenthal can only state that neither he himself nor any of his officials in the Foreign Office knew of or assisted these machinations of Count 'Azev' [430] in Belgrad."

Count Aehrenthal allowed twenty-four hours to elapse before he replied, and then carefully avoided a direct answer. fter calmly affirming that the documents which formed the basis of Dr. Friedjung's article had had "no influence whatever" upon his decisions "either before or after the annexation," he repudiated the aspersions upon Count Forgách, "one of the most estimable of our diplomats," and tried to discredit Professor Masaryk's sources of information on the ground that they were foreign. "If Count Forgách had really done all that is imputed to him, he would not enjoy in serious leading circles in Belgrade his present excellent position," nor would the Servian Government, when rumours of his transference to another post arose, have expressed the wish that he should remain, as "a friend of Servia" (November 9).

Needless to say, these vague phrases satisfied no one, and the Young Czech leader, Dr. Kramarz, was voicing the opinion of many even among his political opponents, when next day he summoned Count Aehrenthal to publish the facts regarding the forgeries. The vigorous criticism of the whole annexation policy with which he accompanied this summons does not concern us here. On November 11 Professor Masaryk returned to the charge, and after rebutting the personalities in which Count Aehrenthal had indulged two days earlier, declared

[430] A reference to the infamous Russian *agent-provocateur* and spy who played a leading part in the counsels of the revolutionaries, but was at last detected and made away with.

with renewed emphasis, "that Count Forgách knew of the forging of the documents." Count Aehrenthal, in reply, referred to the charge against Forgách as "insinuations of a general nature" (sic !), and treated the whole matter as an intrigue of foreign journals against Austro-Hungarian diplomacy and as an attempt to disturb the relations of the Monarchy with Servia. To this Professor Masaryk rejoined, amid a scene of great tension, "Count Aehrenthal dares not and cannot say that his officials had no relations with Vasić, he cannot deny that Count Forgách knew of these forgeries. . . . I ask His Excellency to say in so many words : Had Count Forgách relations with this individual Vasić ? Is Count Aehrenthal aware that Count Forgách knew of these forgeries and wittingly had relations with their forger ? In other words, Count Forgách is the forger. I await an answer."

To the general astonishment Count Aehrenthal remained seated, and the President of the Delegation announced that, as no one else desired to speak, he would put the Foreign Estimates to the vote. At the last moment an official of the Foreign Office whispered something to his chief, and it was only then that Count Aehrenthal rose in great excitement and made the following brief statement :—" In answer to the direct question addressed to me by Professor Masaryk, I have to declare that Count Forgách has never had dealings with this man " (mit diesem Manne nie in Verkehr gestanden ist). As his opponent took care to point out on a later occasion, this was not an answer to the question asked. That Count Forgách was on terms of personal friendship with an individual like Vasić, no sane person would maintain : that under given circumstances an ambassador may have to meet a spy or a forger, is not necessarily discreditable. But that an embassy should deal in forged documents on a large scale, in a matter which might involve Europe in war, is a crime for which no adequate words of condemnation can be found ; and that a Foreign Minister should meet such a charge with evasion and silence, is suspicious in the highest degree.

On November 15 the Servian Foreign Minister, Dr. Milovanović, answered an interpellation in the Skupština, regarding Aehrenthal's statement that Servia had wished to retain Forgách in Belgrad. His statement put a new complexion on the matter : all that had happened was that Servia had formally dissociated itself from a campaign against Forgách which was then raging in the Servian press, and had denied that it was dissatisfied with the Minister. Meanwhile Vasić himself had surrendered himself to the police in Belgrad and confessed his share in the forgeries : pending trial, he was kept in prison, and absolute reticence was shown by those entrusted with his examination. Towards the end of November Count Forgách gave direct official assurances to the Servian Government, that neither he nor Count Aehrenthal had had any connexion with Vasić or his forgeries. On December 6 a skilfully worded communiqué appeared in *Samouprava*, the Servian official gazette, stating that Servia " must attach credence to these assurances, so long as no facts arise to change the standpoint of one or other of the two Governments."

To this communiqué and to further details published by Masaryk in the *Zeit* (December 4), Aehrenthal published a rejoinder in the official *Fremdenblatt* (December 6) which contains the first definite admission of relations between Vasić and the Belgrad Legation. " It must be clear to every one," it says, " that he (Vasić) belongs to a category of individuals which . . . in critical times presses its information on diplomatic agents. His statements were received *by a subordinate clerk* of the Legation in Belgrad, until their worthlessness became apparent. If the article of the *Samouprava* neglects to mention the assurances which the Servian Government gave to Count Forgách—to the effect that authoritative circles in Belgrad never gave the slightest credence to the absurd slanders of a Vasić, according to which Count Forgách or one of his subordinates committed forgery or had forgeries prepared— we fill in this gap in the Belgrad statements all the more readily, because we are convinced that we are thus complying with the Servian Government's intention to maintain friendly relations." Three days later Dr. Milovanović repudiated this version of the case [431] ; and Count Aehrenthal, who eighteen months before had dictated to the Servian Government the most humiliating admissions, now saw himself constrained to swallow this rebuff in silence, thus supplying a fresh presumption in favour of Professor Masaryk's contention. His official press sought to veil its discomfiture by attacks upon Masaryk ; typical of its tactics was the publication of extracts from an article against Masaryk in the Belgrad " *Štampa* "—*an article which had never appeared in that newspaper* ! [432]

[431] *Samouprava*, December 9, 1910.
[432] Masaryk, *Vasić-Forgách-Aehrenthal*, p. 31. It had presumably been written in Vienna for publication in the *Štampa*, but for some

THE VASIĆ TRIAL

On December 22, 1910, the trial of Vasić opened at Belgrad. By orders of the Government, it was conducted behind closed doors, and the Belgrad press was not allowed to publish the evidence, lest public opinion in Servia should be still further inflamed against Austria-Hungary. But reporters of the foreign press, and interested parties were admitted on special application; and among those who availed themselves of this permission, were Professor Masaryk and Dr. Hinković, who watched the case in the interests of the victims of the Agram trial. Vasić was charged with treason and injury to State interests, on the ground that "he helped to prepare reports referring to an imaginary revolutionary activity of the Slovenski Jug in Southern Slav territories outside the Kingdom of Servia and a connexion of this club with the Servian authorities, which reports were made over to the Austro-Hungarian Legation and afterwards figured in the well-known Friedjung trial as proofs of Servia's dishonourable attitude to the neighbouring Monarchy." After a two days' trial Vasić was condemned to five years' imprisonment. The main foundation for this verdict was the full confession of Vasić himself. But while Count Aehrenthal and his supporters were fully justified in treating Vasić's bare assertions as far from reliable,[433] it is obvious that the fellow, when once in court, had no inducement whatever to tell lies which would compromise him still more deeply. The chief interest in his confession lies in the fact that it proved possible to control his statements on seventeen points of detail,[434] and in each case he was found to have spoken the truth. A forged telegram which Vasić produced and which he alleged to have been written by the Austrian Secretary of Legation, Svientochovski, was compared with the latter's handwriting and found to correspond. A man living in the same house as Svientochovski was able to confirm Vasić's assertion that he had been busy working there in February, 1909, and had been alarmed by the appearance of a police official on some errand in the house. Above all, the houseowner confirmed the assertion that the documents had been photographed against the study door :

reason refused by the editor at the last moment, before a reference to it elsewhere could be suppressed.

[433] On the other hand, the bare assertions of Nastić were treated as amply sufficient and Nastić had about as much right to the name of "journalist" as the wretched Vasić.

[434] See Masaryk, op. cit. pp. 35–9 (translation of the indictment).

313

for he had himself seen small holes on the inside of the door, such as are made by drawing pins. Vasić had further alleged that Svientochovski supplied him with a key to the study door, so that he could enter at any time during the owner's absence, without attracting notice. The proprietor now deposed that he had been requested by Svientochovski to add a second outer door at the very entrance to which the missing key gave admission—presumably to prevent its possessor from continuing to gain access. The Court in passing judgment argued that various proofs quite independent of the prisoner's confession established "his connexion with the organs of a foreign Legation," though his accomplices could not be called to account before the law.

If the matter of the forgeries had rested at this point, it might have been possible to treat Professor Masaryk's charges as not proven, and to give Count Aehrenthal the benefit of the doubt, on the ground that the Belgrad Court acted under pressure from a government which had an eminent interest in throwing discredit upon Austro-Hungarian diplomatic methods. At this stage, however, Count Aehrenthal committed a grave tactical error, of which Professor Masaryk naturally took full advantage. An official communiqué appeared in the *Neue Freie Presse* of December 24, admitting the forged telegram produced at the Vasić Trial to be really in Svientochovski's handwriting, but maintaining it to be a mere copy of a document which Vasić had palmed off upon him as genuine.[435] This admission supplied the solitary link

---

[435] Lest I should be accused of putting a wrong interpretation upon it I quote it *in extenso*.

"Vasić brought the alleged original documents of the Slovenski Jug only on the condition that they must be returned to him soon, so that their abstraction should not be noticed by the officials of the Slovenski Jug. The result of this condition was that the Legation Secretary (dragoman) *copied the documents*. Obviously Vasić succeeded in getting hold of *one of these copies, which he has now used before the Court*. To speak of the share of a legation official in Vasić's forgeries, will, as may be seen, hardly be possible. The simple and easily transparent facts invalidate Vasić's assertions on this point.

"Meanwhile the Servian Government is aware that Vasić, even after the Legation had broken off relations with him owing to the discovery of the worthlessness of his assertions, made renewed offers to the Austro-Hungarian Legation, but was this time refused and therefore threatened revelations. Vasić then employed the same threats at our Belgrad Consulate, in Semlin and in Agram, each time without result. It is the excessive cunning of a half-educated person, who finally lost control

which had been missing in the chain of evidence at the Vasić trial. Hitherto it had been allowable to doubt whether the experts had established the identity of Svientochovski's writing : now this doubt was dispelled.

Even Count Aehrenthal's admirers could not fail to be unfavourably impressed with his behaviour. When Professor Masaryk first put forward his charges, the Minister had categorically denied all connexion between Vasić and the Legation. On December 6 he admitted Vasić's relations with " a subordinate clerk " ; after the Belgrad trial, the " clerk " became a secretary of legation, who had actually copied with his own hand all that Vasić brought him. How were such conflicting statements to be reconciled on any other hypothesis than that of a gradual surrender of an untenable position ?

On December 29 the duel between Aehrenthal and Masaryk was renewed in the Austrian Delegation, when the latter produced a photograph of the fatal telegram, showing that it was not a " copy " at all, but an original forgery of Svientochovski. It purported to be despatched from Loznica, a small place on the Servian frontier, by the leader of an irregular Serb " band " to Professor Markoviç, the president of the Slovenski Jug in Belgrad ; it stated that money had been sent to Sarajevo, and made somewhat cryptic references to frontier villages and the Bosnian garrison of Bjelina. If genuine, it would naturally have established a strong presumption· that Marković had the supervision of guerilla bands operating against Austria.

By producing this photograph, Masaryk annihilated Aehrenthal's theory of a " copy " ; for this " copy " was written in Cyrilline characters, *on an official Servian telegram form,* and at the foot had been added an imitation of the official postmark, purposely rendered half illegible ! [436] As Professor Masaryk was able to point out, even the phraseology of this brief telegram of thirty-four words betrays its author as a foreigner : no Servian could conceivably have employed phrases which at once suggest having been translated from German into Serb, like most of the Friedjung " documents." [437] " But the telegram form itself," says the inexorable Professor,

---

of his own plans and affairs, that has now led Vasić to destruction." A very similar communiqué appeared on December 25 in *Pester Lloyd.*

[436] See Appendix I (facsimile) of Masaryk's *Vasić-Forgách-Aehrenthal.*

[437] One phrase, " na " sigurno, Professor Masaryk claims as a " Polonism," and Svientochovski is a Germanized Pole.

" also betrays the forger. The Servain Telegraph Office, like all others, uses two kinds of form, one for handing in telegrams (these the public can have gratis), and one on which telegrams are written at the office and which are sent to the addressees. The Loznica telegram, if Vasić had brought it from the Slovenski Jug, must have been a telegram handed in at Loznica and received in Belgrad, but it is really written on a handing-in form ! (Imagine our getting a telegram from the office on one of our green forms !) Mr. Svientochovski very easily got the forms laid out for the public, and on one of them he forged the telegram which was supposed to have been officially received and delivered. That Vasić could not have brought to our Legation Secretary an official telegraph form from Loznica, is obvious. Mr. Svientochovski simply reckoned on the Servian telegraph forms being unknown in Vienna."

The telegraph form was in itself sufficiently damning evidence. But Professor Masaryk, wishing to prove his charges up to the very hilt, produced further " documents " from the forgers' laboratory. The first of these was one of the notorious minutes of the Slovenski Jug—a gigantic sheet of paper whose exact dimensions were 97·7 by 34·6 centimetres ! [438] That no society in Europe, least of all a band of revolutionaries, would write its minutes on paper of this size, is abundantly clear, and effectively disposes of the argument that these " documents " were brought by Vasić from the Slovenski Jug to the Legation. Not even the veriest tyro in diplomacy would have accepted such a document from the most plausible of spies or robbers. Only one explanation is possible—that the size of these monster-documents was chosen to facilitate photography : and here again, without accepting the evidence of Vasić himself, we are confirmed in the belief by the incident of the drawing pins, which transpired at the Belgrad trial.

The next " document " produced by the Professor was the notorious balance-sheet of the Slovenski Jug, which played its part at the Friedjung trial [439] and seemed to convict Mr. Supilo of having received 6,000 francs from Servia. Here

[438] See Appendix II (life-size facsimile) in Masaryk's pamphlet; already cited.
[439] Strictly speaking the Friedjung " document " in question was the minutes of the Slovenski Jug in which the payment of the 6,000 francs was approved (see p. 217, see also Friedjung, *Aktenstücke*, No. II, pp. 9–10), while the " document " now 'produced was the balance sheet showing actual payment.

again its absurd size [440] makes it quite impossible to believe in its genuine character.

Finally Professor Masaryk produced a sheet of paper containing three signatures of Davidović, alleged to be a leading member of the Slovenski Jug (see pp. 217, 261) and establishing beyond the possibility of doubt that some person unknown had been practising the imitation of Davidović's signature.[441] According to Vasić this person was Svientochovski, and even if we refuse to accept the evidence of such a man, the circumstantial evidence is very strong.

Professor Masaryk concluded his speech before the Delegation by a scathing comparison of Count Aehrenthal's methods with those of Napoleon, Metternich and Bismarck, and declared that as Count Aehrenthal had challenged him, he would carry the matter *usque ad finem* when the session was resumed in January. He had not said all he knew nor the worst of what he knew, and he would prove Count Aehrenthal's own complicity. Count Aehrenthal contented himself with repeating the denial that Count Forgách had ever had dealings with Vasić, " who had forced himself upon the Legation and offered documents for sale at a critical moment when no Legation would have taken the responsibility of refusing to receive them. As soon as their entire worthlessness had been recognized—Count Aehrenthal did not say whether this was before or after the Friedjung trial—all further communications with Vasić were broken off." [442] He tried to minimise the effect of the Belgrad trial by arguing that the only information about it came from the newspapers, and went so far as to insinuate that Professor Masaryk's attendance at the trial had been unpatriotic.[443] In short, he clung desperately to the old tale, which no longer deceived any one. But anything that he might say, or any further onslaught upon him, were now of comparatively minor interest. By his rash communiqué of December 24, he had himself exploded the idea that the forgeries depended on Vasić's mere word ; and the production of the forgeries in the Delegation and their publication in pamphlet form in February, 1911, finally dispelled all doubt

[440] See Masaryk, op. cit., Appendix. III (life-size facsimile).
[441] See facsimile on p. 60 of Masaryk, op. cit.
[442] *Times*, December 30, 1910.
[443] Count Aehrenthal has always taken the line that opposition to his person is unpatriotic, just as his ally Baron Rauch argued that demonstrations against *his* person were anti-dynastic (cf. p. 156).

THE VASIĆ FORGERIES

as to their real authorship. The guilt of the Austro-Hungarian Legation in Belgrad had been fully established, and the fact that the incriminating " documents " had been stolen by Vasić, does not really affect the question. Theft with a view to blackmail, was an action such as might be expected from such an individual ; though as Professor Masaryk caustically remarks in his pamphlet, " compared with the forgers of the Embassy, Vasić is a man of honour ! " [444] The real point in this connexion is that Vasić could not have had an opportunity of stealing such precious papers, unless he had reached a considerable degree of intimacy with the Legation staff : and an independent proof of this intimacy is actually supplied by the incident of the study door key, authenticated by the house proprietor's evidence at the Vasić trial.

Count Aehrenthal's attempt to invalidate all the evidence of Vasić, is far from convincing. Two years ago, he and his officials, according to his own version, accepted " documents " *en masse* [445] from Vasić, knowing him to be a thief and a spy, yet basing a whole policy upon the authenticity of what Vasić brought ; but none the less he claims the right to rule out all the evidence of Vasić, as soon as it becomes inconvenient. Yet nothing has occurred to render Vasić's words either less or more reliable. The statements of a thief and a spy are already tainted ; confession of his crimes may not make him worthier, but most certainly does not make him less worthy. *We* have the right to reject Vasić's evidence as tainted : Count Aehrenthal, whose tool he was, does not possess that right. None the less, we have endeavoured to allow Count Aehrenthal's contention, and have not accepted the statements of Vasić except where they are confirmed by other evidence. On these lines, it is still possible to regard it as not proven, that Count Forgách had personal relations with Vasić, since the sole definite proofs are the evidence of Vasić himself and of a park-keeper in Belgrad. But that Count Forgách was in ignorance of the tactics of his subordinates, that Vasić's salary was paid out of Svientochovski's private purse and

[444] Op. cit. p. 63.
[445] Prof. Masaryk writes of 80 to 100 Slovenski Jug minutes, 20 to 30 secret " resolutions," 20 more minutes of the combined Slovenski Jug and Bands Committee, 5 or 6 balance sheets and about 20 telegrams (see Masaryk, op. cit. p. 67). We need not accept this merely on *Vasic's* word. Dr. Friedjung laid great stress on the fact that his " documents " were only quite a small selection.

318

not out of Embassy money, that the " documents " and photo-graphs were sent wholesale to Vienna without Count Forgách's knowledge and approval, and that he entertained no doubts as to the genuine character even of " the three-foot minutes " —all this is absolutely incredible. We need not accept, unless we please, Vasić's story of his reception by Count For-gách in the house of the Legation usher Tiefenbach : that is quite immaterial. Even if he never set eyes upon Vasić, Count Forgách cannot be acquitted of moral responsibility for the forgeries.

Count Forgách's position in Belgrad had become really pitiable. On all sides he was regarded with amused suspicion, and most embassies in the little capital knew the inner history of the forgeries, and were reporting it to their respective head-quarters. But Count Forgách is not a man to submit tamely to such treatment, and he apparently took no pains to conceal his opinion that the moral responsibility for the whole affair lay with Count Aehrenthal. Indeed he is said to have openly declared that he had not carried out nearly all that had been demanded of him. His growing resentment was soothed by the title of a Privy Councillor, and at length, amid the inspired eulogies of the Aehrenthal press, he was transferred to the less frigid atmosphere of Dresden, where opportunities for diplomatic forgery are scarcely likely to present themselves. His successor is placed before the unpleasant alternative of cleaning up the Augean stable at the Belgrad Legation, or of continuing to act upon the principles of Bomba's Neapolitan police.

If it is incredible that the members of the Belgrad Legation should have supplied the Foreign Office with masses of docu-ments, whether forged or genuine, without the knowledge of their chief, then still more incredible is it that the Foreign Office should have dealt with stolen articles on so large a scale, without Count Aehrenthal's knowledge and approval. It is glaringly obvious that unless the Belgrad Legation had acted upon direct instructions from Vienna, Count Aehrenthal would at once have disavowed not merely Svientochovski and Tiefen-bach, but Forgách himself, and not content with a disavowal, would have instituted the strictest possible inquiry into the whole affair. Instead of this, Count Aehrenthal resorted to prevarication and legal quibbles, answered direct questions by evasion and personal innuendos, and deliberately blocked all inquiry. The jealous care with which the forgeries have always been guarded from the public eye, in itself suggests most strongly that they cannot bear inspection. From the very first Count Aehrenthal has done everything in his power to suppress, not to further, the truth. Indeed from his attitude throughout this sordid affair, only two conclusions can be drawn. Either he has been deluded by the clumsiest of methods, or he has not been deluded at all ; either he is naïve to the point of incapacity, or unscrupulous to an alarming degree. The reader who has studied the evidence of the preceding chapters, should have no difficulty in forming his own opinion on this point.

It may be added, as a final comment on this aspect of the case, that two prominent officials, one at the Ballplatz, one in Bosnia, who received the " documents " with scepticism, were placed on the retired list in a manner which caused the general public no little surprise.

Dr. Friedjung said of the informer Nastić, that decent people can only touch him with the tongs. But Nastić and Vasić have been proved to be mere tools ; and the patriotic efforts of Professor Masaryk have fixed the responsibility in the proper quarter. In seeking to hush up the scandal and shield the real culprit, Austrian politicians are not acting in the true interests of their country, but are merely saddling ustria with the discredit which is really due to a single individual. The man whose foreign policy was based upon the forgeries of the Agram and Friedjung trials, has become an European danger. Cordial diplomatic relations with Austria-Hungary are impossible for any Power, so long as he remains at the head of affairs ; for so long as such methods remain unpunished, there is no guarantee that they will not be employed again, perhaps against some other Power than Servia. So far as Great Britain is concerned, it must be remembered that the imaginary relations of Servia and Great Britain played an important part in the forged Report of Dr. Milovanović.[446] In no other country could a Foreign Minister have survived for twenty-four hours such revelations as those of the Friedjung trial, still less the surgical demonstration of Professor Masaryk ; and the fact that such a survival is possible for eighteen months in Austria-Hungary, proves conclusively how inimical the existing Dual System is to all parliamentary control of foreign affairs.

[446] pp. 28–29 in Dr. Funder's dossier. See Appendix XIV.

In this connexion it is no longer possible to ignore a further aspect of the whole scandal, whose importance is only equalled by its delicate nature. The forged documents upon which Count Aehrenthal relied to justify his Balkan policy in the eyes of Europe, had a still more sinister surpose. It was necessary to win the approval of the Emperor and the Heir Apparent ; and no better means could be devised for winning it. The venerable Emperor's sincere devotion to the cause of peace naturally rendered him reluctant to sanction anything in the nature of aggression and adventure ; but if it could be proved to him that disaffection and treachery were rife among large sections of his subjects, then he might be induced to consent to the adoption of drastic measures. Not a shadow of blame can fall upon Francis Joseph. A monarch may surely be excused for assuming that the documents submitted by his ministers for his perusal, are genuine. It is not his function to test them, but to draw from them the necessary deductions and to base upon them his future course of action. There can be little doubt that the Emperor was won over to Count Aehrenthal's policy by the tales of Pan-Serb propaganda with which he was primed ; just as it is well known that when he once realized the direction in which matters were drifting, his whole personal influence was exerted to repair blunders and to preserve peace.

Other tactics had to be adopted to win the Archduke Francis Ferdinand. As a younger and more energetic man, he was naturally less averse than his uncle to a forward policy, and consequently more ready to take the risks which it involved. But Count Aehrenthal and the Magyar statesmen with whom he was in touch were well aware that the Archduke regarded the Southern Slavs with sympathy, as the natural bulwark of Austrian power in the Balkans. A determined effort had to be made to undermine those sympathies by proving them to be ill-placed, to alienate the future Emperor from the idea of Trialism by convicting the Southern Slavs of anti-dynastic tendencies. Just as the refusal of an audience to the Dalmatian deputies in 1903 had rendered the Southern Slavs suspicious of the dynasty, so the Heir Apparent's cold reception at Ragusa in 1906 [447] had aroused in his mind the first

[447] On the occasion of the Austro-Hungarian manœuvres in Dalmatia in September, 1906, the Heir Apparent visited Ragusa. Through some muddle, he did not arrive at the time arranged, and the official reception at the harbour of Gravosa consequently fell through. Those

doubts as to their loyalty and reliability. When we consider how much more formidable are the barriers which separate members of the House of Habsburg from their people than are those which surround our own Royal family, we shall easily realize that despite his ability and political acumen, the task of misleading the Archduke Francis Ferdinand was by no means hopeless. Indeed, nothing was better calculated to succeed than the production of a dossier of documents proving treason and conspiracy to be rife among the very race in whom he was disposed to trust.[448]

In this connexion it is necessary to point out that strategic considerations had their influence upon the development of affairs. The General Staff had finally rejected the Sandjak as useless, and regarded the valley of the Morava, through the heart of Servia, as the true strategic line of advance upon Salonica; and the proclamation of martial law in Croatia would of course have greatly simplified the task of the military authorities in the event of complications with Servia. This was also favoured by the Magyar Government, who would have profited by the opportunity to bring Croatia to heel; and it is an open secret that the proclamation would have been followed by the most summary measures against the most obnoxious leaders of the alleged Pan-Serb movement.

In effect, Count Aehrenthal invited the Sovereign and the Heir Apparent to build up their whole policy on a substructure of lies and gross fraud. In the Middle Ages ministers have lost their heads for far less grave offences; and even to-day, if anything is to be heard of the mediaeval charge of treason,

who had charge of the programme made no apology to the Mayor of Ragusa, and next day a special audience was provided for the head of the Trieste police, but the mayor was not received at all. This caused general offence, and the Heir Apparent, who was doubtless never informed of the muddle, was received in dead silence by the crowd, when he drove down the Stradone (the chief street of Ragusa). On the other hand, Prince Danilo of Montenegro, who was in Ragusa at the time, was received with deafening cheers. The difficulties raised by the Hungarian Government as to the appointments of the three sectional chiefs in Agram had already caused wide discontent, and Mr. Supilo, in the name of the Coalition, had warned Dr. Wekerle that " unless the appointments were made forthwith, the reception of the Imperial visitor in Dalmatia might lack enthusiasm." All this is well described in an article entitled " Austria-Hungary and the Southern Slavs " by the Vienna correspondent of the *Times* (*Times*, December 31, 1909).

[448] That he also took the authenticity of the " documents " for granted, is only natural, and cannot expose him to any criticism.

it should be directed, not against the fifty-three unhappy Serbs who languished so long in the prisons of Agram, nor against the much-maligned leaders of the Croato-Serb Coalition, but against the statesmen who deliberately set themselves to alienate the dynasty from one of the chief races of the Empire, and created a situation in which all constitutional government was suspended, and even liberty became a mere farce.

The venerable Emperor may be excused if at the age of eighty he is satisfied with the aversion of a catastrophe, and if amid the dearth of outstanding statesmen he leaves the culprit at his post. But the Heir Apparent is scarcely likely to forget the gross manner in which he has been imposed upon. He is far too acute a statesman to air his opinions on the subject, and for action he must still wait ; but the lessons of the Agram, Friedjung and Vasić trials can hardly have been lost upon him, and there is little danger of his again permitting unscrupulous statesmen to exploit his person for their own aims. By cultivating a closer contact with the people, he will doubtless be able to prevent the recurrence of such deception.

" Count Aehrenthal," wrote an able Southern Slav newspaper, " has been forgiven for excluding morality from politics. Will he also be forgiven for destroying by his tricks the reputation of the Monarchy ? " [449] This must not be taken too literally. The prestige of a great Empire cannot be destroyed by the misdeeds of a single individual ; but it can indeed suffer temporary eclipse, and so long as its foreign policy is conducted by Count Aehrenthal's method, this eclipse is likely to continue. It is Austria's misfortune, that despite the enormous progress which she has made during the last five years in every department of public life—and especially in her conception of political liberty—she is still gravely handicapped by the reactionary influences of the ruling oligarchy in Hungary. These influences, more than anything else, hamper the much-needed diplomatic reforms and prevent the infusion of a more healthy and modern spirit into the realm of foreign politics. The introduction of Universal Suffrage in Hungary, which is the essential preliminary to all true progress in the Habsburg Monarchy, cannot now be delayed indefinitely, and is likely to lead to a revision of the obsolete Dual System. Meanwhile the shortcomings of Austro-

[449] *Agramer Tagblatt*, November 10, 1910.

Hungarian diplomacy and the anachronous principles which underlie it, must not blind us to the fact that Austria is a genuinely progressive state, full of new and promising life, and that the inevitable changes of the immediate future will usher in a new era in which such events as have been the subject of the present volume will speedily become utterly impossible.

The complete secret history of the "documents" may perhaps never be known. The original charges against Mr. Supilo had, as we have already seen, appeared in the organ of the Frank party, under the pseudonym of Argus, as early as the autumn of 1905. In Agram their authorship is generally credited to a certain individual named Pjerotić, who has for some years past played a mysterious part behind the scenes of Southern Slav politics, and with whom the leaders of the Frank party have latterly broken off all relations.[450] That the forgers of the Friedjung "documents" used the articles of Argus as a groundwork, is hardly open to doubt, especially to those who have compared the latter with the former. That even a considerable time before the Annexation mysterious forces were at work in Budapest, in Agram, in Vienna, to undermine Mr. Supilo's influence, will be obvious to those who remember the ominous incident which I have related on page 301. This view is strikingly confirmed by the admission of Lieutenant-Field-Marshal Steeb, that the nature of the charges against Mr. Supilo had been known to the Emperor himself before the beginning of 1908.[451]

The direct influence of the Rauch Government on the High Treason trial and also upon the intrigues which preceded the Friedjung trial, has also been established beyond all

---

[450] Their enemies of course assert that they acted *mala fide* ; but there is no reason why they should not have been the victims of an imposture. They at any rate recognized the Friedjung documents to be forgeries, from the first day on which they became known in Agram. One of their leaders has described to me how one editor of *Hrvatsko Pravo*, on reading through the "documents," at once pointed out to his colleagues the impossible nature of their contents. My informant told me that he had himself warned Dr. Friedjung that he was the victim of a Balkan gang.

[451] This officer made the statement to Mirko v. Pisačić in August, 1908 ; the latter published the information in a pamphlet which has never been contradicted. Steeb's relationship to Baron Rauch makes the incident all the more significant.

question. We have already had occasion to refer to the relations which existed between the Croatian Chief of Police, Mr. Sporčić and the informer Nastić—relations which went far beyond the precautions demanded by interests of state, and indeed, according to Professor Masaryk's positive assertion,[452] actually went so far as an order to the *juge d'instruction* for a modification of the evidence given by Nastić at the preliminary inquiry. These relations, however, are best summed up in the words of a leading article in *Agramer Tagblatt* (March 15, 1911), entitled " Anarchy from Above "—an article which Mr. Sporčić has not dared to challenge. " He (Sporčić)," it says, " has sent them (i.e. Nastić and other kindred spirits) thousands of crowns in order to get articles into Austrian, Hungarian and German papers, articles of political bearing, in closest connexion with the High Treason trial. He has gone still further. He has had meetings with the Crown witness Nastić before his examination in that trial ; he informed him when to come to Agram and gave him advice how to conduct himself there ; he sent him the Public Prosecutor's indictment and wrote him a letter in which he says that he— the Chief of Police—has made inquiries ' at the Court ' (*beim Gerichte*), whether it would be well if Nastić in a forthcoming pamphlet (which however did not appear) were to reply to the speech made by Professor Masaryk during the High Treason trial in the Austrian Parliament ; and that he—the Chief of Police—was informed ' at the Court ' that it would be better if Nastić kept what he had to say of Masaryk's speech, for his cross-examination at the trial."

There were the very best of reasons why Sporčić could take no action against such an article ; for it was merely based upon the original correspondence of Sporčić, Nastić and the journalists Steinhardt and Mandl, which had been laid before the Croatian Diet by Dr. Srgjan Budisavljević the day before, and which caused a profound sensation throughout Croatia.[453]

---

[452] Masaryk, op. cit. p. 88 (*Ich weiss sehr genau*). It is hardly necessary to point out that Professor Masaryk still has a good many revelations in reserve.

[453] How Dr. Budisavljević obtained possession of these documents I have no idea ; can they have been bought from Nastić after he had been cast off by the authorities in Vienna and Agram ? Their contents throw a hideous light upon the dark corners of the stage. In one letter, dated February 28, 1909 (the week before the Agram trial opened), Sporčić tells Nastić that he is sending him 150

(Needless to say, Count Aehrenthal's inspired press took care that little was heard of them in Austria.) That Sporčić simply acted upon superior orders in distributing money to spies and "journalists," was abundantly clear ; and Baron Rauch was openly accused in the Sabor of having inspired the whole intrigue. That Baron Rauch's policy was directly inspired from Vienna and Budapest, he himself would not be concerned to deny.

A further proof of Rauch's connexion with the forgeries was the Kandt incident, exposed by the Croat Progressive deputy Professor Šurmin, on March 6, 1909, in the Hungarian Parliament. Baron Rauch had from the moment of his appointment as Ban, laboured to compromise the Croato-Serb Coalition, and one of the methods which he employed was to commission a self-styled "journalist" named Max Kandt to collect material against the Coalition leaders. In the year following February, 1908, this individual is believed to have received 7,000 crowns for the "documents" which he supplied, to say nothing of payments from Mr. Accurti, the Public Prosecutor. Professor Šurmin was able to put a stop to the intrigue, by sketching in his interpellation, [454]

crowns and a copy of the indictment, bids him talk over with Steinhardt the matter of newspaper articles and to try " to get Mandl also," and says that he (the Chief of Police) will come to Vienna if necessary for a talk (with Nastić the Crown witness) ! A letter dated April 21, 1909, to Carl Langer in Vienna, says that he already has the money, but cannot send it through the Agram post without arousing suspicion ! and asks Mandl not to publish any article without previous intimation. Another letter, dated April 20, 1909, and signed " Nikola," refers with visible annoyance to the statement just published by the Croatian Press, that the writer had " conferred with you in Pest, and that we went together with His Excellency to Vienna." " Tell me if these lies come from Mandl. Or did Steinhardt blab ? " (cf. p. 172). In a letter of May 23, Sporčic says that as he cannot write all he has to say, he will arrive in Vienna on the 26th, and stop at Ronacher's under the name of Štefanović. He sends 100 crowns for Steinhardt's railway expenses. In an unsigned letter of May 29, the same writer refers to Nastić's projected pamphlet, and the idea of mentioning in it their journey together from Pest to Vienna and Agram. " I have inquired at the Court, whether it would be well to write about this just now and I was told that it would *not* be good, for it would be best that it should come up first in court." Most of the other letters are from Steinhardt to Nastić or to Mandl—some being signed under false names—and deal with cash payments.

[454] See report of interpellation, March 7, 1909. See also Leopold Mandl, *Oesterreich-Ungarn und Serbien*, p. 46 (the official apologist for Aehrenthal). He states as a fact, that Rauch bought a secret

the methods adopted by Kandt, in conjunction with a certain Kukić and a photographer called Simić. He actually produced Kandt's money receipts, and certain letters of Kukić reporting to Kandt the result of his journeys of inquiry.

Yet another intrigue in Agram came to light at the time of Professor Masaryk's Delegation speeches. Just as a connexion had been established between Nastić and the military authorities in Bosnia (see note 272), so now a connexion was established between the forger Vasić and the General-Commando in Agram. Vasić, when sent to Agram in February, 1910, at the instance of the Belgrad Legation, went to Captain Cvitaš, an officer of the Agram garrison, visited the theatre in his company, and actually lodged with him during part of his stay. Captain Cvitaš, so far from denying this, admitted that he had placed Vasić under observation from the moment of his arrival in Agram (in other words, before the fellow announced himself) and that in doing so he merely acted on the orders of his superiors. The only possible inference is that the military authorities in Croatia had their share in the game of intrigue, and were acting in collusion with the Belgrad Legation. It had already transpired that the General Staff in Vienna was basing its plans upon the information of Vasić and other spies, the genuine portions of which were calculated as a bait to secure acceptance of the false. In short, it is virtually certain that Vasić was playing fast and loose with both the Austro-Hungarian and Servian authorities, and betraying each according to his fancy. Such a game would not have lasted very long, even if Vasić had been a genius instead of a man of very limited intelligence. Yet at a critical moment in the relations of the two countries, he definitely succeeded in leading the Austrian General Staff upon a false trail ; and in the event of war, the result might have been very serious.

It seemed advisable to describe in considerable detail the odious methods which underlay Count Aehrenthal's policy of annexation ; for without detailed treatment the whole story might well seem to be incredible. The reader is now in a position to understand the heartfelt exclamation of the Christian Socialist deputy Hrvoj in the Croatian Diet, " We do not want to live any longer in a moral morass." [455] For-

dossier of documents from " Kandt alias Kohn." On the same page he describes Rauch as " an honourable cavalier."

[455] See *Agramer Tagblatt*, March 14, 1911. A Southern Slav politician

tunately the bankruptcy of the Police State has been proclaimed before the eyes of Europe : organized diplomatic
theft is recognized to be an anachronism in the twentieth
century ; and all honest men will echo the words of the ultra-
loyal Austrian *Armee-Zeitung*, " Zum Teufel mit dem Spitzel-
system " (To the devil with the police spies).

in conversation with the present writer, used a still more drastic expression, reproaching Count Aehrenthal for his " dunghill policy."

CHAPTER XIII

Magyar Railway Policy

THE desperate quarrels so frequently kindled in Austria-Hungary by such apparent trifles as the inscription over an office, the address of a post-bag, or the coloured ribbons worn by a child, seem merely ludicrous to the foreigner, who is unaware of the importance of external trappings in a country where each race upholds a rival theory of constitutional law. But that the quarrel between the Magyar and Croato-Serb Coalitions originated over the provisions of a Railway Bill, was no mere accident ; for underlying the whole struggle is the fact that the Railway Policy which Budapest has advocated and enforced for many years past, is the chief factor in checking Croatia's natural economic development, and hence also the political development of the Southern Slavs.

The whole railway system of Croatia-Slavonia is exploited in the selfish interests of Budapest, to which the most crying needs of the country itself are deliberately sacrificed. A glance at any railway map of Europe will show that Croatia only contains two railways which can be described as main lines—that from Gyekényes viâ Agram to Fiume, and that from Zombor viâ Dálja to Bosnisch-Brod. The former links Budapest with the sea, the latter links Budapest with Bosnia. Everything has been done to connect agricultural Croatia with its most formidable agricultural rival, Hungary, and to hamper its connexions with its best customers in Carniola, Carinthia and Styria.

The connexions between Agram and Budapest are excellent, because Agram of necessity lies on the main line from the Hungarian capital to Fiume. The connexions between Agram and Vienna are wretched, every effort being made to keep Croatia and Austria apart. Between Fiume and Agram—a distance of 142 miles—there is no branch line of any kind leading towards Austria. Yet a connexion is badly needed between Laibach, the capital of Carniola, and the town of Karlovac (Karlstadt), on this very line ; and though Karlovac is the chief market of Western Croatia and a centre for agricultural produce, and though Austria has built her share of the necessary line as far as Rudolfswerth, work has not even been commenced on the Croatian side of the frontier. The explanation is very simple : the Hungarian Ministry of Commerce does not wish to encourage trade and intercourse between Croatia and the Slovene districts.

From Agram itself a branch railway connects with Steinbrück, a junction of the Austian Südbahn situated in the upper valley of the Save between Cilli and Laibach. But though trains do run on this line in connexion with the most important express trains between Vienna and Trieste, they are wretchedly slow, taking two hours and a half where less than two-thirds of the time would not be rapid travelling.

A more direct route from Agram to Graz, Vienna and the chief Austrian towns is that viâ Zaprešić and Krapina to Pragerhof on the main Südbahn south of Marburg. On the Austrian side of the frontier the line has been carried as far as the growing watering-place of Rohitsch ; but the nine miles of line still necessary to connect Rohitsch with Krapina, have purposely not been built by the Hungarian Ministry of Commerce.

Until, then, this much-needed route is completed, the sole alternative routes from Agram to Vienna are that viâ Stein· brück and that viâ Gyekényes, Nagy-Kanizsa, Szombathely (Steinamanger), Sopron (Oedenburg), Wiener – Neustadt. Yet incredible as it may seem, there is no express train connexion on this line during the daytime ; it is necessary either to leave Agram after midnight, or to start early in the morning by an extremely slow train, which crawls until it reaches Magyar territory. Even then there is a delay of over an hour at Nagy-Kanizsa before a quick train can be had ; with the result that the tiresome journey to Vienna has been prolonged three or four hours longer than need have been the case.

Meanwhile the direct route, which would materially shorten the journey from Agram to Vienna, is also awaiting Magyar pleasure. In Austrian territory from Wiener Neustadt to Aspang, Friedberg, Fehring the line already exists ; but from Fehring southwards to Varaždin no pretence has been made at building it.

In short, the settled policy of Budapest is to discourage intercourse between Croatia and Austria, and to tempt those travellers to whom ease and comfort appeal, to make the long detour through Budapest, rather than follow the direct and natural route.

The connexions of Agram eastwards to Belgrad are somewhat better : there are at least quick trains and through-carriages. But Magyar opposition has hitherto prevented one of the great international routes from passing through Agram. Since the opening of the Simplon tunnel, the shortest route from Paris to Belgrade and Constantinople would be viâ Lausanne, Milan, Verona, Venice, Trieste, Laibach, Agram. Over 100 kilometers would thus be saved. The Paris-Lyon-Méditerranée had already accepted the scheme, when it was blocked by the Magyar authorities insisting upon the new route touching Fiume. It is true that this modification while excluding Laibach from the benefits of the scheme would not affect Agram and would not increase the mileage of the route. But on the other hand the configuration of the country between Trieste and Agram supplies a fatal objection. From Trieste the new express would have to climb steadily as far as St. Peter-in-Karst, from which point viâ Laibach and Steinbrück to Agram the gradients present no difficulty whatever. In order to go by Fiume, however, the express would still have to climb to St. Peter, but would then be compelled to descend again steadily to the level of the Adriatic at Fiume and then to mount once more to a height of several thousand feet to Ogulin, before it could descend from the mountainous Karst to Agram and the plain of the Save. From a financial point of view the diversion of the route to Fiume was a fatal objection to the whole scheme : and when the Magyars suggested that the passengers should be shipped from Trieste to Fiume, it became obvious that they were trifling with the idea, and it collapsed altogether.

But it is when we turn to consider the connexions of Croatia with Dalmatia and Bosnia, that the full enormity of the situation becomes apparent. The Magyars have consistently opposed the building of any railway into Dalmatia, and thus to this day the greater part of the latter province is inaccessible to the rest of Europe by rail and can only be reached by steamer. Austria is cut off from her southernmost province by the Western half of Croatia, and for many years supinely tolerated this situation, despite the repeated protests of the Dalmatians themselves. When the commercial Ausgleich between Austria and Hungary was renewed in the winter of 1907, a special clause was inserted, binding Hungary to push on the necessary work for a railway extension from Ogulin, on the main line between Fiume and Agram, and Knin, the most northerly point of the local Dalmatian railway. But since then, Hungary has made no effort to execute its pledges ; the railway is no nearer completion than it was four years ago, and the Austrian Government, in spite of speeches and official statements in the Reichsrat, has been too weak-kneed to hold Hungary to its bargain. Dalmatia remains isolated from Europe, and suffers accordingly ; a vital link in the chain of Croato-Serb unity remains unforged, and Southern Croatia is stagnant and neglected.

At present only two railway lines enter Bosnia from the north. The older route, crossing the frontier at Doberlin, connects Agram with Banjaluka, the third largest town in the annexed provinces. It was originally constructed by the Turks, as the commencement of a strategic line connecting the Bosnian frontier with the Aegean. Like so many Turkish projects, it was abandoned long before its completion, and Banjaluka remained a terminus. Though the distance by rail from Agram to Banjaluka is only 133 miles, it involves a journey of eight or nine hours ! The direct route from Agram and Austria to Sarajevo thus remains incomplete, owing to the absence of a railway connexion along the defile of the River Vrbas, from Banjaluka to Jajce ; and this is mainly due to the influence of the Hungarian Government, which has known how to prevent the erection of a line which would tend to direct Bosnian traffic away from Budapest.

The other entrance to Bosnia is by Bosnisch-Brod, on the River Save, and on the main line between Agram and Belgrad. Here passengers must change onto the narrow-gauge railway which leads to the Bosnian capital, Sarajevo. Travellers from Vienna and the West find it easier and quicker to go to Bosnia through Budapest, though that is far from being the shortest route in mere mileage : both trains and tariffs are arranged in such a way as to divert as much traffic as possible through Budapest, and in this case Croatia suffers very materially. Not long ago the Chamber of €ommerce in Agram urged the Südbahn and the Bosnian railways to arrange a new express train service to connect Graz with Sarajevo, viâ Steinbrück, Agram and Brod, on the ground that under present conditions it is virtually necessary to go from Graz to Sarajevo viâ

Budapest, a detour of about 200 miles.   Both railways readily entertained the idea, but the Hungarian Ministry of Commerce withheld its consent, on the ground of special interests. This incident helps to explain the badness of the railway connexions between Agram and Vienna.

Meanwhile, the most pressing railway connexions between Bosnia and Dalmatia have hitherto been frustrated in the same manner.   The Bosnian railway runs southwards from Sarajevo to Mostar and then through the defile of the Narenta to the fever-swamps of Metković ; but it does not reach a port worthy of the name until it arrives at Gravosa, the harbour of Ragusa. Meanwhile, the rising seaport of Spalato, in Central Dalmatia, has no railway connexion with its natural Hinterland in Bosnia : and indeed, with the exception of Ragusa and Cattaro, the situation of Dalmatia in respect of trade-routes with the interior is relatively far more unfavourable than it was in the Middle Ages.   Then it could boast as good highroads of communication as the rest of South-East Europe : now it is fatally handicapped by the lack of what all its neighbours enjoy. The need for an extension of the Spalato-Sinj railway across the Bosnian frontier viâ Aržano-Livno to the present terminus in Bugojno, has long been apparent to the Dalmatians, but the supine attitude of the Austrian and Bosnian Governments has hitherto allowed them to clamour for it in vain.   But we shall not go far wrong in ascribing this delay at least in part to the influence of the Magyars, who know that Spalato-Sinj-Bugojno would inevitably lead to Spalato-Knin-Ogulin and are anxious to maintain Dalmatia and Croatia in their present isolation. Good railway connexions would naturally involve closer intercourse between the various Southern Slav provinces, and would thus foster the movement in favour of political union.   Hence it is considered necessary in Budapest to maintain as long as possible the present anomalous position, by which the journey from Spalato to Banjaluka actually takes 44 hours, although the distance could be covered by a quick train in 3 or 4 hours.

The tariff system is conducted on similar principles.   Every effort is made to concentrate trade and commerce in Budapest and to hinder Croatia's commercial progress towards the East and still more towards the West.   The unfair results of this essentially Magyar tariff are best illustrated by a comparison of the situation of Agram and Fiume—the Croatian capital and the Magyar seaport.   A few examples will suffice.   From the station of Novska the transport of a truck containing foodstuffs to the amount of 10,000 kilograms, costs 331 crowns as far as Fiume—a distance of 347 kilometers, whereas to Agram, a distance of only 220 kilometers, it costs 348 crowns, or 17 crowns more for the shorter distance. The tariff for a similar truck between Osijek (Essek) and Agram—a distance of 317 kilometers—is 365 crowns, but between Osijek and Fiume—a distance of 534 kilometers—it is only 341 crowns, or 24 crowns less for the longer distance.

In order to divert Croatian timber to Budapest, instead of the sawmills of Croatia, the tariff has been manipulated in the most incredible manner. For example, the distance from Brod (an important timber-centre) to Dugoselo (a large Croatian saw-mill) is recorded in the tariff as 330 kilometers and the distance from Brod to Budapest as 366 kilometers. In reality Brod is only 171 kilometers from Dugoselo ; but the compilers have reckoned the distance by all kinds of roundabout side-routes. Obviously the wood merchants of Brod are driven by this trick to send their wood to Budapest rather than select a route which is so unnaturally expensive. Similar examples could be given of the devices by which goods from Budapest are placed at an advantage over Croatian goods in Croatia itself ; while in Herzegovina it is sometimes cheaper to send goods from Bosnia by way of Budapest than by the direct route ! The railway tariff has been drawn up with the deliberate intention of hampering Croatian exports and leaving a free field to Hungarian industry.

Croatian public opinion has gradually become alive to the fact that the country is exploited economically by Hungary and prevented from developing its natural export trade with Austria and Italy. This exploitation renders still more imperative the need for Croato-Serb Unity, for joint action against Magyar aggression. By helping the Southern Slavs in their economic struggle, Austria would be helping those with whom her own economic interests are identical, and would be paving the way for Austrian economic influence throughout the Balkans. The whole Southern Slav world is at present the victim of a selfish policy of monopoly and favouritism directed from Budapest. It rests with Austria to put an end to this economic thraldom.

CHAPTER XIV

Croat and Serb — The Problem of Unity

"Er sah (die Besten Oesterreichs) verdorren am Felsgrund des Unglaubens an eine bessere Zeit."—

Rudolf Hans Bartsch.

IN the present volume I have attempted to summarize, for the first time in English, the history of the Croat and Serb race under the sway of the House of Habsburg, and to treat in greater detail the constitutional position of the Triune Kingdom of Croatia-Slavonia-Dalmatia, its theoretical relations to the Crown of St. Stephen and its practical relations to the Hungarian Government. The fulfilment of this task led inevitably to an account of the part played by Croatia in the Bosnian Crisis and the political scandals which followed in its train. The reader is thus in a position to judge of the importance of the Southern Slav question in its bearings upon Austrian policy in the Balkans and upon the balance of power within the Monarchy itself. In the following pages, therefore, I shall confine myself to a general survey of the problem, leaving it as far as possible to the reader himself to point the moral and adorn the tale.

The problem of Croato-Serb Unity may be described without exaggeration as the decisive problem of the Habsburg Monarchy ; for it supplies the eventual key alike to external and to internal policy. On the one hand, no forward policy on the part of Austria can succeed, which ignores the wishes and aspirations of the eight million Southern Slavs who now own Habsburg sway ; while on the other hand, they occupy a position which would enable them, under certain circumstances, to destroy the internal balance upon which the Dual System rests, by throwing their whole influence upon the side of Austria or of Hungary.

The situation of the Southern Slavs illustrates in a striking manner the old conflict between history and geography. A wide territory which forms a natural geographical unit and is peopled by a homogeneous population, speaking a single language, has been split up by an unkindly fate into a large number of purely artificial fragments. Passing these fragments in brief review, we find that Croatia-Slavonia forms an autonomous kingdom under the Crown of Hungary : Dalmatia and Istria are two provinces of the Austrian Empire, each with its separate Diet and administration ; the town of Fiume forms an unit of its own, under a Governor appointed direct from Budapest ; close upon 500,000 Serbs inhabit the three most southerly counties of Hungary proper : Bosnia and Herzegovina are administered jointly by Austria and Hungary with a provincial Government and Diet in Sarajevo : Servia and Montenegro form two independent kingdoms, while Old Servia is the most northerly vilayet of European Turkey. This intolerable situation has naturally been rendered more acute than ever by economic developments and by the changed conditions of life in the twentieth century. Political boundaries hamper the progress of the race at every turn, and serve as a handicap in favour of its rivals, notably the Magyars, the Bulgarians and even the more backward Albanians. Thus for purely economic reasons the ground was ready for a movement towards national unity, even if national feeling had been entirely dead, and as a matter of fact, so far from being dead, it is growing in intensity.

The movement in favour of Croato-Serb Unity has many obstacles to surmount, and the backward state of the country and the people may delay its achievement. But as surely as Germany and Italy have won their liberty and unity, so surely will it be won by the Croato-Serb race. The real problem is the manner of its achievement ; and here we are at once faced by two alternatives. Unity can be attained either inside or outside the Habsburg Monarchy, either by the latter's aid and under its auspices, or in defiance of its opposition. Let us consider the latter alternative first.

The Pan-Serb ideal may be briefly defined as the union of all members of the Serb and Croat race under the sceptre of the Karageorgevitch dynasty, with Belgrad as the capital of the new state. That this ideal should appeal to the Chauvinists of the Servian Kingdom is natural enough ; but no one who has had an opportunity of comparing Belgrad and Agram need make the mistake of supposing that it could be greeted with enthusiasm by any Croat, or even by educated Serbs within the Monarchy. The triumph of the Pan-Serb idea would mean the triumph of Eastern over Western culture, and would be a fatal blow to progress and modern development throughout the Balkans.

But even if for the moment we assume that the fulfilment of Pan-Serb dreams is desirable, we must consider the steps by which it could be attained. It is obvious that Servia cannot hope to obtain by peaceful means the cession of Bosnia, still less of Croatia and Dalmatia, by Austria-Hungary. Such a surrender can only follow the break-up of the Habsburg Monarchy and the European conflagration which such an event would inevitably produce. It has long been an axiom of European diplomacy that if Austria-Hungary did not exist, it would be necessary to create it ; and the maintenance of its territorial integrity has justly been regarded as a pressing European interest. Until the international crisis of 1908 many superficial observers believed Austria-Hungary to be a decadent state, which would fall to pieces on the death of the present Emperor, or as the result of any determined onslaught from outside.[456] But the action of Count Aehrenthal during that eventful winter, however open to criticism from other points of view, has at least this sterling merit, that it has for ever dispelled the myth of Austrian decadence. Now that foreign publicists have recovered from the rude shock administered to their pet theories and can see the general situation in better perspective, it is widely recognized that Austria-Hungary, so far from being decadent, is a powerful and progressive state, with one of the finest and best-prepared armies in the world—a state which would be even more powerful and progressive were it not hampered by the reactionary influences of the Magyar oligarchy and its racial and class policy in Hungary. That Servia and Montenegro, even if the former's army were as perfect as it is known to be defective, could measure forces with the Monarchy, is utterly out of the question ; war could only end in the fall of their independence.

Thus the Pan-Serb solution may be dismissed as altogether outside the realm of practical politics. The corruption of public life in Servia, the stagnation caused by embittered party factions and by crushing armaments (which overburden the Budget, without producing the desired effect) and the interests

[456] In a small volume published in 1907 (*The Future of Austria-Hungary and the Attitude of the Great Powers*), I endeavoured to demonstrate the absurdity of this belief.

of European peace combine to render such a solution highly undesirable.

Even among those Austrians who fully realize that Pan-Serbism need not be taken too seriously, there are many who are easily frightened by the bogey of Pan-Slavism, and who seriously suspect Russia of designs for uniting the entire Slav race under the sceptre of the Czar. So far as the Southern Slavs, at any rate, are concerned, this fear can only be described as fantastic. Their union to Russia presupposes the conquest of Hungary, and its corollaries, the destruction of Austrian military power and the defeat of the allied German armies. But in any case, before she could turn to so formidable a task, Russia is faced by enough internal problems of a racial character, to occupy her for many years. Her intolerant attitude to the Polish and Ukraine questions makes it wellnigh impossible for Russia to pose as the champion of Pan-Slavism ; for the Pan-Slav movement, in any save a mere Pan-Muscovite sense, is in direct conflict with the oppressive Chauvinism which the governing classes in Russia at present favour. The Bosnian crisis revealed the fact that Russia is not yet strong enough for a genuine Pan-Slav policy, or at least that she must for the present be content with a policy of peaceful intrigue in Sofia and Constantinople.

As we have seen, Croato-Serb Unity outside the Habsburg Monarchy can only be attained through universal war and a thorough revision of the map of Europe. The achievement of that unity *inside* the Habsburg Monarchy is a far more practical policy. Pan-Serbism is faced by a rival Pan-Croat theory, which aims at the erection, on a strictly Croat and Catholic basis, of a Croatian kingdom under Habsburg sway, as a third state on equal terms with Austria and Hungary. This state would comprise Croatia, Slavonia, Dalmatia, Istria, Bosnia and Herzegovina, and its natural capital would be in Agram. The policy of Trialism, as it has come to be called, has been widely advocated, not merely among the Southern Slavs themselves, but even in German Austria ; and if rumour may be trusted, it is favoured in the highest quarters. While the Christian Socialists regard Croatia as a valuable ally against the Magyar oligarchy and in the cause of the Austrian Imperial idea, the Czechs look upon Trialism as a step towards Federalism, and many Germans are inclined to approve of any scheme which would reduce the Slav element in the Austrian Parliament. The desire of the Pan-Croats that Carniola, and even parts of

Carinthia and Styria, should be incorporated with the new state need not concern us further here ; for it is obvious that no Austrian party could sanction an arrangement which would cut off Vienna from its direct connexion with the sea. Even the extremists are wise enough to realize the impracticable nature of this demand ; and it is certain that even were Trialism to be realized in the near future, the Slovene districts would not be included in the new complex.

The most zealous exponents of the Pan-Croat ideal are to be found in the Party of Pure Right, led by Dr. Joseph Frank. This politician has the great merit of having clearly perceived and consistently advocated an Austro-Croatian alliance at a time when public opinion in Croatia was hostile to Vienna. But on the other hand his policy is marred by the absurd theory—equally untenable from a historic and an ethnographic standpoint—that the Serbs of Croatia are no true Serbs, but merely Orthodox Croats, and by an absolute refusal to recognize their racial and national identity within the bounds of the Triune Kingdom. In a Southern Slav state created in accordance with such views, the Serbs would at best be tolerated, but would in no case be accorded equal rights ; and thus to enforce such a policy (even if it were practicable) would merely be equivalent to driving the Serbs into alliance with the Magyars.

The theories of the Party of Right are merely those of the Magyar Party of Independence, translated into Croatian terms ; the same juggling with high-sounding constitutional phrases, the same narrow racial intolerance, characterize the adherents of Kossuth and of Frank. A state which took such theories for its foundation would be as little deserving of sympathy, and as unstable, as a state based upon the rival Pan-Serb theory of which Belgrad politicians dream. The only true basis for such a state is the recognition of the absolute equality of Croat and Serb, and of their essential unity as two inseparable elements in the life of a single nation. Fortunately, a growing body of opinion throughout the Southern Slav world, is adopting this view ; and the linguistic unity which has been wrought by philologists and men of letters, may be regarded as a happy omen for the achievement of that wider unity upon which the future of the race depends. That a Southern Slav should prefer to call himself Croat rather than Serb, or Serb rather than Croat, ought to be a matter with which the State or society are in no way concerned. The larger Southern Slav patriotism should include and transcend the sense of racial individuality, just as Southern Slav patriotism is in no way inconsistent with a loyal pride in the possession of Austrian Imperial citizenship. The brutally narrow conception of the state advocated by Magyar statesmen, the desire to absorb and assimilate all rival elements and to enforce a dull uniformity of type, must be replaced by the British conception of citizenship, which takes a delight in creating new nations and combining an endless diversity of race and type with the essential unity which encourages rather than hampers individuality.

The chief obstacles to Trialism are the hostility of the Magyars, and the absence of any statesman in Austria capable of guiding the movement to a successful issue. Yet a firm and active alliance between Vienna and Agram would bear down the opposition of the Magyars, hampered as they are by the presence of a strong non-Magyar minority and a discontented and neglected proletariat. For over forty years the Magyars have monopolized all political power in Hungary and have arrested all development in Croatia ; but to-day they have little or nothing to show for this monopoly. The nationalities are embittered and alienated, but not assimilated ; a Magyarophil party has become a virtual impossibility in the Croatia of to-day ; in Hungary the Jews alone are triumphant, in politics, in the Press, in finance, in commerce. Dr. Lueger's offensive gibes at the " Judaeo-Magyars " contain a painful element of truth ; for Hungary is in danger of becoming a Zionist rather than a Magyar national state.

The policy of a whole generation has resulted in the bankruptcy of Unionism in Croatia. The Compromise has been violated time after time by the Hungarian Government ; the financial and commercial relations of the two countries have become intolerable to Croatia : the legal position of Fiume is still in suspense. To-day the Hungaro-Croatian Compromise must be pronounced a lamentable failure, for two main reasons. On the one hand, the Magyars have not kept their side of the bargain ; on the other hand, all such bargains, to be successful, must rest on common interests, and the interests of Hungary and Croatia are diametrically opposed.

Thus the present situation has no solid foundations ; resting as it does upon force, not upon inclination, it might collapse in a moment. It is bolstered up by the power of the Magyar oligarchy, which does not even represent the wishes and interests of the Magyar race, still less of the polyglot Hungarian nation as a whole, and by the support of the Sovereign, who has earned nothing but ingratitude for his wonderful loyalty alike to the letter and to the spirit of that Dual System which he and his advisers created. But it is scarcely conceivable that that system, which after fulfilling a useful part in the evolution of the Monarchy, is to-day effete and anachronous, will long survive the accession of a new sovereign. Without in the faintest degree detracting from the splendid services of the present Emperor-King in the political development of his dominions, it is allowable to point out that an equally splendid task awaits his successor—the destruction of political and racial monopoly in Hungary and the erection of a free community of equal nations, bound by indissoluble ties to a central Throne and Parliament.

It was the short-sighted folly of Austrian statesmen that drove the Croats into the arms of their enemies in Budapest. The alliance was brief and ended in disillusionment; it now rests with " Vienna " to prevent the Croats in their despair from appealing once more for Magyar help. At present Magyar Chauvinism renders such a solution impossible; but if Vienna delays too long, and wastes the psychological moment, a Magyar statesman might arise who, commencing with a bold and thorough advocacy of electoral and administrative reform, might make peace with the non-Magyar nationalities and carry into practical effect that Balkan confederation under Magyar leadership, of which Louis Kossuth dreamed when exile had taught him the folly of racial aggression.

Unquestionably the ideal solution lies in the direction of a moderate form of Trialism, under the auspices of Austria. But so long as Count Aehrenthal remains in office, no such development can be expected. His well-known reactionary sentiments render him averse to political change : cordial relations between him and the Southern Slavs are obviously impossible after the Nastić and Vasić scandals; and he is already giving fresh proof of his cynical view of all national aspirations by his attitude in the Albanian question. A radical revision of diplomatic and secret service methods in the Balkans can hardly be expected from a statesman with Count Aehrenthal's antecedents : and until such a revision occurs, no Southern Slav can regard official circles in Vienna with anything but extreme suspicion and reserve.

In Vienna the Christian Socialist party is not unconscious of the task which awaits Austria in the South ; but its extreme clerical leanings have unhappily obscured its very genuine sense of Austrian Imperial patriotism, and the bluff genius of its founder, Dr. Lueger, is sadly lacking to his divided party. On the other hand, a growth of statesmanlike feeling is noticeable among the German Liberals of Austria, who for so many years were content to regard their country merely as an inferior imitation of Germany, and who by their offensive attitude to all the other races of the Monarchy did so much to arrest the growth of " Austrian " patriotic feeling.

The triangular game between Vienna, Budapest and Agram will inevitably have fresh developments to show in the course of the next few years. Perhaps the key to the whole situation lies in the fact that the two provinces of Bosnia and Herzegovina have been definitely annexed, without any clear arrangement having been made as to their future status and ownership. Sooner or later a conflict must arise between Austria and Hungary for their possession—if only because by their new constitution no legislation of the Diet can pass into effect without the sanction of both Vienna and Budapest ! Count Andrássy's aim in occupying Bosnia in 1878 was to prevent in the narrow interest of the Magyars, the formation of a Serb national state. But in reality his action laid the seeds of a Croato-Serb state, far more dangerous to Hungary than any purely Serb state could be. The annexation brings the aspirations of Croato-Serb Unity within the range of practical politics, by transferring the centre of gravity among the Southern Slavs from the Serbs to the Croats, from Belgrad to Agram. Henceforth Agram must tend more and more to become the centre of Southern Slav life ; its culture is already greatly superior to that of Belgrad, and the removal of political restraint would be the signal for a fresh national revival.

The Serbs in Bosnia are as yet impervious to the new idea. Skilfully encouraged by Baron Kállay for many years to remain in narrow provincial grooves, but accustomed, in their ignorance of the world at large, to regard Belgrad with blind admiration, their leaders in the new Diet are intransigeant to a degree ; and nothing illustrates better their complete lack of perspective, than the impossible demands which they put forward in the land question and the futile obstruction to which they resorted when they saw those demands to be unattainable. But this slavish and unfounded belief in Belgrad is already on the wane in Bosnia. The influence of the Serbs of Croatia and

Slavonia is growing steadily stronger, and already a new Serb party, with capable leaders, has been founded in Bosnia to promote the idea of Croato-Serb brotherhood and union under the Habsburg sceptre.

The formation of a Trialist state would enormously strengthen Austria's prestige in the Western Balkans, and might well produce a reaction of feeling in Servia, where the barrenness of a Russophil policy has long been evident to far-sighted observers. In such an event, it is by no means impossible that Servia and Montenegro might be ready to conclude a military convention and Customs Union with the reconstructed Monarchy. The true obstacle to cordial relations between Austria and the Southern Slav world lies in the pretensions of the Magyar oligarchy.

For Austria the advantages from such a solution are very great ; and her future as a great Power depends upon it. Her permanent retention of Dalmatia depends upon her treatment of the Dalmatian Hinterland, Bosnia and Herzegovina. The population of Dalmatia, Istria and Croatia form the best recruiting ground for the Navy and the merchant service, and must therefore be propitiated by a Power which seeks to retain command of the Adriatic, and so paralyse any efforts of Italian Irredentism. Above all, Croatia and Dalmatia control Hungary's sole means of access to the sea, and thus from a strategic and geographical point of view, are of the first importance in Austria's struggle against Hungary—a struggle which cannot be averted in the near future.

The whole Eastern coast of the Adriatic still remains an unsolved equation in the arithmetic of Europe, and its solution depends upon the course of events among the Southern Slavs. If Vienna has at last realized her Imperial mission, if her statesmen have the courage and ability to identify the movement for Croato-Serb Unity with the requirements of Austrian patriotism, then the situation along the Adriatic and throughout the Western and Northern Balkans may undergo a speedy and beneficial change. By abandoning the old motto of " Divide et Impera " and by directing into her own channels a movement which is already too formidable to be permanently repressed, Austria will go far towards finding a solution for the complicated problem of nationality.

Croato-Serb Unity must and will come. It rests with Austria to delay its attainment for another generation and reap the disastrous fruits of such a policy, or by resolutely encouraging Southern Slav aspirations, to establish Austrian influence in the Northern Balkans by lasting bands of sympathy and interest. Upon Austria's choice of alternative depends the future of the Habsburg Monarchy.

Appendices

APPENDIX I

THE ELECTION OF FERDINAND I AS KING OF CROATIA

THIS document, drawn up by the Croatian Estates at Cetin on January 1, 1527, has been extracted from Kukuljevic *Jura Regni Croatiae Dalmatiae et Slavoniae*, Pars ii, vol. i, pp. 20–22.

Nos Andreas dei et Apostolice Sedis gratia Episcopus Tiieensis et Abbas Toplicenses, Joannes Torquatus Corbavie, Nicolaus Zrinij, Christophorus et Wolfgangus fratres ac Georgius de Frangepanibus Segnie, Veglie et Modrusie . . . (here follow the names of fifteen Croatian nobles) ceterique universi Nobiles et proceres nec non Nobilium Comitatuum, civitatum et districtuum, populorum, universitas Regni Croatie, ad perpetuam rei memoriam fatemur et recognoscimus, notumque facimus tenore presentium universis. Cum Serenissimus et potentissimus Princeps et Dominus Ferdinandus, Dei gratia Bohemie et Croatie Rex, Infans Hispaniarum sacri Romani Imperii Princeps Elector. Archidux Austrie. . . . (here follow his other titles, but no reference is made to Hungary), Princeps et Dominus noster gratiosissimus, miserit his diebus ad nos sacre sue Regie Majestatis consiliarios et oratores, Reverendum in Christo patrem et Dominum Do. Paulum de Oberstain, dei gratia Prepositum Viennensem, artium Philosophie et utriusque Juris Doctorem, Nicolaum Juritschiz Supremum Capitaneum, Joannem Cacziner et Joannem Puchler arcis Mechou Prefectum, Capitaneos, Dominos et Amicos nostros singulares ; et ipsi prefate Regie Majestatis nomine, tanquam pleno et sufficienti Mandato ab ea suffulti, nos requisierint, ut suam Majestatem pro nostro legittimo et naturali Rege et Domino, et Serenissimam Principem et Dominam Dominam Annam Hungarie, Bohemie et Croatie Reginam Principem et Dominum nostram gratiosiossimam pro nostra legitima et naturali Regina et Domina recognoseremus, illisque desuper debitum fidelitatis et homagii Juramentum prestaremus, quod nos exacte perpensis et diligenter consideratis Juribus, quibus idem Rex noster Serenissimus, una cum dicta Serenissima Domina Regina sua consorte, etc., pro sacro Regno Hungarie Jure hereditario obtinendo ad plenum et sufficienter fulcitus et provisus est, precipue vigore plurium inconvincibilium tractatuum, quos nos ex fundamento vidimus, legimus et relegimus, et postremo vigore electionis juxta Decreta et Sanctiones Regni Hungarie, in generali Statuum et ordinum illius Regni Conventu die xvi Mensis Decembris proxime elapsi in Oppido Posoniensi rite et legittime facte et publicate, nec non attentis pariter tot gratiis, opibus et emolumentis, quibus nos (et) Croatie Regnum sua Sacra Regina Majestas sola inter tot Christianos Principes pluribus annis contra immanissimos Thurcas, ne nos illorum seva tyrannide a fide orthodoxa et christiana republica deficere compelleremur, benigne conservavit, ac infinitis aliis beneficentiis et nos et universas res nostras pro singulari sua clementia et liberalitate sibi continue commendatas habuit : idcirco prefatorum Dominorum Oratorum juste et honeste requisitioni, tam devote quam reverenter annuimus, et hodie ante sumptum prandium, quum adhuc jejuni essemus, omnes et singuli unanimitate una voce et proclamatione nobis in generali nostro Conventu existentibus, prenominatum Serenissimum Dominum Regem Ferdinandum, in verum legittimum indubitatum et naturalem nostrum et tocius hujus inclyti Regni Croatie Regem et Dominum, nec non prefatam Serenissimam Dominam Reginam Annam in veram legittimam indubitatam et naturalem nostram et tocius Regni Croatie Reginam et Dominam, felici omine elegimus et recognovimus, assumpsimus, publicavimus, fecimus, constituimus et proclamavimus, proclamarique fecimus per vicos et plateas, prout tenore presentium eligimus, recognoscimus, assumimus, facimus, constituimus proclamamus et veneramur ambas suas Majestates in nostrum (ut premittitur) Regem et Dominum, Reginam et Dominam, omni meliori et alacriori via forma jure consuetudine et solenitate, quibus melius et efficacius facere potuimus (et) possumus, debuimus et debemus, una cum prestatione debiti fidelitatis et homagii juramenti, quod similiter publice alta et intelligibili voce, ut nobis dictus Reverendus D. Viennensis Prepositus sua quoque voce preibat, elevatis in altum digitis et manibus, cum summo gaudio prestitimus in forma, ut de verbo ad verbum sequitur, et est tale, videlicet : " Juramus et promittimus, quod ex nunc in antea erimus fideles semper et obedientes Serenissimo Principi et Domino Domino Ferdinando Bohemorum Regi, ejusque Consorti Serenissime Domine Anne, Nate Regine Hungarie et Bohemie, etc., Dominis nostris clementissimis et gratiosissimis, tanquam veris legittimis et naturalibus heredibus, ac Regi et Regine Regni Croatie, eorumque heredibus et locumtenentibus sive gubernatoribus, bonumque et commodum ac salutem eorum cogitabimus et pro virili nostra promovebimus, damna vero et prejudicia eorum pro posse nostro avertemus et precavebimus, aliaque omnia et singula faciemus, que bonis subditis et fidelibus servitoribus erga Dominum suum conveniunt, et ad que tenentur et astringuntur, quodque nullo unquam tempore deinceps aliquem

THE CROATIAN PRAGMATIC SANCTION (1712)

alium in Dominum aut Regem nostrum acceptare vel recognoscere velimus preter Majestates suas earumque heredes. Quodsi vero conjunctim vel divisim comperiremus unam aut plures personas, sive ecclesiastici sive secularis status et conditionis, que in prejudicium Majestatum suarum vel verbo aut facto alii vel aliis in bonum eorundem adherere vellent, Nos, ubi tales resciremus, continuo Majestates suas, vel superioritatem nobis per eas datam, admonebimus et avisabimus, juvabimusque omnes tales sic inobedientes ad debitam obedientiam reducere, omni penitus dolo et fraude remotis. Ita nos Deus adjuvet et sancta ejus evangelia."

Decantato desuper solemniter in Ecclesia hic Monasterii S. Marie visitationis fratrum minorum de observantia ad omnipotentis Dei laudem honorem et gratiarum actionem Cantico Te Deum laudamus, etc. cum campanarum frequenti sonitu et pulsatione. Quo fit inter cetera, quod nos omnes et singuli, una cum Heredibus posteris et successoribus nostris in infinitum, sumus facti veri naturales legittimi et indubitati subditi prefati Serenissimi Domini Regis et Serenissime Domine Regine nostre ac suorum Heredum in infinitum ex lumbis eorum descendentium. In quorum omnium supradictorum inconcussam et integram fidem et sufficiens testimonium, has literas fieri fecimus et ereximus, quas sigillis nostris solitis partim propriis partim communibus perpetuo valituras munimine roboravimus. Datum in Oppido Cetinensi in generali nostro Conventu in supranominato Monasterio celebrato die prima Mensis Januarii a Nativitate Domini Jesu Christi Salvatoris nostri Millesimo quingentesimo Vicesimo septimo.

APPENDIX II

THE CROATIAN PRAGMATIC SANCTION (1712) [457]

ACTA et Articuli Dominorum Statuum et Ordinum Regnorum Croatiae et Sclavoniae, in generali eorundem congregatione, Zagrabiae, in Arce Episcopali, Praesidente Illustrissimo et reverendissimo Domino Comite Emerico Eszterhazy de Galantha, Episcopo Zagrabiensi, Abbate B. Mariae Virginis de Thopuszka, Sacrae Caesareae Regiaeque Maiestatis Consiliario, et officii Banalis in Politicis Locumtenente, pro Die 9 et sequentibus Mensis Martii Anni 1712 celebrata, conclusi.

* * * *

Articulus Septimus.

Solicitudine atque zelo, quo Domini Status et Ordines ad assecurandam Patriam suam, consideratis tot et tantis eiusdem praeteritis periculis, et periculosis, evenibili quo casu Interregni tempore, revolutionibus, et praeterea ad promerendam ampliorem hoc suo facto Benignitatem atque benignum Regimen Augustissimae

[457] Extracted from Kukuljević, *Jura Regni Croatiae, Dalmatiae et Slavoniae*, Pars II, pp. 101–2.

349

APPENDIX III

Domus Austriacae, cuius deficiente Masculino (quem ut Divina bonitas in omne aevum superesse et florere admitat, optant) foeminini etiam Sexus retinendum, in eosdem Regium Jus, praerogativa, et Jure Regis et Regni exercendum subire cupient, eidemque se confidere, illius nimirum et talis foeminini Sexus, Augustissimi sanguinis Austriaci, qui videlicet non modo Austriae sed Provinciarum etiam Styriae Carinthiae et Carniolae possessionem habebit, et in modo fata Austria residebit : sinceris et unanimibus votis moti et dispositi, statuunt, declarant et resolvunt, suosque Dominos Ablegatos ad suam Sacratissimam Maiestatem Caesaream et Regiam exmittendos, in eo etiam et principaliter se instructuros decernunt, imo protinus instruunt ; ut nimirum hanc eandem praefatorum Dominorum Statuum et Ordinum, *motu eorum proprio*, *atque liberi arbitrii sensu*, expressam et manifestatam resolutionem ac fiduciam Sacratissimae Caesareae et Regiae Maiestati, nomine Dominorum Statuum et Ordinum praesentent et offerant ; et vicissim Sacratissimae Caesareae et Regiae Maiestatis, suorumque Augustissimorum Haeredum Gratiam, et pro tenore Clementissimarum resolutionum promissionum et assecurationum, Augustae reminiscentiae Austriacorum Principum et Regum Hungariae, publicis Diaetalibus Regni Hungariae et Partium eidem annexarum Actis, et privatis quoque, pro parte mentionatorum Dominorum Statuum et Ordinum emanatis Testimoniis insertis, benignam effectuationem, cum assecuratione Diplomatica, manutenendorum et conservandorum horum omnium, et quae praeterea pro bono et emolumento, atque Interesse securitatis, petenda ipsis occurrerint, petere et obtinere non intermittant.

APPENDIX III

ADDRESS OF THE CROATIAN DIET TO HIS MAJESTY, JUNE, 1848 [458]

YOUR MAJESTY,—

It is a well-known fact, that the three united kingdoms of Dalmatia, Croatia and Slavonia, though united with Hungary during seven and a half centuries in good and bad fortune, have yet always preserved their former rights and national liberty, and up to the present day have never recognized the usurped hegemony of Hungary. For even at the very beginning of their momentous union with Hungary, Coloman, the first joint King of Hungary and Croatia, was specially crowned with the crown of Croatia, and in later times the three united kingdoms elevated to the Hungarian throne several kings whom they had elected of their own accord, notably Charles Robert and Charles the Less. In Zara the nation

[458] Translated from Pejaković, *Aktenstücke*, p. 79 sqq. ; Šulek, *Naše Pravice* pp. 300–334.

of these kingdoms, assembled in the Diet, elected as Kings Ladislas of Naples and Tvrtko I of Bosnia, and in that decisive epoch when the House of Habsburg began to assert its rights to Hungary's throne, the Croats in the year 1527 at Cetin elected Ferdinand I as their King (after the Hungarians and Bohemians had already done this), and thereby of themselves established the fortune and fame of the present glorious dynasty. In the same way our nation proved our national and parliamentary independence, when, under Charles VI, it adopted the Pragmatic Sanction several years earlier than the Hungarians or any other people of the Austria of to-day ; for which it was loaded with praise by that monarch. It also signed quite independently of Hungary, the so-called Pacification of Vienna and the document of the Pragmatic Sanction. Thus these kingdoms were governed in every way as a free nation, absolutely equal to the Hungarian, as is proved not only by the above facts but also by the circumstance that these kingdoms received from several kings special Coronation diplomas, and that our Kings pledged themselves on oath, to protect not merely Hungary but also these three kingdoms in their rights and liberties.

The independent position of these three kingdoms is proved still more clearly by their own Diet, which has survived up to the present day quite independent of the Hungarian (Diet) ; in which up to the days of Ferdinand I the Kings themselves presided, and where they were generally elected and proclaimed also as Kings of Croatia and Dalmatia. In this Diet these kingdoms still possess their own legislature and preserved into recent times their own government, which was formerly entrusted to Voivodes of royal blood and later to Bans depending from the King. Envoys of these kingdoms often did not appear at all at the Hungarian Diet, and when they did, were regarded there as representatives of these kingdoms solely in respect of our joint Hungaro-Croatian state affairs, while the laws passed there were regarded as not binding within the boundaries of these Kingdoms, until they were recognized as binding in a special Diet of these Kingdoms. Consequently it often happened that such laws for our countries were drawn up in the Hungarian Diet solely by the representatives of these Kingdoms with their protonotary, and then submitted to the King for sanction. From this one can easily see the reason why those laws which relate exclusively to these Kingdoms are always entered separately in the Corpus Juris. In the same way resolutions of our own Diet were not seldom recognized as laws, though they had been neither drawn up nor debated in the Hungarian Diet ; as is sufficiently proved by our laws of 1492 and 1538, which occur in the Corpus Juris under the name " constitutiones et articuli Slavoniae."

The dignity of Ban, as is proved by countless charters and laws, extended from the Drave and Danube to the Adriatic Sea, and was always exercised, independently of the Kingdom of Hungary and its dignitaries, by Bans who were subject to the King alone. Indeed it is an uncontested fact that while Hungarian judges were forbidden to exercise their office on this side of the Drave, our Voivodes and Bans coined money distinct from the Hungarian. The political administration of the internal affairs of these countries, though the Council of Lieutenancy was introduced in Hungary much earlier, was none the less never subject to Hungary up to the year 1779 (when the specially introduced Royal Council for these countries was abolished), but was until the institution of this Croato-Slavonian Council, exclusively subject to the Ban with the Diet. It was only under Maria Theresa and Joseph II that the office of Ban and the Diet of these Kingdoms began gradually to lose their old glamour and their former power. But even then, when in the year 1790–1, by Law lviii, the powers of the now dissolved Hungarian Council of Lieutenancy were extended to these Kingdoms, such affairs as specially concerned these Kingdoms, were none the less reserved to our Diet, and thus the autonomy of these Kingdoms was recognized and transmitted to posterity, on the basis of the conditions of mutual union and of several fundamental laws, especially that of 1715 (Article cxx).

We have always been accustomed to see the best guarantee for the national independence of these Kingdoms in our noble Kings, whose innate sense of justice, as well as their solemn coronation oath imposed on them the duty of maintaining not only the Kingdom of Hungary but also these united Kingdoms in their rights and liberties. And so it happened that this unimpaired Royal power, which seemed threatening to the Magyars' desire for separation, was for us a sacred refuge, to which we could always appeal for help against our oppressors. Moreover these benefits of the Royal power were always repaid by our loyal nation with heroic self-sacrifice, when the rights and glory of the dynasty had to be defended ; as is sufficiently proved by countless charters in our archives.

But Your Majesty! the days of last March have robbed us loyal Croats, Slavonians and Dalmatians even of this our sole though powerful support. Our former oppressors have also become oppressors of your Majesty's Royal power. The old Hungary is falling to dust before the breath of the new age, and with it goes the old bond between Austria and Hungary. Austria and Hungary are no longer one State, but there is between the two states only the ephemeral bond, that one Monarch might rule over Austria and Hungary, if it were physically possible for him to be enthroned at one and the same time in Vienna and in Buda-Pest. Hungary's trade, her finances and Army, after being administered for centuries by the irresponsible Austrian government, have at present by a strange contrast their own ministers quite distinct from the Austrian (ministers), governmental responsibility being a fundamental law in Austria. And as it is physically impossible to be in two different places at the same time, Hungary has in its Palatine a real ruler, but in its hereditary sovereign—if we call things by their real names—merely a titular shadow-King, with whom it has intercourse through a Foreign Minister, who is in reality only in attendance upon Your Majesty's sacred person in order to prevent any wish of the loyal Slav peoples of Austria which may diverge from the intentions of the Magyars, from gaining access to Your Majesty's fatherly heart.

Your Majesty! The Croat clings stubbornly to that freedom which has been transmitted to him by his ancestors for so many centuries, and he understands too well the requirements of modern times, not to be heartily grateful to his sovereign for the ever memorable concessions made during the March days to the peoples of the unitary state (*Gesammtstaat*). But we confess that a cold shudder ran through our veins, and a dull foreboding came over us, when towards the end of last March we unexpectedly learnt that Hungary's new position towards Austria, instead of being complete amalgamation in the unitary state (as we could not but expect in view of the prevailing constitutional regime in Austria) is that of a state which is entirely independent and separate from Austria. This our alarm is easily explained, for if Austria be compared to a strong rock towering above the seashore, Hungary and our Kingdoms linked to it may be regarded as two different ships of unequal tonnage but under separate commands, which are bound by a strong cable to each other and also to the rock, which by its strength offers equal protection and safety to them both. If then while the sea runs high the larger ship unexpectedly attempts to slip its cable and put out onto the stormy ocean, it is clear that the smaller vessel, even though quite different, is in danger, if the towing cable is stronger than the shore cable, of being dragged out into the foaming sea, or if both cables are equally strong and the axe is not used, of being torn asunder. In such a dangerous position it is the duty of the smaller vessel to summon the larger to stop, and if that is of no avail, self-preservation bids it seize the axe and sever the cable, in order to let its dangerous neighbour go and so secure the safety it desires from the landward side.

This, Your Majesty, is the menacing situation of these three Kingdoms.

We loyal Croatians, Slavonians and Dalmatians neither can nor will recognize for these countries any Ministry which seeks to loosen the bands which have hitherto connected us with the State as a whole (*Gesammtstaat*). Let Hungary separate from the Monarchy, and consequently from these Kingdoms, if it has the inclination and the strength; but Croatia, Slavonia and Dalmatia are independent countries, and as such they not merely do not wish to loosen the existing bond with Austria, but far rather declare openly and unreservedly that they wish to enter into a still closer connexion with the now constitutional Empire of Austria, on the basis of complete equality of all nationalities. For if we and our fathers were only deterred from a similar step by the fact that the old Austria was governed absolutely, we for our part no longer see any obstacle to such a rapprochement, in view of (Austria's) metamorphosis to-day. We therefore submit in all humility for Your Majesty's sanction the following resolutions of our Diet, composed of elected representatives and meeting on June 5, 1848 :—

1. Since for the above reasons we do not recognize the present Hungarian Government for these countries, we regard all decrees, issued by the Hungarian Ministry in violation of our rights and with insult to the dignity of Ban, as unlawful and illegal, and at the same time would beg Your Majesty to declare invalid all such actions of the Hungarian Ministry as are injurious to us, and to shield and protect us in future from its fatal influences. Consequently the present provisional Government—augmented by certain individuals, especially from Lower Slavonia—should continue its present activity for which we confidently await your Majesty's approval, and for the future requests, that a Government may be formed for these Kingdoms, under the presidency of the Ban, consisting of several councillors, secretaries and other individuals, and responsible to the Diet of these Kingdoms, the councillors to be nominated by Your Majesty on the recommendation of the Ban, the others to be appointed by the Ban himself. But in order to better ensure the unity of the Monarchy as a whole, we are ready to subordinate even this our own provincial Government, in matters affecting the whole State, to the responsible Central Government of the Monarchy as a whole. These Kingdoms have all the more reason to hope that this resolution will be sanctioned, since it can be gathered from the above that they were administered since remote times independently of Hungary, and indeed from 1767 to 1779 possessed their own Chancellory, whose restoration they expressly reserved in 1791, when the Hungarian Council's sphere of action was extended to these countries. This shows that these Kingdoms do not aspire to anything new, but simply wish to revive their former inalienable rights, the more so as now the old joint Hungaro-Croatian Dicasteries, through which Your Majesty governed the so-called Hungarian territorial complex, have ceased to exist.

2. The conduct of finance and matters of defence and trade are to be assigned to the responsible Joint Ministry of the whole Empire. But that our provincial interests may be duly represented there, a Council of State responsible to the Diet of these Kingdoms and supplied with the necessary staff, should be appointed by Your Majesty in connexion with the central power, and should counter-

sign every measure of the Central Government relative to these Kingdoms.

3. The entire Military Frontier of these Kingdoms should also be subordinated, in the spirit of complete constitutional freedom, to the proposed provincial Government in all matters other than purely military, and only in purely military matters should be left under the Central War Ministry. The chief command over the entire military forces of these Kingdoms should, however, in accordance with ancient rights, be entrusted to the Ban of these countries.

4. The official language in the entire public life without any exception shall be the national Slav language (spoken) in these countries; and in such a way that even the decrees of the Central Government relative to these countries shall be published exclusively in this language.

5. All matters relating to internal administration will fall within the sphere of the Diet of these Kingdoms. But in respect of those affairs which proceed from the mutual relation of these Kingdoms to the State as a whole, these Kingdoms submit to the decisions of the Central Parliament, to which also the Central Ministry will be responsible for its actions.

But in order to prove that they definitely adhere to the Unitary State, these Kingdoms have already elected their deputies for the Central Parliament of the whole Monarchy, which is to be held on June 26; and these (deputies) are to convey, in the name of the whole nation, to the representatives of the other allied peoples of Austria, our just and earnest wishes of support and greeting.

6. Since it is natural that kindred nationalities should exercise a mutual attraction on each other, and since the Kingdom of Dalmatia, both in view of ancient chartered rights and the coronation oath and solemn promises of Your Majesty, forms an integral part of these Kingdoms, the said Kingdom of Dalmatia shall, both in respect of legislation and administration, be completely reunited to these Kingdoms, while the remaining Southern Slav portions of the Monarchy—namely the restored Serb Voivody, which we desire to see confirmed by Your Majesty in accordance with the old rights conferred upon the Serb nation, and then Lower Styria, Carinthia, Carniola, Istria and Görz—shall be brought into closer connexion with these Kingdoms.

7. These Kingdoms wish to maintain still further their friendly relation with the peoples inhabiting the Kingdom of Hungary in the sense of the Pragmatic Sanction and on the basis of the liberty, equality and fraternity of all nationalities living under the Crown of Hungary. But how this is to be carried out, the nation of these Kingdoms will decide when these its just wishes have been fulfilled

by Your Majesty, and when the true situation of Hungary in relation to the state as a whole, has become clearer.

8. All political and judicial officials, whose appointment lies with Your Majesty alone, are to be only provisionally appointed by the Ban, and such appointments are to be submitted to Your Majesty for approval.

9. Until a new legal procedure is introduced, appeal cases from these Kingdoms to the high courts in Hungary are not to be allowed.

10. With a view of furthering a fulfilment of our nation's wishes, Baron Francis Kulmer has been unanimously elected as representative of these Kingdoms at Your Majesty's Throne, which election we beg your Majesty graciously to confirm.

11. Finally we most solemnly declare that since under Article XI of 1608 the power of the Ban extends from the Drave to the Adriatic Sea, we regard as integral parts of these Kingdoms the counties of Požega, Virovitica and Syrmia, as also the regiments of Gradiška, Brod and Peterwardein, which are known legally and historically under the name of Lower Slavonia—further the districts of Fiume, Buccari and Vinodol, which according to Royal privileges, history and so many laws, belong to Croatia : and we shall manfully defend and protect all these as our lawful inheritance, against every hostile attack.

These are the just resolutions hitherto passed in our Diet, and the wishes expressed by our nation, which we desire to see sanctioned and fulfilled by Your Majesty.

Your Majesty ! More than once since the memorable days of March we sent our deputies to Your Majesty with wishes and grievances, but Your Majesty always saw fit to console us by referring them graciously to the Diet of these three united Kingdoms and bidding us in this Diet lay bare our wounds to the fatherly heart of Your Majesty, where we might certainly expect them to be healed. It is this which now happens in this our most dutiful representation, and we confidently hope, that Your Majesty will not withhold your royal sanction from the urgent and just resolutions of a loyal and brave people. For even though it be assumed that Your Majesty as King of Hungary felt prompted to various generous concessions, and hence as such could not make any disposition without the Hungarian nation, yet this very true though sad assumption does not in any way exist in respect to our three united Kingdoms : for the Kingdoms of Dalmatia, Croatia and Slavonia also have their own King, who has by a solemn oath pledged himself to defend unimpaired their rights and liberties, just as those of the Kingdom of Hungary, and who, having nowhere and never nor through our action been deprived of his traditional Royal authority, also enjoys the full power, in accordance with his oath and at the wish of his Kingdoms, to grant them his fatherly support where and as he pleases. And this King of Dalmatia,

ARTICLE XLII OF THE CROATIAN DIET

Croatia and Slavonia we honour and appeal to for help, in the crowned and exalted person of Your Majesty.

We respectfully remain Your Majesty's loyal subjects,

THE BAN AND DEPUTIES OF THE KINGDOMS OF DALMATIA, CROATIA AND SLAVONIA.

AGRAM, 5th and following days of June, 1848.

APPENDIX IV

ARTICLE XLII (1861) OF THE CROATIAN DIET [459]

On the ground of the Royal proposition (*predlog*) of February 26, 1861, No. 152, and on the basis of the proposals accepted in the Central Committee, after several weeks' deliberation and in consideration of the relations of the Triune Kingdom towards the Crown and Kingdom of Hungary, and after a provisional resolution passed in defence of its national liberty. . . .

The Sabor of the Triune Kingdom resolves as follows :—

§ 1. The Triune Kingdom of Dalmatia, Croatia and Slavonia in its present territorial extent—counting in this the counties of Fiume (with the town of Fiume, its district and the rest of the coast), Zagreb, Varaždin, Križevci, Požega, Virovitica and Syrmia, and the existing Military Frontiers, viz., eight Croatian and three Slavonian regiments, namely, those of Lika, Otočak, Ogulin, Slunj, the first and second Banal, and those of Križevci and St. George, then those of Gradiška, Brod and Peterwardein : likewise understanding as included in this the right to Medjumurje and the remaining virtual and territorial rights of these kingdoms—declares and announces, by way of its Sabor sitting in the capital Zagreb, that since the events of the year 1848 every other link, whether legislative or administrative or judicial, between the Triune Kingdom of Dalmatia-Croatia-Slavonia and the Kingdom of Hungary has legally entirely ceased ; except that His Majesty, their joint King, in accordance with their joint laws up to 1848, has, after the conclusion of a special Coronation diploma for the Triune Kingdom and the Kingdom of Hungary, to be crowned as King of Dalmatia-Croatia-Slavonia, and that by the free wish of the nation of the Triune Kingdom, with the identical crown and coronation ceremony by which he is crowned as King of Hungary ; and that to the Triune Kingdom, apart from its special fundamental status and constitutional rights, there also still belong all those public rights which belonged to the Kingdom of Hungary till the end of the year 1847, and in so far as these do not conflict indirectly or directly with their autonomy and independence as proclaimed above.

[459] Translated from B. Šulek, *Naše Pravice* (Our Rights), pp. 400–403.

357

§ 2. But bearing in mind its joint past history with the Hungarian Kingdom and its former joint constitutional life with it, and likewise bearing in mind the community of interests in respect of the maintenance and development of constitutional freedom : the Triune Kingdom of Dalmatia, Croatia and Slavonia, bringing under discussion His Majesty's Royal Proposition (*predlog*) of February 28, 1861 (No. 152), by which it is invited to express its wishes and ideas regarding its relations with the Kingdom of Hungary, declares valid the resolution of its Sabor, to the effect that the latter is ready, in view of the advantage and requirements which it has in common with the Kingdom of Hungary, to enter upon a still closer constitutional (*staatsrechtliche* : *državo-pravan*) connexion, as soon as on the part of the Kingdom of Hungary the above-mentioned independence and autonomy, as also the above-cited real and theoretical territorial extent of the Triune Kingdom, shall have been legally recognized.

§ 3. The above-mentioned constitutional bond between the Triune Kingdom of Dalmatia, Croatia and Slavonia would have to be—on the basis of their (i.e. the Triune Kingdom's) complete traditional constitution and the already mentioned independence of the Triune Kingdom and its equal rights as a state (*državne ravno pravnosti*)—founded on the joint legislature and the administration created by it, limited to those affairs of state which shall be specified more precisely by the terms of the alliance (*savez* [460]).

§ 4. The legislature and supreme executive in political affairs, and in matters of education, religion, and justice, as also the jurisdiction over all petitions, cannot be the subject of closer connexion between the Triune Kingdom and the Kingdom of Hungary, and, in the question of the mutual relations of these kingdoms, does not come into the discussion.

§ 5. As soon as the Parliament of the Kingdom of Hungary expresses itself on the principles of this resolution, committees shall be delegated by both sides, containing equal numbers and consisting of members of parliament ; for the purpose of meeting at the place fixed for special mutual discussion, and working out the details regarding this constitutional contract, and then submitting it to the said Sabor for approval.

§ 6. With regard to His Majesty's Royal Rescript of October 20, 1860, to the Ban, Baron Šokčevič, as also in view of the mutual intercourse of 700 years, this resolution will have to be communicated to the Hungarian Parliament for its information, and likewise laid before His Majesty on the occasion of the presentation of the Sabor's address, with the request that he may deign to send it, like a Royal proposition, to the Hungarian Parliament for deliberation, or if that Parliament should exercise its own power of initiative, that he may submit the latter's proposals to this Parliament for further deliberation.

[460] i.e. the agreement with Hungary.

APPENDIX V

THE INSTRUCTIONS OF THE CROATIAN DELEGATES DURING THE NEGOTIATIONS WITH HUNGARY (1867)

(Translated from Pliverić, *Beiträge zum ungarisch-kroatischen Bundesrechte*, pp. 265–269.)

As soon as legal conditions such as prevailed up to April, 1867, shall have been restored in the town of Fiume and its district and in the remainder of the Croatian coast lands, and as soon as the Hungarian Parliament declares its willingness to elect on its side a Regnicolar Deputation which would have to enter into negotiations with the delegates of the Diet of the Triune Kingdom, and as soon also as His Majesty, on the removal of those hindrances which disturb confidence towards the present Government, shall have commissioned his Government to enter into negotiations respecting the contents of the Coronation Diploma ; a deputation is to be elected from the Diet of the Triune Kingdom of Dalmatia, Croatia and Slavonia, according to the wording of the Diet's Address of May 18, 1867, and is to be sent to Pest, in order to attend the Coronation ceremony.

This Deputation has to adhere to the following Instructions :—

ARTICLE I. Since the constitutional relations between the Triune Kingdom and the Kingdom of Hungary have up till now not been regulated, the Deputation of the Triune Kingdom has, after its arrival in Pest, to enter into relations with that Deputation of the Hungarian Diet to which the composition of the Coronation Diploma has been entrusted, as with a Deputation enjoying equal position and equal rights with itself ;

ARTICLE II. The Deputation of the Diet of the Triune Kingdom of Dalmatia, Croatia and Slavonia has above all to declare to the Deputation of the Hungarian Diet, that it has been appointed in order to negotiate with the latter as representing the Hungarian Diet, respecting the contents of the Coronation Diploma, and to lay the result of this negotiation before the Diet of the Triune Kingdom from whom it received its commission, for definite decision ;

ARTICLE III. So long as the relations between the Triune Kingdom and the Kingdom of Hungary are not regulated, the Triune Kingdom of Dalmatia, Croatia and Slavonia stands on a constitutional basis of its own, differing from the constitutional basis of the Kingdom of Hungary. The Joint Relations between these two Kingdoms, based upon the Pragmatic Sanction, find their expression in the fact of their having a common Crown and Coronation. But since by Article XLII of 1861 the mode and form in which these Joint Relations were to be expressed has been left to further negotiations, the Deputation of the Triune Kingdom has

APPENDIX V

to inform the Deputation of the Hungarian Diet beforehand : that the Triune Kingdom can take part in the Coronation ceremony in no other way save by guarding itself against all legal consequences which might follow to its disadvantage, in regulating its future relations to the Kingdom of Hungary, and at the same time by demanding that as a legal guarantee the following clause should be inserted in the Coronation Diploma ; (*a*) that the Triune Kingdom even after the Coronation remains unimpaired in its present constitutional position, as laid down by its Diet in the year 1861 in Article XLII with His Majesty's consent ; and this until the relations between the one Kingdom and the other shall be definitely regulated by a free agreement between the two equal Diets. (*b*) That also neither in this manner nor in this case can the constitutional bond between the two Kingdoms be extended to the legislation and administration of such affairs (with their respective Budgets) as are under all circumstances reserved by § 4, Article XLII, 1861 to the autonomy of the Triune Kingdom as the minimum of independence necessary for the national development of this Kingdom ; and further that the territorial extent defined in § 1, Article XLII, 1861—including the town and district of Fiume— is to be regarded unquestionably as the indivisible and inalienable basis and condition of this Kingdom's existence and position as a state.

Therefore our Deputation will distinctly indicate to the Deputation of the Hungarian Diet, that these points are regarded as preliminary conditions, upon which even the possibility of any negotiation between one Kingdom and the other is made entirely dependent.

ARTICLE IV. As a consequence of the preceding articles, the Deputation of the Triune Kingdom will demand of the Deputation of the Kingdom of Hungary, its equal, that as a legal guarantee and assurance there be included in the Coronation Oath (a clause to the effect) that the Hungarian Laws of the year 1848 cannot even after the Coronation has taken place, be extended to the Triune Kingdom.

ARTICLE V. Since the Coronation is not a mere ceremony, but the legal and sworn guarantee for the accurate observance of mutual rights and duties, our Deputation will regard the preparations for the Coronation as incomplete and unfinished until, in agreement with the Crown or with His Majesty's Government, there be included in the Coronation diploma a guarantee possessing the validity and importance of a fundamental law, to the effect :

(*a*) that in the Triune Kingdoms of Dalmatia, Croatia, Slavonia henceforward the Government shall be conducted solely by such organs as are responsible to the Diet of this Kingdom.

(b) that the Croatian-Slavonian Frontier, as an exclusively
military institution, is regarded as at an end, and is united
with the Motherland—viz. the Kingdom of Dalmatia,
Croatia, Slavonia—in the legislation and administration
of political affairs and matters of religion and instruction.

(c) that Dalmatia in accordance with the constitutional law of
the Triune Kingdom of Dalmatia, Croatia, Slavonia is
united with the sister lands of Croatia and Slavonia.

(d) that the responsible Government of His Majesty is bound
to introduce in the next session of the Diet of the Triune
Kingdom a bill relating to the immediate execution of
the provisions recited under *a*, *b*, *c*, and relating to the
manner in which, in harmony with the loyal representation of Dalmatia the union referred to under *d* (?*c*)
is to be carried out.

ARTICLE VI. The Deputation will in the name of this Diet
decline to associate itself with the Resolution laid down between
His Majesty's Government and the Hungarian Diet respecting
Joint affairs and their management ; and it will on the contrary
issue the declaration that the Triune Kingdom of Dalmatia, Croatia,
Slavonia is a Kingdom of the Hungarian Crown enjoying in
every respect equal rights with the Kingdom of Hungary, and
that the above mentioned Resolution cannot possibly be applied
to it in a legal manner without its consent ; and in this respect the
Deputation will have to adhere to the views expressed in the
Address of May 18, 1867, both in dealing with His Majesty's
Government and also with the Hungarian Regnicolar Deputation.

ARTICLE VII. In general the Deputation has to adhere to the
principles and tendency expressed in the Address of May 18, 1867,
and to put forward the demand that the Coronation Diploma
shall be drawn up for the Triune Kingdom in a special original
copy in the Croato-Serb language.

APPENDIX VI

THE HUNGARO-CROATIAN COMPROMISE (1868)

ARTICLE XXX of 1868.

AN agreement having been reached between the Parliament of
Hungary on the one hand and the Parliament of Croatia, Slavonia
and Dalmatia on the other hand, with regard to composing by a
joint enactment the constitutional questions at issue between them :
this agreement, after being also confirmed, enforced and sanctioned
by His Imperial and Apostolic Royal Majesty, is hereby inarticulated as a joint fundamental law of Hungary and of Croatia, Slavonia
and Dalmatia, in the following terms :

APPENDIX VI

Since Croatia and Slavonia have alike *de 'jure* and *de facto* belonged for centuries to the Crown of St. Stephen, and since it is laid down in the Pragmatic Sanction also, that the lands of the Hungarian Crown are indivisible from one another: Hungary on the one hand, and Croatia and Slavonia on the other hand have upon this basis concluded the following agreement with a view to composing the constitutional questions at issue between them :—

§ 1. Hungary and Croatia, Slavonia and Dalmatia form one and the same state complexity, alike towards the other territories under His Majesty's rule and towards other countries.

§ 2. From this unity and coherence as a state it follows that the King of Hungary and of Croatia, Slavonia and Dalmatia is crowned with one and the same Crown and with one and the same Coronation ceremony, and that for all territories under the Crown of St. Stephen a joint Coronation Diploma is drawn up and published in the joint Parliament of these territories.

The original of this Coronation diploma, meanwhile, is in addition to the Magyar text to be drawn up in the Croat language also, and in it also the integrity and provincial constitution of Croatia, Slavonia and Dalmatia are to be guaranteed.

The Coronation Diploma of the year 1867 is also to be drawn up (now after the event) in the original Croat text and to be sent as soon as possible to the Sabor [461] of Croatia, Slavonia and Dalmatia.

§ 3. From the above mentioned indivisible unity of state it further follows that—in respect of all affairs which are common to all the territories of the Hungarian Crown and to the other territories of His Majesty, or which are disposed of by joint agreement—Hungary and Croatia, Slavonia and Dalmatia must possess one and the same representation and legislature, as also, as regards the executive power, a Joint Government.

§ 4. Croatia, Slavonia and Dalmatia recognize as valid and binding Article XII of the Hungarian Parliament of 1867, which defines the Joint Affairs existing between the territories of the Crown of St. Stephen and the other territories of His Majesty, or the affairs which are not actually Joint, but are to be disposed of by joint agreement, and also the manner in which such affairs are to be administered : and in the same way the agreements which have already come into effect on the basis of this law, especially Articles XIV, XV and XVI of 1867 ; but under the express condition that in future similar fundamental laws and agreements can only come into effect subject to the legal participation of Croatia, Slavonia and Dalmatia.

The fundamental law mentioned in this paragraph, as also the

[461] For the sake of clearness, I use the word " Sabor " to denote the Croatian Diet, the word " Parliament " to denote the Hungarian Parliament ; in the original, the same word is used for both.

Articles quoted, are to be now after the event drawn up in Croat original text and to be sent as soon as possible to the Croatian-Slavonian-Dalmatian Sabor for promulgation.

§ 5. Apart from those subjects which are common to the territories of the Crown of St. Stephen and to the other territories of His Majesty, there are also other affairs which are of common interest to Hungary and to Croatia, Slavonia and Dalmatia, and regarding which the joint character of legislature and government is by this agreement recognized as necessary for all territories of the Hungarian Crown.

§ 6. Such a Joint Affair of all territories of the Crown of St. Stephen is above all the adoption of the expenses of the Civil List.

§ 7. A further Joint Affair is the sanction of recruiting, the legislation on the Army system and liability to military service, and control of the quartering and victualling of the Army. In these respects however the following provision is made for Croatia, Slavonia and Dalmatia :—

(a) Out of the contingent of recruits which has to be sanctioned jointly, the portion falling to Croatia, Slavonia and Dalmatia is fixed according to the proportion of the total population : but it goes without saying that if the prevailing system of defence be revised, the details of the new system which is to be enforced will be applied to Croatia, Slavonia and Dalmatia also ;

(b) The recruits falling to the share of Croatia, Slavonia and Dalmatia will be enlisted in the regiments of these territories ;

(c) At the enlistment consideration will be had for the category to which the recruits are best suited, and the recruits of the sea coast will be for the most part assigned to the Navy.

§ 8. The financial system is a Joint Affair between Hungary and Croatia, Slavonia and Dalmatia, alike in respect to legislation and administration, in the manner described below. Consequently the Joint Parliament for all territories of the Crown of St. Stephen is entrusted with the regulation of the whole system of taxation; the ratification of direct and indirect taxes, both with respect to the categories of taxation and to tax-assessments; similarly the calculation, manipulation and collection of taxes ; the introduction of new taxes ; the ratification of the Joint Budget Proposals, as also the examination of balances respecting the Joint expenditure : the contracting of new State debts or the conversion of already existing debts : the administration, conversion, burdening or sale of immovable State property ; control over monopolies and royalties (*jura regalia majora*) and generally all provisions relating to any financial matter common to all territories of the Crown of St. Stephen. This holds good in respect to the sale of Croatian-Slavonian state lands (under which State forests are also included, § 2 Article XXXIV 1873), with the limitation that the Diet of Croatia, Slavonia and Dalmatia is also to be heard on this point, and that without its approval such a sale may not take place. With regard to all these affairs the Joint Financial executive—which is exercised by the Royal Hungarian Minister of Finance, responsible to the Joint Parliament—extends to Croatia, Slavonia and Dalmatia also.

§ 9. Joint Affairs of all territories of the Hungarian Crown are coinage—metal currency—and the banknote system : further, decisions as to minting and the general monetary standard ; examination and approval of commercial and State treaties, such as equally affect the territories of the Crown of St. Stephen : provisions respecting banks, institutions of credit and insurance ; concessions : weights and measures : the protection of patents and trademarks, official stamps,[462] the rights of literary and artistic property : Sea Law, Commercial Law, the law of Bills of Exchange and Mining Law, and generally matters of commerce, customs, telegraphs, Post Office, railways, harbours, shipping, and those roads and rivers which jointly concern Hungary and Croatia, Slavonia and Dalmatia.

§ 10. With regard to the regulation of Trade matters, including hawking, likewise with regard to societies which do not exist for public gain, and also with regard to passports, frontier police, citizenship and naturalization, the legislation is Joint, but the executive in respect of these affairs is reserved to Croatia, Slavonia and Dalmatia.

§ 11. Croatia, Slavonia and Dalmatia recognize that they are bound to contribute in proportion to their taxable capacity, to those expenses which are involved on the one hand by those affairs which are recognized as Common between the territories of the Hungarian Crown and the other territories of His Majesty, and on the other hand by the affairs described above as Common between all territories of the Hungarian Crown themselves.

§ 12. This proportion is—according to the same data, on the basis of which the proportion to be contributed by the territories of the Hungarian Crown to the expenses of the affairs common to them and the other territories of His Majesty was fixed for 10 years—for the like period

for Hungary 93·5,592,201 per cent.
for Croatia and Slavonia 6·4407799 per cent.

(for revision of this, see p. 374).

§ 13. Since however the total net income of Croatia and Slavonia could at present only cover the sum which according to the standard of taxable capacity contained in the preceding paragraph, would fall to the share of these countries out of the expenditure for Joint Affairs, only in the event of these countries making over the greater part of the sum required for their internal administration ; Hungary, having regard to the renewal of the fraternal relation which subsisted for centuries between it and Croatia and Slavonia, willingly agrees that at the very beginning a fixed sum, which is to be fixed from time to time

[462] I.e. the stamping of hallmarks, etc.

by an agreement for the costs of internal administration of these countries, shall be deducted and that the sum which remains over after satisfying the needs of the internal administration, shall be employed for the expenses involved by Joint Affairs.

§ 14. On the basis of the principle laid down in the preceding paragraphs the following financial arrangement has been reached between Hungary on the one hand and Croatia and Slavonia on the other hand :—

§ 15. The needs of internal administration of Croatia and Slavonia are fixed at 2,200,000 florins for these ten years during which the existing agreement between the territories of the Hungarian Crown and the other territories of His Majesty lasts.

§ 16. This sum is above all covered by 45 per cent. of the direct and indirect taxes and other public sources of income of Croatia and Slavonia ; that is, out of the total income of those countries 45 per cent. are paid over to whatever provincial or municipal bank the legislature or government of these countries [463] shall request.

§ 17. Fifty-five per cent. of the total income of Croatia and Slavonia are assigned to the Joint Treasury to cover the Joint expenses.

By § 3 of Article XXXIV, 1873, these paragraphs (15, 16, 17) and also §§ 25 and 26 (see below) were repealed and superseded by the following provision :—

The needs of the internal administration of Croatia-Slavonia, from January 1, 1873, for the period during which the agreement concluded between the territories of the Hungarian Crown and the other kingdoms and territories of His Majesty concerning the proportional contribution to the cost of Joint Affairs lasts, are in the first place covered by 45 per cent. of the direct and indirect taxes and other public sources of income of Croatia and Slavonia ; that is, out of the net public income of these countries 45 per cent. are paid over to whatever Croatian Slavonian provincial or municipal bank the Legislature or Government of these provinces shall request.

Fifty-five per cent. of the total income of Croatia and Slavonia are assigned to the Joint Treasury to cover the Joint expenses.

The 45 per cent. of the total income of Croatia and Slavonia are reckoned in this manner, that from the total direct and indirect taxes of Croatia and Slavonia, from the income of the State lands in Croatia and Slavonia and from other public sources of revenue only such disbursements are deducted, as are connected with the calculation and collection of taxes—in which the cost of the Joint financial adminstration is not included—with the administration of State lands, with the collection and direct manipulation of indirect taxes, monopolies and other public sources of revenue.

[For the modification of § 3, XXXIV, 1873, see § 4, XL, 1889 (p. 374).]

§ 18. From those sources of income which are, in accordance with §§ 16 and 17, to be divided between the demands of Croatia and Slavonia's internal administration and the Joint Expenses, are excluded the following :—

(a) Octroi taxes on wine and meat, which can in future also be used in Croatia-Slavonia to cover communal expenses, according to the practice which has hitherto prevailed.

(b) The income from frontier Custom dues, in accordance with Article XII of 1867.

[See § 5 of Article XL, 1889, p. 375, and also Article X, 1906, p.375–8.]

§ 19. Should the administrative territory of Croatia and Slavonia be increased by the actual reincorporation of Dalmatia or by the administrative union of the Military Frontiers, the revenues of the territories united to Croatia-Slavonia will similarly be divided between the requirements of the Croatian-Slavonian internal

[463] In the Croat text *sdruženih kraljevinah* (united Kingdoms).

administration and those of Joint Affairs, according to the scale fixed in §§ 16 and 17.

§ 20. The "additional tax" which at present exists both in Hungary and in Croatia-Slavonia, will be added to the State taxes.

§ 21. The Mortgage Redemption charge, however, will so far as Croatia-Slavonia are concerned continue to be administered by the Mortgage Redemption office of these countries until the Land Tax Redemption Debt has been entirely paid off, and will be paid by the Department of Finance to the account of that office. The joint guarantee of the territories of the Hungarian Crown for this Redemption Debt continues in future also, and any help which may be required for this purpose will be advanced from the Joint Treasury according to the practice adopted hitherto.

By Law XXVII of 1891 (only one paragraph) this was modified as follows :—

The annual requirement for the amortisation, payment of interest and administration of the Croatian-Slavonian Mortgage Redemption Debt is, until this Debt has been completely wiped out, to be met from the income of the combined direct taxes and Land Redemption charges of Croatia and Slavonia, and the sums corresponding to this requirement are to be paid over to the account of the Croatian-Slavonian Land Redemption Office. This provision has also to be followed in the reckoning which has to be made with Croatia-Slavonia for the year 1890. A special law, in the sense of subsections 1 and 2 of § 5 of Article LIV of 1890, deals with the surpluses which have accrued up to December 31, 1889, out of the proceeds of the Croatian-Slavonian Land Redemption charges, and whose amount was fixed by joint agreement at 2,660,000 florins.

The joint guarantee of the territories of the Hungarian Crown for this Land Redemption Debt remains in force.

§ 22. The Royal Hungarian Minister of Finance exercises the executive in Croatia-Slavonia in respect of direct and indirect taxes, monopolies, stamps, dues and charges and also of the State lands through the Finance Department in Agram, which is to be appointed by him.

§ 23. Those sections of the Provincial Treasury in Agram, which deal with matters belonging to Croatia and Slavonia's autonomous sphere of influence, are in every respect subject to the control of the said countries. The balances drawn up by the said Provincial Treasury sections are however to be communicated to the Joint Finance Minister, in order that the financial data of all the territories of the Hungarian Crown may be compiled in their entirety.

§ 24. The autonomous Provincial Government and the executive authorities of Croatia-Slavonia are entirely ready to assist the organs of the Joint Finance Minister in securing and collecting the revenues of State, and carefully comply with the legal decrees of the Finance Minister, as responsible to the Joint Parliament.

§ 25. Should the 45 per cent. of the total income in certain years not suffice to cover the requirements of the internal administration of Croatia-Slavonia, as laid down above (§ 15), then Hungary advances the balance.

§ 26. If, on the contrary the said 45 per cent. amount to a larger sum than that which was fixed by agreement for the requirements of Croatia-Slavonia's internal administration, then the surplus is employed to cover Joint expenses.

[§§ 25 and 26 were superseded by § 3, XXXIV, 1873, see above, p.365.]

§ 27. Should however the revenues of Croatia and Slavonia, in consequence of increase in taxable strength, exceed that portion of the Joint expenses which would fall upon them according to the standard of taxable strength contained in § 12, then the surplus is at the disposal of Croatia-Slavonia, without Croatia and Slavonia being bound to cover those sums with which they have fallen into arrears in previous years in respect to the Joint expenses.

§ 27 was repealed by Article X, 1906 (quem vide).

§ 28. The statement of the revenues of Croatia and Slavonia is drawn up on the basis of the principles contained in the above paragraphs, and is submitted to the Joint Legislature of the territories of the Hungarian Crown at the same time as the statement of accounts of all the territories of the Hungarian Crown.

The statements, after being examined there are also communicated to the Diet of Croatia and Slavonia for its cognizance.

[See § 6, XL, 1889, revised by X, 1906, see p. 375].

§ 29. The keeping of special returns as to the revenues of Croatia and Slavonia can only come into effect after the agreement has been reached, viz., from January 1, 1869. Until the agreement has been accepted by both legislatures and sanctioned by His Majesty, the Estimates for 1867 are authoritative so far as Croatia and Slavonia are concerned, in assigning the expenses of internal administration.

§ 30. Of Croatia and Slavonia's arrears of taxation up to the end of 1867 inclusive and still claimable, 63 per cent. are to be applied for the requirements of the said countries, while 37 per cent. fall to the Joint Treasury.

§ 31. With regard to those affairs which are Common between the territories of the Hungarian Crown and the other territories of His Majesty, as also with regard to those which have been described in the above paragraphs as common for the territories of the Hungarian Crown themselves, the legislative right belongs to the Joint Parliament of all the territories of the Hungarian Crown, which is to be summoned annually to Pest.

§ 32. In this Joint Parliament Croatia and Slavonia are represented, in proportion to the number of their population, by twenty-nine deputies. The town of Fiume and the coast district are not included in this, in consideration of the reason mentioned in § 66. Should the number of the Hungarian deputies alter in course of time, the number of the deputies of Croatia-Slavonia will be fixed according to the same principles as are followed in fixing the number of the Hungarian deputies, the proportion to the population being retained.

§ 33. If the population of Croatia-Slavonia should be increased, whether by the administrative union of the Military Frontiers, or by the reincorporation of Dalmatia, then the number of deputies of the said countries will likewise be increased in proportion to the increase of the population.

By § 2 of Article XV, 1881, these §§ 32 and 33 were repealed, and the following clause was substituted :—

§ 2. The number of the deputies to be sent by Croatia-Slavonia to the House of Deputies of the Joint Hungarian Parliament is for the future—beginning at the date when the population of the Military Frontiers, after their administrative union with the said countries, shall actually take its place in constitutional life—fixed at the definite number of 40, irrespective of the proportion of population. In this the town of Fiume and the Coast district are not included, in accordance with the reason adduced in § 66 of Article XXX of 1868. Should the number of members of the House of Deputies of the Joint Hungarian Parliament in general be altered by a subsequent law, then the above mentioned number of Croatian-Slavonian members of the Hungarian House of Deputies will be altered in the same proportion in which the total number of members to be fixed by the new law will stand towards the present total number of members.

§ 34. Croatia, Slavonia and Dalmatia elect their deputies to the Joint Parliament from the midst of their own Sabor, for the whole period for which the mandate of the Joint House of Deputies is valid.

In the event of the Croatian-Slavonian Dalmatian-Sabor being dissolved in the interval, the deputies of Croatia, Slavonia and Dalmatia remain members of the Joint Parliament until the newly summoned Croatian-Slavonian-Dalmatian Sabor elects new deputies.

[To this clause the following addition was made by § 4, XXXIV, 1873 :—

In the said event the Diet of Croatia, Slavonia and Dalmatia is to be convoked within three months reckoned from the dissolution.]

§ 35. The deputies of Croatia, Slavonia and Dalmatia exercise their right of personal expression of opinion and voting during the debating of those affairs which have been declared as common in the above paragraphs, and further they do so independently, without instructions, in exactly the same way as the other members of the Joint Parliament.

§ 36. Croatia, Slavonia and Dalmatia also send to the Upper House of the Joint Parliament two deputies from their midst.

[This paragraph was repealed by § 3 of Article XV, 1881, which runs as follows :—]

Beginning from the date indicated in § 2 of the present law (see above, § 33), Croatia and Slavonia send to the Upper House of the

Joint Parliament three deputies from the midst of their own Diet.

§ 37. The Magnates, as also those temporal and ecclesiastical dignitaries of Croatia, Slavonia and Dalmatia who possessed seats and votes in the Upper House of the Hungarian Parliament previous to 1848, will in future also be members of the Upper House with equal rights, for so long as this House is not organized on a different basis.

[This reorganization was carried out by Article VII of 1885].

§ 38. The Joint Affairs will, so far as possible, be discussed in the Joint Parliament first of all and one after the other ; in any case care will be taken that the deputies of Croatia, Slavonia and Dalmatia shall be left at least three months' time annually for the treatment of their internal affairs in their own Diet.

§ 39. The total costs of the Joint Parliament and consequently also the salaries and board allowance of the deputies of Croatia, Slavonia and Dalmatia are to be covered from the Joint Treasury.

§ 40. Since the Joint Parliament of the territories of the Hungarian Crown exercises one part of its functions, namely the fixing of the estimates for those Joint Affairs which are recognized as originating from the Pragmatic Sanction, through a Delegation sent from its midst, there shall be elected to the Hungarian Delegation by the Joint Parliament out of the deputies of Croatia, Slavonia and Dalmatia as many members as fall to their share according to the standard by which the said countries are represented in the Joint Parliament.

[§ 40 was repealed by Article XV of 1881.}

§ 41. It is consequently established that from among the deputies of Croatia-Slavonia four members are to be elected to the Delegation from the House of Deputies, and one member from the Upper House.

§ 42. Should the number of the deputies of the Croatian-Slavonian-Dalmatian Diet increase as a result of the extension of territory mentioned in § 33, then the number of those members who are elected to the Delegation from among the deputies of Croatia, Slavonia and Dalmatia will be increased in corresponding proportion.

[Repealed by Article XV of 1881.]

§ 43. With regard to all those affairs which in Article XII of 1867 and in the present agreement have been declared as common for all territories of the Hungarian Crown—with the exception of the affairs contained in § 10—the executive power is exercised in Croatia, Slavonia and Dalmatia also, by the Central Government residing in Budapest, through its own organs.

§ 44. From the standpoint of the representation of Croatia, Slavonia and Dalmatia's interests, a special Croatian-Slavonian-Dalmatian Minister without portfolio is nominated for these countries as part of the Central Government residing in Budapest. This

Minister is a member of the Joint Cabinet Council, with the right to vote in it, and is responsible to the Joint Parliament. He likewise forms the connexion between His Majesty and the Provincial Government of Croatia, Slavonia and Dalmatia.

[To this paragraph the following addition was made by § 5 of Article XXXIV, 1873 :—

In this capacity he submits to His Majesty unaltered and without delay the reports of the Ban ; and only in the event of doubts arising from the standpoint of the State community or community of interests laid down by Article XXX. of 1868, and in case it should not be possible to remove these doubts after the Ban has been consulted, he submits, simultaneously but separately, to His Majesty his own remarks regarding them, or as the case may be the remarks of the Joint Hungarian Government.

§ 45. The Central Government makes a point of acting on the territory of Croatia, Slavonia and Dalmatia in harmony with the special Government of these countries ; as, however, it is responsible for its action to the Joint Parliament, in which Croatia, Slavonia and Dalmatia are also represented, its measures must consequently be supported by the Croatian-Slavonian-Dalmatian Provincial Government and Courts, and indeed must be directly carried into execution by them, in so far as the Central Government possesses no organs of its own.

§ 46. At the request of Croatia-Slavonia and Dalmatia an assurance is given to these countries, that the Central Government shall appoint natives of Croatia-Slavonia-Dalmatia alike to the Croatian-Slavonian departments of the central offices, and to their organs in the territory of the said countries, so far as is at all possible, in consideration of the necessary technical training.

§ 47. With regard to all those subjects which are not reserved in this agreement to the Joint Parliament and the Central Government, Croatia-Slavonia and Dalmatia enjoy full autonomy alike in the legislative and the executive domain.

§ 48. Consequently the autonomy of Croatia, Slavonia and Dalmatia extends, alike in respect of legislature and administration, to matters of Administration, Religion and Instruction in these countries, as also to (matters of) Justice, under which is also to be understood the administration of justice in every instance, with the exception of Admiralty courts.

§ 49. With regard to the requirements of the Fund for Religion and Schools, the debts will be disposed of, so far as the past is concerned, by mutual agreement.

[To which the following addition was made by § 6 of Article XXXIV, 1873.]

After this mutual agreement has been reached, the part relating to Croatia and Slavonia will be separated from the jointly administered funds and paid over to the Autonomous Government of the said countries.

§ 50. At the head of the Autonomous Provincial Government in Croatia-Slavonia and Dalmatia stands the Ban, who is responsible to the Croatian-Slavonian-Dalmatian Diet.

§ 51. The Ban of Croatia, Slavonia and Dalmatia is appointed by His Imperial and Apostolic Royal Majesty, on the proposal and under the signature of the Royal Hungarian Joint Premier.

§ 52. The civil dignity of the Ban, however, is in future separated from the military, and it is established as a rule, that for the future a military person may not exercise any influence upon the civil affairs of Croatia, Slavonia and Dalmatia.

[§ 52 was superseded by § 7 of Article XXXIV, 1873, as follows :— The Ban may not possess any military position (sphere of interest).]

§ 53. The Ban in his civil position bears in future also the title " Ban of Croatia, Slavonia and Dalmatia," and enjoys all privileges and dignities of the Banal office, which are compatible with his new position. Consequently he remains in future also a member of the Upper House of the Joint Parliament.

[§ 53 was repealed by § 8 of Article XXXIV, 1873, and replaced by the following provision :—

The Ban bears in future also the title " Ban of Croatia, Slavonia and Dalmatia," and remains a member of the Upper House of the Joint Parliament.]

§ 54. The future organization of the autonomous Provincial Government is to be fixed by the Croatian-Slavonian and Dalmatian Diet, on the proposal of the Ban and with the sanction of His Imperial and Apostolic Royal Majesty.

§ 55. After this agreement has been sanctioned, the Croatian-Slavonian Aulic Chancellory will be at once dissolved.

§ 56. In the whole territory of Croatia-Slavonia the Croatian language is the language alike of the Legislature, the Administration and the Judicature.

§ 57. Inside the frontiers of Croatia-Slavonia the Croatian language is prescribed as the official language for the organs of the Joint Government also.

§ 58. Croatian-Slavonian applications and petitions from Croatia-Slavonia are to be accepted by the Joint Government also, and the decision respecting them is to be issued in the same language.

§ 59. It is further declared that the deputies of Croatia-Slavonia, as the deputies of a political nation posssessing a special territory of its own, and of a country which in its internal affairs possesses a Legislature and Government of its own, may use the Croatian language also, alike in the Joint Parliament and in its Delegation.

§ 60. The laws enacted by the Joint Legislature for Croatia-Slavonia and Dalmatia are to be drawn up also in a Croatian original text, signed by His Majesty, and are to be sent to the Diet of the said countries.

§ 61. Croatia, Slavonia and Dalmatia can, within their own frontiers, in their internal affairs, use their own combined colours and coat of arms, the latter, however, being surmounted by the Crown of St. Stephen.

§ 62. The emblem of the Joint Affairs of the territories of the Hungarian Crown is formed by the combined arms of Hungary and of Croatia, Slavonia and Dalmatia.

§ 63. At times when Joint Affairs are being debated, the combined Croatian-Slavonian-Dalmatian flag is to be hoisted beside the Hungarian flag, upon the building in which the Joint Parliament of the territories of the Hungarian Crown is being held.

§ 64. On the coinage which is struck by the territories of the Hungarian Crown, the title " King of Croatia, Slavonia and Dalmatia is also to be included in the Royal title.

§ 65. Hungary recognizes the territorial integrity of Croatia, and promises to promote its completion. It will in future be specially insistent that that portion of the Military Frontiers which belongs to Croatia-Slavonia and the military communes situated therein shall be united with these countries alike in legislative, administrative and judicial matters ; and just as Hungary has hitherto made representations with regard to this matter on repeated occasions, so in future also it will demand the reincorporation of Dalmatia, on the ground of the rights of the Holy Hungarian Crown, and will promote its union with Croatia. Regarding the conditions of this reincorporation, however, Dalmatia also is to be consulted.

§ 66. In the sense of the preceding paragraph the following are recognized as belonging to the territory of Croatia, Slavonia and Dalmatia :—

1. That territory which together with the town and district of Buccari, at present belongs to the County of Fiume, with the exception of the town and district of Fiume. The town, harbour and district of Fiume form a separate body attached to the Hungarian Crown (*separatum sacrae regni coronae adnexum corpus*), with regard to whose special autonomy and the legislative and administrative conditions relating thereto, an agreement is to be reached by means of negotiations between the Hungarian Parliament, the Diet of Croatia-Slavonia and Dalmatia and the town of Fiume in joint understanding.
2. The County of Agram with the towns of Agram and Karlovac (Karlstadt) and the free district of Turopolje.
3. The County of Varaždin with the town of Varaždin.
4. The County of Križevci (Kreuz), with the town of Križevci.
5. The County of Požega with the town of Požega.
6. The County of Virovitica with the town of Virovitica.

7. The County of Syrmia.
8. The County of Bjelovar.
  [Point 8 was added by § 9 of Article **XXXIV**, 1873.]
Further the following frontier regiments :—
  1. That of the Lika.
  2. That of Otočak.
  3. That of Ogulin.
  4. That of Slunj.
  5. The first Banal Regiment.
  6. The Second Banal Regiment.
  7. That of Varaždin-Križevci.
  8. That of Varaždin-St. George.
  9. That of Gradiška.
  10. That of Brod.
  11. That of Peterwardein.
finally the present Dalmatia.

  [Points 7 and 8 drop off, under § 8, XXXIV., 1873.)

§ 67. Until the territorial integrity of Croatia, Slavonia and Dalmatia, as described in the preceding paragraphs, has been restored, Hungary consents that the Customs Offices in Semlin, Mitrovica, Rača, Klenak and Jakova be separated from their present direct administrative control and subordinated to the Agram Finance Department, as recognition of the territorial link.

§ 68. After this agreement has been sanctioned, those laws and existing resolutions which conflict with it, cease to be valid.

§ 69. On the contrary all those constitutional rights and fundamental laws, whose enjoyment and protection have in the past extended equally to Hungary and Croatia-Slavonia, and which do not conflict with this agreement, are regarded in future also as joint rights and fundamental laws of the territories of the Hungarian Crown.

§ 70. This agreement is, after receiving the Royal sanction, to be inarticulated as a Joint Fundamental Law of Hungary and Croatia, Slavonia and Dalmatia.

———————

The financial provisions of the Compromise were revised by *Law XL of* 1889, which ran as follows :—

Since the period of duration of the financial portion of the Agreement contained in Article XXX of 1868 (as laid down in § 12 of this law), and also the period of its provisional extension under Articles XLIII of 1887 and XXXIV of 1888 have expired ; a new financial agreement has been reached by joint consent, between the Hungarian Parliament on the one hand and the Diet of Croatia, Slavonia and Dalmatia on the other hand, in the manner prescribed in § 70 of Article XXX of 1868. This agreement, having also been confirmed, enforced and sanctioned by His Imperial and Apostolic Royal Majesty, it is hereby inarticulated as a Joint Fundamental Law of Hungary and of Croatia, Slavonia and Dalmatia, as follows :—

§ 1. According to the principle recognized on the part of Croatia, Slavonia and Dalmatia in § 11 of Article XXX of 1868, that these countries are bound to contribute, in proportion to their taxable capacity, to those costs which on the one hand the territories of the Hungarian Crown and the other territories of His Majesty have recognized as Common, and on the other hand to those which are involved by the Affairs declared as Common by all the territories of the Hungarian Crown in the said Article XXX of 1868 ; this proportion of taxable capacity has—according to the same data on the basis of which the quota to be contributed by the territories of the Hungarian Crown towards the expenses incurred jointly with the other territories of His Majesty was fixed by Article XXIII of 1887 up to the end of 1897—been fixed for the same period at

92·064805 for Hungary.

7·935195 for Croatia and Slavonia.

§ 2. Since, however, the considerations indicated in § 13 of Article XXX of 1868 still hold good, Hungary hereby willingly consents, that out of the revenues of Croatia and Slavonia there shall first of all be deducted a certain portion which is fixed in this Agreement for the period of its validity for the expenses of internal administration of these countries, and that the sum which remains after the requirements of internal administration have been satisfied shall be employed for the expenses of Joint Affairs.

§ 3. On the basis of the principles laid down in the preceding paragraphs, the following financial agreement has been reached between Hungary on the one hand and Croatia and Slavonia on the other hand.

§ 4. From January 1, 1890, up to the date till which the agreement regarding the quota to be contributed to the expenses of the Joint Affairs of the territories of the Hungarian Crown and of the other kingdoms and territories of His Majesty lasts, the requirements of the internal administration of Croatia-Slavonia is to be covered first of all by 44 per cent. of the direct and indirect taxes, as also of the other public income of Croatia and Slavonia, in so far as these do not fall under the provisions of § 5 of the present law ; that is, 45 per cent. of the net public income of these territories are to be paid over to whichever provincial or local treasury the legislature or government of these territories shall request.

56 per cent. of the total revenue of Croatia and Slavonia are to be paid over to the Joint Treasury, to cover the joint expenses.

The 44 per cent. of net public revenue of Croatia and Slavonia are calculated in such a way that from the total direct and indirect taxes of Croatia and Slavonia, from the revenue of the statelands situated in Croatia and Slavonia and from the other public sources of revenue (so far as these do not fall under § 5 of the present law) only such expenses are to be deducted as are connected with the calculation and collection of taxes (under which the cost of the joint financial administration is not included), with the administration of statelands, with the collection and direct administration of indirect taxes, dues and other public sources of income.

Arrears of taxes due up to the end of 1867 and collected since January 1, 1890, are to be dealt with in future under § 30, XXX, 1868.

Paragraphs 5 and 6, having been subsequently repealed, need not be given here. The latest Financial Compromise between Hungary and Croatia was concluded in 1906 and runs as follows :—

Article X, 1906.

The period of the financial Compromise as laid down in Article XL of the year 1899 and also the period for which this was extended by Articles XLII, 1897, V, 1899, XLVII, 1899, XXXII, 1900, XXIX, 1901, and XXV., 1902, having lapsed, a new Financial Compromise has been concluded by joint agreement, in accordance with § 70, XXX, 1868, between the Parliament of the kingdom of Hungary on the one hand and the Parliament of the kingdom of Croatia Slavonia and Dalmatia on the other hand. This agreement having been approved, confirmed and sanctioned by His Imperial and Royal Apostolic Majesty, is hereby enacted as a joint fundamental law of the Kingdom of Hungary and the kingdoms of Croatia-Slavonia and Dalmatia, as follows :—

§ 1. All claims or debts of Hungary towards Croatia and Slavonia or of Croatia and Slavonia towards Hungary in the past— including the year 1903, up to December 31—are to be regarded as mutually cancelled, so that from the period previous to January 1, 1904, no debt of any kind exists any longer between Hungary and Croatia and Slavonia.

§ 2. According to the principle recognized by the Kingdom of Croatia-Slavonia and Dalmatia in § 11, XXX, 1868, that these territories are bound to contribute, according to their taxable capacity, to those expenses which are necessitated on the one hand by the affairs recognized as common between the territories of the Hungarian Crown and the other territories of His Majesty and on the other hand by the affairs described in the aforesaid Article XXX, 1868, as common to all the territories of the Hungarian Crown ; this proportion of taxable capacity is fixed for the period from January 1, 1904, to December 31, 1913, on the basis of the total revenues of Hungary on the one hand and Croatia-Slavonia on the other hand during the years 1893 to 1902, from the direct taxes—excluding the military exemption tax and the transport tax—from the stamp and law duties and from the tobacco and salt monopolies, in the proportion of

91·873 per cent. for Hungary.

8·127 per cent. for Croatia and Slavonia.

§ 3.   Since, however, the considerations laid down in § 13, XXX, 1868, are still in force, the Kingdom of Hungary gladly consents now also, that first of all a fixed amount—which will be fixed in this Compromise for the period of its duration, for the internal administration of these territories—shall be deducted from the revenues of Croatia and Slavonia and that what remains over after the requirements of internal administration, shall be devoted to the expenditure involved by Joint affairs.

§ 4.   On the basis of the principles stated in the above paragraphs the following financial compromise has been concluded between Hungary on the one side and Croatia and Slavonia on the other.

§ 5.   From January 1, 1904, to the end of 1913, the requirements of the internal administration of Croatia are met out of the public revenues of Croatia and Slavonia as defined below—in so far as these revenues do not fall under § 6 of this law—namely, out of the public revenues of these territories the portion fixed below is to be paid over to whatever Croatian-Slavonian provincial or municipal treasury the legislature or government of these territories [464] shall prescribe.

The remainder of the net public revenue of Croatia and Slavonia is to be paid into the Joint Treasury (§§ 12 and 27, XXX, 1868) in payment of the proportion due for Joint Expenses.

In order to render it possible to calculate the net public revenue of the kingdom of Croatia and Slavonia, a distinction must be drawn

(1) between those sources of revenue in respect of which the joint public revenue drawn from them can be fixed as undoubtedly belonging to Croatia and Slavonia, and

(2) those sources of revenue, in respect of which the joint public revenue drawn from them cannot be fixed as undoubtedly belonging to Croatia and Slavonia.

The net public revenue of Croatia and Slavonia derived from sources of income which fall under (1) is calculated in such a manner that from the income of state lands situated in Croatia and Slavonia and from other public revenue (such as does not fall under § 6 of this law) only such expenses are to be deducted as are connected with the calculation and collection of taxes (in which the expense of the joint financial administration is not included), with the administration of state lands, and with the collection and direct manipulation of the remaining public revenue.

The revenue of Croatia and Slavonia derived from sources of income which fall under (2)—especially from the transport duty

[464] In the Croat text, "sister-kingdoms."

(under Law XX, 1875), from the existing octroi duties on wine and meat, from lotteries and from such revenue as, accruing in the future, would fall under the sources of income mentioned in (2)—is calculated in such a manner that from the joint gross revenue of the territories of the Hungarian Crown falling under these heads, the expenses of collection and direct administration of this revenue—in which the expense of the joint financial administration is not included—are deducted ; and out of the net yearly revenue of the territories of the Hungarian Crown 8·127 per cent. is reckoned as the revenue which Croatia and Slavonia derives from these sources, in proportion to taxable capacity.

Forty-four per cent. form that portion of the net public revenue of Croatia and Slavonia which (by alinea 1 of this §) is to be applied to the requirements of internal administration ; but with this limitation, that the 44 per cent. quota of the net revenue falling under (2) may not exceed that sum which would be realized, if this revenue had exceeded the revenue of the previous year (beginning with 1905) by 5 per cent. The surplus over that sum is to be employed firstly in meeting a deficit, if the net revenue from the state forests situate in Croatia and Slavonia should fall below the net revenue of 1902, or if the revenue from one of the sources specified under (1) should cease as the result of legislation, or be so affected thereby as to fall beyond the net revenue of 1902. But the sum which is not required for this purpose is to be paid into the Joint Treasury, together with 56 per cent. of the net revenue of Croatia and Slavonia calculated on the above basis.

§ 6. Paragraph 18, XXX, 1868 is amended in such a way that the following are excluded from the revenue which under § 5 has to be divided between the requirements of the internal administration of Croatia and Slavonia and the expenditure for Joint Affairs :—

(a) revenue from frontier Customs, which in future also are to be calculated as contributing towards the payment of the affairs recognized as Common between the territories of the Crown of St. Stephen and the other territories of His Majesty.

(b) excise duties on wine and meat, which are in future also to be applied to meeting communal expenditure.

(c) The clergy tithes paid by the Catholic population of the county of Bjelovar, which can also be applied to meeting the autonomous expenditure of Croatia and Slavonia.

(d) The military exemption tax (under Art. XXVII, 1880) which as revenue devoted to a particular purpose, cannot be a subject for division.

§ 7. The annual settlement of accounts between the kingdom of Hungary and the kingdom of Croatia and Slavonia is to be made in the manner developed by § 5, XL, 1889, with the following alterations :—

APPENDIX VI

I. The actual revenue derived by Croatia and Slavonia from transport duty (under XX, 1875), excise duties on wine and meat, and lottery monopolies, and the expenses incurred in connexion with them, are to be omitted from this settlement; in their place, the net revenue of Croatia and Slavonia derived from such sources of income as are subject to dispute, is fixed in such a way that, when the transport duty (under XX, 1875) excise duties on wine and meat and lottery monopoly have been finally calculated, the actual joint revenue of the territories of the Hungarian Crown are reckoned up, the following deductions being made in the particular year :—

(1) The joint expenses connected with the administration of the transport duty (under XX, 1875) and those specified in the final settlement as direct taxes and Land Redemption charges for all the territories of the Hungarian Crown.

(2) The joint expenses connected with the administration of the excise duties on wine and meat, for all the territories of the Hungarian Crown, with the exception of

  (a) the actual expenses incurred on the basis of § 1, VI, 1899 and § 1, XVIII, 1901, in towns with municipal rights and open communes throughout the territories of the Hungarian Crown.

  (b) the actual expenses incurred on the basis of XXXV, 1888, in redemption of and interest on the Indemnity Fund for Croatian and Slavonian inn licences.

(3) the joint actual revenue obtained on the basis of excise duties imposed in Hungary upon meat.

(4) that part of the actual revenue obtained by taxes imposed in Hungary upon wine, coming under the taxes on wine regulated by XLVII, 1887.

(5) the actual expenses incurred by the administration of lotteries throughout the territories of the Hungarian Crown, described in the final state settlement as lottery dues. Of the revenue obtained on this basis in the territories of the Hungarian Crown, 8·127 per cent. is to be regarded as the revenue which Croatia and Slavonia derive from these sources (i.e. from disputable sources). On the basis of § 50, XXXV, 1888, Croatia and Slavonia have to meet out of this revenue the expenses of amortization and interest on the indemnity fund for Croatian-Slavonian inn licences, in such a way that the sum remaining after these expenses have been met forms the net revenue of the kingdom of Croatia and Slavonia from the sources specified above.

II. As the public revenue of Croatia and Slavonia from stamp dues obtained (under Art. XXIII, 1868) from railway and steamer enterprises, is to be reckoned that sum which has actually flown into the Croatian-Slavonian State treasury and revenue office under this title.

III. As Joint Expenses between Hungary and Croatia and Slav-

378

onia are to be reckoned those expenses which are applied to such affairs as are recognized by §§ 5–10, XXX, 1868 as common between Hungary and Croatia-Slavonia and Dalmatia. Accordingly, departing from the method hitherto adopted in the annual settlement of accounts,

(1) the following are not to be regarded as Joint Expenses :—

(a) the costs of industrial and commercial technical education.

(b) the costs of agricultural and economic statistics for the Ministry of Agriculture.

(c) the expenditure in interest on, and amortization of those capital sums raised on the basis of Art. XIV, 1904, or of any state loans which may be raised in the future, and these capital sums are to be applied to such public works as cannot be regarded as Joint within the meaning of §§ 5–10, XXX, 1868.

(2) Only that percentage of the expenses of the central administration of the Ministry of Agriculture is to be regarded as joint expenses of Hungary and Croatia and Slavonia, which is formed by the expenses falling jointly upon Hungary and Croatia and Slavonia, in proportion to the total expenses of the Ministry of Agriculture.

§ 8. Those sections of Articles XXX, 1868 and XXXIV, 1873, which are not repealed by the present statute are maintained unaltered.

APPENDIX VII

THE CROATIAN GOVERNMENT [465]

LAW II (1869) of the Croatian Diet, regulating the organization of the autonomous Croatian Government, runs as follows :—

§ 1. On the basis of §§ 47, 48, 50 and 54 of Article I (1868) of the Croatian-Slavonian-Dalmatian Diet and Article XXX (1868) of the Hungarian Parliament, relative to the constitutional compromise with the Kingdom of Hungary, a supreme administrative authority for the kingdoms of Croatia and Slavonia, for the sphere of constitutional autonomy, is erected with its seat in the capital Agram, under the name " Royal Croatian-Slavonian-Dalmatian Provincial Government."

§ 2. To the Provincial Government's sphere of action belong all those affairs of the above-mentioned kingdoms, which are not expressly assigned, under the Law of Compromise referred to in § 1, to the competence of the joint Hungaro-Croatian-Slavonian-Dalmatian Ministry.

§ 3. In all affairs alluded to in the preceding § 2, the executive power is exercised by His Imperial and Royal Apostolic Majesty, through the responsible Provincial Government.

[465] Translated from Steinbach. *Die Ungarischen Verfassungsgesetze*, pp 126–31.

§ 4. The Provincial Government is divided into three departments :—

I. The Department of Home Affairs and affairs of the Provincial Estimates.

II. The Department for Religion and Instruction.

III. The Department of Justice.

Each of these three departments bears the title : " Royal Croatian-Slavonian-Dalmatian Government Department," its special competence being also indicated.

§ 5. At the head of the Provincial Government stands the Ban, and the departments under him are in their sphere of action independent of each other.

§ 6. To the sphere of action of the department for Home Affairs and Finance belong all those matters which refer to the internal administration of the country, with the exception of those which fall under the competence of other departments, and especially all matters of the public security and of those institutions whose aim is the defence and maintenance of public security : the supervision of societies, theatres and all public institutions devoted to comfort and amusement ; affairs of the Press, matters relating to passports, the administration and supervision of public law as a whole, but especially the control and supervision of subordinate organs and the State executive, the county and communal authorities ; the control of the civil rights of the individual ; the control of the laws relating to elections to the Diet and to autonomous representation ; the preserving the frontier inviolate ; the supreme management of sanitation, including medical matters, of the Poor system and public charitable institutions ; of industry and trade, in so far as matters of the latter kind do not belong to the category of Joint Affairs : credit institutions, land cultivation, settlements on the land and the control of water rights ; the supreme administration of agricultural instruction, as also matters relating to credit on landed property, agricultural insurance and agricultural societies ; mining matters and matters relating to the conversion of mortgages, as also land valuation matters in so far as these are all to be decided through the medium of the administration ; collaboration in carrying out the legal provisions for the recruiting, catering, loan of spare horses and quartering both of the army and the militia ; collaboration in the enforcement of the law relative to Chambers of Commerce and Industry ; census statistics ; public works, including also public roads and canals, so far as they do not belong to the category of Joint Affairs, the preparation of bills relative to subjects of legislation belonging to the above categories—especially the drafting of agrarian laws, so far as concerns the regulation of peasant conditions, of bills for the amelioration, draining and improvement of the land, and of bills concerning water rights, colonization, regulation of woods and forests, game regulations and fishing ; prisons, archives.

Moreover, there is further combined with this department the administration of the Estimates as sanctioned by the Diet, including all those matters, whether of receipts or expenditure, which refer to the provincial Budget existing under the legal autonomy of these kingdoms ; and especially as regards receipts, the administration of the annual sum of 2,200,000 florins [466] assigned under §§ 13, 14, 15 and 16 of the Compromise Law to cover the needs of the autonomous Provincial administration—which sum is made over by the Joint financial administration out of the public receipts of the country. Finally, there also falls under the competence of this Department the compilation of annual accounts relative to this administration : the administration of all provincial funds and also the supreme control of money payments and book balances.

§ 7. To the sphere of action of the provincial Government Department for Religion and Instruction belong : matters relating to all legally recognized Churches and religious societies, the supreme administration and control of the entire educational system, instruction, and all institutions of learned societies, of societies and institutions for art and science, as also generally of all institutions which have influence upon general culture : the administration of the properties of religious bodies and schools, in so far as other provisions have not been made in respect of the Greek Oriental Church : control over the administration of the funds and pious legacies which deal with matters of religion and instruction : and the preparation of bills relating to this Department.

§ 8. To the sphere of action of the provincial Government Department for Justice belong the administration and supervision of the entire judicial system, the supreme supervision of all courts and Crown attorneyships, the supreme control of the enforcement of criminal sentences ; care for the uninterrupted legal exercise of justice, proposals and reports to the Crown in matters relating to the right of pardon : the preparation of bills dealing with judicial matters, and the editing of the laws.

§ 9. The Ban, who stands at the head of the provincial government (§ 5), is responsible to the Diet for the constitutional nature of the governmental acts falling under his competence and of his official actions.

This responsibility, as also the composition of the Court which shall have to decide upon the impeachment of the Ban or his deputy, as also the proceedings at this court, are to be fixed by a special law.

§ 10. If the Ban is absent or is in any other way prevented, or if the dignity of Ban is vacant, his functions in the provincial government are performed by the Chief of the Department for Home Affairs, under his own responsibility.

§ 11. All proposals and motions, which refer to the above men-

[466] This sum was modified by Art. XXXIV, 1873.

tioned affairs, the Ban has to lay before His Majesty through the medium of the Dalmatian-Croatian-Slavonian Minister (§ 44 **Art.** I of the Croatian-Slavonian-Dalmatian Diet, or Art. XXX of the Hungarian Parliament of 1868) and the decisions issued upon them by His Majesty or other orders, including appointments, have to be signed by the Minister named and by the Ban.

§ 12. The Ban is authorized to attend, either personally or through his deputy, all debates of the Diet, including debates in committees and departments, but only to vote if he is member of the Diet. He is bound, whether personally or through his deputy, to answer interpellations of the Diet, to supply the information demanded and to produce the documents relative to them.

§ 13. The Provincial Government lays annually before the Diet for constitutional discussion, the annual Budget dealing with the demands of the whole administration of the country, which is covered by the grant mentioned in §6 and by the provincial funds.

These estimates, however, are to be introduced sufficiently early and in such a manner, as to make it possible for them to be examined and finally fixed at any rate before the beginning of the year for which it holds good.

In the same way the Provincial Government annually lays before the Diet for examination and sanction the final accounts and the results of the annual financial position.

§ 14. The Ban is nominated and appointed in the manner prescribed in the Law upon the constitutional Compromise.

§ 15. With a view to covering the needs of offices and bureaux, the costs of travelling and transference and office disbursements, a suitable contribution is to be assigned with the Diet's approval to the individual Departments and to the Ban, and the accounts of this are to be laid before the Diet with the remaining administrative expenses.

§ 16. The Ban enjoys the right of filling all official posts in all branches of the Provincial Government, in so far as it is not a question of such posts as are reserved to His Majesty in the sense of existing regulations, or such as are to be filled in any other manner in accordance with existing legal practice.

§ 17. The internal regulations in the various Governmental Departments are fixed by the Ban.

§ 18. The officials and servants of the former Croatian-Slavonian-Dalmatian Aulic Chancellory and of the Royal Council of Lieutenancy, which is to be dissolved when this law receives the Royal Sanction, are, in so far as places are not found for them at this reorganization, to remain for a year in undiminished enjoyment of their salaries, and they are then to be treated according to existing regulations.

If meanwhile they are appointed to a position, which is connected with a smaller salary and a lower class of allowance than was their former post, then they are to be left with their former salary and in their former class.

§ 19. The existing Courts in the country, and also the county and town assemblies, retain their present organization and activity until other provisions are made by law.

§ 20. The activity of the newly-formed Provincial Government has to begin within the space of one month after this law has received the Royal sanction.

§ 21. The Ban is entrusted with the execution of this law.

APPENDIX VIII

THE CROATIAN DIET

ARTICLE II, 1870 (of the Croatian Diet), on the organization of the Diet of the Kingdoms of Croatia, Slavonia and Dalmatia.[467]

§ 1. The Diet of the Kingdoms of Croatia, Slavonia and Dalmatia is summoned by His Majesty the King to the capital, Agram.

§ 2. The legal duration of the Diet is fixed at five years.
(See further § 1 of April 24, 1887.)

§ 3. The Diet's session is closed by His Majesty the King, who possesses the right to prorogue the Diet or to dissolve it before the legislative period has elapsed. But in this case new elections must be ordered at once, and the new Diet must meet not later than three months after the Dissolution of the last.

§ 4. The mandate of a deputy lasts as long as the period of legislation. If a deputy's seat become vacant before the close of this period, at a time when the Diet is not sitting, then the new election is to be carried out before the Diet resumes its sittings. If the vacancy occurs during its sittings, the new election is to take place within three weeks at latest.

§ 5 (was superseded by the Law of September 29, 1888. See p. 384.)

§ 6. The Diet is opened and closed by His Majesty or by His Majesty's representative specially nominated for this act ; but the presidency is held by the President whom the Diet elects or by one of the two Vice-presidents of the Diet.

§ 7. The term of office of the President and Vice-presidents, whose election is to be brought to His Majesty's knowledge, lasts for the whole period of a Diet.

§ 8. The Diet elects every year the Clerks and Usher of the House.

§ 9. The deputies receive in addition to travelling expenses a salary of five florins and a further sum of one florin a day for lodgings.

§ 10. As a deputy of the Diet is eligible any one who was born in the Kingdom of Croatia or Slavonia, or who has been admitted

[467] Translated from Steinbach, *Die ungarischen Verfassungsgesetze*, pp. 120-125.

into a commune of these kingdoms as domiciled resident, provided
that he enjoys the franchise, has reached the age of twenty-four
and can read and write ; but no one is eligible who is under guardians or in bankruptcy, or who is the object of a special inquiry or
has been sentenced for any crime or punishable offence committed
for love of gain.

§ 11. The deputies receive no instructions and exercise their
rights in person.

§ 12. Under the competence of the Diet there fall all affairs,
which directly and exclusively affect the Kingdoms of Croatia and
Slavonia and whose extent is defined by the Compromise Law
of November 5, 1868.

§ 13. The right of initiative belongs to the Crown and the Diet.

§ 14. The activity of the Diet is to be regulated by special standing orders, in so far as these do not conflict with the provisions of
this law.

§ 15. The Government has the right and the duty to send its
representatives to the Diet, and they are at all times free to speak,
but only to vote if they are members of the Diet.

§ 16. For the Diet to be duly constituted, a majority of more
than half the duly verified members of the Diet is necessary.

For the validity of any decision the presence of thirty-five duly
verified members of the Diet is necessary.

The Croatian Article of September 29, 1888, introduced the
following modifications into the above law :—

§ 1. The Diet of the Kingdoms of Croatia, Slavonia and Dalmatia consists of ninety elected representatives and of members
who enjoy personal votes in the Diet.

§ 2. Personal votes in the Diet are enjoyed by—

(a) The Archbishop of Agram, the Serb Patriarch and Metropolitan in Karlovitz, the diocesan Bishops, and the Prior of
Aurana ;

(b) The High Sheriffs standing at the head of the counties, and
the Count of Turopolje ;

(c) Male members of those princely, countly and baronial families which have hitherto through their members enjoyed
personal votes in the Diet. These members must have
completed their twenty-fourth year, be able to speak the
Croatian language, and be in possession of estates within
the territory of the Kingdoms of Croatia and Slavonia or of
a family entail [468] (*fidei commissum*) in the same kingdoms,
of such an extent that its state ground taxes, as fixed on
the basis of the new Ground Tax Valuation, in addition

[468] I.e. a property held under a joint entail by all members of a family.

to the House Taxes due for its dwelling houses and farm buildings, amount to not less than 1,000 florins for the year 1885.

§ 3. With regard to such members of the families mentioned in § 2 c, as do not possess the property qualification thus fixed, or subsequently lose it, their personal vote in the Diet falls into abeyance from that date onwards, but it is revived if they subsequently attain to this qualification.

§ 4. Those Hungaro-Croatian Magnate families, or such of their members as are, after this law comes into force, settled on the territory of the Kingdoms of Croatia and Slavonia, as also those who shall in future be made magnates by His Majesty the King, enjoy votes in the Croatian-Slavonian-Dalmatian Diet, in so far as they possess the other qualifications fixed by this law.

They can, however, only exercise this right, if the total number of members fixed by § 5, who possess personal votes in the Diet, is not exceeded by the number of those in possession of this right at the time.

§ 5. The total number of members enjoying personal votes in the Diet may not exceed the half of the elected representatives. If this number is exceeded, then the number of Virilists mentioned in § 2 c is to be reduced to the extent necessary to restore the proportion mentioned. In this event precedence for the exercise of personal votes in the Diet is decided by the tax-contribution, and if two or several pay the same amount in taxation, the precedence falls to the eldest among them.

§ 6. Neither military nor civil service, nor a Church office forms a hindrance to the exercise of the personal vote in the Diet.

§ 7. The personal vote in the Diet is forfeited by—

(1) any member who has been sentenced to hard labour or for any crime or offence due to love of gain ;

(2) any one who loses his citizenship ;

(3) any one exercising this right by reason of his dignity or office, if he no longer possesses such dignity or office.

§ 8. The personal vote is in abeyance—

(1) in respect of those members who have been sentenced for any such punishable offence as does not come under point 1 of § 7, for the whole period prescribed by the Criminal Code.

(2) in respect of those who are under guardians or in bankruptcy.

§ 9. After this law has been proclaimed the Diet is to elect a committee consisting of eleven members, who, on the basis of information submitted by the Provincial Government,

(a) is to draw up the list of those families, whose members have hitherto enjoyed the personal vote in the Diet ;

(b) is to draw up a special register of all those members of these families, to whom the personal vote in the Diet falls under § 2, c.

The list of names drawn up under § 9, and approved by the Diet, is to be published, and the Royal Provincial Government then has to submit to the Diet a Bill for the inarticulation of this list, while taking into account such complaints as may be brought against it.

§ 10.   The list drawn up under § 9 is to be published as soon as it receives the sanction of the Diet, those who regard themselves as illegally omitted being at the same time summoned to submit within three months from the day of this publication the documents calculated to prove their right, to the President of the Diet, if it be sitting, and otherwise to the Ban.

§ 11.   The Diet decides as to whether the individual in question is to be placed on the list.

§ 12.   Those members of the Diet who enjoy the personal vote, will, in future also, receive writs of summons from the Ban, which will serve as the basis of their verification by the Diet.

§ 13.   The provision of § 5 of Article II (1870) on the organization of the Diet of the Kingdoms of Croatia, Slavonia and Dalmatia, is hereby placed out of force.

§ 14.   This law comes into force with the commencement of the next legislative period.

§ 15.   The Ban is entrusted with the execution of this law.

APPENDIX IX

THE CROATIAN BUDGET [469]

Main Groups of Expenditure, 1907

	Total.	Of this, there fell to	
		Hungary.	Croatia.
		(In crowns.)	
Civil List	11,477,000	11,477,000	
Parliament	4,113,000	4,113,000	
Joint Expenses (ordinary) . .	69,193,000	69,193,000	
Do. (extraordinary) . . .	40,278,000	40,278,000	
State Debt	288,089,000	288,089,000	
Railway Guaranteed Interest .	1,748,000	1,748,000	
Internal Admin.	74,239,000	74,239,000	—
Finance Admin.	82,082,000	75,535,000	6,547,000 7·9 p.c.
Internal Admin. of Croatia. .	23,925,000	—	23,925,000
Pensions	27,592,000	26,066,000	1,526,000 5·4 p.c.
Education.	73,119,000	73,119,000	—
Justice.	54,474,000	54,474,000	—
Militia	42,668,000	42,668,000	
Commercial Admin.	26,536,000	26,434,000	102,000 0·3 p.c.
Agricultural Admin.	29,082,000	29,082,000	
Roads, Canals, Bridges, Harbours	27,589,000	26,410,000	1,179,000 4·0 p.c.
Monopolies (Tobacco, Salt, Lotteries)	73,583,000	72,489,000	1,094,000 1·3 p.c.
Post Office and Telegraph . .	60,673,000	55,729,000	4,944,000 8·08 p.c.
Miscellaneous.	14,051,000	14,051,000	
State Expenditure proper . .	1,024,511,000	1,024,511,000	
Expenses of Collection, etc. .	374,962,000	373,617,000	1,345,000 3·4 p.c.
	1,399,473,000	1,358,811,000	40,662,000 2·9 p.c.

[469] From *Ungarisches Statistisches Jahrbuch,* xv (1907), p. 498.

APPENDIX X

CROATIA'S ECONOMIC POSITION

CROATIA is above all an agricultural country. The value of its agricultural products has been estimated for the year 1908 at 381,900,000 crowns. This was divided as follows :—

Cereals	.	.	.	.	.	.	11,172,547 quintals.
Vegetables .	.	.	.	.	.	4,085,037	,,
Flax, tobacco, chicory, etc. .	.	.	.	448,871	,,
Meal, etc. .	.	.	.	.	.	1,763,942	,,
Hay .	.	.	.	.	.	.	11,743,051	,,

29,213,448 ,,

Live Stock.—In 1908 the total number of fairs was 5,566. The sales for three years totalled as follows :—

	1908.		1907.		1906.
Bulls	17,184	..	18,145	..	18,707
Cows	102,982	..	108,429	..	151,429
Heifers . . .	60,222	..	58,995	..	78,425
Oxen	193,318	..	192,451	..	164,681
Calves. . . .	80,003	..	70,261	..	76,271
Sheep	129,458	..	113,372	..	123,310
Pigs	539,844	..	560,655	..	547,801
Horses . . .	72,741	..	63,555	..	84,240

The value of the horses sold, as above, amounted in 1908 to 8,900,000 crowns.

The export of live stock is almost entirely to Austria—to a large extent en route for Italy, Switzerland and Germany. Its value reached in 1908 the sum of 36,700,000 crowns.

The exportation of chickens and eggs was as follows :—

	Chickens. Quantity in kilogrammes and value in crowns.		Eggs. Quantity in kilogrammes.		Value in crowns.
1907 . . .	1,879,996	..	5,693,469	..	3,415,698
1906 . . .	1,915,213	..	6,309,226	..	3,785,533
1905 . . .	3,326,033	..	7,109,271	..	4,265,551
1904 . . .	1,685,706	..	3,419,204	..	2,051,526

The total production of wine was 27,000,000 crowns in 1907, as compared with 20,000,000 in 1906 and 22,000,000 in 1905.[470]

Industry.—How insignificant a part industry plays in Croatia, compared with agriculture, may be gathered from the two following tables, which show the number of persons engaged in each.

[470] All the above statistics are drawn from *Rapport de la Chambre de Commerce et d'Industrie à Zagreb pour* 1908 (Zagreb, 1909). There are three Chambers of Commerce in Croatia, in Agram, Osijek, and Senj (Zengg).

CROATIA'S ECONOMIC POSITION

A. Occupations of the Population.[471]

	Earning.		Dependent.		Total.
Agriculture . . .	1,095,223	..	886,053	..	1,981,276
Industry . . .	89,052	..	113,106	..	202,158
Trade and Finance. .	15,876	..	19,784	..	35,660
Public Service and Private	19,361	..	28,368	..	47,729
Day Labourers . .	15,036	..	18,812	..	33,848
Capitalists, etc. . .	10,241	..	9,719	..	19,960
Total . . .	1,299,244	..	1,117,060	..	2,416,304

B. Percentage of Population engaged in Agriculture.[472]

County of Bjelovar	88·9 p.c.
,, ,, Lika. . . .	92·6 ,,
,, ,, Modruš . . .	76·8 ,,
,, ,, Požega . . .	82·7 ,,
,, ,, Syrmia . . .	77·2 ,,
,, ,, Varaždin . . .	93·8 ,,
,, ,, Virovitica . . .	80·2 ,,
,, ,, Zagreb . . .	90·1 ,,
All Croatia	82·0 ,,

Wood is an important industry ; 145,870 cubic metres of oak were sold for 4,759,587 crowns in 1908. Walking sticks to the number of 8,100,000 were exported (especially the so-called Congo-wood sticks). In the tanning trade, one factory employs 770 workmen. Brewing and distilling are very backward, though "slivovitz" (plum brandy) is exported to a considerable extent. There is a small chemical trade ; three soap factories producing 42,768 quintals.

Textiles were produced of a total value in—

1908	8,573,407 crowns.
1907	7,500,000 ,,
1906	6,250,000 ,,

The state of Croatian industries may be gathered from table C on the following page.[473]

[471] *Ungarisches Statistiches Jahrbuch*, xv p. 30.
[472] Ibid., p. 32.　　　[473] Ibid., pp. 176–7.

C. Croatian Industries.

	Total Value of Property.	Face Value of Shares issued.	Paid-up Capital.	No. of Limited Co.'s.	No. in which Profits were made.			Total Profits.	Dividends	Payment of Staff and Workmen.
	In thousands of crowns.	In thousands of crowns.			Below 5 p.c.	Above 10 p.c.	Nil.	In thousands of crowns.		
Machinery.	501	270	270	1	—	—	—	16	13	17
Stone, earthenware, glass, etc..	2,131	1,360	1,360	6	3	1	1	109	60	96
Wood	1,804	1,200	1,200	1	—	—	—	89	60	18
Leather, brushes, hair, etc.. .	10,242	3,400	3,400	1	—	—	1	302	—	—
Textiles	1,784	680	680	3	—	2	—	37	26	182
Paper	2,113	600	600	1	—	1	—	96	45	—
Articles of Food, etc. . . .	24,187	5,302	5,302	17	2	7	—	381	226	749
Chemicals	226	183	166	2	1	—	4	4	1	18
Printing and Art. . . .	1,690	482	439	8	3	2	2	12	4	164
	44,678	13,477	13,417	40	9	13	8	1,046	435	1,244

The progress made by Croatian banking institutions is shown as follows :—[474]

D. Croatian Finance.

	Banks.	Agricultural Credit Institutions.	Savings Banks.	Co-oper. Societies.	Total.
1899	18	1	75	110	204
1901	19	1	77	257	354
1903	23	1	86	526	636
1905	32	1	97	642	772
1907	42	1	125	674	842

In 1906 there were 38,583 deposits in the Savings Banks, totalling 7,693,214 crowns.

E. The Croatian Press (1904–1907).[475]

Newspapers.	1904.	1905.	1906.	1907.
Political	34	29	33	46
Local	11	13	18	12
Belletristic	19	18	18	19
Technical	64	56	67	74
Comic	1	2	1	1
Total.	129	118	137	152

These newspapers were written in the following languages :—

	1904.	1905.	1906.	1907.	p.c. in 1907.
Croat	104	97	108	124	81·5
Serb.	14	10	15	15	9·8
German	9	9	12	11	7·2
Croat and Latin	1	1	1	1	·6
Other	1	1	1	1	·6

F. Croatian Primary Education.[476]

In the school year 1906–7 the elementary schools were distributed as follows :—

	Number of Schools.	Language of Instruction. Serbo-Croat.	Magyar.	Total.	Teachers. with diploma.
State.	24	24	—	146	111
Communal .	1,405	1,381	4	2,608	2,430
Catholic	2	1	1	7	7
Orthodox .	24	24	—	47	45
Protestant .	17	—	9	21	21
Jewish	4	4	—	16	16
Private	57	19	30	187	168
Total .	1,533	1,453	43	3,032	2,798

The attendances were as follows :—[477]

	1896–1900. (Average.)	1901–1905. (Average).	1906.	1907.
Children liable to attend	323,025	338,766	355,093	370,725
Children actually attending .	196,926	210,474	232,993	241,262
	61 p.c.	62 p.c.	65·6 p.c.	65·1 p.c.

[474] *Ungarisches Statistiches Jahrbuch*, p. 269.　　[475] Ibid., p. 386.
[476] Ibid., p. 336.　　[477] Ibid., p. 320.

APPENDIX XI

G. Croatian Secondary Education.[478]

(i.) Number of pupils in secondary schools :—

	1901-2.		1903-4.		1905-6,
Catholic	4,419	..	4,474	..	4,365
Orthodox	1,232	..	1,182	..	1,103
Protestant	63	..	65	..	73
Jewish .	580	..	583	..	555
Total	6,294	..	6,304	..	6,096

(ii.) Number of schools and professors in 1906-7.

	SCHOOLS.		PROFESSORS, With diplomas.		Total.
Upper Gymnasia.	9	..	116	..	188
Upper Real-Gymnasia	6	..	101	..	173
Lower Real-Gymnasia.	4	..	16	..	49
Girls Lycée.	1	..	17	..	23
Total.	20	..	250	..	433

In 1900 63 per cent. of the population (1,512,888 out of 2,400,766) were still illiterates, as compared to 73·3 per cent. in 1890.[479]

APPENDIX XI

PROGRAMME OF THE PARTY OF PURE RIGHT (SEE p. 109)

THE Party of Right aims at the realization of Croatian constitutional law, and of the natural rights of the Croatian nation, in the sense of the following Articles :—

ART. I. 1. Erection of the Unified Kingdom of Croatia, by the incorporation of Slavonia, Dalmatia, the town of Fiume and its territory, the Littoral, Bosnia, Herzegovina, Istria, Carniola, Carinthia and Styria, within the bounds of the Habsburg Monarchy.

2. Constitutional guarantee of the freedom and independence of this unified Croatian Kingdom.

ART. II. The constitution, liberty and independence of the unified Croatian Kingdom is to be secured by special fundamental laws, to be passed by the Croatian Parliament and sanctioned by His Majesty.

ART. III. The legislation for this unified Croatian Kingdom is to be carried out for all branches of the life of the State, by the Croatian Parliament, in direct agreement with His Majesty.

ART. IV. The affairs which result from the Pragmatic Sanction and the unity of the Monarchy, shall be treated by the Croatian Kingdom on equal terms with the Kingdom of Hungary and with the other lands of His Majesty.

[478] *Ungarisches Statistiches Jahrbuch*, p. 363.   [479] Ibid., p. 306.

ART. V.   The executive power shall be exercised by the Government responsible to the Croatian Parliament and at its head shall stand the Ban, who is to be appointed by His Majesty on the proposal of this Parliament.

AGRAM,
   November 3, 1893.

APPENDIX XII

THE RESOLUTION OF FIUME (OCTOBER 4, 1905) (SEE p. 147)

IN view of the political position into which the Monarchy has fallen as a consequence of the crisis in Hungary, the Croat deputies met together for the purpose of defining their attitude towards this situation and determining the direction of the political work of the Croat nation in the questions which are undisputed and common to all, and which do not prejudice the theoretical standpoint which they uphold in parliamentary life, whether as members of the Club or as individuals.

The Croat deputies hold that the public events of to-day in Hungary arose in consequence of the struggle which aimed at gradually securing for the Kingdom of Hungary complete State independence.

The Croat deputies regard these efforts as justified by the very fact that every nation has the right to decide freely and independently concerning its existence and its fate.

The Croat deputies are convinced that the two nations, the Croatian and the Hungarian, not only in view of their historic relations, but still more in view of the fact of direct neighbourhood and the real needs of their life and mutual aid are thrown upon each other, and that therefore they must avoid every cause and ground for mutual friction.

Starting from these premisses, the Croat deputies consider it to be their duty to fight side by side with the Hungarian nation for the fulfilment of all constitutional rights and liberties, in the conviction that the said rights and liberties will be of advantage to the Croatian and Hungarian nations : and thus will be laid the basis of a lasting understanding between the two nations.

These aims—namely the mutual advantages defined above— having been attained, there is laid down as a condition the speediest reincorporation of Dalmatia in the Kingdoms of Croatia, Slavonia and Dalmatia, to whom it already falls both virtually and lawfully.

With a view to approaching to the realization of the reincorporation of Dalmatia, it is necessary that an end shall be put as soon as possible to the present intolerable parliamentary and constitutional political conditions in Croatia and Slavonia, and that such conditions shall be introduced as shall correspond to the needs of civilized countries and to the claims of constitution and liberty, to the guaranteed liberal constitutional institutions, such as, for example :

An electoral law such as will render possible and assure the election of such national representatives as shall be the true expression of the unhindered and free national will ;

Complete press freedom, with the abolition of objective proceedings and the introduction of juries for political and press offences ;

Freedom of Assembly and Association and free expression of opinion ;

Realization of judicial independence, the guarantee to every judge that he cannot be removed or held responsible for his judicial acts ;

Organization of the special institution of a court of constitutional law for the protection of the interests and political rights of the citizens against the arbitrary action of the authorities ;

Organization of a special court for the criminal responsibility of all public officials for violation of the law.

The Croat deputies are convinced that a lasting understanding between the Croat and Hungarian nations can be most speedily attained by the punctual and strict fulfilment of the rights of the Croatian nation, as contained in the existing Croato-Hungarian Compromise, and by the alteration of the relation which belongs to the sphere of affairs which are to-day common alike to Croatia and Hungary, and to the Western half of the Monarchy—in such a way that an independent political, cultural, financial and general economic existence and development may be assured to the Croatian nation.

As a natural consequence of events, every advance made by the people of Croatia, Slavonia and Dalmatia will exercise a favourable influence upon the condition of those of our race who live in other lands, particularly at the most exposed point, namely in the sisterland of Istria.

With a view to examining and, previous to realisation, revising the principles, aims and demands here enunciated, a committee of five deputies has been elected, who will have the further task of advancing and preparing for decision those questions which are common to all our countries or are of advantage to the general national wellbeing.

From the meeting of Croatian National deputies

FIUME, *October* 3, 1905

(Translated from V. Milič, *Postanak Rijecki Resolucije).*

APPENDIX XIII

THE RESOLUTION OF ZARA (Oct. 17, 1905)

THE aspiration of every nation to dispose over its own existence and destinies, must arouse the sympathies of every one who himself aspires to liberty ; and we greet all the more heartily the present struggle of the Magyar nation, because the structure of the very State against which that struggle is aimed, has obstructed and still obstructs to-day the development of our fatherland, of the Croat and Serb people. Moreover, the autonomy of Hungary, which would then live its own life and dispose of its own forces, would create political conditions in which the Magyar nation would tend to seek, in its own interest, an agreement with the non-Magyar nations of Hungary, to see in the strength of these nations their own strength, and then, with the support of the Triune Kingdom of Dalmatia, Croatia and Slavonia, to take steps to ensure their national future and safety.

Therefore, the undersigned Serb deputies and delegates of Serb parties, conscious of the importance of the present general political situation in the Monarchy, and bearing in mind the attitude adopted by the Croatian deputies at the Conference of Fiume, hereby declare : that they will support the present movement of the Magyar nation, and would even offer it active assistance, if real guarantees could be given on the part of the Magyar Coalition parties, that side by side with their own just claims, effect will also be given to the aspirations of Croatia and Slavonia towards a widening of their autonomy, so that they may be guaranteed a more independent political, cultural, economic and financial existence and development.

At the same time the undersigned deputies and delegates demand, and will work to secure, the introduction of democratic institutions in Croatia and Slavonia, such as should guarantee their constitutional life and development and remove the present intolerable parliamentary administrative and social conditions.

Standing upon this basis, they expect that the Magyar Coalition parties will in their turn place their relations with the non-Magyar nations of Hungary upon a just basis, with a view to guaranteeing the latter's national cultural existence and development.

With regard to the demand of our Croat brethren for the reincorporation of Dalmatia with Croatia and Slavonia, which is actually guaranteed by the existing law,[480] the Serb parties are also ready to use their influence for the realization of this demand, if the Croats on their part remove the obstacle which has hitherto pre-

---

[480] See Appendix VI, Article XXX, 1868, § 65.

vented the Serb party of the Littoral from declaring itself in favour of annexation—if, namely, the Croats give a binding recognition of the equality of the Serb and Croat peoples. With a view then to reaching an agreement for joint action with our Croat brethren, a committee of three, with three proxies, is (hereby) elected ; and they will communicate this decision to the executive committee of the Conference of Fiume, and enter into negotiations with them in the sense of this decision.

As a sequel to the Resolutions of Fiume and Zara, the Croatian Party (for many years the dominant factor in Dalmatian politics) and the National Serb Party of Dalmatia, met at a conference in Zara on November 14, 1905, during the sittings of the Dalmatian Diet. The following declaration was drawn up between them ; and in order to give it added weight, it was read in the Diet on November 18, by Dr. Pero Čingrija, the Mayor of Ragusa, as President of the Croatian party.

" The Clubs of the Croatian Party and the Serb National Party rest upon the principle *that the Croats and Serbs are one nation,* that each enjoys equal rights with the other, and that especially to-day, when in the world at large and still more so in the Monarchy momentous events directly affecting their vital interests are looming large on the horizon, they must summon up their strength and national resources, lest events should take them unawares.

Therefore the Croats and Serbs of Dalmatia will work shoulder to shoulder, as brethren enjoying equal rights in national political questions, and especially they will endeavour with united forces to achieve at the earliest possible date the annexation of Dalmatia to Croatia and Slavonia, as the principal condition for assuring a better national future to those countries.

In order that the principles of brotherly union and equality between the Croats and Serbs of Dalmatia may be applied in a durable form not only among the national representatives, but also within the sphere of the Government's activity, I have the honour in the name of both Clubs to propose to the Diet for acceptance the following resolutions :—

I. The Imperial and Royal Government is invited, in accordance with this Diet's resolution of July 21, 1883, to use its influence, that all Government authorities and offices, in their references to the national language, should always employ the term ' Croat or Serb ' ; that in the schools of Dalmatia the Croat and Serb name should be assigned an honourable position, and that in school textbooks account should be taken of Croat and Serb history, so that the pupils may learn its principal events ; and that the Latin and Cyrilline alphabets should both be studied in such a way that the pupils may be able to read and write both characters.

II. The Provincial Committee (Zemaljski Odbor of Dalmatia) is invited to use its influence to ensure that all written decisions be issued in the same characters in which the (original) application was presented."

APPENDIX XIV

THE FORGED REPORT OF DR. SPALAJKOVIĆ [481]

MINISTRY OF FOREIGN AFFAIRS (POLITICAL DEPARTMENT)
BELGRADE, *June* 4, 1907 (i.e. *June* 17, N.S.).
Confidential, No. 3027.

SIR, [482]

In accordance with orders received, the undersigned, with the cashier of this Ministry, Mr. Božović, was in Semlin, where we visited the Croatian deputy Svetozar Pribičević with a view to coming to terms for the purpose of agreement about the Letter which reached us through Mr. Petković [483] from Budapest from the Croatian delegates in the Hungarian Parliament, Messrs. Supilo, Potočnjak, Pribicević, Lukinić and others.

Mr. Pribičević, who on this day was engaged with his comrades upon the organization of his party in Semlin, declared that it was this time unfortunately impossible for him to come to Belgrad, thankfully received our intimation that Servia will punctually fulfil those obligations which it took over in the sense of the Fiume Resolution, so long as the present Cabinet is in power in Servia ; but that the proposed subsidy is determined by the height (extent) of those means which can be separated from the budgetary contributions, without other needs of the State being thereby impaired.

This motive, as also *the circumstance that there is for this year as yet no sanctioned Budget at the disposal of the Servian Government,* [484] impose on the Servian Government certain limits respecting disbursements for foreign political action ; and as further the Government is also faced by the burning necessity of proceeding without delay to the organization of the army and the supplementing of the armaments of the Servian Army, which will in any case have to take place under control of a Committee of the Skupština, the Servian Government will probably for some time to come find it

[481] See pp. 46–52. *Aktenstücke zur grossserbischen Bewegung in Oesterreich-Ungarn.* Vorgelegt von Dr. Heinrich Friedjung. N.B. The clumsy grammatical constructions are as in the German version.
[482] The German version, " Herr Minister," is untranslatable.
[483] Servian Consul-General in Budapest.
[484] See p. 265.

impossible to increase the pecuniary support which it hitherto put at the disposal of the Croato-Serb *Party*.

All this I explained to Mr. Pribičević in the name of the Minister, but at the same time assured him that in the event of new elections being ordered for the Croatian Diet, the Servian Government was ready to let the Coalition have a considerable contribution ; for the Servian Government is firmly convinced that no other political combination could assure a more certain support to the aims of Southern Slav joint action (*Gemeinschaft*) than that which acquired its basis in the Resolution of Fiume, and which through the agreement reached in Fiume by the Minister and Mr. Protič with Messrs. Supilo and Medaković, was extended to Servia also.

I have not neglected the opportunity of pointing out also to Mr. Pribičević that in view to the unfavourable relations in which Servia at present stands to Bulgaria, and which are proved to be the fruit of Viennese diplomacy's systematic action, further in view of the Servian State's insufficient readiness for war, and finally in view of Servia's important need of reducing its internal political and economic difficulties, the Servian Government is compelled to aim above all else at the restoration of treaty conditions with *the Habsburg Monarchy* and thereby to attain once again more confidential and better political conditions with Vienna. For this very reason Servia is compelled to assume for a time a certain reserve in all matters which could rouse the susceptibilities of Viennese circles, and above all to advise its friends in Bosnia and Herzegovina, to be more moderate in their political work, so that they should not make difficulties for Servia or involve it against its will at a time when Servia is gathering itself together in military, political and financial respects, in order to be able to take up the more strongly the interests of the Bosnian-Herzegovinian people and of the remaining elements of Pan Slav kinship in the south.

The political friends and compatriots must keep in view in their political work the present wretched situation of Servia, as also its momentary great lack of unappropriated means. This situation will not last long, this will change radically by March of next year. For by then the Servian Army will be fully equipped with all war material, cannon, rifles and ammunition, besides the Government will dispose over a new extended Budget, and what is the main thing, over large contributions from *the new State Loan, regarding which the preliminary negotiations are already closed and which the Skupština will vote in the autumn.*[485]

Mr. Pribičević deferred to the line of argument which at present fixes the decisions of the Servian Government, but he noted with discontent, that the Servian Government is at present unable to comply with his and his political friends' demand and to place at their disposal 50,000 francs from Servia's resources for the mainten-

[485] See p. 265.

ance of their political position *in the Triune Kingdom* and for the support of their action in the Hungarian Parliament.[486] But as I informed him, according to my instructions, that the Servian Government was ready, despite its lack of money, to help his political friends and allies in the most necessary needs (*sic*) so far as possible, Mr. Pribičević reduced the present demand of his comrades to 20,000, and in the course of further negotiations to 12,000. In discussing the treatment of this money, *Mr. Božović and I came to the conclusion* that this payment should be made now, in case the state of the funds at this moment permits. As the need and hence also the decision in this matter is urgent, we have given the assurance through Mr. Pribičević to his friends in the Diet, that the money, so far as it is sanctioned, will be paid over, in return for a receipt, and according to Mr. Pribičević's request, into the hands of Peter Jelovac, a Semlin merchant of good standing, within two days at latest.

On the ground of the authorization received, we have at the same time informed Mr. Pribičević that the subvention promised to the Serbo-Croat organs was assigned till further notice for the current year in the secret credit of the Servian Foreign Office, and that the sums still outstanding will be paid *as soon as the Budget is sanctioned*. In view of the fact that an increase of this subvention is impossible, the number of subsidized papers cannot be increased. The Independent Serb Party places at the disposal of our Press bureau the following newspapers : *Srbobran* and *Srpsko Kolo* in Agram, *Srbin* in Gospič, *Sloboda* in Mitrovica and *Srpska Misao* in Karlovitz.

We have arranged that all Bosnian news and correspondence shall be so far as possible sent first to our Press bureau for perusal—so that no traces of our connexions with the political action there (*sic*) may appear and the reprisals of the Bosnian authorities, which the political workers here draw on themselves through lack of caution, may be avoided.

Mr. Pribičević has demanded in his own name and in that of his colleagues, that the Servian Press bureau and the Servian Ministers abroad should support in the large foreign newspapers the action carried on in the Hungarian Parliament by the Coalition deputies.

It was, however, pointed out to him that Servia had need of correct relations to the Hungarian Parliament, mainly owing to our delicate complicated relations to the Viennese Ballplatz, and that consequently the foreign publicist campaign must still continue *in the hands of Mr. Polit-Dezančić*, who has for this purpose definite means at his disposal, and to whom the deputies of the Coalition should turn in this connexion. At the same time Mr. Pribičević was informed, that Mr. Polit had already made certain disbursements in their interest out of our means, mainly for certain persons in the entourage of the Minister Josipovich.

Finally, Mr. Pribičević inquired *of us*, whether it would not be

[486] See p. 154 re obstruction.

possible to manage through our Viennese Minister, that through the medium of the Russian ambassador in Vienna, who in his turn has intimate relations with the German ambassador there, the latter should secure help for the Serbo-Croat Coalition in the entourage of the Emperor against the Hungarian Government.

In accordance with the orders received from the Minister, the first undersigned pointed out to Mr. Pribičević, that the Servian Government considers it to be a great political error if the Serbo-Croatian Coalition should succumb to the influence of Vienna, and if in return for services received it should submit to the policy of the Monarch's entourage. Even if this *could be justified on the part of the deputies of Croat nationality*, the Serb deputies at any rate must bear in mind that the realization of the aims of Serbdom in regard to Bosnia and Herzegovina would be finally compromised, as soon as Viennese circles acquire unlimited power to regulate the fate of the occupied provinces definitely according to their wish. In this connexion the existence of a parliamentary government in Budapest such as the present, forms for Serbdom a guarantee of decisive and undoubted value.

The Servian Government also counts upon the Serb deputies in the Serbo-Croat Coalition always taking care not to undermine the interest which Servia, as such, and with its resources by reason of its purely national interests, (*sic*) through which the interests of all the Southern Slavs are best guaranteed, takes in remaining in connexion with the *Croato-Serb* Coalition.

In view of the fact that latterly events have taken another turn, on the one hand owing to the clouding over of Croato-Hungarian relations, on the other owing to the still unsettled Hungarian relations to Austria, and equally in view of the whole international situation, which offers Servia absolutely no guarantee regarding the national tasks of its policy ; the Servian Government takes up the attitude that it would certainly be best if the parliamentary parties in Croatia could come to an agreement as to their special interests with the leading persons of the Hungarian Parliament.

The Servian Government leaves its political friends in Croatia an entirely free hand, but it cannot suppress the fear that such a further development of events might lead up to the decisive influence of Stadler [487] and his Viennese allies upon the fate of Bosnia and Herzegovina.

But the whole complex of these questions is so comprehensive that, in order to draw the necessary consequences, it seems absolutely essential to clear up all this by means of a personal conversation.

An opportunity is offered for this during the time which the Servian Premier is to spend on the *Hungarian* Riviera from July 2 of this year for several weeks.

[487] The ultra-Clerical Archbishop of Sarajevo.

THE FORGED DESPATCH OF DR. MILOVANOVIĆ

On ground of orders received, we informed Mr. Pribićević for further use, that the head of the Servian Government has fixed upon Crkvenica for his holiday, as recommended by Mr. Supilo ; where he will await his political friends with a view to closer agreement.

While submitting this report upon the mission entrusted to us, with the request that on the above grounds the payment of 12,000 dinars may be made to the credit of No. 190 of point xxxviii. B of Chapter V of the Budget, we remain most obediently,

DR. MIROSLAV SPALAJKOVIĆ.
BOŽOVIĆ.

APPENDIX XV

THE FORGED INSTRUCTIONS OF DR. MILOVANOVIĆ [488]

ROYAL SERVIAN MINISTRY OF FOREIGN AFFAIRS.
POLITICAL DEPARTMENT, P. No. 5,703.

Belgrad, *April* 4 (17), 1909.
To the Royal Servian Minister Extraordinary and Plenipotentiary in Vienna.

SIR, [489]

At yesterday's meeting of the Cabinet Council held under the presidency of His Majesty, on the written wish of the Skupština the resolution, approved by the Crown also, was adopted, that the continuance of the business of State should be left in the hands of the present Coalition Cabinet, until certain legislative work is completed, such as shall serve for the reorganization of the State administration, the fitting combination of constitutional principles and the organization of the army, which in its present form does not give complete expression to the strength of the nation, and therefore forms the obstacle for the foreign policy of every government which sees in a vigorous foreign policy of Servia the sole guarantee for the future of the Servian people. In taking over the conduct of the Servian State for a further period with a programme of this kind, the Cabinet Council in this meeting turned to the general consideration of those principles according to which Servia's policy is to be conducted in relation to the neighbouring Austro-Hungarian Monarchy, to which you are accredited. In order that you may be in a position to adjust your action strictly to the policy adopted by the Royal Government, I shall in the following mention all that you require for your knowledge and guidance.

An important point in our foreign relations is the hearty agreement of the Servian Government with the Cabinet of St. James, which

---

[488] (See pp. 28–35, of Dr. Friedrich Funder's *Aktenstücke zur grossserbischen Propaganda in Oesterreich-Ungarn.*)
[489] Herr Gesandter.

already dates back to two Treaties (Traktate) from the years 1906 and 1908, which are known to you. From this the direction of our future foreign policy receives its definition, but also the support of the Kingdom of Great Britain and the Cabinets of Petersburg and Paris, which are in agreement with it. This support at present best protects our State and national interests in the Balkans, and assures us a great vital guarantee against the policy of the Central European *bloc* with its economic and political aggression towards the Slavonic South.

Through this support economic and financial aid was afforded us, such as seems to us beneficial for the strengthening and further development of the Servian kingdom. The Royal Government is firmly resolved not only to hold out in this policy, but in it to await the moment at which Servia will be able with the best prospects of success, to proceed to the realization of its legitimate interests in the Balkans and in the whole Slavonic South.

The Royal Government has already at its formation, said clearly enough in the declaration addressed to the Skupština, that Servia's policy embraces the interests of the whole Serb race. This axiom rules out all possibility of any political combination with Vienna, which would restrict this our purpose.

The Royal Government is resolved to give a definite form to this axiom for a longer period of time, as soon as conditions in the kingdom have definitely calmed down and the political conditions in Petersburg show a favourable terrain for such action. In this connexion the Cabinet of St. James has assumed the rôle of initiator, to whom we have completely subordinated ourselves. The knowledge of these connexonis and actions of ours will render easy your relations and possibly combined action with the ambassadors of the friendly Powers in Vienna. In proportion as these connexions assume a concrete form or provisional business measures, the Ministry will not fail to have further information sent to you in its instructions.

Hence the Royal Government wishes purely business relations with Vienna, scrupulously correct, attentive, even friendly, but without political engagements of any kind. As little diplomatic activity as possible, as little cause as possible for diplomatic steps— that would best correspond to the intentions of the Royal Government, so that it may not be exposed to the necessity of unmasking by its denials or unfavourable answers the main direction of our policy.

In accordance with this standpoint of principle, the Royal Government will endeavour by no steps on its part to regulate by a fresh contract its disturbed commercial relations with Austria-Hungary, so long as conditions in the neighbouring Monarchy do not undergo change, so that Servia might be offered such a basis for a commercial treaty, as offers (*sic*) distinct advantages to Servia's economic and financial interests. The Royal Government finds for this its decision

—even though it demands certain sacrifices from the State and the nation—a further excuse in the fact that in this way—so far as Servia is concerned—a barrier is erected at least against the *economic* advance of Austria-Hungary in the Balkans. This ground too dictated the termination of all conventions which Servia possessed with Austria-Hungary. And in so far as we shall gain time until the development of conditions, of affairs and of relations (*sic*) shall lead anew to treaty obligations to the neighbouring Monarchy, we are in the position, on the one hand to decline the proposals for railway connexions through Austro-Hungarian territories, and on the other hand, to engage the friendly Powers more actively in favour of those railway projects, which would lead us to the sea while avoiding Austria-Hungary, whereby we should not only realize the guarantees for our economic independence, but also should materially further the interests of those Powers, whose interests (*sic*) [490] are directly opposed to the advance of Austria-Hungary in the Balkans.

After all that has been adduced here, you will without difficulty be able to regulate the activity of the Legation under you, and of the Servian consulates assigned to you, which we shall place under your immediate control, under new instructions which are at present being drawn up.

Fundamental reserve in all undertaken by the Viennese Government, and furtherance of those tendencies and *incitement* of those social and political factors in the Monarchy which completely subordinate to their particularist and entirely one-sided interests the question of the contractual relations of the Monarchy with Servia—this should form the best guide to your activity.

The axiom that we demand nothing from Austria-Hungary, must be upheld, since this forms an obligation which we have taken over by the policy which will only appear justified by the ripeness of the results which are to be prepared in the course of time—this is being steadily worked at—and which obligation we have unreservedly fulfilled up to the last consequence.[491] The Legation under you has in this policy an eminently important task. Any error might react fatally upon the final aims.

So much on the question of our political and commercial relations to the Monarchy. In the question of our national activity in the territory of the Habsburg Crown lands, the Cabinet has laid down the following lines which find their explanation in all the above.

All official circles of the Kingdom of Servia, as also all political collaborators of our legations and consulates, have to hold aloof from all objective and personal share in this activity, which does not however exclude the obligation to record conscientiously in

[490] These verbal repetitions and obscure and clumsy phrases are carefully translated from the German "original."

[491] How could any serious diplomat have taken this dreadful jargon for a genuine State document?

their periodical reports all that might contribute to a knowledge of those events and conditions which might be made at all useful for Southern Slav interests. The Royal Government has decided to suppress every trace of relations and connexions of the political department of the Foreign Office on the territory of the Habsburg Crownlands, and for this purpose to break off all direct relations with persons, politicians and party organizations in Austria-Hungary, including those in Bosnia and Herzegovina, in such a way that the entire correspondence hitherto conducted shall be definitely suspended and that even private letters shall in future not be treated in any official form.[492]

Consequently all subventions and payments are to be stopped from the 15 (28) inst., both in the Foreign Office· and also in the Legation under you and in consulates which we maintain on the territory of the Austro-Hungarian Monarchy. This suspension is to be carried out absolutely and without regard to previously existing engagements. In so far, however, as it is inevitable to make sacrifices in order that Servia should free itself honourably from these engagements, the Cabinet has authorized 25,000 *crowns* [493] from the credit for confidential purposes authorized by the Skupština ; with the help of which you will carry out this liquidation in accordance with the documents and instructions which a special courier of the Ministry will bring you, and observing so far as possible the State interests and finances of our country. From the extent of this credit you will see that the Royal Government is very anxious so far as possible to allay those wounds and misfortune which have been caused or may still be caused by the High Treason trial in Agram.

It of course goes without saying that the credit assigned to your Legation for confidential purposes will not thereby be suspended, but this will now be rounded off at 30,000 dinars. The Legation will not have to make the payments for military news out of this credit ; since for them the necessary sum will be placed by the War Office at the disposal of the military representative in question. Since in all probability it will soon prove possible to replace those gentlemen who hitherto did this work without being accredited, by an officially accredited officer, this branch of our relations will then receive its normal correct form.

With reference to the fact that the development of political conditions in Hungary and the condition of constraint (Zwangslage) in which the disturbed connexions and relations with the Monarchy

[492] This, if genuine, could only have one meaning—that the Austro-Hungarian Foreign Office is in the habit of tampering with the correspondence of foreign embassies. That such a phrase should have passed muster at Vienna, if that practice does not exist, is obviously incredible.

[493] The Austrian word "crowns" slips out instead of the Servian dinar or franc.

place us, render peremptory our unabated influence upon the press in both halves of the Monarchy, the Ministry has placed at your disposal, in addition to the credit for confidential purposes, 4,000 dinars more, which you will receive regularly after the 15th inst. in four quarterly instalments paid in advance.

The Royal Government has subordinated Servia's national propaganda in the Slavonic South to the Pan Slav national propaganda, which with our eager co-operation is being organized just at present in brotherly Russia, and whose organization will receive its definite shape before July 15. This organization will be in a position to unfold its activity with disproportionate strength, and to protect its collaborators, apart from the fact that it will control far more important means than the little Servia could save from its modest income. If in this activity we have assured to Servia a far reaching influence and a stronger share, in such a way that the aims of the Serb race as a whole will be powerfully furthered by this activity, the official Servia will not always require to enter upon any direct engagements such as might lead to conflicts. In the *brother Czech Kingdom*, a new focussing point is projected, far more powerful than that which was formed in Servia, and round which all can gather who wish to or have to seek in the victory of the Pan Slav idea the preservation of their national individuality. May then the means, the political solutions and actions, come from henceforth and from there, behind which will stand all classes of society in *Russia*, with the members of the Duma at their head.[494] The more active all Slavs are, wherever their fate may chain them, the more will our organization in Russia promote a lively committal of official Russian policy in the Slavonic South, where we lost the first battle merely because Slav solidarity is really only maintained in the South. This organization, with its headquarters in Russia, we shall do all we can to chain to all those interests which hitherto we alone have championed ; this organization will dispose over considerable means, both for the national press and also for the intellectual life of the Southern Slavs, which if prosperous and flourishing forms the strongest barrier against the plotting designs of Austrian Imperialism. To Belgrad, as intellectual centre of the Slavonic South, important sums of money are assured, in order to combat by this influence all separatist or foreign aspirations and actions, such as might estrange the official Agram, Ragusa, Neusatz or Sarajevo from intellectual community with Servia.

With these means we shall proceed to the strengthening and organization of the liveliest activity of all our cultural and social institutions and organizations, which may be capable of binding the broad masses of the people in all Serb territories to itself.[495]

[494] This sentence is more than usually clumsy and ungrammatical.
[495] Here again the construction and the style are not mine, but the forger's.

In this domain our action will, even if visible, be unexceptionable. In so far, however, as side by side with it *political revolutionary propaganda* should seem necessary, it should henceforth be managed from *Petersburg* or from *golden Prague*. We also wish to further this activity through the relations which the Servian General Staff will in future make it its business to maintain.

The sketch of our plans drafted above will give you a sufficiently clear picture of all you require to know in order, when opportunity offers, to convince most emphatically, whether directly or indirectly, every such friend of Servia, the Serb race and Slavdom as a whole, as seems worthy of our confidence, that the Government of the Kingdom of Servia, under the irresistible pressure of power has received Austro-Hungarian dictations (?) (and ?) is more than ever resolved not to leave one inch of Servian national territory which is in the forcible possession of the Habsburg Crown, under the latter's permanent sway.

In accordance with this action our Legation has a further field of action, but one which is in the highest degree delicate. While recommending this activity to your care, I take this opportunity of assuring Your Excellency of my high consideration.

The Minister for Foreign Affairs,
DR. M. G. MILOVANOVIĆ.

APPENDIX XVI

THE CONDITION OF DALMATIA

> In allen Wipfeln spürest du
> Kaum einen Hauch. . . .
> Warte nur. Balde. . . .
>
> GOETHE.

IT was my original intention to include in this volume a separate account of the political situation in Dalmatia, instead of treating it in close relation with Croatia. But I have decided to leave this task to a more eloquent and competent spokesman than myself. The following speech was delivered in the Austrian Parliament on December 3, 1910.[496] The speaker, Dr. Joseph Smodlaka, the founder of the Croat Democratic Party in Dalmatia, and member of Parliament for Spalato, is one of the ablest and most attractive Southern Slav politicians, and what is still better, " a modern of the moderns " in the midst of medieval conditions.

The well-known Austrian novelist, Hermann Bahr, in his *Dalmatinische Reise* (pp. 109–117), gives an admirable character sketch of Dr. Smodlaka. He tells us how he had learnt of Dr. Smodlaka as

[496] Translated from the *Stenographische Protokolle* of that date.

THE CONDITION OF DALMATIA

"the general pride of Dalmatia, the new St. Blaise[497] of the Dalmatian youth," and how he expected to find a kind of miniature Croat Gambetta. " And here in front of me sits a kind of Roosevelt, a lover of fresh air, an engineer, showing in his ideas strong traces of the peasant, one who wastes no words, but sets his hand to the work, one who does not dream but calculate, who cares less for phrases than for real needs, who listens to no programme save distress, a road-builder who begins before his own front door, one who is bent on cutting down and letting in light and air."

Dr. Smodlaka is no lover of panegyrics, and I must apologize to him for thus revealing him to the reader. I value Dr. Smodlaka's friendship too highly to add words of my own, such as would be superfluous to all who know him.

" *Vox clamantis in deserto,* I am tempted to exclaim, as I look upon the empty benches. If it were a question of my private affairs, I would naturally withdraw ; but as my duty as a patriot, and the defence of my country are at stake, I must remain and speak. . . .

I may say at once that I shall vote against the Budget, not from tactical reasons, but on purely practical grounds, irrespective of the Government which may chance to be in power. For just as I feel bound now to vote against this Budget of the Bienerth Cabinet, so I would have to do the same, as representative of Dalmatia, if a similar budget were introduced by Bienerth's bitterest enemy.

My reason . . . is the neglect of Dalmatia, on the part of all Austrian Governments, including the present, the way in which my native land's most vital needs are ignored. . . . The crumbs thrown to Dalmatia are still scantier in this Budget. But even were they larger, and even if Dalmatia received richer alms I should still have to vote against the Budget : for in Dalmatia's present serious condition neither crumbs nor alms can help. Besides, I am firmly convinced, and with me, I believe all Dalmatia, that the policy of Crumbs cannot help us materially, while it kills us morally.

Since the desperate condition of Dalmatia forces me to treat this important matter of State from the standpoint of Dalmatian interests, I can hardly expect to succeed in arousing general interest in this cause. . . . One request only I make : let me not be reproached with a narrow local patriotism or ' Campanilism.' [498] Let it not be said that we Dalmatians are petty egotists, without comprehension for the general well-being. Apart from the fact that exceptional conditions prevail in our country, unlike those in any Austrian Crown land,[499] Dalmatia occupies, thanks to its geographical, political and strategic position an exceptional place in the State, so that we can fairly say that the Dalmatian question is not local but Imperial, and should be so regarded both by Government and Parliament.

[497] The patron saint of the Republic of Ragusa.
[498] The Campanile or Church tower is the Southern equivalent of our " village pump."
[499] Dalmatia is only one of seventeen Austrian provinces or Kronländer.

To return to the Budget, which this year is far more unfavourable and meagre for Dalmatia than last year's. . . . Let me quote a few figures and add comments upon them.

While the total State expenditure shows an increase of over 37,000,000 (= £1,155,000), Dalmatia not only receives no increase of contribution in favour of its cultural and economic progress, but on the contrary the balance is restored to the Budget largely at the expense of my poor and neglected country. In order to cover the increased demands for police, gendarmerie, reorganization, etc., almost all the items from which Dalmatia might have gained something have been cut down. For instance, for harbour works we are to get 728,000 crowns instead of 856,000 in 1910, or 127,900 less. . . . For the encouragement of fishery we get barely a third of last year's sum, only 25,000 instead of 82,000 crowns. For lighthouses and signalling stations only a quarter, or 75,000 instead of 300,000 crowns. For roads Dalmatia gets a clear £4,000 less than last year. In short, not to be wearisome, almost all expenses in favour of Dalmatia have been cut down, even the sum for agricultural improvements, for combating phylloxera, for nautical education—and that in a budget which shows an increased grant for all other schools in the country, and in a state which aims at seapower, at least on a small scale.

I may be told that other provinces are also cut down, under Mr. Bilinski's proposals.[500] But I answer : no other province is in such a condition as Dalmatia. The others lack many things, we lack every thing . . . indeed, all the conditions of life. Have you noticed, gentlemen, that at the debate on the increased cost of living, four out of the five Dalmatian deputies present voted for the unlimited import of Argentine meat ? And do you know what it means when the representatives of a peasantry vote on this question with the Social Democrats and the town representatives ? (Deputy Gostinčar : In Carniola we have not even enough potatoes, far less meat !) Potatoes are in Dálmatia a luxury, they are only eaten by the better classes. I invite you to come to Spalato, and you will be able to convince yourself that we have no meat, no potatoes and no bread. If the question of the free importation of corn should be raised in the House, you will find that all Dalmatian deputies will vote in favour of it, and yet Dalmatia is almost exclusively inhabited by peasants and has no industry. But we not only have no bread, but no drinking water ; out of 600 Dalmatian villages more than half have none. The people drink what you might call mud.

But we also have no wood. If our peasants are not to die of cold, they have to steal wood in the woods of their own commune, and the townspeople, not only workmen but officials . . . have to shiver with cold in winter, for with us a stove is a luxury.

But we not only have no wood, no water and no bread, we also have no land for agriculture. The whole surface of productive land

[500] The Austrian Finance Minister in the late Bienerth Cabinet.

is flooded—the plains of the Narenta, of Vrgorac, Sinj, Imotski, the so-called poljes. . . . We could even export corn, but our only fertile land lies under water.

We have no roads, no communications. The health of the population is being ruined. While the Dalmatians under French rule a century ago were a remarkably healthy and powerful race of men, the population is to-day decaying—especially in the north, where there is malaria—and is dying out.

We also have no education. Over 300 Dalmatian villages have no school at all ; in half the country the number of illiterates is not 50 or 60, not 80 or 90 per cent., but 99 and 100 per cent.

I have the honour to represent the central district of Dalmatia, relatively the richest and most progressive of all ; and in my constituency, gentlemen, there are forty-eight villages, of which twenty-eight have no school and no teacher, and only twenty a school with one class, and two or three a school with two classes. If that is the case in what is called the richest and most progressive district, you can imagine what it is like on the edge of the mountains, on the Bosnian frontier.

We also have other specialities such as the system of Coloni or Kmets, according to which the peasant, without getting anything from the owner of the land, has to see to all improvements and expenses and yet to pay the proprietor half or a third of his annual income. How can these people live anything but a wretched existence under such circumstances ? The year 1848 freed the peasants of Austria, but the Austrian Government of that day forgot that Dalmatia also belongs to Austria. With us medieval conditions have survived to the present day. . . .

Besides all this there is the isolation of Dalmatia, which is not natural, since it is not an island, but part of the Continent of Europe, belonging to a Great Power. And yet we have been artificially made into an island. Not only Dalmatia, but also the neighbouring districts of South Croatia and West Bosnia have no railway connexion with the Monarchy or with the rest of Europe.

It is not a question of a tiny piece of land, but of territories larger than the kingdom of Württemberg, with more inhabitants than Istria, Carniola and South Styria. And the communications in this forgotten land are such, that if, for instance, we want to go from Spalato to Banjaluka, which could be reached in a quick train in three or four hours, we require forty-four hours, and can get quicker to St. Petersburg than to the immediate *Hinterland* on which our poor country depends for nourishment. It is just as if we were to go from Trieste to Laibach and were obliged to go first by steamer to Ancona, in order to reach Laibach via Bologna, Padua and Tarvis.[501] Just look at the map, and you will see that this is so.

[501] As if in order to get from Newcastle to Hull, it were necessary to take a steamer to Leith, and then go *via* Glasgow, Carlisle, Crewe, Rugby across to Hull, but taking twice as long as such a journey would actually take.

Under such circumstances, I ask, is it just, is it human, to save in the way in which this Budget saves ? Was this to be expected from the Government which recognized that Austria has great duties towards Dalmatia, and that as it has been neglected by the State for a whole century, something must be done to help it ? Will it be helped by reducing still further the crumbs and alms which it receives ? In the programme of this Government and of the last, is included the Reconquest of Dalmatia. I must remind the House that one cannot speak of a reconquest, since Dalmatia was never conquered by Austria. After the collapse of the Venetian Republic our fathers voluntarily recognized the Emperor Francis I as their sovereign, and invited him to send his officials and his soldiers. We were not conquered, then. But even if one talks of a reconquest in a good sense, everything remains merely in words ; in practice programmes and promises are laid aside. . . . What does the State or Government do to help the country ? . . . I must admit that of late years there has been a lively interest for Dalmatia, and ways of helping it have been sought, but the right way is still not found. Committees sit for months and years, but there is no result. They make excursions to Dalmatia at Easter, and the best season of the year. New bureaucratic posts are created, and a few new sinecures, but Dalmatia gains nothing. I will not deny that money has been spent on the country in recent years. It has, but how ! The agricultural school at Spalato may serve as an example : it has cost the State 400,000 crowns, but it has no land for agricultural instruction and only twenty pupils. Instead of building it in an agricultural district like Sinj or Knin, it is built in a town. . . .

In years of distress the Government buys hay and sells it to poor people, but not to the poor peasantry, but to the poor money-lenders, who buy at 8 heller, in order to sell to the peasants at 16. . . .

We have agricultural teachers, who, to put it mildly, act as clerks in the Prefectures ; we have eight secondary schools, but in over 300 villages not a single elementary school. Every year 200 to 400 more youths from Gymnasia and *Realschulen*, and 100 per cent. of illiterates in hundreds of villages. Are those not unhealthy conditions ? In the little town of Zara, with hardly 18,000 inhabitants, two upper Gymnasia and one Upper *Realschule*—two Italian and one Croat ; and in all Dalmatia, only two industrial schools, and a single lower commercial school. . . .

Not merely is the Diet refused the means for improving the country, but the system is also bad. There is no plan, no organization, the needs of the country are not put first or are not understood.

Here is a classical example. In Spalato a private company has been founded, to build an electric tramway line from Spalato to the little town of Traù. The Government also wants to build a useless railway from Kastel-Sučurac to Traù, which will cost 2,000,000 crowns. The two towns hold together economically as *mutatis mutandis* Vienna and Klosterneuburg.[502] . . . This private company applied to the Government for the concession. The railway would, it said, only run twice a day at the most, and this is no use for the people, who want a proper service. . . . Besides, the railway does not run along the shore, where the villages are, but high up on the side of the hill. . . . What happened in Vienna ? The company (who do not belong to my party, but are business men in the town) were told they would not get the concession even for prospecting ! In astonishment they asked why, and were told, ' because it would compete with the future State railway ' !

At this rate, gentlemen, all the trams running from Vienna to the suburbs would have to be done away with, because they all compete with the State railways. . . . The real reason is, if we get the tram connexion the railway is superfluous ; therefore, they won't grant the concession, because they want to build the railway. It is not a question of State money ; we have the money, the commune would join the company, and the small local banks would do so too. We don't ask a farthing from the State, only the concession, but we cannot get even this. . . .

Near Spalato we have a waterfall, which apart from Scandinavia, is the highest in Europe—over 100 meters high, with 75,000 horse-power. Here a company formed mainly of Italian capitalists has built water-works and invested millions. From this not only Spalato but the whole province expects a great future ; it might supply tramways, aqueducts and so on, with electricity. What happens ? All at once the work is stopped. Spalato, my native town, is greatly embarrassed ; for our contract with the Augsburg Gas Company runs out next year, and we don't know what to do. From these water-works we might get the necessary power for lighting the town, but the work is suspended for months. . . . Why ? Once more there are reasons of high politics. The capitalists are Italians. I repeat, we do not mind ; we are not in love with Italian capital, we would certainly prefer our own capital or help from other Crown-lands. But it does not come, and the help of foreign capital has come. And for Dalmatia a question of life and death is at stake. . . .

A further point must be considered. From so great a distance Dalmatia cannot be governed on centralist lines. I do not wish to speak from a constitutional standpoint or to break a lance for Federalism. I merely refer to the administration in its economic aspect. . . . I can understand that Linz and Upper Austria can easily be governed from Vienna on the same principles. But we are too far off. In this Empire there is a complete difference between the North and this little province which has not even a geographical connexion with this state—climate, people, needs, etc. (Deputy Dr. Bartoli : ' Away from Vienna, then ? ') I shall not draw that conclusion.

[502] Cf. Southampton and Portsmouth.

. . . I do not say ' Away from Vienna,' but I am of opinion that the organization and plan of work in this state are wrong, and that their centre must be not in Vienna but in Dalmatia itself. I do not ask that the State should give us money and that we Dalmatians should manage it as we please. No, gentlemen, unfortunately we are not ripe for that. Let Dalmatia still be administered by men from Vienna. Give us one of your best, a capable, modern, energetic man, and he need not be a Dalmatian, we shall not mind if he is a German Austrian. Give us what the great Napoleon gave us, a Dandolo, who in five years did more for the country than Austria in 105 years. I repeat . . . without regard for nationality : that is a matter of indifference. . . . In our towns during the Middle Ages, the head of the town might never be a native, but always had to be a stranger. Gentlemen, the Government which seeks to further the interests of the State, should take an example from the English. England does not send to its important colonies its most incapable men, does not ask whether the man belongs to an old aristocratic family. . . . Have you an Austrian Cecil Rhodes, a Cromer, a Curzon ? If you have, or even men of lesser calibre, then send them to Dalmatia. But give the man to whom you entrust the fate of the province and the task of its regeneration, also the power to effect something : do not make him a mere marionette of the central authorities, who has not even £4 at his disposal if a village is burnt down. I am not speaking against Vienna. But do you know, gentlemen, the methods of procedure in Vienna ? In 1835 a small road was planned from Almissa eastwards, and after sixty-five years this road was at last built. If one wants to build a church or a harbour in some tiny village, it takes twenty, thirty, forty years, till the plans come back from Vienna, and one is at last free to build. . . . I repeat, the only way to help Dalmatia, is to give a wider sphere of action to the Statthalter—call him Governor or what you will—and to surround him with practical men who know the life of the people. Let the Central Government appoint half these men, and the Diet the other half. Some of them need not be natives ; we shall be glad if you send us some of your capable men. . . . It is not a matter of federalism, but of a healthy decentralization, which not only Dalmatia but I believe all the Crown lands want. . . . Just make the experiment with us, and if it succeeds, all the others will be grateful. If you do not care to learn from the English, let us look into the past . . . give us Proconsuls, propraetors, like those of the ancient Romans, men with initiative who were petty rulers. To-day no one can be jealous of the ancient Romans.

It is absolutely necessary to fulfil what has been promised, to give out of State money the sums for Dalmatia's barest needs. It may be objected that it might help itself, that something could be done with provincial funds. Gentlemen, we are not able for this. . . . Give

THE CONDITION OF DALMATIA

us land, schools, means of communication, bring us out of the Middle Ages, and then we shall do the rest. It is the State's duty to do this much. To-day—I am ashamed to admit it, but it is the sad truth— Dalmatia has become a land of beggars, through no fault of its own. For centuries it has been systematically plundered and ruined, both by Turks and Venetians, merely to prevent the Turks from reaching the Adriatic coast, which would have been equivalent to the conquest of Italy and other countries too. In our coast towns the Venetian Republic allowed no industry, lest it should compete with Venice ; our Hinterland was turned to a desert, lest the Turks should settle there. Our national nobility . . . was rooted out by foreign governments. But the country was not always in so lamentable a condition. I need only remind you of the greatness of Roman Illyria when Salona was one of the greatest industrial towns of the Roman Empire, when the country was intersected by trade roads, when Illyria was a centre of culture for the whole Balkan Peninsula. I need only remind you of the little republic of Ragusa, and of the fact that this country, to-day poor and abandoned, gave to the Roman Empire its wisest organizer, the Emperor Diocletian, to the Church its greatest father, St. Jerome, to the Southern Slav literature its first poet, Gundulic, to Italian literature the best master of the language, Tomaseo. . . . Our past, our contributions to general culture, are the titles on the basis of which we demand of a *Kultur-staat*, that it should do its duty towards us. We ask it too, because Austrian Governments have dealt us the last blow. Our fields have decayed in recent years, our cattle industry has gone back compared to the French period, public health is far worse than then. Our little towns, which had no industry but at least a lively trade with Bosnia and Herzegovina, are to-day ruined, because these countries are only connected by railway with distant Hungary, and thus the main arteries of our towns are severed. Remember too the wine duty on the commercial treaty with Italy, by which we were sacrificed to the interests of the other Crown lands and lost millions.

What we ask of the state to-day, is not alms, not a present, but compensation for the damage which this state has done us. Above all, we demand the necessary railway connexion : without which we cannot live or develop economically. They say, Hungary does not allow that. But if Austria only chooses, she has means to compel Hungary to agree to Dalmatia's railway connexion. Hungary is surrounded by Austria, has no other way to West and North Europe ; and there lies Austria's strength and Hungary's weakness, which we can use for our purposes, which are not provincial, but state aims. But we see that the state has not the serious will to help us in this way. Formerly our good people thought the Magyars were responsible for everything ; the poor Austrian Government would build the railways, but Hungary will not allow it. To-day no one is so naïve as to believe that. For we see that Austria can carry through more difficult and important things when she chooses, even against the will of an overwhelming majority in the Magyar Parliament. If that is not done in Dalmatia's favour, we must draw the logical conclusion, that there is no serious intention, but merely sweet words and fine promises.

They say : ' After all, we need Hungary.' But we Dalmatians ask the state, ' Does Austria not need Dalmatia, or the ten million Serbo-Croats ? ' I think this state needs Dalmatia, that without a province whose coast is 500 kilometres long and dominates the Adriatic with its hundred harbours, it cannot maintain its present position. Without Dalmatia, we say, you have no sea and no sailors ; for of the Austrian sailors, but for the Croats of Istria and Croatia, two-thirds are Dalmatians, who serve two years longer than other men, and even in future will have to serve longer than the others, because in Austria there are not many such smart recruits. If then thousands of our young people must serve two years extra, in order to defend the coast and this state's highest interests, it is only just that the state should give something as compensation. . . .

Gentlemen, it is not enough to be able to exercise material brutal force over a country. A state must endeavour to win over all peoples and provinces in its territory ; is it possible then, that the Dalmatian population should be grateful and devoted to this Government, and even (I say it quite openly) to this state, when we are left 100 years in this sad condition ? There is no Irredentism in Dalmatia, neither on Serbo-Croat nor on Italian side, and this last you will surely believe from me as a Slav. But it is not the Servian nor the Italian Governments which work against the interests of this state but . . . the Austrian Government, which by neglecting the country directly produces discontent against it. Our peasants emigrate to America, to Australia, to New Zealand, to Canada, and some return, after seeing in the great world how one lives in modern states. It is these people who create, and inevitably create, a permanent discontent with present conditions. What can be the feelings of these thousands who, in order not to starve, have had to leave homes and families, and seek their living abroad. . . .

This discontent cannot be cured by ' Flogging Patents,' [503] nor by review articles,[504] least of all by High Treason trials (applause), but the state must at last do its duty in matters of culture and in its own interests remove discontent. Millions will now be expended on Dreadnoughts, but it might perhaps be better for the defence of the state to expend these millions, I will not say on Dalmatia,

[503] A phrase invented to describe the Imperial Patent which inaugurated the absolutist Bach regime (1850–1859).

[504] Probably a reference to the *Oesterreichische Rundschau's* fierce attacks upon Dalmatia.

but on the future sailors of these Dreadnoughts. It is certainly more useful to the state, to satisfy the country and to give it means of existence, than, as still happens, to disburse money from various secret sources for military spies, who watch for years for the alleged smuggle of weapons from Italy, merely to elicit the fact that no weapons are imported, but that there is a lively export trade in human flesh, Dalmatia's sole article of export to-day. . . . Dalmatia is getting depopulated. Quite close to its chief town Spalato lies the island of Brazza, Austria's largest island. On it the fields are already lying fallow, a large section of the population is already missing. . . . In the interests of the state it is regrettable that this population, so smart, so honest, so hard-working and saving, cannot live at home, but has to emigrate and help other states, as, for instance, in the case of Punta Arena, the southernmost town in the world, where the inhabitants of Brazza form a relative majority of the population and are the smartest workmen, as has been repeatedly admitted by the Chilian Government. It is a pity that the state does nothing to check this misery. We cannot be satisfied at the state regulating two or three torrents a year, if hundreds of other torrents do a hundred times greater damage. . . . One cannot wait one or two centuries until the 300 or 400 villages which have no schools get one new school a year. . . . We hear recently of sympathy felt in various quarters for Dalmatia. We are thankful for the sympathy extended to us by Government organs and by members of this House ; but we cannot live on sympathy alone. Besides, these are dangerous sympathies. Dalmatia is regarded as something exotic, it is only regarded from the standpoint of archæology and tourist traffic. We have no wish to play the part of an archæological cemetery or an " Indian reservation " with the authentic Dalmatian Red Indians in their gay costume. No, gentlemen, we want to be able to live and work, to earn our living honestly by agriculture, trade and industry and thus serve the interests of the state as a whole. The necessary conditions are there ; for if the torrents are regulated and the swamps drained, we could not only have enough corn and bread for our own use, but could even export it. We have a splendid situation on the sea, with so many hundred harbours, only five or six hours by steamer from Italy ; a rich Hinterland—Bosnia, Herzegovina, Servia ; admirable trade conditions ; the biggest and strongest water power in Europe, so that industry might be promoted as nowhere else. Just consider all these branches of economic life, the rich supplies of minerals, the sea with its fisheries, and you might say, that could be the richest land in Europe. And this might be attained at a relatively small expense, by investments which would bear a hundredfold to the state.

Gentlemen, in fulfilment of my duty, I have endeavoured to show the Government the means of helping Dalmatia. Not only capital and investments are needed, but also organization and a sensible plan . . . not made in Vienna, but transplanted to the country itself. And so long as the Government and every future Government fails to fulfil this duty towards my native country, I shall vote against the Budget proposals . . . just as I shall gladly acknowledge the Government, if it helps us with deeds, instead, of words and promises. . . . In my opinion we (Dalmatian deputies) shall best serve our country, if we follow the lines I have indicated, with all possible energy and without regard to the Government or any one at all. I believe that we shall thus also best serve the national cause of the Serbo-Croats, to whom Dalmatia belongs as one of their noblest provinces, and who will certainly be stronger if Dalmatia is 'freed from its present wretched conditions." (Loud applause.)

APPENDIX XVII

THE CORRESPONDENCE OF BISHOP STROSSMAYER AND MR. GLADSTONE [505]

I AM indebted to the great kindness of the Trustees of Mr. Gladstone for permission to publish the following letters which he received from Bishop Strossmayer during the Eastern crisis of 1876–8 and the years that followed. I have also been fortunate enough to obtain copies of Mr. Gladstone's replies, and these are included in their proper place in the correspondence.

The connecting link between the Bishop and the statesman was Lord Acton, who had become intimate with Strossmayer during their memorable opposition to the dogma of Papal Infallibility, at the Vatican Council of 1869–70. Lord Acton knew Strossmayer and Gladstone to be spiritually akin, and made more than one effort to arrange a meeting between them. But some obstacle invariably arose, and the modern Bossuet never met the modern Leibniz (*see* page 431). As late as 1886 there appears to have been some idea of the Bishop paying a visit to Hawarden, in company with Lord Acton, but the Bishop's advanced age made the journey impossible (*see* Lord Morley's *Life of Gladstone*, vol. II).

The correspondence reveals one of Mr. Gladstone's sources of information during the Eastern crisis, but it is no less interesting for its references to Church affairs. It throws an equally attractive light upon two of the most striking personalities of their time.

From Professor Kršnjavi, of Agram—whose father-in-law entertained Bishop Strossmayer for some weeks at his house in Mödling

---

[505] Where an asterisk occurs, the particular sentence in the original letter has been specially marked in pencil, presumably by Mr. Gladstone himself. We thus have an indication of what specially interested the receiver of Strossmayer's communications.

near Vienna at the time of the Bosnian rising—I learn that the Bishop set great store upon his communications with Mr. Gladstone, and hoped that they would not be without influence upon the fate of the Balkans.

I have preferred to print the letters so far as possible without comment, leaving the reader to pass his own verdict upon their contents.

I. *Bishop Strossmayer to Mr. Gladstone.* October 1, 1876. (Written in German.)

[All the other letters I have myself translated from the originals, but this version is transcribed from a MS., on the back of which are the words, " Translation in Lord Acton's hand." Needless to say, Lord Acton's version is at once scholarly and accurate. R.W.S.W.]

Allow me to thank you from my inmost soul for the generous initiative you have taken,[506] before your own glorious nation and the whole civilized world, for the rights of humanity and freedom, for which the unfortunate Southern Slavs are suffering so much and are pouring forth their blood in an unequal conflict. We have rejoiced at it the more, because of our sincere admiration for your country, which has succeeded so well in reconciling order and stability with liberty and with every description of progress, and the noble movement which has recently taken possession of a part of the English people [507] fills us with hope, because the force of public opinion is irresistible when it is directed towards noble ends, and is guided by men of your services and reputation. Therefore I thank you again heartily, and will add a few words, not to say anything that is new, but to relieve the pressure that is on my heart.

The Koran has manifested before God and man its absolute incapacity to govern Christian nations, by making itself the basis not only of religious but of social and political life. Its fatal purpose is either to force Islamism upon them, or to deprive them for ever of political rights, and to plunge them into an intolerable oppression. No power in the world can change this inherent mission of the Koran, for it comes, in the belief of the Moslem, from God Himself. To rule and aggrandise, and to indulge undisturbed in all those unnatural vices which, before they bring about the death of nations. are always the source of dreadful cruelties, that is the appointed mission which the Mussulman has received from God. Between the slavery of the Koran and all other slavery there is this difference, that the one is commonly the result of evil custom, of vice and passion, of causes that are destitute of divine sanction, whilst the other claims

---

[506] Mr. Gladstone's famous pamphlet on *The Bulgarian Horrors and the Question of the East*, appeared on September 5, 1876.

[507] Through the correspondence both Strossmayer and Gladstone invariably use the words " England " and " English " for " Britain " and " British."

to be directly sanctioned by God Himself, and must therefore be unchangeable and perpetual. Hence the evident truth, that all attempted reforms are fruitful of nothing but increase of suffering to the Christian. The Turks have the right to say that they must obey the voice of God rather than the precepts of human policy. They regard compulsory reforms as sacrilegious follies, calculated to disturb the rights and enjoyments assured to them by Heaven, and take their revenge on the Christians who occasion the demand for reform. They are cunning enough to abound with treacherous promises in the hour of trouble; but we can truly say of such hollow pledges— "mentita est iniquitas sibi" and "quae societas lucis cum tenebris aut Christi cum Belial." It is impossible that their promises should ever be sincere.* It is pitiful that there should be men who have the courage to allow themselves to be so openly deceived; and it is sad especially that the European diplomacy should be among them. Diplomacy ought to be the highest and safest tribunal, full of wisdom and experience; but it exhibits itself now in a light that does not deserve the confidence of the world. Instead of simplifying problems it makes them obscure, and supplies solutions which instead of peace and tranquillity produce new complications, new delusions, new animosities and new conflicts. Of this kind are assuredly all the reforms now spoken of.

To make the situation of the Christians in some measure bearable, it is requisite that the Turkish Government should be able to give them securities for their personal safety, for intellectual progress, and for a decently upright administration. Turkey is manifestly unable to satisfy any one of these requirements. Not the first, for Turkey cannot grant to Christians the right of serving with Mohammedans in the regular army.* The Christian cannot remain a slave whose liberty, property and life are at the disposal of his Turkish master. He must be unarmed, because he is not his own master, and has no country of his own. In consequence of the undeserved protection it enjoys, and perhaps of secret suggestions, Turkey intends to create an universal militia or Landwehr, to deliver it once and for all from European influence and from proposals of reform. If, to the disgrace of Europe, this should be accomplished, then woe to the Christians! God knows whether in that event the self-constituted protectors and advisers would not afterwards suffer for it themselves.

Turkey cannot satisfy the second requirement, because it absolutely contradicts its nature and its divinely appointed mission to pay for Christian schools and institutions. Islam regards this as the greatest crime, whereas the destruction of the Alexandrian library was a holy and religious work. Lastly, the Turkish administration is the incurable spot in the Turkish State. We know by our own experience, the character of the Asiatic bureaucracy which the Turks have, for many years, sent into our Slavonic provinces. They have not an atom of the laboriousness and integrity necessary to a decent administrative system. They are so covetous and so vicious that they can only be compared to swarms of locusts that devastate a country, and leave nothing but desolation and disease behind ; and I cannot help observing the contrast between the Arabs, who left splendid traces of their mental activity in Europe, and the Turkish race, which is utterly incapable of creating anything and is only skilful to destroy. They will leave nothing behind them in the fairest regions of Europe, after four centuries of occupation, but destitution and misery, without a sign of any loftier or better purpose.* All that is spoken about reform is an illusion, founded very often on bad faith. For there are men who foolishly conceive that the resurrection of the Slavonic race in these parts would be the ruin of their own people.[508] Hence the cry, that the Slavonians must not be free, that the germs of an independent commonwealth must not be suffered to take root in that country. These men are blind to the truth that, by a providential law, the deliverance and revival of an oppressed nation is a pledge of future benefit for others.* That is the true secret of the solidarity of nations. That must be a truly wretched and intolerable existence, which requires as its condition, that a neighbouring people should be crushed and enslaved. There is a process of union going on among the Slavonian people, which, in spite of many obstacles and errors, God seems to have taken in His hands. The issue is a secret of Providence. But I hope with my whole heart that it will be for the advantage of the state to which I belong, and which seems to have the exalted mission of interponing between great nations, to prevent conflict and to bring about a solution of the most intricate questions, that shall be for the advantage and happiness of Europe. The result depends on this : whether that Power remains true without swerving to that law of Justice which is the daily bread of the nations that live for the achievement of great ends. We Croats can truly say, that in this little group of Slavonian brethren, we represent the Tuscan element. Under great difficulties and in a short course of years, we have called into existence institutions which justify us in claiming the lead in the path of intellectual progress and of high ideals. We have a great duty to perform, and we are conscious of our function in this region, and in the questions which are stirring the world. It is in the power of others either to frustrate our action, or to free and consolidate us.

The Bulgarians are an extremely quiet, sensible and hardworking people, rich in domestic virtues. A moral and hardworking people is *eo ipso* fit for self-government.* An independent administration, if it was granted to this fine Slavonian race, would set free forces that would soon do much for material and for moral civilization ; and ecclesiastical self-government, partially introduced, would serve them as a school for political self-government.*

---

[508] A reference to the popular view prevalent among the Magyars.

The Servians are a warlike and very enterprising race, full of vitality. It would be a just reward of their sanguinary sacrifices in a sacred cause, to put the autonomy of Bosnia under the protection of their energy and their fifty years' experience. A valuable security for the success of Bosnian self-government would be due provision for the moral influences which are never more important than in a primitive condition of society. A good Catholic and Orthodox Bishop could do a great work in that country.

Such a system of self-government in its European provinces would suit the true interest of Turkey far better than the continual intervention of Europe in its internal affairs, which is injurious to its honour and reputation. I am thoroughly convinced that any solution of the Eastern question which does not include full administrative autonomy in the European provinces of Turkey will increase the confusion and the danger.

Once more I thank you most sincerely, and hope that I shall soon be able to thank you personally and to shake you warmly by the hand. Two distinguished Englishmen, Dr. Liddon and Mr. Malcolm Mac-Coll, visited me lately, and gave me courage to write to you. I need not say that if you should ever visit this country, you will find the heartiest and most fraternal reception at my house.

STROSSMAYER, *Bishop of Bosnia.*

DIAKOVO, *October* 1, 1876.

II. *Bishop Strossmayer to Mr. Gladstone*, October 24, 1876.
(In German.)

Most esteemed sir, and permit me to add, my very dear friend! for all those who champion truth and justice in this world, are united by the bands of a truly sacred union in a higher friendship and alliance, with the task of using every effort that poor humanity may never lack the daily bread of truth and justice, for on this depends their moral life just as their physical life on material bread.

Your letter greatly honoured, rejoiced and encouraged me. You have done well in leaving your retirement, for, my dear friend, God has placed you on such a height, that even the evening of your life belongs not to yourself, but to your distinguished nation and to all mankind. Let me now give you my opinion upon the events which have occurred since my first letter.

The truce has been caused by Russia's energetic intervention. It seems to me that your Premier[509] did not act in a wise and statesmanlike manner in making his last speech. All those who are anxious that great questions should not be confused, but decided by reason and peaceful agreement rather than by arms, should surely avoid prematurely making warlike speeches, which are calculated to kindle passions and to awake vain hopes. The opinion is

[509] Disraeli.

general that the speech of your Premier provoked that of the Russian Emperor in Moscow. Both speeches have contributed nothing towards calming opinion. It is my conviction, then, that the preservation of peace and the attainment of the great aim which all friends of mankind have before their eyes, *mainly depends upon England's attitude.* But to this end England would have to lay aside all petty scruples, and support honestly and whole-heartedly the efforts of Russia. No doubt it is said that Russia, apart from its openly acknowledged aims, also follows certain special aims in the Eastern Question, such as are injurious to the common weal. I do not know whether there is any truth in this ; but I do know that by an ill-timed opposition one does not counteract such injurious aims. Only if England with complete devotion espouses the cause of suffering Christendom, does she acquire before God and the world the right to watch Russia and in case of need to call to her, " Thus far and no farther " ; while in the contrary case she will be responsible before God and the world for war and for the shattering of those hopes which the Eastern Christians cherish. England is in this respect on a dangerous path to-day. She has probably already allied herself too closely with a state, whose fortunes unhappily rest in the hands of a nation which is full of conceit and which by emphasizing in the most foolish and presumptuous manner its kinship with the Turks [510] and by approving all Turkish atrocities simply because they are committed against the poor Slav Christians, is steering towards a war against Russia in alliance with England and Turkey. If as seems to be the case England really listens unduly to this nation, then war in the direction indicated above is inevitable. The consequences of such a war no one to-day can calculate : but one thing seems to be certain—that England in that case will have for ever sacrificed its moral authority and influence among the Southern Slavs.[511] It is equally clear that in this case the Southern Slavs will but attach themselves to Russia more closely and unreservedly than ever. It is England's natural mission to introduce for the future the *most far-reaching* improvements in the lot of the Christians in Turkey, and if possible to *overtrump* Russia in this respect. The matter, it is true, involves great difficulties, but only weaklings shrink from difficulties ; to a truly enlightened reason, if accompanied by honest intentions, the solution of every difficulty is possible. It is said that the Christians have sunk too low to be capable of any wide autonomy. Yes, the Christians in Turkey indeed have sunk low, but whose doing is that ? It is a most inverted logic, to deduce from the decayed condition of the Christians the right of the Koran, which by its rule of four

[510] Here of course Strossmayer refers to the Magyars, who through Count Andrassy dominated the whole foreign policy of Austria-Hungary.
[511] Strossmayer invariably uses the word Southern Slav in its widest sense to include all the Slavs of the Southern group.

centuries is responsible for their low estate, to continue still further its work of humiliation and desolation. Europe's first duty is to free the poor Christians as speedily and completely as possible from that nightmare which weighs upon their breast. The Christians have sunk low, but have happily not yet died out ; while the Koran is by its inmost nature tyrannical and quite incapable of showing justice towards Christians. Latterly a comedy is being played, called " the Turkish Constitution." But every serious person knows what to think of that ! Where in Turkey are those social and moral seeds which might be capable of life and of those beneficial functions, which a constitution performs in England, for instance. As every innovation hitherto, so also this newly-devised constitution would merely render the lot of the Christians still worse. We see this already before our eyes. At present in Bosnia and Herzegovina, probably in Bulgaria also, papers are being carried round by the Turks and given for signature to the heads of both Christian confessions ; these contain the assertion that the Turks are entirely satisfied with the Rayah, and the poor Rayah with the Turks, and *that they protest against any other modus vivendi than the present.* You can easily imagine the position of the poor clergy of both confessions towards the Turkish proposal. They are not even allowed to see the contents of the papers which they are to subscribe, for that would be an insult to the haughty Ottomans. If the poor priest signs, he has for ever confirmed his own and his people's servitude. But if he does not, he has exposed their lives to obvious danger, if not now, when the Turks are somewhat more cautious, at any rate for the future. The Turks, like all Oriental races, are wily and cunning. Everything in a constitution that guarantees the rights of the population, they will contrive to evade and make illusory ; while all that can serve as a handle to human wickedness and arrogance towards the poor Christians, will be exploited to the full.

A further remark is, that a real and wide autonomy is the beginning of the end. Strengthen the Christian peoples in their autonomy and the Turks in Europe are done for. I answer, Yes, that is so ! As a statesman, I would never deny this aim in granting the autonomy of the Christian provinces of Turkey. Turkey is clearly a rotting Lazarus, with the difference that the Turkish Lazarus, while bodily he merely vegetates, is in spirit already in the tomb and spreads an odour of death in all directions. There is no power which can waken this Lazarus to life. Europe's problem simply consists in making the Turks disappear from Europe, if possible without bloodshed and great upheavals. The sole means is to grant Autonomy to the Christian Provinces. My dear friend ! If Christian Europe were conscious of its higher mission, it would not for a moment tolerate those atrocities, whose saddened witnesses we are. Humane Europe has by international obligations ensured that instruments of war which mangle and annihilate may not be used in modern war, but it has forgotten to note that Man, the savage and fanatic, is the most cruel and fearful engine of war. Otherwise it could not allow the fiercest and most savage peoples of Asia and Africa to be let loose on unhappy Christian peoples. These are more cruel than hyænas, more pitiless than the most dread instrument of war. No child, no old man, no woman is spared by them. They know nothing of consideration towards prisoners, wounded and unarmed men. To them the Red Cross on ambulances and hospitals is a sign not of mercy, but of hate and loathing, which goads him to cruelty and bestiality. Either Europe will at last do its duty, or God will employ the dying Ottoman race as a fearful scourge to Europe, which has sunk in discord and petty disputes and needs a bloody rejuvenation. On England to-day rests a great responsibility. Either it will be a blessing to the world, by its calm and its genuine devotion to Christendom, or by unchaining the fury of war it will be a misfortune to the world. As the world stands to-day the biblical phrase applies to England, " positus hic in resurrectionem vel ruinam multorum in Israel." But above all, if it preserves its calm and judgment and bewares of ill-timed suggestions, England *will render my dear Austria a great service.*

The fear that England's road to India might be blocked is, according to my deep conviction, childish. My friend ! God has obviously placed in the hands of proud Albion the keys to those splendid sea-paths which connect Europe with the rest of the world, and no power on earth can snatch these keys from England's hands. England's Primacy on the sea is a disposition of God, to which in the general interest all must submit. The English are the natural protectors of the freedom of the sea, which is necessary to promote that unity of the human race which clearly lies in God's design. If any one should presume to try to block England's road to India, he would be crushed by the weight of England's power amid the applause of all civilized peoples. I regard this fear for India as groundless and artificial. England and Russia have great aims to fulfil in Asia. The period to which this providential mission extends, is reckoned not by hundreds but by thousands of years. During all this time both Empires should live in peace and mutual esteem. So far as Europe is concerned, a new order of things seems to be in birth-throes. God has so placed England in Europe, that it is bound to it by a thousand ties, but at the same time by its insular position is set apart from Europe's petty passions and disputes, and is best qualified to play the part of arbiter in all difficult questions. Resurrectio multorum ! Such a part is splendid, but also very delicate and responsible. In this great Eastern question also the eyes of all are turned towards England. All feel that almost all depends on England's attitude. From my very soul I wish that England may realize and fulfil its lofty task. This requires firmness and entire devotion to the Christian principle. Especially England has in my opinion to guard against foreign suggestions, which assail every Power on such an occasion, as once the infernal suggester assailed Our Lord.

I shall be immensely delighted if I should be privileged to entertain you in my house, with the distinguished Lord Acton, who is my friend and with whom I shared joy and sorrow during the Vatican Council. . . .

III. *Mr. Gladstone to Bishop Strossmayer.* Hawarden, November 5, 1876. (Written in French.)

It is more than three weeks since I received the letter which your Grace * was good enough to address to me. Neither indifference nor laziness was the cause of my silence. At the moment when this letter arrived, the Turkish Press (as it has been very justly named) of London was endeavouring to poison the public mind by means of a quantity of lies (nothing less) on the subject of Russian " atrocities " in Turkestan. It was not a question of humanity ; it was a very skilful attempt to diminish the public feeling which had been so keenly aroused, by suggesting, " Russian and Turk are a couple of scoundrels (*pendards*) : don't take away from the one, to give to the other." At the present moment, when the English Government has strayed so deplorably from its duty and the Russians almost alone championed the cause of the afflicted provinces, that seemed to me a sufficiently serious matter. Consequently—though against my will—I devoted myself to examining the question, and the result of my work has been published a few days ago in the *Contemporary Review*. I send you a copy of this ; but it is really a *brochure d'occasion*, and is not worth reading on your part : although I think it ought to be of some use for the English public.

My first idea, after the arrival of your letter, was this. I was greatly desirous of the permission to give to the public so interesting a document : even anonymously, in case its publication under your name, which would carry such weight with my countrymen, should not be possible.

I cannot tell you how much I associate myself with the internal feeling (*sentiment intime*) of that letter. The question of the suffering provinces of Turkey is for me a question of the first rank. It has dragged me from my retirement, which to some extent I was beginning to enjoy, after forty-four years of continual struggle in English political life, and after almost reaching the term of sixty-seven years of age. I can indeed assure you that in many respects it is for me a sacrifice, thus to change the current of my ideas and of my daily work, and to trust myself once more to a stormy sea.

Nunc agilis fio, et mersor civilibus undis. It is a sacrifice which

I gladly make, and which one ought not to make by halves. I must then follow the question through all its detours, up to the point where by God's grace it shall have reached its port, its adequate solution.

And I hope, I can almost say, I believe that henceforth this great question is going to have a prosperous journey. Not that the English Government has definitely been converted. But it seems to me that this Government—though perhaps unwittingly—has taken a definite and very important step at the moment when it submitted to the other Powers a project for the administrative autonomy of the Provinces, however inadequate this may be. For every project of this kind is essentially based on the principle of foreign interference in the internal affairs of Turkey. In my opinion there can be no question that once the six Powers have committed themselves to this interference by a solemn act, they are bound in honour, and according to the elementary idea of their office as preservers of European peace and order, to follow their own path to the very end, and to find effective means to secure its success. Hope then outweighs fear in my mind, and I give thanks to God (*au bon Dieu*) for what He has done up to to-day, amid a crowd of dangers and difficulties, of folly and meanness.

Do not imagine, Monseigneur, that the English people has repented, either wholly or partially, of what it has said and done during the past two months. If at the present moment there is less noise, the two chief causes are these ; first of all, almost all the towns (*communautés*) in the country have expressed their opinion, and they do not wish to say the same thing twice : in the second place, it is thought that the Government, *nolens volens*, has felt the impulse from outside, and does not dare now, even if it wishes, to persevere in the false course which it has so long followed. However, what is needed is still far from being accomplished. Without doubt, our Anglo-Turks (and there are only too many of them) count, not altogether without reason, upon the lassitude, rather than upon any possible changes, of the public mind. But on the one hand, I believe that they are mistaken, and on the other hand, that we have gained ground enormously, in the manner I have explained above. No, this national movement, so fresh, so simple, and, I venture to say, so noble, has not been without fruit.

What we always have to fear, are the mutual jealousies of the Powers. It is the strangest of all queer things (*bizarreries*) ; but among us English those who complain incessantly of the aggressive behaviour, whether real or supposed, of Russia, always have an *arrière pensée* themselves, and sometimes are very near suggesting (*la tiennent sur leur langues* that England must seize Egypt, perhaps also Crete, in order to safeguard the route to the East Indies. In present circumstances, this would, in my opinion, be a crime and a piece of folly. It is the English Navy which ought, and will long be able, to safeguard the route to India ; and the British Empire has neither the right nor the need to injure the liberty of any one.

I have written too late, and at too great length. It is in your indulgence and sympathies that I find my excuse. I do not wish to close without begging you to help me in my search for better information as to the capacity for and methods of securing local autonomy in the provinces of Bosnia, Herzegovina and Bulgaria.

As I grow old, I feel lazier or less capable of travelling. Besides, I believe that your Grace is younger than I ; and I hope that you will pay a visit to England, where you will find all the sympathy and respect which we owe you. None the less, I cannot renounce the hope of coming to see you in your own home. I have even discussed the matter with my friend Lord Acton. We have the idea of travelling together at some favourable time to * * *.[512] Perhaps it is a dream, but it is a charming dream, which I shall not willingly dispel. I remain, with every sentiment of respect and affection,

Your Grace's devoted servant,

W. E. GLADSTONE.

P.S. One more small request : please to write German in Italian characters. I cannot read German characters very easily.

IV. *Mr. Gladstone to Bishop Strossmayer.* Hawarden, December 15, 1876. (In French.)

ILLUSTRIOUS MONSEIGNEUR AND DEAR FRIEND !

Since the arrival of your warmly appreciated letter, we have not slept over our work. In the month of October, when the popular meetings had almost come to an end in all parts of the country, the nucleus of an association was formed ; and this body having reached the point of a sufficient organization, we met last Friday, to the number of 2,500 persons, at St. James's Hall, Westminster.

As for the idea of a supposed reaction, I think that we are done with it. In all respects this assembly has been most satisfactory. We have not altogether reached the point of governing the Government. We still have to fear from day to day some evil step (*démarche*). It is more than difficult to make ill-disposed persons act as though they were well-disposed, and up to the present we are uncertain as to whether the Ministers are prompted by their best or worst inspiration. It is the strangest and most incredible of all the political situations which I have known in all my life. Individuals, numerous it is true, but still only individuals, dissatisfied with the proceedings of the existing Government, have contrived to fashion *ab intra* the foreign policy of the country, in the most difficult of all questions. God grant that in the future we may not see a similar

---

[512] Here a word is missing. The appearance of the original suggests that Mr. Gladstone had for the moment forgotten the name of Djakovo, left a blank space, and then forgot to fill it in.

evil nor a similar remedy! They have succeeded up to a certain point ; they have prevented a great deal of positive evil, by frightening the Ministers, above all Disraeli, and by strengthening a little the feebleness of those colleagues of his who did not whole-heartedly share his ideas. But as for the negative evil, that is another matter. It is said that Lord Salisbury and General Ignatieff are in agreement, but it is not known whether they are co-operating frankly or are bargaining with each other nor whether they have come to essential points. Hence we still have uncertainty instead of light ; and in such circumstances one must speak and act, and not trust to accidents. That is in outline the present situation of English opinion and of the movement in England.

As for the object to be attained, the essential in my opinion is, that a new regime and a new source of public authority should succeed the Ottoman. Without a substitution of this kind, all reforms even the most radical, are null and indeed mere talk (*des nullités et des prêcheries*) : but on the other hand, when it has been accomplished, it will be possible to hope great things even from plans which are imperfect in themselves. Once expelled, the Turk will never be able to return. After the expulsion, there will be either autonomy, or the intermediary and provisional state of a foreign regime. In this I see much evil and much danger. If Russia is to be feared, it is then that she will have her opportunity. However, we may hope that all, or almost all, the European world will make an effort to save itself from so troublesome a situation, and to hasten on as far as possible the final and perfected autonomy, whose task it will be to lay the foundations of a better future.

I do not know whether Your Grace, master of so many languages, includes among them English also, and I do not wish to load your library with what might be totally useless. This is the only reason why I do not send you a pamphlet on Hellenism and its function in the Eastern Question, which I wrote for the last number of the *Contemporary Review*.

One more word on what you said regarding my age and my occupations. It was not distaste, nor laziness which has led me to covet the faculty of slightly changing my trade, at a time when I can scarcely cope with the labour of political life pure and simple, in the House of Commons. I should like to serve my country and humanity till death. But this service can be rendered in more than one way. If I ask myself where in our day most is done for the good of humanity, I answer that it is not in the sphere of ordinary politics ; these struggles may be serious, but there is another far graver struggle, the struggle of *Credo* and *Non Credo*, which in my country sounds continually like thunder in our ears. The question of the Christian faith and of its relations to Reason, to Liberty, to the Sciences, to Human Life, is the question, equally menacing and fruitful, alike of the present day and of the future. What a joy and an honour it would be for me, if, by returning to the studies which I have always loved and never entirely abandoned, God might help me to say, were it but a few words, which might advance even the smallest of these questions towards its necessary and desired solution. That is my last hope. None the less for the moment, and for as many moments as may be needed, I take the Eastern Question as an imperious *mot d'ordre.*

I beg to remain, with profound respect,

Your Grace's very affectionate
W. E. GLADSTONE.

V. *Bishop Strossmayer to Mr. Gladstone,* February 10, 1877, Djakovo. (In German.)

Above all pardon me for answering so late. Partly a prolonged indisposition, partly endless work which accumulates before Lent, prevented me. Believe me, each of your letters is a new consolation to me and a further ground for deeply revering and loving you.

Many thanks for the lucid exposition of the situation of your country towards the Eastern Question. To be honest : I have not been at all satisfied by the conferences in Constantinople. They were too temporizing and not decided enough, in view of the wily and malicious subterfuges of Turkey. It seems to me that the result of the conferences is not such as to fill the world with great respect for the wisdom and firmness of European diplomacy. The most essential fault of this conference seems to me to have been *the latent disunion of the Powers*, which the wily Orientals contrived to exploit to the full. There are unhappily in Europe white Turks, who in their dislike for the Slav Christians, emulate the " black " Turks. I do not know whether I take the right view, but it seems to me that more agreement prevailed between the English and Russian ambassadors than could have been hoped. This is mainly *your* doing, my dear friend. At any rate, it seems to me most desirable that agreement, and if possible intimacy, should be restored between England and Russia, respecting the aims to be reached in Turkey. You are a thousand times right ; nothing can be made of the Turkish element. Only the grant of autonomy to the Turkish provinces and a Christian Government, however incomplete at first, can produce seed leading to the rebirth of the Turkish territories. We have here been immensely pleased by the idea recently developed by you, that Turkey, by refusing to accept the unanimous resolutions of Europe, has forfeited the advantages secured to her by the Paris Convention.* Cessante ratione, cessat rationatum. Turkey was only included in the European Concert, on condition that it would enforce in its own house those principles of state upon which humanity and culture largely rest.* If it remains savage and barbarous, and behaves contemptuously and repulsively towards the public opinion of Europe, then it is unworthy of European protection and good-will. Europe would be forgetful of her higher mission and would deserve the divine chastisement, if in this case she did not use absolute force, to quench for ever the inflammable material which threatens a general conflagration.

Only one more point in this direction. When a few months ago I told my kind English guests something of the unheard of cruelties committed by the Turks in Bosnia, and when what I said found its echo in the papers, the English and Austrian Consuls in Sarajevo saw fit virtually to call me to question for this.* The Austrian Consul-General, who is a Slav, I answered in Slav. Now according to our papers the English Red Book has published a greatly watered down extract of my letter. I now venture to give you a correct extract, so that you, and if necessary the English public also, may know exactly what I have written. I wrote to the Austrian Consul, that I had learned of those cruelties from many absolutely reliable witnesses, especially from my priests, who have parishes on the banks of the Save and were eyewitnesses of such cruelties. I then added the remark : " The representatives of foreign powers always serve a certain tendency, and among us it is believed that they do not always possess the capacity of preserving towards their chiefs that independence which is necessary in order to reveal events in their true light. Besides, it is not a question whether this or that event took place in this or that form, but mainly whether it is possible that Christians should remain under the rule of the Koran and its fanatical followers free from tyranny and every kind of cruelty. Every thinking man must answer this question with a decided ' No.' The Koran orders in God's name that the Christian dogs should be exterminated by the sword ; where this is quite impossible, it condemns them, once more in God's name, to shameful servitude, and excludes them for ever from every right and power and property. The whole history of the Christians among the Turks is written in three dreadful words : stupid arrogance and laziness ; shameless and often unnatural lust, and finally the horrible cruelty and tyranny which go with it.* All that Europe has done hitherto to improve the lot of the Christians, has not merely remained ineffective but has made it worse, because the Turks, and rightly from their standpoint, are angry at their Christians giving cause for Europe to interfere in their internal affairs, to disturb them in their enjoyment and to seek impiously to impose on them her own will instead of the divine and unalterable law. I cited, for example, the little town of Brod, which lies on the banks of the Save in our immediate neighbourhood, where the poor rayah in the presence of our authorities hurled thousands of reproaches in the face of the Turks who urged them to return, regarding incredible cruelties such as the murder of innocent children and old men, and the most infamous violation of girls, boys and women, as was related to me by a reliable and learned witness. I added ; if to these cruelties of a single place and a single occasion be added the whole extensive Turkish empire and four whole centuries, then every Christian heart will be convinced that the bitter cup of suffering of the poor Christians in Turkey is already overfull and that we are justified in at last expecting from the justice and wisdom of Europe that it should take pity on them and hasten to their aid, the more so as their own interest demands this, in order that the inflammable material in Turkey may not produce an universal European conflagration." This is the true sense of my letter, which I send you with the request that if your " Red Book " shall have given a false extract, you will be kind enough to correct it.

Unhappily, I do not speak English, but I shall be most grateful if you send me something for my library. I have a niece, my sister's daughter, seventeen years old, who knows English well. I am also anxious that my young clergy should learn English for the sake of its rich and splendid literature.

The final remark in your letter has made you still dearer to me and still more worthy of respect. It is the privilege of great minds to deal with those religious questions which touch the whole world's deepest interests. Christianity is the innermost principle of human life. Only the grace of Him Who died for us all and by His death opened for us the unquenchable sources of higher life, can renew mankind and fit it for the attainment not only of its immortal but also of its earthly destiny. The question of " credo " or " non credo " is for every nation a question of life and death. You are right, my friend, the relations of belief and grace to reason and science, to liberty and the whole complex of earthly life are the most important questions, at once fearful and fruitful. Such questions very often form the subject of my thought, but my weak health and the burdens of my practical calling leave me little leisure for it. If God some day grants that I should see you, and prove to you my respect and admiration, then we will exchange our views on this subject in all love and openness. The human mind can achieve much in such questions. But just as the last word of the secret of the Union of Divine and human nature in one Divine Person will only be clear to us when we are ripe to look upon God, so also the whole secret of those holy and tender relations which subsist between Faith and Reason and Science, between Grace and Freedom and the moral value of practical life, will only be clear to us when we have thrown off our earthly shell and have attained to a higher outlook. Faith stands clearly and firmly enough before our spiritual vision, to bend our reason beneath the yoke of divine Truth ; but so long as we wander in this life, there will always be some dark places in Faith, that with our zeal in the recognition of divine truth and with the humility of the heart the merit of our faith may increase. For some time my mind has specially busied itself with that Unity of Faith and of the Church, which is at once the most precious fruit of our redemption and its final aim. I have indeed chosen this as the subject of this year's pastoral address to my clergy. It seems to me that mankind, despite its errors and numerous frailties, is tending towards this unity. God formerly converted the great Roman Empire into a preface and a true introduction to Christianity ; to-day I think that God wishes to make those wonderful instruments of communication and traffic between the most distant parts of our globe, which steam and electricity offer, into a preface and introduction to that ideal unity which Our Lord made the subject of His noblest prayer to His Eternal Father before His death (St. John xvii.). How gladly I shall some day discuss these lofty subjects with you, if God will ! It is true that for this to be done successfully, Bossuet would have to arise in the Bishop, just as the famous Leibnitz has arisen in my dear and valued friend. Forgive my verbosity. Ex abundantia cordis os loquitur. In deep respect and esteem, I embrace you and am proud to call you my friend.

STROSSMAYER,
Bishop.

VI. *Bishop Strossmayer to Mr Gladstone.* Djakovo, September 3, 1877. (In German.)

I know very well that there are many claims on your time. I watch with great care your splendid activity, and assure you that I admire you more and more, You may be convinced that I shall bless the day when I am permitted to see you face to face.

I was absent about three months, partly in Italy, partly at a bath for my health. In Florence I visited my friend, the Duke of Sermoneta, whose wife is a distinguished Englishwoman. In his house we also spoke of you. As everywhere, so also in the Duke's house you are admired and respected. He sent you his kind regards.

How matters stand at the seat of war in Europe and in Asia, you know as well as and perhaps better than I. No one could have thought that the Turks would have defended themselves so bravely and heroically. None the less they remain a wild horde, not worthy of consideration, because they possess no qualities such as might found a commonwealth worthy of existence. They regard themselves as the tormentors of Christian peoples, and Christian Europe certainly has the duty of at length freeing the Christian peoples from centuries of pain and torture. Those men who contribute to this, cover themselves with eternal fame.

You were good enough to promise to send me one of your works for my library. I applied to my Vienna bookseller, Braumüller, in the matter ; in his answer he mentions the London agent who will send the book to Vienna, so that it may be sent me from there. I send my kindest regards to your family and bless you from the bottom of my heart. If you have the opportunity, please greet my friend Lord Acton from me. With my most distinguished regards, etc.

STROSSMAYER,
Bishop.

VII. *Bishop Strossmayer to Mr. Gladstone,* October 28, 1877.
(In German.)

A thousand thanks for the beautiful gifts which you have sent me. I cannot understand how you can find time to be so unceasingly active, and also to write so much. God bless you henceforth and spare you for many years to your nation and to humanity. This winter I shall read some of your works. Your high ideals and generous disposition lead you habitually to interest yourself in the suffering and oppesrsed. Your German biographer, in a translation of your work on Homer, says with entire truth that in future the neglected Slavs will also be under the obligation of hailing you as their supporter, defender and saviour. Believe me, my dearest friend, the Southern Slavs will never forget what you have done for them under the most difficult circumstances. Your name will be blessed and praised among us from generation to generation.

According to the papers you are now in Ireland. I hope that the Irish will show to the whole world on this occasion, what they owe to their greatest benefactor.

The unexpected course of the war in Europe makes us somewhat anxious, and yet the more difficult the Russian position and the greater the resisting power of the Turks, the more necessary it is that the Russians should win, and that the Christians should once and for all be free of the rough and brutal domination of the Turks. If the poor Christian peoples are not to go under altogether, their fate must be put into their own hands through a full and comprehensive autonomy. The highly industrious Bulgar, who is thoroughly amenable to any civilized discipline, the noble and highly gifted Bosniak and Herzegovinian, will certainly convert their country, which has lain waste for centuries, but is beautiful and fertile by nature, into smiling and fruitful fields, in a short space of time, to their own benefit and to the advantage of such civilized nations as come into contact with them. It is an unavoidable postulate of humanity and Christianity that these countries should at last be set free from the intolerable burden which presses on them. It seems to me to be the Voice of God which is speaking through these events, and at the same time warning the Russians to put many things in order in their own house, if they wish to remain worthy of the favour of the best European nations and able to fulfil the ends of Providence in Europe and Asia alike.

In India, as the papers report, rages a terrible famine. Would it not be possible to anticipate such calamities, or, at any rate,

432

where they are unavoidable, greatly to mitigate them ? This would be a work worthy of the great English nation. Has the Government of England always done her duty in this respect ?

My dear friend ! Again a thousand thanks for the gifts which will always be the chief ornaments of the episcopal library and of my own. God bless you abundantly in all your works and ways. Please give my kind regards to your distinguished family, and remember me in your prayers. With distinguished affection, etc.

STROSSMAYER,
Bishop.

October 28, 1877.

VIII. *Bishop Strossmayer to Mr. Gladstone*, February 13, 1878. (In German.)

Forgive me for writing to you once more and taking up your valuable time. First of all I thank you again and again for the splendid proofs of your courage and devotion to the cause of the unhappy Christians of the Illyrian Peninsula. God will reward you and your family for it. By your noble conduct you have done a great service to your own nation also, and even to your Government. To-day the Congress is accepted by all the Powers, the work of peace and pacification begins. Let me make a few observations.

(1) I think it would be worthy not only of this or that party in England, but of the whole great and glorious English nation, to represent at the Congress the principles of humanity and liberty and to allow no petty considerations to divert one from this. I must confess that in this respect I am not without anxiety. When there was a talk in the English Parliament of liberating all North and South Bulgaria, your Premier spoke in a very frivolous and unwise manner. He exclaimed in a somewhat threatening and mocking tone, " So far as the liberation of Bulgaria is concerned there are others there, who will also have a say in the matter in their own interests." Every one among us knows what that means ; but every one asks if this is the language of the great England, which seeks to pass in the whole world as the school and stronghold of freedom, morality, humanity and noble activity. Every individual and community lives not merely from material but far more from spiritual bread. Truth and justice is the best policy which peoples and states can follow ; this policy triumphs even when it is apparently defeated ; while falsehood and injustice lead peoples and states to ruin, even when they seem to triumph. That is what we call Divine Providence, the final hope and often the sole support of oppressed and unhappy peoples. Great peoples possessing culture and the Divine favour (and to these England especially belongs) are called before all others to represent truth, justice and liberty in the world : otherwise they are untrue to themselves and to God. If then I compare this with the statement of your Premier, he seems to me to say : the liberation of the Bulgarian nation is a just cause, and England as a free nation

433

has nothing against it ; but for other considerations England will be glad, if others do so. That is surely, to some extent, imitating Pilate, who thought that it is as easy to cleanse one's guilty conscience as to cleanse one's dirty hands with water.

I know, in this country there are people who think it is in the interest of their own freedom and culture, not to permit the freedom and culture of their neighbours to flourish.* But my God, does this principle, or better said, this absurdity, deserve to be supported ? Freedom and culture can never be injurious to freedom and culture. What *is* injurious to them, is slavery and barbarism. Hence all really noble men and all truly free peoples must endeavour that every trace of slavery and barbarism may disappear as soon as possible from the Continent of Europe. The sooner the poor and unhappy peoples of European Turkey are freed from their yoke and restored to liberty and culture, the better for all European peoples without exception. Hence England will not only act in conformity with its natural destiny, if at the Congress it represents to the full the interests of the oppressed peoples ; but also will do a material service to those who to-day from blindness and passion oppose the liberation of the peoples of the Thracian Peninsula. England will win morally in the eyes of the whole world, but especially of the oppressed peoples, whose liberation is in question. Moreover, I think that England by representing openly and unreservedly the oppressed peoples, will lend fresh weight to every argument for the protection of its own interests. A contrary attitude on England's part might obviously cause a general conflagration, whose ravages none can foresee. I beg you then, if possible, to work upon your Government in this direction. This will be the crown of your activity hitherto. There are, as you well know, moments in human life when one earns scant recognition in defence of the great principles of truth and justice ; but very often it is just such moments which are the loveliest wreath for the memory of the man who did not shrink from staking his own popularity in the service of truth and justice and exposing himself to much abuse.

If I am eager for the liberation of the oppressed peoples of European Turkey, I mean by that not only the Slavs but also the Greeks. This time, it is true, they have behaved most unworthily ; just as their behaviour was truly unworthy and shameful when like cowards they lost their capital Constantinople to the advancing Turks. Nonethe less, their liberation also should be achieved to-day, in the interest of humanity and the permanent pacification of these parts of Europe.

Secondly, my noble friend, I have to recommend to you the Serbs and the Montenegrins. So far as the former are concerned, it would be very desirable that all Old Servia should be handed over to them. I do not know how far at present they have victoriously penetrated by force of arms ; but this I know for certain, that the Serbs will only be permanently pacified and deprived 'of every excuse for revolting, when they are assigned Pristina in the south, then Ipek (or Petsch) in a westerly direction, then further south Prizren, or " Prisrendt " as is written to-day. Each of these towns has for the Serbs a dear and sacred memory. For instance, Prizren was long the residence of their kings. Ipek was long the seat of their supreme Church authority, their Patriarch and a famous monastery. No people on earth easily forgets such precious traditions. Every Serb carries them in his heart and also in his mouth, in the shape of splendid popular songs. In the present excited state of feeling quiet could hardly be reckoned on for a week, if these places so sacred to every Serb were still left in the hands of the Turks.

The Montenegrins with their splendid and truly heroic prince, I hardly need to recommend to you. If any little people deserves the world's admiration, it is this splendid Montenegrin people, which has taken up its abode like an eagle on a lofty and barren crag, in order to buy its freedom and independence by a thousand sacrifices and renunciations for centuries.

Thirdly, I recommend to you, and to your Government if you have any influence in this direction, the Bosnians and Herzegovinians. I am lawfully Bishop of Bosnia, and am therefore in some ways a Divinely appointed defender of Bosnia and Herzegovina. How happy I should be, if it were possible to grant me a place, however modest, at the Congress, so that I might represent the interests of this very worthy, but also much neglected, people.* Since, however, this is impossible, I venture to recommend them most earnestly to you and if possible to your Government. What is just and fair for the Bulgarians, Roumanians and Greeks, is equally just and fair for the poor Bosnians and Herzegovinians, since it was from them that the first impetus came for the present movement and liberation of these peoples. These districts deserve to be freed from their present yoke and to be entrusted with adequate autonomy. In present conditions it would be impossible to entrust the administration of these countries to the hands of the Serbs, with reservation of the Turkish suzerainty—a course which I regard as the most practical ; on the other hand, it is not easy to imagine any other suzerainty or influence on an international basis, without great confusion. There is then nothing left, in my opinion, but to make these countries quite autonomous and to retain Turkish suzerainty, perhaps defined by international law. What I consider to be extremely important for these countries, is that the Eastern Orthodox Church should be freed as soon as possible from the shameful yoke of Phanariotism. Till now the Bishops here have been Phanariots, who bought their office for hard cash from the Patriarch in Constantinople, in order to compensate themselves a hundredfold for this price by more than Turkish exactions.* That such Bishops did not understand the language of the people, and that they kept the

Orthodox clergy in ghastly ignorance, and entirely neglected all the duties of their calling, goes without saying.* Henceforth this people ought to have a Bishop from among itself, who, knowing its language and customs and loving it, will attend to its spiritual interests better than before.* So far as the Catholic Church is concerned, it has been hitherto far better served, but even in this respect changes are absolutely necessary, and these I shall discuss with Rome quite openly. I know you are too much occupied to reply : I only ask you to see that some one acknowledges the due receipt of this letter.

With true respect and admiration, I remain your admirer and friend,

STROSSMAYER

IX. *Bishop Strossmayer to Mr. Gladstone*, April 11, 1878.
(In German.)

I thank you most heartily for your last letter. It was a great comfort to me. Since then things have grown so much worse that we seem to stand on the verge of a terrible conflagration. God be merciful to poor humanity ! According to my most sincere conviction, England is about to commit a gigantic crime. Before the war, during the war, England could have made a peaceful compact with Russia ; she could do so even now, if she really wished it, and so safeguard her own interests as well as those of Europe. Instead of that she prefers to ally herself with the Hungarians, who know no policy save that of blind hate and aversion towards the Slavs. A strange business ! The words of your new Minister for Foreign Affairs come straight from the soul of every true Magyar, from the very mouth of Count Andrássy. In the Austrian monarchy the Slavs are oppressed by the Magyars and the Germans ; in the Balkan peninsula the Greeks are to take over the task of subjugating and oppressing the Slavs. That is the gist of your Minister's pronouncements. What a monstrosity ; and how unworthy of a great and free nation !

You know that we Slavs wish the Greeks every happiness and every freedom. If it depended on us Greek aspirations would soon be fulfilled, within their just limits ; but one thing strikes me forcibly. The Greeks exist rather by virtue of the fame of their ancestors than by their own deserts. I cannot but hold them very largely to blame that the Turkish hordes have penetrated so far into Europe. The fall of Constantinople is an eternal and irreparable disgrace to the Greeks. Foreign peoples had to defend Constantinople against the attacks of the Turks, while the Greeks busied themselves with senseless religious hair-splittings, and while they in their churches were praying God, in stupid and indolent fashion, to save them by a miracle, the Turks were ˌbreaking into Constantinople, massacring the degenerate inhabitants, and turning the Christian churches into mosques. Hardly even did the heroic death of their emperor, Constantine XIV., atone for the stupidity and degeneracy of his people. A second crime committed by the Greeks is, in my opinion, this : that they very easily became accomplices in every way of the Turkish tyranny. The attitude of the Greek Church and the Greek Patriarch towards the Bulgars and Bosniaks has been until quite lately a horrible one. The Phanariot Bishops [513] and priests with their simony and their corruption were during centuries a far worse plague and tyranny for the poor Bulgars and Bosniaks than the Turks themselves.* Finally, their behaviour even latterly has been senseless. While the Turks had the Russians, Roumanians and Serbs by the throat, they did not stir ; now they begin to make war. All this, of course, does not prove that one should not grant them their freedom, within just limits, but it does indubitably prove that it would positively be a crime to make use of them to hinder the freedom and independent development of the Slav nation in the Balkan peninsula. An idea fostered by the Magyars, and pressed by them on the Government of the great, free and famous English nation. At such critical moments only one comfort remains to any enlightened friend of justice and humanity, that under a just God every injustice is sooner or later avenged upon its perpetrator. To you and your friends will always remain the glory of having defended the cause of truth, justice and humanity with the utmost self-sacrifice in circumstances of the greatest difficulty.

I can assure you that you have secured our eternal gratitude. As to your comment, my most honoured friend, that often the most pious people work against you, while other less pious support you, let me remark this : that, as the Apostle Paul complains, in every man there are, in our present state, two opposing laws, the " anima naturaliter christiana," as Tertullian calls it, and the " anima pagana." Unfortunately, even in the best and noblest souls the " anima pagana " often triumphs.

As to the new Pope, my dear friend, I know nothing of him. In the last Council he remained absolutely silent. It seems to me, nevertheless, that he is a learned and moderate man. His Secretary of State I know well. He certainly is a fair-minded, cultivated and moderate man. As to the necessary reforms in the Catholic Church we must have patience. It seems to me that Divine Providence has already begun those reforms, through the suspension of the Temporal Power of the Popes, which at any rate in its later developments I held to be harmful rather than useful to the eternal and imperishable calling of the Church. The necessary consequence of this will be, sooner or later, the universalization of the Roman Church, not only in the College of Cardinals, but also in the various Congregations, and the whole apparatus called " Curia Romana." The further logical consequence will be the more frequent, and perhaps periodical, meeting of the oecumenical councils, and their re-organization, which

[513] So called, because appointed from the Phanar, the residence of the Greek Patriarch in Stambul.

is absolutely necessary in order that they may become the true expression of the motto : " Quod semper, quod ubique, quod ab omnibus." I cannot relinquish the hope that God will grant to this ancient Church the power, so sorely needed in the present day, to bring about that unity in the human race which lay so close to the heart of our Lord and Saviour (John xiv.) for which every noble soul here below already longs so ardently, and which is the necessary prelude to that peaceful accord and brotherly feeling which is so sadly lacking in the world to-day ; as also to that blessed unity with God in eternity to which we are called. I am but a weak man, belonging to an obscure nation which I love greatly ; but so long as there is life left in me I will devote all my poor powers to the attainment of this end. I have kept you too long already with my talk. With sincerest respect, etc.

STROSSMAYER,
Bishop.

April 11, 1878.

X. *Bishop Strossmayer to Mr. Gladstone,* March 13, 1879. (In German.)

I thank you greatly for the friendly letter you have just sent me. Certainly England has not realized her task in the least with regard to recent events. A great people like the English, who have been free for centuries, should never be unfaithful to its task of defending freedom, truth, justice and culture throughout the world. England is chiefly to blame that the Turco-European question has not been solved, at any rate, not entirely, and that its present solution holds many seeds of anxiety, of unrest, and unavoidable war. Meanwhile you, my most honoured friend, and your noble and enlightened friends have saved the honour and the flag of England. Every one over here is convinced that you and your friends have on this occasion represented the true England and her natural and glorious vocation. We are all, therefore, eternally grateful to you, and hope with all our hearts that your noble intentions and efforts will very shortly become the intentions and efforts of your Parliament and Government. We also put our cause into your hands for the future, and undertake most solemnly to prove ourselves always worthy of our English friends and protectors by our truth, justice, love and good-will towards all men. In my pastoral letters I preach (the doctrine) over and over again that we can only become worthy of freedom and culture by extending the same freedom to all with whom we come into contact, of whatever faith or race they may be, and by letting them partake equally with ourselves of the benefits of freedom and civilization. This is the teaching of the Cross and the law of every community which wishes to be worthy of the fruits of the Redemption.

I also am of the opinion that the Slavs should remain quiet, and take full advantage of their newly-won position in developing themselves (*zu ihrer Ausbildung.*) This is the best way to prove themselves worthy of those aspirations for the future which they very rightly carry in their hearts. I am pleased to note that the very noble Prince of Montenegro, with whom I am in correspondence, is of the same opinion. What in the meanwhile is going to happen in Roumelia, God alone knows. Things there are built upon so unnatural a foundation that any unlucky chance may cause a conflagration. In that country not only are the Turks and Bulgars in opposition to each other, but there are also all kinds of external . . . influences, so that it looks as though things had to a certain extent been purposely so arranged that the peace and quiet of the world might at any moment be disturbed. Ah, how weak and shortsighted is human wisdom, when it strays from the path of justice and love ! Your estimate of Austria is quite correct, and it is much to be feared that she will not maintain her internal system in the newly-acquired provinces. My dear friend ! I would give my life to save that great country. She has a magnificent task to perform in the new situation of the world. Austria should be a great neutral state between the German and Slav empires, whose mission is eventually to prevent conflict between these two states, and to help on the peaceful solution of the Eastern complications. But as this state stands at present, it is becoming daily weaker, and less able to solve any large question happily. The latest events have shown, and future events will show still more plainly, that the Austria of to-day, instead of assisting through her mediation in the settlement of the European confusion, is much more inclined to add to it, and to sow the seeds of future dissension and unavoidable fresh complications in every question which she touches. You know that Count Andrássy, before the outbreak of the war, considered far-reaching agrarian reforms necessary, in order to deprive the insurrection of incentive and support (*Halt und Nahrung*). Now he is master in the land, and not only is there no further talk of improvements, but the Christians complain more than ever. It seems that the new regime wishes to play off the Turkish element against the Slavonic, Orthodox as well as Catholic. A truly petty policy, dictated by an unreasonable fear of the Slavs, which can benefit no one, but must be harmful in all quarters. Although I am Bishop of Bosnia, no influence over Bosnia is granted me. On the contrary, they fear me, and say a thousand damaging things against me. Nevertheless, I have a moral influence in Bosnia, of which no one can deprive me, and I shall make it felt in the sense which you indicate in your letter.

The Pope is really a learned and distinguished man. His chief task is, in my opinion, the reformation of the Roman Church, that is, its universalization. The Church of Rome should become an universal Church, not only by nature and vocation, but also in her

439

outer form. This applies not only to the College of Cardinals, but to all Congregations and courts. Only thus will the Papacy and the Roman Church attain their immortal destination, and fulfil the expectations and the needs of the whole world. Among other abuses to which the present system leads is the following : When one has to choose men for purposes of an universal nature always from¹ one and the same nation, for the most part at any rate (as in this case, from the Italian nation) the supply soon becomes exhausted, and one ends by getting men who are able and well-drilled, but who are quite unequal to their high destination. But the questions which the Roman prelacy have to deal with are of so important a nature that they demand quite exceptional men, in whom natural genius is so harmoniously allied with the inspiration given from above, that the most delicate and important questions which touch the universal conscience of mankind may be happily solved, in accordance with the true needs of society. God grant that the present Pope, who undoubtedly is inspired by holy intentions, may fully grasp this, and have the courage to carry it out. Moreover, it seems as though Providence had already taken the matter into His hands and will sooner or later find a suitable instrument for its fulfilment. . . .

STROSSMAYER,
Bishop of Bosnia and Syrmia.

DIAKOVO, *March* 13, 1879.

XI. *Bishop Strossmayer to Mr. Gladstone*, April 11, 1879.
(In French.)

A certain artist named Kaiser asks me to recommend him to you. I do it willingly, as I know that he is really an artist of great merit. He has already worked a great deal for England, especially for the Arundel Society, which occupies itself with the reproduction of old masterpieces. The best water-colour paintings done for this Society are the work of Kaiser. Therefore, you would oblige me greatly if you could in any way be of service to him.

The state of Bosnia is now worse under the Magyars than it was formerly under the Turks.* Allow me to sign myself, etc., etc.

STROSSMAYER, *Bishop.*

April 11, 1879.

P.S.—The alliance of England and Austria, celebrated by M. Károlyi [514] a few days ago, aims at hindering the freedom and progress of the Slavs. This alliance is, in my opinion, unworthy of a great and free nation. The vocation and the glory of England should be, as I think, always to protect the feeble against their oppressors.

[514] Austro-Hungarian ambassador in London.

XII. *Bishop Strossmayer to Mr. Gladstone.*[515] (Written in French.)

My dear and Venerable Friend,—

I have a most ardent desire to see you on the occasion of your journey to Germany and Italy ; but, unhappily, in present circumstances it is almost impossible. If I could have foreseen your very kind and flattering invitation, I should willingly have arranged my affairs in such a way as to be able to be absent for a time. At present I am already engaged upon enterprises which cannot be deferred. None the less, I do not despair of some day having the honour of seeing and venerating you in your home in England. At present I am extremely busy with the building of my Cathedral church, which will be finished and probably consecrated in 1882 at the feast of St. Peter.[516] If God preserves my life, I shall then be freer. Either before or immediately after the dedication of my church, I shall visit Germany and France, and England expressly to have the good fortune to see you.

I quite realize that your presence will soon be necessary in England, because the electoral struggle which is about to commence, will be decisive for England's prestige, in my opinion gravely compromised by the present Government. May God help you and give you the victory you deserve ! Your victory will be that of your glorious country. We shall all rejoice, who love liberty and progress and who were accustomed from childhood to see England fostering liberty and defending the fate of oppressed peoples.

As to the state (*état*) of which you would like to talk with me more intimately,[517] it has, I am convinced, a providential destiny. It must become, amid the events which have already come to pass and which will still occur towards the end of our century, a great neutral state, strictly based upon truth and justice, to prevent in Europe the clash between the German element and the Slav element : to form the guarantee of a durable peace : to assist sincerely and efficaciously the peoples of the Balkans in their just and meritorious aims. If it were possible, I would secure for it at the cost of my life a juster organization, and one more suited to its eternal destiny. Let us hope that the force of its pressing needs and the course of nature will prove stronger than the blindness of the men who have guided it hitherto. From what is being done to-day and from what is not being done at all in Bosnia and Herzegovina, one cannot as yet believe in the aptitude of this state [517] to win a moral influence over new peoples, and to penetrate by wisdom and by studying their needs,

---

[515] This letter bears no exact date, but various internal references would seem to place it in the summer of 1879. Mr. Gladstone visited Munich and Italy in September and October of that year, and on his return plunged into the great electoral campaign, which ended with his return to power in April, 1880.

[516] *See* page 124.

[517] This of course refers to Austria.

their hearts and consciences. Give my cordial greetings to your family, and my blessing to your children.

Your friend always,

STROSSMAYER, *Bishop*.

XIII. *Bishop Strossmayer to Mr. Gladstone*, April 17, 1880.[518]
(In German.)

You have won the victory. God bless you! My best and warm-est good wishes go with you. Your victory stands, in my eyes, for truth, justice, true freedom, and magnanimous good-will towards suffering and oppressed nationalities. You are quite right; the Austrian Slavs and the Slavs of the Thracian peninsula are most sincerely glad that you have won. But I am also convinced that the empire to which I belong must also rejoice, for otherwise that feverishly-restless man in Berlin (*der krankhaft-unruhige Mann in Berlin*)[519] whose ambition and arbitrary temper know no bounds, might easily have plunged into a war which might have proved fatal to the state. Your victory means: Peace in the world, and a good understanding with the great Slav power in Europe and Asia alike. Your opinion regarding the nationalities of Turkey-in-Europe is entirely correct. They should be left quite free to win and establish such forms as seem to them best adapted for securing and develop-ing their freedom and their culture. Allow me to add one more thought. The glorious victory which you have just won seems to me a sign that Providence has reserved one more special honour for you at the end of your career, namely, to make an end of the brutal domination of the Turks in Europe, and moreover, to do it in a manner which causes no general conflagration, and involves no real injury to any Christian power whatever. I can hardly tell you how happy I should be if I ever lived to see Christian worship celebrated in the magnificent Aga Sofia.[520]

Forgive me, my distinguished friend, that I was not able to see you and pay my respects to you in Venice. You know that I am tied by quite special considerations. Please make my excuses also to my old friend Lord Acton. I still hope to see you in England in the course of this year, or the next. It is the dearest wish of my heart to be able to express to you in person my respect, gratitude, and admiration. Once more, God bless you! May He grant you the realization of all your just and noble aspirations, to the eternal glory of your great country and distinguished name, and to the

---

[518] The original of this letter is marked " Secret," in Mr. Gladstone's hand-writing.

[519] An allusion to Bismarck, against whom Strossmayer had a natural Slav prejudice.

[520] The Church of St. Sofia in Constantinople, which has been a Turkish mosque since the Conquest in 1453.

advantage and comfort of the nations who are still striving after freedom and civilization.

STROSSMAYER,
DIAKOVO, *April 17,* 1880.   *Bishop.*

XIV. *Bishop Strossmayer to Mr. Gladstone,* Sept. 19, 1882.
(In French.)

(Congratulates him on the " great and decisive victory " of the British army in Egypt. British policy " guided by your consummate wisdom " signifies " truth, justice, freedom and progress all the world over.")

. . . " You wield a great and well deserved authority in Europe ; therefore, allow me, my dear and venerable friend, to recommend to you the great and just cause of the Southern Slavs. They will assuredly prove themselves worthy in future of the eminent services which you may render them in the Areopagus of Europe. They have already, though living under very difficult circumstances, given indubitable proofs of their love for true liberty and progress."

(Announces that he has finished his Cathedral church after sixteen years of uninterrupted labour, and would greatly like to show it to Mr. Gladstone.)

September 19, 1882. DIAKOVO.

XV. *Mr. Gladstone to Bishop Strossmayer.*   Hawarden, October 12, 1882. (In French.)

VENERABLE BISHOP AND DEAR FRIEND,—

I thank you with all my heart for your very kind letter, and regret as keenly as possible that the daily burden of public affairs, which is always growing and threatening to overwhelm my poor powers, prevents me from replying to it as I should like to.   In a few words, I do not say that I shall discharge my debt, but at least I shall acknowledge it.

It is by the inexpressible goodness of God that the English operations in Egypt have succeeded in a manner more than satisfactory in every respect.   It remains to be seen whether we are faithful not only to the *Protocole de Désintéressement* drawn up at Constantinople, but also to all our professions and declarations which accord with it.   What we desire in Egypt, is security without, liberty and prosperity within.   A Mohammedan people, it is not far advanced : but it is neither ill to govern nor incapable of learning the practical exercise of a reasonable and growing autonomy.   Let us then do our best : the civilized and Christian world will give us encouragement and support.

As for the Southern Slavs, we may hope for much progress in the future, and may congratulate ourselves upon the great work of emancipation which has to a great extent been accomplished.

And the Cathedral, magnificent in the opinion of all who have seen it, which Your Grace has built and dedicated, to the honour of

God and the salvation of souls, and perhaps to inspire in others a noble emulation, by showing that the lofty spirit of past centuries is not yet entirely extinguished. How I should have liked to profit by your gracious invitation ; but it was impossible. In one way or another, in what place I know not, I still hope to meet you before I die.

I remain, always your friend and most devoted servant,

W. GLADSTONE.

XVI. *Bishop Strossmayer to Mr. Gladstone*, September 26, 1886. (In French.)

I regret infinitely that I should have missed the chance of meeting you at our mutual friend, Lord Acton's house at S. Martin ; but you were right to hasten your return to England. The causes to which you have devoted your illustrious and immortal energies are the best and holiest of causes ; they touch the welfare and interests of all humanity. This last one, touching unhappy Ireland, oppressed for centuries, is the most glorious of all. It is the cause of justice, intimately allied to justice triumphant in the passion and death of our Saviour. Such a cause cannot die ; it triumphs usually at the very moment when the unjust and blind world believes it about to be lost and buried. The triumph of the Irish cause will, I am firmly convinced, be the crown of your glorious career. I appreciate most keenly all the nobility of your devotion, because the present condition of my nation is almost analogous to that of Ireland. Although I am very old and my health very frail, I still hope some day perhaps to see and pay you my homage in England.

STROSSMAYER, *Bishop*.

September 2, 1886.

The correspondence is concluded by three further letters from Bishop Strossmayer, which need not be quoted *in extenso*. The first (dated September 26, 1886) merely introduces Madame Marlet, a Bulgarian authoress, who is anxious for a letter to the French President, M. Grévy. The second (dated 1888, month unreadable) is a letter of praise and congratulation to Mr. Gladstone on his Jubilee ; it contains compliments which are unquestionably heartfelt and genuine, but it contains nothing else save compliments.

The last letter, written on July 25, 1892 (at the height of the Khuen regime), in shaky handwriting, is devoted to congratulations on the Liberal victory at the polls. It contains the following interesting passage :—

. . . " The Hungarians are a proud, egotistical and in the highest degree tyrannical race, and my poor nation is persecuted, oppressed and ill-treated, but I hope that the cause of the Slavs in general, restored by providential events to its natural destiny, to the advantage of universal culture and liberty, will also deliver my own nation, which is worthy of all the favour of God and men." It, is signed, " Your servant and admirer, Joseph George Strossmayer, Bishop."

BIBLIOGRAPHY

THE following bibliography makes no pretence to be complete, but it to some extent supplies a want in English. Here and there I have added brief comments, which are only intended for the guidance of any reader who may be approaching the subject for the first time. Only books of the first importance have been marked with an asterisk.

I. HISTORICAL

*Smičiklas, T. Codex Diplomaticus (7 vols., up to 1300). Zagreb, 1904–8.
——— Poviest Hrvatska (History of Croatia), 2 vols. Zagreb, 1882 (up to 1848).
Rački, Don Franjo. Documenta historiae chroaticae periodam antiquam illustrantia. Zagreb, 1877.
*Klaić, Prof. Vjekoslav. Povjest Hrvata (History of the Croats), 5 vols. Zagreb, 1899, seq. The standard modern history, with numerous original documents and illustrations.
Šišić, Prof. Ferdo. Hrvatska Povijest (History of Croatia), 2 vols. (to 1790). Zagreb, 1906, 1908. An ideal textbook.
Horvat, Dr. Rudolf. Najnovije Doba Hrvatske Povjesti (The Latest Period of Croatian History). Zagreb, 1906.
Pauler. A Magyar Nemzet története Árpádházi Királyok alatt (History of the Hungarian Nation under the Kings of the House of Arpád), 2 vols. Budapest, 1899.
Theiner, Aug. Vetera Monumenta Slavorum meridionalium. I. Romae, 1843.
Chmel. Aktenstücke zur Geschichte Croatiens. Vienna, 1846.
Szalay. Geschichte Ungarns. 3 Bde. Pest, 1866–74.
Helfert, Jos. Alex. Freiherr von. Geschichte der österreichischen Revolution. 2 Bde. Freiburg i. B., 1907–1909.
Friedjung, Heinrich. Oesterreich von 1848 bis 1860. Bd. I. (1848–51). Stuttgart, 1908.
Marczali, Henrik. A legújabb kor története (History of the Most Recent Times). Budapest, 1892.

2. CONSTITUTIONAL.

Andrássy, Gróf Gyula (Count Julius). Beszédei (Speeches). Ed. Lederer, 2 vols. Budapest.
Beksics, Gusztav. A Dualismus. Budapest, 1892.
Bojničić, Dr. Ivan. Zakoni o ugarsko-hrvatskoj Nagodi (Laws relating to the Hungaro-Croatian Compromise). Zagreb, 1907.
*Corpus Juris Hungarici. Editio Millenaria. Ed. Márkus. 7 vols. Leipzig, 1902.

BIBLIOGRAPHY

Deák, Ferencz. Denkschrift über das Verhältnis zwischen Ungarn und Croatien. Vienna, 1861.
*—— Beszédei (Speeches). Ed. Kónyi. 6 vols. Budapest, 1886–98.
Eisenmann, Louis. Le Compromis Austro-Hongrois de 1867. Paris 1904. Indispensable : but does not treat Croatia in any detail.
Farlati, Daniele. Illyricum Sacrum. 7 vols. Venetiis, 1751–1819.
Horn, M. Le Compromis de 1868 entre la Hongrie et la Croatie. Paris, 1907. A useful analysis of the Compromise, from the Croat standpoint.
Kmety. A Magyar Közjog Tankönyve (Manual of Hungarian Public Law). 2nd ed. Budapest, 1902.
*Kukuljević, Joannes. Jura Regni Croatiae Dalmatiae et Slavoniae. 3 vols. Zagrabiae, 1862. The best collection of Croatian historical documents.
Montbel, Guy de. La Condition Politique de la Croatie-Slavonie dans la Monarchie Austro-Hongroise. Paris, 1910. Useful for those who only know French.
*Pejaković, Stephan. Aktenstücke zur Geschichte des Kroatisch-Slavonischen Landtages. Vienna, 1861. A useful collection of Croatian documents, from 1848 to 1860.
Pesty, Fr. Die Entstehung Croatiens (Ungarische Revue, vol. i. 1882). The Magyar view in its most uncompromising and unreasoning form ; for that very reason, worth reading.
*Pliverić, Prof. Joseph. Beiträge zum ungarisch-kroatischen Bundesrechte. Agram, 1886. The best available book, despite its faulty form.
—— Der kroatische Staat. 1887.
—— Das rechtliche Verhältniss Kroatiens zu Ungarn. Agram, 1885. (With the answers of Professor Jellinek, who took a different view.)
Polić, Martin.. Parlamentarna Povjest Kraljevina Hrvatske-Slavonije i Dalmacije (Parliamentary History of the Kingdoms of Croatia, Slavonia and Dalmatia, 1860–1880). 2 vols. Zagreb, 1899, 1900.
*Šulek, Bogoslav. Naše Pravice (Our Rights). Zagreb, 1868. Supplements Kukuljević and Pejaković.
Szalay, Ladislaus von. Zur ungarisch-Kroatischen Frage. Pest, 1863. A sane and thorough statement of the Magyar standpoint.
Timon, Prof. Akos von. Ungarische Verfassungs und Rechtsgeschichte. Berlin, 1904. A standard Magyar work, in which Croatia is assigned a very subordinate place.
Tomasić, Dr. Nikola. Temelji Državnoga Prava Hrvatskoga Kraljevstva (Fundamenta Juris Publici Regni Croatiae). Zagreb, 1910. An able study of Croatian Staatsrecht, published by the present Ban just before his accession to office.
*Verfassungsgesetze, Ungarische. Ed. by Gustav Steinbach. Vienna (Manz), 1900. Useful pocket edition.
Virozsil, Dr. Anton von. Das Staatsrecht des Königreichs Ungarn, 3 vols. Pest, 1865.
Vrbanić, Prof. Fran. Financijalna Nagoda izmedju Hrvatskoj i Ugarskoj (The Financial Compromise between Croatia and Hungary). Agram, 1897. The standard Croat work.

BIBLIOGRAPHY

Živković, Baron Ivan. Zur Sanirung der Verletzungen des kroatisch-ungarischen Ausgleiches. Vienna. Important.

3. PAMPHLETS

Bošković. La mission du peuple Serbe. Paris, 1886.

Cvijić, Prof. J. L'annexion de la Bosnie et la Question Serbe. Paris, 1909. The Belgrade standpoint at its best.

*Fournier, Prof. August. Wie wir zu Bosnien kamen. Vienna, 1909. An historical sketch by one of Austria's best historians.

Gentilizza, Giuseppe. Il Mare Adriatico e la Questione Balcanica. Rome, 1909. Written from a somewhat original standpoint.

Georgević, Dr. Vladan. Die Serbische Frage. Stuttgart, 1909. A statement of the Servian view, by a former Premier of Servia, the friend of King Milan and the Austrian alliance.

Horvát, Stephan. Ueber Croatien als eine durch Unterjochung erworbene ungarische Provinz und des Kön. Ungarn| wirklichen Theil. Leipzig, 1844. Typical of the Magyar attitude in 1848.

Hron, Karl. Die Wahrheit über die Wiener Orientpolitik. Graz, 1909. Though intended as an exposure of Jesuit misdeeds, and hopelessly overstated, it contains an interesting review of the Rauch era in Croatia.

Klaić, Prof. V. Hrvati i Hrvatska (Croats and Croatia). Zagreb, 1890. An historical account of the name and its origin, by the leading Croat historian.

Kvaternik, Eugen. Das historisch-diplomatische Verhältniss des Königreichs Kroatien zu der ungarischen St. Stephans-Krone. Agram, 1861. Ultra-Croat.

Lupis, J. F. O Iseljivanju našega naroda i o Americi (The Emigration of our Nation, and America). Zadar (Zara), 1910.

Mandl, Leopold. Oesterreich-Ungarn und Serbien. Vienna, 1911. A defence of Count Aehrenthal, by the editor of the semi-official *Wiener Allgemeine Zeitung*.

Marjanović, Milan. Hrvatski Pokret (The Croatian Movement). 2 vols. Dubrovnik (Ragusa), 1903–4.

Marković, Prof. Božidar. Die serbische Auffassung der bosnischen Frage. Berlin, 1908.

*Masaryk, Prof. T. G. Vasić-Forgách-Aehrenthal. Einiges Material zur Charakteristik unserer Diplomatie (5 facsimiles), Prag, 1911.

Milić, Vicko. Postanak Riečke Resolucije e njezine Posljedice (The Genesis of the Fiume Resolution and its Consequences).

Nastić, Georg. Finale. Budapest and Sarajevo, 1908.

—— Wo ist die Wahrheit? do. 1908.

Potočnjak, Dr. Franko. Aus dem Lande der Rechtlosigkeit und Demoralisation (Schmachvolle Justizzustände in Kroatien). Fiume, 1905. Violent.

Rapport de la Chambre de Commerce et de l'Industrie à Zagreb. Zagreb, 1909.

Riedl, Richard. Sandschakbahn und Transversallinie (Vortrag). Vienna, 1908. By one of the ablest Austrian permanent officials, a recognized authority on Balkan questions.

*Samassa, Paul. Der Völkerstreit im Habsburgerstaat. Leipzig, 1910. Perhaps the ablest summary of Austro-Hungarian problems in any language. Good chapter on the Southern Slavs.

447

BIBLIOGRAPHY

Sax, Carl Ritter von. Die Wahrheit über die serbische Frage und das Serbentum in Bosnien. Vienna, 1909. An answer to Georgević (see above), by a high Austrian official, author of a good book on "the Decline of Turkey."

Scotus Viator. Absolutismus in Kroatien. Vienna, 1909. Confiscated by the Rauch Government.

Šišić, Prof. Ferd. Nach der Annexion. Erörterungen geogr. ethnogr. histor. u. staatsrechtlicher Fragen, Herzeg-Bosnien betreffend. Zagreb, 1909.

Anonymous :—

Die "Ritterliche Affaire" des Baron Paul Rauch (Aktenmaterial). Zagreb, 1908.

*Enthüllungen über die Künste der Kroatischen Regierung. (Extraabdruck aus der Prager "Politik." No. 121 vom 2 Mai 1872).

Iz crnoga Lista nedavne Prošlosti (Iz dobe Barona Levina Raucha). "From a Black Page of the Recent Past (From the time of Baron Levin Rauch)." Reprint. Varaždin, 1904.

*Kroatien und dessen Beziehungen zu Bosnien. Von einem Kroatischen Abgeordneten. Vienna, 1909. A very able summary.

Veridicus. Kroatien im Jahre 1907–1908. Budapest, 1909. Inspired by Baron Rauch.

4. PAMPHLETS DEALING WITH THE AGRAM TRIAL

*Masaryk, Prof. T. G. Der Agramer Hochverratsprozess und die Annexion von Bosnien und Herzegovina. Vienna, 1909.

Der Agramer Hochverratsprozess : Die Verteidiger über den Prozess. Budapest, 1909. Published by the defence, owing to the campaign of calumny in the Rauch press and its sympathisers abroad.

Die Serbenfrage und der Hochverratsprozess in Agram. Von A-Z. Vienna, 1909.

Lasst die Kroaten reiten! Was uns der Agramer Hochverratsprozess lehrt. Vienna, 1909. These two are worthless, except from the psychological point of view.

Supilo, Frano. Le Procès de Friedjung—"Reichspost" et de la Coalition Croato-Serbe (Lettre à ses Électeurs). Fiume, 1910.

5. CROAT AND SERB LITERATURE

Šafařik, P. J. Geschichte der südslawischen Literatur. 3 Bde. Prag, 1864.

*Murko, Matthias. Die südslavischen Literaturen (in Die Kultur der Gegenwart, Teil I., Abteilung ix., pp. 194–244). Berlin, 1908.

*Jagić, Vatroslav von. Die slavischen Sprachen (ibid. pp. 1–40).

Talvj (Mrs. Robinson, née Theresa von Jacob). Historical View of the Languages and Literature of the Slavic Nations. New York and London, 1850. Now rather out of date.

Andrić, Nikola. Kroatische Literaturgeschichte (Die österreichisch-ungarische Monarchie in Wort und Bild, vol. on Croatia, pp. 125–148).

Kušar, Marcell. Die serbischkroatische Sprache und Literatur (ibid. vol. on Dalmatia, pp. 231–252).

BIBLIOGRAPHY

Hörmann, Konstantin. Literatur in Bosnien (ibid. vol. on Bosnia, pp. 391–412).

*Šurmin, Dr. Gjuro. Povjest Književnosti hrvatske i srpske (History of Croat and Serb Literature). Agram, 1898.

Novaković, Stojan. Istorija Srpske Književnosti (History of Serb Literature). Belgrad, 1871.

Bowring, Sir John. Servian Popular Poetry. London, 1827.

Meredith, Owen (Robert, Earl of Lytton). Serbski Pesme : or National Songs of Servia. London, 1861.

Hrvatske Narodne Pjesme (Croat National Songs). Published by the Matica Hrvatska. 5 vols. Agram. . . .

Mijatović, Elodie Lawson. Kossovo : an Attempt to bring Serbian National Songs about the Fall of the Serbian Empire at the Battle of Kossovo into one Poem. London, 1881.

Kapper, Siegfried. Die Gesänge der Serben. 2 Bde. Leipzig, 1852. Translations.

Goethe. Serbische Lieder (Schriften zur Literatur, iii. Theil, pp. 1–15). Jubiläums-Ausgabe, Bd. xxxviii. See also his fine version of "Hassan Aga's Wife."

Minns, E. H. Article "Slavs" in Encyclopædia Britannica, 11th edition, vol. xxx. (pp. 228–237).

6. MISCELLANEOUS

Auerbach, Bertrand. Les Races et les Nationalités en Autriche-Hongrie. Paris, 1898.

Balch, Emily G. Our Slavic Fellow-Citizens. New York, 1910. An extremely interesting study of Slav immigrants in America ; good chapters on the Croats.

Cepelić, Monsignor, and Pavić. Josip Juraj Strossmayer. Zagreb, 1904. The standard biography.

Chlumecky, Leopold Freiherr von. Oesterreich-Ungarn und Italien : Das westbalkanische Problem und Italiens Kampf um die Vorherrschaft in der Adria. Leipzig, 1907.

Drage, Geoffrey. Austria-Hungary. London, 1909.

Henry, René. Questions d'Autriche-Hongrie et Question d'Orient. Paris, 1903.

—— Des Monts de Bohême au Golfe Persique. Paris, 1908.

Hirtenfeld, J. Ban Jellačić. Vienna, 1861. Short sketch.

Knatchbull-Hugessen, Hon. C. M. The Political Evolution of the Hungarian Nation. 2 vols. London, 1908. An able exposition of the extreme Magyar view.

Laveleye, Emile de. The Balkan Peninsula. Preface by W. E. Gladstone. London, 1886.

Leger, Louis. Le Monde Slave. Paris, 1885.

—— La Save, le Danube et le Balkan. Paris, 1884.

—— Études Slaves.

Loiseau, Charles. Le Balkan Slave et la Crise Autrichienne. Paris, 1898. Few foreigners know so much of Croatia as M. Loiseau.

—— L'Equilibre Adriatique. Paris, 1901.

—— La Hongrie et l'Opposition Croate (Revue des 2 Mondes, cxxxi., pp. 101–129). 1895.

—— Strossmayer (article in Le Correspondant, 1905).

BIBLIOGRAPHY

Maurice, C. E. The Revolutionary Movement of 1848–9. London, 1887.
Pinon, René. L'Europe et l'Empire Ottoman. Paris, 1909. An able monograph by the editor of the Revue des 2 Mondes.
Polić, Martin. Banus Graf Karl Khuen-Héderváry und seine Zeit. Essek, 1901. A hymn of praise.
Ritter, W. Évêques Artistes. 1890.
Staré, Joseph. Die Kroaten (Die Völker Oesterreich-Ungarns). Vienna, 1881.
Tkalac, Dr. E. I. von. Jugenderinnerungen aus Kroatien (to 1843). Leipzig, 1894.
Wachsmuth, W. Geschichte des Illyrismus. Leipzig, 1849.
Zagorsky, Vladimir. Francois Rački et la Renaissance Scientifique et politique de la Croatie (1828–1894). Paris, 1909. An admirable monograph, with a very full bibliography.

7. DALMATIA

*Jackson, T. G. Dalmatia, the Quarnero and Istria. 3 vols. Oxford, 1887.
Freeman, E. A. Subject and Neighbour Lands of Venice. London, 1881.
Neale, Rev. J. M. Dalmatia. London, 1850. Not very accurate.
Wilkinson, Sir Gardner. Dalmatia and Montenegro. 2 vols. London, 1840.
Paton, A. A. The Highlands and Islands of the Adriatic. London, 1849.
Lucius. De Regno Dalmatiae et Croatiae a gentis origine ad an. 1480. Amsterdam, 1666.
Erber, Tullio. Storia della Dalmazia. Zara, 1886.
Pisani, P. La Dalmatie de 1797 à 1815. Paris, 1893.
Villari, Luigi. The Republic of Ragusa. London, 1904.
Bahr, Hermann. Dalmatinische Reise. Berlin, 1909. Treats the Croat race with great sympathy and insight.
Marczali, Prof. H. Les Relations de la Dalmatie et de la Hongrie du XIe au XIIIe siècle. Paris, 1899.
Bulat, G. Die Sprachenfrage in K. Dalmatien. Vienna, 1900.
Studien über Dalmatien und Oesterreichs Politik: von einem öst. Offizier. Graz, 1869.
Der Aufstand in der Herzegovina, Süd-Bosnien und Süd-Dalmatien, 1881–2. Vienna (Kriegsarchiv), 1883.
Denkschrift der Bauern von Spalato an die K. K. Regierung. Spalato, 1899.
Die Wahl in Spalato, 14 und 23 Mai, 1907. Wiedergabe des Protestes der Wähler. Vienna, 1907.

8. BOSNIA-HERZEGOVINA

*Klaić, Vj. Geschichte Bosniens. Leipzig, 1885.
Komlossy, Dr. Franz von. Das Rechtsverhältnis Bosniens und der Herzegovina zu Ungarn. Budapest, 1909. Historical. Moderate.
Jireček, Const. Die Handelsstrassen und Bergwerke von Serbien und Bosnien während des Mittelalters. 1853.

BIBLIOGRAPHY

Spalajkovič, M. La Bosnie et l'Herzégovine. Paris, 1899.
The best treatment of Bosnia from the standpoint of Belgrad.
Vasiljević, Dušan. O Bosni i Hercegovini. Belgrad, 1909. Austrophobe.
Barre, André. La Bosnie-Herzégovine (Administration Autrichienne de 1878 à 1903). Paris, 1904. Violently anti-Austrian ; its facts are far from trustworthy. Preface is an open letter to the Emperor Francis Joseph, in the worst possible taste.
Petrinjensis. Bosnien und das Kroatische Staatsrecht. Vienna, 1898.
Baernreither, Dr. J. M. Bosnische Eindrücke. Vienna, 1908.
Evans, A. J. Through Bosnia on Foot. 2nd ed. London, 1877.
——— Illyrian Letters. London, 1878.
Muir-Mackenzie, G., and Irby, A. P. Travels in the Slavonic Provinces of Turkey in Europe. Preface by W. E. Gladstone. 2 vols. London, 1877.
Somogyi, Oskar von. Das bosnische Kreditwesen (lecture 16 Feb. 1909).
Juristisches aus Bosnien (lecture, printed 1909).

9. THE SERBS OF HUNGARY

*Picot, Emile. Les Serbes de la Hongrie. Prague, 1873.
Bartenstein, Freih. von. Kurzer Bericht von der Beschaffenheit der illyrischen Nation in den kk. Erblanden.
Stefanović Vilovsky. Die Serben in Ungarn, Dalmatien, Bosnien und Herzegovina (Die Völker Oesterreich-Ungarns). Vienna, 1884.
Stojacskovics, Alex. Ueber die staatsrechtlichen Verhältnisse der Serben in der Wojwodina und überhaupt in den Ländern der ungarischen Krone. Temesvár, 1860.
Die serbische Bewegung in Süd-Ungarn. Berlin, 1851.
Helfert, Freiherr J. A. von. Vad Rácz. Geschichte der süd-ungarischen Bewegung und Kämpfe gegen die Zumuthungen des Pan-Magyarismus. (Oesterr. Jahrbuch, 1907–8).
Schlesinger, Max. The War in Hungary 1848–9. Preface by Fr. Pulszky. London, 1850.
Schwicker, J. H. Politische Geschichte der Serben in Ungarn. Budapest, 1880.
Szentkláray, Jenö. 100 Years of the History of South Hungary (in Magyar). Budapest, 1880.

10. SERVIA, MONTENEGRO

Chiudina, G. Storia del Montenero da tempi autichi fino ai nostri. Spalato, 1880.
Coquelle, F. Histoire du Monténégro et de la Bosnia. Paris, 1895.
Denton, W. Montenegro, its People and their History. London, 1877.
Georgewitsch, Dr. Wladan. Die serbische Frage. Stuttgart, 1909.
——— Das Ende der Obrenovitch. Leipzig, 1905. The author, formerly Premier of Servia, was imprisoned on a charge of revealing State secrets in this book.
Gopčević, Spiridion. Montenegro. Leipzig, 1877.
——— Serbien und die Serben. Leipzig, 1888.
*Kallay, Benjamin von. Geschichte der Serben. Budapest, 1878. Written by the famous administrator of Bosnia, in his younger days.

BIBLIOGRAPHY

*Kanitz, F.   Das Königreich Serbien.   2 Bde.   Leipzig, 1904–9.
Mallat, J.   La Serbie contemporaine.   Paris, 1902.
Mijatovich, Chedo.   Servia and the Servians.   London, 1908.
Mijatovich, E. L.   History of Modern Servia.   London, 1872.
Miller, W.   The Balkans.   London, 1896.   An admirable historical
    survey.
*Ranke, Leopold von.   History of Servia and the Servian Revolution.
    London, 1853.   Still valuable.
Vivian, Herbert.   Servia, the Poor Man's Paradise.   London, 1897.

11. THE SERBS OF TURKEY.

Bérard, Victor.   Pro Macedonia.   Paris, 1903.
*Brailsford, H. N.   Macedonia, its Races and their Future.   London,
    1906.
Cvijić, Prof. J.   Grundlinien der Geographie und Geologie von Maze-
    donien und Alt-Serbien.   Gotha, 1908.
*Odysseus (Sir C. N. Elliot).   Turkey-in-Europe.   London, 1900.
*Villari, Luigi (editor).   The Balkan Question.   London, 1905.

THE SOUTHERN SLAVS

(dark gray)━━━━ Frontier between Austria-Hungary and other states.

(dark gray)........ Frontier between Austria, Hungary, Croatia and Bosnia.

(dark gray)·············· Frontier between various provinces of Austria.

(light gray)━━━ Boundary of the Croato-Serb race.

(light gray) .... Boundary between Roman Catholic and Orthodox population. (This cannot of course be drawn with absolute accuracy; but with trifling exceptions, there are no Orthodox Serbs west of this line, though there are a considerable number of Catholic Croats east of the line, in Bosnia. It has been found impossible to indicate the position of the Mohammedan population of Bosnia, which is not geographically separate from its Catholic and Orthodox neighbours and varies in density according to the district.

(light gray)   *(light gray)*

G = German   I = Italian   ⎫ These letters indicate the presence of

M = Magyar   R = Roumanian ⎬   racial minorities, amounting to

S = Slovak   A = Albanian   ⎭   not less than 10 per cent. of the total population of the district.

INDEX

A

Abdul Kerim, 94
Absolutism, Austrian, 50, 52
—— in Croatia, 110, 159
Academy, Southern Slav, 120, 121
Accurti, Mr., 165, 180, 307, 326
Acton, Lord, 127, 416
Adrianople, 38, 40
Adriatic, 331, 332, 343, 351, 356
Aehrenthal, Baron (then Count),
    151, 157, 164, 174, 175, 177, 195,
    196, 199, 201, 207, 211, 240, 253,
    256, 276, 282, 287, 297, 308, 310–
    328, 337, 341
Agram (Zagreb), 3, 30, 33, 45, 48,
    51, 55, 88, 111, 120, 123, 140, 144,
    150, 153, 161, 165, 278, 329–34, 336,
    340
—— University of, 92, 123
—— Treason Trial, 170, 179–192,
    201, 207, 224, 233, 270, 277, 324,
    325, 329, 330, 332, 404
Agriculture, Croatian, 388
Albania, 10, 37, 341
Albert, Archduke, 58
Albini, Felix, 140
Alexander of Servia, 9, 202, 259, 302
Alföld, 42
Ambros, Mr., 209, 228
Andrássy, Count Julius, 59, 60, 61,
    76, 89, 90, 97, 117, 127, 274, 342
Anthologies, 130
Antivari, 10
Apponyi, Count Albert, 143, 149,
    151
Aranicky, Mr., 306
" Argus," 280, 300, 324
Article XLII of 1861, 58, 63, 357–9
Aržano, 333
Athos, Mount, 36
Audience, the rejected Dalmatian,
    114, 115, 321
Aulic Chancellory, 24, 44, 91
—— Council, Illyrian, 44, 352
Austerlitz, 26
Austria-Hungary as Great Power,
    177, 337

Austria versus Hungary, 343
Autonomy, Croatian, 68, 72–3, 366,
    371, 379–86
Avars, 15
Axentinović, 95

B

Bácska, the, 44, 45, 50
Bach, Alexander, 35, 50, 52, 156
——, Louis, 87
Baernreither, Dr. J. M., 282, 299
Bahr, Hermann, 289, 406
Balkan policy of Austria, 174, 343,
    403
Ballads, Serb, 131, 135
Ballplatz, 149, 150, 153, 161, 173, 202,
    205, 245, 297, 303, 319, 399
Ban, office of, 20, 24, 33, 70, 73, 78–
    80, 351, 371, 381, 382
Banal Table, 20
Banat of Temesvár, 31, 43, 49, 134
Bánffy, Baron, 142
Banjaluka, 20, 409
Banks, Croatian, 391
Barčić, Mr. Erasmus, 106, 158
Batthyány, Count Louis, 33, 35
Becskerek, 44
Bedeković, Coloman, 87, 98
Belcredi, Count, 59
Belgrad, 8, 37, 41, 51, 89, 95, 125,
    135, 170, 202, 203, 215, 245, 295,
    300, 319, 336, 337, 342, 405
Belgrad Legation, Austro-Hungarian,
    219, 228, 310–20
Benedikt, Dr., 209, 227, 242, 243,
    247, 250, 261, 283, 291
Berlin, Congress and Treaty of, 96,
    127, 176, 177, 201
Beust, Count, 59
Bienerth, Baron, 199, 407
" Black Days," 114
Black Legion, 42
Bogomile heresy, 16
Bosnia, 6–8, 17, 38, 40, 93, 94, 96,
    110, 119, 126, 150, 153, 162, 165,
    175, 196–202, 217, 220, 231, 241,
    261, 262, 331, 340, 342, 413

455

INDEX

Bosnia, annexation of, 194–201, 342
Bosnian police, 171, 262
Bosnian Railways, 330–34
Branković, George, 40, 42, 49
——, Stephen, 42
——, Vuk, 39, 131
Brazza, 415
Brod, 194, 332, 429
Buchlau, 205
Buda, 41, 42
Budapest, 59, 73, 94, 178, 329, 330
Budget, Croatian, 75, 79, 387
Budisavljević, Bude, 167, 214, 219, 252, 257, 275, 281
—— Dr. Srgjan, 186, 191, 325
Bugojno, 332
Bukovac, 140
Bukowina, 6
Bulgaria, 37, 175, 177, 194, 197
Bulgarian Horrors, Mr. Gladstone on, 417
Bulgars, 1, 36, 419
Burian, Baron, 217
Buxton, Mr. Noel, 195
Byzantium, 16, 36

C

Carinthia, 26, 239
Carniola, 26, 329, 338
Carpaccio, 140
Catherine, Queen of Bosnia, 40
Catholics in Servia, 125
Cattaro, 5, 18, 38, 113
Čengić Aga, 91, 137
Černomen, battle of, 38
Černović, Ivan, 42
Cetin, Diet of, 19, 347, 351
Cetinje Treason Trial, 168, 171, 203
Charles the Great, 16
Charles Robert, 17, 350
Charles of Durazzo, 17, 350
Charles III (VI), 23, 43
Chlopy Army Order, 142
Chlumecky, Baron Leopold, 235–40, 288–300, 303
Christian Socialist Party, 155, 200, 209, 256, 338, 341
Čingrija, Dr. Melko, 293
—— Dr. Pero, 146, 289
Clissa, 20, 39
Coalition, Croato-Serb, 152, 154, 155, 156, 159, 162, 178, 183, 199, 202, 205, 206, 209, 223, 226, 229, 239, 256, 300, 303, 400
—— Hungarian, 143, 146, 201
Collar, Dr. Gjurić's, 189
Coloman of Hungary, 16
Commissioner, Royal, 99

Common Affairs, Austro-Hungarian, 68–70
—— —— Hungaro-Croatian, 70–72
Compromise, Austro-Hungarian, 59, 65, 68, 157, 331
—— Hungaro-Croatian, 62, 64, 65–84, 98, 108; violation of, 80, 98, 152, 340, 361–79
Concordat, 52
Confiscation, 113, 193
Coronation, 20, 59, 61, 359, 360
Corruption, Electoral, 66, 88, 102, 104, 110
Court of Appeal, 73
Crnojević, Arsen, 43
Croatia-Slavonia, 3–4
—— economic position of, 388–92
Croats, total number of, 1, 12
Croat dialects, 130
—— language, 2, 73, 154, 371, 372
—— and Serb literature, 129–40
Croatian Art, 124
—— Music, 124
—— Press, 391
Croato-Serb Unity, 144, 163, 178, 201, 334, 336–43
Crown of St. Stephen, 67, 72, 146
Crvena Hrvatska, 236
Customs, 373, 377
Cvijić, Professor, 224
Cvitaš, Captain, 327
Cyprus Convention, 176
Cyril, St., 15
Cyrilline alphabet, 2, 129, 233
"Czech Kingdom, the brother," 405
Czech Realists, 241, 251

D

Dalmatia, 3, 4–5, 18, 26, 53, 55, 58, 81, 113, 131, 144, 146, 147, 162, 213, 331–34, 355, 361
—— present condition of, 406–16
—— emigration from, 6, 415
—— "reconquest of," 410
—— reincorporation of, 80
Damjanović, Mr., 220, 269, 272
Daničić, George, 120, 123, 135
Danilo, Prince, 322
Danzers Armee Zeitung, 286, 328
David, Antony, 97, 98
—— Baron, 291
Davidović, Ljubomir, 216, 217, 223, 261, 317
Deák, Francis, 50, 54, 56, 59, 63, 76, 85, 97
Delegates at Budapest, Croat, 71, 369
Delegations, 69, 308
Despots of Servia, 39

INDEX

Diploma Inaugurale, 18
Disraeli, 127, 176
Dissidents, 161
Djaković, Isaias, 43
Djakovo, Bishopric of, 3, 118, 122, 124
Dog, a Croat, 189
Dorotka, Mr., 239, 288, 290
Draga, Queen, 9, 295
Drave river, 3
Dualism, 24, 60, 66, 308, 320, 340
Dugoselo, 334
Dulcigno, 10

E

Education in Croatia, 92, 116, 391, 392
Edward VII, 177
Electoral Law, 104, 105, 156
Elegović, Mr., 158
Eötvös, Baron, 50, 76
Erdödy, Ban John, 33
Essek (Osijek), 3, 44
Eugene, Prince, 43
" Exponent " of Budapest, the Ban as, 79

F

Fackel, Die, 286
February Patent of 1861, 53
Federalism, 338
Fejérváry, Baron Géza, 144, 151
Ferdinand I of Austria, 19, 42, 347, 351
—— II, 21
—— V, 48
—— of Bulgaria, 175
Filipović, General, 96, 99
Finale, 167, 204
Finance, Croatian, 74–78, 363–67, 373–78, 391
—— Office in Agram, 75, 98
Fiume, 3, 32, 56, 81, 82, 142, 144, 146, 153, 213, 331, 333, 356, 359, 372
—— Resolution of, 146–50, 213, 225, 229, 255, 276, 279, 393–94
Foreign Office, Austro-Hungarian, *see* Ballplatz
Forgách, Count, 191, 197, 198, 309, 310–19
Forgeries, under Baron Levin Rauch, 89
—— the Vasić, 304–28
Franchise, Croatian, 66
Francis I, 27

Francis Joseph, Emperor-King, 62, 94, 97, 114, 123, 126, 145, 176, 321, 337, 340
Franciscans in Bosnia, 8
Frank Party, *see* Right, Party of
Frank, Dr. Joseph, 102, 110, 111, 146, 149, 152, 161, 165, 181, 297, 305, 339
Frankopan family, 25, 133
—— Krsto, 19
Fremdenblatt, 255, 312
French in Illyria, 26, 409
Friedjung, Dr. Heinrich, 33, 200, 202–6, 209–87, 318
Friedjung Trial, 209–87
Frontiers, Croatian Military, 20, 23, 27, 44, 86, 93, 96, 97, 355, 372
Funder, Dr. Friedrich, 209, 228, 230, 233, 245, 256, 279

G

Gaj, Ljudevit, 27, 29, 30, 32, 136, 137
Gavrila, Dr., 269, 271
George of Servia, Prince, 167, 170, 195, 200, 218, 221, 244
Germanization, 24, 35, 52, 55
Gessmann, Dr., 256
Gjalski, L. Babić, 139, 220
Gjurgjević, Vaso, 108
Gjurić, Dr., 188, 189
Gladstone, Mr., 125, 127 ; correspondence with Bishop Strossmayer, 416–44
Glagolitic rite, 6, 13, 122, 126, 131
Glavni Odbor, 47
Goethe, 135
" Golden Prague," 406
Goluchowski, Count, 174
Görz, 1
Granitschars, 44, 93
Graz, 4, 330, 332
Great Britain, 201
Gregory VII, 16
Grey, Sir Edward, 175
Gül Baba, 94
Gundulić, Ivan, 18, 132, 413

H

Habsburg, House of, 34, 41, 42, 45, 335
Harambašić, Mr., 146
Harpner, Dr., 207, 209, 228, 235, 238, 243, 244, 247, 260, 263, 283, 296
Haulik, Cardinal, 53, 110, 122

INDEX

Havas, Dr. Rudolf, 147
Haynau, 50
Heir Apparent, (Archduke Francis Ferdinand) 256, 258, 282, 297, 309, 321
Heraclius, 15
Herder, 133
Herzegovac, Father, 179
Herzegovina, 7, 41, 131
Hinković, Dr., 185, 191, 193, 208, 313
Hodža, M. M., 127
Hohenwart, Count, 87
Hoitsy, Paul, 147
Hörmann, Father, 28
—— Sectional Chief in Bosnia, 217, 262
Hötzendorf, Gen. Conrad von, 241
Hrabowsky, General, 48
Hrvat, Mirko, 102, 103
Hrvatska, 106
Hrvatsko Pravo, 161, 165, 229, 300
Hrvoj, Mr., 327
Hungary, conquest of, 41
Hunyády, John, 40

I

Illiterates, 392
Illyria, 15, 26, 29, 52, 134, 136
Illyrian Aulic Council, 44, 45
Illyrica lingua, 25
Imperial mission of Austria, 343
Independence, Hungarian Party of, 142, 143, 148, 157, 163, 202
Independent National Party, 97, 101
Industries, Croatian, 390
Innocent III, 36.
Innsbruck, 34, 48
Ipek, 1, 41, 43
Istria, 2, 4, 26, 114
Isvolsky, M., 196, 197, 200, 205
Italians in Dalmatia, 5, 6, 55, 82
Italy, 200

J

Jagić, Professor von, 62, 122, 235
Jajce, 20, 40, 41
Jaksić, George, 138
Janković, Count Julius, 86
Jeftanović, Mr., 269
Jellačić, Baron Joseph, 33, 34, 35, 49, 56, 108
Jelovac, Peter, 226, 260
Jemeršić, Father, 117
Jerome, St., College of, in Rome, 120
Jesuits in Bosnia, 167
John, Archduke, 33

Joint Affairs, 72, 351, 359, 362–67
—— Ministries, 69, 70
Joseph II, 25, 45, 352
Josika, Baron, 33
Josipovich, Mr., 166, 226, 399
Jovanović, General, 96
—— Ljubomir, 162, 216, 221, 242, 254
—— Zmaj Jovan, 51, 138
Julian Society, 5, 116

K

Kačić, Andrew, 133
Kállay, Baron, 7, 85, 236, 342
Kandt, Max, 326
Karadžić, *see* Vuk
Kara George, 45, 134
Karageorgevitch dynasty, 9, 182, 215
Karčanski, 288, 293, 294
Karlovac, 22, 28, 330
Karlowitz, 3, 33, 45, 47, 50, 51
Kaspinović, 95
Khuen-Hedérváry, Count Charles, 79, 99, 100, 101, 104, 109, 110, 111, 114, 115, 117, 142, 155, 303, 308
Kikinda, 44
Kničanin, Gen., 48
Knin, 332, 410
Kollar, Slovak poet, 28
Königgrätz, 59
Königinhof MS., 251
Kopitar, 134
Koran, the, 417
Kossovo, battle of, 12, 39, 41, 131, 136, 181
Kossuth, Mr. Francis, 148, 149, 152, 223, 229, 274
Kossuth, Louis, 31, 35, 47, 49, 88, 341 ; and the Croats, 31
Kostajnica, 165
Kostić, Alexander, 46
Košutić, Mr., 185, 192
Kragujevac arsenal, 203
Kraljević, Marko, 47, 131
Kramarž, Dr., 310
Kraus, Karl, 286
Križevci (Kreuz), 19, 22
Krka river, 5
Kršnjavi, Professor, 416
Kuhać, Franjo, 140
Kulmer, Baron Francis, 33
—— Count, 276
Kulpa river, 22
Kumičić, Eugene, 139
Kvaternik, Eugene, 87

L

Ladislas I, 16

INDEX

Laginja, Mr., 256
Laibach, 27, 330, 331
Language Question, 25, 31
Latin in Hungarian Parliament, 28
Laveleye, Emile de, 127
Lazar Brankovic, 40
—— Grbljanović, 38
Lazarević, Laza, 140
Leger, M. Louis, 120
Lengyel, Mr. Zoltan, 213
Leo XIII, 6, 126
Leopold I, 43, 47
—— II, 45
Lesina, 6
Liberal Party in Hungary, 143, 144
Linz Programme, 210
Lisinsky, 29, 140
Lissa, battle off, 58
Liszt, Professor von, 246
Loan, Servian, 398
Loans, public, 78
London, Treaty of, 176
Lonjski Polje marshes, 86
Lonyay, Count, 89, 90, 97
Lorković, Dr., 221, 252
Lorraine, Duke of, 43
Louis the Great, 17, 37
—— II, 19, 41
—— of Baden, 43
Lueger, Dr., 295, 340
Lukács, Dr. Ladislas, 303
Lukinić, Dr., 206, 209, 214, 232, 397

M

Macedonia, 12
Magdić, Dr., 231, 257
Magnates, Croatian, 369
Magyar language, 29, 73
—— Railway Policy, 328–34, 409
—— State idea, 101
—— tariffs, 334
Magyars, 25, 27, 33, 34, 55, 57, 58,
   70, 126, 145, 153, 164, 340, 352
—— Are we to become ? 28
Magyarones, 53, 62, 99, 158
Mailáth, Count George, 57
Makanec, 94
Makarska, 132, 236
Maklakov, 223
Mamelukes, 99, 101, 109
Mandić, Dušan, 165
Mandl, Leopold, 172
Mandl, journalist in Semlin, 326
Manuel, Emperor, 36
March Laws, 31
Maria Theresa, 24, 43, 56
Marković,Professor Božidar, 216 sqq.,
   244–48, 277, 283, 296, 315

Marmont, Marshal, 26
Martić, Fra Grga, 138
Marulić, Marko, 131
Masaryk, Professor T. G., 112, 192,
   240, 241, 243, 250–55, 270, 283,
   299, 300, 303, 308–28
Matica Srpska, 51
Matthias Corvinus 40, 42,
Mažuranić, Ivan, 53, 61, 89, 90, 93,
   95, 122, 137, 278
Medjumurje, 4, 56, 58, 357
Medović, 140
Meštrović, Ivan, 141
Methodius, St., 15, 126
Metternich, 27
Michael of Servia, Prince, 9
Mihalović, Archbishop, 86, 123
Miladinović, 120
Milan, King, 9, 95
Miletić, Svetozar, 50, 95, 259
Milić, Vicko, 146
Militia, 73
Miljutin, 89
Milosch, Obilić, 39, 131
Milovanović, Dr., 196, 219, 222, 232,
   241, 242, 254, 264, 276, 283, 285,
   311, 320
—— Forged Instructions of, 401–6
Minghetti, Marco, 118
Mirko, Prince, 221
Mirtsea of Wallachia, 39
Mogan, Dr. Julius, 291
Mohács, battle of, 19, 41
Mohammed II, 20, 40
Mollináry, General, 87, 95
Monastir, 1
Montecuccoli, 43
Montenegro, 2, 10–11, 36, 94, 96,
   162, 171, 195, 197, 215, 302, 337,
   342
Montenegrin police, 168, 170
Morava river, 8, 174
Mostar, 7
Mrazović, 63, 90, 97
Murad I, 38
Mürzsteg programme, 175

N

Napoleon, 26, 134, 317, 412
Nardelli, Baron, 289
Narodna Misao, 112
Narodna Obrana, 232, 246
Nastić, George, 151, 166, 168–72,
   204, 248, 255, 320, 325
National Liberal(afterwards National)
   Party, 53, 63, 86, 87, 88, 97, 145,
   156, 280, 304
Nemanja dynasty, 38

INDEX

Nenadović, Captain, 167, 203
Neue Freie Presse, 198–99, 205, 206, 211, 213, 240, 255, 314
Neusatz (Ujvidék), 4, 46, 47, 51, 259
Nicholas I, Czar, 35.
Nicholas, King of Montenegro, 11, 136, 168, 203, 291
Nikolić, Dr. Vladimir, 277
Niš, 9, 39
Novaković, Stojan, 198
Novibazar, 174
Novi List, 144, 213, 229, 237, 289, 292, 301
Novo Doba, 112
Novosel, Father, 194
Nuntium, 69

O

Obilić, Miloš, 39, 131
Obradović, Dositej, 51, 134
Obrenović dynasty, 9
Obstruction, Croatian, 154
Obzor, 112, 147, 193
October Diploma (1860), 53
Odavić, Rista, 216, 263
Offices in Croatia, 79
Ogulin, 87, 331
Oliva, 88
Omladina, 95
Orthodox Church, in Bosnia, 8 ; in Croatia, 3, 45, 92, 125, 181 ; in Servia, 10
Osman of Gundulić, 132, 137
Ožegović, 32
—— Bishop, 48

P

Paču, Dr., 266
Palacky, Francis, 127
Pan-Croat ideal, the, 339
Pancsova, 44, 46
Pan-Germans, 210, 282
Pan-Serbism, 153, 161, 162, 163, 165, 170, 177, 181, 200, 203, 205, 215, 241, 268, 280, 321, 336, 337
Pan-Slavism, 30, 89, 94, 126, 127, 196, 253, 338, 398, 405
Parliament, see Sabor
Partes Adnexae, 24
Pašarić, Professor, 110, 117
Pašić, Dr., 162, 203, 216, 218, 229, 230, 245, 254, 259, 281, 295, 400
Patriarch, Serb Orthodox, 3, 41, 43, 166, 181
Pavečić, Mr. 183
Pavić, Mr., 291
Pavlović, Mile, 216, 223, 224, 261

Pejačević, Count Ladislas, 88, 97
—— Count Theodore, 116, 144, 152, 154, 214, 224, 225, 272, 274, 277, 297
Pester Lloyd, official campaign in, 162
Peter II of Montenegro, 11, 136
Peter, King of Servia, 9, 162, 170, 186, 202, 207, 213
Petković, Mr., 214, 224, 397
Petrović dynasty, 11
Pinon, M. René, 269
Pokret, 167, 193
Pola, 5
Polit, Dr. Michael, 63, 226, 233, 259, 260, 281, 285, 399
Politika, 198, 301
Popović, Dr. Dušan, 186, 233, 280
—— M., 222
Potočnjak, Dr. F., 224, 276, 397
Pragmatic Sanction, Croatian, 23, 67, 349–50, 359
—— Hungarian, 24, 61, 67
Prague University, 112
Premier, Hungarian, 78
Preradović, Peter, 137
Press, liberty of, 92
Pressburg, Diet of, 30, 32, 46
Pribičević, Adam, 167, 187, 207
—— Milan, 167, 168, 204
—— Svetozar, 206, 209, 214, 219, 233, 252, 260, 265, 305, 397–400
—— Valerian, 167, 179, 190, 207
Progressive Party, Croat, 252
Protić, Mr., 398
Pučić, Count Medo, 138
Punta Arena, 415

Q

Quarnero, the, 5
Quota, the, 74, 364, 366, 374, 376

R

Rački, Fr., 53, 57, 63, 89, 91, 97, 120, 122
Radetzky, 34
Radić, Mr. Stephen, 117, 150, 158
Ragusa, 5, 18, 26, 113, 131, 235, 288, 298, 321, 413
Railway Bill of Mr. Kossuth, 152, 230, 272, 304
—— Policy, Magyar, 329–34, 409–12
Railways of Croatia, 4, 152
Rajačić, Patriarch, 33, 47, 48, 49
Rákoczy, Francis, 21
Rakodczay, Dr. Alexander, 154, 155
Ramberg, Baron Hermann, 99
Rasciana, Natio, 43

INDEX

Rauch, Baron Levin, 53, 62, 86, 88, 95, 278
—— Baron Paul, 155, 157, 159, 160, 166, 173, 177, 179, 192, 193, 201, 214, 223, 234, 280, 304, 326
Ravenna, Exarchate of, 15
Reichherzer, 89, 278
Reichspost, 200, 206, 209, 228, 258, 283, 300
Reichsrath, Austrian, 54, 57, 145, 192
Reljković, Matthew, 133
Rešetar, Professor, 275
Reval meeting, 175
Revolution of 1848, 32
Revolutionary Statute, 169, 204
Right, Party of, 54, 99, 101, 103, 104, 107, 109, 152, 156, 165, 181, 182, 306, 324, 339
—— programme, 392
Ristić, Regent of Servia, 89
Rode, Dr. Walter, 240, 289, 291
Rohitsch, 330
Rudolf II, 20
Russia, 175, 196, 197, 199, 200, 338, 405
Ružić, Dr., 291

S

Sabor (Parliament) of Croatia, 25, 28, 30, 32, 34, 53, 58, 61, 63, 66, 71, 90, 101, 102, 103, 155, 158, 212, 305, 306, 362, 383–86
—— Address of (June 1848), 350–57 (Appendix III)
St. James, Cabinet of, 401–2
St. Gotthard, battle of, 43
Salonica, 205
Samouprava, 198, 282, 312
Sandjak of Novibazar, 8, 12, 174, 195
Sarajevo, 3, 7, 41, 51, 96, 135, 204, 269, 272, 315, 332
Sava, St., 36
Save river, 3
Schiavone, 140
Schlegel, Mr., 193
Schmerling, 50, 55, 57
Sebenico, 5
Seitz, frescoes of, 124
Semendria, 40
Semlin, 46, 191, 203
September Manifesto (1871), 87
Serb dictionary, 135
—— Independent Party, 111, 156, 159, 178, 203, 252, 279
—— Radicals, 166, 256, 281
Serbs and Khuen Regime, 107

Serbs of Bosnia, 301, 342
—— of Hungary, 42, 43, 45, 48, 94, 95, 181, 203
Serb Voivody, 3, 31, 34, 45, 50
Servia, 2, 8–10, 36–40, 45–6, 89, 94, 96, 125, 127, 134, 162, 185, 195, 196–204, 215, 216 *sqq*,. 243, 313, 337, 397 *sqq*., 401 *sqq*.
—— Old, 14, 127, 163, 214, 218
Servian Loan, 269, 271, 398
Sigismund, Emperor, 18, 39, 41
Simeon, Czar, 36
Simić, Dr., 242
Sinj, 332, 410
Skrejsovsky, 88
Skupština, 194, 197, 226, 397
Slav Congress in Prague, 47
Slavonia, 3
Slavonian Group, 306
Slovenes, 5, 134
Slovenski Jug, 167, 168, 170, 186, 203, 204, 214, 216–27, 244–49, 264, 284–86, 317
Smodlaka, Dr. Joseph, 406
Šokčević, Ban, 53, 56, 60, 358
Sokol Societies, 108
Somssich, Baron Paul, 54
Southern Slavs, definition, 1
Spalajković, Dr. M., 163, 203, 204, 206, 222, 225, 229, 241, 259, 263–71
Spalajković, the Forged Report of, 206, 225, 260, 263–71, 275, 285, 297–401
Spalato, 5, 16, 18, 113, 330–33, 408–12 ; art in, 141
Sporčić, Mr., 172, 204, 325
Srbobran, 166, 193, 219, 226, 281, 399
Srpska Matica, 135, 259
Srpski Riječ, 164, 218, 232, 269, 272
Staatsrecht, 65, 87
Stadler, Archbishop, 8, 167, 400
Stampa, 312
Standing Orders, Revision of, 102, 103
Stahremberg, 43
Starčević, Antony, 53, 63, 87, 99, 101, 103, 107, 109
—— Dr. Mile, 147, 161, 256
Stefanović, General Nicholas, 227, 247
—— Milan, 227, 228, 246, 308
Steeb, Lieut. F. Marshal, 324
Steinhardt, 172, 326
Stephen Dušan, 17, 37 ; laws of, 131
—— Dabiša, 39
—— Milutin, 37
—— Nemanja, 36
—— Saint, of Hungary, 16

INDEX

Stephen Thomas of Bosnia, 40
—— Uroš, 36
Stratimirović, General, 31, 34, 47, 95, 290
Strossmayer, Bishop, 6, 10, 52, 53, 57, 60, 61, 63, 88, 91, 106, 118–28, 278 ; description, 128 ; correspondence with Mr. Gladstone, 416–44
Šumanović, Dr., 116
Supilo, Mr. Francis, 144, 145, 150, 206, 209, 212, 214, 223, 229, 235–40, 252, 257, 280–82, 303, 309, 317, 322
Supilo-Chlumecky Incident, 235–40, 288–300
Šuplikac, Voivode, 47, 49
Šurmin, Professor, 160, 193, 231, 252, 305, 326
Svientochowski, 199, 309, 310–20
Syrmia, 3, 20, 42, 45, 119, 307
Szapáry, Count Ladislas, 142
Szeged, 35
Széll-Cabinet, 115, 142
Szterényi, Dr., 230

T

Tarabocchia, Mr., 182, 187, 190–91, 307
Tariffs in Croatia, Magyar, 333–34
Tarnóczy, 32
Tasso, 132
Telegram, Forged, 314–17
Temporal Power, 125, 437
Territorial Questions between Hungary and Croatia, 80–82
Theiner, August, 120
Tiefenbach, 319
Tisza, Coloman, 94, 98, 99, 126, 143
—— Count Stephen, 143, 151
Tököly, Sava, 45
Tomanović, Dr., 168
Tomić, J., 280, 285
—— Joseph, 139
Tomislav, D., 16
Tončić, Mr., 261, 288, 292
Traü, 39
Treason Trial in Agram, 179–92, 207
Treasury, Hungaro-Croatian, 77, 91, 365–75
Tresić-Pavičić, Antony, 138
Trialism, 81, 108, 338, 339, 342, 353
Trieste, 5
Triple Entente, 174, 176
Triune Kingdom, 34, 47, 55, 57, 60, 67, 81, 94, 335, 350–57, 359, 399
Trumbić, Dr. Antony, 146, 149
Tschernajev, 95

Turkey, Serbs in, 12
Turkish Revolution, 175
Turks, 94, 95, 126, 195, 197, 412, 418
—— conquer Hungary, 19
Tuškan, Dr., 205, 212, 231, 276
Tvrtko I of Bosnia, 17, 38, 351
—— II, 39

U

Uebersberger, Dr., 235, 275
Uniate Churches in Hungary, 44
Unionist Party in Croatia, 53, 87, 88, 99
" United Opposition," 107
Uroš the Great, 37
—— III, 37
—— IV, 38
Uskok Pirates, 22
Ustavnost, 159, 192, 239

V

Vakanović, Antony, 28, 88, 91
Vakuf, the, 8
Varaždin, 42
Varna, battle of, 40
Vasić, 151, 199, 303–328
—— Trial, 312, 314
Vatican Council, 124, 416
Vazov, Ivan, 139
Velbužd, battle of, 37
Velebit Mountains, 3
Velimirović, Servian Premier, 221
Venice, 18, 26, 37, 132, 413
Versecz, 44
Világos, capitulation of, 35
Virilists, 88
Virpazar, 10
Vladislav, I, 40 ; II, 18
" Vlah," 182
Voivody, see Serb
Vojnović, Count Ivo, 138
Vončina, 89
Vraz, Stanko, 137
Vrbanić, Professor, 110, 146
Vrhovac, Bishop, 25
Vorner, Captain, 171
Vuk Karadžić, 29, 51, 108, 120, 127, 129, 133, 134, 135
Vukašin, 38
Vukotić, General, 194, 220
Vuković, Saba, 48

W

Water power in Dalmatia, 411
Wach, Dr., 209, 234, 239, 267, 270, 277, 283

INDEX

Wekerle, Dr., 79, 149, 151, 155, 157, 166, 177, 193, 225, 267, 303, 305, 322

Wolf, Karl Hermann, 281

Z

Zagorac, Father, 147, 255, 299
Zajc, Ivan, 140
Zajnko, Father, 258
Zapolya, John, 19, 42
Zaprešica riot, 112

Zara, 5, 15, 350, 410
Zara, Resolution of, 149, 213, 279, 395–97
Zastava, 50, 281, 282
Zatočnik, 86
Zengg, 22
Zenta, 43
Zichy, Count Aladar, 143
Živković, Baron, 90
Žrinski, Count Nicholas, 21, 123
—— Count Peter, 21, 25, 133
Zvonimir, King of Croatia, 16, 81